Andrew R. Fausset, Benjamin M. Smith

The Poetical Books of the Holy Scriptures

Andrew R. Fausset, Benjamin M. Smith

The Poetical Books of the Holy Scriptures

ISBN/EAN: 9783337284800

Printed in Europe, USA, Canada, Australia, Japan

Cover: Foto ©Lupo / pixelio.de

More available books at **www.hansebooks.com**

THE

POETICAL BOOKS

OF THE

HOLY SCRIPTURES.

WITH
A CRITICAL AND EXPLANATORY COMMENTARY.

BY THE REV. A. R. FAUSSET, A.M.,
RECTOR, ST. CUTHBERT'S, YORK, ENGLAND,

AND

REV. B. M. SMITH, D.D.,
PROFESSOR OF ORIENTAL LITERATURE AND BIBLICAL INSTRUCTION
IN UNION THEOLOGICAL SEMINARY.

PHILADELPHIA:
JAMES S. CLAXTON,
SUCCESSOR TO WM. S. & ALFRED MARTIEN,
1214 CHESTNUT STREET.
1867.

List of Abbreviations.

A. NEWTON	Miss Adelaide Newton.
BO.	Bochart.
BENG.	Bengel.
BUR.	Burrowes.
COCC.	Cocceus.
DE. W.	De Wette.
DUR.	Durham.
EICH.	Eichorn.
GES.	Gesenius.
GROT.	Grotius, Annott. in Act. Apost.
HOL.	Holden.
HENGST.	Hengstenberg.
LINN.	Linnæus.
MICH.	Michaelis.
MAUR.	Maurer of Heiligstedt.
M. STUART	Moody Stuart.
NOY.	Noyes.
PARKH.	Parkhurst.
RAWL.	Rawlinson.
ROS.	Rosenmuller.
SCH.	Schuttens.
SOUTH.	Southey.
TALM.	Talmud
UMBR.	Umbreit
O. T.	Old Testament.
N. T.	New Testament.
N. S. E. W.	North, South, East, West.
Cf.	(confer, meaning *Compare*
LIT.	Literally.
FIG.	Figuratively
SING.	Singular.
PLUR.	Plural.
EX. GR.	For example's sake.
TRANSL.	Translate, Translation.
NOM.	Nominative
GR.	Greek.
E. V.	English Version.
LXX.	The Septuagint Greek Version of the O. T., written at Alexandria for Hellenistic Jews.
ARAB.	Arabic Version.
SYR.	The Syriac Version.
VULG.	Vulgate, Latin Version of Jerome.

INTRODUCTION TO THE POETICAL BOOKS.

ACCORDING to a division of the Old Testament Scriptures, now very generally received, Job, Psalms, Proverbs, Ecclesiastes, and the Song of Solomon are termed POETICAL BOOKS. Large portions of the Prophecies also present specimens of poetic composition, but these books alone, are almost, and some exclusively, composed in that style. By the Jews they were reckoned in that division of the Old Testament Scriptures, to which the title *Hagiographa*, or *Holy Writings*, was applied, because they were thought to have been inspired by direct communications of the Holy Spirit, and not through the medium of dreams and visions.

I. 1. In reading the Bible in the English version, we discover that there is an obvious difference in the tone we insensibly adopt in reading the books of Genesis and Samuel, for instance, and that we use in reading Job and Psalms. We also observe a marked peculiarity in the structure of the sentences in these latter books, and also in Proverbs, Ecclesiastes, and the Song of Solomon, so that one part of a sentence corresponds, by repetition, comparison, or contrast, with the other. These and some other peculiarities, to be more fully stated below, constitute what is called the *poetic style* of the Old Testament. This differs in many respects from that of Western and modern writings. Some, whose associations with the word Poetry suggest compositions of equal lines, sometimes terminating in like sounds, called Rhyme, are disposed to question the poetic character of writings devoid of such marks. But it is quite obvious that as there may be poetry without Rhyme, so there may be poetry without Rhythm or Metre. The compositions ascribed to Ossian are conceded to be highly poetic, though devoid of both Rhyme and Rhythm. A translation of the most celebrated ancient and modern poets generally destroys these artificial distinctions, but there will remain a poetic sentiment or style of thought. This constitutes ultimately the marked distinction between prose and poetry in all languages, a distinction which arises from an essential difference in the mental conceptions of the writers. The mind of the poet is excited. His conceptions are greatly influenced by the imagination and the passions, which are often kindled into enthusiasm. The associations are rapid, so rapid as often to obscure connecting links. The objects of his attention are often highly exaggerated in his apprehension. Every faculty of the soul becomes, more or less, affected by the imagination. His language reflects his mental condition. It abounds in metaphors, comparisons, and strong contrasts. It is abrupt, concise, and filled with expressions of surprise, exultation, joy, grief or despair, of a highly coloured character. The mind of the purely prose writer, on the other hand, is ordinarily calm and tranquil, and his language, as a vehicle for expressing regular and progressive trains of thought, exhibits, in the choice of words and the structure of sentences, nothing unusual or extraordinary.

In all nations we find that poetry has preceded prose. It is more the language of nature. The poet was also a prophet, and in most languages the same title was employed to designate both. He was the instructor of the people. He incited them to deeds of valour, and celebrated those deeds in their festive gatherings. It was also his office to pourtray great and virtuous deeds, to embellish and commend the precepts of religion, and celebrate the beneficence, wisdom, and power of Deity. These general characteristics of poetry and poets belong in common to the poetry of thought, in whatever language or age its monuments exist. But in respect to the poetic sentiment developed by the ancient Hebrews, and especially as illustrated in these books, there are peculiarities, the delineation of which may serve to enhance our appreciation of these parts of revelation, and, at the same time, aid in the effort to understand them.

2. Whether the more natural province of poetry and poets is men's moral instruction or not, there is good reason for believing that poetic forms of composition are well adapted to such purposes, as they were selected by God as the medium by which some of the most solemn and important truths of divine revelation have been made known to man. Indeed, in view of what has been already said, we may see the reasons for this fact. By its vivid and impressive delineations, poetry is well adapted to excite the strongest emotions, and produce the most lively and permanent conceptions. We have been so accustomed to regard the Greek and Roman poets as models of ancient, and the great English, Italian, and German poets, as models of modern poetry, that since their most celebrated works are pictures of the imagination, we have insensibly adopted the opinion that there is a necessary connection between fiction and poetry; that it is only when the "poet's eye" is "in a fine phrenzy rolling," and "imagination bodies forth the forms of things unknown," that we can expect the "poet's pen" to charm and instruct the soul by words of beauty, sublimity, and pathos. But though most of the Hebrew poets are more ancient than those of Greece and Rome, and so lived nearer the ages of that fabulous antiquity, esteemed so favourable to poetry, they did not deal in fiction. Their inspiration was no work of phrensy, and yet their compositions evince a true poetic fervor. The elevated conceptions, gorgeous imagery, tenderness and sweetness of expression, bold metaphor, vivid comparisons and contrasts, exclamations, interrogations, and apostrophes which distinguish the book of Job, the Psalms, Isaiah, and Habakkuk, and many other parts of the Old Testament, are unequalled by the compositions of any uninspired men. The splendid conceptions which imagination furnished Homer, Virgil, and Shakspeare are exceeded by the grand ideas which the Spirit of God imparted to the Hebrew poets from the facts of creation, providence, and redemption. The themes thus supplied, taught in the words which the Holy Ghost teaches, were in themselves of the most sublime character, and calculated to excite those very feelings, the existence of which gives rise to the loftiest poetic style. God, in his infinite and incomprehensible nature, attributes, and perfections, the displays of his creative power and the "might of his terrible acts," in his "most holy, wise, and powerful" government; the creation, in all the vastness, variety, grandeur, harmony, beauty, and usefulness of its parts; the ordering of the processes of nature, in the storms, floods, volcanoes, and earthquakes, as well as in the usual, though not less magnificent, courses of the sun, moon, and stars, and the changes of the seasons; the special providence of God to his chosen people, his miraculous interventions for their deliverance, his judgments on their enemies, the brilliant future depicted for them, and more especially the coming glories and prevalence of the mediatorial kingdom, with the foreshadowing of the majestic reign of his illustrious incarnate Son as head over

all principality and power and eternal King in Zion, are examples of the topics on which, long before the period of the most celebrated classic literature, the Hebrew poets were employed to instruct mankind.

3. Growing out of the origin and nature of Hebrew poetry, and the character and relation of the writers, are some distinguishing peculiarities.

(1.) It is eminently national. The country, clime, peculiar institutions, with all their rites and ceremonies, and the singular national history of the people are so vividly reflected in these poems, that they can belong to no other people.

(2.) It is peculiarly original. Even Homer's great poems may have had their predecessors in the unrecorded legends and songs of an earlier day. But the song of triumph over Pharaoh's destruction could have had no model. The predictions of Jacob, Gen. xlix., had no type in any precedent history. David's lament for Saul and Jonathan could find no example in other than a people's history, who had received the lessons of inspiration, and the rapt songs in which David mourns the past, or triumphs in the future history of the church, found no precedents in the records of a world which knew but one Zion. On the Hebrew muse, it has been well said, "the rose of Sharon blushed with its first loveliness, and the dews of Hermon were first disturbed by her unsandled feet."

(3.) Hebrew poetry is the spontaneous effusion of the heart. There is neither "constraint, effort, nor affectation." With this is united a winning simplicity. The artificial methods of critics and rhetoricians did not incite or guide, curb or confine the poet. "He lisped in numbers for the numbers came." There is no effort to supply the deficiencies of fancy by the labours of culture. Patriarchs, legislators, kings, prophets, priests, herdsmen, warriors, and ploughmen were the bards of this wonderful age.

(4.) Lastly, Hebrew poetry possesses an undying power. Though Hebrew, it is universal. Its pure religious element, divine truth, fulness and energy have given it perpetual existence. These books, after the lapse of so many ages, "the rise and fall of so many modes of thought and forms of social life," are read by increasing hundreds. Even through the medium of translations, they are regarded with profound admiration. The passions which they pourtray still exist in men's souls, and whether the mourning and sighs of the penitent or the triumphant praises of hearts joyful in God, these writings are found to be more expressive of religious sentiment than any other compositions. They still exercise a moulding influence over men greater than any other religious teachings within the range of human literature, excepting only the words of Him, "who spake as never man spake."

II. 1. It is evident that no artificial structure is essential to true poetry. The external form of a poem in one language is necessarily laid aside in a literal translation. Illustrations of this remark are afforded by attempts to translate the Greek and Latin poets into our own tongue. Those versions of the Psalms of David which are most literal have least of the external form of poetry, as the versions of Sternhold and Hopkins and of Rouse fully testify. Hence, if we find in the poetical books of the Bible an entire want of artificial structure, our foregoing remarks are not at all affected. Still, it is true, that though not presented in the poetic forms of other languages, there is an obvious peculiarity of structure which distinguishes some portions of Scripture from others, and, as already observed, this is so perceptible, even through the medium of a translation, that we insensibly fall into a different tone of voice in reading such portions. Let any one, for instance, read the first verse of the first chapter of Isaiah and then proceed to read the second. It will be discovered that without any design the voice assumes a tone in reading the latter unlike that used in reading the former. Compare thus Job xlii. 1-6 with what follows from verse 7th through the chapter. So also read Deut. xxxi. 30, and follow by reading chap. xxxii. 1, and following. This difference in external form corresponds very strongly with the difference in the style of thought. The passionate feeling gives rise to passionate expression. The excited and vivid conception and animated style of sentiment produces a corresponding mode of speech.

2. A distinguishing peculiarity of poetry is sententiousness. This, however, is combined with another feature which may be called repetition. The ardour of mind in the writer, leads him to express himself in a brief form of speech, and the desire to impress what he says, induces a repetition of the idea in very similar language. Thus Isaiah says, "Israel does not know," by which he very briefly states the unwillingness of the people to receive or retain instruction; then he adds, repeating the same idea, "my people doth not consider." So in the Psalms, 'What is man that Thou art mindful of him, or the son of man that Thou visitest him?" In this verse the idea of the first part is repeated in the second. We may observe this same tendency in poets of other languages. Thus Pope in his "Messiah,"

"'Tis he the obstructed paths of sound shall clear,
And bid new music charm the unfolding ear."

So Shakespeare in King John,

"Our discontented countries do revolt,
Our people quarrel with obedience."

So also Milton, Paradise Lost, b. 1, l. 591-4,

"His form hath not yet lost
All her original brightness; nor appeared
Less than archangel ruined, and th' excess
Of glory obscured."

Similar examples could be easily adduced in great numbers, illustrating the tendency of poetic sentiment to such modes of expression.

3. To this prominent characteristic of poetry, as it appears in the Scriptures, has been given the title of PARALLELISM. It presents examples of various forms, and in their classification some difference exists among critics. We may, however, offer what follows as a fair representation of the views which are now generally received.

There are three forms of Parallelism, the Synonymous, the Antithetic, and the Synthetic.

(1.) *The Synonymous Parallelism.*—In this the two members express substantially the same thought. Sometimes this involves the use, in part, of the same terms, and sometimes of different terms throughout. It occasionally presents a very accurately adjusted arrangement of members, in which each word in one member has a correspondent term in the other. This has, by some, been called the original parallelism. Thus, "The heavens declare the glory of God, and the firmament showeth his handywork." Ps. xix. 1. See a series of such in this Psalm, verses 7-11. To those forms in which the same words occur, in part, in both members, the term *identical* has been applied. Ps. cxviii. 8-9,

"It is better to trust in the Lord than to put confidence in man.
It is better to trust in the Lord than to put confidence in princes."

Other examples of parallelism occur in Gen. iv. 23, Job xviii. 13, Ps. lxviii. 32, Ps. xxxvi. 6, Ps. xl. 9, Ps. xlviii. 1, Ps. xxxi. 10, Ps. xl. 16.

(2.) *The Antithetic Parallelism.*—Here the two members express an opposition or contrast of sentiment and also of terms, or only in sentiment. Prov. x. 1,

"A wise son maketh a glad father;
But a foolish son is the heaviness of his mother."

In this, as in the foregoing species, one of the members may be extended so as to form a complex idea, as in Ps. xv. 4. So also there is sometimes a double set of contrasts, as in Is. liv. 10.

(3.) *The Synthetic Parallelism* is indicated by a resemblance in the form of construction and progression of the thoughts. This is subject to a similar variety to that presented in the other species. In its simpler form we have an example in Ps. xci. 7,

"Though a thousand fall at thy side,
And ten thousand at thy right hand,
It shall not come nigh thee."

In which there is a great similarity to one kind of Synonymous Parallelism, in that the last member is extended. But this extension, it will be observed, introduces a new thought, which pertains equally to both the previous members. There may be an equality in terms, as in Ps. xix. 8,

"The law of the Lord is perfect, converting the soul,
The testimony of the Lord is sure, making wise the simple."

And by reference to the Psalm it will be seen how this parallel is continued through several verses. So also in many other cases, as in Ps. i. 1 and 3; lxv. 10; lxviii. 31, &c.

On the fundamental idea of Parallelism, as a distinguishing feature in the external form of Hebrew poetry, we thus see at least three leading varieties in that form, and these again subject to several modifications. Different modes of classification have been suggested by different critics, but the considerations which are adduced in the favour of any one, by its advocates, are not of a very important character, and the sketch now given may be regarded as sufficiently accurate and comprehensive. Modifications, however, of the general principles now explained, might be cited, in which, while the traces of parallelism are distinctly found, an adherence to the specified forms which most usually occur does not exist.

4. A careful perusal of the poetical books and other portions of the Old Testament, written in poetry, will afford full illustrations of the views which have now been given, even to the English reader. It will appear very clearly that "the primitive and fundamental characteristics of poetry in general, viz., a constant brevity of expression, and a reinforcing of the sentiment by means of repetition, comparison, and contrast, have ever remained the principal and almost the sole distinguishing features of the poetry of the ancient Hebrews." It is true, there are a few passages, in which, at the close of two connecting clauses, there are syllables of like sound, and the clauses having the purest form of parallelism, each consisting of a like number of syllables, such passages have been cited as instances of rhyme. But not only are these very few, and then occurring incidentally, as it were, but the so-called rhymes are formed, in most instances, by the recurrence of the same pronoun forms, added to nouns or verbs. We may safely say, there was no rhyme in Hebrew poetry. Even the appearance of rhythm or metre must be regarded

rather as an incidental accompaniment of parallelism than a designed form of writing.

5. On the other hand, the poetry of Western nations may have had, in their origin, a character analogous to the Hebrew. But these languages were more cultivated. Writers, not content with the harmony of sentiment and a corresponding fitness in sound, produced by the arrangement already described, undertook to establish, as an attribute of poetry, a farther degree of harmony, by not only requiring a certain number of syllables in each line, but also a regular and sometimes complicated arrangement of such syllables. To this was subsequently added the ornament of rhyme. Whether these artificial methods of expression have added anything more than a pleasing impression through the ear, may well be questioned. The English reader may so far find the means of forming an opinion as the perusal of some of the most distinguished English poets will allow, by comparing the best productions in blank verse and rhyme either of the same author or of different authors. It is believed that the result of such a comparison will not greatly favour the opinion that rhyme has improved poetry. There is often required some sacrifice of sense and sound; and so, even in blank verse, there may be a requisition on the writer for similar subordination of the higher elements of poetry to the demands of verses of equal syllabication, and a prescribed recurrence of syllables of like quantity.

6. To the English reader, what has now been offered on the subject of the external form of Hebrew poetry, is as much as seems important or can be made intelligible. A question at once arises, relating to the practical advantage accruing to the students of divine truth, from its presentation to the mind in the garb of poetry. Everything has been made by God beautiful in its time. God has garnished the heavens and the earth with the elegant as well as useful monuments of his power and skill. It would, therefore, be not only no reflection on his wisdom, but only analogous to his providential orderings, that he should clothe the thoughts of Eternal Truth in the forms of an attractive beauty. Could we then discover no other advantage arising from the poetical compositions of the Scriptures, this might seem sufficient reason for their existence.

But we know by our own observation and experience that the memory both acquires and retains sentiments expressed in poetic form with greater ease than it does those expressed in prose. And when we find, as in the Book of Psalms, that most of these compositions are really Liturgical and adapted to the purposes of divine worship, and have been so used ever since their existence, and consider that there is an apparent adaptation of poetic forms to the expression of devotional sentiments, we discover another most admirable mark of divine wisdom.

Farther, to the interpreter of scripture, the particular feature of Hebrew poetry which has been discussed is not without its value. When a sentiment has been expressed in two or three forms, each substantially of the same meaning, obscure words or clauses in one are often elucidated by the clearer corresponding terms of the other. Even in the absence of exact correspondence of terms, the meaning, which may clearly attach to one member, will aid in apprehending the otherwise obscure idea of the other. Thus we are often guided to the settlement of the proper significations of words and idioms, for which an extensive usage may be lacking. So the member of an antithetic parallelism which is in contrast with another, becomes a guide of similar utility. It is only in the constant practice of the art of interpretation that the student will fully appreciate and enjoy the benefits here set forth.

Again, as the mind thus learns more clearly to perceive, and fully appreciate the truths addressed to the understanding in a mode at once pleasing and improving to the taste, it is not unfrequently a consequence that a greater, love for the Scriptures, and more zeal in the effort to become wise in the words and teachings of the Spirit, will arise.

III. A very interesting topic of inquiry is the *doctrinal character* of the Poetical Books. The word, *doctrinal*, is used in its widest sense as synonymous with teaching. It may be observed, in the outset, that we would not properly look to these or indeed to any of the Old Testament writings for as full expositions of the distinguishing truths of revealed religion as to the New Testament writers. For during the greater part of the time occupied with the formation of the Old Testament, the Jews enjoyed the instructions of Prophets or living inspired teachers, and had thus access to supernatural sources of instruction. For our benefit there was needed no more explicit discoveries of the truths of Christianity than would serve to show that Old and New Testaments declare the same great system, and to supply the material whence the advocates and defenders of Divine Revelation might derive their arguments. In the New Testament life and immortality are brought fully to light. Now, not to dwell on the special teachings of each of these books in order, which more properly belongs to the special Introductions to them, it may be profitable to point out, how, as a whole, they unfolded for the ancient church, as fully as was then needed, the essential teachings of that Christian faith which Christ and his apostles have more fully set before their own, and all succeeding ages. It will be remembered that four of these books—Psalms, Proverbs, Ecclesiastes, and the Song of Solomon—were the productions of two consecutive generations, thus belonging to the same age; and that, most probably, the book of Job, of far more ancient origin, had been brought to light by Moses not more than a few centuries previously. Thus before the decline of the nation in piety, before responses had ceased to emanate from between the cherubim, and before the spirit of prophecy had taken its flight from a corrupt and hardened church, God provided a collection of writings, by which the faith of his true people might be fed with sound doctrine, on the great themes of his moral government, and especially the scheme of redemption through his Son. This will appear from such considerations as follow, in which these books are regarded as a whole, presenting as such, in distinction from the Historical, on the one hand, and the Prophetical on the other, those religious views which more peculiarly teach what "man is to believe concerning God, and what duty God requires of man." It may be proper further to say that while, as will be seen, the Song of Songs, as part of the collection, has a most important place, in respect of the one great truth it unfolds, it cannot properly, as it is an allegory for the illustration and enforcement of that truth, be quoted as contributing to the general system presented in other books.

1. The being and attributes of God are most fully set forth, especially in Job and the Psalms. In no portion of the Scriptures is the religion of a pure *Theism* more clearly unfolded. The religious systems of the Eastern nations, other than Jews, very generally favoured the idea, afterwards so distinctive of the Manicheans, that the universe was governed by a *good* and an *evil* principle; and we know how Greek and Roman Mythology peopled Hell, as well as Heaven, with Deities, the one class

(ix)

to be deprecated as much as the other were to be supplicated. God is revealed especially in the Book of Job as ONE: and this is the more remarkable, in that the great theme of discussion, by Job and his friends, was that very feature of Divine providence, the mingled good and evil of the present state, which, misapprehended, furnished the argument for the *Dualism* of heathen religions. This one God is described as infinite in his attributes of omnipresence, omniscience, omnipotence, wisdom, justice, holiness, mercy, and truth. He is eternal, the supreme ruler of the world, the hearer of prayer, and the gracious dispenser of good, or the indignant vindicator of his government, and the avenger of his broken laws, or of his oppressed people.

2. He is set forth as the creator, and the sole creator of the world. He founded it on the seas, and established it on the floods. It was no work of chance, or of created beings; nor was it eternal. The heavens declare his glory, and the firmament showeth his handywork.

3. The *fact* that God governs all men, both good and evil, is everywhere clearly taught, and the Book of Job, more specially, is occupied with an illustration of the wisdom and justice with which this government is administered, as against the crude theories of them, who saw in affliction no other than an evidence of Divine hatred, and in prosperity, only an evidence of Divine love. Through the Psalms and Ecclesiastes, as well as by occasional notices in Proverbs, this, to unaided man— to the natural man—most inexplicable and perplexing topic, God's government of the wicked as well as the good, is most frequently presented, as well in the forms of a simple didactic teaching, as in the melting strains of devotion, both in the language and sentiment of prayer and praise.

4. The existence of good angels, and their service to the heirs of salvation, and of bad, and their agency in the production of evil, are most explicitly announced, and illustrations of the benevolence of the one, and the malevolence of the other are afforded, as if in advance of the poor theories of groping heathen or semi-Christian philsophers.

5. "Of man's first disobedience," and its mournful and memorable results, in the condemnation, as well as the spiritual death of the world, we may not have the clear and explicit teaching presented in the forms of a logical discussion such as Paul gives us, but the whole tenor of these writings implies the belief of these great and awful truths. In no book, inspired or uninspired, are there more clearly exhibited the power and workings of sin, or more fully opened up the depravity and deceitfulness of the heart of man than in many memorable passages of David's inspired declarations of the character and conduct of his enemies, and his equally inspired declarations of his personal convictions and his personal penitence. The Divine mercy to the truly humbled and contrite soul, along with the spiritual import of a divinely appointed ritual, is more than a mere inference, but comes to us in as explicit and encouraging declarations as ever fell from apostolic lips.

6. The great truth of New Testament revelation, though not expounded in the forms of dogmatic statement, is fully presented in the doctrine of a Divine mercy to those who confess and forsake their sins, and approach God for his mercy through those mediums of access, which typified a nobler Victim, a costlier Sacrifice, and a more worthy and exalted Priest and Intercessor.

7. In no portions of Scripture is more light shed on the duties of daily life,

even of the humblest; on the conduct proper in every age and especially in youth; on the intercourse of man, in business as well as the various relations of domestic, social, and civil life, than in these books, especially in Proverbs and Ecclesiastes, though not exclusively; for in Job and Psalms also, we are constantly reminded that the religion of the Bible is not a system of mysticism for anchorites and monks, but of faith and practice for men of like passions, temptations, trials, and duties as ourselves. Even the minor morals, which have respect to men's outward behaviour, gentleness, kindness, politeness, cleanliness, industry, diligence, patience, and perseverance are enforced by the precepts of a Divine teaching, and under the sanctions of a Divine authority.

8. It has been questioned very strongly, whether the doctrines of a future life, and especially of a resurrection, are taught in these books. Time and space allow no discussion of the subject. But the celebrated passage in Job xix. 25-27, we think, admits of no sound interpretation other than that which teaches the doctrine of a resurrection, and Psalms xvi. 9-11, in foretelling, as inspired apostles have declared, the Resurrection of Christ, was doubtless recorded in language capable of application, by those he represented, to their own future, for their comfort and peace in view of the common lot, which they knew they must experience. Of a future state of rewards and punishments, not only must the readers of these books become convinced they teach, by many portions through their general tenor, but the whole view they give of men's relations to God, their subjection to his government, in that their destiny, whether for good or evil, must be contemplated as reaching beyond time, and especially the sublime foreshadowing of a general judgment in Ps. l., and the allusions of Ps. xlix. and xvii., xv., all together seem sufficient to establish in our minds the belief, that the ancient church was not left in ignorance of these awful and glorious truths.

These books, in their attractive dress, more than any other poetic writings preserving that attraction in its native beauty and simplicity, even in a translation, are now presented to the reader with a brief explanation, which, it is hoped, will cast light on many obscure and doubtful passages, enforce the lessons of divine wisdom on the minds of those who peruse it, and thus encourage and promote the successful study of this, as well as other portions of the inspired volume. Brevity and fulness combined have been sought, that, for those whose time and occupations allow them but little leisure for sacred studies, the means of understanding God's word may be afforded. To the authors and publishers of this Commentary no higher reward can be found, no purer pleasure afforded, than will be obtained in the knowledge that the blessing of the author of the Bible may have rested on their labours. To him be glory and dominion evermore.

THE BOOK OF JOB.

INTRODUCTION.

JOB A REAL PERSON.—It has been supposed by some that the Book of Job is an allegory, not a real narrative, on account of the artificial character of many of its statements. Thus the sacred numbers, *three* and *seven*, often occur. He had *seven* thousand sheep, *seven* sons, both before and after his trials; his *three* friends sit down with him *seven* days and *seven* nights; both before and after his trials he had *three* daughters. So also the number and form of the speeches of the several speakers seem to be artificial. The name of Job, too, is derived from an Arabic word signifying *repentance*. But Ez. 14. 14 (cf. *v.* 16, 20.), speaks of "Job" in conjunction with "Noah and Daniel," real persons. St. James (5. 11,) also refers to Job as an example of "patience," which he would not have been likely to do had Job been only a fictitious person. Also the names of persons and places are specified with a particularity not to be looked for in an allegory. As to the exact *doubling* of his possessions after his restoration, no doubt the *round* number is given for the exact number, as the latter approached near the former: this is often done in undoubtedly *historical* books. As to the studied number and form of the speeches, it seems likely that the arguments were *substantially* those which appear in the Book, but that the *studied and poetic form* were given by Job himself guided by the Holy Spirit. He lived 140 years after his trials, and nothing would be more natural, than that he should, at his leisure, mould into a perfect form the arguments used in the momentous debate, for the instruction of the Church in all ages. Probably, too, the debate itself occupied several sittings; and the number of speeches assigned to each was arranged by preconcerted agreement, and each was allowed the interval of a day or more to prepare carefully his speech and replies: this will account for the speakers bringing forward their arguments in regular series, no one speaking out of his turn. As to the name Job—*repentance*—(supposing the derivation correct) it was common in old times to give a name from circumstances which occurred at an advanced period of life, and this is no argument against the reality of the person.

WHERE JOB LIVED.—Uz, according to [*Ges.*] means a light sandy soil, and was in the N. of Arabia Deserta, between Palestine and the Euphrates, called by Ptolemy (*Geog.* 19) *Ausitai* or *Aisitai*. In Gen. 10. 23; 22. 21; 36. 28; and 1 Chr. 1. 17. 42, it is the name of a man: in Jer. 25. 20; Lam. 4. 21; and Job 1. 1, it is a country. Uz, in Gen. 22. 21, is said to be the son of Nahor, brother of Abraham, a different person from the one mentioned (Gen. 10. 23,), a grandson of Shem. The probability is, that the country took its name from the latter of the two; for this one was the son of Aram, from whom the Aramæans take their name, and these dwelt in Mesopotamia, between the rivers Euphrates and Tigris. Cf. as to the dwelling of the sons of Shem in Gen. 10. 30, "a mount *of the East*," answering to "men *of the East*" (Job, 1. 3.). *Rawl.*, in his deciphering of the Assyrian inscriptions, states that " Uz is the prevailing name of the country at the mouth of the Euphrates." It is probable that Eliphaz the Temanite and the Sabeans dwelt in that quarter; and we know that the Chaldeans resided there, and not near Idumea, which some identify with Uz. The tornado from "the wilderness" (ch. 1. 19,) agrees with the view of it being Arabia Deserta. Job (ch. 1. 3,) is called " the greatest of the men of the East ;" but Idumea was not E., but S. of Palestine: therefore in Scripture language, the phrase cannot apply to that country; but probably refers to the N. of Arabia Deserta, between Palestine, Idumea, and the Euphrates. So the Arabs still show in the Houran, a place called Uz, as the residence of Job.

THE AGE WHEN JOB LIVED.—*Eusebius* fixes it two ages before Moses: *i.e.* about the time of Isaac; eighteen hundred years before Christ, and six hundred after the deluge. Agreeing with this are the following considerations:—1. Job's length of life is patriarchal, 200 years. 2. He alludes only to the earliest form of idolatry, viz., the worship of the sun, moon, and heavenly hosts (called *Saba*, whence arises the title Lord of *Sabaoth*, as opposed to Sabeanism,) (ch. 31. 26-28.). 3. The number of oxen and rams sacrificed, *seven*, as in the case of Balaam. God would not have sanctioned this *after* the giving of the Mosaic law, though He might graciously accommodate Himself to existing customs *before* the law. 4. The language of Job is Hebrew, interspersed occasionally with Syriac and Arabic expressions, implying a time when all the Shemitic tribes spoke one common tongue and had not branched into different dialects, Hebrew, Syriac, and Arabic. 5. He speaks of the most ancient kind of writing, viz., sculpture. Riches also are reckoned by cattle. The Hebrew word, translated a *piece of money*, ought rather to be rendered a *lamb*. 6. There is no allusion to the exodus from Egypt and to the miracles that accompanied it: nor to the destruction of Sodom and Gomorrah (*Patrick*, however, thinks there is.); though there is to the flood (ch. 22. 15,); and these events, happening in Job's vicinity, would have been striking illustrations of the argument for God's interposition in destroying the wicked and vindicating the righteous, had Job and his friends known of them. Nor is there any *undoubted* reference to the Jewish law, ritual, and priesthood. 7. The religion of Job is that which prevailed among the patriarchs previous to the law; sacrifices performed by the head of each family; no officiating priesthood, temple, or consecrated altar.

THE WRITER.—All the foregoing facts accord with Job himself having been the author. The style of thought, imagery, and manners, are such as we should look for in the work of an Arabian emir. There is precisely that degree of knowledge of primitive tradition (see ch. 31. 33, as to Adam) which was universally spread abroad in the days of Noah and Abraham, and which was subsequently embodied in the early chapters of Genesis. Job, in his speeches, shows that he was much more competent to compose the work than Elihu, to whom *Lightfoot* attributes it. The style forbids its being attributed to Moses, to whom its composition is by some attributed, "whilst he was among the Madianites, about B. C. 1520." But the fact, that it, though not a Jewish book, appears among the Hebrew sacred writings, makes it likely that it came to the knowledge of Moses during the forty years which he passed in parts of Arabia, chiefly near Horeb; and that he, by Divine guidance, introduced it as a sacred writing to the Israelites, to whom, in their affliction, the patience and restoration of Job were calculated to be a lesson of especial utility. That it is inspired appears from the fact that Paul (1 Cor. 3. 19) quotes it (Job, 5. 13,) with the formula, "It is written." Our Saviour, too (Mat. 24. 28,),

INTRODUCTION—JOB.

plainly refers to Job. 29 30. Cf. also Jam. 4, 10, and 1 Pet. 5. 6, with Job. 22. 29; Rom. 11. 34, 35 with Job, 15. 8. It is probably the oldest book in the world. It stands among the Hagiographa in the threefold division of Scripture into the Law, the Prophets, and the Hagiographa ("Psalms," Luke. 24. 44.).

DESIGN OF THE BOOK.—It is a public debate in poetic form on an important question concerning the Divine government; moreover the prologue and epilogue, which are in prose, shed the interest of a living history over the debate, which would otherwise be but a contest of abstract reasonings. To each speaker of the three friends three speeches are assigned. Job having no one to stand by him is allowed to reply to each speech of each of the three. Eliphaz, as the eldest, leads the way. Zophar, at his *third* turn, failed to speak, thus virtually owning himself overcome (ch. 27.); and therefore, Job continued his reply, which forms *three* speeches (ch. 26; 27, 28; 29-31.). Elihu (ch. 32-37.) is allowed *four* speeches. Jehovah makes *three* addresses (ch. 38-41.). Thus, throughout there is a tripartite division. The whole is divided into *three* parts:—the prologue, poem proper, and epilogue. The *poem*, into three:—1. The dispute of Job and his three friends; 2. The address of Elihu; 3. The address of God. There are *three* series in the controversy, and in the same order. The epilogue (ch. 42.,) also is threefold; Job's justification, reconciliation with his frien s, restoration. The speakers also in their successive speeches *regularly advance from less to greater vehemence*. With all this artificial composition, everything seems easy and natural.

The question to be solved, as exemplified in the case of Job, is, Why are the righteous afflicted consistently with God's justice? The doctrine of retribution after death, no doubt, is the great solution of the difficulty. And to it Job plainly refers in ch. 14. 14. and ch. 19. 25. The objection to this, that the explicitness of the language on the resurrection in Job is inconsistent with the obscurity on the subject in the early books of the O.T., is answered by the fact, that Job enjoyed the Divine vision (ch. 38. 1; 42. 5,). and therefore, *by inspiration*, foretold these truths. Next, the revelations made outside of Israel being few needed to be the more explicit; thus Balaam's prophecy (Num. 24. 17,), was clear enough to lead the wise men *of the East* by the star (Mat. 2.1; and in the age before the written law, it was the more needful for God not to leave himself without witness of the truth. Still Job evidently did not fully realise the significance designed by the Spirit in his own words (cf. 1 Pet. 1, 11, 12.). The doctrine, though existing, was not plain'y revealed, or at least understood. Hence he does not *mainly* refer to this solution. Yes, and *even now*, we need something *in addition* to this solution. David, who firmly believed in a future retribution (Ps. 16. 10; 17. 15,), still felt the difficulty not *entirely* solved thereby (Ps. 83.). The solution is not in Job's or in his three friends' speeches. It must, therefore, be in Elihu's. God will hold a final judgment, no doubt, to clear up all that seems dark in his present dealings; but He also *now* providentially and morally governs the world *and all the events of human life.* Even the comparatively righteous are not without sin which needs to be corrected. The justice and love of God administer the altogether deserved and merciful correction. Affliction to the godly is thus mercy and justice in disguise. The afflicted believer on repentance sees this. "*Via crucis, via salutis.*" Though afflicted, the godly are happier *even now* than the ungodly, and when affliction has attained its end, it is removed by the Lord. In the O.T., the consolations are more temporal and outward; in the N.T., more spiritual; but in neither to the entire exclusion of the other. "Prosperity," says Bacon, "is the blessing of the O.T.; adversity that of the N.T., which is the mark of God's more especial favour. Yet even in the O.T., if you listen to David's harp, you shall hear as many hearse-like airs as carols; and the pencil of the Holy Ghost has laboured more in describing the afflictions of Job than the felicities of Solomon. Prosperity is not without many fears and distastes; and adversity is not without comforts and hopes." This solution of Elihu is seconded by the addresses of God, in which it is shown God *must* be just (because He *is* God) as Elihu had shown *how* God can be just and yet the righteous be afflicted. It is also acquiesced in by Job, who makes no reply. God reprimands the three friends, but not Elihu. Job's general course is approved; he is directed to intercede for his friends; and is restored to double his former prosperity.

POETRY.—In all countries poetry is the earliest form of composition as being best retained in the memory, and in the East especially it was customary to preserve their sentiments in a terse, proverbial, and poetic form (called *maschal,*). Hebrew poetry is not constituted by the rhythm or metre, but in a form peculiar to itself:—1. In an alphabetical arrangement somewhat like our acrostic. For instance, Lam. 1. 2. The same verse repeated at intervals; as Ps. 42; 107. 3 Rhythm of gradation. *Psalms of degrees*, 120-134; in which the expression of the previous verse is resumed and carried forward in the next (Ps. 121.). 4. The chief characteristic of Hebrew poetry is *parallelism*, or the correspondence of the same ideas in the parallel clauses. The earliest instance is Enoch's prophecy (Jude, 14.), and Lamech's parody of it (Gen. 4. 23.). These kinds occur. (1.) The synonymous parallelism, in which the second is a repetition of the first, with or without increase of force (Ps. 22. 27; Isa. 15. 1,); sometimes with double parallelism (Isa. 1. 15.). (2.) The antithetic, in which the idea of the second clause is the converse of that in the first (Pro. 10. 1.). (3.) The synthetic, where there is a correspondence between different propositions, noun answering to noun, verb to verb, member to member, the sentiment, moreover, being not merely echoed, or put in contrast, but enforced by accessory ideas (Job. 3. 3-9.). Also *alternate* (Isa. 51. 19,), "Desolation and destruction famine and sword," *i.e.*, desolation by famine, and destruction by the sword. *Introverted*; where the fourth answers to the first, and the third to the second (Mat. 7. 6.). Parallelism thus often affords a key to the interpretation. For fuller information, see Lowth (Introduction to Isaiah, and Lecture on Hebrew Poetry) and Spirit of Hebrew Poetry by Herder, *transl.* by Marsh. The simpler and less artificial forms of parallelism prevail in Job—a mark of its early age.

THE
BOOK OF JOB.

GENERAL ANALYSIS OF THE BOOK.

Part I. The *historical introduction*, ch. i. ii. Part II. The *argument or controversy*, ch. iii.-xlii. 6. 1. The *first* series of the controversy. Job opens the discussion by cursing his day, and by a bitter complaint of his calamity, ch. iii. Speech of Eliphaz, iv. v. Answer of Job, vi. vii. Speech of Bildad, viii. Answer of Job, ix x. Speech of Zophar, xi. Answer of Job, x i.-xiv. 2. The *second* series in the controversy. Speech of Eliphaz, ch. xv. Answer of Job, x i. xvii. Speech of Bildad, xviii. Answer of Job, xix. Speech of Zophar, xx. Answer of Job, xxi. 3. The *third* series in the controversy. Speech of Eliphaz, ch xxii. Answer of Job, xxiii. xxiv. Speech of Bildad, xxv. Answer of Job, xxv.-xxxi. 4. Speech of Elihu, ch. xxxii.-xxxvii. 5. The close of the discussion. The address of *the Almighty*, ch. xxxviii.-xli. The response and penitential confession of Job, ch. xlii. 1-6. III. The *conclusion*, chap. xlii. 7-17.

CHAPTER I.

1 *The holiness of Job; his wealth; his religious care for his children;* 6 *Satan, appearing before God, falsely accuses Job, and obtains leave to tempt him.* 13 *Job in affliction blesses God.*

B. C. 1520.

CHAP. 1.
a Gen. 22. 20.
b Exo. 14. 14.
Jam. 5. 11.
c Gen. 6. 9.
Gen. 17. 1.
ch. 2. 3.
d Pro. 8. 13.
Pro. 16. 6.
1 Or, cattle.
2 Or, husbandry.
3 sons of the east.
Gen. 25. 6.
e Gen. 8. 20.
ch. 42. 8.
f 2 Cor. 11. 2.
g 1 Kin. 21. 10, 13.
4 all the days.
h ch. 2. 1.
i 1 Kin. 22.
19.
ch. 38. 7.
Dan. 7. 10.
5 the adversary.
1 Chr. 21. 1.
Rev. 12. 9.
6 in the midst of them.
j Mat. 12. 43.
1 Pet. 5. 8.
7 Hast thou set thy heart on.
h Ps. 34. 7.
Isa. 5. 2.
i Ps. 128. 1.
Pro. 10. 22.
8 Or, cattle.
9 *if he curse thee not to thy face.*
10 hand.
Gen. 16. 6.
m Ecc. 9. 13.
n Gen. 10. 7.
11 Or, a great fire.
12 rushed.
13 from aside, etc.
14 Or, *a coat.*
o 1 Pet. 5. 6.
p Jam. 1. 21.
q Mat. 20, 15.
r Eph. 5. 20.
15 Or, attributed folly to God.

THERE was a man ^{a} in the land of Uz, whose name was ^{b} Job; and that man was ^{c} perfect and upright, and one that feared ^{d} God, and eschewed evil.

2 And there were born unto him seven sons and three daughters.

3 His ^{1} substance also was seven thousand sheep, and three thousand camels, and five hundred yoke of oxen, and five hundred she-asses, and a very great ^{2} household; so that this man was the greatest of all the ^{3} men of the east.

4 And his sons went and feasted *in their* houses, every one his day; and sent and called for their three sisters, to eat and to drink with them.

5 And it was so, when the days of *their* feasting were gone about, that Job sent and sanctified them, and rose up early in the morning, ^{e} and offered burnt offerings *according to* the number of them all: for Job said, ^{f} It may be that my sons have sinned, and ^{g} cursed God in their hearts. Thus did Job ^{4} continually.

6 ¶ Now ^{h} there was a day ^{i} when the sons of God came to present themselves before the LORD, and ^{5} Satan came also ^{6} among them.

7 And the LORD said unto Satan, Whence comest thou? Then Satan answered the LORD, and said, From ^{j} going to and fro in the earth, and from walking up and down in it.

8 And the LORD said unto Satan, ^{7} Hast thou considered my servant Job, that *there is* none like him in the earth, a perfect and an upright man, one that feareth God, and escheweth evil?

9 Then Satan answered the LORD, and said, Doth Job fear God for nought?

10 ^{h} Hast ^{k} not thou made an hedge about him, and about his house, and about all that he hath on every side? ^{i} Thou hast blessed the work of his hands, and his ^{8} substance is increased in the land:

11 But put forth thine hand now, and touch all that he hath, ^{9} and he will curse thee to thy face.

12 And the LORD said unto Satan, Behold, all that he hath *is* in thy ^{10} power; only upon himself put not forth thine hand. So Satan went forth from the presence of the LORD.

13 ¶ And there was a day ^{m} when his sons and his daughters *were* eating and drinking wine in their eldest brother's house:

14 And there came a messenger unto Job, and said, The oxen were plowing, and the asses feeding beside them;

15 And the ^{n} Sabeans fell *upon them*, and took them away; yea, they have slain the servants with the edge of the sword; and I only am escaped alone to tell thee.

16 While he *was* yet speaking, there came also another, and said, ^{11} The fire of God is fallen from heaven, and hath burnt up the sheep, and the servants, and consumed them; and I only am escaped alone to tell thee.

17 While he *was* yet speaking, there came also another, and said, The Chaldeans made out three bands, and ^{12} fell upon the camels, and have carried them away, yea, and slain the servants with the edge of the sword; and I only am escaped alone to tell thee.

18 While he *was* yet speaking, there came also another, and said, Thy sons and thy daughters *were* eating and drinking wine in their eldest brother's house:

19 And, behold, there came a great wind ^{13} from the wilderness, and smote the four corners of the house, and it fell upon the young men, and they are dead; and I only am escaped alone to tell thee.

20 Then Job arose, and rent his ^{14} mantle, and shaved his head, and ^{o} fell down upon the ground, and worshipped,

21 And said, Naked came I out of my mother's womb, and naked shall I return thither: the LORD ^{p} gave, and the LORD hath ^{q} taken away; ^{r} blessed be the name of the LORD.

22 In all this Job sinned not, nor ^{15} charged God foolishly.

CHAPTER II.

1 *Satan, appearing again before God, obtains further leave to tempt Job;* 7 *he smites him with sore boils.* 9 *Job reproves his wife.*

AGAIN there was a day when the sons of God came to present themselves before the LORD, and Satan came also among them, to present himself before the LORD.

2 And the LORD said unto Satan, From whence comest thou? And Satan answered the LORD, and said, From going to and fro in the earth, and from walking up and down in it.

3 And the LORD said unto Satan, Hast thou considered my servant Job, that *there is* none like him in the earth, a perfect and

THE
BOOK OF JOB.

CHAPTER I.

PART I.—PROLOGUE OR HISTORICAL INTRODUCTION IN PROSE—CHAPTERS I., II.

Ver. 1-5. THE HOLINESS OF JOB, HIS WEALTH, &c. 1. Uz—N. of Arabia Deserta, lying towards the Euphrates; it was in this neighbourhood, and not in that of Idumea, that the Chaldeans and Sabeans who plundered him dwelt. The Arabs divide their country into the N. called *Sham*, or "the left;" and the S. called Yemen, or "the right;" for they faced E. and so the W. was on their left, and the S. on their right. Arabia Deserta was on the E., Arabia Petræa on the W., and Arabia Felix on the S. Job—The name comes from an Arabic word meaning *to return*, viz., to God, *to repent*, referring to his end: [ETCH.] or rather from a Heb. word signifying one to whom *enmity* was shown, *greatly tried*. [GES.] Significant names were often given among the Hebrews, from some event of the after life (cf. Isa. 8. 18; Gen. 4. 2). Abel—*a feeder* of sheep. So the emir of Uz was by general consent called *Job*, on account of his *trials*. The only other person so called was a son of Issachar (Gen. 46. 13.). perfect—Not absolute or faultless perfection (cf. 9. 20; Eccl. 7. 20.), but *integrity, sincerity*, and *consistency* on the whole, in all relations of life (Gen. 6. 9; 17. 1; Prov. 10. 9; Matth. 5. 48.). It was the *fear of God* that kept Job from evil (Prov. 8. 13. . 3. she asses—Prized on account of their milk, and for riding Judg. 5. 10.). Houses and lands are not mentioned among the emir's wealth, as nomadic tribes dwell in moveable tents, and live chiefly by pasture, the right to the soil not being appropriated by individuals. The "five hundred yoke of oxen" imply, however, that Job tilled the soil. He seems also to have had a dwelling in a town, in which respect he differed from the patriarchs. Camels are well called *ships of the desert*, especially valuable for caravans, as being able to lay in a store of water that suffices them for days, and sustaining life on a very few thistles or thorns. household—(Gen. 26. 14.). The other rendering, which the Heb. admits, *husbandry*, is not so probable. men of the east—Denoting in Scripture those living east of Palestine; as the people of North Arabia Deserta (Judg. 6. 3; Ez. 25. 4.). his day—viz., the birth-day (ch. 3. 1.). Implying the love and harmony of the members of the family, as contrasted with the ruin which soon broke up such a scene of happiness. The *sisters* are specified, as these feasts were not for revelry, which would be inconsistent with the presence of sisters. These latter were invited by the brothers, though they gave no invitations in return. 5. when the days of feasting were gone about—*i.e.*, at the end of all the birth-days collectively, when the banquets had gone round through all the families. Job sanctified them —By offering up as many expiatory burnt-offerings as he had sons (Lev. 1. 4.). This was done *in the morning* (Gen. 22. 3: Lev. 6. 12.). So Jesus began devotions early (Mk. 1. 35.). The holocaust, or burnt-offering, in patriarchal times, was offered (*lit., caused to*

ascend, referring to the smoke ascending to heaven,) by each father of a family officiating as priest in behalf of his household. cursed God—The same Hebrew word means to curse, and to bless; GES. says, the original sense is to *kneel*, and thus it came to mean bending the knee in order to *invoke* either a blessing, or a curse. Cursing is a perversion of blessing, as all sin is of goodness. Sin is a degeneracy, not a generation. It is not, however, likely that Job should fear the possibility of his sons *cursing* God. The sense *bid farewell to*, derived from the *blessing* customary at parting, seems sufficient (Gen. 47. 10.). Thus UMBR. translates "may have dismissed God from their hearts;" viz. amidst the intoxication of pleasure (Prov. 20. 1.). This act illustrates Job's "fear of God." v. 1.

6-12. SATAN, APPEARING BEFORE GOD, FALSELY ACCUSES JOB. 6. sons of God—Angels (ch. 38. 7; 1 Ki. 22. 19,). They present themselves to render account of their "ministry" in other parts of the universe Heb. 1. 14). the Lord—*Heb.*, JEHOVAH—the self-existing God, faithful to His promises. God says (Ex. 6. 3, that He was not known to the patriarchs by this name. But, as the *name* occurs previously in Gen. 2. 7-9, &c., what must be meant is, not until the time of delivering Israel by Moses was He known peculiarly and publicly in the *character* which the name means, viz., *making things to be*, fulfilling the promises made to their forefathers. This name, therefore, here, is no objection against the antiquity of the book of Job. The tradition was widely spread that *he* had been the agent in Adam's temptation. Hence his name is given without comment. The feeling with which he looks on Job is similar to that with which he looked on Adam in Paradise: emboldened by his success in the case of one not yet fallen, he is confident that the piety of Job, one of a fallen race, will not stand the test. He had fallen himself (ch. 4. 19; 15. 15; Jude. 6.). In the book of Job first Satan is designated by *name*: Satan, in *Heb.*, one who lies in wait; an *Adversary* in a court of justice (1 Chron. 21. 1; Ps. 109, 6; Zech. 3. 1.). The *accuser* (Rev. 12. 10.). He has got the law of God on his side by man's sin, and against man. But Jesus Christ has fulfilled the law for us; justice is once more on man's side against Satan (Isa. 42. 21,); and so Jesus Christ can plead as our *Advocate* against the *adversary* (Rom. 8. 33.). Devil is the Greek name—the *slanderer*, or *accuser*. He is subject to God, who uses his ministry for chastising man. In Arabic *Satan* is often applied to a *serpent* (Gen. 3. 1.). He is called Prince of this world (John, 12, 31,); the God of this world (2 Cor. 4. 4.); Prince of the power of the air (Eph. 2. 2.). God here questions him, in order to vindicate His own ways before angels. 7. going to and fro—Rather, hurrying rapidly *to and fro*. The original idea in Arabic is the *heat* of haste (1 Pet. 5. 8; Matth. 12. 43.). Satan seems to have had some peculiar connexion with this earth. Perhaps he was formerly its ruler under an upright man, one that feareth God, and escheweth evil? and still he *holdeth fast his integrity, although thou movedst me against him, ¹to destroy him ᵇ without cause.

4 And Satan answered the LORD, and said, Skin for skin, yea, all that a man hath will he give for his life:

5 But put forth thine hand now, and touch his ᶜ bone and his flesh, and he will curse thee to thy face.

6 And the LORD said unto Satan, Behold, he is in thine hand; ᵍ but save his life.

7 ¶ So went Satan forth from the presence of the LORD, and smote Job with sore boils from the sole of his foot unto his crown.

8 And he took him a potsherd to scrape himself withal; ᵈ and he sat down among the ashes.

9 ¶ Then said ᵉ his wife unto him, ᶠ Dost thou still retain thine integrity? curse God, and die.

10 But he said unto her, Thou speakest as one of the foolish women speaketh. What! shall ᵍ we receive good at the hand of God, and shall we not receive evil? In all this did not Job ʰ sin with his lips.

11 ¶ Now when Job's three friends heard of all this evil that was come upon him, they came every one from his own place; Eliphaz the ⁱ Temanite, and Bildad ʲ the Shuhite, and Zophar the Naamathite: for they had made an appointment together to come ᵏ to mourn with him and to comfort him.

12 And when they lifted up their eyes afar off, and knew him not, they lifted up their voice, and wept; and they rent every one his mantle, and ˡ sprinkled dust upon their heads toward heaven.

13 So they sat down with him upon the ground ᵐ seven days and seven nights, and none spake a word unto him: for they saw that his grief was very great.

CHAPTER III.

1 *Job curses the day of his birth.* 13 *and wishes for the ease of death:* 20 *he complains of life because of his anguish.*

AFTER this opened Job his mouth, and cursed his day.

2 And Job ¹ spake, and said,

3 Let ᵃ the day perish wherein I was born, and the night *in which* it was said, There is a man child conceived.

4 Let that day be darkness; let not God regard it from above, neither let the light shine upon it.

5 Let darkness and ᵇ the shadow of death ² stain it; let a cloud dwell upon it; ³ let the blackness of the day terrify it.

6 *As for* that night, let darkness seize upon it; ⁴ let it not be joined unto the days of the year; let it not come into the number of the months.

7 Lo, let that night be solitary; let no joyful voice come therein.

8 Let them curse it that curse the day, who ᶜ are ready to raise up ⁵ their mourning.

9 Let the stars of the twilight thereof be dark; let it look for light, but *have* none; neither let it see ⁶ the dawning of the day:

10 Because it shut not up the doors of my *mother's* womb, nor hid sorrow from mine eyes.

11 Why died I not from the womb? *why*

B. C. 1520.

CHAP. 2.
ᵃ ch. 27. 5. 6.
1 to swallow him up.
ᵇ Gen. 22. 1.
Mat. 7. 11.
John 9. 2.
Heb. 2. 14.
Heb. 12. 5-11.
ᶜ ch. 19. 20.
2 Or, only.
ᵈ Ezek. 27. 30.
ᵉ Gen. 3. 6.
ᶠ ch. 21. 15.
ᵍ Rom. 12. 12.
Jam. 5. 10.
ʰ Ps. 39. 1.
Jam. 1. 12.
ⁱ Gen. 36. 11.
Jer. 49. 7.
ʲ Gen. 25. 2.
ᵏ Rom. 12. 15.
ˡ Neh. 9. 1.
Lam. 2. 10.
Eze. 27. 30.
ᵐ Gen. 50. 10.

CHAP. 3.
1 answered.
ᵃ Jer. 20. 14.
ᵇ Ps. 44. 19.
Amos 5. 8.
2 Or, challenge it.
3 Or, let them terrify it, as those who have a bitter day.
4 Or, let it not rejoice among the days.
ᶜ Jer. 9. 17.
5 Or, a leviathan.
6 the eyelids of the morning.
7 wearied in strength.
ᵈ Jer. 20. 18.
ᵉ wait.
ᶠ Prov. 2. 4.
ᵍ Lam. 3. 7.
9 before my meat.
10 I feared it came upon me.

CHAP. 4.
1 a word.
2 who can refrain from words?
3 the bowing knee.
ᵃ Luke 4. 23.
ᵇ ch. 1. 1.
ᶜ Prov. 3. 3.
ᵈ Ps. 7. 14.
Pro. 22. 6.
4 That is, by his anger.
Is. 30. 33.
2 Thes. 2. 8.
ᵉ Ps. 58. 6.
ᶠ Ps. 34. 10.
5 by stealth.
ᵍ ch. 33. 15.

did I *not* give up the ghost when I came out of the belly?

12 Why did the knees prevent me? or why the breasts that I should suck?

13 For now should I have lain still and been quiet, I should have slept: then had I been at rest

14 With kings and counsellors of the earth, which built desolate places for themselves;

15 Or with princes that had gold, who filled their houses with silver:

16 Or as an hidden untimely birth I had not been; as infants *which* never saw light.

17 There the wicked cease *from* troubling and there the ⁷ weary be at rest.

18 *There* the prisoners rest together; they hear not the voice of the oppressor.

19 The small and great are there; and the servant *is* free from his master.

20 Wherefore ᵈ is light given to him that is in misery, and life unto the bitter *in* soul;

21 Which ⁸ long for death, but it *cometh* not; and dig for it more than ᵉ for hid treasures;

22 Which rejoice exceedingly, *and are* glad, when they can find the grave?

23 *Why is light given* to a man whose way is hid, ᶠ and whom God hath hedged in?

24 For my sighing cometh ⁹ before I eat, and my roarings are poured out like the waters.

25 For ¹⁰ the thing which I greatly feared is come upon me, and that which I was afraid of is come unto me.

26 I was not in safety, neither had I rest, neither was I quiet; yet trouble came.

CHAPTER IV.

1 *Eliphaz reproves Job for want of religion:* 7 *he shews that God's judgments are not for the righteous, but for the wicked:* 12 *his fearful vision, designed to humble the vain opinion of man's excellency in the sight of his Maker.*

THEN Eliphaz the Temanite answered and said,

2 *If* we assay ¹ to commune with thee, wilt thou be grieved? but ² who can withhold himself from speaking?

3 Behold, thou hast instructed many, and thou hast strengthened the weak hands.

4 Thy words have upholden him that was falling, and thou hast strengthened ³ the feeble knees.

5 But now it is come upon thee, and thou ᵃ faintest; it toucheth thee, and thou art troubled.

6 *Is* not this ᵇ thy fear, ᶜ thy confidence, thy hope, and the uprightness of thy ways?

7 Remember, I pray thee, who *ever* perished, being innocent? or where were the righteous cut off?

8 Even as I have seen, ᵈ they that plow iniquity, and sow wickedness, reap the same.

9 By the blast of God they perish, and ⁴ by the breath of his nostrils are they consumed.

10 The roaring of the lion, and the voice of the fierce lion, and ᵉ the teeth of the young lions, are broken.

11 The ᶠ old lion perisheth for lack of prey, and the stout lion's whelps are scattered abroad.

12 Now a thing was ⁵ secretly brought to me, and mine ear received a little thereof.

13 In ᵍ thoughts from the visions of the night, when deep sleep falleth on men,

God. Man succeeded to the vice-royalty (Gen. 1. 26; Ps. 8. 6.). Man lost it, and Satan became Prince of this world. The Son of man (Ps. 8. 4,)—the representative man, regains the forfeited inheritance (Rev. 11. 15.). Satan's replies are characteristically curt and short. When the angels appear before God, Satan is among them, even as there was a Judas among the apostles. 8. considered—*Marg., set thine heart on; i.e.,* considered *attentively*. No true servant of God escapes the eye of the Adversary of God. 9. fear God for nought—It is a mark of the children of Satan to sneer and not give credit to any for disinterested piety. Not so much God's gifts, as God Himself is "the reward" of His people (Gen. 15. 1.). 10. his substance is increased—*Lit., spread out like a flood:* Job's herds covered the face of the country. 11. curse thee to thy face—In antithesis to God's praise of him *v.* 8,), "one that feareth God." Satan's words are too true of many. Take away their prosperity and you take away their religion (Mal. 3. 14.). 12. in thy power—Satan has no power against man till God gives it. God would not touch Job with His own hand, though Satan asks this (*v.* 11, thine), but *allows* the enemy to do so.

13-22. JOB, IN AFFLICTION, BLESSES GOD, &c. 13. wine—Not specified in verse 4. The mirth inspired by the *wine* here contrasts the more sadly with the alarm which interrupted it. 14. the asses feeding beside them—*Heb., she-asses.* A graphic picture of rural repose and peace; the more dreadful, therefore, by contrast is the sudden attack of the plundering Arabs. 15. Sabeans—Not those of Arabia Felix, but those of Arabia Deserta, descending from Sheba, grandson of Abraham and Keturah (Gen. 25. 3.). The Bedouin Arabs of the present day resemble, in marauding habits, these Sabeans (cf. Gen. 16. 12.). I alone am escaped—Cunningly contrived by Satan. One in each case escapes (*v.* 16, 17, 19.), and brings the same kind of message. This was to *overwhelm* Job, and leave him no time to recover from the rapid succession of calamities—"misfortunes seldom come single." 16. fire of God—Hebraism for *a mighty fire;* as *cedars of God—lofty cedars.* Not *lightning*, which would not consume *all* the sheep and servants. UMBR. understands it of *the burning wind* of Arabia, called by the Turks "wind of poison." The prince of the power of the air" is permitted to have control over such destructive agents. 17. Chaldeans — Not merely robbers as the Sabeans; but experienced in war, as is implied by "they *set in array* three bands," (Hab. 1. 6-8.). RAWL. distinguishes three periods: '1. When their seat of empire was in the S., towards the confluence of the Tigris and Euphrates. The Chaldean period, from 2300 B.C., to 1500 B.C. In this period was Chedorlaomer (Gen. 14.), the Kudur of Hur or Ur of the Chaldees, in the Assyrian inscriptions, and the conqueror of Syria. 2. From 1500 to 625 B.C., the Assyrian period. 3. From 625 to 538 B.C. (when Cyrus the Persian took Babylon,), the Babylonian period. Chaldees in Heb.—*Chasdim.* They were akin, perhaps, to the Hebrews, as Abraham's sojourn in Ur, and the name Ches*e*d, a nephew of Abraham, imply. The *three* bands were probably in order to attack the three separate thousands of Job's camels (*v.* 3.). 19. wind from the wilderness—S. of Job's house. The tornado came the more violently over the desert as being uninterrupted (Isa. 21. 1; Hos. 13. 15.). the young men — Rather, *the young people;* including the daughters (so in Ruth 2. 21.). 20. Job arose—Not necessarily *from sitting.* Inward *excitement* is implied, and the *beginning* to do anything. He had heard the other messages calmly, but on hearing of the death of his children, *then* he arose; or, as [EICH.] translates, he *started up* 2 Sam. 13. 31.). The rending of the mantle was the conventional mark of deep grief (Gen. 37. 34.). Job herein wear a tunic or shirt, and loose pantaloons: and over these a flowing mantle (especially great persons and women,). Shaving the head was also usual in grief (Jer. 41. 5; Mic. 1. 16.). 21. naked—(1 Tim. 6. 7.). "Mother's womb" is poetically the earth, the universal mother (Ec. 5. 15; 12. 7; Ps. 139. 15.). Job herein realizes God's assertion (*v.* 8,) against Satan's (*v.* 11.). Instead of *cursing*, he *blesses* the name of JEHOVAH (the Heb.). The *name* of Jehovah, is Jehovah *himself*, as manifested to us in His attributes (Isa. 9. 6.). 22. nor charged God foolishly—Rather, *allowed himself to commit no folly against God.* [UMBR.] Ch. 2. 10 proves that this is the meaning. Not as marg. *attributed no folly to God.* Hasty words against God, though natural in the bitterness of grief, are *folly;* lit., an *insipid, unsavoury* thing (ch. 6. 6; Jer. 23. 13, margin.). *Folly* in Scripture is continually equivalent to *wickedness*. For when man sins, it is himself, not God, whom he injures (Prov. 8. 36.). We are to submit to trials, not because we see the *reasons* for them, nor yet as though they were matters of *chance,* but because *God wills* them, and has *a right* to send them, and has *His own* good reasons in sending them.

CHAPTER II.

Ver. 1-9. SATAN FURTHER TEMPTS JOB. 1. a day—Appointed for the angels giving an account of their ministry to God. The words *to present himself before the Lord* occur here, though not in 1. 6, as Satan has now a special report to make as to Job. 3. integrity—*lit., completeness;* so "perfect," another form of the same *Heb.* word, ch. 1. 1. movedst . . . against—So 1 Sam. 26. 19; cf. 1 Chr. 21. 1, with 2 Sam. 24. 1. 4. Skin for skin —A proverb. Supply, *He will give. The skin* is figurative for *any outward good.* Nothing outward is so dear that a man will not exchange it for some other outward good; *but* not *yea) life*, the inward good, cannot be replaced, a man will sacrifice every thing else for its sake. Satan sneers bitterly at man's egotism, and says, Job bears the loss of property and children, because these are mere *outward and exchangeable* goods, but he will give up all things, even his religion, in order to save his life, if you touch his bones and flesh. Skin and *life* are in antithesis. [UMBR.] The martyrs prove Satan's sneer false. Ros. explains it not so well, A man willingly gives up *another's* skin (life) for *his own* skin (life.). So Job might bear the loss of his children, &c., with equanimity so long as he remained unhurt himself; but, when touched in his own person, he would renounce God. Thus the first "skin" means the *other's* skin, *i.e.,* body; the second "skin," *one's own,* as in Ex. 21. 23. 6. but save—Rather, *only spare.* Satan shows his ingenuity in inflicting pain, and also his knowledge of what man's body can bear without vital injury. **7.** sore boils — Malignant boils. Rather, as it is singular in the *Heb.*, *a burning sore*. Job was covered with one universal inflammation. The use of the potsherd agrees with this view. It was that form of leprosy called *black* to distinguish it from the *white* or *Elephantiasis*, because the feet swell like those of the elephant. The Arabic *judham* (Deu. 28. 35,), where *sore botch* is rather the *black burning boil* (Isa. 1. 6.). **8.** a p:sherd—Not a piece of a broken earthen vessel, but an instrument made for scratching, the root of the *Heb.* word is *scratch*; the sore was too disgusting to touch. "To sit in the ashes" marks the deepest mourning (Jonah 3. 6,); also humility, as if the mourner were nothing but *dust and ashes*; so Abraham (Gen. 18. 27.).

9-13. JOB REPROVES HIS WIFE. **9.** curse God — Rather *renounce* God. Note, 1. 5. [UMBR.] However, it was usual among the heathens, when disappointed in their prayers accompanied with offerings to their gods, to reproach and *curse* them. and die—*i.e.,* take thy farewell of God and so die. For no good is to be got out of religion, either here or hereafter; or, at least, not in this life. [GILL.] Nothing makes the ungodly so angry, as to see the godly under trial not angry. **10.** the foolish women—*Sin* and *folly* are allied in Scripture (1 Sam. 25. 25; 2 Sam. 13. 13; Ps. 14. 1.). receive evil—Bear willingly (Lam. 3. 39.). **11.** Eliphaz—The view of RAWL. that "the names of Job's three friends represent the Chaldean times, about 700 B.C.," cannot be accepted. Eliphaz is an Idumean name, Esau's eldest son (Gen. 36. 4,); and Teman, son of Eliphaz, 15,' called "duke." EUSEB. places Teman in Arabia Petræa (but see Note 6, 19.). *Teman* means *at the right hand;* and then the S., viz., part of Idumea, capital of Edom (Amos, 1. 12.). Hebrew geographers faced the E., not the N. as we do; hence with them *the right hand* was the S. Temanites were famed for wisdom (Jer. 49. 7.). BARUCH mentions them as "authors of fables (viz., proverbs embodying the results of observation,), and searchers out of understanding." Bildad the Shuhite—Shuah (a pit) Son of Abraham and Keturah (Gen. 25. 2.). PTOL. mentions the region Syccea, in Arabia Deserta, E. of Batanea. Zophar the Naamathite—Not of the Naamans in Judah (Josh. 15. 41,), which was too distant; but some region in Arabia Deserta. FRETELIUS says there was a Naamath in Uz. **12.** toward heaven—They threw violently ashes upwards, that they might fall on their heads and cover them. The deepest mourning (Josh. 7. 6; Acts 22. 23.). **13.** seven days ... nights—They did not remain in the one posture and without food, &c., all this time, but for the most of this period daily and nightly. Sitting on the earth marked mourning (Lam. 2. 10.). Seven days was the usual length of it (Gen. 50. 10; 1 Sam. 31. 13.). This silence may have been due to a rising suspicion of evil in Job; but chiefly because it is only ordinary griefs that find vent in language; extraordinary griefs are too great for utterance.

CHAPTER III.

THE POEM OR DEBATE ITSELF, 2-42. 6; FIRST SERIES IN IT, 3-14.; JOB FIRST 3.

Ver. 1-19. JOB CURSES THE DAY OF HIS BIRTH, AND WISHES FOR DEATH. **1.** opened his mouth—The Orientals speak seldom, and then sententiously. Hence this formula expressing deliberation and gravity (Ps. 78. 2.). *Formally began.* cursed his day—The strict *Heb.* word for *cursing;* not the same as in ch. 1, 5. Job cursed his birth-day, but not his God. **2.** spake—*Heb,* an:wered, *i.e.,* not to any actual question that preceded, but to the question virtually involved in the case. His outburst is singularly wild and bold (Jer. 20. 14.). To desire to die so as to be free from sin is a mark of grace; to desire to die so as to escape troubles is a mark of corruption. He was ill fitted to die, who was so unwilling to live. But his trials were greater, and his light less, than ours. **3.** the night in which—Rather "the night which said." The words in Italics are not in the *Heb.* Night is personified and poetically made to speak. So in v. 7, and Ps. 19. 2. The birth of a male in the East is a matter of joy; often not so, of a female. **4.** let not God regard it—Rather, more poetically, *Seek it out.* "Let not God stoop from his bright throne to raise it up from its dark hiding-place." The curse on *the day* in v. 3, is amplified in v. 4, 5; that on *the night,* in v. 6-10. **5.** let the shadow of death—(deepest darkness, Isa. 9. 2,) stain it—This is a later sense of the verb, [GES,] better the old and more poetic idea, "Let darkness the ancient night of chaotic gloom resume its rights over light (Gen. 1. 2,), and *claim* that day as its own." a cloud —Collectively, *a gathered mass of dark clouds.* the blackness of the day terrify it — *lit., the obscurations;* whatever darkens the day. [GES.] Th verb in *Heb.* expresses *sudden terrifying.* May it be suddenly affrighted at its own darkness. UMBR. explains it of *magical incantations that darken the day,* forming the climax to the previous clauses; v. 8, speaks of *cursers of the day* similarly. But the former view is simpler. Others refer it to the poisonous Simoom wind. **6.** seize upon it—As its prey; *i.e.,* utterly dissolve it. joined unto the days of the year—Rather, by poetic personification, "Let it not *rejoice* in the circle of days and nights, and mouths, which form the circle of years." **7.** solitary —Rather, *unfruitful.* "Would that it had not *given birth* to me." **8.** them ... that curse the day—If *mourning* be the right rendering in the latter clause of this verse, these words refer to the hired mourners of the dead (Jer. 9. 17.). But the *Heb.* for *mourning* elsewhere, always denotes *an animal,* whether it be the *crocodile* or some huge *serpent* (Isa. 27. 1,) that is meant by *leviathan.* Therefore, the expression, *cursers of day,* refers to magicians who were believed to be able by charms to make a day one of evil omen. So Balaam, Num. 22. 5. This accords with UMBREIT'S view v. 7,); or, to the Ethiopians and Atlantes who "used to curse the sun at his rising for burning up them and their country." [HEROD.] Necromancers claimed power to control or rouse wild beasts at will; as the Indian serpent-charmers at this day (Ps. 58. 5.). Job does not say they had the power they claimed, but, supposing they had, may they curse the day. SCH. renders it by supplying words (? Let those that are ready *for anything,* call it the day) the raiser up of leviathan, *i.e., of a host of evils.* **9.** dawning of the day—*lit., eyelashes o.' morning.* The Arab poets call the sun the *eye of day.* His early rays, therefore, breaking forth before sunrise, are the opening *eye-*

lids or *eyelashes* of morning. 12. Why did the knees prevent me?—Old English for *anticipate* my wants. The reference is to the solemn recognition of a new-born child by the father, who used to place it on his knees as his own, whom he was bound to rear (Gen. 30. 3; 50. 23; Isa. 66. 12.). 13. lain . . . quiet . . . slept —A gradation. I should not only have *lain*, but been *quiet*, and not only *been quiet* but *slept. Death* in Scripture is called *sleep* (Ps. 13. 3.); especially in the New Testament, where the Resurrection-awaking is more clearly set forth (1 Cor. 15. 51; 1 Thess. 4. 14; 5. 10.). 14. With kings . . . which built desolate places for themselves—Who built up for themselves what proved to be (not *palaces*, but) *ruins!* The wounded spirit of Job, once a great emir himself, sick of the vain struggles of mortal great men after grandeur, contemplates the *palaces* of kings, now *desolate heaps of ruins*. His regarding the repose of death the most desirable end of the great ones of the earth, wearied with heaping up perishable treasures, marks the irony that breaks out from the black clouds of melancholy. [UMBR.] The *for themselves* marks their *selfishness*. MICH. explains it weakly of *mausoleums*, such as are found still, of stupendous proportions, in the ruins of Petra of Idumæa. 15. filled their houses with silver—Some take this of the treasures which the ancients used to bury with their dead. But see last verse. 16. untimely birth—(Ps. 58. 8.). Preferable to the life of the restless miser (Eccles. 6. 3-5.). 17. the wicked—The original meaning, *those ever restless, full of desires* (Isa. 57. 20, 21.). weary—lit., *those whose strength is wearied out* (Rev. 14. 13.). 18. There the prisoners rest—From their chains. 19. servant—The *slave* is there manumitted from slavery.

20-26. HE COMPLAINS OF LIFE BECAUSE OF HIS ANGUISH. 20. Wherefore giveth He light—*viz.*, God. Often omitted reverentially (ch. 24. 23; Eccles. 9. 9.). Light, *i.e.* life. The joyful light ill suits the mourner. The grave is most in unison with their feelings. 23. whose way is hid—The picture of Job is drawn from a wanderer who has *lost his way*, and who is hedged in, so as to have no exit of escape (Hos. 2. 6; Lam. 3. 7, 9.). 24. my sighing cometh before I eat—*i.e.*, prevents my eating. [UMBR.] Or, conscious that the effort to eat brought on the disease, Job must sigh before eating. [ROS.] Or, sighing takes the place of good (Ps. 42. 3.). [GOOD.] But the first explanation accords best with the text. my roaring is poured out like the waters—An image from the rushing sound of water streaming. 25. the thing which I . . . feared is come upon me —In the beginning of his trials, when he heard of the loss of one blessing, he feared the loss of another, and when he heard of the loss of that, he feared the loss of a third. that which I was afraid of is come unto me— *viz.*, the ill-opinion of his friends, as though he were a hypocrite on account of his trials. 26. I was not in safety, . . . yet trouble came—Referring, not to his former state, but to the *beginning* of his troubles. From that time *I had no rest* there was no intermission of sorrows. And (not, *yet*) a fresh trouble is coming, *viz.*, my friends' suspicion of my being a hypocrite. This gives the starting point to the whole ensuing controversy.

CHAPTER IV.

Ver. 1-21. FIRST SPEECH OF ELIPHAZ. Eliphaz—The mildest of Job's three accusers. The greatness of Job's calamities, and his complaints against God, and the opinion that calamities are proofs of guilt, led the three to doubt Job's integrity. 2. If we essay to commune—Rather, two questions, "May we attempt a word with thee? Wilt thou be grieved at it?" Even pious friends often count that only a touch which we feel as a wound. 3. weak hands—Isa. 35. 3; 2 Sam. 4. 1. 5. thou art troubled—Rather, *unhinged*, hast lost thy self-command (1 Thess. 3, 3.). 6. Is not this thy fear, thy confidence, &c.—Does thy fear, thy confidence, &c., come to nothing? Does it come only to this, that thou faintest now? Rather, by transposition, "Is not thy fear (of God) thy hope? and the uprightness of thy ways, thy confidence? If so, bethink thee, who ever perished being innocent?" [UMB.] But Luke 13. 2,3, shows that, though there *is* a retributive divine government even in this life, yet *we* cannot judge by the mere outward *appearance*. "One event is outwardly to the righteous and to the wicked" (Eccl. 9. 2.); but yet we must *take it on trust*, that God deals righteously *even now* (Ps. 37. 25; Isa. 33. 16.). Judge not by *a part*, but by *the whole* of a godly man's life, and by *his end*, even here (James 5. 11.). The one and the same outward event is altogether a different thing in its inward bearings on the godly and on the ungodly even here. Even prosperity, much more calamity, is a *punishment* to the wicked Prov. 1. 32.). Trials are *chastisements* for their good (to the righteous.) (Ps. 119.; 67.; 71.; 75.). See Preface on the *Design* of this Book. 8. they that plow iniquity, . . . reap the same—(Prov. 22. 8; Hos. 8. 7; 10. 13; Gal. 6. 7, 8.). 9. breath of his nostrils—God's anger. A figure from the fiery winds of the East (ch. 1. 16; Isa. 5. 25; Ps. 18. 8, 15.). 10. lion—*i.e.*, Wicked men, upon whom Eliphaz wished to show that calamities come in spite of their various resources, just as destruction comes on the lion in spite of his strength (Ps. 58. 6; 2 Tim. 4. 17.). Five *different* Heb. terms here occur for *lion*. The raging of *the lion (the tearer,)*, and the roaring of *the bellowing lion*, and the teeth of *the young lions*, not *whelps*, but grown up enough to hunt for prey. The *strong* lion (E. V., *old.*), &c., the whelps of the *lioness* (not *the stout lion*, as *E. V.*). [BARNES and UMBR.] The various phases of wickedness are expressed by this variety of terms: obliquely Job, his wife, and children, may be hinted at by the lion, lioness, and whelps. The one verb, *are broken*, does not suit both subjects: therefore, supply "the roaring of the bellowing lion *is silenced.*" The *strong* lion dies of want at last, and the *whelps*, torn from the mother, are scattered, and the race becomes extinct. 12. a thing—Heb., *a word*. Eliphaz confirms his view by a divine *declaration* which *was secretly and unexpectedly imparted* to him. a little—*lit., a whisper*. Implying the still silence around, and that more was conveyed than articulate words could utter (ch. 26. 14; 2 Cor. 12. 4.). 13. In thoughts from the visions—(So WINER and *E. V.*] Whilst revolving night *visions previously* made to him Dan 2. 29.). Rather, "In my manifold (Heb., *divided*) thoughts, *before* the visions of the night commenced;" therefore not a delusive

14 Fear came upon me, and trembling, which made all my bones to shake.
15 Then a spirit passed before my face; the hair of my flesh stood up:
16 It stood still, but I could not discern the form thereof: an image was before mine eyes; there was silence, and I heard a voice, saying,
17 Shall mortal man be more just than God? shall a man be more pure than his Maker?
18 Behold, he put no trust in his servants; and his angels he charged with folly:
19 How much less in them that dwell in houses of clay, whose foundation is in the dust, which are crushed before the moth?
20 They are destroyed from morning to evening: they perish for ever without any regarding it.
21 Doth not their excellency which is in them go away? they die, even without wisdom.

CHAPTER V.

1 Harm of inconsideration. 3 Misery the end of the wicked. 6 Man born to trouble. 8 God is to be regarded in affliction. 17 Happy end of God's correction.

CALL now, if there be any that will answer thee; and to which of the saints wilt thou turn?
2 For wrath killeth the foolish man, and envy slayeth the silly one.
3 I have seen the foolish taking root: but suddenly I cursed his habitation.
4 His children are far from safety, and they are crushed in the gate, neither is there any to deliver them.
5 Whose harvest the hungry eateth up, and taketh it even out of the thorns, and the robber swalloweth up their substance.
6 Although affliction cometh not forth of the dust, neither doth trouble spring out of the ground;
7 Yet man is born unto trouble, as the sparks fly upward.
8 I would seek unto God, and unto God would I commit my cause:
9 Which doeth great things and unsearchable; marvellous things without number:
10 Who giveth rain upon the earth, and sendeth waters upon the fields:
11 To set up on high those that be low; that those which mourn may be exalted to safety.
12 He disappointeth the devices of the crafty, so that their hands cannot perform their enterprise.
13 He taketh the wise in their own craftiness: and the counsel of the froward is carried headlong.
14 They meet with darkness in the day-time, and grope in the noon-day as in the night.
15 But he saveth the poor from the sword, from their mouth, and from the hand of the mighty.
16 So the poor hath hope, and iniquity stoppeth her mouth.
17 Behold, happy is the man whom God correcteth: therefore despise not thou the chastening of the Almighty:
18 For he maketh sore, and bindeth up; he woundeth, and his hands make whole.
19 He shall deliver thee in six troubles: yea, in seven there shall no evil touch thee.

20 In famine he shall redeem thee from death; and in war from the power of the sword.
21 Thou shalt be hid from the scourge of the tongue; neither shalt thou be afraid of destruction when it cometh.
22 At destruction and famine thou shalt laugh; neither shalt thou be afraid of the beasts of the earth.
23 For thou shalt be in league with the stones of the field; and the beasts of the field shall be at peace with thee.
24 And thou shalt know that thy tabernacle shall be in peace; and thou shalt visit thy habitation, and shalt not sin.
25 Thou shalt know also that thy seed shall be great, and thine offspring as the grass of the earth.
26 Thou shalt come to thy grave in a full age, like as a shock of corn cometh in in his season.
27 Lo this, we have searched it, so it is; hear it, and know thou it for thy good.

CHAPTER VI.

1 Job shows that his complaints are not causeless: 8 he wishes for death, wherein he is assured of rest and comfort: 14 he reproves his friends of unkindness.

BUT Job answered and said,
2 Oh that my grief were throughly weighed, and my calamity laid in the balances together!
3 For now it would be heavier than the sand of the sea: therefore my words are swallowed up.
4 For the arrows of the Almighty are within me, the poison whereof drinketh up my spirit: the terrors of God do set themselves in array against me.
5 Doth the wild ass bray when he hath grass? or loweth the ox over his fodder?
6 Can that which is unsavoury be eaten without salt? or is there any taste in the white of an egg?
7 The things that my soul refused to touch are as my sorrowful meat.
8 Oh that I might have my request; and that God would grant me the thing that I long for!
9 Even that it would please God to destroy me; that he would let loose his hand, and cut me off!
10 Then should I yet have comfort; yea, I would harden myself in sorrow: let him not spare; for I have not concealed the words of the Holy One.
11 What is my strength, that I should hope? and what is mine end, that I should prolong my life?
12 Is my strength the strength of stones? or is my flesh of brass?
13 Is not my help in me? and is wisdom driven quite from me?
14 To him that is afflicted pity should be showed from his friend; but he forsaketh the fear of the Almighty.
15 My brethren have dealt deceitfully as a brook, and as the stream of brooks they pass away;
16 Which are blackish by reason of the ice, and wherein the snow is hid:
17 What time they wax warm, they vanish: when it is hot, they are consumed out of their place.
18 The paths of their way are turned aside; they go to nothing, and perish.
19 The troops of Tema looked, the companies of Sheba waited for them.

dream (Ps. 4. 4.). [UMB.] deep sleep—(Gen. 2. 21; 15. 12.). 16. It stood still—At first the apparition glides before Eliphaz, then stands still, but with that shadowy indistinctness of form which creates such an impression of awe; a gentle murmur! not (E. V.: there was silence: For in 1 Kings, 19. 12, the voice, as opposed to the previous storm, denotes a gentle still murmur. 17. mortal man . . . a man—Two Heb. words for man are used; the first implying his feebleness; the second his strength. Whether feeble or strong, man is not righteous before God. 17. more just than God . . . more pure than his Maker—But this would be self-evident without an oracle. 18. folly—Imperfection is to be attributed to the angels, in comparison with Him. The holiness of some of them had given way (2 Pet. 2. 4.), and at best is but the holiness of a creature. Folly is the want of moral consideration. [UMBR.] 19. houses of clay—2 Cor. 5. 1.). Houses made of sun-dried clay bricks are common in the East; they are easily washed away (Matth. 7. 27.). Man's foundation is this dust (Gen. 3. 19.). before the moth—Rather, as before the moth, which devours a garment (ch. 13. 28; Ps. 39. 11; Isa. 50. 9.). Man, who cannot, in a physical point of view, stand before the very moth, surely cannot, in a moral, stand before God. 20. from morning to evening—Unceasingly; or, better, between the morning and evening of one short day (so Ex. 18. 14; Isa. 38. 12.). "They are destroyed" better, "they would be destroyed," if God withdrew His loving protection. Therefore man must not think to be holy before God, but to draw holiness, and all things else, from God (v. 17.). 21. their excellency—(Ps. 39. 11; 146. 4; 1 Cor. 13. 8.). But UMBR., by an Oriental image from a bow useless, because unstrung. "Their nerve or string would be torn away." MICH., better, in accordance with v. 19, makes the allusion be to the cords of a tabernacle taken down (Isa. 33. 20.). they die, even without wisdom—Rather, "They would perish, yet not according to wisdom," but according to arbitrary choice, if God were not infinitely wise and holy. The design of the Spirit is to show that the continued existence of weak man proves the inconceivable wisdom and holiness of God, which alone save man from ruin. [UMBR.] BENG. shows from Scripture, that God's holiness Heb. Kadosh,) comprehends all his excellencies and attributes. DE W. loses the scope in explaining it, of the shortness of man's life contrasted with the angels "before they have attained to wisdom."

CHAPTER V.

Ver. 1-27. ELIPHAZ'S CONCLUSION FROM THE VISION. 1. if there be any, &c.—Rather, Will He God,) reply to thee? Job, after the revelation just given, cannot be so presumptuous as to think, God or any of the holy ones (Dan. 4. 17; angels,) round His throne, will vouchsafe a reply (a judicial expression) to his rebellious complaint. 2. wrath, . . . envy —Fretful and passionate complaints; such as Eliphaz charged Job with (ch.4.5; so Prov.14. 30.). Not, the wrath of God killeth the foolish, and His envy, &c. 3. the foolish—The wicked. I have seen the sinner spread his roots wide in prosperity, yet circumstances suddenly occurred which gave occasion for his once prosperous dwelling being cursed as desolate (Ps. 37. 35, 36; Jer. 17. 8.) 4. His chil- dren . . . crushed in the gate—A judicial formula. The gate was the place of judgment, and of other public proceedings (Ps. 127. 5; Prov. 22. 22; Gen. 23. 10; Deut. 21. 19.). Such calamity have been found in the Assyrian remains. Eliphaz obliquely alludes to the calamity which cut off Job's children. 5. even out of the thorns—Even when part of the grain remains hanging on the thorn bushes or, is growing among thorns, Matth. 13. 7,), the hungry gleaner does not grudge the trouble of taking even it away, so clean swept away is the harvest of the wicked. the robber--As the Sabeans, who robbed Job. Rather translate, the thirsty, as the antithesis in the parallelism, the hungry, proves. 6. Although—Rather, for truly. [UMBR.] affliction cometh not forth of the dust—Like a weed, of its own accord. Eliphaz hints that the cause of it lay with Job himself. 7. Yet—Rather, Truly, or, But. Affliction does not come from chance; but is the appointment of God for sin; i.e., the original birth-sin of man. Eliphaz passes from the particular sin and consequent suffering of Job to the universal sin and suffering of mankind. Troubles spring from man's common sin by as necessary a law of natural consequence as sparks, Heb., sons of coal,) fly upward. Troubles are many and fiery, as sparks (1 Pet. 4. 12; Isa. 43. 2.). UMBR., for sparks has birds of prey; lit., sons of lightning, not so well. 8. Therefore (as affliction is ordered by God, on account of sin,) I would have you to seek unto God (Isa. 8. 19; Amos, 5. 8; Jer. 5. 24,). 11. Connected with v. 9. His unsearchable dealings are with a view to raise the humble and abase the proud,). Luke, 1. 52. Therefore Job ought to turn humbly to Him. 12. enterprise—lit., realization, The Hebrew combines in the one word the two ideas, wisdom and happiness, enduring existence being the etymological and philosophical root of the combined notion. [UMBR.] 13. Paul (1 Cor. 3. 19,) quoted this clause with the formula establishing its inspiration, it is written. He cites the exact Hebrew words, not as he usually does the LXX. Greek version (Ps. 9. 15.). Haman was hanged on the gallows he prepared for Mordecai (Esth. 5. 14; 7. 10.). The wise—the cunning. is carried headlong—Their scheme is precipitated before it is ripe. 14. Judicial blindness often is sent upon keen men of the world (Deut. 28. 29; Isa. 59. 10; John, 9. 39.). 15. From the sword which proceedeth from their mouth (Ps. 59. 7; 57. 4.). 16. the poor hath hope—of the interposition of God. iniquity stoppeth her mouth — Ps. 107. 42; Mic. 7. 9, 10; Isa, 52. 15.. Especially at the last day, through shame Jude, 15; Matth. 22. 12.). The mouth was the offender (v. 15,), and the mouth shall then be stopped (Isa. 25. 8,) at the end. 17. happy—Not that the actual suffering is joyous; but the consideration of the righteousness of Him who sends it, and the end for which it is sent, make it a cause for thankfulness, not for complaints, such as Job had uttered (Heb. 12. 11.). Eliphaz implies that the end in this case is to call back Job from the particular sin, of which he takes for granted that Job is guilty. Paul seems to allude to this passage in Heb. 12. 5; so James, 1. 12. Prov. 3. 12. Eliphaz does not give due prominence to this truth, but rather to Job's sin. It is Elihu alone 32.-37.) who fully dwells upon the truth, that affliction is mercy and justice

Job reproves his friends. JOB, VII, VIII, IX. *The address of Bildad.*

20 They were confounded because they had hoped; they came thither, and were ashamed.
21 ¹² For now ye are ¹³ nothing; ye see my casting down, and are afraid.
22 Did I say, Bring unto me? or, Give a reward for me of your substance?
23 Or, Deliver me from the enemy's hand? or, Redeem me from the hand of the mighty?
24 Teach me, and I will hold my tongue; and cause me to understand wherein I have erred.
25 How forcible are right words! but what doth your arguing reprove?
26 Do ye imagine to reprove words, and the speeches of one that is desperate, *which are* as wind?
27 Yea, ¹⁴ ye overwhelm the fatherless, and ye dig *a pit* for your friend.
28 Now therefore be content; look upon me: for *it is* ¹⁵ evident unto you if I lie.
29 Return, I pray you, let it not be iniquity; yea, return again, my righteousness *is* ¹⁶ in it.
30 Is there iniquity in my tongue? cannot ¹⁷ my taste discern perverse things?

CHAPTER VII.

1 *Job accuses his desire of death, by representing his extreme restlessness:* 17 *he expostulates with God.*

IS there not ¹ an appointed time to man upon earth? *are not* his days also like the days of an hireling?
2 As a servant ² earnestly desireth the shadow, and as an hireling looketh for *the* reward *of* his work;
3 So am I made to possess months of vanity, and wearisome nights are appointed to me.
4 When I lie down, I say, When shall I arise, and ³ the night be gone? and I am full of tossings to and fro unto the dawning of the day.
5 My flesh is clothed with worms and clods of dust; my skin is broken, and become loathsome.
6 My days are swifter than a weaver's shuttle, and are spent without hope.
7 O remember that ᵃ my life *is* wind: mine eye ⁴ shall no more ⁵ see good.
8 The ᵇ eye of him that hath seen me shall see me no *more*: thine eyes *are* upon me, and ⁶ I *am* not.
9 *As* the cloud is consumed and vanisheth away; so ᶜ he that goeth down to the grave shall come up no *more*.
10 He shall return no more to his house, neither shall his place know him any more.
11 Therefore I will ᵈ not refrain my mouth; I will speak in the anguish of my spirit; I will complain in the bitterness of my soul.
12 *Am* I a sea, or a whale, that thou settest a watch over me?
13 When I say, My bed shall comfort me, my couch shall ease my complaint;
14 Then thou scarest me with dreams, and terrifiest me through visions;
15 So that my soul chooseth strangling, *and* death rather than my ⁷ life.
16 I ⁸ loathe *it*; I would not live alway: let me alone; for ᶠ my days *are* vanity.
17 What ᵍ *is* man, that thou shouldest magnify him? and that thou shouldest set thine heart upon him?
18 And *that* thou shouldest visit him every morning, *and* try him every moment?
19 How long wilt thou not depart from

B. C. 1520.

CHAP. 6.
12 Or, For now ye are like to them.
13 not.
14 ye cause to fall upon.
15 before your face.
16 That is, in this matter.
17 my palate.

CHAP. 7.
1 Or, a warfare.
2 gapeth after.
3 the evening be measured.
ᵃ Ps. 78. 39. Jam. 4. 14.
4 shall not return.
5 To see, that is, to enjoy.
ᵇ ch. 20. 9.
6 That is, I can live no longer.
ᶜ 2 Sa. 12. 23.
ᵈ Ps. 39. 1, 9. Ps. 40. 9.
7 bones.
ᵉ ch. 10. 1.
ᶠ Ps. 62. 9.
ᵍ Ps. 8. 4. Ps. 144. 3. Heb. 2. 6.
ʰ Ps. 35. 6.
8 Or, observer, Ps. 11. 4.

CHAP. 8.
ᵃ Gen. 18. 25. Deut. 32. 4. 2 Chr. 19. 7. ch. 34. 12. Dan. 9. 14. Rom. 3. 5.
1 in the land of their transgression.
ᵇ Deu. 4. 32. Deu. 32. 7.
ᶜ Ps. 39. 6.
2 not.
ᵈ Ps. 129. 6. ᵉ ch. 11. 20. Pro. 10. 28.
3 a spider's house.
ᶠ ch. 27. 18.
ᵍ Ps. 37. 35.
ʰ Ps. 113. 7.
ⁱ Ps. 37. 24.
1 Thes. 5. 23, 24.
4 take the ungodly by the hand.
5 shouting for joy.
6 not be.

CHAP. 9.
ᵃ Ps. 143. 2. Rom. 3. 20.
1 Or, before God.

me, nor let me alone till I swallow down my spittle?
20 I have sinned; what shall I do unto thee, ʰ O thou ⁸ Preserver of men? why hast thou set me as a mark against thee, so that I am a burden to myself?
21 And why dost thou not pardon my transgression, and take away mine iniquity? for now shall I sleep in the dust; and thou shalt seek me in the morning, but I *shall* not *be.*

CHAPTER VIII.

1 *Bildad shows God's justice:* 8 *appeals to antiquity to prove the destruction of the hypocrite:* 20 *applies God's just dealing to the case of Job.*

THEN answered Bildad the Shuhite, and said,
2 How long wilt thou speak these *things?* and *how* long *shall* the words of thy mouth *be like* a strong wind?
3 Doth ᵃ God pervert judgment? or doth the Almighty pervert justice?
4 If thy children have sinned against him, and he have cast them away ¹ for their transgression;
5 If thou wouldest seek unto God betimes, and make thy supplication to the Almighty;
6 If thou *wert* pure and upright; surely now he would awake for thee, and make the habitation of thy righteousness prosperous.
7 Though thy beginning was small, yet thy latter end should greatly increase.
8 For ᵇ enquire, I pray thee, of the former age, and prepare thyself to the search of their fathers:
9 (For ᶜ we *are but of* yesterday, and know ² nothing, because our days upon earth *are* a shadow:)
10 Shall not they teach thee, *and* tell thee, and utter words out of their heart?
11 Can the rush grow up without mire? can the flag grow without water?
12 Whilst ᵈ it *is* yet in his greenness, *and* not cut down, it withereth before any *other* herb:
13 So are the paths of all that forget God; and the ᵉ hypocrite's hope shall perish:
14 Whose hope shall be cut off, and whose trust shall be ³ a spider's web.
15 He ᶠ shall lean upon his house, but it shall not stand: he shall hold it fast, but it shall not endure.
16 He *is* green before the sun, and his branch shooteth forth in his garden.
17 His roots are wrapped about the heap, *and* seeth the place of stones.
18 If ᵍ he destroy him from his place, then *it* shall deny him, *saying*, I have not seen thee.
19 Behold, this *is* the joy of his way, and out ʰ of the earth shall others grow.
20 Behold, God will not ⁱ cast away a perfect *man*, neither will he ⁴ help the evil doers;
21 Till he fill thy mouth with laughing, and thy lips with ⁵ rejoicing.
22 They that hate thee shall be clothed with shame; and the dwelling-place of the wicked shall ⁶ come to nought.

CHAPTER IX.

1 *Job, acknowledging God's justice, shows there is no contending with him.* 22 *Man's innocency is not to be judged by his lot in this world.*

THEN Job answered and said,
2 I know it is so of a truth: but how should ᵃ man be just ¹ with God?

in disguise, for the good of the sufferer. **18.** he maketh sore, and bindeth up—(Deut. 32, 39; Hos. 6. 1; 1 Sam. 2. 6.) An image from binding up a wound. The healing art consisted much at that time in external applications. **19.** in six...yea, in seven—(Prov. 6. 16; Amos, 1. 3.). The Hebrew idiom fixes on a certain number (here *six*), in order to call attention as to a thing of importance; then increases the force by adding, with a *yea, nay even*, the next higher number; here *seven*, the sacred and perfect number. In *all* possible troubles; not merely in the precise number *seven*. **20.** power—(Jer. 6. 12.). Heb., *hands*. of the sword—Ezek. 35. 5.) Marg. *Hands* are given to the sword personified as a living agent. **21.** (Ps. 31. 20; Jer. 18. 18.). *Smite* (Ps. 73. 9.). **22.** famine thou shalt laugh—Not, in spite of destruction and famine, which is true Hab. 3. 17, 18.), though not *the* truth meant by Eliphaz, but because *those calamities shall not come upon thee*. A different Hebrew word from that in *v.* 20; there, famine in *general*; here, the *languid state* of those wanting proper nutriment. [BARNES.] **23.** in league with the stones of the field—They shall not hurt the fertility of thy soil; nor the wild beasts thy fruits. Spoken in Arabia Deserta, where stones abounded. *Arabia*, derived from *Arabah*—a desert plain. The first clause of this verse answers to the first clause of verse 22; and the last of this verse to the last of that verse. The full realization of this is yet future (Isa. 65. 23, 25; Hos. 2. 18.). **24.** know—"Thou shalt rest in the assurance, that thine habitation is the abode of peace; and (if) thou numberest thine herd, thine expectations prove not fallacious." [UMBR.] *Sin* does not agree with the context. The Hebrew word—*to miss* a mark, said of archers (Judg. 20. 16.). The Hebrew for "habitation" primarily means *the fold for cattle;* and for "visit," often *to take an account of*, "*to number.*" "Peace" is the common Eastern salutation; including *inward and outward prosperity*. **25.** as the grass—Ps. 72. 16.). Properly, *herb bearing seed* (Gen. 1. 11, 12.). **26.** in full age—So *full of days* (42. 17; Gen. 35. 29.). Not mere length of years, but *ripeness* for death, one's inward and outward full development not being prematurely cut short, is denoted. (Isaiah, 65. 22.). *Thou shalt come*, not *lit.*, but expressing *willingness* to die. Eliphaz speaks from the Old Testament point of view, which made full years a reward of the righteous (Psalm 91. 16; Ex. 20. 12,), and premature death the lot of the wicked (Ps. 55. 23,).) The righteous once in mortal till their work is done. To keep them longer would be to render them less fit to die. God takes them at their best (Isaiah, 57. 1.). The good are compared to *wheat* (Matth. 13. 30.), cometh in—*lit.*, *ascends*. The corn is *lifted up off the earth* and carried home; so the good man "Is raised into the heap of sheaves." [UMBR.] **27.** Searched it . . . . for thy good—*lit.*, *for thyself* (Ps. 111. 2; Prov. 2. 4; 9. 12,).

CHAPTER VI.

FIRST SERIES CONTINUED.

Ver. 1-30. REPLY OF JOB TO ELIPHAZ.—**2.** thoroughly weighed—O that, instead of censuring my complaints when thou oughtest rather to have sympathized with me, thou wouldest accurately compare together my *sorrow*, and my *misfortunes*: these latter *outweigh in the balance* the former. **3.** the sand—(Prov. 27. 3.). are swallowed up—See Marg. So Ps. 77. 4. But Job plainly is apologizing, not for not having had words *enough* but for having spoken *too much* and *too boldly:* and the Hebrew is, *to speak rashly*, [UMBR., GES., ROS.] "Therefore were my words *so rash.*" **4.** arrows . . . within me—have *pierced* me. A poetic image representing the avenging Almighty armed with bow and arrows (Ps. 38. 2, 3.). Here the arrows are poisoned. Peculiarly appropriate, in reference to *the burning pains* which pene trated, like poison, into *the inmost parts* —("spirit;" as contrasted with mere *surface flesh wounds*,) of Job's body. set themselves in array—A military image (Judg. 20. 33.). All the terrors which the divine wrath can muster are set in array against me (Isa. 42. 13.). **5.** Neither wild animals, as the wild ass, nor tame, as the ox, are dissatisfied when well supplied with food. The braying of the one, and the lowing of the other, prove distress and want of palatable food. So, Job argues, if he complains, it is not without cause; viz., his pains, which are, as it were, *disgusting food*, which God feeds him with—end of verse 7. But he should have remembered a *rational* being should evince a better spirit than the brute. **6.** unsavoury—Tasteless, insipid. *Salt* is a chief necessary of life to an Eastern, whose food is mostly vegetable. the white—*lit.*, *spittle*, 1 Sam. 21. 13,) which the white of an egg resembles. **7.** To touch is contrasted with *meat.* "My taste refused *even to touch* it, and yet am I *fed* with such meat of sickness." The second clause *lit.*, is, "Such is like the sickness of my food." The natural taste abhors even to touch insipid food, and such forms my nourishment. For my sickness is like such nauseous food. [UMBR.] (Ps. 42. 3; 80. 5; 102. 9.). No wonder, then, I complain. **8.** To desire death is no necessary proof of fitness for death. The ungodly sometimes desire it, so as to escape troubles, without thought of the hereafter. The godly desire it, in order to be with the Lord; but they patiently wait God's will. **9.** destroy—*lit.*, *grind* or *crush* (Isa. 3. 15.). let loose his hand—God had put forth His hand only so far as to wound the *surface* of Job's flesh (ch. 1. 12; 2. 6,; he wishes that hand to be *let loose*, so as to wound *deeply and vitally*. cut me off—Metaphor from a weaver *cutting off* the web, when finished, from the thrum fastening it to the loom (Isa. 38. 12.). **10.** I would harden myself—Rather, "I would *exult* in the pain," if I knew that that pain would hasten my death. (GES.) UMBR. translates the *Heb.* of "Let Him not spare." *unsparing;* and joins it with *pain.* The *E.V.* is more vivid. concealed—I have not disowned, in word or deed, the commands of the Holy One (Ps. 119. 4 6; Acts, 20. 20.). He says this in answer to Eliphaz' insinuation that he is a hypocrite. God is here called *the Holy One*, to imply man's reciprocal obligation to be holy, as He is holy (Lev. 19. 2.). **11.** *What strength have I*, so as *to warrant the hope* of restoration to health! a hope which Eliphaz had suggested. *And what* but a miserable end of life is before me, *that I should* desire to prolong *life*? [UMBR.] UMBR. and ROS., not so well translate the last words *to be patient*. **12.** Disease had so attacked him, that his strength would need to be hard as *a stone*, and his flesh like *brass*, not to sink under it. But he has only flesh, like other men. It must, therefore, give way; so that the hope of restoration suggested by Eliphaz is vain see Note, 5. 11.). 13. Is not my help in me?—The interrogation is better omitted. "There is no help in me!" For "wisdom," *deliverance* is a better rendering. "And deliverance is driven quite from me." 14. pity—A proverb. *Chased* is *the love* which judges indulgently of our fellowmen: it is put on a par with *truth* in Prov. 3. 3, for they together form the essence of moral perfection. [UMBR.] It is the spirit of Christianity (1 Pet. 4. 8; 1 Cor. 13. 7; Prov. 10. 12; 17. 17.). If it ought to be used towards all men, much more towards *friends*. But he who does not use it *forsaketh* (renounceth) *the fear of the Almighty* (Jam. 2. 13.). 15. Those whom I regarded as *my brethren*, from whom I looked for faithfulness in my adversity, have disappointed me, as the streams failing from drought; wadys of Arabia, filled in the winter, but dry in the summer, which disappoint the caravans expecting to find water there. The fulness and noise of these temporary streams answers to the past large and loud professions of my friends; their dryness in summer, to the failure of the friendship when needed. The Arab proverb says of a treacherous friend, "I trust not in thy torrent" (Isa. 58. 11, *marg.*). streams of brooks—Rather, "*the brook in the ravines* which passes away." It has no perpetual spring of water to renew it (unlike "the fountain of *living* waters," Jer. 2. 13; Isa. 33. 16, at the end; and thus passes away as rapidly as it arose. 16. black-ish—*lit.*, *Go as a mourner in black clothing* Ps. 34. 14.). A vivid and poetic image to picture the stream turbid and black with melted ice and snow, descending from the mountains into the valley. In the next clause, the snow dissolved, is, in the poet's view, *hid* in the flood. [UMBR.] 17. wax warm—Rather, "At the time when. (*But they soon*,) [UMBR.] they *become narrower*, flow in a narrower bed, *they are silent*, cease to flow noisily; in the heat of the sun they are consumed or vanish out of their place. First the stream flows more narrowly,—then becomes silent and still; at length every trace of water disappears by evaporation under the hot sun." [UMBR.] 18. turned aside—Rather, *Caravans* (Heb. *travellers*, *turn aside from their way*, by circuitous routes, to obtain water. They had seen the brook in spring full of water: and now in the summer heat, on their weary journey, they turn off their road by a devious route to reach the living waters, which they remembered with such pleasure. But, when "they go," it is "*into a desert*." [NOY. and UMBR.] Not as E. V. "They go to *nothing*," which would be a tame repetition of the drying up of the waters in v. 17; instead of waters, they find an "*empty wilderness*;" and, not having strength to regain their road, bitterly disappointed, *they perish*. The terse brevity is most expressive. 19. the troops—*i.e.*, *Caravans*. Tema north of Arabia Deserta, near the Syrian desert; called from Tema son of Ishmael (Gen. 25. 15; Isa. 21. 14; Jer. 25 23.). Still so called by the Arabs. Verses 19, 20, give another picture of the mortification of disappointed hopes: *viz.*, those of *the caravans* on *the direct road*, anxiously awaiting the return of their companions from the distant valley. The mention of the locality whence the caravans came gives living reality to the picture. *Sheba* refers here not to the marauders in N. Arabia Deserta, (ch. 1. 15,) but to the *merchants* (Ez. 27. 22,) in the S. in Arabia Felix or Yemen, "afar off," (Jer. 6. 20; M. 12. 42; Gen. 10. 28.). Caravans are first mentioned, (Gen. 37. 25;) men needed to travel thus in companies across the desert, for defence against the roving robbers, and for mutual accommodation. "The companies waited for them," cannot refer to *the caravans who had gone in quest of the waters*: for *v*. 18 describes their utter destruction. 20. *lit.*, *each had hoped, viz.*, that their companions would find water. The greater had been their hopes the more bitter now their disappointment; they came thither, to the place, and were ashamed; *lit.*, their *countenances burn*, an oriental phrase for the shame and consternation of deceived expectation. So *ashamed* as to disappointment Rom. 5. 5. 21. As the dried up brook is to the caravan, so are ye to me, *viz.*, a nothing; ye might as well not be in existence. [UMBR.] The Marg. *like to them* or *it, viz.*, the waters of the brook,) is not so good a reading. ye see, and are afraid—Ye are struck aghast at *the sight* of my misery, and *ye lose presence of mind*. Job puts this mild construction on their failing to relieve him with affectionate consolation. 22. And yet I did not ask you to *bring me* a gift: or to *pay for me* out of *your substance a reward* to the Judge, to redeem me from my punishment ; all I asked from you was affectionate treatment. 23. the mighty—*The oppressor*, or creditor, in whose power the debtor was. [UMBR.] 24. 25. Irony. If you can *teach me the right view*, I am willing to be set right and *hold my tongue; and to be made to see my error*. But then if your words be really *the right view, how is it* that they are so *feeble*. "Yet how feeble are the words of what you call the right view." So the *Heb.* is used in (Mic. 2. 10; 1. 9.). The E. V. "How *powerful*," &c., does not agree so well with the last clause of the *v*. "And what will your arguings reprove?" *lit.*, "the reproofs which proceed *from you*," the emphasis is on *you; you* may find fault, who are not in *my* situation. [UMBR.] 26. Do you imagine, or *mean*, to reprove *words*, and (to reprove) the speeches of one desperate, (which are) as wind, mere nothings, not to be so narrowly taken to task? UMBR. not so well takes the *Heb.* for *as wind*, "as sentiments;" making formal *sentiments* antithetical to mere *speeches*, and supplying, not the word "reprove," but "would you regard," from the first clause. 27. "Ye overwhelm:" *lit.*, *ye cause*, (supply, *your anger*; [UMBR.] *a net, viz.*, of sophistry, [NOY. & SCH.] *to fall upon the desolate*, (one bereft of help, like *the fatherless* orphan ; *and ye dig* a pit *for your friend*," i. e., try to ensnare him, to catch him in the use of unguarded language [NOY.] Ps. 57. 6;) metaphor from hunters catching wild beasts in a pit covered with brushwood to conceal it. UMBR. from the Syr., and answering to his interpretation of the first clause, has "Would you be *indignant* against your friend?" The *Heb.* in ch. 41. 6, means to *feast upon*. As the first clause asks, "Would you *catch him in a net?*" so this follows up the image, "And would you next *feast upon him*, and his miseries?" So LXX. 28. be content—Rather, *be pleased to*,—look. Since you have so falsely judged my words, *look upon me, i. e.,* upon my countenance: *for* (it is *evident* before your faces *if I lie*; my countenance will betray me, if I be the hypocrite that you suppose. 29. Return—Rather, *retract* your charges: "Let it not be iniquity;" *i.e.,* (retract *that injustice may not be done me.* Yea retract, "my righteousness is in it," *i. e.,* my right is involved in this matter. 30. *Will you say that my guilt lies in the organ of speech,* and will you call it to account? or *is it that my taste* (palate, *or discernment is not capable to form a judgment of perverse things?* Is it thus you will explain the fact of my having no consciousness of guilt. [UMBR.]

CHAPTER VII.

Ver. 1-21. JOB EXCUSES HIS DESIRE FOR DEATH. 1. appointed time—Better, *warfare,* hard conflict with evils; so in Isa. 40. 2; Dan. 10.1; and ch. 14. 14;) translate it *appointed time,* (ch. 14. 5, 13; Ps. 39, 4.). Job reverts to the sad picture of man, however great, which he had drawn, (ch. 3. 14;) and details in this ch. the miseries which his friends will see, if, according to his request, (ch. 6. 28,) they will *look on him.* Even the Christian soldier, "warring a good warfare," rejoices when it is completed (1 Tim. 1. 18; 2 Tim. 2. 3; 4. 7, 8.). 2. earnestly desireth—*Heb. pants for the (evening shadow.* Easterns measure time by the length of their shadow. If the servant longs for the evening when his wages are paid, why may not Job long for the close of his hard service, when he shall enter on his *reward?* This proves that Job did not, as many maintain, regard the grave as a mere sle p. 3. Months *of comfortless misfortune.* "I am made *to possess,*" *lit., to be heir to.* Irony. *To be heir to,* is usually a matter of joy; but here it is *the entail of an involuntary and dismal inheritance. Months,* for *days,* to express its long duration. *Appointed, lit., they have numbered to me;* marking well the unavoidable doom assigned to him. 4. *Lit.,* "when shall be *the flight* of the night?" [GES.] UMBR. not so well, "The night is long extended:" *lit., measured out:* so Marg. 5. In Elephantiasis maggots are bred in the sores, (Acts 12. 23; Isa. 14. 11.). clods of dust —Rather, *a crust of dried filth and accumulated corruption* (ch. 2. 7, 8.). my skin is broken and loathsome—Rather, *comes together so as to heal up,* and again breaks out with *running matter.* [GES.] More simply the *Heb.* is, "My skin rests (for a time) and (again) melts away" (Ps. 58. 7.). 6. (Isa. 38. 12.). Every day like the weaver's shuttle leaves a thread behind; and each shall wear, as he weaves. But Job's thought is, that his days must swiftly be cut off as a web: *without hope, viz.,* of a recovery and renewal of life (ch. 14. 19; 1 Chron. 29. 15.). 7. Address to God. *Wind,* a picture of evanescence. (Ps. 78. 39.). shall no more see—Rather, "shall *no more return to see* good." This change from the different wish in ch. 3. 17, &c., is most true to nature. He is now in a softer mood: and a beam from former days of *prosperity* falling upon memory, and the thought of the unseen world, where one *is seen no more* (v. 8), drew from him an expression of regret at leaving this world of *light* (Eccl. 11. 7.). So Hezekiah (Isa. 38. 11.). Grace rises above nature (2 Cor. 5. 8.). 8. The eye of him who beholds me [*present* not *past,* as *E. V.*] *i. e., in the very act of beholding* me, seeth me no more." "Thine eyes are) upon me, and I am not?" He disappears, *even*

while God is looking upon him. Job cannot survive the gaze of Jehovah (Ps. 104. 32; Rev. 20. 11.). Not, "Thine eyes seek me and I am not to be found;" for God's eye penetrates even to the unseen world (Ps. 139. 8.). UMBR. unnaturally takes, *Thine,* to refer to *one of the three friends.* 9. 2 Sam. 12. 23.). the grave—The Sheol, or place of departed spirits, not disproving Job's belief in the resurrection. It merely means, "He shall come up no more" in the *present* order of things. 10. (Ps. 103. 16.) The Oriental keenly loves his dwelling. In Arabian elegies the desertion of abodes by their occupants is often a theme of sorrow. Grace overcomes this also Luke 18. 29; Acts 4. 34.) 11. Therefore, as such is my hard lot, I will at least have the melancholy satisfaction of venting my sorrow in words. The *Heb.* opening words, *therefore I, at all events,* express self-elevation. [UMBR.] 12-14. Why dost thou deny me the *comfort* of care-assuaging sleep? Why *scarcest thou me with* frightful *dreams? Am I,* then, *a sea,* (regarded in O. T. poetry, as a violent rebel against God, the Lord of nature, who therefore curbs his violence, Jer. 5. 22.? *or a whale,* (or some other sea monster (Isa. 27. 1.), *that thou* needest thus *to watch* and curb *me?* The Egyptians "watched" the *crocodile* most carefully to prevent its doing mischief. 14. The frightful dreams resulting from Elephantiasis, he attributes to God; the common belief assigned all night visions to God. 15. UMBR. translates," So that I could wish to strangle myself,—dead by my own hands." He softens this idea of Job's harbouring the thought of suicide, by representing it as entertained only in agonizing dreams, and immediately repudiated with horror next verse, "Yet that (self-strangling) I loathe." This is forcible and graphic. Perhaps the meaning is simply, "My soul chooses (even) strangling (or any violent) death rather than my life," *lit., my bones,* Ps. 35. 10; *i. e.,* rather than the wasted and diseased *skeleton,* left to him). In this view, "I loathe it," *v.* 16, refers to his *life.* 16. "Let me alone:" *i. e.,* cease to afflict me for the few and *vain* days still left to me. 17. (Ps. 8. 4; 144. 3.). Job means "What is man that thou shouldest *make him of so much importance,* and that thou shouldest expend such attention (heart-thought,) upon him," as to make him the subject of so severe trials? Job ought rather to have reasoned from God's condescending so far to notice man as to try him, that there must be a wise and loving purpose in trial. David uses the same words in their right application, to express wonder, that God should do so much as he does, for insignificant man. Christians who know God manifest in the man Christ Jesus still more may use them. 18. With each new day (Ps. 73. 14.). It is rather God's mercies, not our trials, that are "new *every morning*" (Lam. 3. 23.). The idea is that of a shepherd taking count of his flock every morning, to see if all are there. [COCC.] 19. "How long (like a jealous keeper,) wilt thou never *take thine eyes off* (so the *Heb.* for *depart from*) me? Nor let me alone *for a brief respite,*" (lit., *so long as I take to swallow my spittle.* An Arabic proverb, like our, *till I draw my breath?* 20. "I have sinned (I grant): yet what sin can I *do against* (to: ch. 35. 6, , thee (of such a nature that, thou shouldest jealously watch and

3 If he will contend with him, he cannot answer him one of a thousand.
4 *He is* wise in heart, and mighty in strength: who hath hardened *himself* against him, and hath prospered?
5 Which removeth the mountains, and they know not; which overturneth them in his anger;
6 Which shaketh the earth out of her place, and the pillars thereof tremble;
7 Which commandeth the sun, and it riseth not, and sealeth up the stars;
8 Which alone spreadeth out the heavens, and treadeth upon the waves of the sea;
9 Which maketh Arcturus, Orion, and Pleiades, and the chambers of the south;
10 Which doeth great things past finding out; yea, and wonders without number.
11 Lo, he goeth by me, and I see *him* not: he passeth on also, but I perceive him not.
12 Behold, he taketh away, who can hinder him? who will say unto him, What doest thou?
13 *If* God will not withdraw his anger, the proud helpers do stoop under him.
14 How much less shall I answer him, *and* choose out my words *to reason* with him?
15 Whom, though I were righteous, *yet* would I not answer, *but* I would make supplication to my judge.
16 If I had called, and he had answered me; *yet* would I not believe that he had hearkened unto my voice.
17 For he breaketh me with a tempest, and multiplieth my wounds without cause.
18 He will not suffer me to take my breath, but filleth me with bitterness.
19 If *I speak* of strength, lo, *he is* strong: and if of judgment, who shall set me a time to plead?
20 If I justify myself, mine own mouth shall condemn me: *if I say*, I *am* perfect, it shall also prove me perverse.
21 *Though* I were perfect, *yet* would I not know my soul: I would despise my life.
22 This *is* one *thing*, therefore I said *it*, He destroyeth the perfect and the wicked.
23 If the scourge slay suddenly, he will laugh at the trial of the innocent.
24 The earth is given into the hand of the wicked: he covereth the faces of the judges thereof; if not, where, *and* who *is* he?
25 Now my days are swifter than a post: they flee away, they see no good.
26 They are passed away as the swift ships: as the eagle *that* hasteth to the prey.
27 If I say, I will forget my complaint, I will leave off my heaviness, and comfort *myself*;
28 I am afraid of all my sorrows, I know that thou wilt not hold me innocent.
29 *If* I be wicked, why then labour I in vain?
30 If I wash myself with snow water, and make my hands never so clean;
31 Yet shalt thou plunge me in the ditch, and mine own clothes shall abhor me.
32 For *he is* not a man, as I *am*, *that* I should answer him, *and* we should come together in judgment.
33 Neither is there any daysman betwixt us, *that* might lay his hand upon us both.
34 Let him take his rod away from me, and let not his fear terrify me:
35 *Then* would I speak, and not fear him; but *it is* not so with me.

CHAPTER X.

1 *Job, taking liberty of complaint, expostulates with God about his afflictions:* 18 *he complains of life, and craves a little ease before his death.*

MY soul is weary of my life: I will leave my complaint upon myself; I will speak in the bitterness of my soul.
2 I will say unto God, Do not condemn me; show me wherefore thou contendest with me.
3 *Is it* good unto thee that thou shouldest oppress, that thou shouldest despise the work of thine hands, and shine upon the counsel of the wicked?
4 Hast thou eyes of flesh? or seest thou as man seeth?
5 *Are* thy days as the days of man? *are* thy years as man's days,
6 That thou enquirest after mine iniquity, and searchest after my sin?
7 Thou knowest that I am not wicked; and *there is* none that can deliver out of thine hand.
8 Thine hands have made me, and fashioned me together round about; yet thou dost destroy me.
9 Remember, I beseech thee, that thou hast made me as the clay; and wilt thou bring me into dust again?
10 Hast thou not poured me out as milk, and curdled me like cheese?
11 Thou hast clothed me with skin and flesh, and hast fenced me with bones and sinews.
12 Thou hast granted me life and favour, and thy visitation hath preserved my spirit.
13 And these *things* hast thou hid in thine heart; I know that this *is* with thee.
14 If I sin, then thou markest me, and thou wilt not acquit me from mine iniquity.
15 If I be wicked, woe unto me; *and if* I be righteous, *yet* will I not lift up my head. *I am* full of confusion; therefore see thou mine affliction;
16 For it increaseth. Thou huntest me as a fierce lion; and again thou showest thyself marvellous upon me.
17 Thou renewest thy witnesses against me, and increasest thine indignation upon me; changes and war *are* against me.
18 Wherefore then hast thou brought me forth out of the womb? Oh that I had given up the ghost, and no eye had seen me!
19 I should have been as though I had not been; I should have been carried from the womb to the grave.
20 *Are* not my days few? cease *then, and* let me alone, that I may take comfort a little,
21 Before I go *whence* I shall not return, *even* to the land of darkness, and the shadow of death;
22 A land of darkness, as darkness *itself*; *and* of the shadow of death, without any order, and *where* the light is as darkness.

CHAPTER XI.

1 *Zophar reproves Job for justifying himself;* 7 *he shows God's counsel is unsearchable.* 13 *Blessing of repentance.*

THEN answered Zophar the Naamathite, and said,
2 Should not the multitude of words be answered? and should a man full of talk be justified?
3 Should thy lies make men hold their peace? and when thou mockest, shall no man make thee ashamed?

deprive me of all strength, as if thou didst fear me. Yet thou art one who hast men ever in view, ever *watchest* them, —O thou *Watcher*, *v.* 12; Dan. 9, 14,), not as *E. V.*, *Preserver* [GES.] of men." Job had borne with patience his trials, as sent by God: (ch. 1. 21; ch. 2. 10.); (only his reason cannot reconcile the ceaseless continuance of his mental and bodily pains with his ideas of the divine nature. se me as a mark—Wherefore dost thou make me thy point of attack? *i. e.*, ever assail me with new pains. [UMBR.] (Lam. 3. 12. 21. for now—*very soon.* in the morning—Not the *r* s*urrection*: for then Job will be found. It is a figure, from one seeking a sick man in the morning, and finding he has died in the night. So Job implies, that if God does not help him at once, it will be too late, for he will be gone. The reason why God does not give an immediate sense of pardon to awakened sinners is, they think they have a *claim* on God for it.

CHAPTER VIII.
FIRST SERIES.—FIRST SPEECH OF BILDAD, MORE SEVERE AND COARSE THAN ELIFHAZ.
Ver. 1-22. THE ADDRESS OF BILDAD. 2. like a . . . wind—Disregarding restraints, and daring, against God. 3. The repetition of *pervert* gives an emphasis galling to Job (ch. 31. 12.). "Wouldest thou have God as thy words imply) pervert judgment," by letting thy sins go unpunished? He *assumes* Job's guilt from his sufferings. 4. If—Rather "*since* thy children have sinned against Him, and (*since*) He has cast them away for (*Heb.*, *by the* hand of) their transgression, (Yet) if thou wouldest seek unto God, &c., if thou wert pure, &c., surely (even) now He would awake for thee." UMBR. makes the apodosis to, "since thy children," &c., begin at "He has cast them away." Also, instead of *for*, "He gave them up *to lit.*, *into* the hand of) their own guilt." Bildad expresses the justice of God, which Job had arraigned. Thy children have sinned, God leaves them to the consequence of their sin. Most cutting to the heart of the bereaved father. 5. seek unto God betimes—Early. Make it the *first* and chief anxiety Ps. 78. 34; Hos. 5. 15; Isa. 26. 9; Prov. 8. 17; 13. 24.). 6. "He would awake for thee," *i.e.*, arise to thy help. God seemed to be asleep towards the sufferer (Ps. 35. 23; 7. 6; Isa. 51. 9.). make . . . prosperous —Restore to prosperity thy (their) righteous habitation. Bildad assumes it to have been heretofore the habitation of guilt. 7. thy beginning—The beginning of thy new happiness after restoration. latter end—ch. 42. 12; Prov. 23. 18.). 8, 9. The sages of the olden time reached an age beyond those of Job's time (Note 42. 16.); and therefore could give the testimony of a fuller experience. of yesterday —*i.e.*, a recent race. We know nothing as compared with them, from the brevity of our lives. So even Jacob (Gen. 47. 9.). Knowledge consisted then in the results of observation, embodied in poetical proverbs, and handed down by tradition. Longevity gave the opportunity of wider observation. a shadow—Ps. 144. 4; 1 Chr. 29. 15. 10. teach thee — (ch. 6. 24.), had said, "Teach me." Bildad, therefore, says, Since you want *teaching*, Enquire of the fathers, They will teach thee. utter words—more than mere speaking: "put forth well-considered words." out of their heart—From observation and reflection. Not merely *from their mouth*: such as Bildad insinuates, were Job's words. Verses 11, 12, 13, embody in poetic and sententious form (probably the fragment of an old poem, the observation of the elders. The double point of comparison between the ungodly and the paper-reed is, 1. The luxuriant prosperity at first; and, 2. The sudden destruction. 11. rush—Rather, *paper reed*: the papyrus of Egypt, which was used to make garments, shoes, baskets, boats, and *paper* a word derived from it.). It and the flag or bulrush grow only in marshy places such as are along the Nile.). So the godless thrive only in external prosperity; there is in the hypocrite no inward stability; his prosperity is like the rapid growth of water plants. 12. not cut down—Ere it has ripened for the scythe, it withers more suddenly than any herb, having no self-sustaining power, once that the moisture is gone, which other herbs do not need in the same degree. So ruin seizes on the godless in the zenith of prosperity, more suddenly, than on others who appear less firmly seated in their possessions. (UMBR.) (Ps.112.10.). 13. paths—So *ways* Pro. 1. 19.), all that forget God—The distinguishing trait of the godless (Ps. 9. 17; 50. 22.). 14. cut off—So GES. Or, to accord with the metaphor of the spider's *house*, "The confidence on which he *builds*) shall be *laid in ruins*" Isa. 59. 5, 6. . 15. he shall hold it fast—Implying his eager grasp, when the storm of trial comes. As the spider "holds fast" by its web: but with this difference, that the light spider is sustained by that on which it rests, the godless is not, by the thin web on which he rests. The expression, "Hold fast," properly applies to the spider holding his web, but is transferred to the man. Hypocrisy, like the spider's web, is fine-spun, flimsy, and woven out of its own inventions, as the spider's web out of its own bowels. An Arab proverb says, "Time destroys the well-built house, as well as the spider's web." 16. before the sun—*i.e.*, He the godless,) is green only *before the sun rises*: but he cannot bear its heat, and withers So succulent plants like the gourd Jonah, 4. 7, 8.). But the wide-spreading in the garden does not quite accord with this. Better, "in sunshine," the sun representing the smiling fortune of the hypocrite, during which he wondrously progresses. [UMBR.] The image is that of *weeds* growing in rank luxuriance, and spreading over even heaps of stones and walls, and then being speedily torn away. 17. seeth the place of stones—*Heb.*, "*the house* of stones," *i.e.*, the wall surrounding the garden. The parasite plant, in creeping towards and over the wall—the utmost bound of the garden—is said figuratively to "see" or regard it. 18. If He (God,) tear him away (*E. V.*, *destroy*; properly, *to tear away rapidly and violently*,) from his place, "then it the place personified,) shall deny him" (Ps. 103, 16.). The very soil is ashamed of the weeds lying withered on its surface, as though it never had been connected with them. So, when the godless falls from prosperity, his nearest friends disown him. 19. Bitter irony. The hypocrite boasts of joy. This then is his "joy" at the last. and out of the earth— Others immediately, who take the place of the man thus punished. Not *godly* men Matth. 3. 9.). For "the place" of the weeds is among stones, where the gardener wishes no plants. But, *ungodly*: a fresh crop of

weeds always springs up in the room of those torn up; there is no end of hypocrites on earth. [UMBR.] 20. Bildad regards Job, as a righteous man, who has fallen into sin. "God will not cast off for ever a perfect" (or godly man, such as Job was,), if he will only repent. "Those alone who persevere in sin God will not help" (*Heb.*, take by the hand; Ps. 73. 23; Isa. 41. 13; 42. 6,) when fallen. 21. Till—*lit.*, "to the point that:" God's blessing on thee, when repentant, will go on increasing to the point that, or until, &c. 22. The haters of Job are the wicked. They shall be clothed with shame ,Jer. 3. 25; Ps. 35. 26; 109. 29, at the failure of their hope, that Job would utterly perish, and because they, instead of him, come to nought.

CHAPTER IX.

FIRST SERIES.

Ver. 1-35. REPLY OF JOB TO BILDAD. 2. I know that it is so—That God does not "pervert justice" (8. 3.). But (even though I be sure of being in the right,) how can a mere man assert his right—,be just,) with God. The Gospel answers (Rom. 3. 26.). 3. If He (God) will contend with him—lit., "*deign* to enter into judgment." he cannot answer, &c.—He (man) would not dare, even if he had a thousand answers in readiness to one question of God's, to utter one of them, from awe of his Majesty. 4. *Heb.*, Wise in heart understanding)! And mighty in power! God confounds the ablest arguer by His wisdom, and the mightiest by His power. hardened—viz., *himself*, or *his neck* (Prov. 29. 1,); *i.e.*, defied God. To prosper, one must fall in with God's arrangements of Providence and grace. 5. and they know not—*Heb.* for "suddenly, unexpectedly, before they are aware of it" (Ps. 35. 8,); "at unawares;" *Heb.*, which *he knoweth not of* (Joel, 2. 14; Prov. 5. 6.). 6. The earth is regarded, poetically, as resting on pillars, which tremble in an earthquake (Ps. 75. 3; Isa. 24. 20.). The literal truth as to the earth is given (26. 7.). 7. The sun, at His command, doth not rise; viz., in an eclipse, or the darkness that accompanies earthquakes (v. 6.). sealeth up—*i.e.*, totally covers, as one would seal up a room, that its contents may not be seen. 8. spreadeth out—Isa. 40. 22; Ps. 104. 2.). But throughout it is not so much God's creating, as His governing, power over nature that is set forth. A storm seems a struggle between Nature and her Lord! Better, therefore, "Who *boweth* the heavens alone," without help of any other. God descends from the bowed-down heaven to the earth (Ps. 18. 9). The storm, wherein the clouds descend, suggests this image. In the descent of the vault of heaven, God has come down from His high throne, and walks majestic over *the mountain waves* (*Heb.*, *heights*,), as a conqueror *taming their violence*. So *tread upon* (Deut. 33. 29; Amos, 4. 13; Matth. 14. 26.). The Egyptian hieroglyphic for impossibility is a man walking on waves. 9. maketh—Rather, from the Arabic, *covereth up*. This accords better with the context which describes His boundless power as controller, rather than as creator. [UMBR.] Arcturus—The great bear, which always revolves about the pole, and never sets. The Chaldeans and Arabs early named and grouped in constellations the stars; often travelling, and tending flocks by night, they would naturally do so, especially as the rise and setting of some stars mark the distinction of seasons. BRINKLEY *presuming* the stars here mentioned to be those of Taurus and Scorpio, and that these were the cardinal constellations of spring and autumn in Job's time, calculates, by the precession of equinoxes, the time of Job to be 818 years after the deluge, and 184 before Abraham. Orion—*Heb.*, *the fool*; in ch. 38. 31, he appears fettered with "bands." The old legend represented this star as a hero, who presumptuously rebelled against God, and was therefore a *fool*, and was chained in the sky, as a punishment: for its rising is at the stormy period of the year. He is *Nimrod* —(*the exceedingly impious rebel*,) among the Assyrians; *Orion*, among the Greeks. Sabaism (worship of the heavenly hosts,' and hero-worship were blended in his person. He first subverted the patriarchal order of society by substituting a chieftainship based on conquest (Gen. 10. 9, 10.). Pleiades—*lit.*, "the heap of stars:" Arabic, "knot of stars." The various names of this constellation in the East expresses the *close union* of the stars in it Amos, 5. 8.). chambers of the south—The unseen regions of the S. hemisphere, with its own set of stars, as distinguished from those just mentioned, of the N. The true structure of the earth is here implied. 10. Repeated from Eliphaz, ch. 5. 9. 11. I see Him not: He passeth on—The image is that of a howling wind (Isa. 21. 1.). Like it when it bursts invisibly upon man; so God is felt in the awful *effects* of His wrath, but is not *seen* (John, 3. 8.). Therefore, reasons Job, it is impossible to contend with Him. 12. If "He taketh away," as in my case all that was dear to me, still a mortal cannot call him to account. He only takes His own. He is an absolute King Eccl. 8. 4; Dan. 4. 35.). 13. If God—Rather, "God will not withdraw His anger," *i.e.*, so long as a mortal obstinately resists. [UMBR.] the proud helpers—*1 he arrogant*, who would *help* one contending with the Almighty, are of no avail against Him. 14. How much less shall I—Who am weak—seeing that the mighty have to stoop before Him. Choose words (use a *well chosen speech*, in order to reason) with Him. 15. ch. 10, 15.). Though I were conscious of no sin, yet I would not dare to say so, but leave it to His judgment and mercy to justify me (1 Cor. 4 4.). 16. 17. "I would not believe that He had hearkened unto my voice, who breaketh me as a tree stript of (its leaves) with a tempest." 19. UMBR. takes these as the words of God, translating, "What availeth the might of the strong? 'Here (saith he,) behold ! what availeth justice? Who will appoint me a time to plead?'" (so Jer. 49. 19.). The last words certainly apply better to God, than to Job. The sense is substantially the same, if we make "me," with *E. V.* apply to Job. The "lo!" expresses God's swift readiness for battle, when challenged. 20. *it*—ch. 15. 6; Lu. 19. 22.) or, "He," God. 21. *Lit.*, here (and in v. 20.). "I perfect! I should not know my soul! I would despise (disown,) my life;" *i.e.*, Though conscious of innocence, I should be compelled, in contending with the infinite God, to ignore my own soul, and despise my past life, as if it were guilty. [Ros.] 22. one thing—"It is all one; whether perfect or wicked,—He destroyeth." This was the point Job maintained against his friends, that the righteous and wicked alike are afflicted; and that great sufferings *here* do not prove great guilt Lu. 13. 1-5; Eccles. 9. 2.). 25. If—Rather, "While (His scourge slays suddenly the wicked, v. 22,), He laughs at *disregards*; not *derides*,) the pining away of the innocent." The only difference, says Job, between the innocent and guilty is, the latter are slain by a *sudden* stroke, the former *pine away gradually*. The translation, "trial," does not express the antithesis to "slay suddenly," as "pining away" does. [UMBR.] 24. Referring to righteous *judges*, in antithesis to "the wicked," in the parallel first clause, Whereas the *wicked* oppressor often has *the earth given into his hand*, the righteous *judges are led to execution*; culprits had their *faces covered* preparatory to execution (Esth. 7. 8.). Thus the contrast of the wicked and righteous here answers to that in verse 23. if not, where and *who—If* God be *not* the cause of these anomalies, *where* is the cause to be found, and *who* is *he?* 25. a post—A courier. In the wide Persian empire such couriers, on dromedaries, or on foot, were employed to carry the royal commands to the distant provinces (Esth. 3. 13, 15; 8. 14.). My days are, not like the slow caravan, but the fleet post. *The days* are themselves poetically said to *see no good*, instead of Job in them (1 Pet. 3. 10.). 26. swift ships—Rather, *canoes of reeds*, or *papyrus-skiffs*, used on the Nile, swift from their lightness (Isa. 18. 2.). 28. The apodosis to 27,—" If I say, &c." I still am afraid of all my sorrows (returning), for I know that thou wilt (dost) not by removing my sufferings, hold or declare me innocent," How then can *I leave off my heaviness?* 29. The *if* is better omitted: I am treated by God, as) wicked; why then labour I in vain (to disprove His charge.). Job submits, not so much because he is *convinced* that God is *right*, as because God is *powerful*, and he *weak*. [BARNES.] 30. snow water—Thought to be more cleansing than common water, owing to the whiteness of snow (Ps. 51. 7; Isa. 1. 18.,. never so clean—Better, to answer to the parallelism of the first clause which expresses the cleansing material, *lye:* the Arabs used alkali mixed with oil, as *soap* (Ps. 73. 13; Jer. 2. 22.). 32. (Eccl. 6. 10; Isa. 5. 9.). 33. daysman—Mediator or umpire; he imposition of whose hand expresses power to adjudicate between the persons. There might be one on a level with Job, the one party; but Job knew of none on a level with the Almighty, the other party (1 Sam. 2. 25.). We Christians know of such a Mediator (not, however, in the sense *umpire*,) on a level with both, the God man, Christ Jesus (1 Tim. 2. 5.). 34. rod—Not here the symbol of *punishment*, but of *power*. Job cannot meet God on fair terms, so long as God deals with him on the footing of His Almighty power. 35. t is not so with me—As it now is, God not taking His rod away, I am not on such a footing of equality, as to be able to vindicate myself.

CHAPTER X.

Ver. 1-22. JOB'S REPLY TO BILDAD CONTINUED. 1. leave my complaint on myself—Rather, "I will *give loose* to my complaint" (ch. 7. 11.). 2. shew me, &c.—Do not, by virtue of thy mere sovereignty, treat me as guilty, without showing me the reasons. 3. Job is unwilling to think, God can have "pleasure" in using his power to "oppress" the weak, and to "treat" man, "the work of His own hands, as of no value" *v. 8*; Ps. 138. 8.), shine upon—Favour with prosperity Ps. 50. 2.). 4, 5, 6. Dost thou see as bodily as man? *i.e.*, with the same uncharitable eye, as for instance, Job's friends. Is thy time as short? Impossible! Yet one might think, from the rapid succession of thy strokes, that thou hadst no time to spare in overwhelming me. 7. "Although thou the Omniscient knowest," &c. (connected with v. 6.) "thou searchest after my sin." and . . . that none can deliver out of thine hand—Therefore thou hast no need to deal with me with the rapid violence, which "man" would use (Note, v. 6.). 8. "Made" with pains; implying a *work of difficulty and art*; applying to God language applicable only to man. together round about—Implying that the human body is a *complete unity*, the parts of which on all sides will bear the closest scrutiny. 9. clay—Next *v.* proves that the reference here is, not so much to the *perishable* nature of the materials, as to *their wonderful fashioning* by the Divine potter. 10. In the organization of the body from its rude commencements the liquid original gradually assumes a more solid consistency, like milk curdling into cheese Ps. 139. 15, 16.). Science reveals that the chyle circulated by the lacteal vessels is the supply to every organ. 11. fenced—Or "inlaid" (Ps. 1:9. 15.); curiously wrought." [UMBR.] In the fœtus the skin appears first, then the flesh, then the harder parts. 12. visitation—Thy watchful Providence. spirit—Breath. 13. is with thee—Was thy purpose. All God's dealings with Job in his creation, preservation, and present afflictions were part of His secret counsel Ps. 139. 16; Acts, 15. 18; Eccl. 3. 11.). 14, 15. Job is perplexed, because God "marks" every sin of his with such ceaseless rigour. Whether "wicked" *godless* and a *hypocrite*) or "righteous" comparatively: *sincere*,), God condemns and punishes alike. lift up my head—In conscious innocence (Ps. 3. 3.). see thou—Rather, "and seeing I see—I too well see mine affliction," (which seems to prove me guilty.). [UMBR.] 16. increaseth—Rather, (if) I *lift up* my head) thou wouldest hunt me, &c. [UMFR.] and again—As if a lion should not kill his prey at once, but come back and torture it again. 17. witnesses—His accumulated trials were like a succession of witnesses brought up in proof of his guilt, to wear out the accused. changes and war—Rather ("thou settest in array) against me host after host" (*lit., changes and a host, i.e.*, a succession of hosts,), *viz.*, his afflictions, and then reproach upon reproach from his friends. 20. But, since I was destined from my birth to these ills, at least give me a *little breathing time* during the few days left me (ch. 9. 34; 13. 21; Ps. 39. 13.). 22. The ideas of order and light, disorder, and darkness, harmonize (Gen. 1. 2.). Three *Heb.* words are used for darkness; in v. 21 (1,) the common word "*darkness:*" here (2, "a land of gloom" from a Heb. root, *to cover up;* (3,) " as *thick darkness*" or *blackness* from a root, expressing *sunset*.). "Where the light there-of is like blackness." Its only sunshine is thick darkness. A bold figure of poetry. Job is in a better frame which brighter thing is of the unseen world. But his views at best wanted the definite clearness of the Christian's. Compare with his words here Rev. 21. 23; 22. 5; 2 Tim. 1. 10.).

4 For *thou hast said, My doctrine is pure, and I am clean in thine eyes.
5 But oh that God would speak, and open his lips against thee;
6 And that he would show thee the secrets of wisdom, that they are double to that which is! Know therefore that *God exacteth of thee less than thine iniquity deserveth.
7 Canst *thou by searching find out God? canst thou find out the Almighty unto perfection?
8 It is ³as high as heaven; what canst thou do? deeper than hell; what canst thou know?
9 The measure thereof is longer than the earth, and broader than the sea.
10 If he *cut off, and shut up, or gather together, then *who can hinder him?
11 For *he knoweth vain men: he seeth wickedness also; will he not then consider it?
12 For *vain man would be wise, though man be born like a wild ass's colt.
13 If thou *prepare thine heart, and stretch *out thine hands toward him;
14 If iniquity be in thine hand, put it far away, and let not wickedness dwell in thy tabernacles.
15 For *then shalt thou lift up thy face without spot; yea, thou shalt be stedfast, and shalt not fear:
16 Because thou shalt forget thy misery, and remember it as waters that pass away:
17 And thine age ⁷shall be clearer than the noon-day; thou shalt shine forth, thou shalt be as the morning.
18 And thou shalt be secure, because there is hope; yea, thou shalt dig about thee, and thou shalt take thy rest in safety.
19 Also thou shalt lie down, and none shall make thee afraid; yea, many shall *make suit unto thee.
20 But the eyes of the wicked shall fail, and *they shall not escape, and their hope shall be as ¹⁰the giving up of the ghost.

CHAPTER XII.

1 Job censures the arrogant pretension of his friends to superior knowledge: he shows that wicked men often prosper: 13 God's divine wisdom and omnipotency.

AND Job answered and said,
2 No doubt but ye are the people, and wisdom shall die with you!
3 But I have ¹understanding as well as you; ²I am not inferior to you: yea, ³who knoweth not such things as these?
4 I am as one mocked of his neighbour, who *calleth upon God, and he answereth him: the just upright man is laughed to scorn.
5 He *that is ready to slip with his feet is as a lamp despised in the thought of him that is at ease.
6 The tabernacles of robbers prosper, and they that provoke God are secure; into whose hand God bringeth abundantly.
7 But ask now the beasts, and they shall teach thee: and the fowls of the air, and they shall tell thee:
8 Or speak to the earth, and it shall teach thee; and the fishes of the sea shall declare unto thee.
9 Who knoweth not in all these that the hand of the LORD hath wrought this?
10 In *whose hand is the *soul of every living thing, and the breath of *all mankind.

11 Doth not the ear try words? and the *mouth taste his meat?
12 With the ancient is wisdom; and in length of days understanding.
13 With ⁷him is wisdom and strength, he hath counsel and understanding.
14 Behold, he breaketh down, and it cannot be built again; he *shutteth *up a man, and there can be no opening.
15 Behold, he *withholdeth the waters, and they dry up; also he *sendeth them out, and they overturn the earth.
16 With him is strength and wisdom: the deceived and the deceiver are his.
17 He leadeth counsellors away spoiled, and maketh the judges fools.
18 He looseth the bond of kings, and girdeth their loins with a girdle.
19 He leadeth princes away spoiled, and overthroweth the mighty.
20 He removeth away *the speech of the trusty, and taketh away the understanding of the aged.
21 He poureth contempt upon princes, and ¹⁰weakeneth the strength of the mighty.
22 He *discovereth deep things out of darkness, and bringeth out to light the shadow of death.
23 He increaseth the nations, and destroyeth them: he enlargeth the nations, and ¹¹straiteneth them again.
24 He taketh away the heart of the chief of the people of the earth, and causeth them to wander in a wilderness where there is no way.
25 They grope in the dark without light, and he maketh them to ¹²stagger like a drunken man.

CHAPTER XIII.

1 Job reproves his friends of partiality: 14 he professes his confidence in God, etc.

LO, mine eye hath seen all this, mine ear hath heard and understood it.
2 What ye know, the same do I know also: I am not inferior unto you.
3 Surely I would speak to the Almighty, and I desire to reason with God.
4 But ye are forgers of lies, ye are all physicians of no value.
5 O that ye would altogether hold your peace! and *it should be your wisdom.
6 Hear now my reasoning, and hearken to the pleadings of my lips.
7 Will ⁵ye speak wickedly for God? and talk deceitfully for him?
8 Will ye *accept his person? will ye contend for God?
9 Is it good that he should search you out! or as one man mocketh another, do ye so mock him?
10 He will surely reprove you, if ye do secretly accept persons.
11 Shall not his ¹excellency make you afraid? and his dread fall upon you?
12 Your remembrances are like unto ashes, your bodies to bodies of clay.
13 ²Hold your peace, let me alone, that I may speak, and let come on me what will.
14 Wherefore do I take my flesh in my teeth, and *put my life in mine hand?
15 Though *he slay me, yet will I trust in him: *but I will ³maintain mine own ways before him.
16 He also shall be my *salvation: for an hypocrite shall not come before him.
17 Hear diligently my speech, and my declaration with your ears.

First Speech of Zophar. JOB, XI, XII. *Job's Reply to Zophar.*

CHAPTER XI.
FIRST SERIES.
Ver. 1-20. FIRST SPEECH OF ZOPHAR. 2. Zophar assails Job for his empty words, and indirectly, the two friends, for their weak reply. Taciturnity is highly prized among Orientals Prov. 10. 8, 19.). 3. lies—Rather, *rain boasting* Isa. 16. 6; Jer. 48. 30.). The "men" is emphatic; men of sense; in antithesis to "vain boasting." mockest — Upbraidest God by complaints. 4. doctrine— Purposely used of Job's speeches, which sounded like lessons of doctrine Deu. 32. 2; Prov. 4. 2.). thine—Addressed to God. Job had maintained his *sincerity*, against his friends' suspicions, not *faultlessness*. 6. to that which is!—Rather, "they are double to (man's) *wisdom*." [MICH.] So the *Heb.* is rendered (Prov. 2. 7.). God's ways, which you arraign, if you were shown their secret wisdom, would be seen vastly to exceed that of men, including yours (1 Cor. 1. 25.). exacteth—Rather, "God *consigns to oblivion* in thy favour much of thy guilt." 7. Rather, "Penetrate to the perfections of the Almighty" ch. 9. 10; Ps. 139. 6.). 8. It—The "wisdom" of God (v. 6.). The abruptness of the *Heb.* is forcible; "The heights of heaven! What canst thou do" as to attaining to them with thy gaze, Ps. 139. 8.)? know— *viz.*, of His perfections. 10. cut off—Rather, as in ch. 9. 11, *pass over* as a storm; *viz.*, rush upon in anger. shut up—In prison, with a view to trial. gather together—The parties for judgment: hold a judicial *assembly*, to pass sentence on the prisoners. 11. Ps. 94. 11.). consider—So as to punish it. Rather, from the connexion, v. 6, "He seeth wickedness also, which man does not *perceive*;" *lit.*, "But no (other, save He) perceiveth it." [UMBR.] God's "wisdom" (v. 6,) detects sin where Job's human eye cannot reach *v.* 8,), so as to see any. 12. vain—Hollow. wou'd be—*Wants to consider himself* "wise;" opposed to God's "wisdom" note, v. 11,); refuses to see sin, where God sees it Rom. 1. 22.. wild ass's colt—A proverb for untamed wildness ch. 39. 5, 8; Jer. 2. 24; Gen. 16. 12; *Heb.*, "a wild-ass man.") Man wishes to appear *wisely obedient* to his Lord, whereas he is *from his birth, unsubdued in spirit*. 13. The apodosis to the "If" is at v. 15. The "preparation of the heart" is to be obtained (Prov. 16. 1,) by "stretching out the hands" in prayer for it Ps. 10. 17; 1 Chr. 29. 18.). 14. Rather, "if thou wilt put far away the iniquity in thine hand" as Zaccheus did, Luke, 19. 8.). The apodosis or conclusion is at v. 15, "then shalt thou," &c. 15. Zophar refers to Job's own words ch. 10. 15,), "yet will I not *lift up my* head," even though righteous. Zophar declares, if Job will follow his advice, he may "lift up his face." spot—(Deu. 32. 5.. steadfast—*lit.*, *run fast together*, like metals which become firm and hard by fusion. The sinner on the contrary is wavering. 16. Just as when the stream runs dry (ch. 6. 17,), the danger threatened by its wild waves is forgotten (Isa. 16.). [UMBR.] 17. age—*Days* or *life*. the noon-day—*viz.*, of thy former prosperity; which, in the poet's image, had gone on increasing, until it reached its height, as the sun rises higher and higher until it reaches the meridian (Prov. 4. 18.. shine forth—Rather, "though now *in darkness*, thou shalt be as the morning." Or, "thy darkness (if any dark shade should arise on thee, it) shall be as the morning" only the dullness of morning twilight, not nocturnal darkness.). [UMBR.] 18. The experience of thy life will teach thee, there is hope for man in every trial. dig—*viz.*, wells; the chief necessary in the E. Better, "though now *ashamed* (Rom. 5. 5, opposed to the previous "hope," thou shalt then rest safely." [GES.] 19— Ps. 4. 8; Prov. 3. 24; Isa. 14. 30.). Oriental images of prosperity. 19. make suit —*lit.*, "stroke thy face, caress thee" Prov. 19. 6.). 20. A warning to Job, if he would not turn to God. "The wicked." *i. e.*, *obdurate sinners*. eyes . . . fail — *i.e.*, in vain look for relief Deu. 28. 65.). Zophar implies, Job's only hope of relief is in a change of heart. they shall not escape—*lit.*, "every refuge shall vanish from them." giving up the ghost—Their hope shall leave them as the breath does the body (Prov. 11. 7.).

CHAPTER XII.
FIRST SERIES.
Ver. 1-25. JOB'S REPLY TO ZOPHAR. XII, XIII, XIV. 2. wisdom shall die with you!— Ironical. As if all the wisdom in the world was concentrated in them, and would expire when they expired. Wisdom makes "a people;" a foolish nation are "not a people" (Rom. 10. 19.). 3. not inferior—Not vanquished in argument and "wisdom" ch. 13. 2.. such things as these—Such commonplace maxims, as you so pompously adduce. 4. The unfounded accusations of Job's friends were a "mockery" of him. He alludes to Zophar's word, "mockest" (ch. 11. 3.. his neighbour, who calleth, &c.—Rather, "*I who call upon God that he may answer me* favourably. [UMBR.] 5. Rather, "a torch lamp) is an object of contempt in the thoughts of him who rests securely (is at ease,), though it (which) was prepared for the falterings of the feet." [UMBR.] (Prov. 25. 19.). "Thoughts" and "feet" are in contrast; also rests "securely," and "falterings." The wanderer, arrived at his night-quarters, contemptuously throws aside the torch, which had guided his uncertain steps through the darkness. As the torch is to the wanderer, so Job to his friends. Once they gladly used his aid in their need, now they in prosperity mock him in his need. 6. Job shows that the matter of *fact* opposes Zophar's *theory* (ch. 11. 14, 19, 20,), that wickedness causes "insecurity" in men's "tabernacles." On the contrary they who "rob the tabernacles" (dwellings) of others "prosper securely" in their own. into whose hand, &c.—Rather, "who make a god of their own hand," *i.e.*, who regard their might as their only ruling principle. [UMBR.] 7, 8. Beasts, birds, fishes, and plants, reasons Job, teach that the violent live the most securely (v. 6,). The vulture lives more securely than the dove, the lion than the ox, the shark than the dolphin, the rose than the thorn which tears it. speak to the earth— Rather, "*the shrubs of* the earth." [UMBR.] 9. In all these cases, says Job, the agency must be referred to Jehovah ("the Lord," *E.V.*) though they may seem to man to imply imperfection (v. 6; ch. 9. 24.). This is the only undisputed passage of the poetical part, in which the name "Jehovah" occurs: in the historical parts it occurs frequently. 10. The soul, *i.e.*, the animal *life*. Man, reasons Job, is subjected to the same laws as the

lower animals. 11. As the *mouth* by *tasting meats* selects what pleases it, so *the ear tries the words* of others and retains what is convincing. Each chooses according to his taste. The connexion with *v.* 12 is, in reference to Bildad's appeal to the "ancients" (ch. 8. 8.). You are right in appealing to them, since "with them was wisdom," &c. But you select such proverbs of theirs as suit your views, so I may borrow from the same such as suit mine. 12. ancient—Aged (ch. 15. 10.). 13. In contrast to, "with the ancient is wisdom" (*v.* 12.), Job quotes a saying of the ancients which suits his argument, "with Him (God) is (the true) wisdom" (Pro. 8. 14, : and by that "wisdom and strength" He breaketh down," &c., as an absolute Sovereign, not allowing man to penetrate His mysteries: man's part is to bow to His unchangeable decrees ch. 1, 21.). The Mahomedan saying is, "if God will, and how God will." 14. shutteth up—(Isa. 22. 22.). Job refers to Zophar's "shut up" (ch. 11. 10.). 15. Probably alluding to the flood. 16. (Ez. 14. 9.). 18. He looseth the *authority* of kings—the "bond" with which they bind their subjects Isa. 45. 1; Ge. 14. 4; Dan. 2. 21.), a girdle—The *cord*, with which they are bound as captives, instead of the royal "girdle" they once wore (Isa. 22. 21.), and the bond they once bound others with. So "gird,"—put on one the *bonds* of a prisoner, instead of the ordinary *girdle* (Jn. 21. 18.). 19. princes—Rather, *priests*, as the *Heb.* is rendered (Ps. 99. 6.). Even the sacred ministers of religion are not exempt from reverses and captivity. the mighty—Rather, "the firm-rooted in power:" the Arabic root expresses *everflowing water*. [UMBR.] 20. the trusty—Rather, "those secure in their eloquence:" *ex. gr.*, the speakers in the gate (Isa. 3. 3.). [BEZA.] understanding—*lit.*, *taste*, *i.e.*, insight or spiritual discernment, which experience gives the aged. The same *Heb.* word is applied to Daniel's wisdom in interpretation Dan. 2. 14.). 21. Ps. 107. 40 quotes, in its first clause, this *v.*, and, in its second, the 24th *v.* of the ch. weakeneth the strength—*lit.*, *looseth the girdle;* Orientals wear flowing garments: when active strength is to be put forth, they gird up their garments with a girdle. Hence here—"He destroyeth their power" in the eyes of the people. 22. (Dan. 2. 22.). 23. Isa. 9. 3; Ps. 107. 38, 39, which Ps. quotes this ch. elsewhere. (See note *v.* 21.). a raitene h—*lit.*, leadeth in, *i.e.*, reduces. 24. hear—*Intelligence.* wander in a wilderness—Figurative; not referring to any actual fact. This cannot be quoted to prove Job lived after Israel's wanderings in the desert. Ps. 107. 4, 40, quotes this passage. 25. Deu. 28. 29; Ps. 107. 27, again quotes Job, but in a different connexion.

CHAPTER XIII.
Ver. 1-28. JOB'S REPLY TO ZOPHAR CONTINUED. 1. all this—as to the dealings of Providence (ch.12.3.). 3. Job wishes to plead his cause before God ch. 9. 34, 35, as he is more and more convinced of the *valueless* character of his would-be "physicians" ch. 16. 2.). 4. forgers of lies—*lit.*, *artful twisters of vain speeches.* [UMBR.] 5. (Pro. 17, 28.). The Arabs say, "the wise are dumb: silence is wisdom." 7. deceitfully—Use fallacies to vindicate God in His dealings; as if the end justified the means. Their "deceitfulness" for God, against Job, was, they asserted he was a sinner, because he was a sufferer. 8. accept his person—God's: *i.e.*, be partial for Him, as when a judge favours one party in a trial, because of personal considerations. contend for God—viz., with fallacies and prepossessions against Job before judgment (Jud. 6. 31.). Partiality can never please the impartial God; nor the goodness of the cause excuse the unfairness of the arguments. 9. Will the *issue* to you be *good, when He searches out you* and your arguments? Will you be regarded by Him as pure and disinterested? mock—Gal. 6. 7.). Rather, "can you deceive Him as one man?" &c. 10. *If ye do*, though *secretly*, act *partially*. (Note *v.* 8; Ps. 82. 1, 2.). God can successfully vindicate His acts, and needs no fallacious argument of man. 11. make you afraid?—*viz.*, of employing sophisms in His name (Jer. 10. 7, 10.). 12. remembrances—"Proverbial maxims," so called because *well-remembered*, like unto ashes—Or, "parables of ashes;" the image of lightness and nothingness (Isa. 44. 20.). bodies—Rather, "entrenchments;" those of clay, as opposed to those of stone, are easy to be destroyed: so the proverbs, behind which they entrench themselves, will not shelter them, when God shall appear to reprove them for their injustice to Job. 13. Job would wish to be spared their speeches, so as to speak out all his mind as to his wretchedness *v.* 14.). happen what will. 14. A proverb for, "Why should I anxiously desire to save my life?" [EICH.] The image in the first clause is that of a wild beast, which in order to preserve his prey, carries it in his teeth. That in the second refers to men who hold in the hand what they want to keep secure. 15. in him—So the margin or Keri reads. But the textual reading or cetib is "not," which agrees best with the context, and other passages wherein he says he has *no hope* (ch. 6. 11; 7.21; 10.20; 19.10.). "Though He slay me, and I dare *no more hope*, yet I will maintain," &c., *i.e.*, "I desire to vindicate myself before Him," as not a hypocrite. [UMBR. & NOY.] 16. He—Rather, "*This* also already speaks in my behalf [*lit.*, "for my *saving* acquittal,"] for an hypocrite would not wish to come before Him" as I do. [UMBR.] See last clause of *v* 15.). 17. my declaration—*viz.*, that I wish to be permitted to justify myself immediately before God. with your ears—*i.e.*, attentively. 18. ordered—Implying a *constant preparation* for defence in his confidence of innocence. 19. if, &c.—Rather, *Then* would I hold my tongue and give up the ghost," *i.e.*, if any one can contend with me and prove me false, I have no more to say, "I will be silent and die." Like our, "I would stake my life on it." [UMBR.] 20. Address to God. not hide —Stand forth boldly to maintain my cause. 21. Note, 9. 34; Ps. 39. 10.). 22. call—A challenge to the defendant to answer to the charges. answer—The defence begun. speak —As plaintiff. answer—To the plea of the plaintiff. Expressions from a trial. 23. The catalogue of my sins ought to be great, to judge from the severity with which God ever anew crushes one already bowed down. Would that He would reckon them up! He then would see how much my calamities outnumber them, sin?—Sing., "I am unconscious of a *single* particular sin, much less many." [UMBR.] 24. hidest . . . face— A figure from the gloomy impression caused

by the sudden clouding over of the sun. enemy—God treated Job as an enemy who must be robbed of power by ceaseless sufferings ch. 7. 17, 21.). 25. (Lev. 26. 36; Ps. 1. 4.). Job compares himself to a leaf already fallen, which the storm still chases hither and thither. break—lit., *shake with* thy *terrors*. Jesus Christ does not "break the bruised reed" (Isa. 42. 3; 27. 8.). 26. writest—A judicial phrase, to note down the determined punishment. The sentence of the condemned used to be *written* down (Isa. 10. 1; Jer. 22. 30; Ps. 149. 9.). [UMBR.] bitter things—Bitter punishments. makest me to possess—Or inherit. In old age he receives possession of the inheritance of sin thoughtlessly acquired in youth. "To inherit *sins*" is to inherit the *punishments* inseparably connected with them in *Heb*. ideas (Ps. 25. 7.). 27. stocks—In which the prisoner's feet were made fast until the time of execution (Jer. 20. 2.). lookest narrowly—As an overseer would watch a prisoner. print—Either the stocks, or his disease, *marked* his *soles* (Heb. *roots* as the bastinado would. Better, thou drawest or *diggest* [GES.] a line, or *trench* [GES.] round my soles, beyond which I must not move. [UMBR.] 28. Job speaks of *himself* in the third person, thus forming the transition to the *general* lot of man (ch. 14. 1; Ps. 39. 11; Hos. 5. 12.).

CHAPTER XIV.
Ver. 1-22. JOB PASSES FROM HIS OWN TO THE COMMON MISERY OF MANKIND, 1. woman—Feeble and in the E. looked down upon (Gen. 2. 21.). Man being born of one so frail must be frail himself (Matt. 11. 11.). few days— (Gen. 47. 9; Ps. 90. 10.). Lit., *short of days*. Man is the reverse of *full of days and short of trouble*. 2. (Ps. 90. 6; Note, ch. 8. 9.). 3. open . . . eyes upon—Not in graciousness; but, "Dost thou sharply fix thine eyes upon?" Note, 7. 20; also 1. 7.). Is one so frail as man worthy of such constant watching on the part of God? Zech. 12. 4.). me—So frail. thee—So Almighty. 4. A plea in mitigation. The doctrine of original sin was held from the first. "Man is unclean from his birth, how then can God expect perfect cleanness from such a one and deal so severely with me?" 5. determined—ch. 7. 1; Isa. 10. 23; Dan. 9. 27; 11. 36.). 6. Turn—*viz.*, thine eyes from watching him so jealously (v. 3.) hireling—ch. 7. 1.) accomplish—Rather, "enjoy." That he may at least enjoy the measure of rest of the hireling, who though hard-worked reconciles himself to his lot by the hope of his rest and reward. [UMBR.] 7. Man may the more claim a peaceful life, since, when separated from it by death, he never returns to it. This does not deny a future life, but a return to the *present condition* of life. Job plainly hopes for a future state (v. 13; ch. 7. 2.). Still it is but vague and trembling *hope*, not *assurance*; excepting the one bright glimpse in ch. 19. 25. The Gospel revelation was needed to change fears, hopes, and glimpses into clear and definite certainties. 9. scent—*Exhalation*, which, rather than the humidity of water, causes the tree to germinate. In the antithesis to *man* the *tree* is personified, and volition is poetically ascribed to it, like a plant—"as if newly planted." [UMBR.] Not as if trees and plants were a different species. 10. man . . . man—Two distinct *Heb.* words are here used; *Geber*, a *mighty* man; though

mighty, he dies: *Adam*, a man *of earth*: because earthly, he gives up the ghost. wasteth —is reduced to nothing: he cannot revive in the present state, as the tree does. The cypress and pine, which when cut down, do not revive, were the symbols of death among the Romans. 11. sea—*i.e.*, *a lake*, or pool formed from the outspreading of a river. Job lived near the Euphrates: and "sea" is applied to it (Jer. 51. 36; Isa. 27. 1.). So of the Nile Isa. 19. 5.). fail—Utterly disappeared by drying up. The rugged channel of the once flowing water answers to the outstretched corpse—("lieth down," v. 12, of the once living man. 12. heavens be no more—This only implies that Job had no hope of living again in the *present* order of the world, not that he had no hope of life again in a new order of things. Ps. 102. 26, proves that early under the O. T. the dissolution of the present earth and heavens was expected cf. Gen. 8. 22.). Enoch *before* Job had implied that the "saints shall live again Jude, 14; Heb. 11. 13-16.). Even if, by this phrase, Job meant "never" (Ps. 89. 29,) in his gloomier state of feelings, yet the *Holy Ghost* made him unconsciously (1 Pe. 1. 11, 12,) use language expressing the truth, that the resurrection is to be preceded by the dissolution of the heavens. In v. 13-15, he plainly passes to brighter hopes of a world to come. 13. Job wishes to be kept hidden in the grave, until God's wrath against him shall have passed away. So whilst God's wrath is visiting the earth for the abounding apostasy which is to precede the Second Coming, God's people shall be hidden against the resurrection-glory (Isa. 26. 19-21.). set time— A decreed time (Acts, 1. 7.). 14. shall he live?— The answer implied is, *There is a hope that he shall, though not in the present order of life;* as is shown by the words following. Job had denied v. 10-12, that man shall live again in this present world. But hoping for a "set time" when God shall remember and raise him out of the "hiding" place of the grave v. 13.), he declares himself willing to "wait all the days of his appointed time" of continuance in the grave, however long and hard that may be. "Appointed time," *lit., warfare, hard service;* implying the *hardship* of being shut out from the realms of light and God for the time he shall be in the grave ch. 7. 1.). change—My release, as a soldier at his post released from duty by *the relieving guard* Note 10. 17.). [UMBR. & GES.] but elsewhere [GES.] explains it, *renovation*, as of plants in spring (v. 7,), but this does not accord so well with the metaphor in "appointed time" or "*warfare.*" 15. viz., at the resurrection (John, 5. 28; Ps. 17. 15.). have a desire—*lit., become pale with anxious desire*: the same word is translated "sore longedst after" (Gen. 31. 30; Ps. 84. 2.): implying the utter unlikelihood that God would leave in oblivion the "creature of His own hands so fearfully and wonderfully made." It is objected that if Job knew of a future retribution, he would make it the leading topic in solving the problem of the permitted afflictions of the righteous. But 1. "He did not intend to exceed the limits of what was *clearly revealed;* the doctrine was then in a vague form only. 2. The doctrine of God's moral government in *this* life, even *independently of the future*, needed vindication. 16. Rather, Yea, thou wilt number, &c.,

18 Behold now, I have ordered my cause; I know that I shall be justified.
19 Who *is* he that will plead with me? for now, if I hold my tongue, I shall give up the ghost.
20 Only do not two *things* unto me; then will I not hide myself from thee.
21 Withdraw thine hand far from me; and let not thy dread make me afraid:
22 Then call thou, and I will answer; or let me speak, and answer thou me.
23 How many *are* mine iniquities and sins? make me to know my transgression and my sin.
24 Wherefore hidest thou thy face, and holdest me for thine enemy?
25 Wilt thou break a leaf driven to and fro? and wilt thou pursue the dry stubble?
26 For thou writest bitter things against me, and makest me to possess the iniquities of my youth.
27 Thou puttest my feet also in the stocks, and lookest narrowly unto all my paths; thou settest a print upon the heels of my feet.
28 And he, as a rotten thing, consumeth, as a garment that is moth-eaten.

CHAPTER XIV.

1 Brevity of man's life. 13 Job waits for his change.

MAN that is born of a woman is of few days, and full of trouble.
2 He cometh forth like a flower, and is cut down: he fleeth also as a shadow, and continueth not.
3 And dost thou open thine eyes upon such an one, and bringest me into judgment with thee?
4 Who can bring a clean thing out of an unclean? not one.
5 Seeing his days *are* determined, the number of his months *are* with thee, thou hast appointed his bounds that he cannot pass;
6 Turn from him, that he may rest, till he shall accomplish, as an hireling, his day.
7 For there is hope of a tree, if it be cut down, that it will sprout again, and that the tender branch thereof will not cease.
8 Though the root thereof wax old in the earth, and the stock thereof die in the ground;
9 Yet through the scent of water it will bud, and bring forth boughs like a plant.
10 But man dieth, and wasteth away; yea, man giveth up the ghost, and where *is* he?
11 *As* the waters fail from the sea, and the flood decayeth and drieth up;
12 So man lieth down, and riseth not: till the heavens *be* no more, they shall not awake, nor be raised out of their sleep.
13 O that thou wouldest hide me in the grave, that thou wouldest keep me secret, until thy wrath be past, that thou wouldest appoint me a set time, and remember me!
14 If a man die, shall he live again? All the days of my appointed time will I wait, till my change come.
15 Thou shalt call, and I will answer thee: thou wilt have a desire to the work of thine hands.
16 For now thou numberest my steps: dost thou not watch over my sin?
17 My transgression *is* sealed up in a bag, and thou sewest up mine iniquity.

18 And surely the mountain falling cometh to nought, and the rock is removed out of his place.
19 The waters wear the stones: thou washest away the things which grow out of the dust of the earth; and thou destroyest the hope of man.
20 Thou prevailest for ever against him, and he passeth: thou changest his countenance, and sendest him away.
21 His sons come to honour, and he knoweth *it* not; and they are brought low, but he perceiveth *it* not of them.
22 But his flesh upon him shall have pain, and his soul within him shall mourn.

CHAPTER XV.

1 Eliphaz reproves Job for justifying himself. 17 He proves the unquietness of wicked men.

THEN answered Eliphaz the Temanite, and said,
2 Should a wise man utter vain knowledge, and fill his belly with the east wind?
3 Should he reason with unprofitable talk? or with speeches wherewith he can do no good?
4 Yea, thou castest off fear, and restrainest prayer before God.
5 For thy mouth uttereth thine iniquity, and thou choosest the tongue of the crafty.
6 Thine own mouth condemneth thee, and not I; yea, thine own lips testify against thee.
7 *Art* thou the first man *that* was born? or *wast* thou made before the hills?
8 Hast thou heard the secret of God? and dost thou restrain wisdom to thyself?
9 What knowest thou, that we know not? *what* understandest thou, which *is* not in us?
10 With us *are* both the grey-headed and very aged men, much elder than thy father.
11 *Are* the consolations of God small with thee? is there any secret thing with thee?
12 Why doth thine heart carry thee away? and what do thy eyes wink at,
13 That thou turnest thy spirit against God, and lettest such words go out of thy mouth?
14 What *is* man, that he should be clean? and *he which is* born of a woman, that he should be righteous?
15 Behold, he putteth no trust in his saints; yea, the heavens are not clean in his sight;
16 How much more abominable and filthy *is* man, which drinketh iniquity like water?
17 I will show thee, hear me; and that which I have seen I will declare;
18 Which wise men have told from their fathers, and have not hid *it:*
19 Unto whom alone the earth was given, and no stranger passed among them.
20 The wicked man travaileth with pain all *his* days, and the number of years is hidden to the oppressor.
21 A dreadful sound *is* in his ears: in prosperity the destroyer shall come upon him.
22 He believeth not that he shall return out of darkness, and he is waited for of the sword.
23 He wandereth abroad for bread, *saying,* Where *is it?* he knoweth that the day of darkness is ready at his hand.

and wilt not (as now) jealously watch over my sin." Thenceforward, instead of severe watching for every sin of Job, God will guard him against every sin. "Number ... steps," *i.e.*, *minutely attend to* them, that they may not wander. [UMBR.] (1 Sam. 2. 9; Ps. 37. 23.). 17. s aled up—(ch. 9. 7.). Is shut up in eternal oblivion, *i.e.*, God thenceforth will think no more of my former sins. To *cover* sins is to *completely forgive* them (Ps. 32. 1; 85. 2.). Purses of money in the East are usually sealed. sewest up—Rather, "coverest;" akin to an Arabic word "to colour over," to forget wholly. 18. cometh to nought—*lit.*, *fadeth*; a poetical image from a leaf (Isa. 34. 4.). Here Job falls back into his gloomy bodings as to the grave. Instead of "and surely," translate "yet;" marking the transition from his brighter hopes. Even the solid mountain falls and crumbles away, man therefore cannot "hope" to escape decay or to live again in the *present* world *v*. 19.). out of his place—So man (Ps. 103. 16.). 19. The *Heb.* order is more forcible. "Stones themselves are worn away by water." things wlich grow out of—Rather, "*floods* wash away the dust of the earth." There is a gradation from "mountains" to "rocks" (*v*. 18), then "stones," then last "dust of the earth;" thus the solid mountain at last disappears utterly. 20. prevailest—Dost overpower by superior strength. passeth—Dieth. changest countenance—The change in the visage at death. Differently Dan. 5. 9.). 21. One striking trait is selected from the sad picture of the severance of the dead from all that passes in the world (Eccl. 9. 5.), viz., the utter separation of parents and children. 22. "Flesh" and "soul" describe the whole man. Scripture rests the hope of a future life, not on the inherent immortality of the soul, but on the restoration of the *body* with the soul. In the unseen world, Job in a gloomy frame anticipates, man shall be limited to the thought of his own misery. "Pain is by personification, from *our* feelings whilst *alive*, attributed to the flesh and soul, as if the man could feel in his body when dead. It is the dead in general, not the wicked, who are meant here.

CHAPTER XV.

SECOND SERIES.

Ver. 1-35. SECOND SPEECH OF ELIPHAZ. 2. a wise man—which Job claims to be. vain knowledge—*Heb.*, *windy knowledge*; *lit.*, "of wind" ch. 8. 2.). In Eccl. 1. 14, *Heb. to catch wind* expresses to strive for what is vain. east wind—Stronger than the previous "wind." For in that region the East wind is the most destructive of winds Isa 27. 8.). Thus here, —*empty violence.* belly—The inward parts, the breast Pro.18.8.). 4. fear—Reverence for God, (ch. 4. 6; Ps. 2. 11.), prayer—Meditation in Ps. 104. 34; so *devotion*. If thy views were right, reasons Eliphaz, that God disregards the afflictions of the righteous and makes the wicked to prosper, all devotion would be at an end. 5. The sophistry of thine own speeches proves thy guilt. 6. No *pious* man would utter such sentiments. 7. *i.e.*, Art thou *wisdom* personified? Wisdom existed before the hills, *i.e.*, the eternal Son of God (Prov. 8. 25; Ps. 90. 2.) Wast thou in existence before Adam. The farther back one existed, the nearer he was to the Eternal Wisdom. 8. secret—Rather, "Wast thou a listener *in the secret council* of God?" The *Heb.* means

properly *the cushions* on which a divan of counsellors in the E. usually sit. God's servants are admitted to God's secrets (Ps. 25. 14; Gen. 18. 17; John, 15. 15.). restrain—Rather, didst thou take away, *or borrow*, thence *viz.*, from the Divine secret council, thy wisdom? Eliphaz in this (*v*. 8, 9,) retorts Job's words upon himself ch. 12. 2, 3; 13. 2.. 9. in us—Or "with us," Eliphaz is for *we are aware of*. 10. On our side, thinking with us are the aged. Job had admitted that wisdom is with them (ch. 12. 12.). Eliphaz seems to have been himself older than Job; perhaps the other two also were so ch. 32. 6. . Job in ch. 30. 1. does not refer to his three friends; it therefore forms no objection. The Arabs are proud of fulness of years. 11 consolations—*viz.*, the revelation which Eliphaz had stated as a consolatory reproof to Job, and which he repeats in *v*. 14. secret—Hast thou some *secret* wisdom and source of consolation, which makes thee disregard those suggested by me! *v*. 8.). Rather, from a different *Heb.* root, Is the word of *kindness* or *gentleness* addressed by me treated by thee as valueless! [UMBR.] 12. wink—*i.e.*, why do thy eyes *evince pride*? Prov. 6. 13; Ps. 35. 19.). 13. *i.e.*, Frettest against God, and lettest fall rash words. 14. Eliphaz repeats the revelation (ch. 4. 17,) in substance, but using Job's own words (ch. 14. 1, Note on "born of a woman,") to strike him with his own weapons. 15. Repeated from ch. 4. 18; "servants" there are "saints" here, *viz.*, holy angels. heavens—*lit.*, or else answering to "angels" (ch. 4. 18; see Note there, and ch. 25. 5.). 16. filthy—In Arabic *sour* (Ps. 14. 3; 53. 3,), corrupted from his original purity. drinketh—(Prov. 19. 28.). 17. In direct contradiction of Job's position (ch. 12. 6, &c.,) that the lot of the wicked was the most prosperous here, Eliphaz appeals 1, to his own experience, (2, to the wisdom of the ancients. 18. Rather, "and which as handed down from their fathers, they have not concealed." 19. Eliphaz speaks like a genuine Arab when he boasts that his ancestors had ever possessed the land unmixed with foreigners. [UMBR.] His words are intended to oppose Job's (ch. 9. 24,); "the earth" in their case was *not* "given into the hand of the wicked." He refers to the division of the earth by Divine appointment (Gen. 10. 5, 25. 32.). Also he may insinuate that Job's sentiments had been corrupted from original purity by his vicinity to the Sabeans and Chaldeans. [ROS.] 20. travaileth—Rather, "trembleth of himself," though there is no real danger. [UMBR.] and the number of his) years, &c.—This gives the reason why the wicked man trembles continually, *viz.*, because he knows not the moment when his life must end. 21. An evil conscience conceives alarm at every sudden sound, though it be in a time of peace ("prosperity," when there is no real danger Lev. 26. 36; Prov. 28. 1; 2 Ki. 7. 6.). 22. darkness—*viz.*, *danger or calamity*. Glancing at Job who despaired of restoration: in contrast to good men when in darkness Mic. 7. 8, 9.). waited for of—*i. e.*, He is destined for the sword. [GES.] Rather, (in the night of danger) "he *looks anxiously towards* the sword," as if every sword was drawn against him. [UMBR.] 23. Wandereth *in anxious search* for bread. Famine in O. T., depicts sore need (Isa. 5. 13.). Contrast the pious

24 Trouble and anguish shall make him afraid; they shall prevail against him, as a king ready to the battle.
25 For he stretcheth out his hand against God, and strengtheneth himself against the Almighty.
26 He runneth upon him, even on his neck, upon the thick bosses of his bucklers;
27 Because he covereth his face with his fatness, and maketh collops of fat on his flanks.
28 And he dwelleth in desolate cities, and in houses which no man inhabiteth, which are ready to become heaps.
29 He shall not be rich, neither shall his substance continue, neither shall he prolong the perfection thereof upon the earth.
30 He shall not depart out of darkness; the flame shall dry up his branches; and by the breath of his mouth shall he go away.
31 Let not him that is deceived trust in vanity; for vanity shall be his recompence.
32 It shall be accomplished before his time, and his branch shall not be green.
33 He shall shake off his unripe grape as the vine, and shall cast off his flower as the olive.
34 For the congregation of hypocrites shall be desolate, and fire shall consume the tabernacles of bribery.
35 They conceive mischief, and bring forth vanity, and their belly prepareth deceit.

CHAPTER XVI.

1 Job reproves his friends for unmercifulness; 17 he asserts his innocency.

THEN Job answered and said,
2 I have heard many such things: miserable comforters are ye all.
3 Shall vain words have an end? or what emboldeneth thee that thou answerest?
4 I also could speak as ye do: if your soul were in my soul's stead, I could heap up words against you, and shake mine head at you.
5 But I would strengthen you with my mouth, and the moving of my lips should asswage your grief.
6 Though I speak, my grief is not asswaged; and though I forbear, what am I eased?
7 But now he hath made me weary: thou hast made desolate all my company.
8 And thou hast filled me with wrinkles, which is a witness against me: and my leanness rising up in me beareth witness to my face.
9 He teareth me in his wrath, who hateth me: he gnasheth upon me with his teeth; mine enemy sharpeneth his eyes upon me.
10 They have gaped upon me with their mouth; they have smitten me upon the cheek reproachfully; they have gathered themselves together against me.
11 God hath delivered me to the ungodly, and turned me over into the hands of the wicked.
12 I was at ease, but he hath broken me asunder: he hath also taken me by my neck, and shaken me to pieces, and set me up for his mark.
13 His archers compass me round about; he cleaveth my reins asunder, and doth not spare; he poureth out my gall upon the ground.
14 He breaketh me with breach upon breach; he runneth upon me like a giant.

15 I have sewed sackcloth upon my skin, and defiled my horn in the dust.
16 My face is foul with weeping, and on my eyelids is the shadow of death;
17 Not for any injustice in mine hands: also my prayer is pure.
18 O earth, cover not thou my blood, and let my cry have no place.
19 Also now, behold, my witness is in heaven, and my record is on high.
20 My friends scorn me: but mine eye poureth out tears unto God.
21 Oh that one might plead for a man with God, as a man pleadeth for his neighbour!
22 When a few years are come, then I shall go the way whence I shall not return.

CHAPTER XVII.

1 Job appeals from men to God. 6 The unmerciful dealing of men with the afflicted may astonish, but not discourage the righteous. 11 Job's hope.

MY breath is corrupt, my days are extinct, the graves are ready for me.
2 Are there not mockers with me? and doth not mine eye continue in their provocation?
3 Lay down now, put me in a surety with thee; who is he that will strike hands with me?
4 For thou hast hid their heart from understanding: therefore shalt thou not exalt them.
5 He that speaketh flattery to his friends, even the eyes of his children shall fail.
6 He hath made me also a byword of the people; and aforetime I was as a tabret.
7 Mine eye also is dim by reason of sorrow, and all my members are as a shadow.
8 Upright men shall be astonied at this, and the innocent shall stir up himself against the hypocrite.
9 The righteous also shall hold on his way, and he that hath clean hands shall be stronger and stronger.
10 But as for you all, do ye return, and come now: for I cannot find one wise man among you.
11 My days are past, my purposes are broken off, even the thoughts of my heart.
12 They change the night into day: the light is short because of darkness.
13 If I wait, the grave is mine house: I have made my bed in the darkness.
14 I have said to corruption, Thou art my father; to the worm, Thou art my mother, and my sister.
15 And where is now my hope? as for my hope, who shall see it?
16 They shall go down to the bars of the pit, when our rest together is in the dust.

CHAPTER XVIII.

1 Bildad reproves Job for presumption and impatience. 5 Calamities of the wicked.

THEN answered Bildad the Shuhite, and said,
2 How long will it be ere ye make an end of words? mark, and afterwards we will speak.
3 Wherefore are we counted as beasts, and reputed vile in your sight?
4 He teareth himself in his anger: shall the earth be forsaken for thee? and shall the rock be removed out of his place?
5 Yea, the light of the wicked shall be put out, and the spark of his fire shall not shine.

Job Reproves His Friends   JOB, XVI.   *For Unmercifulness.*

man's lot ch. 5. 20-22.). **knoweth—Has the firm** conviction. Contrast the same word applied to the pious ch. 5. 24, 25. . **ready at his hand** —An Arabic phrase to denote a thing's *complete readiness* and *full presence*, as if in the hand. 24. prevail — **break upon him suddenly and terribly, as a king, &c.** Prov. 6, 11.). 25. stretcheth . . . hand—Wielding the spear, as a bold rebel against God ch. 9. 4; Isa. 27. 4.). 26. on his neck—Rather, " with outstretched neck," viz., that of the rebel. [UMBR.] (Ps. 75. 5.) upon . . . bucklers— Rather, "*with*—his the rebel's, not God's' bucklers." The rebel and his fellows are depicted as joining shields together, to form a compact covering over their heads against the weapons hurled on them from a fortress. [UMBR. & GES.] 27. The well nourished body of the rebel is the sign of his prosperity. collops—*Masses* of fat. He pampers and fattens himself with sensual indulgences. Hence his rebellion against God (Deu. 32. 15; 1 Sam. 2. 29.). 28. The class of wicked here described is that of robbers who plunder' cities," and seize on the houses of the banished citizens Isa. 13. 20.). Eliphaz chooses this class, because Job had chosen the same ch. 12. 6.). **hears—Of ruins.** 29. Rather, he shall not *increase* his riches: he has reached his highest point: his prosperity shall not continue. **perfection —Rather,** " His *acquired wealth*—what he possesses—shall not be extended," &c. 30. depart—*i. e.*, escape *v. 23.*. branches—*viz.*, his offspring ch. 1. 18; 19; Ps. 37. 35.. dry up—The " flame" is the sultry wind in the E. by which plants most full of sap are suddenly shrivelled. His **mouth**—*i.e.*, God's wrath (Isa. 11. 4.). 31. Rather, let him not trust in vanity or he will be deceived, &c. vanity — That which is unsubstantial. Sin is its own punishment (Prov. 1. 31; Jer. 2. 19.). 32. *lit.*, "it *(the tree* to which he is compared *v.* 30, or else *his life*, shall not be filled up in its time:" *i.e.*, "he shall be ended before his time." shall **not be green—Image from a withered tree:** the childless extinction of the wicked. 33. Images of incompleteness. The loss of the unripe grapes is poetically made the vine tree's own act, in order to express more pointedly that the sinner's ruin is the fruit of his own conduct Isa. 3. 11; Jer. 6. 19.). 34. Rather, The binding together of the hypocrites wicked shall be *fruitless*. [UMBR.] Tabernacles of bribery, *viz.*, dwellings of unjust judges, often reprobated in the O. T. (Isa. 1. 23.). The "fire of God" that consumed Job's possessions (ch. 1. 16.) Eliphaz insinuates may have been on account of Job's bribery as an Arab sheikh or emir. 35. Bitter irony, illustrating the "unfruitfulness *(v. 34,)* of the wicked. Their conceptions and birth-givings consist solely in mischief, &c. (Isa. 33. 11.). prepareth—Hatcheth.

CHAPTER XVI.

SECOND SERIES.

Ver. 1-22. JOB'S REPLY. 2. (ch. 13. 4.). 3. "Words of wind," *Heb.* He retorts upon Eliphaz his reproach ch. 15. 2.). embuldeneth —*lit.*, What wearies you so that ye contradict? *i.e.*, What have I said to *provoke* you ? &c. [SCH.] Or, as better accords with the first clause, "wherefore do ye weary yourselves contradicting." [UMBR.] 4. heap up —Rather, marshal together (an army of words). shake head—in mockery: it means *nodding*, rather than *shaking*; nodding is not

with us, as in the East, a gesture of scorn (Isa. 37. 22; Jer. 18. 16; Matt. 27. 39. . 5. **st engthen with mouth**—Bitter irony. In allusion to Eliphaz's boasted "consolations" ch. 15. 11.). Opposed to, strengthening with the heart, *i.e.*, with real consolation. *Transl.* "I also like you could strengthen with the *mouth*," *i.e.*, with *heartless* talk: "And the moving of my *lips* (mere lip-comfort could console" in the same fashion as you do. [UMBR.] "*Hearty* counsel" Prov. 27. 9.) is the opposite. 6. eased—*lit.*, What portion of my sufferings) goes from me? 7. But now— Rather, "ah!" he—God. company—Rather, " band of *witnesses*," *viz.*, those who could attest his innocence, his children, servants, &c. So the same *Heb.* is translated next *v.* UMBR. makes his "band of witnesses" *himself*, for alas! he had no other to witness for him. But this is too reconcilite. 8. filled with wrinkles — Rather as also the same *Heb.* word in ch. 22. 16: *E. V.*, " cut down,"). " thou hast *fettered* me, thy witness," *(besides* cutting off my "band of witnesses," *v.* 7, *i.e.*, hast disabled me by pains from properly attesting my innocence. But another "witness" arises against him, *viz.*, his "leanness" or wretched state of body, construed by his friends into a proof of his guilt. The radical meaning of the *Heb.* is to *draw together*, whence flow the double meanings *to bind* or *fetter*, and in *Syr. to wrinkle*. leanness—meaning also *lie;* implying it was a *false* "witness." 9. Image from a wild beast. So God is represented ch. 10. 16. who hate'h me—Rather, "and pursues me hard." Job would not ascribe "hatred" to God (Ps. 50. 22.). mine an eye— Rather, he sharpens, &c., *as an enemy*" (Ps. 7. 12.). Darts wrathful glances at me, like a foe (ch. 13. 24.). 10. gape—not in order to devour, but to mock him. To fill his cup of misery, the mockery of his friends *(v. 10.*) is added to the hostile treatment from God (*v.* 9.). smitten . . . cheek—*fig.*, for contemptuous abuse (Lam. 3. 30; Matt. 5. 39.). gathered themselves—"Conspired unanimously," [SCH.] 11. turned me over—*lit.*, cast me head-long into, &c. the ungodly—*viz.*, his professed friends, who persecuted him with unkind speeches. 12. I was at ease—in past times (ch. 1.). by my neck—as an animal does its prey so ch. 10. 16.). shaken—violently; in contrast to his former "ease" (Ps. 102. 10.). Set me up *(again)*. mark—(ch. 7. 20; Lam. 3. 12.). God lets me always recover strength, so as to torm ent me ceaselessly. 13. his archers—The image of last *v.* is continued. God, in making me His "mark," is accompanied by *the three friends*, whose words wound like sharp arrows. gall—put for a vital part. So the liver (Lam. 2. 11.). 14. The image is from storming a fortress by making breaches in the walls (2 Ki. 14. 13.). a giant—a mighty warrior. 15. sewed—denoting the tight fit of the mourning garment; it was a sack with arm-holes *closely sewed* to the body. horn—image from horned cattle, which when excited tear the earth with their horns. The horn was the emblem of *power;* (1 Ki. 22. 11.). Here, it is " in the *dust*," which as applied to Job denotes *his humiliation* from former greatness. To throw one's self in the dust was a sign of *mourning*: this idea is here joined with that of *excited despair*, depicted by the fury of a horned beast. The Druses of Lebanon still wear horns as

Bildad reproves Job. JOB, XIX, XX. *Job complains of his friends.*

6 The light shall be dark in his tabernacle, and his ³ candle shall be put out with him.
7 The steps of his strength shall be straitened, and his own counsel shall cast him down.
8 For he is cast into a net by his own feet, and he walketh upon a snare.
9 The gin shall take *him* by the heel, *and* the robber shall prevail against him.
10 The snare *is* ⁴ laid for him in the ground, and a trap for him in the way.
11 Terrors ⁵ shall make him afraid on every side, and shall ⁶ drive him to his feet.
12 His strength shall be hunger-bitten, and *d* destruction *shall* be ready at his side.
13 It shall devour the ⁶ strength of his skin: *even* the first-born of death shall devour his strength.
14 His ⁶ confidence shall be rooted out of his tabernacle, and it shall bring him to the king of terrors.
15 It shall dwell in his tabernacle, because it *is* none of his: *f* brimstone shall be scattered upon his habitation.
16 His roots shall be dried up beneath, and above shall his branch be cut off.
17 His *g* remembrance shall perish from the earth, and he shall have no name in the street.
18 He ⁷ shall be driven from light into darkness, and chased out of the world.
19 He *h* shall neither have son nor nephew among his people, nor any remaining in his dwellings.
20 They that come after *him* shall be astonied at his day, as they that ⁸ went before ⁹ were affrighted.
21 Surely such *are* the dwellings of the wicked, and this *is* the place *of him that* knoweth *i* not God.

CHAPTER XIX.

1 *Job complains of his friends' cruelty: 23 his belief in the resurrection.*

THEN Job answered and said,
2 How long will ye vex my soul, and break me in pieces with words?
3 These ten times have ye reproached me: ye are not ashamed *that* ye ¹ make yourselves strange to me.
4 And be it indeed *that* I have erred, mine error remaineth with myself.
5 If indeed ye will magnify *yourselves* against me, and plead against me my reproach;
6 Know now that God hath overthrown me, and hath compassed me with his net.
7 Behold, I cry out of ² wrong, but I am not heard: I cry aloud, but *there is* no judgment.
8 He hath fenced up my way that I cannot pass, and he hath set darkness in my paths.
9 He hath stripped me of my glory, and taken the crown *from* my head.
10 He hath destroyed me on every side, and I am gone; and mine hope hath he removed like a tree.
11 He hath also kindled his wrath against me, and he counteth me unto him as one of his enemies.
12 His troops come together, and raise up their way against me, and encamp round about my tabernacle.
13 He hath put my brethren far from me, and mine acquaintance are verily estranged from me.
14 My kinsfolk have failed, and my familiar friends have forgotten me.

B. C. 1520.
CHAP. 18.
§ Or, lamp.
⁴ hidden.
d Jer. 6. 25.
⁵ scatter him.
d ch. 15. 23.
⁶ bars.
e Pro. 10. 28.
f Gen. 19. 24.
g Ps. 34. 16. Pro. 2. 22. Pro. 10. 7.
⁷ they shall drive him.
h Is. 14. 22. Jer. 22. 30.
⁸ Or, lived with him.
⁹ laid hold on horror.
i Jer. 9. 3. Jer. 10. 25. 1 Thess. 4. 5. 2 Thess. 1. 8. Tit. 1. 16.

CHAP. 19.
¹ Or, harden yourselves against me.
² Or, violence.
³ my belly.
⁴ Or, the wicked.
⁵ the men of my secret.
⁶ Or, as.
⁷ Who will give, etc.
⁸ Or, After I shall awake, though this body be destroyed, yet out of my flesh shall I see God.
a Rom. 8. 23.
b Ps. 17. 15.
1 Cor. 13. 12.
1 John 3. 2.
⁹ a stranger.
¹⁰ Or, my reins within me are consumed with earnest desire [for that day.]
¹¹ in my bosom.
¹² Or, and what root of matter is found in me?

CHAP. 20.
1 my haste is in me.
2 from near.
3 cloud.
⁴ Or, The poor shall oppress his children.
⁵ in the midst of his palate.

15 They that dwell in mine house, and my maids, count me for a stranger: I am an alien in their sight.
16 I called my servant, and he gave me no answer; I entreated him with my mouth.
17 My breath is strange to my wife, though I entreated for the children's *sake* of ³ mine own body.
18 Yea, ⁴ young children despised me; I arose, and they spake against me.
19 All ⁵ my inward friends abhorred me; and they whom I loved are turned against me.
20 My bone cleaveth to my skin ⁶ and to my flesh, and I am escaped with the skin of my teeth.
21 Have pity upon me, have pity upon me, O ye my friends; for the hand of God hath touched me.
22 Why do ye persecute me as God, and are not satisfied with my flesh?
23 ⁷ Oh that my words were now written! oh that they were printed in a book!
24 That they were graven with an iron pen and lead in the rock for ever!
25 For *a* I know *that* my Redeemer liveth, and *that* he shall stand at the latter *day* upon the earth:
26 ⁸ And *though* after my skin *worms* destroy this *body*, yet *b* in my flesh shall I see God:
27 Whom I shall see for myself, and mine eyes shall behold, and not ⁹ another; ¹⁰ *though* my reins be consumed ¹¹ within me.
28 But ye should say, Why persecute we him, ¹² seeing the root of the matter is found in me?
29 Be ye afraid of the sword: for wrath *bringeth* the punishments of the sword, that ye may know *there is* a judgment.

CHAPTER XX.

THEN answered Zophar the Naamathite, and said,
2 Therefore do my thoughts cause me to answer, and for *this* ¹ I make haste.
3 I have heard the check of my reproach, and the spirit of my understanding causeth me to answer.
4 Knowest thou *not* this of old, since man was placed upon earth,
5 That the triumphing of the wicked *is* ² short, and the joy of the hypocrite *but* for a moment?
6 Though his excellency mount up to the heavens, and his head reach unto the ³ clouds;
7 *Yet* he shall perish for ever like his own dung: they which have seen him shall say, Where *is* he?
8 He shall fly away as a dream, and shall not be found; yea, he shall be chased away as a vision of the night.
9 The eye also *which* saw him shall see him no more; neither shall his place any more behold him.
10 ⁴ His children shall seek to please the poor, and his hands shall restore their goods.
11 His bones are full *of the sin* of his youth, which shall lie down with him in the dust.
12 Though wickedness be sweet in his mouth, *though* he hide it under his tongue;
13 *Though* he spare it, and forsake it not, but keep it still ⁵ within his mouth;

Job's Answer Continued. JOB, XVII. *His Hope in Death.*

an ornament. 16. foul—Rather, "is red," *i.e.*, flushed and heated. [UMBR. & NOY.] shadow of death—*i.e.*, darkening through many tears (Lam. 5. 17.). Job here refers to Zophar's implied charge (ch. 11. 14.). Nearly the same words occur as to Jesus Christ (Isa. 53. 9.). So *v.* 10 above answers to the description of Jesus Christ (Ps. 12. 13; Isa. 59. 6; and *v.* 4, to Ps. 22. 7.). He alone realized what Job aspired after, viz., outward *righteousness* of acts and inward *purity* of devotion. Jesus Christ as the representative man is typified in some degree in every servant of God in the O. T. 18. my blood—*i.e.*, my undeserved suffering. He compares himself to one murdered, whose blood the earth refuses to drink up until he is avenged (Gen. 4. 10, 11; Ez. 24. 1, 8; Isa. 26. 21.). The Arabs say that the dew of heaven will not descend on a spot watered with innocent blood (cf. 2 Sam. 1, 21.). no place—no resting-place. "May my cry never stop!" May it go abroad! "Earth" in this *v.* in antithesis to "heaven" (*v.* 19.). May my innocence be as well known to man, as it is even now to God! 19. Also now—even now when I am so greatly misunderstood on earth, God in *heaven* is sensible of my innocence. record—*Heb., my witness*. Amidst all his impatience, Job still trusts in God. 20. *Heb.,* more forcibly, "my mockers—my friends!" A heart-cutting paradox! [UMBR.] God alone remains to whom he can look for attestation of his innocence; plaintively with tearful eye he supplicates for this. 21. one—Rather, He (God). "O that He would plead for a man (viz. me) against God." Job quaintly says, God must support me against God: for He makes me to suffer, and He alone knows me to be innocent. [UMBR.] So God helped Jacob in wrestling against Himself (ch. 23. 6; Gen. 32. 25.). *God* in Jesus Christ does plead with *God* for man (Rom. 8. 26, 27.). as a man—*lit.*, the Son of man. A prefiguring of the advocacy of Jesus Christ—a boon longed for by Job (ch. 9. 33,), though the spiritual pregnancy of his own words, designed for all ages, was but little understood by him (Ps. 80. 17.). for his neighbour—*Heb., friend.* Job himself (ch. 42. 8,) pleaded as intercessor for his "friend," though "his scorners" (*v.* 20.): so Jesus Christ the Son of man (Lu. 23. 34,); "for *friends*" (John, 15. 13-15.). 22. few—*lit.*, "years *of number*" *i.e.,* few, opposed to *numberless* (Gen. 34. 30.).

CHAPTER XVII.
Ver. 1-16. JOB'S ANSWER CONTINUED. 1. breath-corrupt—result of elephantiasis. But [UMBR.] "my strength (spirit) is spent." extinct—Life is compared to an expiring light. "The light of my day is extinguished." graves — *plur.*, to heighten the force. 2. [UMBR.] more emphatically, "had I only not to endure *mockery,* in the midst of their *contentions* I (mine eye) would remain quiet." "Eye continue," or *tarry all night* (Heb.), is a figure taken from sleep at night, to express undisturbed *rest:* opposed to (ch. 16. 20,), when the eye of Job is represented as pouring out tears to God *without rest.* 3. Lay down—viz., a pledge or security, *i.e.*, be my surety; do thou attest my innocence, since my friends only *mock* me (*v.* 2.). Both litigating parties had to lay down a sum as security before the trial. put me in surety—Provide a surety for me (in the trial) with thee. A presage of the "surety" (Heb. 7. 22,), or "one Mediator between God and man"

(see note 16. 21.). strike hands—"who else save God Himself, could strike hands with me?" *i.e.*, be my security (Ps. 119. 122.). The Hebrew strikes the hand of him for whom he goes security (Prov. 6. 1,). 4. their heart—The *intellect* of his friends. shalt . . . exalt—Rather imperative, exalt them not. Allow them not to conquer [UMBR.] (Isa. 6. 9, 10,). 5. The *Heb.* for *flattery* is *smoothness:* then it came to mean a *prey* divided by *lot,* because a smooth stone was used in casting the lots (Deut. 18. 8,), "a portion" (Gen. 14. 24.). Therefore *transl.* "He that delivers up his friend as a prey (which the conduct of my friends implies that they would do), even the eyes," &c. [NOY.] (ch. 11. 20,). Job says this as to the sinner's *children,* retorting upon their reproach as to the cutting off of his (ch. 5. 4; 15. 30.). This accords with the O. T. dispensation of legal retribution (Ex. 20. 5.). 6. He hath made me a *byword*—God. The poet reverentially suppresses the name of God, when speaking of calamities inflicted. byeword—(Deut. 28. 37; Ps. 69. 11.). My awful punishment makes my name execrated everywhere, as if I must have been superlatively bad to have earned it. aforetime . . . tabret—As David was honoured (1 Sam. 18. 6.). Rather from a different *Heb.* root, "I am treated *to my face* as an object *of disgust.*" *Lit., an object to be spit upon in the face* (Nu. 12. 14.). So *Ruca* means (Matt. 5. 22.). [UMBR.] 7. (Ps. 6. 7; 31. 9; Deut. 34. 7,). members—*lit., figures*; all the individual members being peculiar *forms* of the body: opposed to "shadow," which looks like a figure without solidity. 8. astonied—at my unmerited sufferings. against the hypocrite—The upright shall feel their sense of justice wounded ("will be indignant") because of the prosperity of the wicked. By "hypocrite" or "ungodly" he perhaps glances at his false friends. 9. The strength of religious principle is heightened by mis-fortune. The pious shall take fresh courage to persevere from the example of suffering Job. The image is from a warrior acquiring new courage in action (Isa. 40. 30, 31; Phil. 1. 14.). 10. "Return." If you have anything to advance really wise, though I doubt it, re-commence your speech. For as yet I cannot find one wise man among you all. 11. Only do not vainly speak of the restoration of health to me; for "my days are past." broken off—As the threads of the web cut off from the loom (Isa. 38. 12.). thoughts—*lit., possessions, i.e.,* all the feelings and fair hopes which my heart once nourished. These belong to the heart, as "purposes" to the *understanding;* the two together here describe the entire inner man. 12. They — viz., *my friends* would change the night into day, *i.e.*, would try to persuade me of the change of my misery into joy, which is impossible. [UMB.] (ch. 11. 17.) (but) the light of prosperity (could it be enjoyed,) would be short because of the darkness of adversity. Or better for "short." the *Heb.* "near;" "and the light of new prosperity should be near in the face of (before) the darkness of death;" *i.e.,* they would persuade me that light is near, even though darkness approaches. 13. Rather, if I wait for this grave (scheol, or the unseen world) as my house, and make my bed in the darkness (*v.* 14.) and say to corruption," rather, *to the pit, or grave,* &c., (*v.* 15.). Where, then, is my hope! [UMBR.] The apodosis is at *v.* 15. 14. Thou art my father, &c.—Express-

369

ing most intimate connexion (Prov. 7. 4.). His diseased state made him closely akin to the grave and worm. 15. Who shall see it fulfilled? viz., the "hope" (ch. 11. 18,), which they held out to him of restoration. 16. They—viz., my hopes, shall be buried with me. bars—(Isa. 38. 10.). Rather, *the wastes*, or *solitudes* of the pit (scheol, the unseen world.). rest together—The rest of me and my hopes is in, &c. Both expire together. The word "rest" implies that man's ceaseless hopes only rob him of rest.

CHAPTER XVIII.
SECOND SERIES.
Ver. 1-21. REPLY OF BILDAD. 2. ye—*The other two friends of Job*, whom Bildad charges with having spoken *mere* "words," *i.e.*, empty speeches: opposed to "mark," *i.e.*, come to *reason*, consider the question *intelligently*: and then let us speak. 3. beasts—Alluding to what Job said (ch. 12. 7; so Isa. 1. 3.). vile—Rather, from a *Heb.* root *to stop up*. "Stubborn," answering to the stupidity implied in the parallel first clause. [UMBR.] Why should we give occasion by your empty speeches for our being mutually reputed in the sight of Job, and one another, unintelligent? ch. 17. 4, 10.). 4. Rather, turning to Job, "thou that tearest thyself in anger ,ch. 5. 2.). be forsaken—Become desolate. He alludes here to Job's words as to the "rock," &c., crumbling away ,ch. 14. 18, 19, ; but in a different application. He says bitterly "for thee." Wert thou not punished as thou art, and as thou art unwilling to bear, the eternal order of the universe would be disturbed, and the earth become desolate through unavenged wickedness. [UMBR.] Bildad takes it for granted Job is a great sinner (ch. 8. 5-9; Isa. 24. 5, 6.). "Shall that which stands fast as a rock be removed for your special accommodation?" 5. That (*v.* 4,) cannot be. The decree of God is unalterable, the light prosperity) of the wicked shall at length be put out. his fire—Alluding to Arabian hospitality, which prided itself on welcoming the stranger to the fire in the tent, and even lit fires to direct him to it. The ungodly shall be deprived of the means to show hospitality. His dwelling shall be dark and desolate! 6. candle—The *lamp* which in the E. is usually fastened to the ceiling. Oil abounds in those regions, and the lamp was kept burning all night, as now in Egypt, where the poorest would rather dispense with food, than the night-lamp (Ps. 18. 28.). To put out the lamp was an image of utter desolation. 7. "Steps of strength," *Heb.* for, *His strong steps*. A firm step marks health. To be straitened in steps is to be no longer able to move about at will Prov. 4. 12). his own counsel—Or plans shall be the means of his fall (ch. 5. 13.). 8. he walketh upon—Rather, "he *lets himself go into* the net." [UMBR.] If the *E.V.* be retained, then understand "snare" to be the *pit-fall*, covered over with branches and earth, which when walked upon give way (Ps. 9. 15; 35. 8.). 9. robber—Rather answering to "gin" in the parallel clause, "the *noose* shall hold him fast." [UMBR.] 11. terrors — Often mentioned in this book (*v.* 14; ch. 24. 17; &c.). The terrors excited through an evil conscience are here personified. "Magor-missabib," (Jer. 20. 3.). drive ... to his feet—Rather, shall pursue (*lit.*, scatter, Hab. 3. 14,) him close at his heels (*lit.*, immediately after his feet,

Hab. 3. 5; 1 Sam. 25. 42; *Heb.*). The image is that of a pursuing conqueror who scatters the enemy. [UMBR.] 12. The *Heb.* is brief and bold, "his strength is hungry." destruction—*i.e.*, a great calamity (Prov. 1. 27.). ready at his side—Close at hand to destroy him Prov. 19. 29.). 13. UMBR. has "he" for "it," *i.e.*, "in the rage of hunger he shall devour his own body;" or, *his own children* (Lam. 4. 10.). Rather, "destruction" from the last verse is *nom.* to "devour." strength—Rather, "members" (*lit.*, the branches of a tree,). the first-born of death—A personification full of poetical horror. The first-born son held the chief place (Gen. 49. 3,); so here *the chiefest* (*most deadly) disease* that death has ever engendered Isa. 14. 30; "first-born of the poor."—the poorest.). The Arabs call fever "daughter of death." 14. confidence — All that the father trusted in for domestic happiness, children, fortune, &c., referring to Job's losses. rooted out — Suddenly torn away. it shall bring—*i.e.*, he shall be brought; or, as UMBR. better has, "*Thou* God) snalt bring him *slowly*." The *Heb.* expresses, "to stride slowly and solemnly." The godless has a fearful death for long before his eyes, and is at last taken by it. Alluding to Job's case. The King of terrors, not like the heathen Pluto, the fabled ruler of the dead, but Death, with all its terrors to the ungodly, personified. 15. It—*Terror* shall haunt, &c., and not as UMBR. *another*, which the last clause of the verse disproves. none of his—It is his no longer. brimstone— Probably comparing the calamity of Job by the "fire of God" (ch. 1. 16,), to the destruction of guilty Sodom by fire and brimstone (Gen. 19. 24,). 16. "Roots," himself. "Branch," his children (ch. 8. 12; 15. 30; Mal. 4. 1.). 17. street—Men shall not speak of him in meeting in the highways. Rather, in the field, or *meadow*: where the shepherds shall no more mention his name. A picture from nomadic life. [UMBR.] 18. light . . . darkness—Existence—non-existence. 19. nephew—So Isa. 14. 22.). But it is translated "grandson" Gen. 21. 23,), *transl*. "kinsman." 20. after . . . before — Rather, "those in the W.— those in the E.;" *i.e.*, all people; *lit.*, those behind—those before; for Orientals in geography turn with their face to the E. not to the N. as we, and back to the W.; so that *before*—E.; *behind*—N. so Zech. 14. 8.). day—Of ruin (Obad. 12.). affrighted—Seized with terror (ch. 21. 6; Isa. 13. 8.). 21. (ch. 8. 22. *Marg.*).

CHAPTER XIX.
SECOND SERIES.
Ver. 1-29. JOB'S REPLY TO BILDAD. 2. How long, &c.—Retorting Bildad's words (ch. 18. 2.). Admitting the punishment to be deserved, is it kind thus ever to be harping on this to the sufferer? And yet even this they have not yet proved. 3. These—Prefixed to numbers emphatically (Gen. 27. 30.). ten—*i.e.*, often (Gen. 31. 7.). make yourselves strange—Rather, *stun* me. [GES.] (See *Marg.* for a different meaning.). 4. erred—The *Heb.* expresses *unconscious error*. Job was unconscious of wilful sin. remaineth—*lit.*, *passeth the night*. An image from harbouring an unpleasant guest for the night. I bear the consequences 5. magnify, &c.—Speak proudly (Obad. 12; Ez. 35. 13.). against me—Emphatically repeated Ps. 38. 16.). plead ... reproach—*E.V.* makes this part of the protasis "if"

being understood, and the apodosis beginning at v. 6. Better, with UMBR., if ye would become great heroes against me in truth, ye must *prove* (evince) against me my *guilt*, or *shame*, which you assert. In the *E.V.* "reproach" will mean Job's *calamities*, which they " pleaded" against him as a "reproach," or proof of guilt. 6. compassed . . . net—Alluding to Bildad's words ch. 18. 8.). Know, that it is not that *I* as a wicked man have been caught in my " *own* net ;" *it is God* who has compassed me in His—why, I know not. 7. wrong—violence: brought on him by God. no judgment—God will not remove my calamities, and so vindicate my just cause: and my friends will not do *justice* to my past character. 8. Image from a benighted traveller. 9. stripped . . . crown—image from a deposed king, deprived of his *robes* and *crown:* appropriate to Job, once an emir with all but royal dignity (Lam. 5. 16; Ps. 89. 39.). 10. destroyed . . . on every side—"Shaken all round, so that I fall in the dust;" image from a tree uprooted by violent shaking from every side. [UMBR.] The last clause accords with this Jer. 1. 10.). mine hope—As to this life in opposition to Zophar, ch. 11. 18,): not as to the world to come, (v. 25; ch. 14. 15.). removed — Uprooted. 11. enemies — (ch. 13. 24; Lam. 2. 5.). 12. troops—Calamities advance together like hostile troops (ch. 10. 17.). raise up . . . way—An army must *cast up a way* of access before it, in marching against a city (Isa. 40. 3.). 13. brethren—*Nearest kinsmen*, as distinguished from " acquaintance." So " kinsfolk " and " familiar friends" (v. 14,) correspond in parallelism. The Arabic proverb is, " The brother, *i.e.,* the true friend is only known in time of need," estranged—*lit.,* turn away with disgust. Job again unconsciously uses language prefiguring the desertion of Jesus Christ (ch. 16. 10; Lu. 23. 49; Ps. 38. 11.). 15. They that dwell, &c.—Rather, *sojourn:* male-servants, *sojourning* in his house. Mark the contrast. The stranger admitted to sojourn as a dependent treats the master as a stranger in his own house. 16. servant—Born in my house (as distinguished from those *sojourning* in it,), and so altogether belonging to the family. Yet even he disobeys my call. mouth—*i.e.,* calling aloud; formerly a *nod* was enough. Now I no longer look for *obedience*, I try *entreaty.* 17. strange—His *breath* by elephantiasis had become so *strongly altered* and offensive, that his wife turned away as *estranged* from him (v. 13; ch. 17. 1.) children . . . of mine own body—*lit., belly.* But "loins" is what we should expect, not " belly," (womb) which applies to the woman. The " mine" forbids it being taken of his wife. Their children besides were dead. In ch. 3. 10, the same words " my womb" mean, *my mother's womb:* therefore *transl.* " and I must entreat (as a suppliant) the children of my mother's womb ;" *i.e.,* my own brothers. A heightening of force, as compared with last clause of v. 16. [UMBR.] Not only must I entreat suppliantly my *servant*, but my own *brothers* (Ps. 69. 8.). Here too, he unconsciously foreshadows Jesus Christ (John. 7. 5.). 18. young children — So the Heb. means (ch. 21. 11.). Reverence for age is a chief duty in the E. The word means " wicked" (ch. 16. 11.). So UMBR. has it here, not so well. I arose—Rather, supply "if," as Job was no more in a state to stand up. " If I stood up (arose)

they would speak against (abuse) me." [UMBR.] 19. inward — *Confidential: lit.,* " men of my secret "—to whom I entrusted my most intimate confidence. 20. Extreme meagreness. The bone seemed to stick to the skin, being seen through it, owing to the flesh drying up and falling away from the bone. The *Marg. " as to my flesh,"* makes this sense clearer. The *E. V.* however expresses the same; "*And* to my flesh," viz., which has fallen away from the bone, instead of firmly covering it. skin of my teeth—Proverbial. I have *escaped with* bare life; I am whole *only with* the *skin of my teeth, i.e.,* my gums alone are whole, the rest of the skin of my body is broken with sores (ch. 7. 5; Ps. 102. 5.). Satan left Job speech, in hope that he might therewith curse God. 21. When God had made him such a piteous spectacle, his friends should spare him the additional persecution of their cruel speeches. 22. As God has persecuted me. Prefiguring Jesus Christ Ps. 69. 26.). That God afflicts, is no reason that man is to add to a sufferer's affliction (Zech. 1. 15.). satisfied with my flesh —It is not enough that God afflicts my flesh literally (v. 20,), but you must "eat my flesh" metaphorically (Ps.27.2,*:* i.e., *utter the worst calumnies,* as the phrase often means in Arabic. 23. Despairing of justice from his friends in his life time, he wishes his words could be preserved imperishably to posterity, attesting his hope of vindication at the resurrection. printed—Not our modern printing, but *engraven.* pen — Graver. lead — poured into the engraven characters, to make them better seen. [UMBR.] Not on *leaden plates;* for it was " in the rock" that they were engraved. Perhaps it was the *hammer* that was of " lead," as sculptors find more delicate incisions are made by it, than by a harder hammer. [FOSTER.] (*One Primev. Lang.*) has shown, that the inscriptions on the rocks in Wady-Mokatta, along Israel's route through the desert, record the journeys of that people, as Cosmas Indicopleustes asserted, 535 A.D, 24. for ever—As long as the rock lasts. 25. Redeem-r—UMBR., &c., understand this and *v.* 26, of God appearing as Job's Avenger *before his death,* when his body would be wasted to a skeleton. But Job uniformly despairs of restoration and vindication of his cause in this life (ch. 17. 15, 16.). One hope alone was left, which the Spirit revealed, a vindication in a future life: it would be no full vindication, if his soul alone were to be happy *without the body;* as some explain (v. 26,) " *out of* the flesh." It was his body that had chiefly suffered: the resurrection of his body, therefore, alone could vindicate his cause: to see God with *his own eyes,* and in a renovated body (r. 27,), would disprove the imputation of guilt cast on him because of the sufferings of his present body. That this truth is not further dwelt on by Job, or noticed by his friends, only shows that it was *with him* a bright passing glimpse of *O. T. hope,* rather than the steady light of *Gospel assurance; with us* this passage has a definite clearness, which it had not in *his* mind (see Note 21. 30.). The idea in " Redeemer" with Job is *Vindicator* (ch. 16. 19; Nu. 35. 27,), redressing his wrongs; also including at least with *us*, and probably with *him,* the idea of the predicted Bruiser of the Serpent's head. Tradition would inform him of the prediction. FOSTER shows

Zophar describes the wicked.   *Job's reply to Zophar.*

14 Yet his meat in his bowels is turned, it is the gall of asps within him.
15 He hath swallowed down riches, and he shall vomit them up again: God shall cast them out of his belly.
16 He shall suck the poison of asps: the viper's tongue shall slay him.
17 He shall not see *the rivers, *the floods, the brooks of honey and butter.
18 That which he laboured for shall he restore, and shall not swallow it down: according to his substance shall the restitution be, and he shall not rejoice therein.
19 Because he hath *oppressed and hath forsaken the poor; because he hath violently taken away an house which he builded not;
20 Surely *he shall not *feel quietness in his belly, he shall not save of that which he desired.
21 *There shall none of his meat be left; therefore shall no man look for his goods.
22 In the fulness of his sufficiency he shall be in straits: every hand of the *wicked shall come upon him.
23 When he is about to fill his belly, God shall cast the fury of his wrath upon him, and shall rain it upon him *while he is eating.
24 He *shall flee from the iron weapon, and the bow of steel shall strike him through.
25 It is drawn, and cometh out of the body; yea, the glittering sword cometh out of his gall: *terrors are upon him.
26 All darkness shall be hid in his secret places: *a fire not blown shall consume him; it shall go ill with him that is left in his tabernacle.
27 The heavens shall reveal his iniquity; and the earth shall rise up against him.
28 The increase of his house shall depart, and his goods shall flow away in the day of his wrath.
29 This *is the portion of a wicked man from God, and the heritage *appointed unto him by God.

CHAPTER XXI.

1 *Job craves to be patiently heard because of his calamities: he shows that sometimes the wicked do so prosper that they despise God, etc.*

BUT Job answered and said,
2 Hear diligently my speech; and let this be your consolations.
3 Suffer me that I may speak; and after that I have spoken, mock on.
4 As for me, is my complaint to man? and if it were so, why should not my spirit be *troubled?
5 *Mark me, and be astonished, and lay your hand upon your month.
6 Even when I remember I am afraid, and trembling taketh hold on my flesh.
7 Wherefore do the wicked live, become old, yea, are mighty in power?
8 Their seed is established in their sight with them, and their offspring before their eyes.
9 Their houses *are safe from fear, neither is the rod of God upon them.
10 Their bull gendereth, and faileth not; their cow calveth, and casteth not her calf.
11 They send forth their little ones like a flock, and their children dance.
12 They take the timbrel and harp, and rejoice at the sound of the organ.
13 They spend their days *in wealth, and in a moment go down to the grave.

14 Therefore they say unto God, Depart from us; for we desire not the knowledge of thy ways.
15 What is the Almighty, that we should serve him? and what profit should we have, if we pray unto him?
16 Lo, their good is not in their hand: the counsel of the wicked is far from me.
17 How oft is the *candle of the wicked put out? and how oft cometh their destruction upon them? God distributeth sorrows in his anger.
18 They are as stubble before the wind, and as chaff that the storm *carrieth away.
19 God layeth up *his iniquity for his children: he rewardeth him, and he shall know it.
20 His eyes shall see his destruction, and he shall drink of the wrath of the Almighty.
21 For what pleasure hath he in his house after him, when the number of his months is cut off in the midst?
22 Shall any teach God knowledge? seeing he judgeth those that are high.
23 One dieth *in his full strength, being wholly at ease and quiet:
24 His *breasts are full of milk, and his bones are moistened with marrow.
25 And another dieth in the bitterness of his soul, and never eateth with pleasure.
26 They shall lie down alike in the dust, and the worms shall cover them.
27 Behold, I know your thoughts, and the devices which ye wrongfully imagine against me.
28 For ye say, Where is the house of the prince? and where are *the dwelling-places of the wicked?
29 Have ye not asked them that go by the way? and do ye not know their tokens,
30 That *the wicked is reserved to the day of destruction? they shall be brought forth to *the day of wrath.
31 Who shall declare his way to his face? and who shall repay him what he hath done?
32 Yet shall he be brought to the *grave, and shall *remain in the tomb.
33 The clods of the valley shall be sweet unto him, and every man shall draw after him, as there are innumerable before him.
34 How then comfort ye me in vain, seeing in your answers there remaineth *falsehood?

CHAPTER XXII.

1 *Eliphaz shows that God is not profited by man's goodness; he accuses Job of divers sins; 21 he exhorts him to repentance, etc.*

THEN Eliphaz the Temanite answered and said,
2 Can *a man be profitable unto God, *as he that is wise may be profitable unto himself?
3 Is it any pleasure to the Almighty, that thou art righteous? or is it gain to him, that thou makest thy ways perfect?
4 Will he reprove thee for fear of thee? will he enter with thee into judgment?
5 Is not thy wickedness great? and thine iniquities infinite?
6 For thou hast taken a pledge from thy brother for nought, and *stripped the naked of their clothing.
7 Thou hast not given water to the weary to drink, and thou *hast withholden bread from the hungry.

that the fall by the serpent is represented perfectly on the Temple of Osiris at Phylæ; and the resurrection on the tomb of the Egyptian Mycerinus, dating 4000 years back. Job's sacrifices imply sense of sin and need of atonement. Satan was the injurer of Job's body; Jesus Christ his Vindicator, the Living one, who giveth life (John, 5. 21, 26.). at the latter day—Rather, "the Last," the peculiar title of Jesus Christ, though Job may not have known the pregnancy of his own inspired words, and may have understood merely *one that comes after* (1 Cor. 15. 45; Rev. 1. 17.). Jesus Christ is *the last.* The day of Jesus Christ *the last day* (John, 6. 39.). stand—Rather, *arise.* As God is said to "raise up" the Messiah (Jer. 23. 5; Deut. 18. 15.). earth—Rather, *dust:* often associated with the body crumbling away in it (ch. 7. 21; 17. 16.); therefore appropriately here. *Above* that very *dust* wherewith was mingled man's decaying body, shall man's Vindicator arise. "Arise above the dust," strikingly expresses that fact that Jesus Christ *arose* first Himself *above the dust,* and then is to *raise* His people *above* it (1 Cor. 15. 20. 23.). The Spirit intended in Job's words more than Job fully understood (1 Pet. 1. 12.). Though he *seems,* in forsaking me, to be as one *dead:* He now truly "liveth" in heaven; hereafter He shall appear also above the *dust* of earth. The Goel or Vindicator of blood was the nearest kinsman of the slain. So Jesus Christ took our flesh, to be our kinsman. Man lost life by Satan the "murderer" (John 8. 44.), here Job's persecutor (Heb. 2. 14.). Comp. also as to *redemption of the inheritance* by the kinsman of the dead (Ruth, 4. 3-5; Eph. 1. 14.). 26. Rather, "though after my skin (is no more) this (body) is destroyed, "body" being omitted, because it was so wasted as not to deserve the name'; yet *from* my flesh (*from my renewed body,* as the starting point of vision (Song Sol. 2. 9.); "looking out *from* the windows") "shall I see God." Next clause proves *bodily* vision is meant, for it specifies "mine eyes." [ROS. 2nd Ed.] The *Heb.,* opposes "*in* my flesh." The "skin" was the first destroyed by Elephantiasis, then the "body." 27. for myself—For my advantage, as my friend. not another—Mine eyes shall behold Him, but *no longer as* one estranged from me, as now. [BENG.] though— Letter omitted: my reins (inward recesses of the heart) are consumed within me, *i.e.,* pine with longing desire for that day (Ps. 84. 2; 119. 81.). The Gentiles had but few revealed promises: how gracious that the few should have been so explicit (cf. Nu. 24. 17; Matt. 2. 2.). 28. Rather, ye will then (when the Vindicator cometh) say, Why, &c. root... in me—The root of pious integrity, which was the *matter* at issue, whether it could be in one so afflicted, is found in me [UMBR.] with many MSS. and versions reads "in him." "Or how found we in him *ground of contention."* 29. "Wrath the passionate violence with which the friends persecuted Job) bringeth, &c.: *lit., is sin of the sword,* that ye may know—Supply, "I say this," judgment—Inseparably connected with the coming of the Vindicator. The "wrath" of God at His appearing for the temporal vindication of Job against the friends (ch. 42. 7.), is a pledge of the eternal wrath at the final coming to glorify the saints and *judge* their enemies (2 Thess. 1. 6-10; Isa. 25. 8.).

CHAPTER XX.

SECOND SERIES.

Ver. 1-29. REPLY OF ZOPHAR. 2. Therefore—Rather, the more excited I feel by Job's speech, the more *for that very reason* shall my reply be supplied by my calm consideration. *Lit.,* "Notwithstanding; my calm thoughts (as in ch. 4. 13,) shall furnish my answer, because of the excitement (haste) within me." [UMBR.] 3. check of my reproach—*i.e.,* the castigation intended as a reproach (*lit.,* shame) to me. spirit of ... understanding—My rational spirit; answering answer in calm reason. 5. hypocrite—*lit.,* *the ungodly* (Ps. 37. 35, 36.). 6. (Isa. 14. 13; Obad. 3, 4.). 7. dung—In contrast to the haughtiness of the sinner *v.* 6.; this strong term expresses disgust and the lowest degradation (Ps. 83. 10; 1 Ki. 14. 10.). 8. (Ps. 73. 20.). 9. Rather, "the eye followeth him, but can *discern* him no more." A *sharp looking* is meant (ch. 28. 7; cf. ch. 7. 10.). 10. seek to please—"Atone to the poor" (by restoring the property of which they had been robbed by the father.). [DE W.] Better than *E.V.* "The children" are reduced to the humiliating condition of "seeking the favour of those very poor," whom the father had oppressed. But UMBR. translates as *marg.* his hands— Rather, *their* (the childrens) hands. their goods—The goods of the poor. Righteous retribution! (Ex. 20. 5.) 11. (Ps. 25. 7.); so *Vulg.* GES. has "full of youth;" viz., *in the fulness of his youthful strength* he shall be laid in the dust. But "bones" plainly alludes to Job's disease, probably to Job's own words (ch. 19. 20.). UMBR. *transl.* "full of his *secret sins,"* as in Ps. 90. 8; his secret guilt in his time of seeming righteousness, like secret poison, at last lays him in the dust. The *E.V.* is best. Zophar alludes to Job's own words (ch. 17. 16.). with him—His sin had so pervaded his nature that it accompanies him to the grave: for eternity the sinner cannot get rid of it (Rev. 22. 11.). 12. be—"*Taste* sweet." Sin's fascination is like poison sweet to the taste, but at last deadly to the vital organs Prov. 20. 17; ch. 9. 17. 18.). hide... tongue —Seek to prolong the enjoyment by keeping the sweet morsel long in the mouth so *v.* 13.). 14. turned—The *Heb.* denotes a total change into a disagreeable contrary (Jer. 2. 21; cf. Rev. 10. 9. 10.). 14. gall—In which the poison of the asp was thought to lie. It rather is contained in a sack in the mouth. Scripture uses popular language, where no moral truth is thereby endangered. 15. He is forced to disgorge his ill-gotten wealth. 16. shall suck—It shall turn out, that he has sucked the poison, &c. 17. floods—*lit.,* *streams of floods,* plentiful streams flowing with milk, &c. (ch. 29. 6; Ex. 3. 17.). Honey and butter are more fluid in the E. than with us. and are poured out from jars. These "rivers" or *water brooks* are in the sultry E. emblems of prosperity. 18. Image from food which is taken away from one, before he can swallow it. restitution—(So Prov. 6. 31.). The parallelism favours the *E.V.* rather than the *transl.* of GES., "As a possession to be restored in which he rejoices not." he shall not rejoice—His enjoyment of his ill-gotten gains shall then be at an end (*v.* 5.). 19. oppressed—Whereas he ought to have espoused their cause (2 Chr. 16. 10.), forsaken—Left helpless. house — Thus leaving the poor without shelter (Isa. 5. 8; Mic. 2. 2.). 20. UMBR. *transl.* "His inward parts know no rest" from desires. his belly—*i.e.*, peace inwardly, not save—*lit.*, "not *escape* with that which," &c. Alluding to Job's having been stripped of his all. 21. look for—Rather, Because his goods, *i.e.*, prosperity *shall have* no *endurance.* 22. shall be — Rather, "he is (feeleth) straitened." The next clause explains in what respect. wicked — Rather, "the whole hand of the *miserable* whom he had oppressed cometh upon him;" viz., the sense of his having oppressed the poor, now in turn comes with all its power (hand) on him. This causes his "straitened" feeling even in prosperity. 23. Rather, "God shall cast (may God send) [UMBR.] upon him the fury, of His wrath *to fill his belly!*" while eating—Rather, "Shall rain it up on him *for his food!*" Fiery rain, *i.e.*, lightning (Ps. 11. 6; alluding to Job's misfortune ch. 1. 10.). The force of the image is felt by picturing to one's self the opposite nature of a refreshing rain in the desert (Ex. 16. 4; Ps. 68. 9.). 24. steel—Rather, "brass." Whilst the wicked flees from one danger, he falls into a greater one from an opposite quarter. [UMBR.] 25. It is drawn—Rather, "He (God) draweth (the sword, Josh. 5. 13,) and no sooner has He done so, than) it cometh out of (*i.e.*, passes right through) the (sinner's) body", Deu. 32. 41, 42; Ezek. 21. 9, 10.). The *glittering* sword is a happy image for *lightning.* gall—*i.e.*, his life (ch. 16. 13.). "Inflicts a deadly wound," terrors—Zophar repeats Bildad's words (ch. 17. 11; Is. 88. 16; 55. 4.). 26. "All darkness," *i.e.*, every calamity that befalls the wicked shall be *hid* (in store for him *in His* (God's *secret places*, or treasures (Jude, 13; Deu. 32. 34.). not blown—Not kindled by man's hands, but by God's Isa. 30, 33; LXX. in ALEX. MS. read "unquenchable fire" (Mat. 3. 12.). Fact is shown by the friends in not expressly mentioning, but *alluding* under colour of general cases, to Job's calamities; here (ch. 1. 16.) UMBR. explains it, *wickedness* is a "self-igniting fire;" in it lie the principles of destruction. ill ... tabernacle — Every trace of the sinner must be obliterated (ch. 18. 15.). 27. All creation is at enmity with him, and proclaims his guilt, which he would fain conceal. 28. increase—Prosperity. Ill got—ill gone. flow away—Like waters that run dry in summer; using Job's own metaphor against himself (ch. 6. 15-17; 2 Sam. 14. 14; Mic. 1. 4.). his wrath — God's. 29. appointed—Not as a matter of chance, but by the Divine "decree" (*Marg.*) and settled principle.

CHAPTER XXI.
SECOND SERIES.

Ver. 1-34. JOB'S ANSWER. 2. consolations —If you will listen calmly to me, this will be regarded as "consolations;" alluding to Eliphaz' boasted "consolations" (ch. 15. 11,), which Job felt more as aggravations ("mockings," v. 3,) than consolations (ch. 16. 2.). 3. *lit., Begin* your mockings" (ch. 17. 2.'. 4. Job's difficulty was not as to *man,* but as to *God,* why He so afflicted him, as if he were the guilty hypocrite which the friends alleged him to be. VULG. translates it, "my disputation." if it were—Rather, since this is the case. 5. lay ... had hand upon ... mouth— (Prov. 30. 32; Jud. 18. 19.). So the heathen god of silence was pictured with his hand on his mouth. There was enough in Job's case to awe them into silence (ch. 17. 8.). 6. remember — Think on it. Can you wonder that I broke out in complaints, when the struggle was not with men but with the Almighty! Reconcile, if you can, the ceaseless woes of the innocent with the Divine justice! Is it not enough to make one tremble? [UMBR.] 7. The answer is (Rom. 2. 4; 1 Tim. 1. 16; Ps. 73. 18; Eccl. 8. 11-13; Luke, 2. 35 end; Prov. 16. 4; Rom. 9. 22.). old—In opposition to the friends who asserted that sinners are "cut off" early ,ch. 8. 12, 14.). 8. In opposition to (ch. 18. 19; 5. 4.). 9. *Lit.*, *peace from* fear: with poetic force. Their house is *peace itself* far removed from fear. Opposed to the friends' assertion, as to the bad ch. 15. 21-24; 20. 26-28,), and conversely, the good, (ch. 5. 23, 24.). 10. Rather, their *cattle conceive.* The first clause of the verse describes an easy *conception,* the second, a happy *birth.* [UMBR.] 11. "Send forth," viz., out of doors, to their happy sports under the skies, like a joyful flock sent to the pastures. little ones — Like lambkins. children—Son e- what older than the former. dance — Not formal dances; but skip, like lambs, in joyous and healthful play. 12. take— Rather, *lift up the voice* (sing) to the note of. [UMBR.] timbrel — Rather, *tambourine,* organ—Not the modern "organ," but the "pipe" (Gen. 4. 21.). The first clause refers to stringed, the latter, to wind instruments; thus, with "the voice" all kinds of music are enumerated. 13. wealth — Old E.V. for *prosperity,* in a moment—Not by a lingering disease. Great blessings! Lengthened life with prosperity, and a sudden painless death (Ps. 73. 4.). 14. Therefore—Rather, *And yet* they are such as say, &c., *i.e., say,* not in so many words, but virtually, by their conduct (so the Gergesenes, Matth. 8. 34. . How differently the godly (Isa. 2. 3.). ways— The *course of action,* which God points out: as in Psalm 50. 23; *marg.* 15. cf. Jer. 2. 10; *marg.*; Prov. 30. 9; Ex. 5. 2.). what profit— (ch. 35. 3; Mal. 3. 14; Ps. 73. 13.). Sinners ask, not what is *right,* but what is for the *profit of self.* They forget, "if religion cost self something, the want of it will cost self infinitely more." 16. not in their hand — But in the hand of God. This is Job's difficulty, that God who has sinners' prosperity good, in His hand should allow them to have it. is— Rather, "may the counsel of the wicked be far from me!" [UMBR.] This naturally follows the sentiment of the first clause; Let me not hereby be thought to regard with aught but horror the ways of the wicked, however prosperous. 17. Job in this whole passage down to 21 quotes the assertion of the friends, as to the short continuance of the sinner's prosperity, not his own sentiments. In 22 he proceeds to refute them. "How oft is the candle" (lamp &c., quoting Bildad's sentiment (ch. 18. 5, 6,), in order to question its truth cf. Mat. 25. 8.). how oft— "God distributeth," &c., alluding to ch. 20. 23, 29,). sorrows—UMBR. translates "snares," *lit., cords,* which lightning in its twining motion resembles (Ps. 11. 6.). 18. Job alludes to a like *sentiment* of Bildad (ch. 18. 18,), using his own previous *words* (ch. 13. 25,). 19. Equally questionable is the friends' assertion, that if the godly himself is not punished, the children are ch. 18. 19; 20. 10,; and that God *rewardeth him* here for his iniquity, and that *he shall know it to his cost.* So "know" Hos. 9. 7.). 20. Another questionable assertion of the friends, that the sinner sees his own and his children's destruction in his life-time. drink—Ps. 11. 6; Isa. 51. 17; Lam. 4. 21.). 21. The argument of the friends, in proof of *v.* 20, What pleasure can he have from his house (children) when he is dead—("after him;" Eccl. 3. 22.), when the number, &c.—ch. 14. 21.). Or, rather, *What hath he to do with* his children, &c.? (so the *Heb.* in Eccl. 3. 1; 8. 6.). It is therefore necessary *"his eyes* should *see* his and their destruction." cut off — Rather, When the number of his *allotted* months is *fulfilled* (ch. 14. 5.). From an Arabic word, *arrow,* which was used to draw lots with. Hence *arrow* — inevitable destiny. [UMBR.] 22. Reply of Job, "In all these assertions you try to teach God how He *ought* to deal with men, rather than [prove that He does *in fact* so deal with them. Experience is against you. God gives prosperity and adversity as it pleases Him, not as man's wisdom would have it, on principles inscrutable to us." (Isa. 40. 13; Rom. 11. 34.). those . . . high—The high ones, not only angels, but men (Isa. 2. 12-17.). 23. *Lit.,* in the bone of his perfection, *i.e.,* the full strength of unimpaired prosperity. [UMBR.] 24. breasts—Rather, skins or *vessels* for fluids. [LEE.] But [UMBR.] "stations or resting-places of his herds near water :" in opposition to Zophar (ch. 20. 17, the first clause refers to his abundant substance, the second to his vigorous health, moistened—Comparing man's body to a well-watered field (Prov. 3. 8; Isa. 58. 11.). 26. (Eccl. 9. 2.). 27. Their wrongful thoughts against Job are stated by him in *v.* 28. They do not honestly *name* Job, but *insinuate* his guilt. 28. ye say—referring to Zophar (ch. 20. 7.). the house—referring to the fall of the *house* of Job's eldest son (ch. 1. 19, and the destruction of his *family.* prince—The parallel "wicked" in the second clause requires this to be taken in a bad sense, *tyrant, oppressor* Isa. 13. 2,), the same *Heb.* "nobles"—oppressors. dwelling-places — Rather, *pavilions; lit.,* a tent containing many dwellings, such as a great emir, like Job,with many dependents,would have. 29. Job seeing that the friends will not admit him as an impartial judge, as they consider his calamities prove his guilt, begs them to ask the opinion of travellers (Lam. 1. 12,) who have the experience drawn from observation, and who are no way connected with him. Job opposes this to Bildad (ch. 8. 8,) and Zophar (ch. 20. 4.), tokens—Rather, *intimations* (*ex. gr.,* inscriptions, proverbs, *signifying* the results of their observation, *testimony. Lit.,* signs or proofs in confirmation of the word spoken Isa.7.11.). 30. Their testimony (referring perhaps to those who had visited the region where Abraham once enjoyed a revelation then lived is, that "the wicked is now) spared *(reserved)* against the day of destruction" hereafter.. The *Heb.* does not so well agree with [UMBR.] *"in the* day of destruction." Job does not deny sinners' *future* punishment, but their punishment *in this life.* They have their "good things" *now.* Hereafter their lot, and that of the godly, shall be reversed (Lu. 16. 25.). Job, by the Spirit, often utters truths, which solve the difficulty under which he laboured. His afflictions mostly clouded his faith, else he would have seen the solution furnished by his own words. This answers the objection, that if he knew of the Resurrection in ch. 19. 25, and future retribution (ch. 21. 30, why did he not draw his reasonings elsewhere from them, which he does not? God's righteous government, however, needs to be vindicated as to *this* life also, and therefore the Holy Ghost has caused the argument mainly to turn on it, at the same time giving glimpses of a future fuller vindication of God's ways. brought forth—not "carried away safe" or "escape" (referring to *this life*), as UMBR. has it. wrath—*lit.,* "wraths," *i.e.,* multiplied and fierce wrath. 31. *i.e.,* who dares to charge him openly with his bad ways? viz., in this present life. He shall, I grant (*v.* 30,), be "repaid" hereafter. 32. Yet —Rather, *and.* brought—with solemn pomp (Ps. 45. 15.). grave—*lit., graves; i.e.,* the place where the graves are. remain in—Rather, on the tomb, or sepulchral *mound.* Even after death he seems still to live and *watch i.e.,* have his "remembrance" preserved) by means of the monument over the grave. In opposition to Bildad ch. 18.17.). 33. As the classic saying has it, "The earth is light upon him." His repose shall be "sweet." draw—follow. He shall share the common lot of mortals: no worse off than they (Heb. 9. 27.). [UMBR.] Not so well (for it is not true of "*every* man."). "*Most men* follow in his bad steps, as countless such preceded him." 34. talsehood—*lit.,* wickedness. Your boasted "consolations" (ch. 15. 11,) are contradicted by facts, ("vain,") they therefore only betray your *evil intent* ("wickedness" against me.

CHAPTER XXII.

THIRD SERIES.

Ver. 1-30. AS BEFORE, ELIPHAZ BEGINS. 1. Eliphaz shows, that man's goodness does not add to, or man's badness take from, the happiness of God: therefore it cannot be that God sends prosperity to some, and calamities on others, for his own advantage: the cause of the goods and ills sent must lie in the men themselves (Ps. 16. 2; Lu. 17. 10; Acts. 17. 25; 1 Chr. 29. 14.). So Job's calamities must arise from guilt. Eliphaz instead of meeting the *facts,* tries to show that it *could not* be so. 2. as he that is wise—Rather, *yea* the *pious* man profiteth himself. So "understanding" or "wise"—*pious* (Dan. 12. 3, 10; Ps. 14. 2.). [MICH.] 3. pleasure—Accession of happiness: God has pleasure in man's righteousness (Ps. 45. 7.), but He is not dependent on man's character for His happiness. 4. Is the punishment inflicted on thee from fear of thee, in order to disarm thee? as Job had implied (Notes, 7. 12, 20; 10. 17.), will He enter . . . into judgment?—Job had desired this (ch. 13. 3, 21.). He ought rather have spoken as (Ps. 143. 2.). 5. Heretofore Eliphaz had only insinuated, now he plainly asserts Job's guilt; merely on the ground of his sufferings. 6. The crimes alleged, on a harsh inference, by Eliphaz against Job are such as he would think likely to be committed by a rich man. The Mosaic law (Ex. 22. 26; Deut. 24. 10,) subsequently embodied the feeling that existed among the godly in Job's time against oppression of debtors as to their pledges. Here the case is not quite the same: Job is charged with taking a pledge where he had *no just claim to it:* and in the second clause, that pledge *the outer garment* which served the

8 But as for [3]the mighty man, he had the earth; and the [4]honourable man dwelt in it.
9 Thou hast sent widows away empty, and the arms of the fatherless have been broken.
10 Therefore snares are round about thee, and sudden fear troubleth thee;
11 Or darkness, that thou canst not see; and abundance of waters cover thee.
12 Is [c]not God in the height of heaven? and behold [5]the height of the stars, how high they are!
13 And thou sayest, [6]How doth God know? can he judge through the dark cloud?
14 Thick clouds are a covering to him, that he seeth not; and he walketh in the circuit of heaven.
15 Hast thou marked the old way which wicked men have trodden?
16 Which were cut down out of time, [7]whose foundation was overflown with a flood:
17 Which said unto God, Depart from us: and what can the Almighty do [8]for them?
18 Yet he filled their houses with good things: but the counsel of the wicked is far from me.
19 The righteous see it, and are glad; and the innocent laugh them to scorn.
20 Whereas our [9]substance is not cut down, but [10]the remnant of them the fire consumeth.
21 Acquaint now thyself [11]with him, and be [d]at peace: thereby good shall come unto thee.
22 Receive, I pray thee, the law from his mouth, and lay up his words in thine heart.
23 If thou return to the Almighty, thou shalt be built up, thou shalt put away iniquity far from thy tabernacles.
24 Then shalt thou lay up gold [12]as dust, and the gold of Ophir as the stones of the brooks.
25 Yea, the Almighty shall be thy [13]defence, and thou shalt have [14]plenty of silver.
26 For then shalt thou have thy delight in the Almighty, and shalt lift up thy face unto God.
27 Thou shalt make thy prayer unto him, and he shall hear thee, and thou shalt pay thy vows.
28 Thou shalt [e]also decree a thing, and it shall be established unto thee: and the light shall shine upon thy ways.
29 When men are cast down, then thou shalt say, There is lifting up; and he shall save [15]the humble person.
30 [16]He shall deliver the island of the innocent: and it is delivered by the pureness of thine hands.

CHAPTER XXIII.

1 *Job longs to appear before God, 6 in confidence of his mercy.* 13 *God's decree immutable.*

THEN Job answered and said,
2 Even to-day is my complaint bitter: [1]my stroke is heavier than my groaning.
3 Oh that I knew where I might find him! that I might come even to his seat!
4 I would order my cause before him, and fill my mouth with arguments.
5 I would know the words which he would answer me, and understand what he would say unto me.
6 Will [a]he plead against me with his great power? No; but he would put strength in me.

7 There the righteous might dispute with him; so should I be delivered for ever from my judge.
8 Behold, [b]I go forward, but he is not there; and backward, but I cannot perceive him:
9 On the left hand, where he doth work, but I cannot behold him: he hideth himself on the right hand, that I cannot see him:
10 But he knoweth [2]the way that I take: when [c]he hath tried me, I shall come forth as gold.
11 My [d]foot hath held his steps, his way have I kept, and not declined.
12 Neither have I gone back from the commandment of his lips; [3]I have esteemed the words of his mouth more than [4]my necessary food.
13 But he is in one mind, and [e]who can turn him? and what his soul desireth, even that he doeth.
14 For he performeth the thing that is [f]appointed for me: and many such things are with him.
15 Therefore am I troubled at his presence: when I consider, I am afraid of him.
16 For God maketh my heart soft, and the Almighty troubleth me:
17 Because I was not cut off before the darkness, neither hath he covered the darkness from my face.

CHAPTER XXIV.

1 *Sin often goes unpunished in this life.* 12 *Of God's providence in all things, etc.*

WHY, seeing [a]times are not hidden from the Almighty, do they that know him not see his days?
2 Some remove the [b]landmarks: they violently take away flocks, and [1]feed thereof.
3 They drive away the ass of the fatherless, they [c]take the widow's ox for a pledge.
4 They turn the needy out of the way: the [d]poor of the earth hide themselves together.
5 Behold, as wild asses in the desert, go they forth to their work; rising betimes for a prey: the wilderness yieldeth food for them and for their children.
6 They reap every one his [2]corn in the field; and [3]they gather the vintage of the wicked.
7 They [e]cause the naked to lodge without clothing, that they have no covering in the cold.
8 They are wet with the showers of the mountains, and [f]embrace the rock for want of a shelter.
9 They pluck the fatherless from the breast, and take a pledge of the poor.
10 They cause him to go naked without clothing, and they take away the sheaf from the hungry;
11 Which make oil within their walls, and tread their wine-presses, and suffer thirst.
12 Men groan from out of the city, and the soul of the wounded crieth out: [g]yet God layeth not folly to them.
13 They are of those that rebel against the light; they know not the ways thereof, nor abide in the paths thereof.
14 The murderer rising with the light killeth the poor and needy, and in the night is as a thief.
15 The eye also of the adulterer waiteth for the twilight, saying, No eye shall see me; and [4]disguiseth his face.

poor as a covering by day, and a bed by night) is represented as taken from one who ha ! not "changes of raiment" a common constituent of wealth in the East; but was *poorly clad*—"naked" Matt. 25. 36; Ja. 2. 15,): a sin the more heinous in a rich man like Job. 7. Hospitality to the weary traveller is regarded in the East as a primary duty (Isa. 21. 14.). 8. mighty—*Heb.*, "man *of arm*" (Ps. 10. 15; viz.,Job.). honourable—*Heb., accepted of countenance* (Isa. 3. 3; 2 Ki. 5. 1.) *i.e.*, possessing authority. Eliphaz repeats his charge (ch. 15. 28; so Zophar, ch. 20. 19,) that it was by violence Job wrung houses and lands from the poor, to whom now he refused relief (v. 7. 9.. [MICH.] 9. empty—without their wants being relieved (Gen. 31. 42.). The Mosaic law especially protected the widow and fatherless (Ex. 22. 22.); the violation of it in their case by the great is a complaint of the prophets (Isa. 1. 17.). arms—supports, helps, on which one leans (Hos. 7. 15.). Thou hast robbed them of their only stay. Job replies in ch. 29. 11-16.). 10. snares—alluding to Job's admission ch. 19. 6; cf. ch. 18. 10; Prov. 22.5.). 11. that—*So that* thou, abundance —floods. Danger by floods is a less frequent image in this book, than in the rest of the O. T. (ch. 11. 16; 27. 20.). 12. Eliphaz says this to prove that God can from His height behold all things; gratuitously *inferring* that Job denied it, because he denied that the wicked are punished here. height—*Heb., head, i.e.,* elevation (ch. 11. 8.). 13. Rather, *And yet* thou sayest, God does not *concern himself with* (" know") human affairs (Ps. 73. 11.). 14. "In the circuit of heaven" only, not taking any part in earthly affairs. Job is alleged as holding this epicurean sentiment (Lam. 3. 44; Isa. 29. 15; 40. 27; Jer. 23. 24; Ez. 8. 12; Ps. 139. 12.). 15. marked—Rather, Dost thou *keep to? i.e.,* wish to follow (so Heb., 2 Sam. 22. 22.). If so, beware of sharing their end. the old way—The degenerate ways of the world before the flood (Gen. 6. 5.). 16. cut down—Rather, "fettered," as in ch. 16. 8; *i.e.,* arrested by death. out of time—Prematurely, suddenly (ch. 15. 32; Eccl. 7. 17.) *Lit.,* whose foundation was poured out (so as to become) a stream, or flood. The solid earth passed from beneath their feet into a flood (Gen. 7. 11.). 17. Eliphaz designedly uses Job's own words (ch. 21. 14, 15.). do for them— They think they can do everything for themselves. 18. "Yet" you say (ch. 21. 16, see Note) that it is "*He* who filled their houses with good"—"their" "good is not in *their* hand," but comes from *God*. but the counsel ..., &c.—Rather, may the counsel be, &c. Eliphaz sarcastically quotes in continuation Job's words (ch. 21. 16.). Yet, after uttering this godless sentiment, thou dost hypocritically add, "May the counsel," &c. 19. Triumph of the pious at the fall of the recent followers of the antediluvian sinners. Whilst in the act of denying that God can do them any good or harm, they are cut off by Him. Eliphaz hereby justifies himself and the friends for their conduct to Job: not derision of the wretched, but joy at the vindication of God's ways (Ps. 107. 42; Rev. 15. 3; 16. 7; 19. 1, 2.). 20. The triumphant speech of the pious. If "substance" be retained, *transl.,* rather as LXX., "has not their substance been taken away, and" &c.? But the *Heb.* is rather, "Truly our *adversary* is cut down." [GES.] The same opposition exists between

the godly and ungodly seed, as between the unfallen and restored Adam and Satan *adversary*; this forms the groundwork of the book chs. 1. and 2.; Gen. 3. 15.). remnant—all that "is left" of the sinner: repeated from (ch. 20. 26,) which makes [UMBR'S.] rendering "glory" *(marg.),* "excellency" less probable. fire—alluding to Job (ch. 1. 16; 15. 34; 18. 15.). 1. First is mentioned destruction by *water* (v. 16,); here, by *fire* (2 Pet. 3. 5-7.). 21. Eliphaz takes it for granted, Job is not yet "acquainted" with God; *lit.,* become a *companion* of God. Turn with familiar confidence to God. and be—*So* thou *shalt* be: the 2nd *Imperat.* expresses the consequence of obeying the 1st (Ps. 37. 27.). peace—prosperity and restoration to *Job:* true spiritually also to *us* (Rom. 5. 1; Col. 1. 20.). Good— (1 Tim. 4. 8.). 22. lay up—(Psalm 119. 11.). 23. "Built up" anew, as a *restored* house. Thou shalt put away—Rather, *If* thou put away. [MICH.] 24. Rather, containing the protasis from the last clause of v. 23, *If* thou regard the glittering metal *as dust; lit., lay it on the dust;* to regard it of as little value as the dust on which it lies. The apodosis is at v. 25, *Then* shall the Almighty be, &c. God will take the place of the wealth, in which thou didst formerly trust. gold— Rather, "precious" or "glittering metal," parallel to " (gold) of Ophir," in the second clause. [UMBR. & MAUR.] Ophir—Derived from a *Heb.* word—*dust,* viz., gold dust. HEEREN thinks it a general name for the rich countries of the S., on the African, Indian, and especially the Arabian coast, (where was the port Aphar. El Ophir, too, a city of Oman, was formerly the centre of Arabian commerce.). It is curious, the natives of Malacca still call their mines *Ophirs.* stones of the brooks—*If* thou dost *let* the gold of Ophir remain in its native valley *among the stones of the brooks; i.e., regard it as of little worth as the stones,* &c. The gold was washed down by mountain torrents and lodged among the stones and sand of the valley. 25. Apodosis. Yea—Rather, *Then* shall the Almighty be, &c. defence—Rather, as the same *Heb.* means in v. 24 (see note,)—Thy *precious metals;* God will be to thee in the place of riches. plenty of silver—Rather, "And shall be to thee in the place of *laboriously obtained treasures* of silver." [GES.] Elegantly implying, it is less labour to find God than the hidden metals; at least to the humble seeker ch. 28. 12-28.). But [MAUR.] "the shining silver." 26. lift up ... face, &c.—Repeated from Zophar (ch. 11. 15.). 27. (Isa. 58. 9, 14.). pay thy vows—Which thou hast promised to God in the event of thy prayers being heard : God will give thee occasion to pay the former, by hearing the latter. 28. light—Success. 29. Rather, When (*thy ways*; from v. 28,) are cast down (for a time,), thou shalt (soon again have joyful cause to) say, There is lifting up (prosperity returns back to me.). [MAUR.] he—God. humble—*Heb.,* him that is of low eyes. Eliphaz implies, that Job is not so now in his affliction; therefore it continues: with this he contrasts the blessed effect of being humble under it (James, 4. 6; and 1 Pet. 5. 5. probably quote this passage.). Therefore it is better, I think, to take the first clause as referred to by "God resisteth the *proud.*" When (men) are cast down, thou shalt say, (behold the effects of) *pride.* Eliphaz hereby justifies himself for attributing

Job's Confidence in God's Mercy. JOB, XXIII, XXIV. *He Declares His Innocence.*

Job's calamities to his *pride*. "Giveth grace to the humble," answers to the second clause. 30. island—*i.e.*, dwelling. But the *Heb.* expresses the *negative* (1 Sam. 4, 21.), transl. "Thus He (God), shall deliver him who was *not* guiltless," viz., one, who like Job himself on conversion shall be saved, but not because he was, as Job so constantly affirms of himself, guiltless, but because he *humbles* himself *v.* 29.); an oblique attack on Job, even to the last. and *i*—Rather, "*he* the one *not* heretofore guiltless) shall be delivered through the purity acquired since conversion) of thy hands;" by thy intercession (as Gen. 18. 26, &c.). [MAUR.] The irony is strikingly exhibited in Eliphaz unconsciously uttering words which exactly answer to what happened at last; he and the other two were "delivered" by God accepting the intercession of Job for them (ch. 42. 7, 8.).

CHAPTER XXIII.
THIRD SERIES.

Ver. 1-17. JOB'S ANSWER. 2. to-day—Implying, perhaps, that the debate was carried on through more days than one see Introd. bitter—ch. 7. 11; 10, 1,). my stroke—The *hand* of God *on me* (marg.; ch. 19. 21; Ps. 32. 4.. heavier than—Is so heavy that I cannot relieve myself adequately by groaning. 3. The same wish as in ch. 13. 3 cf. Heb. 10. 19-22.). seat —The idea in the *Heb.* is a *well-prepared throne* Ps. 9. 7.). 4. order—State methodically ch. 13. 18; Isa. 43. 26. . fill, &c.—I would have abundance of arguments to adduce. 5. he—Emphatic; it little matters what *man* may say of me, if only I know what *God* judges of me. 6. An objection suggests itself, whilst he utters the wish *v.* 5.). Do I hereby wish, that he should plead against me with His omnipotence? Far from it! (ch. 9. 19, 34; 13. 21; 30, 18,). strength—So as to prevail with Him; as in Jacob's case (Hos. 12. 3, 4.). UMBR. and MAUR. better translate as in ch. 4. 20, I only wish that He) "would *attend* to me," *i.e.*, give me a patient hearing as an ordinary judge, not using His omnipotence, but only His divine knowledge of my innocence. 7. there—Rather, Then ; if God would "attend" to me *v.* 6.); righteous—*i.e.*, the result of my *dispute* would be, He would acknowledge me as *righteous*, deliverd— *From* suspicion of guilt on the part of *my Judge*. 8. But I wish in vain. For "behold," &c. forward . . . backward—Rather, "*to the E.*—to the *W.*" The Hebrew geographers faced the E., *i.e.*, sun rise: not the N., as we do. So "before" means E.: "behind," W. (So the Hindoos.) " Para," *before*— E.; "Apara," *behind*—W.; "Daschina," *the right hand*—S; "Bama," *left*—N. A similar reference to sun-rise appears in the name Asia, *sunrise*; Europe, *sunset*; pure Babylonian names, as RAWL. shows. 9. Rather, "To the N." work—God's glorious *works* are especially seen towards the N. region of the sky by one in the N. hemisphere. The antithesis is between God *working* and yet *not being beheld*; as in ch. 9. 11, between "*He goeth by*," and "*I see* Him *not*." If the *Heb.* bears it, the parallelism to the second clause is better suited by translating, as UMBR., *doth hide himself*; but then the antithesis to *behold* would be lost. right hand—"In the S." hideth—Appropriately, of the *unexplored* S., then regarded as uninhabitable through heat see ch. 34, 20.). 10. But—Correcting himself for the wish that his cause should be known before God. The omniscient One already *knoweth the way in me* my *inward* principles; His *outward* way or course of acts is mentioned in *v.* 11. So *in me*, ch. 4. 21,); though for some inscrutable cause He as yet hides himself (*v.* 8, 9. . when—Let Him only but try my cause, (1 Shall, &c. 11. held—Fast by *His steps*. The law is 'n O. T. poetry regarded as *a way*, God going before us as our guide, in whose footsteps we must tread Ps. 17. 5.). declined —(Ps. 125. 5.). 12. esteemed—Rather, *laid up*, viz., as a treasure found (Matt. 13. 44; Ps. 119. 11,); alluding to the words of Eliphaz ch. 22. 22,). There was no need to tell me so; I have done so already (Jer. 15. 16.). necessary —" Appointed portion" (of food : as in Prov. 30. 8.). UMBR. & MAUR. translate "More than *a g law*," my own will, in antithesis to " the words of His mouth" John 6. 38.). Probably under the general term, " what is *appointed* to me" (the same *Heb.* is in *v.* 14,), all that ministers to the appetites of the body and carnal will is included. 13. on one mind — Notwithstanding my innocence, He is *unaltered* in His purpose of proving me guilty (ch. 9. 12,). soul—His *will* (Ps. 115. 3,). God's sovereignty. He has *one* great purpose ; nothing is hap-hazard ; everything has its proper place with a view to His purpose. 14. many such—He has yet many more such ills in store for me, though hidden in His breast (ch. 10. 13.). 15. God's decrees, impossible to be resis'ed, and leaving us in the dark as to what may come next, are calculated to fill the mind with holy awe. [BARNES.] 16. soft — Faint. Hath melted my c urage. Here again Job's language is that of Jesus Christ (Ps. 22. 11.). 17. Because I was not taken away by death from the evil to come *lit.*, *from before the face of the darkness*, Isa. 57. 1.). Alluding to the words of Eliphaz (ch. 22. 11,), "darkness," *i.e.*, calamity. "Cut off;" rather, in the Arabic sense, *Brought* to the land of *silence*; my sad complaint hushed in death. [UMBR.] "Darkness" in the second clause, not the same *Heb.* word as in the first, *cloud*, *obscurity*. Instead of " covering the cloud (of evil) from my face," He "covers" me with it (ch. 22. 11,).

CHAPTER XXIV.

Ver. 1-25. 1. Why is it that, seeing that the times of punishment (Ezek. 30. 3; "time" in the same sense, are not hidden from the Almighty, they who know Him (His true worshippers, ch. 18. 21,) do not see His days of vengeance ; Joel, 1. 15; 2 Pet. 3. 10,)? Or, with UMBR. less simply, making the parallel clauses more nicely balanced, Why are not times of punishment hoarded up (" laid up;" ch. 21. 19; *appointed*. by the Almighty? *i.e.*, why are they not so appointed as that man many now *see* them ; as the second clause shows. Job does not doubt that they *are* appointed ; nay, he asserts it (ch. 21. 30,); what he wishes is that God would Let *all* now *see* that it is so. 2-24. Instances of the wicked doing the worst deeds with seeming impunity. Some—The wicked. Indo arks -- Boundaries between different pastures (Deu. 19. 14 ; Prov. 22. 28.). 3. pledge—Alluding to ch. 22. 6. Others really do, and with impunity, that which Eliphaz falsely charges the afflicted Job with. 4. *Lit.*, they push the poor out of their road in meeting them. *Fig.*, they take advantage of them by force and injustice (alluding to the charge of Eliphaz, ch. 22. 8; 1 Sam. 8. 3.), poor—In spirit and in circumstances Matt. 5. 3.). hide— From the injustice of their oppressors, who have robbed them of their all and driven them into unfrequented places (ch. 20. 19; 30. 3-6; Prov. 28. 28.). 5. wild asses— ch. 11. 12.). So Ishmael is called *a wild ass-man*; Heb., (Gen. 16. 12.). These Bedouin robbers with the unbridled wildness of the ass of the desert, go forth thither. Robbery is their lawless "work." The desert, which yields no food to other men, yields food for the robber and his children by the plunder of caravans. rising betimes—In the E. travelling is begun very early, before the heat comes on. 6. Like the wild asses *v*. 5,) they (these Bedouin robbers) reap (metaphorically their various grain (so the *Heb*. for "corn" means.). The wild ass does not let man pile up in a stable his *mixed provender* (Isa. 30. 24.); so these robbers find their food in the open air, at one time in the desert (*v*. 5.), at another, in the fields. the vintage of the wicked—The vintage of robbery, not of honest industry. If we translate "belonging to the wicked," then it will imply, that the wicked alone have vineyards, the "pious poor" (*v*. 4.), have none. "Gather" in, *Heb*., is *gather late*: as the first clause refers to the *early* harvest of corn, so the second to the vintage *late* in autumn. 7. UMBR. understands it of the Bedouin robbers who are quite regardless of the comforts of life. "They *pass the night* naked, &c., and uncovered." &c. But the allusion to ch. 22. 6, makes the *E.V.* preferable (see Note below, *v*. 10.). Frost is not uncommon at night in those regions (Gen. 31. 40.). 8. They—The plundered travellers. embrace the rock—Take refuge under it (Lam. 4. 5. . 9. from the breast—Of the widowed mother. Kidnapping children for slaves. Here Job passes from wrongs in the desert, to those done among the habitations of men. pledge—viz., the garment of the poor debtor, as next verse shows. 10. (Note ch. 22. 6.). In *v*. 7, a like sin is alluded to: but *there* he implies open robbery of garments in the desert; *here*, the more refined robbery in civilized life. under the name of a "pledge." Having stripped the poor, they make them besides labour in their harvest-fields, and do not allow them to satisfy their hunger with any of the very corn which they carry to the heap. Worse treatment, than that of the ox, according to Deu. 25. 4. *Trans*. "they (the poor labourers) hungering carry the sheaves." [UMBR.] 11. Which — "They" the poor, "press the oil within their walls:" viz., not only in the open fields (*v*. 10.), but also in the *wall-enclosed* vineyards and olive gardens of the oppressor (Isa. 5. 5.). Yet they are not allowed to quench their "thirst" with the grapes and olives. Here, *thirsty; v*. 10, *hungry*. 12. Men—Rather, "mortals" not the common *Heb*. for "men,"); so the Masoretic vowel points read as *E.V.* But the vowel points are modern. The true reading is, *The dying*: answering to "the wounded" in the next clause, so *Syr*., Not merely in the country *v*. 1.; but also in the city there are oppressed sufferers, who cry for help in vain. "From out of the city;" *i.e.*, they long to get forth and be free outside of it Ex. 1. 11; 2. 23.). wounded—By the oppressor (Ezek. 30. 34.). layeth not folly—Takes no account of (by punishing) their *sin* ("folly" in Scripture; ch. 1. 22.) This is the gist of the whole previous list of sins Acts. 17. 30.). UMBR. with *Syr*. reads by changing a vowel point, "Regards not their *supplication*." 13. So far as to openly committed sins; now, those done in the dark. *Trans*. "There are those among them the wicked who rebel," &c. light—Both *lit*. and *fig*. John. 3. 19, 20: Prov. 2. 13.). paths thereof—Places where the light shines. 14. with the light—At early dawn, whilst still dark, when the traveller in the E. usually sets out, and the poor labourer to his work; the murderous robber lies in wait then (Ps. 10. 8.). is as a thief— *Thieves* in the E steal whilst men sleep at night, *robbers* murder at early dawn. The same man who steals at night, when light dawns not only robs, but murders to escape detection. 15. (Prov. 7. 9; Ps. 10. 11.). disguiseth—Puts a veil on. 16. dig through— Houses in the E. are generally built of sun-dried mud bricks so Matt. 6. 19.). "Thieves break through," *lit*., *dig through* (Ezek. 12. 7.). had marked — Rather as in ch. 9. 7. "They shut themselves up in their *houses*: *lit*., they seal up. for themselves — For their own ends, **viz**., to escape detection. know not—Shun. 17. They shrink from the "morning" light, as much as other men do from *the blackest darkness*, ("the shadow of death." it one know—*i.e.*, recognize them. Rather, "They know well are familiar with the terrors of," &c. [UMBR.] Or, as MATR., "They know the terrors of (this) darkness," *viz*., of morning, the light, which is as terrible to them, as darkness ("the shadow of death") is to other men. 18-21. In these verses Job quotes the opinion of his adversaries, ironically: he quoted them so before (ch. 21. 17-21.). In *v*. 22-24, he states his own observation as the opposite. You say "*The sinner is swift, i.e.*, swiftly passes away as a thing floating *on the surface of the waters*" Eccl. 11. 1; Hos. 10. 7.). is cursed—By those who witness their "swift" destruction. beholdeth not—"Turneth not to:" *fig*., for, He cannot enjoy his pleasant possessions (ch. 20. 17; 15. 33.). the way of the vineyards—Including his *fields*, fertile as vineyards: opposite to "the way of the desert." 19. Arabian image: melted snow, as contrasted with the living fountain, quickly dries up in the sun-burnt sand, not leaving a trace behind ch. 6. 16-18.). The *Heb*. is terse and elliptical to express the swift and utter destruction of the godless; (so: "the grave—they have sinned!" 20. The womb—The very mother that bare him, and who is the last to "forget" the child that *sucked* her (Isa. 49. 15,), shall dismiss him from her memory (ch. 18. 17; Prov. 10. 7.). The worm shall *suck*; *i.e.*, "feed sweetly" on him as a delicate morsel (ch. 21. 33.). wickedness —*i.e.*, the wicked; abstract f r concrete (as ch. 5. 16.). as a tree—Utterly *lit., draweth out at length; Marg*., Ps. 36. 10, the mighty with His (God's) power. He (the wicked) riseth up (from his sick bed

God's power and wisdom.   JOB, XXV–XXVIII.   *Job protests his sincerity.*

16 In the dark they dig through houses, which they had marked for themselves in the day-time: *h* they know not the light.
17 For the morning *is* to them even as the shadow of death: if *one* know *them*, *they are* in the terrors of the shadow of death.
18 He *is* swift as the waters; their portion is cursed in the earth: he beholdeth not the way of the vineyards.
19 Drought and heat *5* consume the snow waters: *so doth* the grave *those which* have sinned.
20 The womb shall forget him; the worm shall feed sweetly on him; *i* he shall be no more remembered; and wickedness shall be broken as a tree.
21 He evil-entreateth the barren *that* beareth not, and doeth not good to the widow.
22 He draweth also the mighty with his power: he riseth up, *6* and no man is sure of life.
23 *Though* it be given him *to be* in safety, whereon he resteth, yet *7* his eyes *are* upon their ways.
24 They are exalted for a little while, but *8* are gone and brought low; they are *9* taken out of the way as all *other*, and cut off as the tops of the ears of corn.
25 And if *it be* not *so* now, who will make me a liar, and make my speech nothing worth?

CHAPTER XXV.

Bildad declares the sovereignty of God, before whom man cannot be justified.

THEN answered Bildad the Shuhite, and said,
2 Dominion and fear *are* with him; he maketh peace in his high places.
3 Is there any number of his armies? and upon whom doth not *a* his light arise?
4 How *b* then can man be justified with God? or how can he be clean *that is* born of a woman?
5 Behold even to the moon, and it shineth not; yea, the stars are not pure in his sight:
6 How much less man, *that is* *c* a worm; and the son of man, *which is* a worm?

CHAPTER XXVI.

1 *Job reproves the uncharitable spirit of Bildad.* 5 *God's power infinite and unsearchable.*

BUT Job answered and said,
2 How hast thou helped *him that is* without power? *how* savest thou the arm *that hath* no strength?
3 How hast thou counselled *him that hath* no wisdom? and *how* hast thou plentifully declared the thing as it is?
4 To whom hast thou uttered words? and whose spirit came from thee?
5 Dead *things* are formed from under the waters, 1 and the inhabitants thereof.
6 Hell *a* is naked before him, and destruction hath no covering.
7 He *b* stretcheth out the north over the empty place, *and* hangeth the earth upon nothing.
8 He *c* bindeth up the waters in his thick clouds; and the cloud is not rent under them.
9 He holdeth back the face of his throne, *and* spreadeth his cloud upon it.
10 He *d* hath compassed the waters with bounds, *2* until the day and night come to an end.
11 The pillars of heaven tremble and are astonished at his reproof.

B. C. 1520.

CHAP. 24.
h John 3. 20.
5 violently take.
4 Pro. 10. 7.
6 Or, he trusteth not his own life.
7 That is, God's.
Heb. 4. 13.
8 are not.
9 closed up.

CHAP. 25.
a Jam. 1. 17.
b ch. 4. 17.
ch. 15. 15.
Ps. 130. 3.
Ps. 143. 2.
c Ps. 22. 6.

CHAP. 26.
1 Or, with the inhabitants.
a Ps. 139. 8.
Pro. 15. 11.
b Ps. 24. 2.
c Prov. 30. 4.
d Jer. 5. 22.
2 until the end of light with darkness.
e Ex. 14. 21.
Is. 51. 15.
Jer. 31. 35.
3 pride, or, Rahab.
f Ps. 33. 6.

CHAP. 27.
1 added to take up.
a ch. 34. 5.
2 made my soul bitter.
3 That is, the breath which God gave him.
b ch. 13. 15.
c ch. 2. 3.
d Acts 24. 16.
4 from my days.
e Mat. 16. 26.
Lu. 12. 20.
f ch. 35. 12.
Ps. 18. 41.
Ps. 109. 7.
Pro. 1. 28.
Jer. 14. 12.
Eze. 8. 18.
Mic. 3. 4.
Jam. 4. 3.
g ch. 22. 26.
5 Or, being in the hand, etc.
h Esth. 9. 10.
i Ps. 78. 64.
j Pro. 23. 8.
Eccl. 2. 26.
k Lam. 2. 6.
l Nu. 20. 26.
6 in fleeing he would flee.

CHAP. 28.
1 Or, a mine.
2 Or, dust.

12 He *e* divideth the sea with his power, and by his understanding he smiteth through *3* the proud.
13 By *f* his Spirit he hath garnished the heavens; his hand hath formed the crooked serpent.
14 Lo, these *are* parts of his ways; but how little a portion is heard of him? but the thunder of his power who can understand?

CHAPTER XXVII.

1 *Job protests his sincerity.* 8 *The hypocrite without hope.*

MOREOVER Job *1* continued his parable, and said,
2 *As* God liveth, *a* who hath taken away my judgment; and the Almighty, *who* hath *2* vexed my soul;
3 All the while my breath *is* in me, and *3* the spirit of God *is* in my nostrils,
4 My lips shall not speak wickedness, nor my tongue utter deceit.
5 God forbid that I should justify you: till I die *b* I will not remove mine integrity from me.
6 My righteousness I *c* hold fast, and will not let it go: *d* my heart shall not reproach *me* *4* so long as I live.
7 Let mine enemy be as the wicked, and he that riseth up against me as the unrighteous.
8 For *e* what *is* the hope of the hypocrite, though he hath gained, when God taketh away his soul?
9 Will *f* God hear his cry when trouble cometh upon him?
10 Will *g* he delight himself in the Almighty? will he always call upon God?
11 I will teach you *5* by the hand of God: *that* which *is* with the Almighty will I not conceal.
12 Behold, all ye yourselves have seen *it*; why then are ye thus altogether vain?
13 This *is* the portion of a wicked man with God, and the heritage of oppressors, *which* they shall receive of the Almighty.
14 If *h* his children be multiplied, *it is* for the sword: and his offspring shall not be satisfied with bread.
15 Those that remain of him shall be buried in death: and *i* his widows shall not weep.
16 Though he heap up silver as the dust, and prepare raiment as the clay;
17 He may prepare *it*, but *j* the just shall put *it* on, and the innocent shall divide the silver.
18 He buildeth his house as a moth, and as *k* a booth *that* the keeper maketh.
19 The rich man shall lie down, but he shall not be *l* gathered: he openeth his eyes, and he *is* not.
20 Terrors take hold on him as waters, a tempest stealeth him away in the night.
21 The east wind carrieth him away, and he departeth; and as a storm hurleth him out of his place.
22 For *God* shall cast upon him, and not spare: *6* he would fain flee out of his hand.
23 *Men* shall clap their hands at him, and shall hiss him out of his place.

CHAPTER XXVIII.

1 *There is a knowledge of natural things,* 12 *but wisdom is an excellent gift of God.*

SURELY there is 1 a vein for the silver, and a place for gold *where* they fine it.
2 Iron is taken out of the *2* earth, and brass is molten *out of* the stone.

Bildad's Reply. JOB, XXV, XXVI. *Job's Reply.*

although he had given up hope of (*lit.*, when he no longer believed in) life" (Deu. 28. 66.). 23. *Lit.*, He (God omitted as often: ch. 3. 20; Eccl. 9. 9; reverentially) giveth to him (the wicked, to be in safety, or security, yet—Job means, How strange that God should so favour them, and yet have his eyes all the time open to their wicked ways! (Prov. 15. 3; I's. 73. 4.). 24. Job repeats what he said (ch. 21. 13.), that sinners die in exalted positions, not the painful and lingering death we might expect, but a *quick and easy death.* Join "for a while" with "are gone," not as *E.V. Transl.* "A moment—and they are no more! They are brought low, as all (others) gather up their feet to die" (so the *Heb.* of "are taken out of the way." A natural death Gen. 49. 33.), ears of corn—In a ripe and full age, not prematurely (ch. 5. 26.), 20, (so ch. 9. 24.).

CHAPTER XXV.
THIRD SERIES.

Ver. 1-6. BILDAD'S REPLY. He tries to show Job's rashness (ch. 23. 3.), by arguments borrowed from Eliphaz (ch. 15. 15.), with which cf. ch. 11, 17. 2. Power and terror, *i.e.*, terror-inspiring power. peace in His high places—Implying that His power is such on high as to quell all opposition, not merely there, but on earth also. The Holy Ghost here shadowed forth Gospel truths (Col. 1. 20; Eph. 1. 10.). 3. armies—Angels and stars (Isa. 40. 26; Jer. 33. 22; Gen. 15. 5; countless Dan. 7. 10.). His light—(Jam. 1. 17.). 4. (ch. 4. 17, 18; 14. 4; 15. 14.). 5. "Look up even unto the moon" (ch. 15. 15.). "Stars" here answer to "saints" (angels) there; "the moon" here, to "the heavens" there. Even the "stars," the most dazzling object to man's eye, and the angels, of which the stars are emblems (ch. 4. 18; Rev. 9. 1,), are imperfect in His sight. Theirs is the light and purity of but creatures; his, of the Creator. 6. (ch. 4. 19-21; 15. 16.). worm ... worm—Two distinct *Heb.* words. The first, a worm bred in putridity; alluding to man's *corruption.* The second, a crawling worm; implying that man is *weak and grovelling.*

CHAPTER XXVI.
THIRD SERIES.

JOB'S REPLY. 2, 3. without power ... no strength ... no wisdom—The negatives are used instead of the positives, *powerlessness,* &c., designedly (so Isa. 31. 8; Deut. 32. 21.). Granting I am, as you say (ch. 18. 7; 15. 2.), *powerlessness* itself, &c. How hast thou helped such a 'one? savest—supportest. plentifully ... the thing as it is—Rather, "abundantly—wisdom." Bildad had made great pretensions to *abundant wisdom.* How has he shown it? 4. For whose instruction were thy words meant? If for me, I know the subject (God's omnipotence) better than my instructor; (*v.* 5-14,) is a sample of Job's knowledge of it, whose spirit—not that of God (ch. 32. 8,; nay rather, the borrowed sentiment of Eliphaz (ch. 4. 17-19; 15. 14-16.). 5-14. As before in chap. 9. and 12., Job had shown himself not inferior to the friends in ability to describe God's greatness, so now he describes it as manifested in Hell the world of the dead 5, 6; on earth 7; in the sky 8-11; the sea 12; the heavens 13. Dead things are formed—Rather, "The souls of the dead (Rephaim) tremble." Not only does God's power exist, as Bildad says ch. 25. 2.), "in high places" (heaven), but reaches to the region of the dead. *Rephaim* here, and Pro. 21. 16; Isa. 14. 9, is from a *Heb.* root, meaning to be *weak,* hence *deceased*; in Gen. 14. 5, it is applied to the Canaanite *giants*; perhaps in derision, to express their *weakness,* in spite of their gigantic size, as compared with Jehovah [UMBR.]; or as the imagination of the living magnifies apparitions, the term originally was applied to *ghosts,* and then to *giants* in general. [MAGEE.] from under—UMBR. joins this with the previous word, tremble *from beneath* (so Isa. 14. 9.). But the Masoretic text joins it "under (the waters." Thus the place of the dead will be represented as *under the waters* Ps. 18. 4, 5,): and the waters as under the earth (Ps. 24. 2,), MAGEE well *transl.* thus, "The souls of the dead tremble: (the places) under the waters, and their inhabitants." Thus the Masoretic connexion is retained; and at the same time the parallel clauses are evenly balanced. "The inhabitants of the places under the waters" are those in Gehenna, the lower of the two parts into which Sheol, according to the Jews, is divided: they answer to "destruction," *i.e.*, the place of the wicked in *v.* 6, as "Rephaim" (*v.* 5,) to "Hell" (Sheol), (*v.* 6.) Sheol comes from a *Heb.* root—*ask,* because it is insatiable Prov. 27. 20,); or *ask as a loan to be returned,* implying Sheol is but a *temporary* abode, previous to the resurrection; so for *E.V.* "formed:" LXX. and Chaldee *transl. shall be born,* or *born again,* implying the dead are to be *given back* from Sheol and *born again into a new state.* [MAGEE.] 6.—(ch. 38. 17; Ps. 139. 8; Prov. 5. 11.) cestruction—*The abode of destruction, i.e.*, of lost souls. *Heb.* Abaddon (Rev. 9. 11.). no covering—from God's eyes. 7. Hint of the true theory of the earth. Its suspension in empty space is stated in the 2nd clause. The N. in particular is specified in the 1st, being believed to be the *highest part of the earth* (Isa. (14. 13.). The N. hemisphere or vault of heaven is included; often compared to a stretched out canopy (Ps. 104. 2.). The chambers of the S. are mentioned (ch. 9. 9,), *i.e.*, the S. hemisphere, consistently with the earth's globular form. 8. in ... clouds—as if in airy vessels, which though light do not burst with the weight of water in them (Prov. 30. 4.). 9. Rather, He *encompasseth* or *closeth.* God makes the clouds a veil to screen the glory not only of His person, but even of *the exterior of His throne* from profane eyes. His agency is everywhere, yet Himself invisible (Ps. 18. 11; 104. 3.). 10. Rather, "He hath drawn a circular bound round the waters" (Prov. 8. 27; Ps. 104. 9.). The horizon seems a circle. Indication is given of the globular form of the earth. until the day, &c.—To the confines of light and darkness. When the light falls on our horizon, the other hemisphere is dark. UMBR. & MAUR. *transl.* "He has *most perfectly* (*lit.* to perfection) drawn the bound (taken from the 1st clause) between light and darkness," (cf. Gen. 1. 4. 6, 9,): where the bounding of the light from darkness is similarly brought into proximity with the bounding of the waters. 11. pillars—poetically for the mountains which seem to bear up the sky (Ps. 104. 32.). astonished—viz., from terror. Personification. His reproof—(Ps. 104. 7.). The thunder, reverberating from cliff to cliff Hab. 3. 10; Nah. 1. 5.). 12. divideth—(Ps. 74. 13.). Perhaps at creation (Gen. 1. 9,

10. The paral'el clause favours UMBR. "He stilleth." But the *Heb.* means *He moves*. Probably such a "moving" is meant as that at the *assuaging* of the flood by the wind which "God made to pass over" it (Gen. 8. 1; Ps. 104. 7.), the proud—Rather, *its pride*, viz., of the sea(ch.9.13. . 13. UMBR. less simply. "By His breath He maketh the heavens to revive." viz., His wind dissipates the clouds, which obscured the shining stars. And so the next clause in contrast, "His hand doth strangle," *i.e.*, obscures the N. constellation, the dragon. Pagan astronomy typified the flood brining to destroy the ark by the dragon constellation about to devour the moon in its eclipsed crescent-shape like a boat (ch. 3. 8, *Marg.*). But better as E. V. Ps. 33. 6.). crooked—Implying the *oblique* course, of the stars, or the ecliptic. "Fleeing" or "swift" [UMBR.] (Isa. 27. 1.). This particular constellation is made to represent the splendour of all the stars. **14.** parts—Rather, "only the extreme boundaries of, &c., and how faint is the *whisper* that we hear of Him!" thunder—The entire fulness. In antithesis to "whisper" (1 Cor. 13. 9, 10, 12.)

CHAPTER XXVII.

Ver. 1-23. It was now Zophar's turn to speak. But as he and the other two were silent, virtually admitting defeat, after a pause Job proceeds. 1. parable—Applied in the E. to a figurative sententious embodiment of wisdom in poetic form, a gnome (Ps. 49. 4.). continued—proceeded to put forth: implying *elevation* of discourse. **2.** (1 Sam. 20. 3.). taken away ... judgment—words unconsciously foreshadowing Jesus Christ (Isa. 53. 8; Acts, 8. 33.). God will not give Job his right, by declaring his innocence. vexed—*Heb. made bitter* (Ruth.1. 20). **3.** Implying Job's knowledge of the fact that the living soul was breathed into man by God (Gen. 2. 7.). "All the while." But MAUR. "as yet all my breath is in me (notwithstanding my trials):" the reason why I can speak so boldly. **4.** (ch. 6. 2, 30.) The "deceit" would be, if he were to admit guilt, against the witness of his conscience. **5.** justify you—approve of your views. mine integrity—which you deny, on account of my misfortunes. **6.** Rather, "my heart" (conscience) reproaches "not one of my days." *i.e.*, I do not repent of any of my days since I came into existence. [MAURER.] **7.** Let . . . be—Let mine enemy be accounted as wicked, *i.e.*, He who opposes my asseveration of innocence must be regarded as actuated by criminal hostility. Not a curse on his enemies. **8.** "What hope hath the hypocrite, notwithstanding all his gains, when?" &c. "Gained" is antithetic to "taketh away." UMBR's. translation is an unmeaning tautology. "When God cuts *off*, when He *taketh away* his life." taketh away—*Lit., draws out* the soul from the body, which is, as it were, its scabbard ch. 4. 21; Ps. 104. 29; Dan.7.15.). Job says, he admits what Bildad said (ch. 8. 13.) and Zophar (ch. 20, 5.). But he says, the very fact of his still calling upon God (v.10.) amidst all his trials which a hypocrite would not dare to do, shows he is no "hypocrite." **9.** (Ps. 66. 18.). **10.** Alluding to ch. 22. 26., always call—he may do so in times of prosperity, in order to be thought religious. But he will not, as I do, call on God in calamities verging on death. Therefore I cannot

be a "hypocrite" (ch. 19.25; 20. 5; Ps. 62. 8.). 11-**23.** These words are contrary to Job's previous sentiments (Notes. ch. 21. 22-33; 24. 22-25.). They therefore seem to be Job's statement, not so much of his own sentiments, as of what Zophar would have said, had he spoken when his turn came (end of ch. 26.). So Job stated the friends' opinion (ch. 21. 17-21; 24. 18-21.). The objection is, why, if so, does not Job answer Zophar's opinion, as stated by himself? The fact is, it is probable that Job tacitly, by giving, in ch. 28., only a general answer, implies, that in spite of the wicked *often* dying, as he said, in prosperity, he does not mean to deny that the wicked are *in the main* dealt with according to right, and that God herein vindicates His moral government *even here*. Job therefore states Zophar's argument more strongly than Zophar would have done. But by comparing v. 13. with ch. 20. 29 ("portion," "heritage,"), it will be seen, it is Zophar's argument, rather than his own, that Job states. Granting it to be true, implies Job, you ought not to use it as an argument to criminate *me*. For (ch. 28.). the ways of Divine wisdom in afflicting the godly are inscrutable: all that is sure to man is, the fear of the Lord is wisdom (v. 28.). by the hand—Rather, *concerning* the hand of God, viz., what God does in governing men. with the Almighty—The counsel or principle which regulates God's dealings. **12.** "Ye yourselves see," that the wicked *often* are afflicted (though often the reverse ch. 21. 33.). But why do you "vainly" make this an argument to prove from my afflictions that I am wicked? **13.** (Note, v. 11.). **14.** His family only increases to perish by sword, or famine (Jer. 18. 21; ch. 5. 20, the converse. **15.** Those that escape war and famine *v.* 14.), shall be buried by *the deadly plague*—"death" (ch. 18. 13; Jer. 15. 2; Rev. 6. 8.). The plague of the middle ages was called "the black death." *Buried by* it implies, that they would have none else, but the death plague itself (poetically personified), to perform their funeral rites, *i.e.*, would have none. his—Rather, *their* widows. Transitions from *Sing.* to *Plur.* are frequent. Polygamy is not implied. **16.** dust . . . clay—Images of multitudes (Zech. 9. 3.). Many changes of raiment are a chief constituent of wealth in the E. **17.** *Introverted parallelism*. My Introd. Of the four clauses in the two verses, 1 answers to 4, 2 to 3 (so Matt. 7. 6.). **18.** (ch. 8. 14: 4. 19.). The transition is natural from "raiment" (v.16,) to the "house" of the "moth" in it, and of it, when in its larva state. The *moth worm's house* is broken whenever the "raiment" is shaken out, so frail is it. booth—A bough-formed hut which the guard of a vineyard raises for temporary shelter (Isa.1. 8.). **19.** gathered—Buried honourably (Gen. 25. 8; 2 Ki. 22. 20.). But UMBR., agreeably to v. 18, which describes *the short continuance of the sinner's prosperity*, "He layeth himself rich in his bed, *and nothing is robbed from him*, he openeth his eyes, and *nothing more is there.*" If E. V. be retained, the first clause probably means, rich though he be in *dying*, he shall not be honoured with a *funeral*; the second, When he opens his eyes *in the unseen world*, it is only to see *his destruction*. LXX. read for "not gathered," *He does not proceed*, *i.e.*, goes to his bed no more. So MAUR. **20.** (ch. 18. 11; 22. 11, 21.). Like a sudden violent flood Isa. 8. 7, 8; Jer. 47. 2,); conversely (Ps. 32. 6.'. 21. (ch. 21. 18; 15. 2; Ps. 58. 9.). 22. cast—viz., thunderbolts ch. 6. 4; 7. 20; 16. 13; Ps. 7. 12, 13). 23. clap hands —for joy at his downfall (Lam. 2. 15; Nah. 3. 19.'. 1 iss—deride Jer. 25, 9.,. Job alludes to Bildad's words (ch. 18. 18.).

CHAPTER XXVIII.

Ver. 1-28. JOB'S SPEECH CONTINUED. In ch. 27., Job had tacitly admitted, that the statement of the friends was often true, that God vindicated His justice by punishing the wicked here: but still the affliction of the godly remained unexplained. Man has, by skill, brought the precious metals from their concealment. But the Divine Wisdom, which governs human affairs, he cannot similarly discover, 12, &c. However, the image from the same metals (ch. 23, 10.), implies Job has made some way towards solving the riddle of his life, viz., that affliction is to him, as the refining fire to gold. vein—A mine, from which it *goes forth*, Heb., *i.e.*, is dug. place for gold — A place where gold may be found, *which* men refine. Not as *E. V.*, "A place—*where*," &c. (Mal. 3. 3.). Contrasted with gold found in the bed and sand of rivers, which does not need refining; as the gold *dug from a mine* does. Golden ornaments have been found in Egypt, of the times of Joseph. 2. brass— *i.e.*, *copper:* for brass is a mixed metal of copper and zinc, of modern invention. Iron is less easily discovered, and wrought, than copper: therefore copper was in common use long before iron. Copper-stone is called "cadmium" by Pliny [NAT. HIST. 34. 1; 36. 21.]. Iron is fitly said to be taken out of the " earth" (dust,), for ore looks like mere earth. 3. " Man makes an end of darkness," by exploring the darkest depths (with torches.). all perfection—Rather, carries out his search to the utmost perfection; most thoroughly searches the stones of darkness and of the shadow of death (thickest gloom,), *i.e.*, the stones, whatever they be, embedded in the darkest bowels of the earth [UMBR.] (ch. 28. 10.). 4 Three hardships in mining : 1. " A stream (flood) breaks out at the side of the stranger ;" viz., *the miner, a strange new-comer* into places heretofore unexplored; his *surprise* at the sudden stream breaking out *beside* him is expressed (*E. V.*, *from the inhabitant :* 2. " For, otten (unsupported, by the foot they *hang*, viz., by pumps, in descending. In the *Heb.*, " Lo there" precedes this clause, graphically placing it as it before the eyes. *The waters* are inserted by *E. V.*, *Are dried up*, ought to be, " hang," " are suspended." *E. V.* perhaps understood, waters of whose existence man was previously *unconscious*, and near which he *never trod;* and yet man's energy is such, that by pumps, &c., he soon causes them to "dry up and go away." [So HERDER.] 3. " Far away from men, they move with uncertain step;" they stagger : not " they are gone." [UMBR.] 5. Its fertile surface yields food : and yet " beneath it is turned up as it were with fire." So PLIN. HIST. NAT. 33, observes on the ingratitude of man who repays the debt, he owes the earth for food, by digging out its bowels. " Fire" was used in mining. [UMBR.] *E. V.* is simpler, which means precious stones which glow *like fire;* and so *v.* 6 follows naturally (Ezek. 28. 14.). 6. Sapphires are found in alluvial soil near rocks and embed- ded in gneiss. The ancients distinguished two kinds : 1. The real, of transparent blue: 2. That improperly so called, opaque, with gold spots, *i.e.*, lapislazuli. To the latter, looking like cold dust UMBR. refers "dust of gold." *E. V.* better, " The *stones* of the earth are, &c., and the *clods* of it (*Vulg.*) are gold :" the parallel clauses are thus neater. 7. fowl — Rather, *ravenous bird*, or *eagle*, which is the most sharp-sighted of birds (Isa. 46. 11.). A vulture will spy a carcass at an amazing distance. The miner penetrates the earth by a way unseen by birds of keenest sight. 8. lion's whelps—*Lit.*, *the sons of pride*, *i.e.*, the fiercest beasts. passed—The *Heb.* implies *the proud gait* of the lion. The miner ventures, where not even the fierce lion dares to go in pursuit of his prey. 9. rock — Flint. He puts forth his hand to cleave the *hardest rock*, by the roots—From their foundations, by undermining them, 10. *He cuts* channels to drain off the waters, which hinder his mining; and when the waters are gone, he is able to see *the precious things* in the earth. 11. floods—"He restrains the *streams* from *weeping;*" a poetical expression for the *trickling* subterranean *rills*, which impede him : answering to the first clause of *v.* 10; so also the two latter clauses in each verse correspond. 12. Can man discover the Divine Wisdom by which the world is governed, as he can the treasures hidden in the earth? Certainly not. Divine Wisdom is conceived as a person (*v.* 12-27,) distinct from God (*v.* 23 ; also in Prov. 8. 23, 27.). The Almighty Word, Jesus Christ, *we know now*, is that Wisdom. The order of the world was originated and is maintained by the breathing forth (Spirit) of Wisdom, unfathomable and unpurchaseable by man. In verse 28, the only aspect of it, which relates to, and may be understood by, *man*, is stated. understanding—Insight into the plan of the Divine goverment. 13. Man can fix no price upon it, as it is nowhere be found in man's abode (Isa. 38. 11.). Job implies both its invaluable worth, and the impossibility of buying it at any price. 15. Not the usual word for "gold :" from a *Heb.* root, *to shut up* with care ; *i.e.*, *purest gold* (1 Ki. 6. 20. *Marg.*). weighed—The precious metals were *weighed* out before coining was known (Gen. 23. 16.). 16. gold of Ophir—The most precious (Note, 22. 24 ; Ps. 45. 9.'. onyx —(Gen. 2. 12.). More valued formerly than now. The term is Greek, meaning *thumb nail*, from some resemblance in colour. The Arabic denotes, of two colours, white preponderating. 17. crystal—Or else *glass*, if then known, very costly. From a root, *to be transparent*. jewels — Rather, *vessels*. 18. Red coral (Ezek 27. 16.). 18. pearls — *Lit.*, *what is frozen*. Probably *crystal;* and *v.* 17 will then be *glass*. rubies—UMBR. *transl*. pears (see Lam. 4. 1; Prov. 3. 15.). The Urim and Thummim, the means of consulting God by the twelve stones on the high priests' breastplate, "the stones of the sanctuary" (Lam. 4. 1., have their counterpart in this chapter ; the precious stones symbolizing the " light" and " perfection " of the Divine wisdom. 19. Ethiopia—*Cush* in the *Heb.* Either Ethiopia, or the S. of Arabia, near the Tigris. 20. Verse 12 repeated with great force. 21. None can tell *whence* or *where*, *seeing it*, &c. fowls—The gift of divination was assigned by the heathen especially to birds. Their

3 He setteth an end to darkness, *and* searcheth out all perfection: the stones of darkness, and the shadow of death.
4 The flood breaketh out from the inhabitant; *even the waters* forgotten of the foot: they are dried up, they are gone away from men.
5 *As for* the earth, out of it cometh bread; and under it is turned up as it were fire.
6 The stones of it *are* the place of sapphires: and it hath *dust of gold.
7 *There is* a path which no fowl knoweth, and which the vulture's eye hath not seen:
8 The lion's whelps have not trodden it, nor the fierce lion passed by it.
9 He putteth forth his hand upon the rock; he overturneth the mountains by the roots.
10 He cutteth out rivers among the rocks; and his eye seeth every precious thing.
11 He bindeth the floods from overflowing; and *the thing that is* hid bringeth he forth to light.
12 But where shall wisdom be found? and where *is* the place of understanding?
13 Man knoweth not the price thereof; neither is it found in the land of the living.
14 The depth saith, It is not in me; and the sea saith, *It is* not with me.
15 It cannot be gotten for gold, neither shall silver be weighed *for* the price thereof.
16 It cannot be valued with the gold of Ophir, with the precious onyx, or the sapphire.
17 The gold and the crystal cannot equal it; and the exchange of it *shall not be for* jewels of fine gold.
18 No mention shall be made of coral, or of pearls: for the price of wisdom *is* above rubies.
19 The topaz of Ethiopia shall not equal it, neither shall it be valued with pure gold.
20 Whence then cometh wisdom? and where *is* the place of understanding?
21 Seeing it is hid from the eyes of all living, and kept close from the fowls of the air.
22 Destruction and death say, We have heard the fame thereof with our ears.
23 God understandeth the way thereof, and he knoweth the place thereof.
24 For he looketh to the ends of the earth, *and* seeth under the whole heaven;
25 To make the weight for the winds; and he weigheth the waters by measure.
26 When he made a decree for the rain, and a way for the lightning of the thunder;
27 Then did he see it, and declare it; he prepared it, yea, and searched it out.
28 And unto man he said, Behold, the fear of the Lord, that *is* wisdom; and to depart from evil *is* understanding.

CHAPTER XXIX.

Job bemoans himself when he remembers his former prosperity and honour.

MOREOVER Job continued his parable, and said,
2 Oh that I were as *in* months past, as in the days *when* God preserved me;
3 When his candle shined upon my head, *and when* by his light I walked through darkness;
4 As I was in the days of my youth, when the secret of God *was* upon my tabernacle;
5 When the Almighty *was* yet with me, *when* my children *were* about me;

6 When I washed my steps with butter, and the rock poured me out rivers of oil!
7 When I went out to the gate through the city, *when* I prepared my seat in the street:
8 The young men saw me, and hid themselves: and the aged arose, *and* stood up.
9 The princes refrained talking, and laid their hand on their mouth.
10 The nobles held their peace, and their tongue cleaved to the roof of their mouth.
11 When the ear heard *me*, then it blessed me; and when the eye saw *me*, it gave witness to me:
12 Because I delivered the poor that cried, and the fatherless, and *him that had* none to help him.
13 The blessing of him that was ready to perish came upon me: and I caused the widow's heart to sing for joy.
14 I put on righteousness, and it clothed me: my judgment *was* as a robe and a diadem.
15 I was eyes to the blind, and feet *was* I to the lame.
16 I *was* a father to the poor: and the cause *which* I knew not I searched out.
17 And I brake the jaws of the wicked, and plucked the spoil out of his teeth.
18 Then I said, I shall die in my nest, and I shall multiply my days as the sand.
19 My root *was* spread out by the waters, and the dew lay all night upon my branch.
20 My glory *was* fresh in me, and my bow *was* renewed in my hand.
21 Unto me *men* gave ear, and waited, and kept silence at my counsel.
22 After my words they spake not again; and my speech dropped upon them.
23 And they waited for me as for the rain; and they opened their mouth wide *as* for the latter rain.
24 *If* I laughed on them, they believed *it* not; and the light of my countenance they cast not down.
25 I chose out their way, and sat chief, and dwelt as a king in the army, as one *that* comforteth the mourners.

CHAPTER XXX.

1 Job's honour turned into extreme contempt: 15 his prosperity into calamity.

BUT now *they that are* younger than I have me in derision, whose fathers I would have disdained to have set with the dogs of my flock.
2 Yea, whereto *might* the strength of their hands *profit* me, in whom old age was perished?
3 For want and famine *they were* solitary; fleeing into the wilderness in former time desolate and waste.
4 Who cut up mallows by the bushes, and juniper roots *for* their meat.
5 They were driven forth from among men, (they cried after them as *after* a thief;)
6 To dwell in the cliffs of the valleys, *in* caves of the earth, and *in* the rocks.
7 Among the bushes they brayed; under the nettles they were gathered together.
8 *They were* children of fools, yea, children of base men; they were viler than the earth.
9 And now am I their song; yea, I am their byword.

Job Bemoaneth himself JOB, XXIX. *of his Former Prosperity.*

rapid flight heavenwards and keen sight originated the superstition. Job may allude to it, Not even the boasted divination of birds has an insight into it (Eccl. 10. 20.). But it may merely mean, as verse 7, It escapes the eye of the most keen-sighted bird. 22. *i.e.,* the abodes of *destruction* and of the *dead.* "Death" put for Sheol (ch. 30. 23; 26. 6, Note; Ps. 9. 13.). We have (only) heard—The *report* of her. We have not *seen* her. In the land of the living (v. 13,) the workings of Wisdom are *seen,* though not herself. In the regions of the dead, she is only *heard* of, her actings on nature not being seen (Eccl. 9. 10.). 23. God hath, and is Himself wisdom. "Seeth (all that is) under." &c. 25. God has adjusted the weight of the winds, so seemingly imponderable, lest, if too weighty, or too light, injury should be caused. He measureth out the waters, fixing their bounds, with wisdom as His counsellor (Prov. 8. 27-31 ; Isa. 40. 12.). 26. The decree regulating at what time and place, and in what quan'ity the rain should fall, a way —Through the parted clouds ch. 38. 25; Zech. 10. 1.), 27. declare—Manifest her, viz., in His works (Ps. 19. 1, 2.). So the approval bestowed by the Character on His works (Gen. 1. 10. 31.; cf. the "rejoicing" of wisdom at the same (Prov. 8. 30; which UMBR. *transl.* "I was the skilful artificer by his side" 31.). prepared—Not, *created,* for wisdom is from everlasting (Prov. 8.); but "established" Her as Governor of the world, searched out—Examined her works to see, whether she was adequate to the task of governing the world. [MAUR.] 28. Rather, *But* unto man, &c., *My* wisdom is that whereby all things are governed : *Thy* wisdom is in *fearing God and shunning evil,* and in feeling assured that my wisdom always acts aright, though thou dost not understand the principle which regulates it : *ex. gr.,* in afflicting the godly (John 7. 17.). The friends, therefore, as not comprehending the Divine Wisdom, should not infer Job's guilt from his sufferings. Here alone in Job the name of God, "Adonai" occurs, *Lord* or *master,* often applied to Messiah in O. T. Appropriately here, in speaking of the Word or Wisdom, by whom the world was made (Prov. 8. ; John 1. ; Ecclus. 24.).

CHAPTER XXIX.

1. Job pauses for a reply. None being made: he proceeds to illustrate the mysteriousness of God's dealings, as set forth (ch. 28.) by his own case. 2. preserved me—From calamity. 3. candle—When His favour shone on me, (Note, 18. 6 ; Ps. 18. 28.). darkness —By His safeguard I passed secure through dangers. Perhaps alluding to the lights carried before caravans in nightly travels through deserts. [NOY.] 4. youth—*Lit., autumn ;* the time of the ripe fruits of my prosperity. Applied tö *youth,* as the Orientalists *began* their year with autumn, the most temperate season in the E. secret— When the intimate friendship of God rested on my tent (Prov. 3. 32; Ps. 31. 20; Gen. 18. 17; John. 15. 15.). The *Lit.* often means a *divan* for *deliberation.* 6. butter—Rather, *cream, lit., thick milk.* Wherever I turned my steps the richest milk and oil flowed in to me abundantly. Image from pastoral life. Literal *washing of the feet in milk* is not meant, as the second clause shows ; *Marg. with me, i.e., near* my path, wherever I walked (Deu.

32. 13.). Olives amidst *rocks* yield the best oil. Oil in the E. is used for food. light, anointing, and medicine. 7-10. The great influence Job had over young and old, and noblemen, through . . . street — Rather, When I went out of my house, in the country (see ch. 1., prologue to the gate, (ascending) *up to* the city (which was on elevated ground,), and when I prepared my (judicial) seat in *the market-place.* The market-place was the place of judgment, at the gate or propylœa of the city, such as is found in the remains of Nineveh and Persepolis (Isa. 59. 14; Ps. 55. 11; 127. 5.). 8. hid—Not *lit.* Rather, *Stepped backwards,* reverent'ally. *The aged,* who were already seated, *arose and remained standing* (Heb.) until Job seated himself. Oriental manners. 9. (ch. 4. 2. Note, 21. 5.). "Refrained," stopped in the middle of their speech. 10. *Marg., voice*—hid, *i.e., hushed* (Ezek. 3. 26.). "Tongue cleaved," &c., *i.e.,* awed by my presence the emirs or sheikhs were silent. 11. blessed— Extolled my virtues (Prov. 31. 28.). Omit *me* after " heard ;" whoever *heard of* me in general, not in the market-place, (7-10,), praised me. gave witness—to my honourable character. Image from a court of justice (Luke 4. 22.). "The eye"—*i.e., face to face ;* antithesis to " ear "—*i.e., report of* me. 12-17. The grounds on which Job was praised ,v. 11,), his helping the afflicted (Ps. 72. 12, who cried to him for help), as a judge, or as one possessed of means of charity. *Transl.* The fatherless who had none to help him. 13. So far was I from sending " widows" away empty (ch. 22. 9.). ready to perish—(Prov. 31. 6.). 14. (Isa. 61. 10; 1 Chron. 12. 18.) *Marg.* judgment—Justice. diadem—Tiara. Rather, *turban, head-dress.* It and the full flowing outer mantle or " robe," are the prominent characteristics of an Oriental's grandee or high-priest's dress (Zech. 3. 5.). So Job's righteousness especially characterized him. 15. *Lit., the blind* (Deu. 27. 18.): lame (2 Sam. 9. 13); *fig.,* also the spiritual support which the more enlightened gives to those less so (ch. 4. 3; Heb. 12. 13; Num. 10. 31.). 16. So far was I from " breaking the arms of the *fatherless,*" as Eliphaz asserts (ch. 22. 9.), I was a " father" to such. the cause which I knew not—Rather—*of him whom I knew not,* the stranger (Prov. 29. 7; [UMBR.] contrast Luke. 18. 1, &c.) Applicable to *almsgiving* (Ps. 41. 1.); but here primarily, *judicial conscientiousness* (ch. 31. 13.). 17. Image from combating with wild beasts (ch. 4. 11; Ps. 3. 7.). So compassionate was Job to the oppressed, so terrible to the oppressor ! jaws— Job broke *his power,* so that he could do no more hurt, and tore from him the spoil, which he had torn from others. 18. I said —In my heart (Ps. 30. 6.). nest—Rather, " *With* my nest ;" as the second clause refers to long life. Instead of my family dying before me, as now, I shall live so long as to die with them : proverbial for long life. Job did realize his hope (ch. 42. 16.). *In* the bosom of my family, gives a good sense. (Num. 24. 21; Obad. 4). Use " nest " for a *secure dwelling.* sand—Gen. 22. 17; Hab. 1. 9.). But LXX., and *Vulg.,* and Jewish Interpreters, favour the *transl.,* " the phœnix bird." " Nest " in the pa allel clause supports the reference to a *bird.* "Sand " for *multitude,* applies to men, rather than to *years.* The myth was, that the Phœnix

Job's Honour turned   JOB, XXX.   *into Extreme Contempt.*

sprang from a nest of myrrh, made by his father before death, and that he then came from Arabia (*Job's country*) to Heliopolis (the city of the Sun) in Egypt, once in every 500 years, and there burnt his father. [HERODOT. 2. 73.] Modern research has shown that this was the Egyptian mode of representing hieroglyphically a particular chronological era or cycle. The death and revival every 500 years, and the reference to the *sun* implies such a grand cycle commencing afresh from the same point in relation to the sun, from which the previous one started. Job probably refers to this. 19. *Lit*, *opened to the waters.* Opposed to ch. 18. 16. Vigorous health. 20. My renown, like my bodily health, was continually fresh. bow—Metaphor from war, for, *My strength*, which gains me "renown," was ever renewed (Jer. 49. 35.). 21. Job reverts with peculiar pleasure to his former dignity in assemblies (v. 7-10.). 22. not again—Did not contradict me. dropped—Affected their minds, as the genial rain does the soil on which it gently drops (Amos, 7. 16; Deu. 32. 2; Song, 4. 11.). 23. Image of v. 22 continued. They waited for my salutary counsel, as the dry soil does for the refreshing rain. opened ... mouth—*Panted for*; Oriental image (Ps. 119. 131.). The "early rain" is in autumn and onwards, while the seed is being sown. The "latter rain" is in March, and brings forward the harvest, which ripens in May or June. Between the early and latter rains, *some* rain falls, but not in such quantities as those rains. Between March and October no rain falls (Deu. 11. 14; James 5. 7.). 24. When I relaxed from my wonted gravity (a virtue much esteemed in the E.) and smiled, they could hardly credit it, and yet, notwithstanding my condescension *they did not cast aside* reverence for *my gravity.* But the parallelism is better in UMBR.'s transl., "I smiled kindly on those who trusted not," *i.e.*, in times of danger I cheered those in despondency. "And they could not cast down (by their despondency) my *serenity of countenance*" (flowing from trust in God, (Prov. 16. 15; Ps. 104. 15.] The opposite phrase (Gen. 4. 5, 6,). "Gravity" cannot well be meant by "light of countenance." 25. I chose ... their way — *i.e.*, I willingly went up to their assembly (from my country residence, v. 7.). in ... army—As a king supreme in the midst of his army. comforteth ... mourners— Here again Job unconsciously foreshadows Jesus Christ (Isa. 61. 2. 3,). Job's afflictions, as those of Jesus Christ, were fitting him for the office hereafter (Isa. 50. 4; Heb. 2. 18.).

CHAPTER XXX.

Ver. 1-31. 1. younger—Not the three friends (ch. 15. 10; 32. 4, 6, 7.). A general description; 1-8, the lowness of the persons who derided him; 9-15, the derision itself. Formerly old men rose to me (ch. 29. 8). Now not only my *juniors*, who are bound to reverence me (Lev. 19. 32,), but even the mean and *base-born* actually *deride* me; opposed to, "smiled upon" (ch. 29. 24.). This goes farther than even the "mockery" of Job by *relations* and *friends* (ch. 12. 4; 16. 10. 20; 17. 2, 6; 19. 22.). Orientals feel keenly any indignity shown by the young. Job speaks as a rich Arabian emir, proud of his descent. dogs—Regarded with disgust in the E. as unclean (1 Sam. 17, 43; Prov. 26.

11.). They are not allowed to enter a house, but run about wild in the open air, living on offal and chance morsels (Ps. 59. 14, 15.). Here again we are reminded of Jesus Christ (Ps. 22. 16.). Their fathers, my co-evals, were so mean and famished that I would not have associated them *with* (not to say, set them *over*) my dogs in guarding my flock." 2. If their fathers, could be of no *profit* to me, much less the sons, who are feebler than their sires; and *in whose case the hope of attaining old age is utterly gone*, so puny are they (ch. 5. 26.). [MAUR.] Even if they had "strength of hands," that could be now of *no use to me*, as all I want in my present affliction is sympathy. 3. solitary—*Lit., hard* as a rock; so *transl.* rather, *dried up*, emaciated with hunger. Job describes the rudest race of Bedouins of the desert. [UMBR.] fleeing—So LXX. Better, as *Syr.*, *Arab.* and *Vulg.*, "*gnawers* of the wilderness." What they gnaw, follows in v. 4. in former time—*Lit.*, the "*yesternight* of desolation: *tion and waste*" (the most utter desolation: Ezek. 6. 14,); *i.e.*, those deserts *frightful as night* to man and even there *from time immemorial.* I think *both* ideas are in the word *darkness* [GES.] and *antiquity* [UMBR.] Isa. 30. 33., *Marg.*). 4. mallows—Rather, *salt-wort*, which grows in deserts and is eaten as a salad by the poor. [MAUR.] by the bushes—Among the bushes. juniper—Rather, a kind of broom, *spartium junceum* [LINN.], still called in Arabia, as in the *Heb*. of Job, *Retem*, of which the bitter roots are eaten by the poor. 5. they cried—*i.e.*, a cry is raised, &c. Expressing the contempt felt for this race by civilized and well-born Arabs. When these wild vagabonds make an incursion on villages, they are driven away, as thieves would be. 6. They are forced "to dwell." cliffs of valleys—Rather, "in the gloomy (*lit.*, gloom of) valleys," or *wadys.* To dwell in valleys, is, in the E. a mark of wretchedness. The Troglodytes, in parts of Arabia, lived in such dwellings as caves, &c. 7. brayed—Like the wild ass (ch. 6. 5,) for food. The inarticulate tones of this uncivilized rabble are but little above those of the beast of the field. gathered together —Rather, sprinkled here and there. *Lit.*, poured out, graphically picturing their disorderly mode of encampment, lying up and down behind the thorn-bushes. nettles—Or brambles. [UMBR.] 8. fools—*i.e.*, the impious and abandoned (1 Sam. 25. 25.). base —Nameless, low-born rabble. viler than, &c.—Rather, they were *driven* or *beaten out of the land.* The Horites in Mount Seir (Gen. 14. 6, with which cf. Gen. 36. 20, 21; Deut. 2. 12, 22,) were probably the aborigines, driven out by the tribe to which Job's ancestors belonged; their name means Troglodytæ, or *dwellers in caves*. To these Job alludes here, v. 1-8, and Gen. 24. 4-8, which cf. together. 9. (ch. 17. 6.). Strikingly similar to the derision Jesus Christ underwent (Lam. 3. 14; Ps. 69. 12.). Here Job returning to the sentiment in v. 1. It is to such I am become a song of "derision." 10. in my face —Rather, refrain not to spit (in deliberate contempt) *before* my face. To spit at all in presence of another is thought in the E. insulting, much more when done to mark "abhorrence." Cf. the further insult to Jesus Christ (Isa. 50. 6; Matt. 26. 67,). 11. *He, i.e.*, God; antithetical to *they, E.V.*, here follows the marginal reading (KERI) "*My* cord;" image from a bow unstrung; opposed to ch. 29. 20. The text (CHETIB: "*His* cord," or "reins," is better: "yea, each lets loose his reins." [UMBR.] 12. youth—Rather, a (low) brood. To rise on the right hand is to *accuse*, as that was the position of the accuser in court (Zech. 3. 1; Ps. 109. 6.). push ... feet —Jostle me out of the way (ch. 24. 4.). ways of—*i.e.*, their ways of (*i.e.*, with a view to my) destruction. Image, as in ch. 19. 12, from a besieging army throwing up a way of approach for itself to a city. 13. Image of an assailed fortress continued. They tear up the path, by which succour might reach me. set forward—(Zech. 1. 15.). they have no helper —Arabic proverb for *contemptible* persons. Yet even such afflict Job. 14. waters—(So 2 Sam. 5. 20.). But it is better to retain the image of *v*. 12, 13. "They came upon me) as through a wide *breach*," viz., made by the besiegers in the wall of a fortress (Isa. 30, 13.). [MAUR.] in the desolation—"Amidst the crash" of falling masonry: or "with a shout like the crash" of, &c. 15. they—Terrors. soul — Rather, my dignity. [UMBR.] welfare — Prosperity. cloud—ch. 7. 9; Isa. 44. 22.). 16-23. Job's outward calamities affect his mind. poured out--In irrepressible complaints Ps. 42. 4; Josh. 7. 5.). 17. In the *Heb.*, night is poetically personified, as ch. 3. 3; "night pierceth my bones, so that they fall) *from* me " (not as *E.V.*, "*in* me,") see *v.* 30. sinews—So the Arabic, *veins*, akin to the *Heb.*; rather, *gnawers*, as in *v*. 3 (Note,), viz., *my gnawing pains* never cease. Effects of elephantiasis. 18. of my disease—Rather, "of God" (ch. 23. 6.). garment changed—From a robe of honour to one of mourning, literally (ch. 2. 8; Jon. 3. 6,) and metaphorically. [UMBR.] Or rather, as SCH., following up *v.* 17, My outer garment is changed into affliction; *i.e.*, affliction has become my outer garment, it also bindeth me fast round (my throat) as the collar of the *inner* coat; *i.e.*, it is both my inner and outer garment. Observe the distinction between the inner and outer garments. The latter refers to his afflictions *from without*, (*v*. 1-13,): the former his personal afflictions (*v*. 14-23.). UMBR. makes "God" subject to "bindeth," as in *v*. 19. 19. God is poetically said to do that, which the mourner had done to himself (ch. 2. 8.). With lying in the ashes he had become, like them, in dirty colour. 20. stand up—The reverential attitude of a suppliant before a king (1 Ki. 8. 14; Luke, 18. 11-13.). not—Supplied from the first clause. But the intervening affirmative "stand" makes this ellipsis unlikely. Rather, as ch. 16. 9 (not only dost thou refuse aid to me "standing" as a suppliant, but) *thou dost regard me with a frown*: eye me sternly. 22. liftest ... to wind—As a "leaf," or "stubble" (ch. 13. 25.). The moving pillars of sand, raised by the wind to the clouds, as described by travellers, would happily depict Job's agitated spirit, if it be to them that he alludes. dissolvest ... substance—The *marg. Heb.* reading KERI,): "my wealth," or else "wisdom." *i.e.*, sense and spirit; or "my hope of *deliverance.*" But the text (CHETIB) is better, "Thou dissolvest me (with fear, Ex. 15. 15,) *in the crash* (of the whirlwind; see *v*. 14, Note.). [MAUR.]. UMBR. *transl.* as a verb, "Thou *terrifiest* me." 23. This shows ch. 19. 25 cannot be restricted to Job's hope of a *temporal*

deliverance. death — as in ch. 28. 22, the realm of the dead (Heb. 9. 27; Gen. 3. 19.). 24. Expressing Job's faith as to the state after death, Though one must go to the grave, yet He will no more afflict *in the ruin* of the body (so *Heb.* for *grave*, there, if one has cried to Him when being destroyed. The "stretching of His hand" to punish after death, answers antithetically to the raising "the cry" of prayer in the second clause. MAUR. gives another *transl.* which accords with the scope of *v*. 24-31; if it be natural for one in affliction to ask aid, why should it be considered (by the friends) wrong in my case? "Nevertheless does not a man in ruin stretch out his hand" (imploring help, *v*. 20; Lam. 1. 17.)? If one be in his calamity (destruction) is there not therefore a "cry" (for aid.)? Thus in the parallelism "cry" answers to "stretch—hand;" "in his calamity," to "in ruin." The negative of the first clause, is to be supplied in the second, as in *v*. 25 (ch. 28. 17.). 25. May I not be allowed to complain of my calamity, and beg relief, seeing that I myself sympathized with those "in trouble" (*lit.*, *hard of day*; those who had a hard time of it.). 26. I may be allowed to crave help, seeing that, "when I looked for good (on account of my piety and charity), yet evil," &c. light—(ch. 22. 28.). 27. bowels —Regarded as the seat of deep feeling (Isa. 16. 11.). boiled—Violently heated and agitated. prevented—Old English for *unexpectedly came upon me, surprised me.* 28. mourning —Rather, I move about *blackened*, though not by the sun; *i.e.*, whereas many are blackened by the sun, I am, by the heat of God's wrath (so "boiled," *v*. 27.); the elephantiasis covering me with blackness of skin (*v*. 30,), as with the garb of mourning (Jer. 14. 2.). This striking enigmatic form of *Heb.* expression occurs, Isa 29. 9. stood up—As an innocent man crying for justice in an assembled court (*v*. 20.). 29. dragons ... owls—Rather, *jackals, ostriches,* both of which utter dismal screams (Mic. 1. 8,); in which respect, as also in their living amidst solitudes, the emblem of desolation, Job is their brother and companion, *i. e.*, resembles them. "Dragon," *Heb.*, *Tannim*, usually means the crocodile; so perhaps here, its open jaws lifted towards heaven, and its noise making it seem as if it mourned over its fate. [Bo.] 30. upon me —Rather, as in 17 (Note), my skin is black (and falls away) *from* me. my bones—(ch. 19. 20; Ps. 102. 5.). 31. organ—Rather, *pipe* (ch. 21. 12.); "My *joy* is turned into the voice of weeping" (Lam. 5. 15.). These instruments are properly appropriated to *joy* (Isa. 30. 29, 32.), which makes their use now in sorrow the sadder by contrast.

CHAPTER XXXI.

Ver. 1-40. 1. Job proceeds to prove, that he deserved a better lot. As in ch. 29., he showed his uprightness as an Emir. or magistrate, in *public* life, so in this chapter he vindicates his character in *private* life. 1-4. He asserts his guarding against being allured to sin by his senses. 1. think—Rather, *cast a* (lustful) *look*. He not merely did not so, but put it out of the question by covenanting with his eyes against leading him into temptation (Prov. 6. 25; Matt. 5. 28.). 2. Had I let my senses tempt me to sin, "what portion would there have been to me, *i.e.*, must I have expected, from (*lit. of*) God above, and what inheritance from (*lit. of*) the Al-

10 They abhor me, they flee far from me, and spare not *a* to spit in my face.
11 Because he *b* hath loosed my cord, and afflicted me, they have also let loose the bridle before me.
12 Upon my right *hand* rise the youth; they push away my feet, and *c* they raise up against me the ways of their destruction.
13 They mar my path, they set forward my calamity, they have no helper.
14 They came *upon me* as a wide breaking in *of waters:* in the desolation they rolled themselves *upon me.*
15 Terrors are turned upon me: they pursue [7] my soul as the wind; and my welfare passeth away as a cloud.
16 And now my soul is poured out upon me; the days of affliction have taken hold upon me.
17 My bones are pierced in me in the night season; and my sinews take no rest.
18 By the great force *of my disease* is my garment changed: it bindeth me about as the collar of my coat.
19 He hath cast me into the mire, and I am become like dust and ashes.
20 I cry unto thee, and thou dost not hear me: I stand up, and thou regardest me not.
21 Thou art [8] become cruel to me: with [9] thy strong hand thou opposest thyself against me.
22 Thou liftest me up to the wind; thou causest me to ride *upon it,* and dissolvest my [10] substance.
23 For I know *that* thou wilt bring me *to* death, and *to* the house appointed for all living.
24 Howbeit he will not stretch out *his* hand to the [11] grave, though they cry in his destruction.
25 Did *d* not I weep [12] for him that was in trouble? was *not* my soul [13] grieved for the poor?
26 When *e* I looked for good, then evil came *unto me;* and when I waited for light, there came darkness.
27 My bowels boiled, and rested not; the days of affliction prevented me.
28 I went mourning without the sun : I stood up, *and* I cried in the congregation.
29 I am a brother to dragons, and a companion to [14] owls.
30 My skin is black upon me, and my bones are burnt with heat.
31 My harp also is *turned* to mourning, and my organ into the voice of them that weep.

CHAPTER XXXI
Job's solemn protestation of his integrity.

I MADE a covenant with mine *a* eyes; why then should I think upon *f* maid?
2 For what portion of God *is there* from above? and *what* inheritance of the Almighty from on high?
3 *Is* not destruction to the wicked? and a strange *punishment* to the workers of iniquity?
4 Doth *b* not he see my ways, and count all my steps?
5 If I have walked with vanity, or if my foot hath hasted to deceit;
6 [1] Let me be weighed in an even balance, that God may know mine integrity.
7 If my step hath turned out of the way, and *c* mine heart walked after mine eyes, and if any blot hath cleaved to mine hands;

8 *Then* let me sow, and let another eat; yea, let my offspring be rooted out.
9 If mine heart have been deceived by a woman, or if I have laid wait at my neighbour's door;
10 *Then* let my wife grind unto another, and let others bow down upon her.
11 For this *is* an heinous crime; yea, it *is* an iniquity *to be punished by* the judges.
12 For it *is* a fire that consumeth to destruction, and would root out all mine increase.
13 If I did despise the cause of my manservant, or of my maid-servant, when they contended with me;
14 What then shall I do when God riseth up? and when he visiteth, what shall I answer him?
15 Did *d* not he that made me in the womb make him? and [2] did not one fashion us in the womb?
16 If I have withheld the poor from *their* desire, or have caused the eyes of the widow to fail;
17 Or have eaten my morsel myself alone, and the fatherless hath not eaten thereof;
18 (For from my youth he was brought up with me, as *with* a father, and I have guided *a* her from my mother's womb;)
19 If I have seen any perish for want of clothing, or any poor without covering;
20 If his loins have not blessed me, and *if* he were *not* warmed with the fleece of my sheep;
21 If I have lifted up my hand against the fatherless, when I saw my help in the gate;
22 *Then* let mine arm fall from my shoulder blade, and mine arm be broken from [4] the bone.
23 For destruction *from* God *was* a terror to me, and by reason of his highness I could not endure.
24 If I have made gold my hope, or have said to the fine gold, *Thou art* my confidence;
25 If I rejoiced because my wealth *was* great, and because mine hand had *b* gotten much;
26 If *c* I beheld *b* the sun when it shined, or the moon walking [7] in brightness;
27 And my heart hath been secretly enticed, or *c* my mouth hath kissed my hand;
28 This also *were an* iniquity *to be punished by* the judge: for *f* I should have denied the God that *is* above.
29 If I rejoiced at the destruction of him that hated me, or lifted up myself when evil found him;
30 Neither *g* have I suffered *h* my mouth to sin by wishing a curse to his soul;
31 If the men of my tabernacle said not, Oh that we had of his flesh! we cannot be satisfied;
32 The *h* stranger did not lodge in the street; *but* I opened my doors [10] to the traveller;
33 If I *i* covered my transgressions [11] as Adam, by hiding mine iniquity in my bosom;
34 Did I fear a great multitude, or did the contempt of families terrify me, that I kept silence, *and* went not out of the door?
35 Oh that one would hear me! [12] behold, my desire *is, that* the Almighty would answer me, and *that* mine adversary had written a book;

mighty," &c. [MAUR.], (ch. 20. 29; 27. 13.). 3. Answer to the question in v. 2. strange—extraordinary. 4. Doth not He see, &c.? Knowing this, I could only have expected "destruction" (v. 3,), had I committed this sin (Prov. 5. 21.). 5. Job's abstinence from evil deeds. v: nity—i.e., falsehood (Ps.12.2.). 6. Parenthetical. Transl., "O that God would weigh me, &c., then would He know," &c. 7. Connected with v. 6. the way—of God (ch. 23. 11; Jer. 5. 5.). A godly life. heart... after... eyes—If my heart coveted, what my eyes beheld (Eccl. 11. 9; Josh. 7. 21.). hands—(Ps. 24. 4.). 8. Apodosis to v. 5 and 7; the curses which he imprecates on himself, if he had done these things (Lev.26.16; Amos 9. 14 ; Ps. 128. 2.). Offspring—Rather, what I plant, my harvests. 9-12. Job asserts his innocence of adultery. deceived—hath let itself be seduced Prov. 7. 8, &c.; Gen. 39. 7-12.). laid wait—until the husband went out. 10. grind—turn the handmill. Be the most abject slave and concubine (Isa. 47. 2; 2 Sam. 12. 11.). 11. In the earliest times punished with death (Gen. 38, 24.). So in later times Deut. 22. 22.). Heretofore he had spoken only of sins against conscience; now, one against the community, needing the cognizance of the judge. 12. (Prov. 6. 27-35 ; 8. 6-23, 26, 27.). No crime more provokes God to send *destruction* as a *consuming fire*. none so desolates the soul. 13-23. Job affirms his freedom from unfairness towards his servants; from harshness and oppression towards the needy. despise the cause —refused to do them justice. 14, 15. Parenthetical; the reason why Job did not despise the cause of his servants. *Transl.*, What then (had I done so) could I have done, when God arose (to call me to account); and when He visited (came to enquire, what could I have answered Him? 15. Slaveholders try to defend themselves by maintaining the *original* inferiority of the slave. But (Mal. 2. 10; Acts,17.26; Eph.6.9,) make the common origin of masters and servants the argument for brotherly love being shown by the former to the latter. 16. to fail—in the vain expectation of relief ch. 11. 20.). 17. Arabian rules of hospitality require the stranger to be helped first, and to the best. 18. Parenthetical: asserting that he did the contrary to the things in v. 16, 17. he—the orphan, guided her—viz., the widow, by advice and protection. On this and "a father" (see ch. 29.16.). 19. perish—*i.e.*, ready to perish (ch. 29. 13.). 20. loins—the parts of the body, benefitted by Job, are poetically described as thanking him, the loins before naked, when clad by me, wished me every blessing. 21. "When (*i.e.*, because I saw, that I might calculate on the "help" of a powerful party in the court of justice—("gate"), if I should be summoned by the injured fatherless. 22. Apodosis to vs. 13, 16, 17, 19, 20, 21. If I had done those crimes, I should have made a bad use of my influence (*my arm, figuratively, v.* 21,); therefore, if I have done them let my *arm* (literally) suffer. Job alludes to Eliphaz's charge ch. 22. 9.). The first "arm" is rather *the shoulder*. The second "arm" is the *forearm*. from the bone—Lit. *a reed:* hence the upper arm, above the elbow. 23. For—*i.e.*, the reason why Job guarded against such sins. *Fear of God*, though he could escape man's judgment (Gen. 39. 9.) UMBR. more spiritedly *transl.* Yea, destruction and ter-

ror from God might have befallen me (had I done so) : mere *fear* not being the motive. highness—majestic might. endure—I could have availed nothing against it. 24, 25. Job asserts his freedom from trust in money (1 Tim. 6. 17.). Here he turns to his duty towards God, as before he had spoken of his duty towards *himself*, and his *neighbour*. Covetousness is covert idolatry, as it transfers the heart from the Creator to the creature (Col. 3. 5.). In v. 26, 27, he passes to overt idolatry. 26. If I looked unto the Sun (as an object of worship), *because* he shined: or to the Moon *because* she walked, &c. Sabaism (from *tsaba*, the heavenly hosts) was the earliest form of false worship. God is hence called in contradistinction "Lord of Sabaoth." The sun, moon, and stars, the brightest objects in nature, and seen everywhere, were supposed to be visible representatives of the invisible God. They had no temples, but were worshipped on high places and roofs of houses (Ezek. 8. 16; Deut. 4. 19; 2 Ki. 23. 5, 11.). The *Heb.* here for "sun" is *light*. Probably *light* was worshipped as the emanation from God, before its embodiments, the sun, &c. This worship prevailed in Chaldea; wherefore Job's exemption from the idolatry of his neighbours was the more exemplary. Our "Sun-day, Monday" or Moon-day, bear traces of Sabaism, 27. enticed—away from God to idolatry. kissed... hand—*Adoration, lit.*, means this. In worshipping they used to kiss the hand, and then throw the kiss, as it were, towards the object of worship (1 Ki. 19. 18; Hos. 13.2.). 28. The Mosaic law embodied subsequently the feeling of the godly from the earliest times against idolatry, as deserving judicial penalties: being treason against the Supreme King (Deut. 13. 9 ; 17. 2-7; Ezek. 8. 14-18.). This passage therefore does not prove Job to have been subsequent to Moses. 29. lifted up myself—in malicious triumph (Prov. 17. 5 ; 24. 17 ; Ps. 7. 4.). 30. mouth—*lit., palate;* ch. 6. 30, Note.) wishing—*lit.*," so as to demand his (my enemy's) soul, *i.e.*, life by a curse." This verse parenthetically confirms v. 30. Job in the patriarchal age of the promise, anterior to the law, realizes the Gospel Spirit, which was the end of the law (cf. Lev. 19. 18; Deut. 23. 6, with Matt. 5. 43, 44.). 31. *i.e.,* Job's household said, O that we had Job's enemy to devour, we cannot rest satisfied till we have! But Job refrained from even wishing revenge (1 Sam. 26. 8 ; 2 Sam. 16. 9, 10.). So Jesus Christ (Lu. 9. 54, 55.). But, better (see v. 32,) *transl.,* "Who can show (*lit., give*) the man who was not satisfied with the flesh (meat) provided by Job?" He never let a poor man leave his gate without giving him enough to eat. 32. traveller —*lit. way, i.e.,* wayfarers; so expressed to include all of every kind (2 Sam. 12. 4.). 33. *Adam—Transl.* by UMBR. "as men do" (Hos. 6. 7, where see *Marg.*). But *E. V.* is more natural. The very same word for "hiding" is used in Gen. 3. 8. 10, of Adam *hiding* himself from God. Job elsewhere alludes to the flood. So he might easily know of the fall, through the two links which connect Adam and Abraham (about Job's time) viz., Methuselah, and Shem. Adam is representative of fallen man's propensity to conceal ment (Prov. 28. 13.). It was *from God* that Job did not "hide his iniquity in his bosom," as on the contrary it was from God

36 Surely I would take it upon my shoulder, *and* bind it *as* a crown to me.
37 I would declare unto him the number of my steps; as a prince would I go near unto him.
38 If my land cry against me, or that the furrows likewise thereof [13] complain;
39 If I have eaten [14] the fruits thereof without money, or have [15] caused the owners thereof to lose their life:
40 Let thistles grow instead of wheat, and [16] cockle instead of barley. The words of Job are ended.

CHAPTER XXXII.
1 *Elihu is angry with Job and his three friends:* 11 *he reproves them for not satisfying Job.*

SO these three men ceased [1] to answer Job, because he *was* righteous in his own eyes.
2 Then was kindled the wrath of Elihu the son of Barachel [a] the Buzite, of the kindred of Ram: against Job was his wrath kindled, because he justified [2] himself rather than God.
3 Also against his three friends was his wrath kindled, because they had found no answer, and *yet* had condemned Job.
4 Now Elihu had [3] waited till Job had spoken, because they *were* [4] elder than he.
5 When Elihu saw that *there was* no answer in the mouth of *these* three men, then his wrath was kindled.
6 And Elihu the son of Barachel the Buzite answered and said, I am [5] young, and ye *are* very old; wherefore I was afraid, and [6] durst not show you mine opinion.
7 I said, Days should speak, and multitude of years should teach wisdom.
8 But *there is* a spirit in man: and [b] the inspiration of the Almighty giveth them understanding.
9 Great men are not *always* wise; neither do the aged understand judgment.
10 Therefore I said, Hearken to me; I also will show mine opinion.
11 Behold, I waited for your words; I gave ear to your [7] reasons, whilst ye searched out [8] what to say.
12 Yea, I attended unto you, and, behold, *there was* none of you that convinced Job, or that answered his words:
13 Lest ye should say, We have found out wisdom: God thrusteth him down, not man.
14 Now he hath not [9] directed *his* words against me: neither will I answer him with your speeches.
15 They were amazed; they answered no more: [10] they left off speaking.
16 When I had waited, (for they spake not, but stood still, and answered no more,)
17 *I said,* I will answer also my part; I also will show mine opinion.
18 For I am full of [11] matter; [12] the spirit within me constraineth me.
19 Behold, my belly *is* as wine *which* [13] hath no vent; it is ready to burst like new bottles.
20 I will speak, that I may [14] be refreshed: I will open my lips and answer.
21 Let me not, I pray you, accept any man's person; neither let me give flattering titles unto man.
22 For I know not to give flattering titles: *in so doing* my Maker would soon take me away.

B.C. 1520.

CHAP. II.
13 weep.
14 the strength thereof.
15 caused the soul of the owners thereof to expire, or, breathe out.
16 Or, noisome weeds.

CHAP. 32.
1 from answering.
a Gen.xx.21.
2 his soul.
3 expected Job in words.
4 elder for days.
5 few of days.
6 feared.
b James 1.5.
7 understandings.
8 words.
9 Or, ordered his words.
10 they removed speeches from themselves.
11 words.
12 the spirit of my belly.
13 is not opened.
14 breathe.

CHAP. 33.
1 in my palate.
2 purely.
3 according to thy mouth.
4 cut out of the clay.
5 in mine ears.
6 he answereth not.
7 he revealeth, or, uncovereth.
8 work.
9 from passing by the sword.
10 meat of desire.
11 Or, an atonement.
12 than childhood.
13 Or, He shall look upon men, and say, I have sinned.
14 Or, He hath delivered my soul, etc., and my life.

CHAPTER XXXIII.
1 *Elihu offers to reason with Job:* 8 *he excuses God from giving men an account of his ways;* 14 *God calls men to repentance by visions, afflictions, and by his ministry.*

WHEREFORE, Job, I pray thee, hear my speeches, and hearken to all my words.
2 Behold, now I have opened my mouth, my tongue hath spoken [1] in my mouth.
3 My words *shall be of* the uprightness of my heart; and my lips shall utter knowledge [2] clearly.
4 The Spirit of God hath made me, and the breath of the Almighty hath given me life.
5 If thou canst answer me, set *thy words* in order before me, stand up.
6 Behold, I am [3] according to thy wish in God's stead: I also am [4] formed out of the clay.
7 Behold, my terror shall not make thee afraid, neither shall my hand be heavy upon thee.
8 Surely thou hast spoken [5] in mine hearing, and I have heard the voice of *thy* words, *saying,*
9 I am clean without transgression, I am innocent; neither *is there* iniquity in me.
10 Behold, he findeth occasions against me, he counteth me for his enemy,
11 He putteth my feet in the stocks, he marketh all my paths.
12 Behold, *in* this thou art not just: I will answer thee, that God is greater than man.
13 Why dost thou strive against him? for [6] he giveth not account of any of his matters.
14 For God speaketh once, yea twice, *yet* man perceiveth it not.
15 In a dream, in a vision of the night, when deep sleep falleth upon men, in slumberings upon the bed;
16 Then [7] he openeth the ears of men, and sealeth their instruction,
17 That he may withdraw man *from his* [8] purpose, and hide pride from man.
18 He keepeth back his soul from the pit, and his life [9] from perishing by the sword.
19 He is chastened also with pain upon his bed, and the multitude of his bones with strong *pain:*
20 So that his life abhorreth bread, and his soul [10] dainty meat.
21 His flesh is consumed away, that it cannot be seen; and his bones *that* were not seen stick out.
22 Yea, his soul draweth near unto the grave, and his life to the destroyers.
23 If there be a messenger with him, an interpreter, one among a thousand, to show unto man his uprightness;
24 Then he is gracious unto him, and saith, Deliver him from going down to the pit; I have found [11] a ransom.
25 His flesh shall be fresher [12] than a child's: he shall return to the days of his youth:
26 He shall pray unto God, and he will be favourable unto him; and he shall see his face with joy: for he will render unto man his righteousness.
27 [13] He looketh upon men; and *if any* say, I have sinned, and perverted *that which was* right, and it profited me not;
28 [14] He will deliver his soul from going into the pit, and his life shall see the light.

that "Adam" hid in his lurking place. This disproves the *transl.* "as men:" for it is *from their fellowmen* that "men" are chiefly anxious to hide their real character as guilty. MAGEE, to make the comparison with Adam more exact, for my "bosom" *transl.* "lurking place." 34. Rather, the apodosis to *v.* 33, "Then let me be fearstricken before a great multitude, let the contempt, &c., let me keep silence (the greatest disgrace to a patriot, heretofore so prominent in assemblies), and not go out," &c. A just retribution, that he who hides his sin from God, should have it exposed before man (2 Sam. 12. 12.). But Job had not been so exposed, but on the contrary was esteemed in the assemblies of the *tribes*—("families"); a proof, he implies, that God does not hold him guilty of hiding sin (ch. 24. 16, contrast with ch. 29. 21-25.). 35. Job returns to his wish ch. 13. 22; 19. 23.). Omit *is;* "Behold my *sign,*" *i.e.*, my mark of subscription to the statements just given in my defence: the *mark* of signature was originally a cross; and hence the letter Tau or T. *Transl.* also," *O that* the Almighty," &c. He marks "God" as the "One" meant in the first clause. Adversary, *i.e.*, he who contends with me, refers also to God. The vagueness is designed, to express "whoever it be that *judicially opposes* me,"—the Almighty if it be He. had written a book— Rather, "would write down his charge." 36. So far from hiding the adversary's "answer" or "charge" through fear, "I would take it on my shoulders" as a public honour (Isa. 9. 6.). a crown—not a mark of shame, but of distinction (Isa. 62. 3.). 37. A good conscience imparts a princely dignity before man and free assurance in approaching God. This can be realized, not in Job's way (ch. 42. 5, 6.); but only through Jesus Christ (Heb. 10. 22.). 38. Personification. The complaints of the unjustly-ousted proprietors are transferred to the lands themselves (*v.*20; Gen. 4. 10; Hab. 2. 11.). If I have unjustly acquired lands (ch. 24. 2; Isa. 5. 8.). furrows —The specification of these makes it likely, he implies in this, "If I paid not the labourer, for *tillage;*" as next verse, "If I paid him not for gathering in *the fruits.*" Thus of the four clauses in *v.* 38, 39, the 1st refers to the same subject as the 4th, the 2d is connected with the 3rd by *introverted parallelism.* Jam. 5. 4, who plainly alludes to this passage: cf. "Lord of Sabaoth" with *v.* 26 here. 39. lose ... life—not *lit.*, but "harassed to death;" until he gave me up his land *gratis* [MAUR.]; as in Judg. 16. 16; "suffered him to languish" by taking away his means of living [UMBR.] (1 Ki. 21. 19.). 40. this'les — or *brambles, thorns.* cockle—*lit.*, *noxious weeds.* The words ... ended—*i.e.*, in the controversy with the friends. He spoke in the book afterwards, but not to *them.* At 37 would be the regular conclusion in strict art. But 38-40 is natural to be added by one whose mind in agitation recurs to its sense of innocence, even after it has come to the point usual to stop at; this takes away the appearance of rhetorical artifice. Hence the transposition by EICH. of 38-40 to follow 25, is quite unwarranted.

CHAPTER XXXII.
Ver. 1-22. SPEECH OF ELIHU (ch. 32-37.).
1-6. Prose (poetry begins with "I am young.")
1. because, &c.—and because they could not prove to him that he was unrighteous. 2. Elihu—meaning "God is Jehovah." In his name, and character as messenger between God and Job, he shadows forth Jesus Christ (ch. 33. 23-26.). Barachel—meaning "God blesses." Both names indicate the piety of the family, and their separation from idolaters. Buzite—Buz was son of Nahor, brother of Abraham. Hence was named a region in Arabia Deserta (Jer. 25. 23.). Ram—Aram, nephew of Buz. Job was probably of an elder generation than Elihu. However the identity of names does not necessarily prove the identity of persons. The particularity with which Elihu's descent is given, as contrasted with the others, led LIGHTFOOT to infer, Elihu was the author of the book. But the reason for particularity was, probably, that Elihu was *less known* than the three called "friends" of Job: and that it was right for the poet to mark especially him who was mainly to solve the problem of the book, rather than God — *i. e.*, was more eager to *vindicate himself than God.* In ch. 4. 17, Job denies that *man can be more just than God.* [UMBR.] *Trans.*, "Before (in the presence of) God," 3. Though silenced in argument, they held their opinion still. 4. had spoken—*Heb. in words,* referring rather to *his own* "words" of reply, which he had long ago ready, but kept back in deference to the seniority of the friends who spoke. 6. was afraid—the root meaning in *Heb.* is *to crawl* (Deut. 32. 24.). 7. days—*i.e.*, the aged (ch. 15. 10.). 8. Elihu claims inspiration, as a divinely-commissioned messenger to Job (ch. 33. 6, 23.); and that claim is not contradicted in ch. 42. *Transl.*," But the spirit (which God puts) in man, and the inspiration, &c., is that which giveth," &c., it is not mere "years" which give understanding (Prov. 2. 6; John, 20. 22.). 9. Great—Rather, *old (v.* 6.). So *Heb.* in Gen. 25. 23, "Greater, less" for *the elder, the younger.* judgment — what is right. 10. Rather, *I say.* opinion—Rather, *knowledge.* 11. Therefore Elihu was present from the first. reasons—*lit., understandings, i.e.*, the meaning intended by words. whilst—I waited *until* you should discover a suitable reply to Job. 13. This has been so ordered, "lest you should" pride yourselves on having overcome him by your "wisdom" Jer. 9. 23, the great aim of the book of Job): and that you may see, "God alone can thrust him down," *i.e.*, confute him, "not man." So Elihu grounds his confutation not on the maxims of sages, as the friends did, but on his special commission from God (*v.* 8; ch. 33. 4, 6.). 14. I am altogether unprejudiced. For it is not I, whom he addressed. "Your speeches" have been influenced by irritation. 15. Here Elihu turns from the friends to Job; and so passes from the second person to the third; a transition frequent in a rebuke (ch. 16. 3, 4.). they left off—words were taken from them. 17. my par:—for my part. opinion—knowledge. 18. "I am full of words," whereas the friends have not a word more to say. the spirit—(*v.* 8; ch. 33. 4; Jer. 20. 9; Acts, 13. 5.). 19. be ly—Bosom: from which the words of orientalists in speaking seem to come more than with us: they speak *gutturally.* "Like (new) wine (in fermentation) without a vent," to work itself off. *New* wine is kept in new goatskin bottles. This fittingly applies to the *youn*

Elihu, as contrasted with the old friends (Matt. v. 17.). 20. refers ed—*lit., that there may be air to me,* 1 Sam. 16. 23. 21. "May I never accept," &c. Elihu alludes to Job's words (ch. 13, 8, 10.), wherein he complains that the friends plead for God partially, "accepting His person." Elihu says, he will not do so, but act impartially between God and Job. "And I will not give flattery," &c. (Prov. 24. 23.). 22. take me away—as a punishment (Ps. 102. 24.).

CHAPTER XXXIII.

Ver. 1-33. ADDRESS TO JOB. AS (ch. 32.) TO THE FRIENDS. 2. mouth—Rather, *palate,* whereby the taste *discerns.* Every man speaks with his mouth, but few, as Elihu try their words with *discrimination* first, and only say what is really good (ch. 6. 30; 12. 11.). hath spoken—Rather, *Proceeds to speak.* 3. I will speak according to my inward conviction. clearly—Rather, *purely;* sincerely, not distorting the truth through passion, as the friends. 4. "The Spirit of God hath made me," as He did thee: latter clause of v. 6, (Gen. 2. 7.). Therefore thou needest not fear me, as thou wouldest God (v. 7; ch. 9. 34.). On the other hand, "the breath of the Almighty hath *inspired* me" (as ch. 32. 8.); not as E. V., "givenme life;" therefore "I am, according to thy wish (ch. 9. 32, 33.) in God's stead" to thee; a "daysman," umpire, or mediator, between God and thee. So Elihu was designed by the Holy Ghost to be a type of Jesus Christ (v. 23-26.). 5. Images from a court of justice. stand up—alluding to Job's words (ch. 30. 20.). 6. (Note, v. 4; ch. 31.35; 13. 3, 20, 21.). formed—though acting as God's representative, I am but a creature, like thyself. Arabic, *pressed together,* as a mass of clay by the potter, in *forming* a vessel. [UMBR.] *Heb.* cut off, as the portion taken from the clay to *form* it. [MAUR.] 7. hand—alluding to Job's words (ch. 13. 21.). 8. thy words—ch. 10, 7; 16. 17; 23, 11, 12; 27. 5, 6; 29. 14. In ch. 9. 30; 13. 23, Job had acknowledged sin; but the general *spirit* of his words was to maintain himself to be "clean;" and to charge God with injustice. He went too far on the opposite side in opposing the friends' false charge of *hypocrisy.* Even the godly though willing to confess themselves sinners in *general,* often dislike sin in *particular* to be brought as a charge against them. Affliction is therefore needed to bring them to feel that sin *in them* deserves even worse than they suffer, and that God does them no injustice. Then at last humbled under God they find, *affliction is for their real good,* and so at last it is taken away either here, or at least at death. To teach this is Elihu's mission. 9. clean—spotless. 10. occasions—for hostility; *lit., enmities* (ch. 13. 24; 16. 9; 19. 11; 30. 21.). 11. (ch. 13.). marketh—narrowly watches (ch. 14. 16; 7. 12; 31. 4.). 12. in this—view of God and His government. It cannot be that God should jealously "watch" man, though "spotless," as an "enemy," or as one afraid of him as an equal. For "God is greater than man." There must be sin in man, even though he be no hypocrite, which needs correction by suffering for the sufferer's good. 13. (Isa. 45. 9.). his matters—ways. Our part is, not to "strive" with God, but to *submit.* To believe, it is right, because He does it, not because we see all the *reasons* for His doing it. 14. *Transl.,* "Yet man *regardeth* it not;" or rather, as UMBR., "Yea twice (He repeats the warning),—if man gives no heed" to the first warning, Elihu implies that God's reason for sending affliction is, because, when God has communicated His will in various ways, man in prosperity has not heeded it: God therefore must try what affliction will effect John. 15. 2; Ps. 62. 11; Isa 28. 10, 13.). 15. slumberings—light, as opposed to "deep sleep." Elihu has in view Eliphaz (ch. 4. 13,) and also Job himself (ch. 7. 14.). "Dreams" in sleep, and "visions" of actual apparitions, were among the ways, whereby God then spake to man (Gen. 20. 3.). 16. *Lit.,* sealeth their ears to himself by warnings, *i.e.,* with the sureness and secrecy of a seal He reveals His warnings. [UMBR.] To seal up securely (ch. 37. 7.). On the "openeth" (see ch. 36. 10.). 17. purpose—*Marg., work.* So ch. 36. 9. So "business" in a bad sense (1 Sam. 20. 19.). Elihu alludes to Job's words (ch. 17. 11.). "Pride" is an open "pit" (v. 18.) which God hides or covers up, lest man should fall into it. Even the godly need to learn the lesson, which trials teach, to "humble themselves under the mighty hand of God." 18. his soul—his life. the pit—the grave; a symbol of hell. perishing by the sword—*i.e.,* a violent death; in the O. T. a symbol of the future punishment of the ungodly. 19. When man does not heed warnings of the night, he is chastened, &c. The new thought suggested by Elihu is that affliction is *disciplinary* (ch. 36. 10.): *for the good of the godly,* multitude—so the *Marg., Heb.,* (KERI). Better with the text (CHETIB,) "And with the perpetual (strong) contest of his bones;" the never-resting fever in his bones (Ps. 38. 3. [UMBR.] 20. life—*i.e.,* the *appetite,* which ordinarily sustains "life" (ch. 38. 39; see Ps. 107. 18; Eccl. 12. 5.). The taking away of desire for food by sickness symbolizes the removal by affliction of lust, for things which foster the spiritual fever of pride. soul—desire. 21. His flesh once prominent "can no more be seen." His bones once not seen now appear prominent. stick out—*lit., are bare.* The *Marg., Heb.,* KERI reading, The text (CHETIB) reads it a noun (are become, "bareness." The Keri was no doubt an explanatory reading of transcribers. 22. destroyers—*angels of death* commissioned by God to end man's life 2 Sam. 24. 16; Ps. 78. 49.). The *death pains* personified may, however, be meant; so "gnawers" (Note, ch. 30. 17.). 23. Elihu refers to himself as the divinely-sent (ch. 32.8; 33.6.), "messenger," the "interpreter" to explain to Job and vindicate God's righteousness: such a one Eliphaz had denied that Job could look for (ch. 5. 1.), and Job (ch. 9. 33.) had wished for such a "daysman" or umpire between him and God. The "messenger" of good is antithetical to "the destroyers" v. 23.). with him—If there be vouchsafed to the *sufferer.* The office of the Interpreter is stated "to show unto man God's uprightness" in His dealings; or, as UMBR., "man's upright course towards God" (Prov. 14. 2.). The former is better; Job maintained his own "uprightness" (ch. 16. 17; 27. 5, 6.). Elihu on the contrary maintains God's, and that man's true uprightness lies in submission to God, "One among a thousand" is a man rarely to be found. So Jesus Christ (Song Sol. 5. 10.). Elihu, the God-sent mediator of a *temporal* deliverance (v. 24-26,), is a type of the God-man Jesus Christ the Mediator of eternal deliverance: "the *messenger* of the covenant" (Mal. 3. 1.). This is the wonderful work of the Holy Ghost, that persons and events move in their own sphere in such a way, as uncon-ciously to shadow forth Him, whose "testimony is the Spirit of prophecy;" as the same point may be centre of a small and of a vastly larger concentric circle. 24. Apodosis to 23. be—God. Deliver—*Lit.*, *redeem*: in it and "ransom" there is reference to the *consideration*, on account of which God pardons and relieves the sufferers; here it is primarily the intercession of Elihu. But the language is too strong for its full meaning to be *exhausted* by this: The Holy Ghost has suggested language which receives its *full* realization only in the "eternal redemption found" by God in the price paid by Jesus Christ for it, *i.e.*, His blood and meritorious intercession (Heb. 9. 12.). "Obtained," *lit.*, *found*: implying the earnest zeal, wisdom, and faithfulness of the *finder*, and the newness and joyousness of the *finding*. Jesus Christ could not but have *found* it, but still His *seeking* it was needed. [BENG.] (Luke, 15. 8.) God the Father, is the Finder (Ps. 89. 19.). Jesus Christ the Redeemer, to whom He saith, *Redeem* (so *Heb.*,) him from going, &c. (2 Cor. 5. 19.) ransom—Used in a general sense by Elihu. but meant by the Holy Ghost in its strict sense as applied to Jesus Christ, of a *price* paid for deliverance (Exod. 21. 30.), an *atonement i.e.*, means of selling *at once*, *i. e.*, reconciling *two* who are estranged,), *a covering*, as of the ark with pitch, typical of what covers us sinners from wrath (Gen. 6. 14; Ps. 32. 1.). The pit. is primarily here the *grave* (Isa. 38. 17.), but the spiritual pit is mainly shadowed forth (Zech. 9. 11.). 25-28. Effects of restoration to God's favour; *lit.*, to Job a temporal revival; spiritually, an eternal *regeneration*. The striking words cannot be restricted to their temporal meaning, as used by Elihu (1 Pet. 1. 11, 12.), fresher than a child's—So Naaman, 2 Ki. 5. 14; spiritually, John, 3. 3-7. 26. Job shall no longer pray to God, as he complains, in vain (ch. 23. 3, 8, 9.). True especially to the redeemed in Jesus Christ (John, 16. 23-27.). He Job) shall see his face—Or *God shall make him to see His face*, [MAUR.] God shall no longer "hide His face" (ch. 13. 24.). True to the believer, now, John, 14. 21, 22: eternally, Ps. 17. 15: John, 17. 24. his God's) righteousness—God will again make the restored Job, no longer ("I perverted—right," *v.* 27,) doubt God's *justice*, but to justify Him in His dealings. The penitent justifies God (Ps. 51. 4.). So the believer is made to see God's righteousness in Jesus Christ (Is. 45. 24; 46. 13.). 27. He looketh—God. Rather, with UMBR., "Now he (*the restored penitent*) singeth *joyfully* answering to "joy" *v.* 26; Ps. 51. 12, before men, and saith," &c., (Prov. 25. 20; Ps. 66. 16; 116. 14.). perverted—Made the straight crooked: as Job had misrepresented God's character. profited—*Lit.*, *was made even* to me; rather, "My punishment was not commensurate with my sin;" (so Zophar, ch. 11. 6,); the reverse of what Job heretofore said (ch. 16. 17; Ps. 103. 10; Ezra, 9. 13.). 28. Note *v.* 21; rather, as *Heb.* text (*E.V.* reads as *Marg.*, *Heb.*, *Keri*, "*his* soul, *his* life,") "He hath delivered *my* soul, &c., *my* life." Continuation of the penitent's testimony to the people. light—(*v.* 30; ch. 3. 16, 20; Ps. 66. 13; Eccl. 11. 7.) 29. *Marg.* *twice and thrice*, alluding to *v.* 14: once, by visions, 15-17; secondly, by afflictions, 19-22; now, by the "messenger," thirdly, 23. 30. Referring to *v.* 29 (Ps. 50. 13.). 32. justify—To do thee justice; and, if I can, consistently with it, to declare thee innocent. At *v.* 33, Elihu pauses for a reply; then proceeds; ch. 34.

CHAPTER XXXIV.

Ver. 1-37. 1. answered — Proceeded. 2. This ch. is addressed also to the "friends," as ch. 33. to Job alone. 3. *Palate*; (Note ch. 12, 11; ch. 33. 2.). 4. judgment—Let us select among the conflicting sentiments advanced, what will stand the test of examination. 5. judgment—My right. Job's own words (ch. 13. 18; 27. 2.). 6. *i.e.*, Were I to renounce my right (*i.e.*, confess myself guilty,), I should lie. Job virtually had said so (ch. 27. 4. 5; 6. 28.). MAUR., not so well, "Notwithstanding my right (innocence) I am treated as a liar by God," by his afflicting me. my wound—*Lit.*, *mine arrow*, viz., by which I am pierced. So "*my* stroke" (hand *Marg.*, ch. 23. 2.). My sickness (ch. 6. 4; 16. 13.). without transgression—Without fault of mine to deserve it (ch. 16. 17.). 7. (ch. 15. 16.). Image from the camel. scorning—Against God ch. 15. 4.). 8. Job virtually goeth in company (makes common cause) with the wicked, by taking up their sentiments (ch. 9. 22, 23, 30; 21. 7-15,), or at least by saying, that those who act on such sentiments are unpunished (Mal. 3. 14.). To deny God's righteous government, because we do not see the reasons of His acts, is virtually to take part with the ungodly. 9. with God—In intimacy (Ps. 50. 18.). 10. The true answer to Job, which God follows up (ch. 38.). Man is to *believe* God's ways are right, because they are His, not because we fully *see* they are so (Rom. 9. 14; Deu. 32. 4; Gen. 18. 25). 11. Partly here; fully, hereafter (Jer. 32. 19; Rom. 2. 6; 1 Pet. 1. 17; Rev. 22. 12.). 12. (ch. 8. 3.). In opposition to Job, *v.* 5. will not—Cannot, 13. If the world were not God's property, as having been made by Him, but committed to His charge by some Superior, it might be possible for Him to act unjustly, as He would not thereby be injuring Himself; but as it is, for God to act unjustly would undermine the whole order of the world, and so would injure God's own property (ch. 36. 23.) disposed — Hath founded (Isa. 44. 7,), established the circle of the globe. 14, 15. "If He were to set His heart on man," either to injure him, or to take strict account of his sins. The connexion supports rather, [UMBR.] "If He had regard to himself (only), and were to gather unto Himself (Ps. 104 29,) man's spirit, &c. (which he sends forth. Ps. 104, 30; Eccl. 12. 7,), all flesh must perish together," &c. (Gen. 3. 19.) God's loving preservation of his creatures proves, He cannot be selfish, and therefore cannot be unjust. 16. In *v.* 2, Elihu had spoken to *all* in general, now he calls Job's special attention. 17. "Can even He who (in thy view) hateth right (justice) govern?" The government of the world be impossible if injustice were sanctioned. God must be just, because He governs (2 Sam. 23. 3.). govern — *Lit.*, *bind*, viz., by authority (so "reign," *Marg.*, 1 Sam. 9, 17.). UMBR. *transl.* for "govern," *repress wrath*, viz., against Job for his accusations. most just—Rather, "Him who is at once

Elihu reproves Job   JOB, XXXIV, XXXV.   *for charging God with injustice.*

29 Lo, all these *things* worketh God oftentimes with man,
30 To bring back his soul from the pit, to be enlightened with the light of the living.
31 Mark well, O Job; hearken unto me: hold thy peace, and I will speak.
32 If thou hast any thing to say, answer me: speak, for I desire to justify thee.
33 If not, hearken unto me: hold thy peace, and I shall teach thee wisdom.

CHAPTER XXXIV.
1 *Elihu accuses Job for charging God with injustice.* 10 *God all-perfect cannot be unjust, etc.*

FURTHERMORE, Elihu answered and said,
2 Hear my words, O ye wise *men;* and give ear unto me, ye that have knowledge:
3 For the ear trieth words, as the mouth tasteth meat.
4 Let us choose to us judgment: let us know among ourselves what *is* good.
5 For Job hath said, I am righteous: and God hath taken away my judgment.
6 Should I lie against my right? my wound *is* incurable without transgression.
7 What man *is* like Job, *who* drinketh up scorning like water?
8 Which goeth in company with the workers of iniquity, and walketh with wicked men.
9 For he hath said, It profiteth a man nothing that he should delight himself with God.
10 Therefore hearken unto me, ye men of understanding: Far be it from God, *that he should do* wickedness; and *from* the Almighty, *that he should commit* iniquity.
11 For the work of a man shall he render unto him, and cause every man to find according to *his* ways.
12 Yea, surely God will not do wickedly, neither will the Almighty pervert judgment.
13 Who hath given him a charge over the earth? or who hath disposed the whole world?
14 If he set his heart upon man, *if* he gather unto himself his spirit and his breath;
15 All flesh shall perish together, and man shall turn again unto dust.
16 If now *thou hast* understanding, hear this; hearken to the voice of my words:
17 Shall even he that hateth right govern? and wilt thou condemn him that is most just?
18 *Is it fit* to say to a king, *Thou art* wicked? *and* to princes, *Ye are* ungodly?
19 *How much less to him that* accepteth not the persons of princes, nor regardeth the rich more than the poor? for they all *are* the work of his hands.
20 In a moment shall they die, and the people shall be troubled at midnight, and pass away; and the mighty shall be taken away without hand.
21 For his eyes *are* upon the ways of man, and he seeth all his goings.
22 *There* is no darkness, nor shadow of death, where the workers of iniquity may hide themselves.
23 For he will not lay upon man more than right, that he should enter into judgment with God.
24 He shall break in pieces mighty men without number, and set others in their stead.

25 Therefore he knoweth their works, and he overturneth *them* in the night, so that they are destroyed.
26 He striketh them as wicked men in the open sight of others;
27 Because they turned back from him, and would not consider any of his ways:
28 So that they cause the cry of the poor to come unto him, and he heareth the cry of the afflicted.
29 When he giveth quietness, who then can make trouble? and when he hideth *his* face, who then can behold him? whether *it be done* against a nation, or against a man only:
30 That the hypocrite reign not, lest the people be ensnared.
31 Surely it is meet to be said unto God, I have borne *chastisement,* I will not offend *any more:*
32 *That which* I see not, teach thou me: if I have done iniquity, I will do no more.
33 *Should it be* according to thy mind? he will recompense it, whether thou refuse, or whether thou choose; and not I: therefore speak what thou knowest.
34 Let men of understanding tell me, and let a wise man hearken unto me.
35 Job hath spoken without knowledge, and his words *were* without wisdom.
36 My desire *is, that* Job may be tried unto the end, because of *his* answers for wicked men.
37 For he addeth rebellion unto his sin; he clappeth *his hands* among us, and multiplieth his words against God.

CHAPTER XXXV.
1 *No comparison to be made with God, because our good or evil cannot extend to him.* 9 *Many cry in their afflictions, but are not heard for want of faith.*

ELIHU spake moreover, and said,
2 Thinkest thou this to be right, *that* thou saidst, My righteousness *is* more than God's?
3 For thou saidst, What advantage will it be unto thee? *and,* What profit shall I have, *if I be cleansed* from my sin?
4 I will answer thee, and thy companions with thee.
5 Look unto the heavens, and see; and behold the clouds, *which* are higher than thou.
6 If thou sinnest, what doest thou against him? or if thy transgressions be multiplied, what doest thou unto him?
7 If thou be righteous, what givest thou him? or what receiveth he of thine hand?
8 Thy wickedness *may hurt* a man as thou *art;* and thy righteousness *may profit* the son of man.
9 By reason of the multitude of oppressions they make *the oppressed* to cry; they cry out by reason of the arm of the mighty.
10 But none saith, Where is God my maker, who giveth songs in the night;
11 Who teacheth us more than the beasts of the earth, and maketh us wiser than the fowls of heaven?
12 There they cry, but none giveth answer, because of the pride of evil men.
13 Surely God will not hear vanity, neither will the Almighty regard it.
14 Although thou sayest thou shalt not see him, *yet* judgment *is* before him; therefore trust thou in him.
15 But now, because *it is* not *so,* he hath

God Omnipotent cannot be Unjust. JOB, XXXV. *Comparison not to be made with God.*

mighty and just" (in His government of the world.. 18. *Lit.,* (Is it fit *to be said* to a king? It would be a gross outrage to reproach thus an earthly monarch, much more, the King of kings (Exod. 22. 28.). But MAUR. with LXX. and *Vulg.* reads (It is not fit to accuse of injustice Him) *who says* to a king, Thou art wicked, Ye are ungodly, *i.e.,* who punishes impartially the great, as the small. This accords with *v.* 19. 19. Acts, 10. 34; 2 Chron. 19. 7; Prov. 22. 2; ch. 31. 15. 20. they—" The rich " and "princes" who offend God. the people—viz., of the guilty princes; guilty also themselves. at midnight—Image from a night-attack of an enemy on a camp, which becomes an easy prey (Ex. 12. 29, 30.). without hand—Without *visible* agency, by the mere word of God (so ch. 20. 26; Zech. 4. 6; Dan. 2. 34.). 21. God's omniscience and omnipotence enable Him to execute immediate justice. He needs not to be long on the "watch," as Job thought (ch. 7. 12; 2 Chron. 16. 9; Jer. 32. 19.). 22. shadow of death— Thick darkness (Amos, 9. 2, 3; Ps. 139. 12.; 23. (1 Cor. 10, 13; Lam. 3. 32; Isa. 27. 8.). Better, as UMBR., " He does not (needs not to) regard (as in *v.* 14; Isa. 41. 20,) man *long* (so *Heb.,* Gen. 46. 29, in order that he may go (be brought by God) into judgment." *Lit.,* " *set* his (attention upon men" (ch. 11, 10, 11.). So *v.* 24, " without number " ought to be *transl.* " without (needing any) searching out," such as has to be made in human judgments. 24. break in pieces — (Ps. 2. 9; ch. 12. 18; Dan. 2. 21.). 25. therefore—Because He knows all things, (*v.* 21,) He knows their works, without a formal investigation, *v.* 24.). in the night—Suddenly, unexpectedly (*v.* 20.). Fitly *in the night,* as it was in it that the godless hid themselves *v.* 22.). UMBR., *less* simply, for "overturneth," *transl.* "walketh ;" *i.e.,* God is ever on the alert, discovering all wickedness. 26. striketh—Chasteneth. as—*i.e.,* because they are wicked. sight of others—Sinners hold themselves in darkness; therefore they are punished before all, in open day. Image from the place of public execution (ch. 40. 12; Exod. 14. 30; 2 Sam. 12. 12.). 27, 28. The grounds of their punishment in *v.* 26; *v.* 28, states in what respect they "considered not God's ways," viz., by *oppression,* whereby "they caused the cry," &c. 29. (Prov. 16. 7; Isa. 26. 3.). make trouble—Rather, *condemn* (Rom. 8, 33, 34,). MAUR. from the reference being only to *the godless,* in the next clause, and *v.* 30. *transl.* " When God keeps quiet (leaves men to *perish*) Ps. 83. 1; (UMBR.) from the Arabic, *strikes to the earth),* who shall *condemn* Him as unjust?" *v.* 17. hideth . . . face—ch. 23. 8, 9; Ps. 13. 1.) it be done—Whether it be against a guilty nation (2 Ki. 18. 9-12.), or an individual, that God acts so. 30. "Ensnared" into sin (1 Ki. 12. 28, 30.). Or rather, *enthralled by further oppression, v.* 26-28. 31. Job accordingly says so (ch 40. 3-5; Mic. 7. 9; Lev. 26. 41.). It was to lead him to this, that Elihu was sent. Though no hypocrite, Job, like all, had sin, therefore through affliction he was to be brought to humble himself under God. *All* sorrow is a proof of the common heritage of sin, in which the godly shares: and therefore he ought to regard it as a merciful correction. UMBR. & MAUR. lose this by *transl.* as the *Heb.* will bear, "Has any. a right to say to God, I have borne chastisement and yet have not sin-

ned ?" (so *v.* 6.) borne—viz., the penalty of sin, as in Lev. 5. 1, 17. offend—*Lit., to deal destructively* or *corruptly* (Neh. 1. 7.). 32. ch. 10. 2; Ps. 32. 8; 19. 12; 139. 23, 24. no more— Prov. 28. 13; Eph. 4. 22. 33. Rather "should God recompense sinners) according to thy mind ? Then it is for thee to reject and to choose, and not me," [UMBR.] or as MAUR. " *For thou hast rejected* God's way of recompensing; state therefore thy way, *for thou must choose, not I," i.e.,* it is thy part, not mine, to show a better way than God's. 34, 35. Rather, men, *words*—(ch. 11. 2; 35. 16.). To his original "sin," to correct which trials have been sent, "he adds *rebellion," i.e.,* words arraigning God's justice.

CHAPTER XXXV.

Ver. 1-16. 2; 25. 4; "I am righteous (*lit.,* my righteousness is) before God." E.V., however agrees with ch. 9. 17; 16. 12-17; 27. 2-6. Ch. 4. 17 is susceptible of either rendering. Elihu means Job said so, not in so many words, but virtually. 3. Rather, explanatory of "this" in *v.* 2, " That thou sayest to tnyself, as if a distinct person,) What advantage is it thy integrity) to thee? What profit have I (by integrity) more than (I should have) by my sin ?" *i.e.,* more than if I had sinned (ch. 34. 9.). Job had said that the wicked, who use *these very words,* do not suffer for it (ch. 21. 13-15,) ; whereby he virtually sanctioned their sentiments. The same change of persons from oblique to direct address occurs (ch. 19. 28; 22. 17.). 4. companions—Those entertaining like sentiments with thee (ch. 34. 8, 36.). 5-8. Elihu like Eliphaz ch. 22. 2, 3, 12,) shows that God is too exalted in nature to be susceptible of benefit or hurt from the righteousness or sin of man respectively : it is themselves that they benefit by righteousness, or hurt by sin. higher than thou—Spoken with irony. Not only are they higher than thou, but thou can not even reach them clearly with the eye. Yet these are not as high as God's seat, God is there ore too exalted to be dependant on man. Therefore He has no inducement to injustice in His dealings with man. When He afflicts, it must be from a different motive ; viz., the good of the sufferer. 6. what doest—How canst thou affect Him ? unto him—That can hurt Him ? (Jer. 7. 19; Prov. 8. 36.). 7. (Ps. 16. 2; Prov. 9. 12; Luke, 17. 10.). 9. (Eccl. 4. 1,). Elihu states in Job's words ch. 24. 12; 30. 20,) the difficulty; the "cries" of "the oppressed" not being heard might lead man to think that wrongs are not punished by Him. 10-13. But the reason is, that the innocent sufferers often do not humbly seek God for succour; so to their "pride" is to be laid the blame of their ruin : also because 13-16 they, as Job, instead of waiting God's time in pious trust, are prone to despair of His justice, when it is not immediately visible ch. 33. 19-26.). If the sufferer would apply to God with an humbled, penitent spirit, He would hear,

Elihu defends God's providence, JOB, XXXVI, XXXVII. *and describes his great works.*

visited in his anger; yet [a] he knoweth it not in great extremity:
16 Therefore [b] doth Job open his mouth in vain; he multiplieth words without knowledge.

CHAPTER XXXVI.

1 *Elihu shows how God is just in all his ways:* 5 *the end of God's chastisements:* 16 *how Job's sins hinder God's blessings.* 22 *God's works to be magnified.*

ELIHU also proceeded, and said,
2 Suffer me a little, and I will show thee [1] that *I have* yet to speak on God's behalf.
3 I will fetch my knowledge from afar, and will ascribe righteousness to my Maker.
4 For truly my words *shall* not be false: he that is perfect in knowledge *is* with thee.
5 Behold, God *is* mighty, and despiseth *not any;* he *is* mighty in strength *and* [2] wisdom.
6 He preserveth not the life of the wicked: but giveth right to the [3] poor.
7 He withdraweth not his eyes from the righteous: but [a] with kings *are they* on the throne; yea, he doth establish them for ever, and they are exalted.
8 And [b] if *they be* bound in fetters, *and* be holden in cords of affliction;
9 Then he sheweth them their work, and their transgressions that they have exceeded.
10 He openeth also their ear to discipline, and commandeth that they return from iniquity.
11 If they obey and serve *him,* they shall spend [c] their days in prosperity, and their years in pleasures.
12 But if they obey not, [4] they shall perish by the sword, and they shall die without knowledge.
13 But the hypocrites in heart heap up wrath: they cry not when he bindeth them.
14 [5] They die in youth, and their life *is* among the [6] unclean.
15 He delivereth the [7] poor in his affliction, and openeth their ears in oppression:
16 Even so would he have removed thee out of the strait *into* a broad place, where there *is* no straitness; and [8] that which should be set on thy table *should* be full of fatness.
17 But thou hast fulfilled the judgment of the wicked: [9] judgment and justice take hold *on thee.*
18 Because *there is* wrath, *beware* lest he take thee away with *his* stroke: then a great ransom cannot [10] deliver thee.
19 Will he esteem thy riches? *no,* not gold, nor all the forces of strength.
20 Desire not the night, when people are cut off in their place.
21 Take heed, regard not iniquity: for this [d] hast thou chosen rather than affliction.
22 Behold, God exalteth by his power: who [e] teacheth like him?
23 Who hath enjoined him his way? or who [f] can say, Thou hast wrought iniquity?
24 Remember that thou [g] magnify his work, which men behold.
25 Every [h] man may see it; man may behold *it* afar off.
26 Behold, God *is* great, and we [i] know *him* not, [j] neither can the number of his years be searched out.
27 For he maketh small the drops of water: they pour down rain according to the vapour thereof,

B. C. 1520.
CHAP. 35.
4 That is, Job.
[g] ch. 34. 35, 37.
ch. 33. 2.
CHAP. 36.
1 that there are yet words for God.
2 heart.
3 Or, afflicted.
[a] Ps. 113. 8.
[b] Ps. 107. 10.
[c] Is 1. 19.
1 Tim. 4. 8.
4 they shall pass away by the sword.
5 their soul dieth.
6 Or, sodomites.
Deu. 23. 17.
7 Or, afflicted.
8 the rest of thy table.
9 Or, judgment and justice should uphold thee.
10 turn thee aside.
[d] Heb. 11. 25.
[e] Is. 40. 13.
Ro. 11. 34.
1 Cor. 2. 16.
[f] Deut. 32. 4.
[g] Ps. 92. 5.
Rev. 15. 3.
[h] Rom. 1. 19.
[i] 1 Cor. 13. 12.
[j] Ps. 90. 2.
Ps. 102. 24, 27.
Heb. 1. 12.
11 the roots.
12 that which goeth up.

CHAP. 37.
1 Hear in hearing.
2 light.
3 wings of the earth.
4 and to the shower of rain, and to the showers of rain of his strength.
[a] Ps. 111. 2.
5 Out of the chamber.
6 scattering winds.
7 the cloud of his light.
8 a rod.
[b] ch. 36. 4.
[c] Is. 44. 24.
9 Gold.
[d] 1 Ti. 6. 16.
[e] ch. 36. 5.
[f] Lam. 3. 33.
[g] Mat. 10. 29.
[h] Mat. 11. 25.
1 Cor. 1. 26.

28 Which the clouds do drop *and* distil upon man abundantly.
29 Also can any understand the spreadings of the clouds, *or* the noise of his tabernacle?
30 Behold, he spreadeth his light upon it, and covereth [11] the bottom of the sea.
31 For by them judgeth he the people; he giveth meat in abundance.
32 With clouds he covereth the light; and commandeth it *not to shine* by *the cloud* that cometh betwixt.
33 The noise thereof sheweth concerning it, the cattle also concerning [12] the vapour.

CHAPTER XXXVII.

1 *God to be feared for his great works:* 15 *his wisdom is unsearchable in them.*

AT this also my heart trembleth, and is moved out of his place.
2 [1] Hear attentively the noise of his voice, and the sound *that* goeth out of his mouth.
3 He directeth it under the whole heaven, and his [2] lightning unto the [3] ends of the earth.
4 After it a voice roareth: he thundereth with the voice of his excellency; and he will not stay them when his voice is heard.
5 God thundereth marvellously with his voice; great things doeth he, which we cannot comprehend.
6 For he saith to the snow, Be thou *on* the earth; likewise to the small rain, and to the great rain of his strength.
7 He sealeth up the hand of every man; that [a] all men may know his work.
8 Then the beasts go into dens, and remain in their places.
9 [5] Out of the south cometh the whirlwind: and cold out of the [6] north.
10 By the breath of God frost is given; and the breadth of the waters is straitened.
11 Also by watering he wearieth the thick cloud: he scattereth [7] his bright cloud,
12 And it is turned round about by his counsels: that they may do whatsoever he commandeth them upon the face of the world in the earth.
13 He causeth it to come, whether for [8] correction, or for his land, or for mercy.
14 Hearken unto this, O Job: stand still, and consider the wondrous works of God.
15 Dost thou know when God disposed them, and caused the light of his cloud to shine?
16 Dost thou know the balancings of the clouds, the wondrous works of [b] him which is perfect in knowledge?
17 How thy garments *are* warm, when he quieteth the earth by the south *wind?*
18 Hast thou with him [c] spread out the sky, *which is* strong, *and* as a molten looking-glass?
19 Teach us what we shall say unto him; *for* we cannot order *our speech* by reason of darkness.
20 Shall it be told him that I speak? If a man speak, surely he shall be swallowed up.
21 And now *men* see not the bright light which *is* in the clouds: but the wind passeth, and cleanseth them.
22 [9] Fair weather cometh out of the north: with God *is* terrible majesty.
23 *Touching* the Almighty, [d] we cannot find him out: [e] *he is* excellent in power, and in judgment, and in plenty of justice: he will [f] not afflict.
24 Men do therefore [g] fear him: he respecteth not any *that are* [h] wise of heart.

377

Where, &c.—(Jer. 2. 6, 8; Isa. 51. 13.). songs—Of joy at deliverance (Ps. 42. 8; 149. 5; Acts, 16. 25.), in the night—*Unexpectedly* (ch. 34. 20, 25.). Rather, *in calamity*. 11. Man's spirit which distinguishes him from the brute, is the strongest proof of God's beneficence: by the use of it we may understand that God is the Almighty helper of all sufferers who humbly seek him; and that they err who do not so seek him. fowls—(ch. 28. 21; Note.). 12. There—Rather, *Then*, (when none humbly casts himself on God, *v.* 10.). They cry proudly *against* God, rather than humbly *to* God. So, as the design of affliction is to humble the sufferer, there can be no answer until " pride" gives place to humble penitent prayer (Ps. 10. 4; Jer. 13. 17.). 13. Vanity, *i.e.*, cries uttered in an unhumbled spirit, *v.* 12. which applies in some degree to Job's cries; still more to those of the wicked (ch. 27. 9; Prov. 15. 29.). 14. Although thou sayest, thou shalt not see Him (as a *temporal* deliverer ; for he did look for a Redeemer *after death:* (ch. 19. 25-27,) which passage cannot consistently with Elihu's assertion here be interpreted of "seeing" a *temporal* " Redeemer,") ch. 7. 7; 9. 11; 23. 3, 8, 9, yet, judgment, &c., therefore trust, &c. But the Heb. favours MAUR. "*How much less* (will God — regard, *v.* 13), since thou sayest, that He does not regard thee." So in ch. 4. 19. Thus Elihu alludes to Job's words (ch. 19. 7; 30. 20.). judgment—*i.e.*, thy *cause*, thy *right*; as in Ps. 9. 16; Prov. 31. 5. 8. trust—Rather, *wait thou* on Him, patiently, until He take up thy cause (Ps. 37. 7.). 15. *As it is, because* Job waited *not* trustingly and patiently (*v.* 14; Num. 20. 12; Zeph. 3. 2; Mic. 7. 9,), *God hath visited*, &c., *yet still he has not taken* (severe) *cognizance of the great multitude* (E. V. wrongly, "extremity") of sins; therefore Job should not complain of being punished with undue severity (ch. 7. 20; 11. 6.). MAUR. *transl.* "Because His anger hath not visited (hath not immediately punished Job for his impious complaints,) nor has He taken *strict* (great) cognizance of his *folly* (sinful speeches,), therefore, &c. For "folly," UMBR. *transl.* with the Rabbins, *multitude*. GES. reads with LXX. and *Vulg.* needlessly " transgression." 16. Apodosis to 15. in vain—Rashly.

CHAPTER XXXVI.

Ver. 1-33. 1, 2. Elihu maintains, that afflictions are to the godly disciplinary, in order to lead them to attain a higher moral worth, and that the reason for their continuance is not, as the friends asserted, on account of the sufferer's extraordinary guilt, but because the discipline has not yet attained its object, viz., to lead him to humble himself penitently before God (Isa. 9. 13; Jer. 5. 3.). This is Elihu's *fourth* speech. He thus exceeds the ternary number of the others. Hence his formula of politeness, *v.* 2. *Lit., Wait yet but a little for me.* Bear with me a little farther. *I have yet* (much ch. 32. 18-20.). There are Chaldeisms in this verse, agreeably to the view that the scene of the book is near the Euphrates and the Chaldees. 3. from afar—Not trite common-places, but drawn from God's mighty works. ascribe righteousness — Whereas Job had ascribed unrighteousness (ch. 34. 10-12.). A man, in enquiring into God's ways, should at the outset *presume* they are all just, be *willing* to find them so, and *expect* that the result of in-

vestigation will prove them to be so; such a one will never be disappointed. [BA.] 4. I will not "speak wickedly for God," as the friends, ch. 13. 4, 7, 8; *i.e.*, vindicate God by unsound arguments. he that is perfect, &c. —Rather, as the parallelism requires, "a man of *integrity in sentiments* is with thee" (is he with whom thou hast to do.). Elihu means himself, as opposed to the dishonest reasonings of the friends (ch. 21. 34.). 5. Rather, *Strength of understanding* (heart) the force of the repetition of "mighty" is, " mighty" as God is, none is too low to be " despised" by Him; for His "might" lies especially in " His strength of understanding," whereby He searches out the most minute things, so as to give to each his right. Elihu confirms his exhortation (ch. 35. 14.). 6. right . . . poor—He espouses the cause of the afflicted. 7. (1 Pet. 3. 12.) God does not forsake the godly, as Job implied, but "establishes," or *makes* them *sit* on the throne as kings (1 Sam. 2. 8; Ps. 113. 7. 8,). True of believers in the highest sense, already in part, 1 Pet. 2. 9.; Rev. 1. 6; hereafter fully, Rev. 5. 10; ch. 22. 5. and they are—*That they may be.* 8-10. If they be afflicted, it is no proof that they are hypocrites, as the friends maintain; or that God disregards them, and is indifferent whether men are good or bad, as Job asserts: God is thereby "disciplining them," and "showing them their sins," and if they bow in a right spirit under God's visiting hand, the greatest blessings ensue. 9. work—Transgression, that . . . exceeded—" In that they behaved themselves mightily," *lit., great; i.e.,* presumptuously, or, at least, self-confidently. 10. (ch. 33. 16-18, 23.) 11. serve—*i.e.*, *worship*; as in Isa. 19. 23, God is to be supplied (cf. Isa. 1. 19, 20.) 12. (ch. 33. 18.) without knowledge—*In, i.e., on account of their foolishness* (ch. 4. 20, 21.). 13-15. Same sentiment, as *v.* 11, 12, expanded. 13. hypocrites—Or, the ungodly [MAUR.]; but "hypocrites" is perhaps a distinct class from the openly wicked (*v.* 12.). heap up wrath—Of God against themselves (Rom. 2. 5.). UMBR. *transl.* " nourish *their* wrath *against God*," instead of "crying" unto Him. This suits well the parallelism and the *Heb.* But *E.V.* gives a good parallelism, "hypocrites" answering to, "cry not" (ch. 27. 8, 10,); "heap up wrath" against themselves, to "He bindeth them" with fetters of affliction (*v.* 8.). 14. Rather, (Deu. 23. 17,) *Their life* is (ended) as that of (*lit., among*) *the unclean,*" prematurely and dishonourably. So the second clause answers to the first. A warning that Job make not common cause with the wicked ch. 34. 36.). 15. poor—*The afflicted* pious. openeth . . . ears—, *v.* 10,); so as to be *admonished* in their straits (" oppression") to seek God penitently, and so be " delivered " ch. 33. 16, 17, 23-27.). 16. Rather, " He *will* lead forth thee also out of *the jaws of* a strait" (Ps. 18. 19; 118. 5.). The "broad place" expresses the *liberty*, and the well-supplied "table" the *abundance* of the prosperous Ps. 23. 5; Isa. 25. 6.). 17. Rather, " But *if* thou art fulfilled (*i.e.*, entirely filled) with the judgment of the wicked (*i.e.*, the judgment due to them ch. 34. 5. 6, 7, 36. He acknowledges as UMBR. referring to ch. 34. 36, that *guilt* incurring judgment [MAUR.]; or rather, as UMBR. referring to ch. 34. 36, *judgment pronounced on God by the guilty* in misfortunes judgment *God's judgment on the wicked;* Jer. 51. 9. playing on the double meaning of "judgment,"), and justice shall closely follow each other. [UMBR.] 18. (Num. 16, 45; Ps. 49, 6, 7; Matt. 16. 26.). Even the "ransom" by Jesus Christ (ch. 33. 24,) will be of no avail to wilful despisers (Heb. 10. 26-29.). with his stroke—(ch. 34. 26.). UMBR. transl. "Beware lest the wrath of God (thy severe calamity) lead thee to scorn" (ch. 34. 7; 27. 23.). This accords better with the verb in the parallel clause, which ought to be transl., "Let not the great ransom (of money, which thou canst give) seduce thee." (Marg., turn thee aside, as if thou couldst deliver thyself from "wrath" by it.) As the "scorn" in the first clause answers to the "judgment of the wicked," v. 17, so "ransom, seduce" to "Will he esteem riches," v. 19. Thus v. 18 is the transition between v. 17 and 19. 19. forces of strength—i.e., resources of wealth (Ps. 49. 7; Prov. 11. 4.). 20. desire—Pant for. Job had wished for death (ch. 3. 3-9, &c.). night—Jo. 9. 4. when—Rather, whereby, cut off—Lit., ascend, as the corn cut and lifted upon the waggon or stack (v. 26,); so cut off, disappear. in their place—Lit., under themselves; so, without moving from their place, on the spot, suddenly (ch. 40. 12.) [MAUR.] UMBR.'S transl., "To ascend (which is really, as thou wilt find to thy cost, to descend) to the people below," (lit., under themselves,) answers better to the parallelism and the Heb. Thou pantest for death as desirable, but it is a "night" or region of darkness, thy fancied ascent (amelioration) will prove a descent (deterioration, ch. 10. 22,); therefore desire it not. 21. regard—Lit., turn thyself to, iniquity—viz., presumptuous speaking against God, ch. 34. 5, and above, v. 17, 18: Note.). rather than—To bear "affliction" with pious patience. Men think it an alleviation to complain against God. But this is adding sin to sorrow; it is sin, not sorrow, which can really hurt us, (contrast Heb. 11. 25.). 22-25. God is not to be impiously arraigned, but to be praised for His might, shown in His works. exalteth—Rather, doeth lofty things, shows His exalted power [UMBR.] (Ps. 21. 13,). teacheth—(Ps. 94. 12, &c.). The connexion is, returning to v. 5. God's "might" is shown in His "wisdom:" He alone can teach; yet, because He, as a sovereign, explains not all His dealings, forsooth Job must presume to teach Him (Isa. 40. 13, 14; Rom. 11. 34; 1 Cor. 2. 16.). So the transition to v. 23 is natural. UMBR. with LXX. transl. "Who is Lord?" wrongly, as this meaning belongs to later Heb. 23. Job dared to prescribe to God, what He should do (ch. 34. 10, 13.) 24. Instead of arraigning, let it be thy fixed principle to magnify God in His works (Ps. 111. 2-8; Rev. 15. 3,): these, which all may "see," may convince us, that what we do not see is altogether wise and good (Rom. 1. 20.). behold—As "see," v. 25 shows; not, as MAUR. "sing," laud (Note 33. 27.). 25. "See" viz., with wondering admiration. [MAUR.] man may behold—Rather, "(yet) mortals (a different Heb. word from "man") behold it (only) from afar off;" see but a small "part" ch. 26. 14.). 26.—ch. 37. 13. God's greatness in heaven, and earth: a reason why Job should bow under His afflicting hand. 26. know him not—Only in part (v. 25; 1 Cor. 13. 12.) his years—(Ps. 90. 2; 102. 24, 27.); applied to Jesus Christ (Heb. 1. 12.) 27, 28. The marvellous formation of rain (so ch. 5. 9, 10.), maketh small—Rather, "He draweth (up) to Him,

He attracts from the earth below: the drops of water; they (the drops of water) pour down rain, which is) His vapour," "Vapour" is in apposition with "rain," marking the way in which rain is formed, viz., from the vapour drawn up by God into the air and then condensed into drops, which fall (Ps. 147. 8.). The suspension of such a mass of water, and its descent not in a deluge, but in drops of vapoury ruin, are the marvel. The selection of this particular illustration of God's greatness forms a fit prelude to the storm in which God appears ch. 40. 1.). 28. abundantly—Lit., upon many men. 29.—ch. 37. 5. God's marvels in thunder and lightnings. 29. spreadings, &c.—The canopy of thick clouds, which covers the heavens in a storm (Ps. 105. 39.). the noise (crashing) of his tabernacle—viz., thunder; God being poetically said to have His pavilion amidst dark clouds (Ps. 18. 11; Isa. 40. 22.). 30. light—Lightning. it—His tabernacle. The light, in an instant spread over the vast mass of dark clouds, forms a striking picture. "Spread" is repeated from v. 29, to form an antithesis, "He spreads not only clouds, but light." covereth the bottom (roots) of the sea—viz., with the light. In the storm the depths of ocean are laid bare; and the light "covers" them, at the same moment that it "spreads" across the dark sky. So in Ps. 18. 14, 15, the discovering of "the channels of waters" follows the "lightnings." UMBR. transl. "He spreadeth His light upon Himself, and covereth Himself with the roots of the sea;" (Ps. 104. 2.) God's garment is woven of celestial light and of the watery depths, raised to the sky to form His cloudy canopy. The phrase "cover Himself with the roots of the sea" is harsh: but the image is grand. 31. These (rain and lightnings) are marvellous and not to be understood, (v. 29,) yet necessary; "For by them He judgeth chastiseth on the one hand) &c., (and on the other,) by them; He giveth meat" (food.) &c. (ch. 37. 13; 38. 23, 27; Acts, 14. 17.). 32. Rather, "He covereth (both) His hands with light (lightning, ch. 37. 3, Marg.), and giveth it a command against his adversary" (it., the one assailing Him; (Ps. 8. 2; 139. 20, 21. 19.) Thus, as in v. 31. the twofold effects of His waters are set forth, so here, of His light; in the one hand destructive lightning against the wicked; in the other, the genial light for good to His friends, &c., v. 33. [UMBR.] 33. noise—Rather, He revealeth it (it., announceth concerning it) to His friend (antithesis to adversary, v. 32, so the Heb. is transl., ch. 2. 11,); also to cattle and plants (lit., that which shooteth up; Gen. 40. 10; 41. 22.). As the genial effect of "water" in the growth of food, is menti ned v. 31, so here that of "light" in cherishing cattle and plants. [UM.] If E.V. "noise" be retained, transl. "His (His coming in the tempest, the cattle too announce concerning Him when He is in the act of rising up" (in the storm.) Some animals give various intimations, that they are sensible of the approach of a storm. (Virg. Georg. I. 373, &c.)

CHAPTER XXXVII.

Ver. 1-24. 1. At this—When I hear the thundering of the Divine Majesty. Perhaps the storm already had begun, out of which God was to address Job ch. 38. 1.). 2. Hear attentively—The thunder, ("noise,") &c., and then you will feel that there is good reason to tremble. sound—*Muttering* of the thunder. 3. directeth it—However, zig-zag the *lightning's* course; or, rather, it applies to the peeling roll of the *thunder*. God's all-embracing power. ends—*Lit., wings, skirts,* the habitable earth being often compared to an extended garment (ch. 38. 13; Isa. 11. 12. 4. The thunder-clap follows at an interval after the flash. stay them—He will not *hold back the lightnings* (v. 3,) when the thunder is heard. (MAUR.] Rather, take "them" as the usual concomitants of thunder, viz., *rain and hail* [UMBR.] ch. 40. 9,). 5. (ch. 36. 26; Ps. 65. 6; 139. 14.), The sublimity of the description lies in this, that God is everywhere in the storm, directing it whither He will. (BA.] See Ps. 29. where, as here, the "voice" of God is repeated with grand effect. The thunder in Arabia is sublimely terrible. 6. Be—More forcible than "Fall," as UMBR. *transl.* (Gen. 1. 3.), to the small rain, &c.— He saith, Be on the earth. The shower increasing from "small" to "great," is expressed by the *plur. showers* (*Marg.,*) following the *sing. shower*. Winter rain (Song Sol. 2. 11.). 7. In winter God stops man's out-of-doors activity. sealeth—Closeth up (ch. 9. 7). Man's "hands" are then tied up. his work —In antithesis to *man's own work* (" hand") which at other times engages men so as to be liable to forget their dependence on God. UMBR. more *lit. transl.*, That all men whom *He has made* (lit., *of His making*) may be brought to acknowledgment. 8. remain— Rest in their lairs. It is beautifully ordered that during the cold, when they could not obtain food, many lie torpid; a state wherein they need no food. The desolation of the fields, at God's bidding, is poetically graphic. 9. south—*Lit., chambers*; connected with the S. (ch. 9. 9.). The whirlwinds are poetically regarded as pent up by God in His S. chambers, whence He sends them forth (so ch. 38. 22; Ps. 135. 7.). As to the S. whirlwinds (see Isa. 21. 1; Zech. 9. 14,), they drive before them burning sands; chiefly from February to May. the north—*Lit., scattering*; the N. wind-*scatters* the clouds. 10. frost— Rather, *ice*. the breath of God—Poetically, for the ice-producing N. wind. straitened— Physically accurate: frost *compresses* or *contracts* the expanded liquid into a congealed mass (ch. 38. 29, 30; Ps. 147. 17, 18.). 11-13. How the thunder-clouds are dispersed, or else employed by God, either for correction or mercy. by watering—By loading it with water. wearieth—*Burdeneth* it, so that it falls in rain; thus "wearieth" answers to the parallel "scattereth". (cf. Note v. 9,); a clear sky resulting alike from both. bright cloud—*Lit., cloud of His light, i.e.,* of His lightning. UMBR. for "watering," &c., *transl.* "*Brightness* drives away the clouds," His *light* scattereth the thick clouds:" the parallelism is thus good, but the *Heb.* hardly sanctions it. 12. it—The cloud of lightning. counsels—Guidance (Ps. 148. 8,); *lit., steering*; the clouds obey God's guidance, as the ship does the helmsman. So the *lightning* Note, 36. 31, 32, ; neither is hap-hazard in its movements. they—*The clouds*, implied in the collective *sing.* "it." face of the world, &c.— In the face of the earth's circle. 13. *Lit., He maketh it* the rain cloud) *find place*, whether for correction, if it be destined) for His land, (*i.e.* for the part *inhabited by man*, with whom God deals, as opposed to the *parts uninhabited,* on which rain is at other times appointed to fall (ch. 38. 26, 27,) or for mercy. "If it be destined for His land" is a parenthetical supposition. [MAUR.] In *E.V.,* this clause spoils the even balance of the antithesis between the "rod" (*Marg.*) and "mercy." (Ps. 68. 9; Gen. 7.). 14. (I's. 111. 2.). 15. wnen—Rather, *how,* disposed them—*Lays His charge on these* "wonders" (v. 14, to arise. light—Lightning. shine—Flash. How is it that *light* arises from the *dark* thunder-cloud? 16. *Heb.* "*Hast thou understanding of the balancings,* &c., how the clouds are poised in the air, so that their watery gravity does not bring them to the earth? The condensed moisture, descending by gravity, meets a warmer temperature, which dissipates it into vapour (the tendency of which is to ascend) and so counteracts the descending force. perfect in knowledge — God : not here in the sense that Elihu uses it of himself (ch. 36. 4.). 17. dost thou know—How, &c. thy garments—*i.e.*, how thy body grows warm, so as to affect thy garments with heat? south wind—*Lit., region of the S.* "When He *maketh still* (and sultry) the earth (*i.e.,* the atmosphere) by (during) the S. wind (Song Sol. 4. 16.). 18. with him—Like as He does (ch. 40. 15,). spread out—Given expanse to. strong—Firm; whence the term "firmament" (Gen. 1. 6; *Marg. expansion*, Isa. 44. 24,). molten looking-glass— Image of the bright smiling sky. *Mirrors* were then formed of molten polished metal, not "glass." 19. Men cannot explain God's wonders; we ought, therefore, to be dumb and not contend with God. If Job thinks we ought, "let him teach us, what we shall say." order — Frame. darkness—Of mind : ignorance. "The eyes are bewilderingly blinded, when turned in bold controversy with God towards the sunny heavens" (v. 18.). [UMBR.] 20. What I a mortal say against God's dealings is not worthy of being told HIM. In opposition to Job's wish to "speak" before God ch. 13. 3, 18-22.). If... surely he shall be swallowed up — The paralellism more favours UMBR. "Durst a man speak (before Him, complaining) *that he is* (without cause) *being destroyed?*" 21. "Cleanseth," *i.e., cleareth* the air of clouds. When the "bright light" *of the sun*, previously "not seen" through "clouds," suddenly shines out from behind them, owing to "the wind clearing them away," the effect is dazzling to the eye; so if God's majesty, now hidden, were suddenly revealed in all its brightness, it would spread "darkness" over Job's eyes, anxious as he is for it (cf. Note, v. 19.). [UMBR.] It is because "now man sees not the bright sunlight" (God's dazzling Majesty,) owing to the intervening "clouds" (ch. 26. 9,), that they dare to wish to "speak" before God (v. 20.). Prelude to God's appearance (ch. 38. 1.). The words also hold true in a sense not intended by Elihu, but perhaps included by the Holy Ghost, Job and other sufferers cannot see the *light* of God's countenance through the *clouds* of trial: but the wind will soon clear them off, and God shall appear again : let them but wait patiently, for He still shines, though for a time they see Him not see Note 23.). 22. Rather, *golden splendour*. MAUR. *transl. gold. It* is found in N. regions. But *God* cannot be "found out," because of His "Ma-

CHAPTER XXXVIII.

1 God challenges Job to answer. 4 God, by enumerating his mighty works, convinces Job of ignorance. 31 and of imbecility.

THEN the LORD answered Job *out of the whirlwind, and said,

2 Who *is* this that darkeneth counsel by words without knowledge?

3 Gird *up now thy loins like a man; for I will demand of thee, and ¹answer thou me.

4 Where *wast thou when I laid the foundations of the earth? declare, ²if thou hast understanding.

5 Who hath laid the measures thereof, if thou knowest? or who hath stretched the line upon it?

6 Whereupon are the ³foundations thereof ⁴fastened? or who laid the corner stone thereof,

7 When the morning stars sang together, and all *the sons of God shouted for joy?

8 Or *who shut up the sea with doors, when it brake forth, *as if* it had issued out of the womb?

9 When I made the cloud the garment thereof, and thick darkness a swaddlingband for it.

10 And ⁵brake up for it my decreed *place*, and set bars and doors,

11 And said, Hitherto shalt thou come, but no further; and here shall ⁶thy proud waves be stayed?

12 Hast thou commanded the morning since thy days; *and* caused the dayspring to know his place;

13 That it might take hold of the ⁷ends of the earth, that the wicked might be shaken out of it?

14 It is turned as clay *to* the seal; and they stand as a garment.

15 And from the wicked their light is withholden, and the high arm shall be broken.

16 Hast thou entered into the springs of the sea? or hast thou walked in the search of the depth?

17 Have *the gates of death been opened unto thee? or hast thou seen the doors of the shadow of death?

18 Hast thou perceived the breadth of the earth? declare if thou knowest it all.

19 Where is the way *where* light dwelleth? and *as for* darkness, where *is* the place thereof,

20 That thou shouldest take it ⁸to the bound thereof, and that thou shouldest know the paths *to* the house thereof?

21 Knowest thou *it*, because thou wast then born? or *because* the number of thy days *is* great?

22 Hast thou entered into the treasures of the snow? or hast thou seen the treasures of the hail,

23 Which I have reserved against the time of trouble, against the day of battle and war?

24 By what way is the light parted, *which* scattereth the east wind upon the earth?

25 Who hath divided a watercourse for the overflowing of waters; or a way for the lightning of thunder;

26 To cause it to rain on the earth, *where* no man *is*; *on* the wilderness, wherein *there is* no man;

27 To *satisfy the desolate and waste *ground*; and to cause the bud of the tender herb to spring forth?

28 Hath ʰthe rain a father? or who hath begotten the drops of dew?

29 Out of whose womb came the ice? and the ⁱhoary frost of heaven, who hath gendered it?

30 The waters are hid as *with* a stone, and the face of the deep ⁹is frozen.

31 Canst thou bind the sweet influences of ¹⁰Pleiades, or loose the bands of ¹¹Orion?

32 Canst thou bring forth ¹²Mazzaroth in his season? or canst thou ¹³guide Arcturus with his sons?

33 Knowest thou *the ordinances of heaven? canst thou set the dominion thereof in the earth?

34 Canst thou lift up thy voice to the clouds, that abundance of waters may cover thee?

35 Canst thou send lightnings, that they may go, and say unto thee, ¹⁴Here we *are*?

36 Who ᵏhath put wisdom in the inward parts? or who hath given understanding to the heart?

37 Who can number the clouds in wisdom? or ¹⁵who can stay the bottles of heaven,

38 ¹⁶When the dust ¹⁷groweth into hardness, and the clods cleave fast together?

39 Wilt thou hunt the prey for the lion, or fill ¹⁸the appetite of the young lions,

40 When they couch in *their* dens, *and* abide in the covert to lie in wait?

41 Who ˡprovideth for the raven his food? when his young ones cry unto God, they wander for lack of meat.

CHAPTER XXXIX.

God shows his power; 1 Of the wild goats and hinds, 5 of the wild ass, 9 the unicorn, 13 the peacock and ostrich, 19 the horse, 26 the hawk, 27 the eagle.

KNOWEST thou the time when the wild goats of the rock bring forth? *or canst thou mark when the hinds do calve?

2 Canst thou number the months *that* they fulfil? or knowest thou the time when they bring forth?

3 They bow themselves, they bring forth their young ones, they cast out their sorrows.

4 Their young ones are in good liking, they grow up with corn; they go forth, and return not unto them.

5 Who hath sent out the wild ass free? or who hath loosed the bands of the wild ass?

6 Whose ᵃhouse I have made the wilderness, and the ¹barren land his dwellings.

7 He scorneth the multitude of the city, neither regardeth he the crying ²of the driver.

8 The range of the mountains *is* his pasture, and he searcheth after every green thing.

9 Will the ³unicorn be willing to serve thee, or abide by thy crib?

10 Canst thou bind the unicorn with his band in the furrow? or will he harrow the valleys after thee?

11 Wilt thou trust him, because his strength *is* great? or wilt thou leave thy labour to him?

12 Wilt thou believe him, that he will bring home thy seed, and gather it *into* thy barn?

13 *Gavest thou* the goodly wings unto the peacocks? or ⁴wings and feathers unto the ostrich?

jesty" v. 23.). Thus ch. 28. corresponds: E.V. is simpler. the north—*Brightness* is chiefly associated with it (Note, 23. 9.). Here, perhaps, because the N. wind clears the air (Prov. 25. 23.). Thus this clause answers to the last of v. 21; as the second of this v. to the first of v. 21: Inverted parallelism. (See Isa. 14. 13; Ps. 48. 2.). with God — Rather, *upon God*, as a garment (Ps. 104. 1, 2.). majesty—Splendour. 23. afflict— Oppressively, so as to "pervert *judgment*" as Job implied (Note, 8. 3, ; but see end of Note, 21. above. The reading "He answereth not," *i.e.*, gives no account of His dealings, is like a transcriber's correction, from ch. 33. 13: *Marg.* 24. do—Rather, *ought*, wise—in their own conceits.

CHAPTER XXXVIII.

Ver. 1-41. 1. Jehovah appears unexpectedly in a whirlwind, (already gathering ch. 37. 1, 2.) the symbol of "judgment," (Is. 50. 3, 4, &c.,) to which Job had challenged him. He asks him now to get himself ready for the contest. Can he explain the phenomena of God's *natural* government? How can he, then, hope to understand the principles of His *moral* government? God thus confirms Elihu's sentiment. that *submission to*, not *reasonings on*, God's ways is man's part. This and the *disciplinary* design of trial to the godly is the great lesson of this book. He does not solve the difficulty by reference to future retribution: for this was not the immediate question: *glimpses* of that truth were already given, in ch. 14. and 19., the *full revelation* of it being reserved for Gospel times: Yet even *now* we need to learn the lesson taught by Elihu and God in Job. 2. this—Job. counsel—Impugning my divine *wisdom* in the providential arrangements of the universe. Such "words" (including those of the friends) rather *obscure*, than throw light on my ways. God is about to be Job's Vindicator, but must first bring him to *a right state of mind* for receiving relief. 3. a man—*Hero*, ready for battle (1 Cor. 16. 13,) as he had wished (ch. 9. 35; 13. 22; 31. 37.). The robe, usually worn flowing, was girt up by a girdle, when men ran, laboured, or fought (1 Pet. 1. 13.). 4. To understand the cause of things, man should have been present at their origin. The finite creature cannot fathom the infinite wisdom of the Creator (ch. 28. 12; 15. 7, 8.). hast (knowest) understanding—(Prov. 4. 1.). 5. measures—Of its proportions. Image from an architect's plans of a building. Line—of measurement (Isa. 28. 17.). The earth is formed on an all-wise *plan*. 6. foundations —Not sockets, as *Marg.* fastened—*Lit., made to sink*, as a foundation-stone let down till it settles firmly in the clay (ch. 26. 7.). Gravitation makes and keeps the earth a sphere. 7. As at the founding of Zerubbabel's temple (Ezra, 3. 10-13.). So hereafter at the completion of the Church, the temple of the Holy Ghost (Zech. 4. 7.); as at its foundation (Luke, 2. 13, 14.). 7. morning stars—Especially beautiful. The creation-*morn* is appropriately associated with these, it being the *commencement* of this world's-*day*. The stars are *fig.* said to sing God's praises, as in Ps. 19. 1; 148. 3. They are symbols of the angels, bearing the same relation to our earth, as angels do to us. Therefore they answer to "sons of God," or angels, in the parallel.

See Note, 25. 5. 8. doors—Flood-gates; these when opened caused the flood (Gen. 7. 2,); or else, *the shores*. womb—of Chaos. The bowels of the earth. Image from child-birth (v. 8, 9.). Ocean at its birth was wrapped in clouds as its swaddling bands (Ezek. 32. 2; Mic. 4. 10.). 10. brake up for—*i.e.*, appointed it. Shores are generally *broken* and abrupt cliffs. The Greek for *shore* means a *broken place*. I *broke off* or measured off for it *my limit*, *i.e.*, the limit which I thought fit ch. 26. 10.). 11. s'ayed—*Heb.*, *a limit shall be set to*. 12-15. Passing from creation to phenomena in the existing inanimate world. 12. hast thou—To rise. since thy days—Since thou hast commanded the morning come into being. its place—It varies in its place of rising from day to day, and yet has its place each day according to fixed laws. 13. take hold of the ends, &c.—Spread itself over the *earth to its utmost bounds* in a moment. wicked—Who hate the light, and do their evil works in the dark ch. 24. 13.). shaken out of it—The corners (*Heb., wings* or *skirts*) of it, as of a garment, are taken hold of by the day-spring, so as to shake off the wicked. 14. Explaining the first clause of v. 13, as v. 15 does the second clause. As the plastic clay presents the various figures impressed on it by a seal, so the earth, which in the dark was void of all form, when illuminated by the day-spring, presents a variety of forms, hills, valleys, &c. "Turned" ("turns itself," *Heb.*) alludes to the rolling cylinder seal, such as is found in Babylon, which leaves its impressions on the clay, as it is *turned about*: so the morning light *rolling on over* the earth. they stand—*The forms of beauty*, unfolded by the dawn, stand forth as a garment, in which the earth is clad. 15. their light—by which *they* work, viz., *darkness*, which is *their day* (ch. 24. 17.). is extinguished by daylight. high — Rather, *The arm uplifted* for murder or other crime is broken; it falls down suddenly, powerless, through their fear of light. 16. springs—Fountains beneath the sea (Ps. 95. 4.). search—Rather, *The inmost recesses, lit., that which is only found by searching*, the deep caverns of ocean. 17. seen—The second clause heightens the thought in the first. Man during life does not even "see" the gates of the realm of the dead ("death," ch. 10. 21,), much less are they "opened" to him. But those are "naked before God" (ch. 26. 6.). 18. Hast thou—As God doth (ch. 28. 24.). 19-38. The marvels in heaven. 19. "What is the way (to the place wherein) light dwelleth?" The origin of light and darkness. In Gen. 1., "light" is created distinct from, and previous to, light-emitting bodies, the luminaries of heaven. 20. Dost thou know its place so well, as to be able to *guide*, "take" as in Isa. 36. 17,) it to (but UMBR. "*reach* it in") its own boundary, *i.e.*, the limit between light and darkness ch. 26. 10.). 21. Or without the interrogation, in an ironical sense. [UMBR.] then — When I created light and darkness (ch. 15. 7.). 22. treasures —*Store-houses*, from which God draws forth snow and hail. Snow is vapour congealed in the air, before it is collected in drops large enough to form hail. Its shape is that of a crystal in endless variety of beautiful figures. Hail is formed by rain falling through dry cold air. 23. against the time of trouble—The time when I design to chastise men (Ex. 9. 18; Josh. 10. 11; Rev. 16. 21; Isa. 28. 17; Ps. 18. 12, 13; Hag. 2. 17.). 24. is ... parted—Parts, so as to diffuse itself over the whole earth, though seeming to come from one point. Light travels from the sun to the earth, ninety millions of miles, in eight minutes. which scattereth—Rather, "And by what way the E. wind (personified) spreads (scattereth) itself," &c. The light and E. wind are associated together, as both come from one quarter, and often arise together (Jon. 4. 8.). 25. waters—Rain falls, not in a mass on one spot, but in countless separate canals in the air marked out for them. way for the lightning—(ch. 28. 26.). 26. Since rain falls also on places uninhabited by man, it cannot be that man guides its course. Such rain, though man cannot explain the reason for it, is not lost. God has some wise design in it. 27. As though the desolate ground thirsted for God's showers. Personification. The beauty imparted to the uninhabited desert pleases God, for whom primarily all things exist, and He has ulterior designs in it. 28. Can any visible origin of rain and dew be assigned by man? Dew is moisture, which was suspended in the air, but becomes condensed on reaching the—in the night—lower temperature, of objects on the earth. 29. ch. 37. 10, 30. The unfrozen *waters are hid* under the frozen, as *with* a covering of *stone*. frozen—*Lit.*, is *taken*: the particles *take hold* of one another so as to cohere. 31. sweet influences—The joy diffused by spring, the time when the Pleiades appear. The E. poets, Hafiz, Sadi, &c., describe them as "brilliant rosettes." GES. transl. "bands" or "knot," which answers better the parallelism. But *E.V.* agrees better with the *Heb.* The seven stars are closely "bound" together. Note, 9. 9. "Canst thou bind or loose the tie?" "Canst thou loose the bonds by which the constellation Orion (represented in the E. as an inipious giant chained to the sky) is held fast." (Note, 9. 9.). 32. *Canst thou bring forth* from their places or *houses* (Mazzaloth. Marg. 2 Ki. 23. 5; to which *Mazzaroth* here is equivalent) into the sky *the signs of the Zodiac at their respective seasons*—the twelve lodgings in which the sun successively stays, or appears, in the sky? Arcturus — Ursa Major. his sons — The three stars in its tail. Canst thou make them appear in the sky? (ch. 9. 9.) The great and less Bear are called by the Arabs "Daughters of the Bier," the quadrangle being the bier, the three others the mourners. 33. ordinances—Which regulate the alternations of seasons, &c. (Gen. 8. 22.) dominion — *Controlling influence* of the heavenly bodies, the sun, moon, &c., on the earth on the tides, weather.). (Gen. 1. 16; Ps. 136. 7-9.) 34. Jer. 14. 22; above, ch. 22. 11, metaphorically. 35. Here we are—At thy disposal (Isa. 6. 8.). 36. inward parts ... heart—But [UMBR.] "dark clouds (" shining phenomena," MAUR.) — meteor," referring to the consultation of these as signs of weather by the husbandman (Eccl. 11. 4.). But *Heb.* supports *E.V.* The connexion is, "Who hath given thee the intelligence to comprehend in any degree the phenomena just specified?" heart—Not the usual *Heb.* word, but one from a root *to view; perception*. 37. Who appoints by his wisdom the due measure of the clouds? stay—Rather, *empty; lit.*, *lay down* or *incline* so as to *pour out*. "Bottles of heaven," rain-filled clouds. 38. groweth, &c.—Rather, *pours itself into a mass* by the rain, like molten metal; then *trans.* 38, "Who is it that *empties*, &c., when," &c.? *E.V.* however is tenable: "Is *caked into a mass*" by heat, like molten metal, *before* the rain falls;" "Who is it that *can empty* the rain vessels, and bring down rain *at such a time?*" (v. 38.). 39. From this v. to ch. 39. 30, the Instincts of animals. Is it thou that givest it the instinct to hunt its prey (Ps. 104. 21.). appetite — *Lit., life*: which depends on the *appetite* (ch. 33. 20.). 40. lie in wait—for their prey (Ps. 10. 9.) 41. Luke, 12. 24. Transition from the noble lioness to the croaking raven. Though man dislikes it, as of ill-omen, God cares for it, as for all His creatures.

CHAPTER XXXIX.

Ver. 1-30. 1. Even wild beasts, cut off from all care of *man*, are cared for by *God* at their seasons of greatest need. Their instinct comes direct from God, and guides them to help themselves in parturition; the very time when the herdsman is most anxious for his herds. wild goats—Ibex (Ps. 104. 18; 1 Sam. 24. 2.). hinds—Fawns: most timid and defenceless animals, yet cared for by God. 2. They bring forth with ease. and do not need to reckon the months of pregnancy, as the shepherd does in the case of his flocks. 3. "Bow themselves" in parturition; bend on their knees (1 Sam. 4. 19.). bring forth—*Lit., cause their young to cleave the womb and break forth*. Sorrows—Their young ones, the cause of their momentary pains. 4. are in good liking—In good condition, grow up strong. with corn—Rather, *in the field*, without man's care. return not—Being able to provide for themselves. 5. wild ass—Two different *Heb.* words are here used for the same animal, *the ass of the woods* and *the wild ass*. (Note 6. 5; ch. 11. 12; 24. 5; Jer. 2. 24.) loosed the bands—Given its liberty to. Man can rob animals of freedom, but not, as God, give freedom, combined with subordination to fixed laws. 6. barren — *Lit., salt, i.e.*, unfruitful. (So Marg. Ps. 107. 34.) 7. multitude—Rather, *din;* he sets it at defiance, being far away from it in the freedom of the wilderness. driver—who urges on the tame ass to work. The wild ass is the symbol of uncontrolled freedom in the E.; even kings have, therefore, added its name to them. 8. The range—*Lit., searching*, "that which it finds by searching is," &c. 9. unicorn—Pliny, H. N. 8. 21, mentions such an animal; its figure is found depicted in the ruins of Persepolis. The *Heb. reem* conveys the idea of *loftiness* and-*power*, cf. *Ramah*, Indian *Ram*, Lat. *Roma*. The rhinoceros was perhaps the original type of the unicorn. The Arab *rim* is a two horned animal. Sometimes "unicorn" or *reem* is a mere *poetical symbol* or abstraction. But the *buffalo* is the animal referred to here, from the contrast to *the tame ox*, used in ploughing, &c., v. 10, 12. crib—Is. 1. 3.) abide—*Lit., pass the night*. 10. his band—fastened to the horns, as its chief strength Obedient to thee; willing to follow, instead of being goaded on *before* thee. 11. thy labour—Rustic work. 12. Believe—Trust. Seed—Produce (1 Sam. 8. 15.). into thy barn—Rather, *gather* (the contents of) *thy thresh-*

ing floor; [MAUR.] the corn threshed on it. 13. feather, " the wing of the *ostrich* hen—(*lit. the crying-*bird; as the Arab name for it means *song;* referring to its night-cries, (ch. 30. 29; Mic. 1. 8.) vibrates joyously. Is it not like the quill and feathers of *the pious bird"* (the stork? [UMBR.] The *vibrating, quivering wing,* serving for sail and oar at once, is characteristic of the ostrich in full course. Its white and black feathers in the wing and tail are like the stork's. But unlike that bird, the symbol of parental love in the E., it with seeming want of natural pious) affection deserts its young. Both birds are poetically called by descriptive, instead of their usual appellative names. 14. Yet unlike the stork she leaveth, &c. Hence called by the Arabs *the impious bird.* However, the fact is, she lays her eggs with great care and hatches them, as other birds do; but in hot countries the eggs do not need so constant incubation: she therefore often leaves them; and sometimes forgets the place on her return: moreover the outer eggs, intended for food, she feeds her young with; these eggs lying separate in the sand, exposed to the sun, gave rise to the idea of her altogether leaving them. God describes her as she *seems to man:* implying, though she may seem foolishly to neglect her young, yet really she is guided by a sure instinct from God, as much as animals of instincts widely different. 16. On a slight noise often she forsakes her eggs, and returns not, *as if* she were "hardened towards her young." her labour—in producing eggs, *is in vain,* (yet) *she has no disquietude* (about her young): unlike other birds, who, if one egg and another are taken away, will go on laying till their full number is made up. 17. wisdom—such as God gives to other animals, and to man: (ch. 35. 11.). The Arab proverb is, "foolish as an ostrich." Yet her very seeming want of wisdom is not without wise design of God, though man cannot see it: just as in the trials of the godly, which seem so unreasonable to Job, there lies hid a wise design. 18. Notwithstanding her deficiencies, she has distinguishing excellencies. lifteth... herself—for running: she cannot mount in the air. (GES. *transl. lashes herself* up to her course by flapping her wings. The old versions favour *E. V.,* and the parallel "scorneth" answers to her *proudly* " lifting up herself." 19. The allusion to " the horse" *v.* 18, suggests the description of him. Arab poets delight in praising the horse; yet it is not mentioned in the possessions of Job (chs. 1. and 42.). It seems to have been at the time chiefly used for war, rather than " domestic purposes." thunder—poetically for, "he with arched neck inspires fear as *thunder* does." *Transl.* " Majesty." [UMBR.] Rather " the trembling, *quivering mane,"* answering to the "vibrating wing" of the ostrich; (Note 13.) [MAUR.] *Mane* in Greek also is from a root meaning *fear. E. V.* is more sublime. 20. make... afraid—Rather, " canst thou (as I do) make him *spring* as the *locust."* So in Joel 2. 4, the comparison is between *locusts* and *war horses.* The heads of the two are so like, that the Italians call the locusts *cavaletta,* "little horse." nostrils—Snorting furiously. 21. valley—Where the battle is joined. goeth on—Goeth forth. (Numb. 1. 3; 21. 23.). 23. quiver—for *the arrows,* which they contain, and which are directed "*against*

him." glittering spear—*lit., glittering of the spear,* like "lightning of the spear," Hab. 3. 11.) shield—Rather, *lance.* 24. swalloweth —Fretting with impatience, he *draws the ground towards him* with his hoof, as if he would *swallow* it. The parallelism shows this to be the sense; not as MAUR., "scours over it," neither believeth—For joy. Rather, " he will not *stand still,* when the note of the trumpet" (soundeth). 25. saith—Poetically applied to his mettlesome neighing, whereby he shows his love of the battle. smelleth— Snuffeth: discerneth *Marg.* Isa. 11. 3.) thunder—Thundering voice. 26. The instinct by which some birds migrate to warmer climes before winter. Rapid *flying* peculiarly characterizes the whole hawk *genus.* 27. eagle —It flies highest, of all birds: Thence called *the bird of heaven.* 28. abideth—Securely, (Ps. 91. 1,); it occupies the *same abode* mostly for life. crag—*lit., tooth* (*Marg.* 1 Sam. 14. 5.). strong place—Citadel, fastness. 29. seeketh—Is on the look out for. behold—the eagle descries its prey at an astonishing distance, by sight, rather than smell. 30. Quoted partly by Jesus Christ, Matt. 24. 28.). The food of young eagles is the blood of victims brought by the parent, when they are still too feeble to devour flesh. slain—as *the vulture* chiefly feeds on carcases, *it* is included probably in the genus *eagle.*

CHAPTER XL.

Ver. 1-24. GOD'S SECOND ADDRESS. He had paused for a reply, but Job was silent. 1. the Lord—*Heb.,* JEHOVAH. 2. he that contendeth—As Job had so often expressed a wish to do. Or, *rebuketh.* Does Job now still (after seeing and hearing of God's majesty and wisdom) wish to set God right? answer it—viz., the questions I have asked. 3. Lord—JEHOVAH. 4. I am (too) vile to reply.). It is a very different thing to vindicate ourselves before God, from what it is before men. Job could do the latter, not the former. lay... hand upon... mouth— I have no plea to offer (ch. 21. 5; Jud. 18. 19.). 5. Once... twice — *Oftentimes, more than once* (ch. 33. 14, cf. with 29; Ps. 62. 11): " I have spoken " viz., against God. not answer—Not plead against thee. 6. the Lord—JEHOVAH. 7. (Note, 38. 3.) Since Job has not only spoken against God, but accused Him of injustice, God challenges him to try, could *he* govern the world, as *God* by His power doth, and punish the proud and wicked (*v.* 7-14.). 8. Wilt thou not only contend with, but *set aside my judgment,* or justice in the government of the world. condemn—Declare me unrighteous, in order *that thou mayest be accounted righteous* (innocent: undeservingly-afflicted.) 9. arm—God's omnipotence (Isa. 53. 1.). thunder—God's voice ch. 37. 4,). 10. See hast thou power and majesty like God's, to enable thee to judge and govern the world. 11. rage—Rather, pour out *the redundant floods of,* &c. behold—Try, canst thou, as God, by a mere *glance* abase the proud (Isa. 2. 12, &c.). 12. proud—high (Dan. 4. 37.). in this place—On the spot: suddenly, before they can move from their place (Note, 34. 26; 36. 20.). 13. (Isa. 2. 10,) *Abase* and remove them out of the sight of men. bind... faces— *i.e., Shut up* their *persons.* [MAUR.] But it refers rather to the custom of *binding* a cloth over the *faces* of persons about to be executed (ch. 9. 21; Esth. 7. 8.). in secret:— Consign them to *darkness.* 14. confess.—

Job humbles himself to God.   JOB, XL., XLI.   *Leviathan described.*

14 Which leaveth her eggs in the earth, and warmeth them in dust,
15 And forgetteth that the foot may crush them, or that the wild beast may break them.
16 She is *hardened* against her young ones, as though *they were* not her's: her labour is in vain without fear;
17 Because God hath deprived her of wisdom, neither hath he *imparted* to her understanding.
18 What time she lifteth up herself on high, she scorneth the horse and his rider.
19 Hast thou given the horse strength? hast thou clothed his neck with thunder?
20 Canst thou make him afraid as a grasshopper? the glory of his nostrils *is* terrible.
21 He paweth in the valley, and rejoiceth in *his* strength: he goeth on to meet the armed men.
22 He mocketh at fear, and is not affrighted; neither turneth he back from the sword.
23 The quiver rattleth against him, the glittering spear and the shield.
24 He swalloweth the ground with fierceness and rage; neither believeth he that it *is* the sound of the trumpet.
25 He saith among the trumpets, Ha, ha! and he smelleth the battle afar off, the thunder of the captains, and the shouting.
26 Doth the hawk fly by thy wisdom, *and* stretch her wings toward the south?
27 Doth the eagle mount up at thy command, and make her nest on high?
28 She dwelleth and abideth on the rock, upon the crag of the rock, and the strong place.
29 From thence she seeketh the prey, *and* her eyes behold afar off.
30 Her young ones also suck up blood: and where the slain *are*, there *is* she.

CHAPTER XL.

1 Job humbles himself to God; 6 God stirs him up to show his righteousness, power, and wisdom. 15 Of the behemoth.

MOREOVER the LORD answered Job, and said,
2 Shall he that contendeth with the Almighty instruct *him?* he that reproveth God, let him answer it.
3 ¶ Then Job answered the LORD, and said,
4 Behold, I am vile; what shall I answer thee? I will lay mine hand upon my mouth.
5 Once have I spoken; but I will not answer: yea, twice; but I will proceed no further.
6 ¶ Then answered the LORD unto Job out of the whirlwind, and said,
7 Gird up thy loins now like a man: for I will demand of thee, and declare thou unto me,
8 Wilt thou also disannul my judgment? wilt thou condemn me, that thou mayest be righteous?
9 Hast thou an arm like God? or canst thou thunder with a voice like him?
10 Deck thyself now *with* majesty and excellency, and array thyself with glory and beauty.
11 Cast abroad the rage of thy wrath: and behold every one *that is* proud, and abase him,
12 Look on every one *that is* proud, *and* bring him low; and tread down the wicked in their place.

13 Hide them in the dust together; *and* bind their faces in secret.
14 Then will I also confess unto thee that thine own right hand can save thee.
15 ¶ Behold now behemoth, which I made with thee; he eateth grass as an ox.
16 Lo now, his strength *is* in his loins, and his force *is* in the navel of his belly.
17 He moveth his tail like a cedar: the sinews of his stones are wrapped together.
18 His bones *are as* strong pieces of brass; his bones *are* like bars of iron.
19 He *is* the chief of the ways of God: he that made him can make his sword to approach *unto* him.
20 Surely the mountains bring him forth food, where all the beasts of the field play.
21 He lieth under the shady trees, in the covert of the reed, and fens.
22 The shady trees cover him *with* their shadow; the willows of the brook compass him about.
23 Behold, he drinketh up a river, *and* hasteth not: he trusteth that he can draw up Jordan into his mouth.
24 He taketh it with his eyes; *his* nose pierceth through snares.

CHAPTER XLI.

Of God's great power in the leviathan.

CANST thou draw out leviathan with an hook? or his tongue with a cord *which* thou lettest down?
2 Canst thou put an hook into his nose? or bore his jaw through with a thorn?
3 Will he make many supplications unto thee? will he speak soft *words* unto thee?
4 Will he make a covenant with thee? wilt thou take him for a servant for ever?
5 Wilt thou play with him as *with* a bird? or wilt thou bind him for thy maidens?
6 Shall thy companions make a banquet of him? shall they part him among the merchants?
7 Canst thou fill his skin with barbed irons? or his head with fish spears?
8 Lay thine hand upon him, remember the battle, do no more.
9 Behold, the hope of him is in vain: shall not *one* be cast down even at the sight of him?
10 None *is* so fierce that dare stir him up: who then is able to stand before me?
11 Who hath prevented me, that I should repay *him?* *whatsoever is* under the whole heaven is mine.
12 I will not conceal his parts, nor his power, nor his comely proportion.
13 Who can discover the face of his garment? *or* who can come to him with his double bridle?
14 Who can open the doors of his face? his teeth *are* terrible round about.
15 *His* scales *are his* pride, shut up together *as with* a close seal.
16 One is so near to another, that no air can come between them.
17 They are joined one to another, they stick together, that they cannot be sundered.
18 By his neesings a light doth shine, and his eyes *are* like the eyelids of the morning.
19 Out of his mouth go burning lamps, *and* sparks of fire leap out.
20 Out of his nostrils goeth smoke, as *out* of a seething pot or caldron.
21 His breath kindleth coals, and a flame goeth out of his mouth.

Rather, *extol;* "I also," who now *censure* thee. But since thou canst not do these works, thou must, instead of censuring, extol *my* government. thine own... hand... save— Ps. 44. 3.). So as to eternal salvation by Jesus Christ (Isa. 59. 16; 63. 6.). 15-24. God shows that if Job cannot bring under control the lower animals of which he selects the two most striking, Behemoth on land, Leviathan in the water), much less is he capable of governing the world. 15. behemoth—The description in part agrees with the hippopotamus, in part with the elephant, but exactly in all details with neither. It is rather a *poetical personification of the great Pachydermata,* or *Herbivora* (so "he eateth grass," &c.), the idea of the hippopotamus being predominant. In v. 17, "the tail like a cedar," hardly applies to the latter: so also v. 20; 23, "Jordan," a river which elephants alone could reach, but see Note 23.). On the other hand, 21, 22 are characteristic of the *amphibious* river-horse. So leviathan (the twisting animal) ch. 41. 1, is a *generalized term for cetacea, pythons, saurians,* of the neighbouring seas, and rivers, including the crocodile which is the most prominent, and is often associated with the river-horse by old writers. "Behemoth" seems to be the Egyptian *Pehemout,* "water-ox," Hebraized, so called as being like an ox, whence the Ital. "bomarino." with tree—As I made thyself. Yet how great the difference! The *manifold* wisdom and power of God! he sateth grass—Marvellous in an animal living so much in the water: also strange, that such a monster should not be carnivorous. 16. navel—Rather, *muscles* of his belly; the weakest point of the elephant, therefore *it* is not meant. 17. like a cedar—As the tempest *bends* the cedar, so it can move its smooth thick tail. [UMBR.] But the cedar implies straightness and length, such as do not apply to the river-horse's short tail, but perhaps to an extinct species of animal see Note 15.). stones—Rather, *thighs.* wrapped—Firmly *twisted together.* like a thick rope. 18. strong pieces—Rather, *tubes* of copper [UMBR.] 19. Chief of the *works* of God : so "ways" (ch. 26. 14; Prov. 8. 22). can make his sword to approach—Rather, *has furnished him with his sword,* harpe,) viz., the *sickle-like* teeth with which he cuts down grain. *E.V.* however, is *lit.* right. 20. The mountain is not his *usual* haunt. Bo. says it is *sometimes* found there (?) beasts... play—A graphic trait: though armed with such teeth, he let the beasts play near him unhurt, for his food is grass. 21. lieth—He leads an inactive life. shady trees — Rather, *lotus-bushes;* as v. 22 requires. 22. *Transl.* lotus-*bushes.* 23. Rather, "Though a river be violent (over flow), he trembleth not;" (for though living on land, he can live in the water too, he is secure, though a Jordan swell up to his mouth." "Jordan" is used for *any great river;* consonant with the "behemoth" being a *poetical generalization* (Note 15.). The author cannot have been a Hebrew as UMBR. asserts, or he would not adduce the Jordan where there were no river horses. He alludes to it as a name for *any* river, but not as one known to him, except by hearsay. 24. Rather, "will any take him by open *force lit., before his eyes),* or pierce his nose with cords?" No : he can only be taken by guile, and in a pitfall 'ch. 41. 1, 2,).

CHAPTER XLI.

Ver. 1-34. 1. leviathan—*Lit., the twisted animal,* gathering itself in folds : a synonym to the Thannin (ch. 3. 8, *Marg.*; see Ps. 74. 14; type of the Egyptian tyrant; Ps. 104, 26; Isa. 27. 1; the Babylon tyrant.). *A poetical generalization* for all cetacean, serpentine, and saurian monsters (Note, 40. 16; hence *all* the description* (Note, 40. 16; hence *all* the description applies to no *one* animal); especially the crocodile : which is naturally described after the *river-horse,* as both are found in the Nile. tongue ... lettest down—The crocodile has no tongue, or a very small one cleaving to the lower jaw. But as in fishing the *tongue of the fish* draws the baited hook to it, God asks, Canst thou in like manner take leviathan? 2. hook—Rather, *a rope of rushes.* thorn—Rather, *a ring* or *hook.* So wild beasts were led about when caught (Isa. 37. 29; Ezek. 29. 4,); fishes also were secured thus, and thrown into the water, to keep them alive. 3. soft words—That thou mayest spare his life. No : he is untameable. 4. Can he be tamed for domestic use? (so ch. 39. 10-12.). 5. a bird—That is tamed. 6. Rather, *partners* (viz., *in fishing.*. make a banquet—The parallelism rather supports UMBR., "Do partners (in trade) *desire to purchase* him? (so the Heb. Deu. 2. 6.) merchants—*Lit., Canaanites,* who were great merchants (Hos. 12 7, *Marg.*). His hide is not penetrable, as that of fishes. 8. If thou *lay,* &c. thou wilt have reason ever to *remember,* &c., and thou wilt never try it again. 9. the hope—*Of* taking him. cast down—With fear "at the (mere) sight of him." 10. fierce—Courageous, If a man *dare* attack one of my creatures (Gen. 49. 9; Num. 24. 9,), who will dare (as Job had wished) oppose himself (Ps. 2, 2) to me, the Creator? This is the main drift of the description of leviathan. 11. prevented —Done me a favour first : anticipated me with service (Ps. 21, 3.). None can call me to account (" stand before me," v. 10, as unjust, because I have withdrawn favours from him (as in Job's case): for none has laid on me under a prior obligation by conferring on me something which was not already my own. What can man give to Him, who possesses all, including man himself? Man cannot constrain the creature to be his "servant," *v.* 4,) much less the Creator. 12. I will not conceal — A resumption of the description broken off by the digression, which formed an agreeable change. his power—*Lit., the way, i.e.,* true proportion or expression *of his strength* (so Heb., Deut. 19. 4.). comely proportion—*Lit., the comeliness of his structure* (his *apparatus:* so "suit of apparel" Jud. 17. 10.). [MAUR.] UMBR. *transl.* "his armour." But that follows after. 13. discover—Rather, *uncover the surface* of his garment *(skin,* ch. 10. 11): strip off the hard *outer* coat with which the inner skin is covered. with—Rather, *within* his double *jaws, lit., bridle:* hence that into which the bridle is put, *the double row of teeth ;* but "bridle" is used to imply that none dare put his hand in to insert a bridle where in other animals it is placed *(v.* 4; ch. 39. 10,). 14. doors of ... face—His mouth. His teeth are sixty in number, larger in proportion than his body, some standing out, some serrated, fitting into each other like a comb. [Bo.] 15. Rather, his *furrows of shields* (as "tubes," "channels," Note, 40. 18,) are, &c., *i.e.,* the rows of *scales,* like *shields* covering him : he

Job submits himself to God. JOB, XLII. *Job restored to prosperity.*

22 In his neck remaineth strength, and sorrow is turned into joy before him.
23 The flakes of his flesh are joined together: they are firm in themselves; they cannot be moved.
24 His heart is as firm as a stone; yea, as hard as a piece of the nether *millstone.*
25 When he raiseth up himself, the mighty are afraid: by reason of breakings they purify themselves.
26 The sword of him that layeth at him cannot hold; the spear, the dart, nor the habergeon.
27 He esteemeth iron as straw, *and* brass as rotten wood.
28 The arrow cannot make him flee: slingstones are turned with him into stubble.
29 Darts are counted as stubble: he laugheth at the shaking of a spear.
30 Sharp stones *are* under him: he spreadeth sharp-pointed things upon the mire.
31 He maketh the deep to boil like a pot; he maketh the sea like a pot of ointment.
32 He maketh a path to shine after him; *one* would think the deep *to be* hoary.
33 Upon earth there is not his like, who is made without fear.
34 He beholdeth all high *things:* he *is* a king over all the children of pride.

CHAPTER XLII.

1 *Job submits himself to God.* 7 *Job's friends submit to him.* 9 *God accepts Job, and doubles his blessings.* 13 *Job's children;* 16 *his age and death.*

THEN Job answered the LORD, and said,
2 I know that thou canst do every *thing,* and that no thought can be withholden from thee.
3 Who *is* he that hideth counsel without knowledge? therefore have I uttered that I understood not; things too wonderful for me, which I knew not.
4 Hear, I beseech thee, and I will speak: I will demand of thee, and declare thou unto me.
5 I have heard of thee by the hearing of the ear; but now mine eye seeth thee:
6 Wherefore I abhor *myself,* and repent in dust and ashes.
7 ¶ And it was so, that after the LORD

B. C. 1520.

CHAP. 41.
6 sorrow rejoiceth.
8 The fallings.
7 Or, breastplate.
8 Sharp pieces of potsherd.
9 Or, who behave themselves without fear.

CHAP. 42.
a Gen. 18. 14. Mat. 19. 26.
3 Job.
1 Or, no thought of thine can be hindered.
b ch. 3b. 2.
c Ps. 40. 5.
Ps. 131. 1.
Ps. 139. 6.
d ch. 33. 3.
ch. 40. 7.
e Ro. 10. 17.
f Eph. 1 17, 18.
g Nu. 23. 1.
h Mat. 5. 24.
i Gen. 20. 17.
Jam 5. 16.
1 John 5. 16.
2 his face, or, person.
3 the face of Job.
4 added all that had been to Job unto the double.
Zech. 9. 12.
j Is. 40. 2.
k ch. 19. 13.
l ch. 8. 7.
Jam. 5. 11.
m ch. 1. 3.
n ch. 5. 26.
Pro. 3. 16.
o Gen. 25. 8.

had spoken these words unto Job, the LORD said to Eliphaz the Temanite, My wrath is kindled against thee, and against thy two friends: for ye have not spoken of me *the thing that is* right, as my servant Job hath.
8 Therefore take unto you now seven bullocks and seven rams, and go to my servant Job, and offer up for yourselves a burnt offering; and my servant Job shall pray for you; for him will I accept; lest I deal with you *after your* folly, in that ye have not spoken of me *the thing which is* right, like my servant Job.
9 ¶ So Eliphaz the Temanite and Bildad the Shuhite *and* Zophar the Naamathite went and did according as the LORD commanded them: the LORD also accepted Job.
10 And the LORD turned the captivity of Job, when he prayed for his friends: also the LORD gave Job twice as much as he had before.
11 Then came there unto him all his brethren, and all his sisters, and all they that had been of his acquaintance before, and did eat bread with him in his house: and they bemoaned him, and comforted him over all the evil that the LORD had brought upon him: every man also gave him a piece of money, and every one an earring of gold.
12 So the LORD blessed the latter end of Job more than his beginning; for he had fourteen thousand sheep, and six thousand camels, and a thousand yoke of oxen, and a thousand she-asses.
13 He had also seven sons and three daughters.
14 And he called the name of the first, Jemima; and the name of the second, Kezia; and the name of the third, Kerenhappuch.
15 And in all the land were no women found so fair as the daughters of Job: and their father gave them inheritance among their brethren.
16 After this lived Job an hundred and forty years, and saw his sons, and his sons' sons, *even* four generations.
17 So Job died, *being* old, and full of days.

THE BOOK OF PSALMS.

PSALM I.

Happiness of the godly. 4 *Misery of the ungodly.*

BLESSED *is* the man that walketh not in the counsel of the ungodly, nor standeth in the way of sinners, nor sitteth in the seat of the scornful:
2 But his delight *is* in the law of the LORD; and in his law doth he meditate day and night.
3 And he shall be like a tree planted by the rivers of water, that bringeth forth his fruit in his season; his leaf also shall not wither; and whatsoever he doeth shall prosper.
4 The ungodly *are* not so: but *are* like the chaff which the wind driveth away.
5 Therefore the ungodly shall not stand

PSALM 1.
a Pro. 4. 14.
1 Or, wicked.
2 fade.
b Gen. 39. 3.
Job 22. 21.
1 Tim. 4. 8.
c John 10. 14.
2 Tim 3.19.

PSALM 2.
1 Or, tumultuously assemble.
2 meditate.
a Ps. 45. 7.
John 1. 41.
b Lu. 19. 14.
c Ps. 11. 4.

in the judgment, nor sinners in the congregation of the righteous.
6 For the LORD knoweth the way of the righteous: but the way of the ungodly shall perish.

PSALM II.

1 *Kingdom of Christ;* 10 *kings and judges exhorted to accept of it.*

WHY do the heathen rage, and the people imagine a vain thing?
2 The kings of the earth set themselves, and the rulers take counsel together, against the LORD, and against his Anointed, *saying,*
3 Let us break their bands asunder, and cast away their cords from us.
4 He that sitteth in the heavens shall laugh: the LORD shall have them in derision.

has seventeen such rows. shut up—Firmly closed together. A musket ball cannot penetrate him, save in the eye, throat, and belly. 18. *Transl.*, "his sneezing causeth a light to shine." Amphibious animals, emerging after having long held their breath under water, respire by violently expelling the breath like one sneezing: in the effort the eyes which are usually direc ed towards the sun. seem to flash fire: or it is the expelled *breath* that, in the sun, seems to emit light. eyelids of morning—The Egyptian hieroglyphics paint the *eyes of the crocodile* as the symbol for *morning*, because the eyes appear the first thing, before the whole body emerges from the deep. [HOR. HIEROG., 1. 65. BO.] 19. burning lamps—*Torches*, viz., in res iring (v. 18,) *seem* to go out. 20. seething—Boiling: *lit.*, *blown under*, under which a fire is blown. 21. kindl th coa s—Poetical imagery (Ps. 18. 8.). 22. remaineth—Abideth permanently. His chief strength is in the neck. sorrow—Anxiety or dismay personified. is turned into joy—Rather, *danceth, exulteth*; wherever he goes, he spreads terror "before him." 23. flakes—Rather, dewlaps. That which *falls* down (*Marg.*). They are "joined" *fast and firm*, together, not *hanging loose*, as in the ox. are firm—UMBR. and MAUR. "Are spread." In themselves—Rather, *upon him.* 24. heart — Bo.. "In large beasts which are less acute in feeling. there is great firmness of the *heart*, and slower motion." [BO.] The nether millstone, on which the upper turns, is especially hard. 25. he—The crocodile: a type of the awe which the Creator inspires, when He rises in wrath. breakings—viz., of the mind, *i.e.*, terror. purify themselves—Rather, *they wander from the way*, *i.e.*, flee away bewildered. [MAUR. & UMBR.] 26. cannot hold —On his hard skin. habergeon—Coat of mail: *avail* must be taken by Zeugma out of "hold," as the verb in the second clause: "hold" cannot apply to the "coat of mail." 27. iron . . . brass—viz., weapons. 28. arrow —*Lit., son of the bow;* Oriental imagery, (Lam. 3. 13; *Marg.*) stubble—Arrows produce no more effect. than it would to throw stubble at him. 29. darts—Rather, *clubs*; darts have been already mentioned. 30. stones—Rather, *potsherds, i.e.,* the sharp and pointed scales on the belly, like broken pieces of pottery. sharp-pointed things — Rather, *a threshing instrument,* but not on the *fruits* of the earth, but "on the *mire;"* irony. When he lies on the mire, he leaves the marks of his scales so imprinted on it, that one might fancy a threshing instrument with its sharp teeth had been drawn over it (Isa. 28. 27.. 31. Whenever he moves, sea—The Nile Isa. 19. 5; Nah. 3. 8,) pot of ointment—The vessel in which it is mixed. Appropriate to the crocodile, which emits a musky smell. 32. path—The foam on his tr ck. ho ry—As hair of the aged. 33. who —Being one who, &c. 34. beholdeth — As their superior. children of pride—The proud and fierce beasts. So ch. 28. 8; *Heb., sons of pride.* To humble the *pride* of man, and to teach implicit submission, is the aim of Jehovah's speech, and of the book: therefore with this as to leviathan, the type of God in His Lordship over creation, he closes.

CHAPTER XLII.

Ver. 1-6. JOB'S PENITENT REPLY. 2. In the first clause he owns God to be omnipotent over nature, as contrasted with his own feebleness, which God had proved ch. 40. 15; 41. 34, ; in the second, that God is supremely just, which, in order to be governor of the world, He must needs be, in all His dealings, as contrasted with his own vileness (v. 6, , and incompetence to deal with the wicked as a just judge (ch. 40. 8-14.). thought—*Purpose*, as in ch. 17. 11; but it is usually applied to *evil devises* ch. 21. 27; Ps. 10. 2.): the ambiguous word is designedly chosen to express, that, whilst to Job's finite view, God's plans seem bad, to the All-wise One, they continue unhindered in their development, and will at last be seen to be as good as they are infinitely wise. No evil can emanate from the Parent of good (Ja. 1. 13, 17,: but it is His prerogative to overrule evil to good. 3. I am the man! Job in *God's own words* (ch. 38. 2,), expresses his deep and humble penitence. God's word concerning our guilt should be engraven on our hearts and form the ground-work of our confession. Most men in confessing sin pall ate, rather than confess. Job in omitting "by words" (ch. 38. 2,), goes even further than God's accusation. Not merely my *words*, but my whole thoughts and ways were "without knowledge." too wonderful—I rashly denied that thou hast any fixed plan in governing human affairs, merely because thy plan was "too wonderful" for my comprehension. 4. When I said, "Hear," &c., Job's *demand* (ch. 13. 22,), convicted him of being "without knowledge." God alone could speak thus to Job, not Job to God: therefore he quotes again God's words as the ground-work of retracting his own foolish words. 5. hearing of ear—(Ps. 18. 44, *Marg.*). *Hearing* and *Seeing* are often in antithesis (ch. 29. 11; Ps. 48. 8.). seeth—not God's *face* (Ex. 33. 20,), but his presence in the veil of a dark cloud (ch. 38. 1.). Job implies also that, besdes this literal *seeing*, he now saw spiritually what he had indistinctly taken on hearsay before God's infinite wisdom. He "now" proves this; he had seen in a *literal* sense before, at the beginning of God's speech. but he had not seen *spiritually* till "now" at its close. 6. myself — Rather, "I abhor," and retract *the rash speeches* I made against thee, v. 3, 4, [UMBR.]

7-17. EPILOGUE, in prose. 7. to Eliphaz—Because he was the foremost of the three friends: their speeches were but the echo of his. right — *Lit., well-grounded*, sure and true. Their spirit towards Job was unkindly, and to justify themselves in their unkindness they used false arguments ch. 13. 7,., (viz., that calamities always prove *peculiar* guilt); therefore, though it was "for God," they spake thus falsely. God "reproves" them, as Job said He would (ch. 13. 10.). like Job—Job had spoken rightly in relation to *them* and their argument, denying their *theory*, and the *fact* which they a leged, that he was peculiarly guilty and a hypocrite; but wrongly in relation to *God*, when he fell into the opposite extreme of almost denying *all* guilt. This extreme *he* has now repented of, and there ore God speaks of him as now altogether "right." 8. seven—See Introd.). The number offered by the Gentile prophet (Num. 23. 1,. Job plainly lived before the legal priesthood, &c. The patriarchs acted as priests for their families; and sometimes as praying mediators (Gen. 20. 17,), thus foreshadowing the true Mediator (1 Tim. 2. 5,, but sacrifice accompanies, and is the ground-work, on which the mediation rests, him — Rather, "His person (face) only" (Note 22. 30.). The "person" must be first accepted, before God can accept his offering and work (Gen. 4. 4,): *that* can be only through Jesus Christ. folly — impiety (ch. 1. 22; 2. 10.). 9. The forgiving spirit of Job foreshadows the love of Jesus Christ and of Christians, to enemies Mat. 5. 44; Luke, 23. 34; Acts 7. 60; 16. 21, 28, :0, 31.). 10. turned ... captivity—Proverbial for *restored*, or *amply indemnified him for all he had lost*. Ez. 16. 53; Ps. 14. 7; Hos. 6. 11.). Thus the future vindication of man, body and soul, against Satan (ch. 1. 9-12,), at the resurrection (ch. 19. 25-27,), has its earnest and adumbration in the temporal vindication of Job at last by Jehovah in person. th rice—So to the afflicted literal and spiritual Jerusalem (Isa. 40. 2; 60. 7; 61. 7; Zech. 9. 12.). As in Job's case, so in that of Jesus Christ, the glorious recompence follows the "intercession" for enemies (Is. 53. 12.). 11. It was Job's complaint in his misery that his "brethren," &c., were "estranged" from him ch. 19. 13,): these now return with the return of his prosperity (Pro. 14. 20; 19. 6, 7.): the true friend loveth at all times Pro. 17. 17; 18. 24,]. "Swallow-friends leave in the winter and return with the spring." [HENRY.] eat bread—in token of friendship (Ps. 41. 9.). piece of m ney—Presents are usual in visiting a man of rank in the E. especially after a calamity 2 Chron. 32 23.). Heb., *Kesita*. MAGEE transl., a *lamb*, (the medium of exchange then, before money was used, as it is in *Mary*. of Gen. 33. 19; Josh, 21. 32. But it is from the Arabic *Kasat*, "weighed out," [UMBR.] not coined; so Gen. 42. 35; 33. 19; cf. with Gen 23. 15, makes it likely it was equal to four shekels: *Heb. kashat*, "pure," viz., metal. The term, instead of the usual "shekel," &c., is a mark of antiquity. ring—whether for the nose or ear (Gen. 35. 4; Isa. 3. 21.). Much of the gold in the E., in the absence of banks, is in the shape of ornaments. 12. Probably by degrees, not all at once. 13. The same number as before ; pei haps by a second wife : in ch. 19. 17, his wife is last mentioned. 14. Names significant of his restored prosperity (Gen. 4, 25; 5. 29.). Jemima, *daylight*, after his "night" of calamity: but MAUR., "a dove." Kezia, *cassia*, an aromatic herb Ps. 45. 8 : instead of his offensive breath and ulcers. Keren-happuch, "horn of *stibium*," a paint with which females dyed their eye-lids; in contrast to his "horn defiled in the dust" (ch. 16. 15.). The names also imply the beauty of his daughters. 15. inherit nce among ... brethren—An unusual favour in the E. to daughters, who, in the Jewish law, only inherited, if there were no sons Num. 27. 8., a proof of wealth and unanimity. 16. LXX. make Job live 170 years after his calamity, and 240 in all. This would make him seventy at the time of his calamity, which added to 140 in *Heb.* text make up 210; little more than the age 205) of Terah, father of Abraham, perhaps his contemporary. Man's length of life gradually shortened till it reached three score and ten in Moses' time (Ps. 90. 10.). 16. sons' sons—A proof of Divine favour (Gen. 50. 23; Ps. 128. 6; Prov. 17. 6.). 17. full of days—*Fully sated and contented* with all the happiness that life could give him : Realizing what Eliphaz had painted as the lot of the godly (ch. 5. 26; Ps. 91. 16; Gen. 25. 8; 35. 29.. LXX. adds, "It is written, that he will rise again with those whom the Lord will raise up." Cf. Mat. 27. 52, 53, from which it perhaps was derived spuriously.

THE BOOK OF PSALMS.

INTRODUCTION.

THE Hebrew title of this book is [Tehilim] *Praises* or *Hymns*, for a leading feature in its contents is praise, though the word occurs in the title of only one Psalm (145). The Greek title (in the Septuagint, a translation made 200 years before Christ,) is *Psalmoi*, whence our word *Psalms*. This corresponds to the Hebrew word *Mizmor*, by which sixty-five Psalms are designated in their inscriptions, and which the Syriac, a language like the Hebrew, uses for the whole book. It means, as does also the Greek name, an ode, or song, whose singing is accompanied by an instrument, particularly the harp, cf. 1 Chr. 16. 4-8; 2 Chr, 5. 12, 13. To some Psalms, the Hebrew word (*shir*) a *song*, is prefixed. Paul seems to allude to all these terms in Eph. 5. 19, "singing ... in *Psalms, Hymns*, and Spiritual *Songs*."

TITLES.—To more than a hundred Psalms are prefixed inscriptions, which give one or more, (and in one case, 60th, all) of these particulars; the direction to the Musician, the name of the author, or the instrument, the style of the music or of the poetry, the subject or occasion. The authority of these inscriptions has been disputed by some writers. They say that the earliest translators, as the Greek and Syriac, evince a disregard for their authority, by variations from a proper translation of some, altering others, and, in several instances, supplying titles to Psalms which, in Hebrew, had none. It is also alleged, that the subject of a Psalm, as given in the title, is often inconsistent with its contents. But those translators have also varied from a right translation or many passages in the Bible, which all agree to be of good authority: and the alleged inconsistency may be shown, on more accurate investigation, not to exist. The admitted antiquity of these inscriptions, on the other hand, and even their obscurity, raise a presumption in their favour, while such preservers on a composition accord with the usages of that age and part of the world, cf. Is. 38 9.

"*The Chief Musician*" was the Superintendent of the Music, cf. 1 Chr. 15. 21, *Marg. To* prefixed to this, means, *pertaining* to in his official character. This Inscription is found in 53 Psalms, and is attached to Habakkuk's prayer, Ha. 3. The same Hebrew preposition is prefixed to the name of the author, and translated *of*, "as a Psalm *of* David," "*of* Asaph," etc., except that to "the sons *of* Korah," it is translated *for*, which is evidently wrong, as the usual direction " *to the chief Musician*" is given, and no other authorship intimated. On the apparent exception to this last remark, see following page, and Psalm 88, *title*. The explanations of other particulars in the titles will be given as they occur.

380 [1]

INTRODUCTION—PSALMS.

AUTHORS.—This book is usually called "The Psalms of David," he being the only author mentioned in the N. T., Lu. 20. 42, and his name appearing in more titles than that of any other writer. Besides about one-half of the Psalms in which it thus appears, the 2nd and 95th are ascribed to him, Acts 4. 25, and Heb. 4. 7. He was probably the author of many others which appear without a name. He used great efforts to beautify the worship of the Sanctuary. Among the 288 Levites he appointed for singing and performing instrumental Music, we find mentioned the "sons of Korah," 1 Chr. 9, 19; including Heman, 1 Chr. 6, 33-38; and also Asaph, 39-44; and Ethan, 15-19. God was doubtless pleased to endow these men with the inspiration of His Spirit, so that they used those poetic talents, which their connexion with the kindred art of Music had led them to cultivate, in the production of compositions like those of their King and patron. To Asaph are ascribed twelve Psalms; to the sons of Korah, eleven, including the 88th, which is also ascribed to Heman, (that being the only instance in which the name of the "son" (or descendant) is mentioned; and to Ethan, one. Solomon's name appears before the 72nd and 127th; and that of Moses before the 90th. Special questions respecting authorship will be explained as they arise.

CONTENTS.—As the book contains 150 independent compositions, it is not susceptible of any logical analysis. The Jews having divided it into five books, corresponding to the Five Books of Moses, (1st, 1-42; 2nd, 43-72; 3rd, 73-89; 4th, 90-106; 5th, 107-150,) many attempts have been made to discover, in this division, some critical or practical value, but in vain. Sundry efforts have been made to classify the Psalms by subject. That of "Angus's Bible Hand-Book" is perhaps the most useful, and is appended.

Still the Psalms have a form and character peculiar to themselves; and with individual diversities of style and subject, they all assimilate to that form, and together constitute a consistent system of moral truth. They are all poetical, and of that peculiar parallelism (Intro. to Poetical Books) which distinguished Hebrew Poetry. They are all lyrical, or songs adapted to Musical instruments, and all religious lyrics, or such as were designed to be used in the Sanctuary worship.

The distinguishing feature of the Psalms is their devotional character. Whether their matter be didactic, historical, prophetical, or practical, it is made the ground or subject of prayer, or praise, or both. The doctrines of theology and precepts of pure morality are here inculcated. God's nature, attributes, perfections, and works of creation, providence and grace, are unfolded. In the sublimest conceptions of the most exalted verse, His glorious supremacy over the principalities of Heaven, Earth, and Hell, and His holy, wise, and powerful control of all material and immaterial agencies, are celebrated. The great covenant of grace resting on the fundamental promise of a Redeemer, both alike the provisions of God's exhaustless mercy, is set forth in respect of the doctrines of Regeneration by the Spirit, Forgiveness of sins, Repentance toward God, and Faith toward Jesus Christ, while its glorious results, involving the Salvation of men from "the ends of the earth," are proclaimed in believing, prophetic prayer and thankful praise. The personal history of the authors, and especially David's, in its spiritual aspects, is that of God's people generally. Christian biography is edifying, only as it is truth illustrated in experience, such as God's Word and Spirit produce. It may be factitious in origin and of doubtful authenticity. But here the experience of the truly pious is detailed, under Divine influence, and "in words which the Holy Ghost" taught. The whole inner life of the pious man is laid open, and Christians of all ages have here the temptations, conflicts, perplexities, doubts, fears, penitent moanings, and overwhelming griefs on the one hand, and the joy and hope of pardoning mercy, the victory over the seductions of false-hearted flatterers, and deliverance from the power of Satan on the other, with which to compare their own spiritual exercises. Here, too, are the fruits of that sovereign mercy, so often sought in earnest prayer, and when found, so often sung in rapturous joy, exhibited by patience in adversity, moderation in prosperity, zeal for God's glory, love for man, justice to the oppressed, holy contempt for the proud, magnanimity towards enemies, faithfulness towards friends, delight in the prosperity of Zion, and believing prayer for her enlargement and perpetuity.

The historical summaries of the Psalms are richly instructive. God's choice of the patriarchs, the sufferings of the Israelites in Egypt, their exodus, temptations of God, rebellions and calamities in the Wilderness, settlement in Canaan, backslidings and reformations, furnish illustrations of God's providential government of His people, individually and collectively, tending to exalt His adorable grace and abase human pride. But the promises and prophecies connected with these summaries, and elsewhere presented in the Psalms, have a far wider reach, exhibiting the relations of the book to the great theme of promise and prophecy.

THE MESSIAH AND HIS KINGDOM.—David was God's chosen servant to rule His people, as the Head, at once, of the State and the Church, the lineal ancestor "according to the flesh," of His adorable Son, and His type, in His official relations, both in suffering and in triumph. Generally, David's trials by the ungodly depicted the trials of Christ, and his final success the success of Christ's kingdom. Typically, he uses language describing his feelings, which only finds its full meaning in the feelings of Christ. As such it is quoted and applied in the N. T. And further, in view of the great promise (2 Sam. 7) to him and his seed, to which such frequent reference is made in the Psalms, David was inspired to know, that though his earthly kingdom should perish, his spiritual would ever endure, in the power, beneficence, and glory of Christ's. In repeating and amplifying that promise, he speaks not only as a type, but "being a prophet, and knowing that God had sworn with an oath to him, that of the fruit of his loins, according to the flesh, he would raise up Christ to sit on his throne," he "foretold the sufferings of Christ and the glory that should follow. His incarnation, humiliating sorrows, persecution, and cruel death are disclosed in the plaintive cries of a despairing sufferer; and his resurrection and ascension, his eternal priesthood, his royal dignity, his prophetical office, the purchase and bestowal of the gifts of the Spirit, the conversion of the nations, the establishment, increase, and perpetuity of the Church, the end of time, and the blessedness of the righteous, who acknowledge, and the ruin of the wicked, who reject, this King in Zion, are predicted in the language of assured confidence and joy." While these great themes have supplied the people of God with a popular theology and a guide in religious experience and Christian morality, clothed in the language of devotion, they have provided an inspired liturgy in which the pious, of all creeds and sects, have, for nearly three thousand years, poured out their prayers and praises. The pious Jew, before the coming of Christ, mourned over the adversity, or celebrated the future glories, of Zion, in the words of her ancient king. Our Saviour, with his disciples, sung one of these hymns on the night on which he was betrayed; he took from one the words in which he uttered the dreadful sorrows of his soul, and died with those of another on his lips. Paul and Silas in the dungeon, primitive Christians in their covert places of worship, or the costly churches of a later day, and the scattered and feeble Christian flocks in the prevalence of

The Messiah's kingdom.   PSALMS III-VI.   *David's complaint in sickness.*

5 Then shall he speak unto them in his wrath, and ³vex them in his sore displeasure.
6 Yet have I ⁴set my King ⁵upon my holy hill of Zion.
7 I will declare ⁶the decree: the LORD hath said unto me, ᵈ Thou *art* my Son; this day have I begotten thee.
8 Ask ⁶of me, and I shall give *thee* the heathen *for* thine inheritance, and the uttermost parts of the earth *for* thy possession.
9 Thou ƒshalt break them with a rod of iron; thou shalt dash them in pieces like a potter's vessel.
10 Be wise now therefore, O ye kings; be instructed, ye judges of the earth.
11 Serve the LORD with fear, and rejoice with trembling.
12 Kiss ᵍthe Son, lest he be angry, and ye perish *from* the way, when his wrath is kindled but a little. Blessed *are* all they that put their trust in him.

PSALM III.
Security of God's protection.
A Psalm of David, when he fled from Absalom his son.

LORD, ᵃhow are they increased that trouble me? many *are* they that rise up against me.
2 Many *there be* which say of my soul, *There* ᵇ *is* no help for him in God. Selah.
3 But thou, O LORD, *art* a shield ᶜ for me; my glory, and ᵈthe lifter up of mine head.
4 I cried unto the LORD with my voice, and he heard me out of his holy hill. Selah.
5 I ᵈ laid me down and slept; I awaked; for the LORD sustained me.
6 I will not be afraid of ten thousands of people that have set *themselves* against me round about.
7 Arise, O LORD; save me, O my God: for thou hast smitten all mine enemies *upon* the cheek-bone; thou hast broken the teeth of the ungodly.
8 Salvation ᵉ *belongeth* unto the LORD: thy blessing *is* upon thy people. Selah.

PSALM IV.
1 *David prays for audience:* 2 *he reproves and exhorts his enemies.* 6 *Man's happiness in God's favour.*
To the ¹chief Musician on Neginoth, A Psalm of David.

HEAR me when I call, O God of my righteousness: thou hast enlarged me when *I was* in distress; ²have mercy upon me, and hear my prayer.
2 O ye sons of men, how long *will ye turn* my glory into shame? *how long* will ye love vanity, *and* seek after leasing? Selah.
3 But know that ᵃthe LORD hath set apart him that is godly for himself: the LORD will hear when I call unto him.
4 Stand ᵇin awe, and sin not: commune with your own heart upon your bed, and be still. Selah.
5 Offer ᶜthe sacrifices of righteousness, and ᵈput your trust in the LORD.
6 *There be* many that say, Who will show us *any* good? ᵉ LORD, lift thou up the light of thy countenance upon us.
7 Thou hast put gladness in my heart, more than in the time *that* their corn and their wine increased.
8 I will both lay me down in peace, and sleep: ƒ for thou, LORD, only makest me dwell in safety.

PSALM 2.
3 Or, trouble.
4 anointed.
5 upon Zion, the hill of my holiness.
6 Or, for a decree.
ᵈ Acts 13.33.
ᵉ Dan. 7. 13.
John 17.4.
John 19.15.
ƒRev. 12. 5.
ᵍJohn 5. 23.

PSALM 3.
ᵃ 2 Sam. 15. 12.
ᵇ 2 Sa. 16. 1.
1 Or, about.
ᶜPs. 27. 6.
ᵈLev. 26. 6.
Pro. 3. 24.
ᵉ Hos. 13. 4.

PSALM 4.
1 Or, overseer.
2 Or, be gracious unto me.
ᵃ 2 Tim. 2. 19.
2 Pet. 2. 9.
ᵇ Eph. 4. 26.
ᶜ Deu. 33. 19.
ᵈ Ps. 37. 3.
ᵉ Ps. 80, 3.
ƒDeu. 12. 10.

PSALM 5.
ᵃ Ps. 30. 5.
ᵇ Jer. 41. 4.
ᶜ Hab. 1. 13.
1 before thine eyes.
2 the man of blood and deceit.
ᵈ 1 Ki. 8. 29.
3 the temple of thy holiness.
4 those which observe me.
5 Or, stedfastness.
6 in his mouth, that is, in the mouth of any of them.
7 wickednesses.
8 Or, Make them guilty.
9 Or, from their counsels.
10 thou coverest over, or, protectest them.
11 crown him.

PSALM 6.
1 Or, upon the eighth.
ᵃ Hos. 5. 1.
ᵇ Ps. 90. 13.
2 Or, every night.
ᵈ Ps. 66. 19.

PSALM V.
1 *David prays, and professes constancy in prayer.* 4 *God favours not the wicked.* 7 *David prays unto God to guide him,* 10 *to destroy his enemies,* 11 *and to preserve the godly.*
To the chief Musician upon Nehiloth, A Psalm of David.

GIVE ear to my words, O LORD; consider my meditation.
2 Hearken unto the voice of my cry, my King, and my God: for unto thee will I pray.
3 My *a* voice shalt thou hear in the morning, O LORD; in the morning will I direct *my prayer* unto thee, and will look up.
4 For thou *art* not a God that ᵇ hath pleasure in wickedness: neither shall evil dwell with thee.
5 The ᶜfoolish shall not stand ¹in thy sight: thou hatest all workers of iniquity.
6 Thou shalt destroy them that speak leasing: the LORD will abhor ²the bloody and deceitful man.
7 But as for me, I will come *into* thy house in the multitude of thy mercy; *and* in thy fear will I worship ᵈtoward ³thy holy temple.
8 Lead me, O LORD, in thy righteousness because of ⁴mine enemies; make thy way straight before my face.
9 For *there is* no ⁵faithfulness ⁶in their mouth; their inward part *is* ⁷very wickedness; their throat *is* an open sepulchre; they flatter with their tongue.
10 ⁸ Destroy thou them, O God; let them fall ⁹by their own counsels; cast them out in the multitude of their transgressions; for they have rebelled against thee.
11 But let all those that put their trust in thee rejoice: let them ever shout for joy, because ¹⁰thou defendest them: let them also that love thy name be joyful in thee.
12 For thou, LORD, wilt bless the righteous; with favour wilt thou ¹¹compass him as *with* a shield.

PSALM VI.
1 *David's complaint in his sickness:* 8 *by faith he triumphs over his enemies.*
To the chief Musician on Neginoth ¹ upon Sheminith, A Psalm of David.

O LORD, rebuke me not in thine anger, neither chasten me in thy hot displeasure.
2 Have mercy upon me, O LORD; for I am weak: O LORD, ᵃheal me; for my bones are vexed.
3 My soul is also sore vexed; but thou, O LORD, ᵇ how long?
4 Return, O LORD, deliver my soul: oh save me for thy mercies' sake!
5 For ᶜin death *there is* no remembrance of thee: in the grave who shall give thee thanks?
6 I am weary with my groaning; ²all the night make I my bed to swim; I water my couch with my tears.
7 Mine eye is consumed because of grief; it waxeth old because of all mine enemies.
8 Depart from me, all ye workers of iniquity; for the LORD hath heard the voice of my weeping.
9 The LORD ᵈ hath heard my supplication; the LORD will receive my prayer.
10 Let all mine enemies be ashamed and sore vexed: let them return *and* be ashamed suddenly.

381

darkness and error through the middle ages, fed their faith and warmed their love with these consoling songs. Now, throughout the Christian world, in untold forms of version, paraphrase, and imitation, by Papists and Protestants, Prelatists and Presbyterians—Independents, Baptists, Methodists—men of all lands and all creeds, in public and private worship, God is still adored in the sentiments expressed in these venerable Psalms. From the tone of sorrow and suffering which pervade their earlier portions, we are gradually borne on amidst alternate conflicts and triumphs, mournful complaints and awakening confidence; as we approach the close the tones of sorrow grow feebler, and those of praise wax louder and stronger—till, in the exulting strains of the last Psalm, the chorus of earth mingles with the Hallelujahs of the multitude which no man can number, in the Sanctuary above.

Angus's or Bickersteth's arrangement may be profitably used as a guide for finding a Psalm on a special topic. It is a little modified, as follows:—

1. Didactic.—Good and bad men, Ps. 1, 5, 7, 9-12, 14, 15, 17, 24, 25, 32, 34, 36, 37, 50, 52, 53, 58, 73, 75, 84, 91, 92, 94, 112, 121, 125, 127, 128, 133.—God's Law, Ps. 19, 119.—Human life vain, Ps. 39, 49, 90.—Duty of Rulers, Ps. 82, 101.—2. Praise. (1) For God's goodness generally to Israel, Ps. 46, 48, 65, 66, 68, 76, 81, 85, 98, 105, 124, 126, 129, 135, 136, 149. (2) To Good Men, Ps. 23, 34, 36, 91, 100, 103, 107, 117, 121, 145, 146. (3) Mercies to Individuals, Ps. 9, 18, 22, 30, 40, 75, 103, 108, 116, 118, 138, 144. (4) For His attributes generally, Ps. 8, 19, 24, 29, 33, 47, 50, 65, 66, 76, 77, 93, 95-97, 99, 104, 111, 113 115, 134, 139, 147, 148, 1 0.—3. Devotional—expression of (1) Penitence, Ps. 6, 25, 32, 38, 51, 102, 130, 143; (2) Trust in trouble, Ps. 3, 16, 27, 31, 54, 56, 57, 61, 62, 71, 86. (3) Sorrow with Hope, Ps. 13, 22, 69, 77, 88—(4) Of Deep Distress, Ps. 4, 5, 11, 28, 41, 55, 59, 64, 70, 109, 120, 140, 141, 143—(5) Feelings when Deprived of Religious Privileges, Ps. 42, 43, 63, 84. (6) Desire for Help, Ps. 7, 17, 26, 35, 44, 60, 74, 79, 80, 83, 89, 94, 102, 129, 137. (7) Intercession, Ps. 20, 67, 1, 2, 132, 144.—4. Historical, Ps. 78, 105, 106.—5. Prophetical, Ps. 2, 16, 22, 40, 45, 68, 69, 72, 97, 110, 118.

Note.—The compiler of the following notes has omitted all references to authors as needlessly encumbering the commentary. He has had before him the works of Calvin, Scott, Poole, Ainsworth, Cobbin, Geier, Vatablus, Tholuck, J. H. Michaelis, Rosenmuller, and Alexander. To the two last named he has been particularly indebted for the parallel passages. He has made a free use of the views advanced by these authors, and claims no credit for any thing in the work except the conciseness united with fulness of exposition. Whoever attempts it will find it far easier to write a long commentary than a brief one.

PSALM I.

Ver. 1-6. The character and condition, and the present and future destiny of the pious and the wicked, are described and contrasted, teaching that true piety is the source of ultimate happiness, and sin, of misery. As this is a summary of the teachings of the whole book, this Psalm, whether designedly so placed or not, forms a suitable preface.

1. Blessed—*lit., oh, the happinesses*—an exclamation of strong emotion, as if resulting from reflecting on the subject. The use of the plural may denote fulness and variety (2 Chr. 9, 7. . counsel ... way ... seat—With their corresponding verbs, mark gradations of evil, as acting on the principles, cultivating the society, and permanently conforming to the conduct of the wicked, who are described by three terms, of which the last is indicative of the boldest impiety cf. Ps. 26. 4, 5; Jer. 15. 17.). 2. law—all of God's word then written, especially the books of Moses cf. Ps. 119. 1, 55, 97, &c.). 3. like a tree—Jer. 17. 7, 8. planted—settled, fast. by —or over. the rivers—canals for irrigation. shall prosper—*lit.,* make prosper, brings to perfection. The basis of this condition and character is given Ps. 32. 1. 4. not so—either as to conduct or happiness. like the chaff—which by eastern modes of winnowing against the wind, was utterly blown away. 5. stand in the judgment—be acquitted. They shall be driven from among the good (M. 25. 45, 46.). 6. knoweth the way—attends to and provides for them (Ps. 101. 6; Pr. 12. 10; Ho. 13. 5). way of the wicked—all their plans will end in disappointment and ruin (Ps. 37. 13; 146. 8; Prov. 4. 19.).

PSALM II.

Ver. 1-12. The number and authorship of this Psalm are stated (Acts. 4. 25 ; 13. 33.). Though the warlike events of David's reign may have suggested its imagery, the scenes depicted, and the subjects presented can only find a fulfilment in the history and character of Jesus Christ, to which, as above cited and Heb. 1. 5; 5. 5, the N.T. writers most distinctly testify. In a most animated and highly poetical style, the writer, in "four stanzas of three verses each," sets forth the inveterate and furious, though futile, hostility of men to God and His anointed, God's determination to carry out His purpose, that purpose as stated more fully by His Son, the establishment of the Mediatorial Kingdom, and the imminent danger of all who resist, and the blessing of all who welcome this mighty and triumphant king.

1. Why do the heathen, &c.—Beholding, in prophetic vision, the peoples and nations, as if in a tumultuous assembly, raging with a fury like the raging of the sea, designing to resist God's government, the writer breaks forth into an exclamation in which are mingled surprise at their folly, and indignation at their rebellion. heathen —nations generally, not as opposed to Jews. people—*or, lit.,* peoples, or races of men. 2. The kings and rulers lead on their subjects. set themselves—take a stand. take counsel—*lit.,* sit together, denoting their deliberation. anointed—*Heb.,* Messiah; *Gr.,* Christ Jo. 1. 41.). Anointing, as an emblem of the gifts of the Holy Spirit, was conferred on Prophets, Isa. 61. 1; Priests, Ex. 30. 30; and Kings, 1 Ki. 1. 39; 1 Sam. 10. 1; 16. 13. Hence this title well suited Him who holds all these offices, and was generally used by the Jews before His coming to denote Him (Dan. 9. 26.). While the prophet has in view men's opposition generally, he here depicts it in its culminating aspect, as seen in the events of Christ's great trial, Pilate and Herod, and the rulers of the Jews (Lu. 23. 1-25; M. 27. 1, with the furious mob are vividly pourtrayed. 3. The rebellious purposes of men are more distinctly announced by this representation of their avowal in words, as well as actions.

bands and cords—denote the restraints of government. 4. By a figure whose boldness is only allowable to an inspired writer, God's conduct and language in view of this opposition are now related. he that sitteth in the heavens—enthroned in quiet dignity cf. Ps. 29. 10; Isa. 40. 22). sh' ll laugh—in supreme contempt: their vain rage excites His derision. He is still the Lord, lit., Sovereign, though they rebel. 5. Then shall he speak— His righteous indignation as well as contempt is roused. For God to speak is for Him to act, for what He resolves He will do (Ps. 33. 9; Gen. 1. 3.). vex them—agitate or terrify them Ps. 83. 15. . 6. The purpose here declared, in its execution, involves their overthrow. yet—lit., and, in an adversative sense. I h ve set—anointed, or firmly placed, with allusion in the Heb., to "casting an image in a mould." The sense is not materially varied in either case. my king—appointed by me and for me Num. 27. 18,). on my holy hill of Zion—Zion, selected by David as the abode of the ark, and the seat of God's visible residence, as 1 Ki. 8. 1,) also of David, the head of the Church and nation, and type of Christ, was called holy, and the Church itself came to be thus named (Ps. 9. 11; 51. 18; 99. 2; Isa. 8. 18; 18. 7, &c.). 7. The king thus constituted declares the fundamental law of His kingdom, in the avowal of His Sonship, a relation, involving His universal dominion. this day have I begotten thee— as 2 Sam. 7. 14, "he shall be my son," is a solemn recognition of this relation. The interpretation of this passage to describe the inauguration of Christ as Mediatorial King, by no means impugns the Eternal Sonship of His divine nature. In Acts, 13. 33, Paul's quotation does not imply an application of this passage to the resurrection; for raised up in v. 32 is used in the sense of Acts, 2. 30; 3. 22, &c., to denote bringing him into being as a man: and not that of resurrection which it has, only when, as in v. 34, allusion is made to His death Ro. 1. 4, which says He was declared as to His divine nature to be the Son of God, by the resurrection, only teaches that that event manifested a truth already existing. A similar recognition of his Sonship is introduced Heb. 5. 5, by these words, and by others in M. 3. 17; 17. 5. 8. The hopes of the rebels are thus overthrown, and not only so, the kingdom they opposed is destined to be co-extensive with the earth. heathen—or nations (v. 1.). and the uttermost parts of the earth—Ps. 22. 27, denote universality. 9. His enemies shall be subject to His terrible power Job, 4. 9; 2 Th. 2. 8), as His people to His grace Ps. 110. 2, 3. . rod of iron —denotes severity Rev. 2. 27.'. a potter's vessel—when shivered cannot be mended, which will describe utter destruction. 10-12, kings... judges—for rulers generally (Ps. 148, 11., who have been leaders in rebellion should be examples of penitent submission, and with fear for His terrible judgments, mingled with trust in. His mercy, acknowledge—kiss—the authority of the Son. perish from the way—i.e., is suddenly and hopelessly. kindled but a little—or in a little time. put their trust in him—or take refuge in Him (Ps. 5. 11.). Men still cherish opposition to Christ in their hearts, and evince it in their lives. Their ruin, without such trust is inevitable (Heb. 10. 29, while their happiness in His favour is equally sure.

PSALM III.

Ver. 1-8. For the historical occasion mentioned, cf. 2 Sam. chs. 15-17. David in the midst of great distress, with filial confidence implores God's aid, and, anticipating relief, offers praise. 1. L rd . . . increased—The extent of the rebellion (2 Sam. chs. 15-13,) surprises and grieves him. 2. say of my soul—i.e., of me (cf. Ps. 25. 3, . This use of soul is common, perhaps it arose from regarding the soul as man's chief part. no help... in God—rejected by Him. This is the bitterest reproach for a pious man, and denotes a spirit of malignant triumph. Selah—This word is of very obscure meaning. It probably denotes rest or pause, both as to the music and singing. intimating something emphatic in the sentiment cf. Ps. 9. 16.. 3. But—lit., and Ps. 2. 6. . He repels the reproach by avowing his continued trust. shield — a favourite and often-used figure for protection. my glory— its source. lifter up of mine head—one who raises me from despondency. 4. cried . . . heard—Such has been my experience. The last verb denotes a gracious heaving or answering. out of (or from) his holy hill— Zion (Ps. 2. 6). His visible earthly residence. 5. the Lord sustained me—lit., will sustain me, as if his language or thought when he laid down and the reason of his composure. 6. ten thousands of people—or myriads, any very great number cf. 2 Sam. 16. 18. . 7. Arise, O Lord—God is figuratively represented as asleep to denote His apparent indifference Ps. 7. 6. . The use of cheek-bone and teeth represents his enemies as fierce, like wild beasts ready to devour (Ps. 27. 2), and smiting their cheek-bone 1 Ki. 22. 24,) denotes violence and insult. thou hast broken —God took his part, utterly depriving the enemy of power to injure. 8. An ascription of praise to a delivering God, whose favour is an efficient benefit.

PSALM IV.

Ver. 1-8. On Neginoth, i.e., Stringed Instruments, as the kind of musical accompaniment on other parts of title cf. Intr.). The historical occasion was probably the same as that of the foregoing. The writer, praying for further relief, admonishes his enemies of the vanity of attacking God's servant, exhorts them to repentance, and avows his confidence and peace in God's favour. 1. Hear—as Ps. 3. 4. God my righteousness — or my righteous God, as my holy hill Ps. 2. 6, who will act toward me on righteous principles. thou has enlarged— expresses relief afforded in opposition to distress, which is expressed by a word denoting straits or pressure. Past favour is a ground of hope for future. 2. Men of note or prominence (cf. 2 Chr. 21. 9, . turn my glory—or royal dignity. to shame— or reproach, vanity— a foolish and hopeless enterprise (Ps. 2. 1.). leasing—a lie. 3. godly—An object as well as subject of divine favour (cf. Ps. 105. 14. 15.). 4. stand in awe Eph. 4. 26, from Sept. be angry. Both clauses are qualified by not. 5. Not only repent, but manifest penitence by sacrifices of righteousness or righteous sacrifices, &c. 6, 7. Contrasts true with vain confidence. light of countenance—figure for favour Ps. 81. 16; 44. 3; Nu. 6. 26.). corn and wine—lit., new corn and wine. increased—an abundant harvest giving great joy (Isa. 9. 3.). 8. both lay me down, &c.—or, will lie down at once, and sleep in sure confidence and quiet repose (Ps. 3. 5.).

PSALM V.

Ver. 1-12. *Upon Nehiloth*—flutes or wind instruments. The writer begs to be heard, on the ground of God's regard for His covenant people, and true worshippers as contrasted with His holy hatred to the wicked. He prays for Divine guidance, on account of his watchful, malignant, and deceitful enemies; and also for their destruction, as being also God's enemies. At the same time he expresses his confidence that God will extend aid to His people.

1. meditation—moanings of that half-uttered form, to which deep feeling gives rise—groanings, as Rom. 8. 26, 27. 2. Hearken—incline 'the ear,' Ps. 10. 17) (cf. Ps. 61, 2)—give close attention. my cry—i.e., for help Ps. 31. 2; Jer. 8. 19.). my King—thus by covenant relation interested in my cause. 3. direct—lit., *set in order*, as the shewbread was placed or set in order Ex. 40. 23.). 4. For, &c.—God only regards sincere worshippers. evil—or the evil man. dwell—lodge, remain under protection. 5. foolish—vain-glorious and insolent. iniquity—especially such as denotes a negation, or defect, i.e., of moral principle. 6. leasing —a lie. the bloody . . . man—lit., *man of blood*—murderer. 7. But—as Ps. 2. 6, lit., and, house—(1 Chr. 9. 23, the tabernacle. temple — lit., *palace*, applied to God's residence, the Holy of Holies (1 Sam. 3. 3; 2 Sam. 22. 7;); the inner part of the tabernacle. toward — not in, the high priest alone was allowed to enter. 8. enemies— lit., *watchers* (Ps. 27. 11), hence special need of guidance. in thy righteousness—an attribute implying faithfulness in promises as well as threatenings. make thy way straight —i.e., make the way of providence plain. 9. The wicked are not reliable, because by nature full of wickedness, or lit., *wickednesses*, of every kind (Rom. 8. 7.). sepulchre—a dwelling-place of corruption, emitting moral putridness. flatter—or make smooth. their tongue—speaks deceitfully. 10. Destroy—or, condemn them to destruction as guilty. 11. defendest—(cf. *Marg.*). love thy name—thy manifested perfections (Ps. 9. 10.). 12. with favour—or acceptance, alluding to the favour shown to an acceptable offering and worshipper (Lev. 7. 18; 19. 7.). shield—(cf. Ps. 3. 3.).

PSALM VI.

Ver. 1-10. *On Neginoth* (cf. Ps. 4.) *upon Sheminith—the eighth*—an instrument for the *eighth* key—or, more probably, the *bass*, as it is contrasted with Alamoth (the treble, Ps. 46.) in 1 Chr. 15. 20, 21. In deep affliction the Psalmist appeals to God's mercy for relief from chastisement, which otherwise must destroy him, and thus disable him for God's service. Sure of a gracious answer, he triumphantly rebukes his foes.

1. He owns his ill desert in begging a relief from chastisement. 2. I am weak—as a wilted plant Isa. 24. 4.). my bones—the very frame. are vexed—(Ps. 2. 5.)—shaken with fear. 3. how long?—shall this be so (cf. Ps. 79. 5.). but—or, and. thou—the sentence is incomplete as expressive of strong emotion. 4. Return—i.e., to my relief—or, *turn*, as now having His face averted. for thy mercies' sake—to illustrate thy mercy. 5. (Cf. Ps. 115.

17, 18; Isa. 38. 18.). There is no incredulity as to a future state. The contrast is between this scene of life, and the grave or *sheol*, the unseen world of the dead. give . . . thanks—or, praise for mercies. 6. By a strong figure the abundance as well as intensity of grief is depicted. 7. consumed—or, has failed, denoting general debility (Ps. 13. 3; 38. 10.). waxeth old—or, dim. grief—mingled with indignation. 8, 9. Assured of God's hearing, he suddenly defies his enemies by an address indicating that he no longer fears them; 10. and knows they will be disappointed and in their turn (cf. v. 1) be terror-stricken or confounded.

PSALM VII.

Ver. 1-17. *Shiggaion*—a plaintive song or elegy. Though obscure in details, this title seems to intimate that the occasion of this Psalm was some event in David's persecution by Saul. He prays for relief, because he is innocent, and God will be glorified in his vindication. He thus passes to the celebration of God's righteous government, in defending the upright and punishing the wicked, whose malignant devices will result in their own ruin; and, confident of God's aid, closes with rejoicing.

1, 2. Though many enemies set upon him, one is singled out as prominent; and compared to a wild beast tearing his prey to pieces (cf. 1 Sam. 26. 19; 20. 1; 23. 23.). 3. if I have done this—i.e., the crime charged in the "words of Cush" (cf. 1 Sam. 24. 9.). 4. If I have injured my friend. yea, I have delivered, &c.—This makes a good sense, but interrupts the course of thought, and hence it is proposed to render—*if I have spoiled my enemy*—in either case cf. 1 Sam. 24. 4 17; 31. 8. 11. 5. This is the consequence, if such has been his conduct. mine honour—(cf. Ps. 3. 3; 4. 2,)—my personal and official dignity. 6. God is invoked as if hitherto careless of him (Ps. 3. 7; 9. 18.). rage—the most violent, like a flood rising over a river's banks. the judgment . . . commanded—or ordained ; a just decision. 7. compass thee—as those seeking justice. return thou on high — assume the judgment-seat, to be honoured as a just Ruler by them. 8. Though not claiming innocence in general, he can confidently do so in this case, and in demanding from the Judge of all the earth a judgment, he virtually asks acquittal. 9. the hearts and reins— the affections and motives of men, or the seat of them (cf. Ps. 16. 7; 26, 2,); as we use *heart* and *bosom* or *breast*. 10. defence—*lit.*, *shield* (Ps. 5. 12.). 11. judgeth—as v. 8. the wicked—though not expressed, is implied, for they alone are left as objects of anger, 12, 13. and here distinctly pointed out, though by changing the person, a very common mode of speech, one is selected as a representative of wicked men generally. The military figures are of obvious meaning. against the persecutors — some render "for burning," but the former is the best sense. Arrows for burning would be appropriate in besieging a town, not in warring against one man or a company in open fight. 14. The first clause expresses the general idea that wicked men labour to do evil, the others carry out the figure fully. 15, 16. 1 Sam. 18. 17; 31. 2, illustrates the statement whether alluded to or not. These verses are expository of v. 14, showing how the devices of the wicked end in disappointment, falsifying

David prayeth against his enemies. PSALMS VII–X. *God praised for his judgments.*

PSALM VII.

1 David prays against the malice of his enemies, professing his innocence: 10 by faith he sees his defence, and derides their vain enterprises.

Shiggaion of David, which he sang unto the LORD, concerning the words of Cush the Benjamite.

1 O LORD my God, in thee do I put my trust: save me from all them that persecute me, and deliver me;
2 Lest he tear my soul like a lion, rending it in pieces, while there is none to deliver.
3 O LORD my God, if I have done this; if there be iniquity in my hands;
4 If I have rewarded evil unto him that was at peace with me; (yea, I have delivered him that without cause is mine enemy;)
5 Let the enemy persecute my soul, and take it; yea, let him tread down my life upon the earth, and lay mine honour in the dust. Selah.
6 Arise, O LORD, in thine anger, lift up thyself, because of the rage of mine enemies; and awake for me to the judgment that thou hast commanded.
7 So shall the congregation of the people compass thee about: for their sakes therefore return thou on high.
8 The LORD shall judge the people: judge me, O LORD, according to my righteousness, and according to mine integrity that is in me.
9 Oh let the wickedness of the wicked come to an end; but establish the just: for the righteous God trieth the hearts and reins.
10 My defence is of God, which saveth the upright in heart.
11 God judgeth the righteous, and God is angry with the wicked every day.
12 If he turn not, he will whet his sword; he hath bent his bow, and made it ready.
13 He hath also prepared for him the instruments of death; he ordaineth his arrows against the persecutors.
14 Behold, he travaileth with iniquity, and hath conceived mischief, and brought forth falsehood.
15 He made a pit, and digged it, and is fallen into the ditch which he made.
16 His mischief shall return upon his own head, and his violent dealing shall come down upon his own pate.
17 I will praise the LORD according to his righteousness: and will sing praise to the name of the LORD most high.

PSALM VIII.

God's glory magnified by his works, and by his astonishing love to man.

To the chief Musician upon Gittith, A Psalm of David.

1 O LORD our Lord, how excellent is thy name in all the earth! who hast set thy glory above the heavens.
2 Out of the mouth of babes and sucklings hast thou ordained strength because of thine enemies, that thou mightest still the enemy and the avenger.
3 When I consider thy heavens, the work of thy fingers, the moon and the stars, which thou hast ordained;
4 What is man, that thou art mindful of him? and the son of man, that thou visitest him?
5 For thou hast made him a little lower than the angels, and hast crowned him with glory and honour.
6 Thou madest him to have dominion over the works of thy hands; thou hast put all things under his feet:
7 All sheep and oxen, yea, and the beasts of the field;
8 The fowl of the air, and the fish of the sea, and whatsoever passeth through the paths of the seas.
9 O LORD our Lord, how excellent is thy name in all the earth!

PSALM IX.

1 David praises God for executing judgment on his enemies; 11 he incites others to praise him; 13 He prays that he may have cause to praise him.

To the chief Musician upon Muth-labben, A Psalm of David.

1 I WILL praise thee, O LORD, with my whole heart; I will show forth all thy marvellous works.
2 I will be glad and rejoice in thee: I will sing praise to thy name, O thou Most High.
3 When mine enemies are turned back, they shall fall and perish at thy presence.
4 For thou hast maintained my right and my cause; thou satest in the throne judging 2 right.
5 Thou hast rebuked the heathen, thou hast destroyed the wicked, thou hast put out their name for ever and ever.
6 O thou enemy, destructions are come to a perpetual end; and thou hast destroyed cities; their memorial is perished with them.
7 But the LORD shall endure for ever: he hath prepared his throne for judgment;
8 And he shall judge the world in righteousness, he shall minister judgment to the people in uprightness.
9 The LORD also will be a refuge for the oppressed, a refuge in times of trouble.
10 And they that know thy name will put their trust in thee: for thou, LORD, hast not forsaken them that seek thee.
11 Sing praises to the LORD, which dwelleth in Zion: declare among the people his doings.
12 When he maketh inquisition for blood, he remembereth them: he forgetteth not the cry of the humble.
13 Have mercy upon me, O LORD; consider my trouble which I suffer of them that hate me, thou that liftest me up from the gates of death;
14 That I may show forth all thy praise in the gates of the daughter of Zion: I will rejoice in thy salvation.
15 The heathen are sunk down in the pit that they made: in the net which they hid is their own foot taken.
16 The LORD is known by the judgment which he executeth: the wicked is snared in the work of his own hands. Higgaion. Selah.
17 The wicked shall be turned into hell, and all the nations that forget God.
18 For the needy shall not alway be forgotten: the expectation of the poor shall not perish for ever.
19 Arise, O LORD; let not man prevail: let the heathen be judged in thy sight.
20 Put them in fear, O LORD; that the nations may know themselves to be but men. Selah.

PSALM X.

1 David complains to God of the outrage of the wicked: 12 he prays for redress: 16 he professes his confidence.

1 WHY standest thou afar off, O LORD? why hidest thou thyself in times of trouble?

God's Love to Man. PSALMS VIII, IX. *God Praised for His judgments.*

their expectations. 17. his righteousness— (Ps. 5. 8.). Thus illustrated in the defence of his servant and punishment of the wicked.

PSALM VIII.

Ver. 1-9. *Upon* or according to the *Gittith*, probably means that the musical performance was directed to be according to a tune of that name; which, derived from *Gath*, a wine-press, denotes a tune (used in connection with gathering the vintage) of a joyous character. All the Psalms to which this term is prefixed are of such a character. The Psalmist gives vent to his admiration of God's manifested perfections, by celebrating His condescending and beneficent providence to man as evinced by the position of the race, as originally created and assigned a dominion over the works of His hands.

1. thy name—perfections (Ps. 5. 11; 7. 17.). **who mast set—***lit.*, *which, set thou thy glory* &c., or, *which glory of thine set thou*, &c., *i.e.*, make it more conspicuous as if earth were too small a theatre for its display. A similar exposition suits the usual rendering. So manifest are God's perfections, that by very weak instruments, He conclusively sets forth His praise. Infants are not only wonderful illustrations of God's power and skill, in their physical constitution, instincts, and early developed intelligence, but also in their spontaneous admiration of God's works, by which they put to shame—s.il — or, silence men who rail and cavil against God. A special illustration of the passage is afforded in Mat. 21. 16, when our Saviour *stilled* the cavillers by quoting these words; for the glories with which God invested His incarnate Son, even in His humiliation, constitute a most wonderful display of the perfections of His wisdom, love, and power. In view of the scope of v. 4-8 see below, this quotation by our Saviour may be regarded as an exposition of the prophetical character of the words. **sucklings—**among the Hebrews were probably of an age to speak cf. 1 Sam. 1. 22-24; Mark, 7. 27.). **ordained—**founded, or prepared, and perfected, which occurs in Mat. 21. 16; taken from the *Sept.* has the same meaning. **strength—**In the quotation in the N.T., *praise* occurs as the consequence or effect put for the cause (cf. Ps. 118. 14.). **avenger—**as in Ps. 44. 16; one desirous of revenge, disposed to be quarrelsome, and so apt to cavil against God's government. **3, 4.** The allusion to the magnificence of the visible heavens is introduced for the purpose of illustrating God's condescension, who, though the mighty creator of these glorious worlds of light, makes man the object of regard and recipient of favour. **man—***lit. frail man*, an allusion to his essential infirmity. **son of man—**only varies the form of speech. **visitest—**in favour (Ps. 65. 10.). This favour is now more fully illustrated. **5-8.** God has placed man next in dignity to angels, and but a little lower, and crowned him with the empire of the world. glory and honour—are the attributes of royal dignity (Ps. 21. 5; 45. 3.). The position assumed in man is that described (Gen. 1. 26-28.) as belonging to Adam, in his original condition, the terms employed in detailing the subjects of man's dominion corresponding with those there used. In a modified sense, in his present fallen state, man is still invested with some remains of this original dominion. It is very evident, however, by the apostle's inspired

expositions (Heb. 2. 6-8; 1 Cor. 15. 27, 28, that the language here employed, finds its fulfilment only in the final exaltation of Christ's human nature. There is no limit to the "*all things*" mentioned, God only excepted, who "puts all things under." Man, in the person and glorious destiny of Jesus of Nazareth, the Second Adam, the head and representative of the race will not only be restored to his original position, but exalted far beyond it. "The last enemy, death," through fear of which, man, in his present estate, is "all his lifetime in bondage," "shall be destroyed." Then *all things* will have been put under his feet, "principalities and powers being made subject to him." This view, so far from being alien from the scope of the passage, is more consistent than any other; for man as a race cannot well be conceived to have a higher honour put upon him, than to be thus exalted in the person and destiny of Jesus of Nazareth. And at the same time, by no other of His glorious manifestations has God more illustriously declared those attributes which distinguish His name than in the scheme of redemption, of which this economy forms such an important and essential feature. In the generic import of the language, as describing man's present relation to the works of God's hands, it may be regarded as typical, thus allowing not only the usual application, but also this higher sense which the inspired writers of the N.T. have assigned it. **9.** Appropriately, the writer closes this brief but pregnant and sublime song of praise with the terms of admiration with which it was opened.

PSALM IX.

Ver. 1-20. *Upon Muth-labben*, or, *after the manner, according to* "*death to the Son*," by which some song was known, to whose air or melody the Musician is directed to perform this Psalm. This mode of denoting a song by some prominent word or words is still common cf. Ps. 22.). The Psalmist praises God for deliverance from his enemies, and celebrates the divine government, for providing security to God's people and punishment to the wicked. Thus encouraging himself, he prays for new occasions to recount God's mercies, and confident of His continued judgment on the wicked and vindication of the oppressed, he implores a prompt and efficient manifestation of the divine sovereignty.

1. Heart-felt gratitude will find utterance. **3-5.** When . . . are turned back—it is the result of God's power alone. He, as a righteous judge (Ps. 7. 11,), vindicates His people. He rebukes by acts as well as words (Ps. 6. 1; 18. 15,), and so effectually as to destroy the names of nations as well as persons. **6.** *Lit.*, *As to the enemy finished are his ruins for ever. Thou* (God) *hast destroyed*, &c. 1 Sam. 15. 3, 7; 27. 8, 9. The wicked are utterly undone. Their ruins shall never be repaired. **7, 8.** God's eternal possession of a throne of justice is contrasted with the ruin of the wicked. **9, 10.** So that the oppressed, and all who know Him (Ps. 5, 3; 7. 1,), find Him a sure refuge. **11.** Cf. Ps. 2. 6; 3. 4. **12.** for blood—*i.e.*, murders (Ps. 5. 6,), including all the oppressions of His people. n aketh inquisition—cf. Gen. 9. 5.). He will avenge their cause. **13.** gates—or, regions—of (e.g., the gates being the entrance) is put for the bounds. **14.** gates . . . Zion—the enclosure of the city (cf.

David complains of the wicked. PSALMS XI–XIV. *David craveth help of God.*

2 ¹ The wicked in *his* pride doth persecute the poor: let them be taken in the devices that they have imagined.
3 For the wicked boasteth of his ² heart's desire, and ³ blesseth the covetous, *whom* the LORD abhorreth.
4 The wicked, through the pride of his countenance, will not seek *after God:* ⁴ God *is* not in all his thoughts.
5 His ways are always grievous; thy judgments *are* far above out of his sight: *as for* all his enemies, he puffeth at them.
6 He hath said in his heart, I shall not be moved: for *I shall* ⁵ never be in adversity.
7 His mouth is full of cursing and ⁶ deceit and fraud: under his tongue *is* mischief and ⁷ vanity.
8 He sitteth in the lurking-places of the villages; in the secret places doth he murder the innocent: his eyes ⁸ are privily set against the poor.
9 He lieth in wait ⁹ secretly as a lion in his den: he lieth in wait to catch the poor: he doth catch the poor, when he draweth him into his net.
10 ¹⁰ He croucheth, *and* humbleth himself, that the poor may fall ¹¹ by his strong ones.
11 He hath said in his heart, God hath forgotten: he hideth his face; he will never see *it.*
12 Arise, O LORD; O God, lift up thine hand: forget not the ¹² humble.
13 Wherefore doth the wicked contemn God? he hath said in his heart, Thou wilt not require *it.*
14 Thou hast seen *it;* for thou beholdest mischief and spite, to requite *it* with thy hand: the poor ¹³ committeth himself unto thee; thou art the helper of the fatherless.
15 Break thou the arm of the wicked and the evil *man:* seek out his wickedness *till* thou find none.
16 The LORD *is* King for ever and ever: the heathen are perished out of his land.
17 LORD, thou hast heard the desire of the humble: thou wilt ¹⁴ prepare their heart, thou wilt cause thine ear to hear;
18 To judge the fatherless and the oppressed, that the man of the earth may no more ¹⁵ oppress.

PSALM XI.

1 *David encourageth himself in God against his enemies; 4 he rejoices in the providence and justice of God.*

To the chief Musician, *A* Psalm of David.

IN the LORD put I my trust: how say ye to my soul, Flee *as* a bird to your mountain?
2 For, lo, the wicked bend *their* bow, they make ready their arrow upon the string, that they may ¹ privily shoot at the upright in heart.
3 If the foundations be destroyed, what can the righteous do?
4 The ᵃ LORD *is* in his holy temple, the LORD's throne *is* in heaven: his eyes ᵇ behold, his eye-lids try, the children of men.
5 The LORD ᶜ trieth the righteous: but the wicked and him that loveth violence his soul hateth.
6 Upon the wicked he shall rain ² snares, fire and brimstone, and ³ an horrible tempest: *this shall be* the portion of their cup.
7 For the righteous LORD loveth righteousness; his countenance doth behold the upright.

PSALM 10.
¹ In the pride of the wicked he doth persecute.
² soul's.
³ Or, the covetous blesseth himself, he abhorreth the LORD.
⁴ Or, all his thoughts are, There is no God.
⁵ unto generation and generation.
⁶ deceits.
⁷ Or, iniquity.
⁸ hide themselves.
⁹ in the secret places.
¹⁰ He breaketh himself.
¹¹ Or, into his strong parts.
¹² Or, afflicted.
¹³ cleaveth.
¹⁴ Or, establish.
¹⁵ Or, terrify.

PSALM 11.
¹ in darkness.
ᵃ Hab. 2. 20.
ᵇ Heb. 4. 13.
ᶜ Gen. 22. 1. Jam. 1. 12.
² Or, quick burning coals.
³ Or, a burning tempest.

PSALM 12.
¹ Or, upon the eighth.
² Or, Save.
³ an heart and an heart.
⁴ great things.
⁵ are with us.
⁶ Or, would ensnare him.
⁷ him: that is, every one of them.
⁸ of the sons of men.

PSALM 13.
¹ Or, overseer.
ᵃ Deut. 31. 17.
ᵇ Ezra 9. 8.
ᶜ Jer. 51. 39.

PSALM 14.
ᵃ Ps. 10. 4.
¹ stinking.
² they feared a fear.
³ Who will give.

PSALM XII.

1 *David, destitute of human comfort, craves help of God; 3 God's judgments on the wicked, 6 his promises to protect the righteous.*

To the chief Musician ¹ upon Sheminith, A Psalm of David.

HELP, ² LORD; for the godly man ceaseth; for the faithful fail from among the children of men.
2 They speak vanity every one with his neighbour: *with* flattering lips, *and* with ³ a double heart, do they speak.
3 The LORD shall cut off all flattering lips, *and* the tongue that speaketh ⁴ proud things:
4 Who have said, With our tongue will we prevail; our lips ⁵ *are* our own: who *is* lord over us?
5 For the oppression of the poor, for the sighing of the needy, now will I arise, saith the LORD; I will set *him* in safety *from him that* ⁶ puffeth at him.
6 The words of the LORD *are* pure words: *as* silver tried in a furnace of earth, purified seven times.
7 Thou shalt keep them, O LORD, thou shalt preserve ⁷ them from this generation for ever.
8 The wicked walk on every side, when the vilest ⁸ men are exalted.

PSALM XIII.

1 *David craves help of God; 3 he prays God to support him, that his enemies may not insult over him; 5 he trusts in the divine mercy.*

To the ¹ chief Musician, A Psalm of David.

HOW long wilt thou forget me, O LORD? for ever? ᵃ how long wilt thou hide thy face from me?
2 How long shall I take counsel in my soul, *having* sorrow in my heart daily? how long shall mine enemy be exalted over me?
3 Consider *and* hear me, O LORD my God: lighten ᵇ mine eyes, ᶜ lest I sleep the *sleep of* death;
4 Lest mine enemy say, I have prevailed against him; *and* those that trouble me rejoice when I am moved.
5 But I have trusted in thy mercy; my heart shall rejoice in thy salvation.
6 I will sing unto the LORD, because he hath dealt bountifully with me.

PSALM XIV.

1 *David describes the general corruption of mankind; 4 the iniquity of the wicked; 7 he prays for God's salvation.*

To the chief Musician, *A* Psalm of David.

THE ᵃ fool hath said in his heart, *There is* no God. They are corrupt; they have done abominable works; *there is* none that doeth good.
2 The LORD looked down from heaven upon the children of men, to see if there were any that did understand, *and* seek God.
3 They are all gone aside, they are all together ¹ filthy; *there is* none that doeth good, no, not one.
4 Have all the workers of iniquity no knowledge? who eat up my people *as* they eat bread, and call not upon the LORD.
5 There ² were they in great fear: for God *is* in the generation of the righteous.
6 Ye have shamed the counsel of the poor, because the LORD *is* his refuge.
7 Oh that the salvation of Israel were come out of Zion! when the LORD bringeth back the captivity of his people, Jacob shall rejoice, *and* Israel shall be glad.

Ps. 48. 12; Isa. 23. 12,) or, church, as denoted by this phrase contrasted with that of death, carries out the idea of exaltation as well as deliverance. Signal favours should lead us to render signal and public thanks. **15, 16.** The undesigned results of the devices of the wicked prove them to be of God's overruling or ordering, especially when those results are destructive to the wicked themselves. Higgaion — means meditation, and, combined with Selah, seems to denote a pause of unusual solemnity and emphasis (cf. Ps. 3. 2.). Though Selah occurs seventy-three times, this is the only case in which Higgaion is found. In the view which is given here of the retribution on the wicked as an instance of God's wise and holy ordering, we may well pause in adoring wonder and faith. **17.** shall be turned—or, shall turn, retreating under God's vengeance, and driven by Him to the extreme of destruction, even hell itself. Those who forget God are classed with the depraved and openly profane. **18.** (Cf. Ps. 13.) *the needy—lit., poor*, as deprived of anything; hence miserable. **expectation** of the poor—or, meek, humble made so by affliction. **19. Arise**—(cf. Ps. 3. 7.). let not man— Ps. 9. 4.). let ... be judged —and of course condemned. **20.** By their effectual subjection, make them to realise their frail nature (Ps. 8. 4.), and deter them from all conceit and future rebellion.

PSALM X.

Ver. 1-18. The Psalmist mourns God's apparent indifference to his troubles, which are aggravated by the successful malice, blasphemy, pride, deceit, and profanity of the wicked. On the just and discriminating providence of God, he relies for the destruction of their false security, and the defence of the needy.

1. These are, of course, figurative terms (cf. Ps. 7. 6; 13. 1; &c.). hidest—supply *thine eyes or face*. **2.** *Lit., In pride of the wicked they* (the poor or humble, v. 17; Ps. 12. 5, *shall be taken in the devices they* (the proud *have imagined*). **3.** his heart's (or *soul's*) desire— *i.e.*, his success in evil, and blesseth, &c.—he (the wicked) *blesseth the covetous, he despiseth the Lord*. **4.** The face expresses the self-conceit, whose fruit is practical atheism (Ps. 14. 1.). **5, 6.** Such is his confidence in the permanence of his way or course of life, that he disregards God's providential government, *(out of sight*, because he will not look, Isa. 26. 11.), sneers at his enemies, and boasts perpetual freedom from evil. **7-10.** The malignity, and deceit (Ps. 140. 3.), of such are followed by acts combining cunning, fraud, and violence cf. Pro. 1. 11, 18,), aptly illustrated by the habits of the lion, and of hunters taking their prey. *Poor* in v. 8, 10, 14, represents a word peculiar to this Psalm, meaning the sad or sorrowful; in v. 9, as usual, it means the pious or meek sufferer. eyes ...)r vily set—he watches with half-closed eyes, appearing not to see. croucheth —as a lion gathers himself into as small compass as possible to make the greater spring. fall by his strong ones—the figure of the lion is dropped, and this phrase means the accomplices of the chief or leading wicked man. **11.** As before, such conduct implies disbelief or disregard of God's government. 12. Cf. Ps. 9. 19; 3. 7.). hu able— cf. v. 17, and *Marg.*. lift up thine hand—exert thy power. **13, 14.** It is in vain to suppose God will overlook sin, however forbearing; for He carefully examines or beholds all wickedness, and will mark it by His providential *(thy hand* punishment. mischief and spite—provocation and trouble of the sufferer cf. Ps. 6. 7;7. 14.). committeth—or leaves (his burden) on thee. **15. arm**—power. til then find none—so far from not requiring r 11. 13.), God will utterly destroy the wicked and his deeds Ps. 9. 5, 6; 34. 16; 37. 36,. **16 18.** God reigns. The wicked, if for a time successful, shall be cut off. He hears, a. d confir us the hearts of His suffering people (Ps. 112. 7.), executes justice for the feeble, and represses the pride and violence of conceited though frail men (cf. Ps. 9. 16.).

PSALM XI.

Ver. 1-7. On title cf. *Intr*. Alluding to some event in his history, as 1 Sam. 23. 13, the Psalmist avows his confidence in God, when admonished to flee from his raging persecutors, whose destruction of the usual foundations of safety rendered all his efforts useless. The grounds of his confidence are God's supreme dominion, His watchful care of His people, His :atred to the wicked, and judgments on them, and His love for righteousness and the righteous.

1. my soul—me (Ps. 3. 2.). **Flee**—*lit., flee ye; i.e.*, he and his companion. as a bird to your mountain—having as such no safety but in flight (cf. 1 Sam. 26. 20; Lam. 3. 52.). **2. privily** —*lit., in darkness*, treacherously. **3.** *Lit., The foundations* (*i.e., of good order and law,) will be destroyed, what has the righteous done* (to sustain them)? All his efforts have failed. **4. temple** ... heaven—the connection seems to denote God's heavenly residence; the term used is taken from the place of His visible earthly abode (Ps. 2. 6; 3. 4; 5. 7.). Thence He inspects men with close scrutiny. **5.** The trial of the righteous results in their approval, as it is contrasted with God's hatred to the wicked. **6.** Their punishment is described by vivid figures denoting abundant, sudden, furious, and utter destruction (cf. Gen. 19. 24; Job, 18. 15; Ps. 7. 15; 9. 15.). **cup** —is a frequent figure for God's favour or wrath (Ps. 11. 5; 23. 5; Mat. 20. 22, 23.) **7.** his countenance—*lit., their faces*—a use of the plural applied to God, like Gen. 1. 26; 3. 22; 11. 7; Isa. 6. 8, &c., denoting the fulness of His perfections, or more probably originating in a reference to the trinity of persons. Faces is used as eyes, (v. 4), expressing here God's complacency towards the upright, (cf. Ps. 34. 15, 16.).

PSALM XII.

Ver. 1-8. On title cf. *Intr*. and Ps. 6. The Psalmist laments the decrease of good men. The pride and deceit of the wicked provokes God's wrath, whose promise to avenge the cause of pious sufferers will be verified even amidst prevailing iniquity.

1. the faithful—or *lit., faithfulness* Ps. 31. 23.). **2.** The want of it is illustrated by the prevalence of deceit and instability. **3, 4.** Boasting (Dan. 7. 25. is, like flattery, a species of lying, lips and ... tongue—for persons. **5.** The writer intimates his confidence by depicting God's actions cf. Ps. 9. 19; 10. 12,' as coming to save the poor at whom the wicked sneers Ps. 10. 5.). **6.** The words—*lit., saying of v. 5.*), seven times—thoroughly Dan. 3 19.). **7. them**—*Marg.*. **8.** The wicked roam undisturbed, doing evil, when vileness or vile men are exalted.

PSALM XV.
David describes a citizen of Zion.
A Psalm of David.

LORD, who shall [1] abide in thy tabernacle? who shall dwell [a] in thy holy hill?
2 He [b] that walketh uprightly, and worketh righteousness, and speaketh the truth in his heart.
3 *He that* backbiteth not with his tongue, nor doeth evil to his neighbour, nor [2] taketh up a reproach against his neighbour.
4 In whose eyes a vile person is contemned; but he honoureth them that fear the LORD. *He that* [c] sweareth to *his own* hurt, and changeth not.
5 *He* [d] *that* putteth not out his money to usury, nor taketh reward against the innocent. He that doeth these *things* shall never be moved.

PSALM XVI.
1 *David, in distrust of merit, and hatred of idolatry, flees to God for preservation;* 5 *he shows the hope of his calling, of the resurrection, and life everlasting.*

1 Michtam of David.

PRESERVE me, O God: [a] for in thee do I put my trust.
2 *O my soul,* thou hast said unto the LORD, Thou *art* my Lord: my goodness *extendeth* not to thee;
3 *But* to the saints that *are* in the earth, and to the excellent, in whom *is* all my delight.
4 Their sorrows shall be multiplied *that* [2] hasten *after* another *god*: their drink offerings of blood will I not offer, nor take up their names into my lips.
5 The LORD *is* the portion [3] of mine inheritance and of my cup: thou maintainest my lot.
6 The lines are fallen unto me in pleasant *places;* yea, I have a goodly heritage.
7 I will bless the LORD, who hath given me counsel; my reins also instruct me in the night seasons.
8 I have set the LORD always before me: because *he is* at my right hand, I shall not be moved.
9 Therefore my heart is glad, and my glory rejoiceth: my flesh also shall [4] rest in hope.
10 For [b] thou wilt not leave [c] my soul in hell; neither wilt thou suffer thine [d] Holy One to see corruption.
11 Thou wilt show me the path of life: in thy presence *is* fulness of joy; at thy right hand *there are* pleasures for evermore.

PSALM XVII.
1 *David prays to God to be saved from his enemies;* 10 *he shows their pride, craft, and eagerness;* 13 *he prays against them in confidence of his hope.*

A Prayer of David.

HEAR [1] the right, O LORD, attend unto my cry, give ear unto my prayer, *that* goeth [2] not out of feigned lips.
2 Let my sentence come forth from thy presence; let thine eyes behold the things that are equal.
3 Thou hast proved mine heart; thou hast visited me in the night; thou hast tried me, *and* shalt find nothing: I am purposed *that* my mouth shall not transgress.
4 Concerning the works of men, by the word of thy lips I have kept *me* from the paths of the destroyer.
5 Hold up my goings in thy paths, *that* my footsteps [3] slip not.

PSALM 15.
1 sojourn.
a Ps. 2. 6.
b Is. 33. 16.
2 Or, receiveth, or, endureth.
c Judg. 11. 35.
d Ezek. 18. 8

PSALM 16.
1 Or, a golden Psalm.
a Ps. 25. 20.
2 Or, give gifts to another.
3 of my part.
4 dwell confidently.
b Ps. 49. 15.
Acts 2. 27.
Acts 13. 35.
c Lev. 19. 29. Nu. 6. 6.
d Dan. 9. 24. Luke 1. 35.

PSALM 17.
1 justice.
2 without lips of deceit.
3 be not moved.
4 Or, that savest them which trust in thee from those that rise up against thy right hand.
5 that waste me.
6 my enemies against the soul.
7 The likeness of him, *that* is, of every one of them) is as a lion that desireth to ravin.
8 sitting.
9 prevent his face.
10 Or, by thy sword.
11 Or, their children are full.
a 1 John 3.2.
b Col. 1. 15.

PSALM 18.
a 2 Sam. 22.
b Ps. 144. 1.
c my rock.
d Heb. 2. 13.
d Ps. 76. 4.
e Ps. 116. 3.
2 Belial.
3 Or, cords.
f Acts 4. 31.
4 by his.
g Is. 64. 1.
h Ps. 99. 1.
i Ps. 104. 3.
j Ps. 97. 2.

6 I have called upon thee, for thou wilt hear me, O God: incline thine ear unto me, *and* hear my speech.
7 Show thy marvellous loving-kindness, O thou [4] *that* savest by thy right hand them which put their trust in *thee* from those that rise up *against them.*
8 Keep me as the apple of the eye; hide me under the shadow of thy wings,
9 From the wicked [5] that oppress me, *from* [6] my deadly enemies, *who* compass me about.
10 They are inclosed in their own fat: with their mouth they speak proudly.
11 They have now compassed us in our steps; they have set their eyes bowing down to the earth;
12 [7] Like as a lion *that* is greedy of his prey, and as it were a young lion [8] lurking in secret places.
13 Arise, O LORD, [9] disappoint him, cast him down: deliver my soul from the wicked, [10] which *is* thy sword:
14 From men *which are* thy hand, O LORD, from men of the world, *which have* their portion in *this* life, and whose belly thou fillest with thy hid *treasure:* [11] they are full of children, and leave the rest of their *substance* to their babes.
15 As for me, [a] I will behold thy face in righteousness: I shall be satisfied, when I awake, with [b] thy likeness.

PSALM XVIII.
David's psalm of thanksgiving for God's manifold and marvellous blessings.

To the chief Musician, A Psalm of David the servant of the LORD, who spake unto the LORD the words of [a] this song in the day *that* the LORD delivered him from the hand of all his enemies, and from the hand of Saul: And he said,

I [b] WILL love thee, O LORD, my strength.
2 The LORD *is* my rock, and my fortress, and my deliverer; my God, [1] my strength, [c] in whom I will trust; my buckler, and the horn of my salvation, *and* my high tower.
3 I will call upon the LORD, [d] *who is* worthy to be praised: so shall I be saved from mine enemies.
4 The [e] sorrows of death compassed me, and the floods of [2] ungodly men made me afraid.
5 The [3] sorrows of hell compassed me about; the snares of death prevented me.
6 In my distress I called upon the LORD, and cried unto my God: he heard my voice out of his temple, and my cry came before him, *even* into his ears.
7 Then [f] the earth shook and trembled; the foundations also of the hills moved and were shaken, because he was wroth.
8 There went up a smoke [4] out of his nostrils, and fire out of his mouth devoured: coals were kindled by it.
9 He [g] bowed the heavens also, and came down: and darkness *was* under his feet.
10 And [h] he rode upon a cherub, and did fly; yea, [i] he did fly upon the wings of the wind.
11 He made darkness his secret place; his [j] pavilion round about him *were* dark waters *and* thick clouds of the skies.
12 At the brightness *that was* before him his thick clouds passed, hail *stones* and coals of fire.

PSALM XIII.

Ver. 1-6. On title cf. *Intr.* The Psalmist, mourning God's absence and the triumph of his enemies, prays for relief ere he is totally destroyed, and is encouraged to hope his trust will not be in vain.

1. The forms of expression and figure here used are frequent (cf. Ps. 9. 12, 18; 10. 11, 12.). How long . . . for ever—shall it be for ever? 2. The counsels or devices of his heart afford no relief. 3. lighten mine eyes—dim with weakness, denoting approaching death (cf. 1Sam. 14. 27-29; Ps. 6. 7; 38. 10.) 4. rejoice—*lit.*, *shout as in triumph*. I am moved —cast down from a firm position (Ps. 10. 6.). 5, 6. Trust is followed by rejoicing in the deliverance which God effects, and, instead of his enemy, he can lift the song of triumph.

PSALM XIV.

Ver. 1-7. The practical atheism, and total and universal depravity, of the wicked, with their hatred to the good, are set forth. Yet, as they dread God's judgments when He vindicates His people, the Psalmist prays for His delivering power.

1. Sinners are termed *fools*, because they think and act contrary to right reason (Gen. 34. 7; Josh. 7. 15; Ps. 39. 8; 74. 18, 22. . in his heart—to himself (Gen. 6. 12.). 2. looked —in earnest inquiry. understand—as opposed to fool. 3. filthy—*lit., spoiled*, or, *soured, corrupted* (Job, 15. 16; Rom. 3. 12). 4-6. Their conduct evinces indifference rather than ignorance of God; for when He appears in judgment they are stricken with great fear. who eat up my people—to express their beastly fury (Pro. 30. 14; Hab. 3. 14;); to *call on the Lord* is to worship Him. 7. captivity—denotes any great evil. Zion—God's abode, from which He revealed His purposes of mercy, as He now does by the Church (cf. 3. 4; 20. 2,), and which He rules, and all other things for the good of His people (Eph. 1. 22.).

PSALM XV.

Ver. 1-5. Those who are fit for communion with God may be known by a conformity to His law, which is illustrated in various important particulars.

1. abide—or, sojourn (cf. Ps. 5. 4,), where it means under God's protection; here, as (Ps. 23. 6; 27. 4, 6,), communion. tabernacle—seat of the ark (2 Sam. 6. 17.), the symbol of God's presence. holy hill—(cf. Ps. 2. 6.). 2. walketh —(cf. Ps. 1. 1,). uprightly—in a complete manner, as to all parts of conduct (Gen. 17. 1,), not as to degree. worketh—or does. righteousness—what is right, in his heart—sincerely (Pro. 23. 7.). 3. He neither slanders nor spreads slander. 4. Love and hate are regulated by a regard to God's. sweareth . . . hurt—or what so results (cf. Lev. 5. 4.). 5. (Cf. Lev. 25. 37; Deut. 23. 19, 20. . usury—is derived from a verb meaning *to bite*. All gains made by the wrongful loss of others are forbidden. taketh reward, &c.,—the innocent would not otherwise be condemned (cf. Ex. 23. 8; Deut. 16. 19.). Bribery of all sorts is denounced. doeth these, &c.,—Such persons admitted to God's presence and favour shall never (Ps. 10. 6; 13. 5,) be moved.

PSALM XVI.

Ver. 1-11. *Michtam* or, by the change of one letter, *Michtab*—a *writing*, such as a poem or song: cf. Isa. 38. 9.). Such a change of the letter *m* for *b* was not unusual. The position of this word in connection with the author's name, being that usually occupied by some term, such as Psalm or Song, denoting the style or matter of the composition, favours this view of its meaning, though we know not why this and Ps. 56.-60. should be specially called *a writing*. *A golden* (Psalm), or a *Memorial*, are explanations proposed by some—neither of which, however, applicable here, appear adapted to the other Psalms where the term occurs. According to Peter (Acts, 2. 25,) and Paul Acts, 13. 35, ,this Psalm relates to Christ, and expresses the feelings of His human nature, in view of His sufferings and victory over death and the grave, including His subsequent exaltation at the right hand of God. Such was the exposition of the best earlier Christian interpreters. Some moderns have held that the Psalm relates exclusively to David, but this view is expressly contradicted by the apostles; others hold that the language of the Psalm is applicable to David as a type of Christ, capable of the higher sense assigned it in the N.T. But then the language of v. 10 cannot be used of David in any sense, for "he saw corruption." Others again propose to refer the first part to David, and the last to Christ; but it is evident that no change in the subject of the Psalm is indicated. Indeed, the person who appeals to God for help is evidently the same who rejoice, in having found it. In referring the whole Psalm to Christ, it is, however, by no means denied that much of its language is expressive of the feelings of His people, so far as in their humble measure they have the feelings of trust in God expressed by Him, their head and representative. Such use of His language, as recorded in His last prayer (John, 17.); and even that He used in Gethsen ane, under similar modifications, is equally proper. The propriety of this reference of the Psalm to Christ will appear in the scope and interpretation. In view of the sufferings before Him, the Saviour, with that instinctive dread of death manifested in Gethsemane, calls on God to "preserve" Him; He avows His delight in holiness and abhorrence of the wicked and their wickedness; and for "the joy that was set before Him, despising the shame," encourages Himself; contemplating the glories of the heritage appointed Him. Thus even death and the grave lose their terrors in the assurance of the victory to be attained and "the glory that should follow."

1. Preserve me—keep or watch over my interests. in thee . . . I . . . trust—as one seeking shelter from pressing danger. 2. my goodness—must be supplied; expressed in similar cases (Ps. 42. 5, 11.). my goodness . . . thee—This obscure passage is variously expounded. Either one of two expositions falls in with the context. *My goodness* or merit is not on account of thee—*i.e.*, is not for thy benefit. Then follows the contrast of v. 3, but is in respect, or for the saints. &c.—*i.e.*, it enures to them. Or *my goodness*—or happiness is not—*besides thee*—*i.e.*, without thee I have no other source of happiness. Then, "to the saints," &c. means that the same privilege of deriving happiness from God only is theirs. The first is most consonant with the Messianic character of the Psalm, though the latter is not inconsistent with it. 3. saints—or persons consecrated to God, set apart from others, to his service. in the earth—*i.e.*, land of Palestine—the residence of God's chosen people—figuratively for the Church. excel-

lent—or nobles, distinguished for moral excellence. 4. He expresses his abhorrence of those who seek other sources of happiness or objects of worship, and, by characterising their rites by drink-offerings of blood, clearly denotes idolaters. The word for sorrows is by some rendered idols; but, though a similar word to that for idols, it is not the same. In selecting such a term, there may be an allusion, by the author, to the sorrows produced by idolatrous practices. 5-7. God is the chief good, and supplies all need. Deut. 10. 9.). portion of mine inheritance and of my cup—may contain an allusion to the daily supply of food, and also to the inheritance of Levi Deut. 18. 1, 2.). maintainest—or, drawest out my lot—enlargest it. The next verse carries out this idea more fully. given me counsel—cared for me. my reins—the supposed seat of emotion and thought (Ps. 7. 9; 26. 2.). instruc me—or, excite to acts of praise Isa. 53. 11, 12; Heb. 12. 2.). 8. With God's presence and aid he is sure of safety (Ps. 10. 6; 15. 5; John. 12. 27, 28; Heb. 5. 7, 8.). 9.'glory—as heart Ps. 7. 5., for self. In (Acts. 2. 26.), after the Sept., my tongue as "the glory of the frame" —the instrument for praising God. flesh—if taken as opposed to soul v. 10., it may mean the body; otherwise, the whole person (cf. Ps. 63. 1; 84. 2., rest in hope—(cf. Marg.. 10. soul—or, self. This use of soul for the person is frequent (Gen. 12. 5; 46 26; Ps. 3. 2; 11. 1; 7. 2.) even when the body may be the part chiefly affected, as Ps. 35. 13; 105. 18.). Some cases are cited as Lev. 22. 4; Num. 6. 6; 9. 6. 10; 19. 13; Hag. 2. 13, &c.) which seem to justify assigning the meaning of body, or dead body; but it will be found that the latter sense is given by some adjunct expressed or implied. In those cases person is the proper sense. wilt not leave... hell— abandon to the power of (Job. 39. 14; Ps. 49. 10.). Hell as (Gen. 42. 38; Ps. 6. 5; Jon. 2. 2., the state or region of death, and so frequently—or the grave itself (Job. 14. 13; 17. 13; Eccl. 9. 10, &c.) So the Greek Hades (cf. Acts. 2. 27. 31.). The context alone can settle whether the state mentioned is one of suffering, and place of the damned (cf. Ps. 9. 17; Pro. 5. 5; 7. 27.). wilt... suffer—lit., give, or, appoint. Holy One— Ps. 4. 3.), one who is the object of God's favour, and so a recipient of divine grace which he exhibits —pious. to see—or, experience—undergo Luke. 2. 26.). corruption—Some render the word, the pit, which is possible, but for the obvious sense which the apostle's exposition (Acts, 2. 27; 13. 36, 37.), gives. The sense of the whole passage is clearly this:—by the use of flesh and soul, the disembodied state produced by death is indicated; but, on the other hand, no more than the state of death is intended; for the last clause of v. 10 is strictly parallel with the first, and Holy One corresponds to soul, and corruption to hell. As Holy One, or David Acts, 13. 36, 37.), which denotes the person, including soul and body, is used for body, of which only corruption can be predicated (cf. Acts, 2. 31.); so on the contrary, soul, which literally means the immaterial part, is used for the person, the language may be thus paraphrased, "In death I shall hope for resurrection; for I shall not be left under its dominion and within its bounds, or be subject to the corruption which ordinarily ensues." 11. Raised from the dead, he shall die no more, death hath no more dominion over him. Thou wilt show me— guide me to attain. the path of life—or, lives— the plural denoting variety and abundance— immortal blessedness of every sort—as life often denotes. in thy presence—or, before thy faces. The frequent use of this plural form for faces may contain an allusion to the Trinity (Num. 6. 25, 26; Ps. 17. 15; 31. 16.). at thy right hand—to which Christ was exalted (Ps. 110. 1; Acts, 2. 33; Col. 3. 1 Heb. 1, 3.). In the glories of this state. He shall see of the travail (Isa. 53. 10, 11; Phil. 2. 9.), of his soul, and be satisfied.

PSALM XVII.

Ver. 1-15. This Psalm is termed a prayer, because the language of petition is predominant. With a just cause since ely presented, the writer prays for a just decision and help and protection. Pleading former mercies as a ground of hope, he urges his prayer in view of the malice, pride, rapacity, and selfishness of his foes, whose character is contrasted with his pious devotion and delight in God's favour. 2. sentence—acquitting judgment. from thy presence—thy tribunal. things that are equal—just and right, do thou regard. 3. proved... visited... tried—his character was most rigidly tested, at all times, and by all methods, affliction and others (Ps. 7. 10.). purposed that, &c.—or, my mouth does not exceed my purpose—I am sincere. 4. works of men—sinful practices. by the word of thy lips—as a guide (Ps. 119. 9, 11, 95.). destroyer— violent man. 5. May he read as an assertion; "my steps or goings have held on to thy paths." 6. wilt hear me—i.e., graciously Ps. 3. 4.). 7. Show—set apart as special and eminent (Ex. 8. 18; Ps. 4. 3.). thy right hand—for thy power. 8. Similar figures denoting the preciousness of God's people in his sight, in Deut. 32. 10-11; Mat. 23. 37. 9. compass me (cf. Ps. 118. 10-12.). 10. inclosed... fat—are become proud in prosperity, and insolent to God Deut. 32. 15; Ps. 73. 7.). 11. They pursue us as beasts tracking their prey. 12. The figure made more special, by that of a lion lurking. 13-15. disappoint—lit., come before, or, encounter him. Supply with before sword (v. 13., and hand (v. 14.). These denote God's power. men... world—all men of this present time. They appear, by fulness of bread and large famil es, to be prosperous but v. 15., he implies this will be transient contrasting his better portion in a joyful union with God hereafter.

PSALM XVIII.

Ver. 1-50. "The servant of the Lord," which in the Hebrew precedes "David," is a significant part of the title and not a mere epithet of David, denoting the inspired character of the song, as the production of one intrusted with the execution of God's will. He was not favoured by God, because he served Him, but served Him because selected and appointed by God in His sovereign mercy. After a general expression of praise and confidence in God for the future, David gives a sublimely poetical description of God's deliverance, which he characterises as an illustration of God's justice to the innocent and His righteous government. His own prowess and success are celebrated as the results of divine aid, and, confident of its continuance, he closes in terms of triumphant praise. 2 Sam. 22. is a copy of this Psalm, with a few unimportant variations, recorded there as a part of the history, and repeated here as part of a collection designed for permanent use.

1. I will love thee—with most tender affection. **2, 3.** The various terms used describe God as an object of the most implicit and reliable trust. rock—*lit.*, *a cleft rock*, for concealment. strength—a firm Immovable rock. horn of my salvation—the horn, as the means of attack or defence of some of the strongest animals, is a frequent emblem of power or strength efficiently exercised (cf. Deut. 33. 17; Luke, 1. 69). tower—*lit.*, *high place*, beyond reach of danger. to be praised —for past favours, and worthy of confidence. **4.** sorrows—*lit.*, *bands as of a net* (Ps. 116. 3.) floods—denotes multitude. death—and hell (cf. Ps. 16. 10, —are personified as man's great enemies (cf. Rev. 20. 13, 14.). prevented—encountered me, crossed my path and endangered my safety. He does not mean he was in their power. **6.** He relates his methods to procure relief when distressed, and his success. temple—(cf. Ps. 11. 4.). **7, 8.** God's coming described in figures drawn from His appearance on Sinai cf. Deut. 32. 22.). smoke out ... of His nostrils—better in his wrath (cf. Ps. 74. 1.). by it—*i.e.*, the fire (Ex. 19. 18.). **9.** darkness—or, a dense cloud Ex. 19. 16; Deut. 5. 22.). **10.** cherub—angelic agents (cf. Gen. 3. 24.), the figures of which were placed over the ark (1 Sam. 4. 4.), representing God's dwelling; used here to enhance the majesty of the divine advent. *Angels* and *winds* may represent all rational and irrational agencies of God's providence cf. Ps. 104. 3, 4. did fly —rapidity of motion adds to the grandeur of the scene. **11.** dark waters—or, clouds heavy with vapour. **12.** Out of this obscurity, which impresses the beholder with awe and dread, He reveals Himself by sudden light and the means of His terrible wrath Josh. 10. 11; Ps. 78, 47.). **13.** The storm breaks forth—thunder follows lightning, and hail with repeated lightning, as often seen, like balls or coals of fire, succeed Ex. 9. 23.). **14.** The fiery brightness of lightning, in shape like burning arrows rapidly shot through the air, well represents the most terrible part of an awful storm. Before the terrors of such a scene the enemies are confounded and overthrown in dismay. **15.** The tempest of the air is attended by appropriate results on earth. The language, though not expressive of any special physical changes, represents the utter subversion of the order of nature. Before such a God none can stand. **16-19.** from above—as seated on a throne. directing these terrible scenes, God—sent—His hand (Ps. 144. 7.), reached down to His humble worshipper and delivered him. many waters—calamities (Job, 30. 14; Ps. 124. 4, 5.). prevented—(*v.* 3.). a large place—denotes safety or relief, as contrasted with the straits of distress (Ps. 4. 1. . All his deliverance is ascribed to God, and this sublime poetical representation is given to inspire the pious with confidence and the wicked with dread. **20-24.** The statements of innocence, righteousness, &c., refer, doubtless, to his personal and official conduct and his purposes, during all the trials to which he was subjected in Saul's persecutions and Absalom's rebellions, as well as the various wars in which he had been engaged as the head and defender of God's Church and people. upright before him—in my relation to God I have been perfect as to all parts of His law. The perfection does not relate to degree,

mine iniquity—perhaps the thought of his heart to kill Saul (1 Sam. 24. 6.). That David does not allude to all his conduct, in all relations is evident from Ps. 51. 1, &c. **25-27.** God renders to men according to their deeds in a penal, not vindictive, sense Lev. 26. 23, 24. . merciful—or, kind Ps. 4.3.). froward—contrary to. the afflicted people—*i.e.*, the humbly pious. high looks—pride (Ps. 101. 5; 131. 1.). **28** To give one light is to make prosperous Job, 18. 5, 6; 21. 17. . thou —is emphatic, as if to say, I can fully confide in *thee* for help. **29.** And this on past experience, in his military life, set forth by these figures. **30-32.** God's perfection is the source of his own, which has resulted from his trust on the one hand, and God's promised help on the other. tried—"as metals are tried by fire and proved genuine." Ps. 12. 6. , *Shield* Ps. 3. 3.). *Girding* was essential to free motion on account of the looseness of oriental dresses. hence it is an expressive figure for describing the gift of strength. **33- 6.** God's help farther described —He gives swiftness to pursue or elude his enemies (Hab. 3. 19,), strength, protection, and a firm footing. thy gentleness—as applied to God—condescension—or, that which He gives, in the sense of *humility* ct. Pro. 22. 4.). enlarged my steps—made ample room (cf. Pro. 4. 12.). **37-41.** In actual conflict, by God's aid, the defeat of his enemies is certain. A present and continued success is expressed. that rose up against me—*lit.*, *insurgents* Ps. 3. 1; 44. 5.). given me the necks —*lit.*, *backs of the necks*—made them retreat Ex. 23. 27; Josh. 7. 8. . **42.** This conquest was complete. **43-45.** Not only does He conquer civil foes, but foreigners, who are driven from their places of refuge, submit, &c.— (cf. *Marg.*)—*i.e.*, show a forced subjection. **46.** The Lord liveth—contrasts Him with idols (1 Cor. 8. 4.). **47, 48.** vengeth me—his cause is espoused by God as His own. livest me up—to safety and honours. **49, 50.** Paul, (Rom. 15. 9,), quotes from this doxology to show that, under the O. T. economy, others than the Jews were regarded as subjects of that spiritual government, of which David was head, and in which character his deliverances and victories were typical of the more illustrious triumphs of David's greater Son. The language of *v.* 50 justifies this view in its distinct allusion to the great promise (cf. 2 Sam. 7.). In all David's successes he saw the pledges of a fulfilment of that promise, and he mourned in all his adversities not only in view of his personal suffering, but because he saw in them evidences of danger to the great interests which were committed to his keeping. It is in these aspects of his character that we are led properly to appreciate the importance attached to his sorrows and sufferings, his joys and successes.

PSALM XIX.

Ver. 1-14.—After exhibiting the harmonious revelation of God's perfections made by His works and His word, the Psalmist prays for conformity to the divine teaching.

1. the glory of God—is the sum of His perfections Ps. 24. 7-10; Rom. 1. 20.). handywork —old English for work of his hands. firmament—another word for heavens Gen. 1. 8.). **2.** uttereth—pours forth—as a stream—a perpetual testimony. **3.** Though there is no articulate speech or words; yet, without these, their voice is heard (cf. *Marg.*). **4.**

for his manifold blessings. **PSALM XIX.** *God's works proclaim his glory.*

13 The LORD also thundered in the heavens, and the Highest gave *his voice; hail stones and coals of fire.
14 Yea, *he sent out his arrows, and scattered them; and he shot out lightnings, and discomfited them.
15 Then the channels of waters were seen, and the foundations of the world were discovered at thy rebuke, O LORD, at the blast of the breath of thy nostrils.
16 He sent from above, he took me, he drew me out of *many waters.
17 He delivered me from my strong enemy, and from them which hated me: for they were too strong for me.
18 They prevented me in the day of my calamity: but the LORD was my stay.
19 He *brought me forth also into a large place; he delivered me, because he delighted in me.
20 The *LORD rewarded me according to my righteousness; according to the cleanness of my hands hath he recompensed me.
21 For I have kept the ways of the LORD, and have not wickedly departed from my God.
22 For all his judgments *were* before me, and I did not put away his statutes from me.
23 I was also upright *before him, and I kept myself from mine iniquity.
24 Therefore *hath the LORD recompensed me according to my righteousness, according to the cleanness of my hands in his eyesight.
25 With *the merciful thou wilt show thyself merciful; with an upright man thou wilt show thyself upright;
26 With the pure thou wilt show thyself pure; and *with the froward thou wilt show thyself froward.
27 For thou wilt save the afflicted people; but wilt bring down *high looks.
28 For *thou wilt light my *candle: the LORD my God will enlighten my darkness.
29 For by thee I have *run through a troop; and by my God have I leaped over a wall.
30 *As for* God, *his way *is* perfect: *the word of the LORD is *tried; he *is* a buckler to all those that trust in him.
31 For *who *is* God save the LORD? or who *is* a rock save our God?
32 *It is* God that girdeth me with strength, and maketh my way perfect.
33 He maketh my feet like hinds' *feet*, and setteth me upon my high places.
34 He teacheth my hands to war, so that a bow of steel is broken by mine arms.
35 Thou hast also given me the shield of thy salvation; and thy right hand hath holden me up, and *thy gentleness hath made me great.
36 Thou hast enlarged my steps under me, that *my feet did not slip.
37 I have pursued mine enemies, and overtaken them; neither did I turn again till they were consumed.
38 I have wounded them, that they were not able to rise: they are fallen under my feet.
39 For thou hast girded me with strength unto the battle: thou hast *subdued under me those that rose up against me.
40 Thou hast also given me the necks of mine enemies, that I might destroy them that hate me.
41 They cried, but *there was* none to save

PSALM 18.
*Ps. 29. 3.
*Is. 30. 30.
*Ps. 144. 7.
*Or, great waters.
*Ps. 118. 5.
*2 Sam. 22. 21.
*with.
*1 Sam. 26. 23.
*before his eyes.
*1 Ki. 8. 32.
*Lev. 2. 23. Pro. 3. 34
*Or, wrestle.
*Pro. 6. 17
*Job 18. 6.
*Or, lamp.
*Or, broken.
*Deu. 32. 4.
*Dan. 4. 37.
*Rev. 15. 3.
*Ps. 12. 6.
*Ps 119.140. Pro. 30. 6.
*Or, refined.
*Deu.32.21.
*Or, with thy meekness thou hast multiplied me.
*mine uncles.
*caused to bow.
*Pro. 1. 28.
*At the hearing of the ear.
*the sons of the stranger.
*lie, or, yield feigned obedience.
*Mic. 7. 17.
*Jer. 10. 10.
*giveth avengements for me.
*Or, destroyeth.
*man of violence.
*Or, confess. Rom.15.9.

PSALM 19.
*Is. 40. 22.
Ro. 1. 19.
*without their voice heard, or, without these their voice is heard.
*Or, Their rule, or, direction.
*Or, doctrine.
*Or, restoring.
*truth.
*the dropping of honeycombs.
*Or, much.
*my rock.

them; *even unto the LORD, but he answered them not.
42 Then did I beat them small as the dust before the wind; I did cast them out as the dirt in the streets.
43 Thou hast delivered me from the strivings of the people; *and* thou hast made me the head of the heathen: a people *whom* I have not known shall serve me.
44 *As soon as they hear of me, they shall obey me: *the strangers shall *submit themselves unto me.
45 The *strangers shall fade away, and be afraid out of their close places.
46 The *LORD liveth; and blessed *be* my Rock; and let the God of my salvation be exalted.
47 *It is* God that *avengeth me, and *subdueth the people under me.
48 He delivereth me from mine enemies; yea, thou liftest me up above those that rise up against me: thou hast delivered me from the *violent man.
49 Therefore will I *give thanks unto thee, O LORD, among the heathen, and sing praises unto thy name.
50 Great deliverance giveth he to his king; and sheweth mercy to his anointed, to David, and to his seed for evermore.

PSALM XIX.
1 The creatures show God's glory. 7 Excellency of God's law. 12 David prays for grace
To the chief Musician, A Psalm of David.

THE *heavens declare the glory of God; and the firmament sheweth his handywork.
2 Day unto day uttereth speech, and night unto night sheweth knowledge.
3 *There is* no speech nor language 1 *where* their voice is not heard.
4 2 Their line is gone out through all the earth, and their words to the end of the world. In them hath he set a tabernacle for the sun;
5 Which *is* as a bridegroom coming out of his chamber, *and* rejoiceth as a strong man to run a race.
6 His going forth *is* from the end of the heaven, and his circuit unto the ends of it: and there is nothing hid from the heat thereof.
7 The 3 law of the LORD *is* perfect, *converting the soul: the testimony of the LORD *is* sure, making wise the simple;
8 The statutes of the LORD *are* right, rejoicing the heart; the commandment of the LORD *is* pure, enlightening the eyes;
9 The fear of the LORD *is* clean, enduring for ever: the judgments of the LORD *are* *true *and* righteous altogether.
10 More to be desired *are they* than gold, yea, than much fine gold; sweeter also than honey, and *the honeycomb.
11 Moreover by them is thy servant warned; *and* in keeping of them *there is* great reward.
12 Who can understand *his* errors? cleanse thou me from secret *faults*.
13 Keep back thy servant also from presumptuous *sins*; let them not have dominion over me: then shall I be upright, and I shall be innocent from 7 the great transgression.
14 Let the words of my mouth, and the meditation of my heart, be acceptable in thy sight, O LORD, *my strength, and my redeemer.

The Church's Confidence in God. PSALMS XX—XXII. *A Thanksgiving for Victory.*

Their line—or, instruction—the influence exerted by their tacit display of God's perfections. Paul, Rom. 10, 8., quoting from the Sept., uses *sound*, which gives the same sense. 5, 6. The sun, as the most glorious heavenly body, is specially used to illustrate the sentiment; and his vigorous, cheerful, daily, and extensive course, and his reviving heat (including light) well display the wondrous wisdom of his Maker. 7-9. The law is described by six names, epithets, and effects. It is a rule, God's testimony for the truth, I's special and general prescription of duty, fear (as its cause), and judicial decision. It is distinct and certain, reliable, right, pure, holy, and true. Hence it revives those depressed by doubts, makes wise the unskilled (2 Tim. 3. 15,), rejoices the lover of truth, strengthens the desponding (Ps. 13. 4; 34. 6,), provides permanent principles of conduct, and by God's grace brings a rich reward. 12-14. The clearer our view of the law, the more manifest are our sins. Still, for its full effect, we need divine grace to show us our faults, acquit us, restrain us from the practice, and free us from the power, of sin. Thus only can our conduct be blameless, and our words and thoughts acceptable to God.

PSALM XX.

Ver. 1-9. David probably composed this Psalm to express the prayers of the pious for his success as, at once, the head of the Church and nation. Like other compositions of which David, in such relations, is the subject, its sentiments have a permanent value —the prosperity of Christ's kingdom being involved, as well as typified, in that of Israel and its king.

1. hear thee—graciously (Ps. 4. 1.). name of —or, manifested perfections, as power, wisdom, &c. defend thee—set thee on high from danger Ps. 9. 9; 18. 3.). 2. strengthen thee— *sustain* in conflict; even physical benefits may be included, as courage for war, &c., as such may proceed from a sense of divine favour, secured in the use of spiritual privileges. 3. all thy offerings—or, gifts, vegetable offerings. accept—*lit.*, *turn to ashes* (cf. 1 Ki. 18. 38.) Selah—Ps. 3. 2.). 4. thy counsel—or, plan. 5. salvation—that wrought and experienced by him. set up our banners—(Num. 2. 3, 10,), in usual sense, or, as some render— *may we be made great*. 6. He speaks as if suddenly assured of a hearing. his holy heaven—or, *lit.*, *the heavens of His holiness*, where He resides Ps. 2. 6; 11. 4.). saving . . . hand—His power which brings salvation. his anointed—not only David personally, but as the specially appointed head of His Church. 7. remember—or, cause to remember, mention thankfully, (1 Sam. 17. 45; Ps. 33. 16.). 8 They—i.e., who trust in horses, &c. stand upright—*lit.*, *we have straightened ourselves up from our distress and fears*. 9. let the King hear—as God's representative, delivered to deliver. Perhaps a better sense is, "Lord, save the king, hear us when we call," or pray.

PSALM XXI.

Ver. 1-13. The pious are led by the Psalmist to celebrate God's favour to the king in the bounties already conferred and in prospective victories. The doxology added may relate to both Psalms; the preceding of petition chiefly, this of thanksgiving, ascribing honour to God for His display of grace and power to His Church in all ages, not only

under David, but also under his last greatest successor, "The King of the Jews." 1. thy strength . . . thy salvation—as supplied by thee. 2. The sentiment affirmed in the first clause is re-affirmed by the negation of its opposite in the second. 3. preventest —*lit.*, *to meet*, *here in good sense*, or, *friendship* Ps. 69. 10,), (cf. opposite, Ps. 17. 13.). crown of pure gold—a figure for the highest royal prosperity. 4-6. Cf. 2 Sam. 7. 13-16.). The glory and blessedness of the king as head of his line, including Christ, as well as in being God's specially selected servant, exceeded that of all others. made him most blessed—or set him *to be blessings*, as Abraham Gen. 12. 2.). with thy countenance—by *sight of thee* (Ps. 16. 11,), or, by thy favour expressed by the light of thy countenance (Num. 6. 25, , or both. 7. The mediate cause is the king's faith, the efficient, God's mercy. 8. The address is now made to the king. hand—denotes power, and—right hand—a more active and efficient degree of its exercise. find out—reach, lay hold of, indicating success in pursuit of his enemies. 9. The king is only God's agent. anger—*lit.*, *face*, as appearing against them. as a fiery oven—as in it. 10. fruit—children Ps. 37. 25; Hos. 9. 16.). 11 This terrible overthrow, reaching to posterity, is due to their crimes (Ex. 20. 5, 6.). 12. turn their back—*lit.*, *place them* [as to the] *shoulder*. against the face of them —The shooting against their faces would cause them to turn their backs in flight. 13. The glory of all is ascribable to God alone.

PSALM XXII.

Ver. 1-31. The obscure words *Aijeleth Shahar* in this title have various explanations. Most interpreters agree in translating them by "Hind of the morning." But great difference exists as to the meaning of these words. By some they are supposed (cf. Ps. 9.) to be the name of the tune to which the words of the Psalm were set; by others, the name of a musical instrument. Perhaps the best view is to regard the phrase as enigmatically expressive of the subject—the sufferer being likened to a hind pursued by hunters in the early morning, *lit.*, *the dawn of day*,) —or that, while *hind* suggests the idea of a meek, innocent sufferer, the addition of *morning* denotes relief obtained. The feelings of a pious sufferer in sorrow and deliverance are vividly portrayed. He earnestly pleads for divine aid on the ground of his relation to God, whose past goodness to His people encourages hope, and then on account of the imminent danger by which he is threatened. The language of complaint is turned to that of rejoicing in the assured prospect of relief from suffering and triumph over his enemies. The use of the words of the first clause of *v.* 1, by our Saviour on the cross, and the quotation of *v.* 18 by John, (19. 24,), and of *v.* 22 by Paul, (Heb. 2. 12,), as fulfilled in His history, clearly intimate the prophetical and Messianic purport of the Psalm. The intensity of the grief, and the completeness and glory of the deliverance and triumph, alike appear to be unsuitable representations of the fortunes of any less personage. In a general and modified sense, (cf. on Ps. 16.), the experience here detailed may be adapted to the case of all Christians suffering from spiritual foes, and delivered by divine aid, inasmuch as Christ, in His

A thanksgiving for victory. PSALMS XX.–XXII. *Sufferings of the Messiah.*

PSALM XX.

1 *The church blesses the king in his exploits: 6 she expresses a confidence in God's favour.*

To the chief Musician, A Psalm of David.

THE LORD hear thee in the day of trouble; the name of the God of Jacob ¹ defend thee.
2 Send ² thee help from the sanctuary, and ³ strengthen thee out of Zion.
3 Remember all thy offerings, and ⁴ accept thy burnt sacrifice. Selah.
4 Grant thee according to thine own heart, and fulfil all thy counsel.
5 We will rejoice in thy salvation, and in the name of our God we will set up *our* banners: the LORD fulfil all thy petitions.
6 Now know I that the LORD saveth his anointed: he will hear him ⁵ from his holy heaven ⁶ with the saving strength of his right hand.
7 Some *trust* in chariots, and some in horses: but we will ᵃ remember the name of the LORD our God.
8 They are brought down and fallen; but we are risen, and stand upright.
9 Save, LORD: let the King hear us when we call.

PSALM XXI.

1 *A thanksgiving for victory, 7 with confidence of further success.*

To the chief Musician, A Psalm of David.

THE king shall joy in thy strength, O LORD; and in thy salvation how greatly shall he rejoice!
2 Thou hast given him his heart's desire, and hast not withholden the request of his lips. Selah.
3 For thou preventest him with the blessings of goodness: thou settest a crown of pure gold on his head.
4 He asked life of thee, *and* thou gavest *it* him, *even* length of days for ever and ever.
5 His glory *is* great in thy salvation: honour and majesty hast thou laid upon him.
6 For thou hast ¹ made him most blessed for ever: thou hast ² made him exceeding glad with thy countenance.
7 For the king trusteth in the LORD; and through the mercy of the Most High he shall not be moved.
8 Thine hand shall find out all thine enemies: thy right hand shall find out those that hate thee.
9 Thou shalt make them as a fiery oven in the time of thine anger: the LORD shall swallow them up in his wrath, and the fire shall devour them.
10 Their fruit shalt thou destroy from the earth, and their seed from among the children of men.
11 For they intended evil against thee: they imagined a mischievous device, *which* they are not able *to perform:*
12 Therefore ³ shalt thou make them turn their ⁴ back, *when* thou shalt make ready *thine arrows* upon thy strings against the face of them.
13 Be thou exalted, LORD, in thine own strength: *so* will we sing and praise thy power.

PSALM XXII.

1 *David complains in great discouragement: 9 he prays in great distress: 21 he promises public thanksgiving and praise.*

To the chief Musician upon ¹ Aijeleth Shahar, A Psalm of David.

MY ᵃ God, my God, why hast thou forsaken me? *why art* thou so far ² from helping me, and from ᵇ the words of my roaring?
2 O my God, I cry in the day-time, but thou hearest not; and in the night season, and ³ am not silent.
3 But thou *art* ᶜ holy, O thou that inhabitest the praises of Israel.
4 Our fathers trusted in thee: they trusted, and thou didst deliver them.
5 They cried unto thee, and were delivered: they trusted in thee, and were not confounded.
6 But I *am* a worm, and no man; ᵈ a reproach of men, and despised of the people.
7 All ᵉ they that see me laugh me to scorn: they ⁴ shoot out the lip, they shake the head, *saying,*
8 ⁵ He trusted on the LORD *that* he would deliver him; let him deliver him, ⁶ seeing he delighted in him.
9 But thou *art* he that took me out of the womb: thou ⁷ didst make me hope *when I was* upon my mother's breasts.
10 I was cast upon thee from the womb: thou *art* my God from my mother's belly.
11 Be not far from me, for trouble *is* near; for *there is* ⁸ none to help.
12 Many bulls have compassed me: strong *bulls* of Bashan have beset me round.
13 They ⁹ gaped upon *me with* their mouths, *as* a ravening and a roaring lion.
14 I am poured out like water, and all my bones are ¹⁰ out of joint: my heart is like wax; it is melted in the midst of my bowels.
15 My ᵍ strength is dried up like a potsherd; and my tongue cleaveth to my jaws; and thou hast brought me into the dust of death.
16 For dogs have compassed me; the assembly of the wicked have enclosed me: they ʰ pierced my hands and my feet.
17 I may tell all my bones: they look and stare upon me.
18 They ⁱ part my garments among them, and cast lots upon my vesture.
19 But be not thou far from me, O LORD: O my strength, haste thee to help me.
20 Deliver my soul from the sword; ¹¹ my darling ¹² from the power of the dog.
21 Save me from the lion's mouth: for thou hast heard me from the horns of the unicorns.
22 I will declare thy name unto ᵏ my brethren: in the midst of the congregation will I praise thee.
23 Ye that fear the LORD, praise him; all ye the seed of Jacob, glorify him; and fear him, all ye the seed of Israel.
24 For he hath not despised nor abhorred the affliction of the afflicted; neither hath he hid his face from him; but when he cried unto him, he heard.
25 My praise *shall be* of thee in the great congregation: I will pay my vows before them that fear him.
26 The ˡ meek shall eat and be satisfied: they shall praise the LORD that seek him: your heart ᵐ shall live for ever.
27 All ⁿ the ends of the world shall remember, and turn unto the LORD: and all the kindreds of the nations shall worship before thee.
28 For ᵒ the kingdom *is* the LORD's; and he *is* the governor among the nations.
29 All *they that be fat* upon earth shall eat and worship: ᵖ all they that go down to the dust shall bow before him: and none can keep alive his own soul.

human nature, was their head and representative.
1. A summary of the complaint. Desertion by God, when overwhelmed by distress, is the climax of the sufferer's misery. *words of my roaring*—shows that the complaint is expressed intelligently, though the term *roaring* is figurative, taken from the conduct of irrational creatures in pain. **2.** The long distress is evinced by—*am not silent*—*lit., not silence to me*, either meaning, I continually cry; or, corresponding with *thou hearest not*, or, answerest not, it may mean, there is no rest or quiet to me. **3.** Still he not only refrains from charging God foolishly, but evinces his confidence in God by appealing to him. *thou art holy*—or possessed of all the attributes which encourage trust, and the right object of the praises of the Church; hence the sufferer need not despair. **4, 5.** Past experience of God's people is a ground of trust. The mention of "our fathers" does not destroy the applicability of the words as the language of our Saviour's human nature. **6.** He, who was despised and rejected of His own people, as a disgrace to the nation, might well use these words of deep abasement which express not His real, but esteemed, value. **7, 8.** For the Jews used one of the gestures, (Mat. 27. 39,), here mentioned, when taunting Him on the cross, and (v. 43,) reproached Him almost in the very language of this passage. *trusted in the Lord*—*lit., rolled*—*i.e.*, his burden, (Ps. 37. 5; Pro. 16. 3.), on the Lord. This is the language of enemies sporting with his faith in the hour of his desertion. *sho t cut* [or, *open*] *the lip*—(cf. l's. 35. 21.). **9, 10.** Though ironically spoken, the exhortation to trust was well founded on his previous experience of divine aid, the special illustration of which is drawn from the period of helpless infancy. *didst make me hope*—or *lit., made me secure.* **11.** From this statement of reasons for the appeal, he renews it, pleading his double extremity, the nearness of trouble, and the absence of a helper. **12, 13.** His enemies, with the vigour of bulls and rapacity of lions, surround him, eagerly seeking his ruin. The force of both figures is greater without the use of any particle denoting comparison. **14, 15.** Utter exhaustion and hopeless weakness, in these circumstances of pressing danger, are set forth by the most expressive figures: the *solidity* of the body is destroyed, and it becomes like water; the bones are parted; the heart, the very seat of vitality, melts like wax; all the juices of the system are dried up; the tongue can no longer perform its office, but lies parched and stiffened cf. Gen. 49. 4; 2 Sam. 14. 14; Ps. 58. 8.). In this, God is regarded as the ultimate source, and men as the instruments. *the dust of death*—of course denotes the grave. We need not try to find the exact counterpart of each item of the description in the particulars of our Saviour's sufferings. Figurative language resembles pictures of historical scenes, presenting substantial truth, under illustrations, which, though not essential to the facts, are not inconsistent with them. Were any portion of Christ's terrible sufferings specially designed, it was doubtless that of the garden of Gethsemane. **16.** Evil-doers are well described as dogs, which, in the East, herding together, wild and rapacious, are justly objects of great abhorrence. The last clause has been a subject of much discussion, involving questions as to the genuineness of the Hebrew word translated *pierce*, which cannot be made intelligible to the English reader. Though not quoted in the N. T., the remarkable aptness of the description to the facts of the Saviour's history, together with difficulties attending either mode of explaining the clause in the Hebrew, justify an adherence to the terms of our version and their obvious meaning. **17.** His emaciated frame, itself an item of his misery, is rendered more so, as the object of delighted contemplation to his enemies. The verbs, *look* and *stare*, often occur as suggestive of feelings of satisfaction (cf. Ps. 27. 13; 54. 7; 118. 7.). **18.** This literally fulfilled prediction closes the sad picture of the exposed and deserted sufferer. **19, 20.** He now turns with unabated desire and trust to God, who, in His strength and faithfulness, is contrasted with the urgent dangers described. *my soul*—or, self cf. Ps. 3. 2; 16. 10. . *my darling*—*lit., my only one*, or, *solitary one*, as desolate and afflicted (Ps. 25. 16; 35. 17.). **21.** Deliverance pled in view of former help, when in the most imminent danger, from the most powerful enemy, represented by the unicorn or wild buffalo. *the lion's mouth*—(cf. v. 13.). The lion often used as a figure representing violent enemies; the connecting of the *mouth* intimates their rapacity. **22-24.** He declares his purpose to celebrate God's gracious dealings and publish His manifested perfections (name, Ps. 5. 11,), &c., and forthwith invites the pious, those who have a reverential fear of God, to unite in special praise for a deliverance, illustrating God's kind regard for the lowly, whom men neglect. *To hide the face or eyes* expresses a studied neglect of one's cause, and refusal of aid or sympathy (cf. Ps. 30. 7; Isa. 1. 15.). **25, 26.** My praise shall be of thee—or, perhaps better, *from thee*—*i.e.*, God gives grace to praise him. With offering praise, he farther evinces his gratitude, by promising the payment of his vows, in celebrating the usual festival, as provided in the law, (Deut. 12. 18; 16. 11,), of which, the pious or humble, and they that seek the Lord, His true worshippers, shall partake abundantly, and join him in praise. In the enthusiasm produced by his lively feelings, he addresses such in words, assuring them of God's perpetual favour. *The dying of the heart* denotes death (1 Sam. 25. 37;); so its *living* denotes life. **27-31.** His case illustrates God's righteous government. Beyond the existing time and people, others shall be brought to acknowledge and worship God; the *fat ones*, or the rich as well as the poor, the helpless who cannot keep themselves alive, shall together unite in celebrating God's delivering power, and transmit to unborn people the records of his grace. *it shall be accounted to the Lord for, &c.*—or, it shall be told of the Lord to a generation. God's wonderful works shall be told from generation to generation. *that he hath done*—supply *it*, or *this*—*i.e.*, what the Psalm has unfolded.

PSALM XXIII.

Ver. 1-6. Under a metaphor borrowed from scenes of pastoral life, with which David was familiar, he describes God's providential care in providing refreshment, guidance, protection, and abundance, and so affording grounds of confidence in His perpetual favour.

David's confidence in God.   PSALMS XXIII-XXVII.   *His faith in God's protection.*

30 A seed shall serve him; it shall be accounted to the LORD for a generation.
31 They shall come, and shall declare his righteousness unto a people that shall be born, that he hath done *this*.

PSALM XXIII.

David's confidence in God's grace.
A Psalm of David.

THE LORD *is* ᵃ my shepherd, I shall not want.
2 He maketh me to lie down in ¹ green pastures: ᵇ he leadeth me beside the ² still waters.
3 He restoreth my soul: he leadeth me in the paths of righteousness for his name's sake.
4 Yea, though I walk through the valley of the shadow of death, I will fear no evil: for ᶜ thou *art* with me; thy rod and thy staff they comfort me.
5 Thou preparest a table before me in the presence of mine enemies: thou ³ anointest my head with oil; my cup runneth over.
6 Surely goodness and mercy shall follow me all the days of my life; and I will ᵈ dwell in the house of the LORD ⁴ for ever.

PSALM XXIV.

1 *God's lordship over the world: 3 citizens of his spiritual kingdom, 7 The Lord's solemn entrance into his sanctuary.*
A Psalm of David.

THE ᵃ earth *is* the LORD's, and the fulness thereof; the world, and they that dwell therein.
2 For he hath founded it upon the seas, and established it upon the floods.
3 Who shall ascend into the hill of the LORD? and who shall stand in his holy place?
4 ¹ He that hath clean hands, and ᵇ a pure heart; who hath not lifted up his soul unto vanity, nor sworn deceitfully.
5 He shall receive the blessing from the LORD, and righteousness from the God of his salvation.
6 This *is* the generation of them that seek him, that seek thy face, ² O Jacob. Selah.
7 Lift up your heads, O ye gates; and be ye lift up, ye everlasting doors; ᵈ and the King of glory shall come in.
8 Who *is* this King of glory? The LORD strong and mighty, the LORD mighty in battle.
9 Lift up your heads, O ye gates; even lift them up, ye everlasting doors; and the King of glory shall come in.
10 Who *is* this King of glory? The LORD of hosts, he *is* the King of glory. Selah.

PSALM XXV.

1 *David's confidence in prayer, 2 being grieved at the malice of his enemies: 16 he prays for help in affliction.*
A Psalm of David.

UNTO ᵃ thee, O LORD, do I lift up my soul.
2 O my God, I ᵇ trust in thee: let me not be ashamed; let not mine enemies triumph over me.
3 Yea, let none that wait on thee be ashamed: let them be ashamed which transgress without cause.
4 Show ᶜ me thy ways, O LORD; teach me thy paths.
5 Lead me in thy truth, and teach me: for thou *art* the God of my salvation; on thee do I wait all the day.
6 Remember, O LORD, ¹ thy tender mercies and thy loving-kindnesses; for they have been ever of old.

PSALM 23.
ᵃ John 10. 11.
1 Ps. 2. 25.
Rev. 7. 17.
1 pastures of tender grass.
ᵇ Rev. 7. 17.
2 waters of quietness.
ᶜ Is. 43. 2.
3 makest fat.
ᵈ 2 Cor. 5. 1.
4 to length of days.

PSALM 24.
ᵃ Ex. 9. 29.
Job 41. 11.
1 The clean of hands.
1 Tim. 2. 8.
ᵇ Mat. 5. 8.
2 Or, O God of Jacob.
ᶜ Hag. 2. 7.
Mal. 3. 1.
1 Cor. 2. 8.

PSALM 25.
ᵃ Lam. 3. 41.
ᵇ Ro. 10. 11.
ᶜ Ex. 33. 13.
1 thy bowels.
ᵈ Ps. 51. 1.
ᵉ Ps. 31. 3.
Ps. 79. 9.
Ps. 109. 21.
Ps. 143. 11.
ᶠ Rom. 5. 20.
ᵍ Ps. 37. 23.
2 shall lodge in goodness.
Pro. 19. 23.
ʰ Ps. 37. 11,
22, 29.
ⁱ Prov. 3. 32.
John 7. 17.
John 16. 15.
2 Cor. 4. 2-6.
3 Or, and his covenant to make them know it.
ʲ Ps. 141. 8.
4 bring forth.
ʰ Ps. 69. 16.
ⁱ 2 Sam. 16. 12.
5 hatred of violence.
ᵐ Ps. 130. 8.

PSALM 26.
ᵃ Ps. 7. 8.
ᵇ Ps. 28. 7.
ᶜ Ps. 1. 1.
Jer. 15. 17.
ᵈ Ps. 31. 5.
ᵉ Ex. 30. 19.
Ps. 73. 13.
1 Ti. 2. 8.
1 of the tabernacle of thy honour.
2 Or, Take not away.
1 Sam. 25. 29.
ᵍ men of bloods.
4 filled with.

7 Remember not the sins of my youth, nor my transgressions: ᵈ according to thy mercy remember thou me for thy goodness' sake, O LORD.
8 Good and upright *is* the LORD: therefore will he teach sinners in the way.
9 The meek will he guide in judgment; and the meek will he teach his way.
10 All the paths of the LORD *are* mercy and truth unto such as keep his covenant and his testimonies.
11 For ᵉ thy name's sake, O LORD, pardon mine iniquity; ᶠ for it *is* great.
12 What man *is* he that feareth the LORD? him ᵍ shall he teach in the way that he shall choose.
13 His soul ² shall dwell at ease; and his ʰ seed shall inherit the earth.
14 The ⁱ secret of the LORD *is* with them that fear him; ³ and he will show them his covenant.
15 Mine ʲ eyes *are* ever toward the LORD; for he shall ⁴ pluck my feet out of the net.
16 Turn ʰ thee unto me, and have mercy upon me; for I *am* desolate and afflicted.
17 The troubles of my heart are enlarged: O bring thou me out of my distresses.
18 Look ⁱ upon mine affliction and my pain; and forgive all my sins.
19 Consider mine enemies, for they are many; and they hate me with ⁵ cruel hatred.
20 O keep my soul, and deliver me: let me not be ashamed; for I put my trust in thee.
21 Let integrity and uprightness preserve me; for I wait on thee.
22 Redeem ᵐ Israel, O God, out of all his troubles.

PSALM XXVI.

1 *David, in confidence of his integrity, resorts to God: 8 his love to God's house.*
A Psalm of David.

JUDGE ᵃ me, O LORD; for I have walked in mine integrity: ᵇ I have trusted also in the LORD; *therefore* I shall not slide.
2 Examine me, O LORD, and prove me; try my reins and my heart.
3 For thy loving-kindness *is* before mine eyes; and I have walked in thy truth.
4 I ᶜ have not sat with vain persons, neither will I go in with dissemblers.
5 I have ᵈ hated the congregation of evil-doers; and will not sit with the wicked.
6 I ᵉ will wash mine hands in innocency; so will I compass thine altar, O LORD;
7 That I may publish with the voice of thanksgiving, and tell of all thy wondrous works.
8 LORD, I have loved the habitation of thy house, and the place ¹ where thine honour dwelleth.
9 ² Gather not my soul with sinners, nor my life with ᵍ bloody men;
10 In whose hands *is* mischief, and their right hand *is* ⁴ full of bribes.
11 But as for me, I will walk in mine integrity: redeem me, and be merciful unto me.
12 My foot standeth in an even place: in the congregations will I bless the LORD.

PSALM XXVII.

1 *David sustains his faith by the power of God, 4 by his love for the service of God, 8 by prayer.*
A Psalm of David.

THE LORD *is* my light and my salvation; whom shall I fear? the LORD *is* the strength of my life; of whom shall I be afraid?

1. Christ's relation to His people is often represented by the figure of a shepherd (John, 10. 14; Heb. 13. 20; 1 Pet. 2. 25; 5. 4,), and therefore the opinion that He is *the Lord* here so described, and in Gen. 48.15; Ps. 80. 1; Isa. 40. 11, is not without some good reason. 2. green pastures—or, pastures of tender grass, are mentioned, not in respect to food, but as places of cool and refreshing rest. the still waters—are, *lit., waters of stillness,* whose quiet flow invite to repose. They are contrasted with boisterous streams on the one hand, and stagnant, offensive pools on the other. 3. To restore the soul is to revive or quicken it (Ps. 19. 7,), or relieve it (Lam. 1. 11, 19.). paths of righteousness—those of safety, as directed by God, and pleasing to Him, for his name's sake—or, regard for His perfections, pledged for His people's welfare. 4. In the darkest and most trying hour God is near. the valley of the shadow of death—is a ravine overhung by high precipitous cliffs, filled with dense forests, and well calculated to inspire dread to the timid, and afford a covert to beasts of prey. While expressive of any great danger or cause of terror, it does not exclude the greatest of all, to which it is most popularly applied, and which its terms suggest. thy rod and thy staff—are symbols of a shepherd's office. By them he guides his sheep. 5, 6. Another figure expresses God's provident care, a table—or, food, anointing oil—the symbol of gladness, and the overflowing cup—which represents abundance—are prepared for the child of God, who may feast in spite of his enemies, confident that this favour will ever attend him. This beautiful Psalm most admirably sets before us, in its chief figure, that of a shepherd, the gentle, kind, and sure care extended to God's people, who, as a shepherd, both *rules and feeds them.* The closing verse shows that the blessings mentioned are spiritual.

PSALM XXIV.

Ver. 1-10. God's supreme sovereignty requires a befitting holiness of life and heart in His worshippers; a sentiment sublimely illustrated by describing His entrance into the sanctuary, by the symbol of His worship—the ark, as requiring the most profound homage to the glory of His Majesty.

1. fulness—every thing, world—the habitable globe, with, they that dwell—forming a parallel expression to the first clause. 2. poetically represents the facts of Gen. 1. 9. 3, 4. The form of a question gives vivacity. *Hands, tongue,* and *heart* are organs of action, speech, and feeling, which compose character. lifted up his soul—is to set the affections (Ps. 25. 1) on an object; here, vanity—or, any false thing, of which swearing falsely, or *fo falsehood,* is a specification. hill of the Lord —cf. Ps. 2. 6, &c.). His Church—the true or invisible. as typified by the earthly sanctuary. 5. righteousness—the rewards which God bestows on His people, or the grace to secure those rewards as well as the result. 6. Jacob— by Jacob, we may understand God's people (cf. Isa. 43. 22; 44. 2, &c.,), corresponding to "the generation," &c., as if he had said, "those who seek thy face who they chosen people." 7-10. The entrance of the ark, with the attending procession, into the holy sanctuary is pictured to us. The repetition of the terms gives emphasis. Lord of hosts—or fully, *Lord God of hosts* (Hos. 12. 5; Amos, 4. 13,) describes God by a title indicative of supremacy over all creatures, and especially the heavenly armies (Josh. 5. 14; 1 Ki. 22. 19.). Whether, as some think, the actual enlargement of the ancient gates of Jerusalem be the basis of the figure, the effect of the whole is to impress us with a conception of the matchless majesty of God.

PSALM XXV.

Ver. 1-22. The general tone of this Psalm is that of prayer for help from enemies. Distress, however, exciting a sense of sin, humble confession, supplication for pardon, preservation from sin, and divine guidance, are prominent topics. 1. lift up my soul—(Ps. 24. 4; 86. 4,) set my affections (cf. Col. 3. 2.). 2. not be ashamed— by disappointment or hopes of relief. 3. The prayer generalised as to all who *wait on* God —*i.e.,* who expect His favour. On the other hand, the disappointment of the perfidious, who, unprovoked, have done evil, is invoked (cf. 2 Sam. 22. 9.). 4, 5. On the ground of former favour, he invokes divine guidance, according to God's gracious-ways of dealing and faithfulness. 6, 7. Confessing past and present sins, he pleads for mercy, not on palliations of sin, but on God's well-known benevolence. 8, 9. upright—acting according to His promise. sinners—the general term, limited by the meek—who are *penitent.* in judgment—rightly. the way—and his way— God's way of providence. 10. paths—similar sense—his modes of dealing (cf. *v.* 4.). mercy and truth—(Job, 14,), God's grace in promising and faithfulness in performing. 11. God's perfections of love, mercy, goodness, and truth are manifested (*his name,* cf. Ps. 9. 10,) in pardoning sin, and the greatness of sin renders pardon more needed. 12, 13. What he asks for himself is the common lot of all the pious. The phrase—inherit the earth—(cf. Mat. 5. 5,), alluding to the promise of Canaan, expresses all the blessings included in that promise, temporal as well as spiritual. 14. The reason of the blessing explained—the pious enjoy communion with God cf. Pro. 3. 21, 22,), and, of course, learn His gracious terms of pardon. 15. His trust in God is fixed. net—is frequently used as a figure for dangers by enemies (Ps. 9. 15; 10. 9.). 16-19. A series of earnest appeals for aid, because God had seemed to desert him (cf. Ps. 13. 1; 17. 13, &c.,), his sins oppressed him, his enemies had enlarged his troubles and were multiplied, increasing in hate and violence (Ps. 9. 8; 18. 48.). 20. keep my soul— (Ps. 16. 1.). put my trust—flee for refuge (Ps. 2. 12.). 21. In conscious innocence of the faults charged by his enemies, he confidently commits his cause to God. Some refer—integrity, &c.—to God, meaning His covenant faithfulness. This sense, though good, is an unusual application of the terms. 22. Extend these blessings to all thy people in all their distresses.

PSALM XXVI.

Ver. 1-12. After appealing to God's judgment on his avowed integrity and innocence of the charges laid by his enemies, the Psalmist professes delight in God's worship, and prays for exemption from the fate of the wicked, expressing assurance of God's favour.

1. Judge—decide on my case—the appeal of innocence. in mine integrity—freedom from blemish (cf. Ps. 25. 21.). His confidence of perseverance results from trust in God's sus-

2 When the wicked, *even* mine enemies and my foes, ¹ came upon me to eat up my flesh, they stumbled and fell.
3 Though an host should encamp against me, my heart shall not fear: though war should rise against me, in this *will* I be confident.
4 One *thing* have I desired of the LORD, that will I seek after; that I may dwell in the house of the LORD all the days of my life, to behold ² the beauty of the LORD, and to enquire in his temple.
5 For *ª* in the time of trouble he shall hide me in his pavilion: in the secret of his tabernacle shall he hide me; he shall set me up upon a rock.
6 And now shall mine head be lifted up above mine enemies round about me: therefore will I offer in his tabernacle sacrifices ³ of joy; I will sing, yea, I will sing praises unto the LORD.
7 Hear, O LORD, *when* I cry with my voice: have mercy also upon me, and answer me.
8 ⁴ *When thou saidst*, Seek ye my face; my heart said unto thee, Thy face, LORD, will I seek.
9 Hide not thy face *far* from me; put not thy servant away in anger: thou hast been my help; leave me not, neither forsake me, O God of my salvation.
10 When my father and *ᵇ* my mother forsake me, then the LORD *ᵇ* will take me up.
11 Teach me thy way, O LORD, and lead me in ⁶ a plain path, because of ⁷ mine enemies.
12 Deliver me not over unto the will of mine enemies: for *ᶜ* false witnesses are risen up against me, and such as breathe out cruelty.
13 *I had fainted*, unless I had believed to see the goodness of the LORD in the land of the living.
14 Wait on the LORD; be of good courage, and he shall strengthen thine heart: wait, I say, on the LORD.

PSALM XXVIII.

1 *David prays against his enemies;* 6 *he blesses God;* 9 *he prays for the people.*

A Psalm of David.

UNTO thee will I cry, O LORD my rock; be not silent ¹ to me: lest, *if* thou be silent to me, I become like them that go down into the pit.
2 Hear the voice of my supplications when I cry unto thee, when I lift up my hands ² toward thy holy oracle.
3 Draw me not away with the wicked, and with the workers of iniquity, which speak peace to their neighbours, but mischief *is* in their hearts.
4 Give *ª* them according to their deeds, and according to the wickedness of their endeavours: give them after the work of their hands; render to them their desert.
5 Because they regard not the works of the LORD, nor the operation of his hands, he shall destroy them, and not build them up.
6 Blessed *be* the LORD, because he hath heard the voice of my supplications.
7 The LORD *is* *ᵇ* my strength and my shield; my heart trusted in him, and I am helped: therefore my heart greatly rejoiceth; and with my song will I praise him.
8 The LORD *is* ³ their strength, and he *is* the ⁴ saving strength of his anointed.

PSALM 27.
1 approached against me.
2 Or, the delight.
ª Is. 4. 5.
3 of shouting.
4 Or, My heart said unto thee, Let my face seek thy face.
ᵇ Is. 49. 15.
5 will gather me.
Is. 40. 11.
6 a way of plainness.
7 those which observe me.
ᶜ 1 Sa. 22. 9.

PSALM 28.
1 from me.
2 Or, toward the oracle of thy sanctuary.
ª 2 Tim. 4. 14.
ᵇ Ps. 18. 2.
3 Or, his strength.
4 strength of salvations.
5 Or, rule.

PSALM 29.
1 ye sons of the mighty.
2 the honour of his name.
3 Or, in his glorious sanctuary.
4 Or, great.
5 in power.
6 in majesty.
ª Deu. 4. 46.
7 cutteth out.
8 Nu. 13. 26.
9 Or, to be in pain, and so bring forth.
9 Or, every whit of it uttereth, etc.

PSALM 30.
1 Or, to the memorial.
2 there is but a moment in his anger.
ª Ps. 68. 3.
3 in the avenging.
4 singing.
5 settled strength for my mountain.
ᵇ Psalm 104. 29.
ᶜ Psalm 115. 17.
Is. 38. 18.
6 That is, my tongue, or, my soul.

9 Save thy people, and bless thine inheritance: ⁵ feed them also, and lift them up for ever.

PSALM XXIX.

1 *David exhorts princes to give glory to God,* 3 *by reason of his power,* 11 *and protection of his people.*

A Psalm of David.

GIVE unto the LORD, O ¹ ye mighty, give unto the LORD glory and strength.
2 Give unto the LORD ² the glory due unto his name; worship the LORD ³ in the beauty of holiness.
3 The voice of the LORD *is* upon the waters: the God of glory thundereth: the LORD *is* upon ⁴ many waters.
4 The voice of the LORD *is* ⁵ powerful; the voice of the LORD *is* ⁶ full of majesty.
5 The voice of the LORD breaketh the cedars; yea, the LORD breaketh the cedars of Lebanon.
6 He maketh them also to skip like a calf; Lebanon and *ª* Sirion like a young unicorn.
7 The voice of the LORD ⁷ divideth the flames of fire.
8 The voice of the LORD shaketh the wilderness; the LORD shaketh the wilderness of *ᵇ* Kadesh.
9 The voice of the LORD maketh the hinds ⁸ to calve, and discovereth the forests: and in his temple ⁹ doth every one speak of *his* glory.
10 The LORD sitteth upon the flood; yea, the LORD sitteth king for ever.
11 The LORD will give strength unto his people; the LORD will bless his people with peace.

PSALM XXX.

1 *David praises God for his deliverance;* 4 *he exhorts others to praise him, by the example of God's dealing with him.*

A Psalm and Song at the dedication of the house of David.

I WILL extol thee, O LORD; for thou hast lifted me up, and hast not made my foes to rejoice over me.
2 O LORD my God, I cried unto thee, and thou hast healed me.
3 O LORD, thou hast brought up my soul from the grave: thou hast kept me alive, that I should not go down to the pit.
4 Sing unto the LORD, O ye saints of his, and give thanks ¹ at the remembrance of his holiness.
5 For ² his anger *endureth but a moment;* *ª* in his favour *is* life: weeping may endure ³ for a night, but ⁴ joy cometh in the morning.
6 And in my prosperity I said, I shall never be moved.
7 LORD, by thy favour thou hast ⁵ made my mountain to stand strong: thou *ᵇ* didst hide thy face, *and* I was troubled.
8 I cried to thee, O LORD; and unto the LORD I made supplication.
9 What profit *is there* in my blood, when I go down to the pit? *ᶜ* Shall the dust praise thee? shall it declare thy truth?
10 Hear, O LORD, and have mercy upon me: LORD, be thou my helper.
11 Thou hast turned for me my mourning into dancing: thou hast put off my sackcloth, and girded me with gladness;
12 To the end that *ᵇ* my glory may sing praise to thee, and not be silent. O LORD my God, I will give thanks unto thee for ever.

David Sustaineth his Faith. PSALMS XXVII—XXX. *God's Glory and Majesty.*

taining grace. 2. He asks the most careful scrutiny of his affections and thoughts (Ps. 7. 9,), or motives. 3. As of en, the ground of prayer for present help is former favour. 4-8. As exemplified by the fruits of divine grace, presented in his life, especially in his avoiding the wicked and his purposes of cleaving to God's worship. wash mine hands—expressive symbol of freedom from sinful acts (cf. Mat. 27. 24.). the habitation of thy house—where thy house rests—as the tabernacle was not yet permanently fixed. honour dwelleth—conveys an allusion to the Holy of Holies. 9. Gather not, &c.—bring me not to death. bloody men—(cf. Ps. 5. 6.). 10. Their whole conduct is that of violence and fraud. 11, 12. But, &c.—He contrasts his character and destiny with that of the wicked (cf. v. 1, 2.). even place—free from occasions of stumbling—safety in his course is denoted. Hence he will render to God his praise publicly.

PSALM XXVII.
Ver. 1-14. With a general strain of confidence, hope, and joy, especially in God's worship, in the midst of dangers, the Psalmist introduces prayer for divine help and guidance.
1. light—is a common figure for comfort. strength—or stronghold—affording security against all violence. The interrogations give greater vividness to the negation implied. 2. eat... my flesh—(Job, 19. 22; Ps. 14. 4.). The allusion to wild beasts illustrates their rapacity. they stumbled—"they" is emphatic; *not I*, but *they* were destroyed. 3. In the greatest dangers. in this—i.e., then, in such extremity. 4, 5. The secret of his confidence is his delight in communion with God (Ps. 16. 11; 23. 6;) beholding the harmony of His perfections, and seeking His favour in His temple or *paluce;* a term applicable to the tabernacle (cf. Ps. 5. 7.). There he is safe (Ps. 31. 21; 61. 5.). The figure is changed in the last clause, but the sentiment is the same. 6 head be lifted up—I shall be placed beyond the reach of my enemies. Hence he avows his purpose of rendering joyful thank-offerings. 7. Still pressing need extorts prayer for help. cry with my voice—denotes earnestness. Other things equal, Christians in earnest pray audibly, even in secret. 8. The meaning is clear, though the construction in a literal translation is obscure. The E. V. supplies the implied clause. To *seek God's face* is to seek His favour (Ps. 105. 4.). 9. Hide not, &c.—(Ps. 4. 6; 22. 24.). Against rejection he pleads former mercy and love. 10. In the extremity of earthly destitution (Ps. 31. 11; 38. 11.). God provides (cf. Mat. 25. 35.). 11. thy way—of providence, a plain path—(Ps. 26. 12.). enemies—*lit., watchers for my fall,* (Ps. 5. 8.). 12. will—*lit., soul, desire* (Ps. 35. 25.). enemies—*lit., oppressors.* False-hood aids cruelty against him. breathe out—as being filled with it (Acts. 9. 1.). 13. The strong emotion is indicated by the incomplete sentence, for which the *E. V.* supplies a proper clause; or, omitting that, and rendering, *yet I believed,* &c., the contrast of his faith and his danger is expressed. to see—is to experience Ps. 22. 17,). 14. Wait, &c.—in confident expectation. The last clause is, *lit., and wait,* &c., as if expecting new measures of help.

PSALM XXVIII.
Ver. 1-9. An earnest cry for divine aid against his enemies, as being also those of God, is followed by the Psalmist's praise in assurance of a favourable answer, and a prayer for all God's people.
1. my rock—(Ps. 18. 2, 31.). be not sile t to me—*lit., from me,* deaf or i attentive. become like them, &c.—share their fate. go down into the pit—or, grave (Ps. 30. 3.). 2. lift up my hands—a gesture of prayer (Ps. 63. 4; 141. 2.). oracle - place of *speaking* Ex. 25. 22; Num. 7, 89., where God answered His people (cf. Ps. 5. 7.). 3. Draw me not, &c.- implies punishment as well as death (cf. Ps. 26. 9.). Hypocrisy is the special *wickedness* mentioned. 4. The imprecation is justified in v. 5. The force of the passage is greatly enhanced by the accumulation of terms describing their sin. endeavours—points out their deliberate sinfulness. 5. Disregard of God's judgments brings a righteous punishment. destroy... build... up—The positive strengthened by the negative form. 6. supplications—or, cries for mercy. 7. The repetition of heart denotes his sincerity. 8. The distinction made between the people. their strength—and the anointed—may indicate Absalom's rebellion as the occasion. 9. The special prayer for the people sustains this view. feed them—as a shepherd (Ps. 23. 1, &c.).

PSALM XXIX.
Ver. 1-11. Trust in God is encouraged by the celebration of his mighty power as illustrated in his dominion over the natural world, in some of its most terrible and wonderful exhibitions.
1. Give—or, ascribe (Deut. 32. 3.). mighty—or, sons of the mighty Ps. 89. 6.). Heavenly beings as angels. 2. name—as (Ps. 5. 11; 8. 1.). beauty of holiness—the loveliness of a spiritual worship, of which the perceptible beauty of the sanctuary worship was but a type. 3. The voice of the Lord—audible exhibition of His power in the tempest, of which thunder is a specimen, but not the uniform or sole example. the waters—are the clouds or vapours (Ps. 18. 11; Jer. 10. 13.). 4. powerful... majesty—*lit., in power, in majesty.* 5, 6. The tall and large cedars, especially of Lebanon, are *shivered,* utterly broken. The waving of the mountain forests before the wind is expressed by the figure of skipping or leaping. 7. divideth—*lit., hews off.* The lightning, like flakes and splinters, hewed from stone or wood, flies through the air. 8. the wilderness—especially Kadesh, south of Judea, is selected as another scene of this display of divine power, as a vast and desolate region impresses the mind, like mountains, with images of grandeur. 9. Terror-stricken animals and denuded forests close the illustration. In view of this scene of awful sublimity, God's worshippers respond to the call of, (v. 2,). and speak or cry, "glory!" By temple, or palace (God's residence, Ps. 5. 7,\`.) may here be meant, heaven, or the whole frame of nature, as the angels are called on for praise. 10, 11. Over this terrible racing of the elements God is enthroned, directing and restraining by sovereign power; and hence the comfort of His people. "This awful God is ours, our Father and our Love."

PSALM XXX.
Ver. 1-12. *Lit., A Psalm-song*—a composition to be sung with musical instruments, or without them—or, "*Song of the dedication,*" &c., specifying the particular character of the Psalm. Some suppose that "*of*

A prayer in calamity. PSALMS XXXI–XXXIII. *Blessedness of the pardoned.*

PSALM XXXI.

1 *David, showing his confidence in God, craves his help;* 19 *he extols God's goodness to them that fear him.*

To the chief Musician, A Psalm of David.

IN thee, O LORD, do I put my trust; let me never be ashamed: deliver me in thy righteousness.

2 Bow down thine ear to me; deliver me speedily: be thou my strong rock, for an house of defence to save me.

3 For thou *art* my rock and my fortress; therefore for thy name's sake lead me, and guide me.

4 Pull me out of the net that they have laid privily for me; for thou *art* my strength.

5 Into thine hand I commit my spirit: thou hast redeemed me, O LORD God of truth.

6 I have hated them that regard lying vanities: but I trust in the LORD.

7 I will be glad and rejoice in thy mercy: for thou hast considered my trouble; thou hast known my soul in adversities;

8 And hast not shut me up into the hand of the enemy: thou hast set my feet in a large room.

9 Have mercy upon me, O LORD, for I am in trouble: mine eye is consumed with grief, *yea*, my soul and my belly.

10 For my life is spent with grief, and my years with sighing: my strength faileth because of mine iniquity, and my bones are consumed.

11 I was a reproach among all mine enemies, but especially among my neighbours, and a fear to mine acquaintance: they that did see me without fled from me.

12 I am forgotten as a dead man out of mind: I am like a broken vessel.

13 For I have heard the slander of many: fear *was* on every side: while they took counsel together against me, they devised to take away my life.

14 But I trusted in thee, O LORD: I said, Thou *art* my God.

15 My times *are* in thy hand: deliver me from the hand of mine enemies, and from them that persecute me.

16 Make thy face to shine upon thy servant: save me for thy mercies' sake.

17 Let me not be ashamed, O LORD; for I have called upon thee: let the wicked be ashamed, *and* let them be silent in the grave.

18 Let the lying lips be put to silence; which speak grievous things proudly and contemptuously against the righteous.

19 Oh how great *is* thy goodness, which thou hast laid up for them that fear thee; *which* thou hast wrought for them that trust in thee before the sons of men!

20 Thou shalt hide them in the secret of thy presence from the pride of man; thou shalt keep them secretly in a pavilion from the strife of tongues.

21 Blessed *be* the LORD; for he hath showed me his marvellous kindness in a strong city.

22 For I said in my haste, I am cut off from before thine eyes: nevertheless thou heardest the voice of my supplications when I cried unto thee.

23 O love the LORD, all ye his saints: *for* the LORD preserveth the faithful, and plentifully rewardeth the proud doer.

24 Be of good courage, and he shall strengthen your heart, all ye that hope in the LORD.

PSALM XXXII.

1 *Blessedness of him whose sins are forgiven.* 8 *The psalmist exhorts to a well-regulated conduct by its many blessings.*

A Psalm of David, Maschil.

BLESSED *is he whose* transgression *is* forgiven, *whose* sin is covered.

2 Blessed *is* the man unto whom the LORD imputeth not iniquity, and in whose spirit *there is* no guile.

3 When I kept silence, my bones waxed old through my roaring all the day long:

4 For day and night thy hand was heavy upon me: my moisture is turned into the drought of summer. Selah.

5 I acknowledged my sin unto thee, and mine iniquity have I not hid. I said, I will confess my transgressions unto the LORD; and thou forgavest the iniquity of my sin. Selah.

6 For this shall every one that is godly pray unto thee in a time when thou mayest be found: surely in the floods of great waters they shall not come nigh unto him.

7 Thou *art* my hiding-place; thou shalt preserve me from trouble; thou shalt compass me about with songs of deliverance. Selah.

8 I will instruct thee and teach thee in the way which thou shalt go: I will guide thee with mine eye.

9 Be ye not as the horse, *or* as the mule, which have no understanding; whose mouth must be held in with bit and bridle, lest they come near unto thee.

10 Many sorrows *shall be* to the wicked: but he that trusteth in the LORD, mercy shall compass him about.

11 Be glad in the LORD, and rejoice, ye righteous: and shout for joy, all ye that are upright in heart.

PSALM XXXIII.

1 *God to be praised for his goodness,* 6 *for his power,* 12 *and for his providence.* 20 *Confidence is therefore to be placed in him.*

REJOICE in the LORD, O ye righteous; for praise is comely for the upright.

2 Praise the LORD with harp; sing unto him with the psaltery and an instrument of ten strings.

3 Sing unto him a new song; play skilfully with a loud noise.

4 For the word of the LORD *is* right; and all his works *are done* in truth.

5 He loveth righteousness and judgment: the earth is full of the goodness of the LORD.

6 By the word of the LORD were the heavens made; and all the host of them by the breath of his mouth.

7 He gathereth the waters of the sea together as an heap: he layeth up the depth in storehouses.

8 Let all the earth fear the LORD: let all the inhabitants of the world stand in awe of him:

9 For he spake, and it was *done;* he commanded, and it stood fast.

10 The LORD bringeth the counsel of the heathen to nought: he maketh the devices of the people of none effect.

11 The counsel of the LORD standeth for ever, the thoughts of his heart to all generations.

A Prayer in Calamity.   PSALMS XXXI, XXXII.   *Blessedness of the Pardoned.*

David" shou d be connected with the name of the composition, and not with "*house;*" and refer for the occasion to the selection of a site for the temple 1 Chr. 21. 26-30; 22. 1.). But "*house*" is never used absolutely for the temple, and *dedication* does not well apply to such an occasion. Though the phrase in the *Heb.,* "dedication of the house of David" is an unusual form; yet it is equally unusual to disconnect the name of the author and the composition. As a "dedication of David's house" as provided, Deut. 20, 5,\, the scope of the Psalm well corresponds with the state of repose and meditation on his past trials, suited to such an occasion (2 Sam. 5. 11; 7. 2.). For beginning with a celebration of God's delivering favour in which he invites others to join, he relates his prayer in distress, and God's gracious and prompt answer.

1. lifted me up—as one is drawn from a well (Ps. 40. 2.). **2. healed me—affliction is often described as disease** Ps. 6. 2; 41. 4; 107. 20,), **and so relief by healing. 3.** The terms describe extreme danger. **soul—or, myself. grave**—*lit., hell,* as in Ps. 16. 10. **hast kept me ... pit—quickened or revived me from** the state of dying (cf. Ps. 28. 1.). **4. remembrance—the thing remembered or memorial. holiness**—as the sum of God's perfections (cf. Ps. 22. 3,\, used as *name* (Ex. 3. 15; Ps. 135, 13.). **5.** Relatively, the longest experience of divine anger by the pious is momentary. These precious words have consoled millions. **6, 7.** What particular prosperity is meant we do not know. Perhaps his accession to the throne. In his self-complacent elation he was checked by God's *hiding His face* (cf. Ps. 22. 24; 27. 9.). **troubled—confounded with fear** (Ps. 2. 5.). **8-11.** As in Ps. 6. 5; 88. 10; Isa. 38. 18, the appeal for mercy is based on the destruction of his agency in praising God here, which death would produce. . The terms expressing relief are poetical, and not to be pressed, though *dancing* is the translation of a word which means a *lute,* whose cheerful notes are contrasted with *mourning,* or, (Amos, 5. 16,), wailing. **sackcloth—was used,** even by kings, in distress (1 Chr. 21. 16; Isa. 37. 1,); but *gladness,* used for a garment, shows the language to be figurative. **12.** Though—my—is supplied before—**glory**—it is better as Ps. 16. 10, to receive it as used for *tongue,* the organ of praise. The ultimate end of God's mercies to us is our praise to Him.

PSALM XXXI.

Ver. 1-24. The prayer of a believer in time of deep distress. In the first part, cries for help are mingled with expressions of confidence. Then the detail of griefs engrosses his attention, till, in the assurance of strong but submissive faith, he rises to the language of unmingled joyful trust, and exhorts others to like love and confidence toward God.

1. expresses the general tone of feeling of the Psalm. **2-4.** He seeks help in God's righteous government Ps. 5. 8,\, and begs for an attentive hearing, and speedy and effectual aid. With no other help and no claim of merit, he relies solely on God's regard to his own perfections for a safe guidance and release from the snares of his enemies. On the terms "*rocks,*" &c., cf. Ps. 17. 2; 18. 2, 50; 20. 6; 23. 3; 25. 21. **5, 6.** commit my spirit —my life, or, myself. Our Saviour used the words on the cross, not as prophetical, but, as many pious men have done, as expressive of his unshaken confidence in God. The Psalmist rests on God's faithfulness to His promises to His people, and hence avows himself one of them, detesting all who revere objects of idolatry cf. Deut. 32. 21; 1 Cor. 8. 4. . **7. hast known my soul,** &c.—had regard to me in trouble. **8. shut me up . . . enemy—abandon** to 1 Sam. 23. 11,). **large room—place of safety** (cf. Ps. 18. 19.). **9, 10. mine eye,** &c.—denotes extreme weakness (cf. Ps. 6. 7.). **grief—** mingled sorrow and indignation (Ps. 6. 7.). **soul and . . . belly—the whole person.** Though the effects ascribed to grief are not mere figures of speech. **spent . . . consumed—must** be taken in the modified sense of *wasted* and *decayed.* **iniquity—or, suffering by it** cf. on v. 8. **make . . . shine**—cf. Num. 6. 25; Ps. 4. 6.). Deprecating from himself, he imprecates on the wicked, God's displeasure, and prays that their virulent persecution of him may be stopped. **19-21.** God displays openly His purposed goodness to His people. the secret of thy presence—or, *covering* of thy countenance: the protection He thus affords; cf. Ps. 27. 5 for a similar figure; "dwelling" used there for "presence" here. The idea of security farther presented by the figure of a tent and a fortified city. **22.** For I said—*lit., and I said,* in an adversative sense. I, thus favoured, was despondent. in my haste—in my terror. cut off . . . eyes—from all the protection of thy presence. **23, 24.** the Lord . . . proud doer—*lit., the Lord is keeping faith*— *i.e.*, with His people, and is repaying, &c. Then let none despair, but take courage, their hopes shall not be in vain.

PSALM XXXII.

Ver. 1-11. *Maschil—lit., giving instruction.* The Psalmist describes the blessings of His forgiveness, succeeding the pains of conviction, and deduces from his own experience instruction and exhortation to others.

1, 2. (Cf. Rom. 4. 6.). **forgiven**—*lit., taken away,* opposed to *retain* (John, 20. 23.). **covered**—so that God no longer regards the sin (Ps. 85. 3.). **imputeth—charge to him, and treat him accordingly. no guile—or, *deceit,*** no false estimate of himself, nor hypocrisy before God (cf. Rom. 8. 1.). **3, 4.** A vivid description of felt, but unacknowledged, sin. when—*lit., for,* as v. 4, the hand—of God, or, power in distressing him (Ps. 38. 2.). moisture—vital juices of the body, the parching heat of which expresses the anguish of the soul. On the other figures (cf. Ps. 6. 2, 7; 31. 9-11.). If composed on the occasion of the fifty-first Psalm, this distress may have been protracted for several months. **5.** A prompt fulfilment of the purposed confession is followed by a prompt forgiveness. **6.** For this —*i.e.,* my happy experience. godly—pious in the sense of Ps. 4. 3. a time—(Isa. 55. 6.), when God's Spirit inclines us to seek pardon. He is ready to forgive. **floods,** &c.—denote great danger (Ps. 18. 17; 69. 12.). **7. His ex-** perience illustrates the statement of v. 6, **8.**

Blessedness of the righteous. PSALMS XXXIV, XXXV. *An appeal for God's protection.*

12 Blessed is the nation whose God is the LORD; and the people whom he hath chosen for his own inheritance.
13 The LORD looketh from heaven; he beholdeth all the sons of men.
14 From the place of his habitation he looketh upon all the inhabitants of the earth.
15 He fashioneth their hearts alike; he considereth all their works.
16 There is no king saved by the multitude of an host: a mighty man is not delivered by much strength.
17 An horse is a vain thing for safety: neither shall he deliver any by his great strength.
18 Behold, the eye of the LORD is upon them that fear him, upon them that hope in his mercy;
19 To deliver their soul from death, and to keep them alive in famine.
20 Our soul waiteth for the LORD: he is our help and our shield.
21 For our heart shall rejoice in him; because we have trusted in his holy name.
22 Let thy mercy, O LORD, be upon us, according as we hope in thee.

PSALM XXXIV.

David praises God, and exhorts others thereto by his experience. 8 They blessed who trust in God. 11 He exhorts to the fear of God, etc.

A Psalm of David, when he changed his behaviour before Abimelech; who drove him away, and he departed.

I WILL bless the LORD at all times: his praise shall continually be in my mouth.
2 My soul shall make her boast in the LORD: the humble shall hear thereof, and be glad.
3 O magnify the LORD with me, and let us exalt his name together.
4 I sought the LORD, and he heard me, and delivered me from all my fears.
5 They looked unto him, and were lightened; and their faces were not ashamed.
6 This poor man cried, and the LORD heard him, and saved him out of all his troubles.
7 The angel of the LORD encampeth round about them that fear him, and delivereth them.
8 O taste and see that the LORD is good: blessed is the man that trusteth in him.
9 O fear the LORD, ye his saints: for there is no want to them that fear him.
10 The young lions do lack, and suffer hunger: but they that seek the LORD shall not want any good thing.
11 Come, ye children, hearken unto me; I will teach you the fear of the LORD.
12 What man is he that desireth life, and loveth many days, that he may see good?
13 Keep thy tongue from evil, and thy lips from speaking guile.
14 Depart from evil, and do good; seek peace, and pursue it.
15 The eyes of the LORD are upon the righteous, and his ears are open unto their cry.
16 The face of the LORD is against them that do evil, to cut off the remembrance of them from the earth.
17 The righteous cry, and the LORD heareth, and delivereth them out of all their troubles.
18 The LORD is nigh unto them that are of a broken heart; and saveth such as be of a contrite spirit.

19 Many are the afflictions of the righteous: but the LORD delivereth him out of them all.
20 He keepeth all his bones: not one of them is broken.
21 Evil shall slay the wicked; and they that hate the righteous shall be desolate.
22 The LORD redeemeth the soul of his servants: and none of them that trust in him shall be desolate.

PSALM XXXV.

1 David prays for his own safety, and his enemies' confusion: 22 he pleads with God to do him right.

A Psalm of David.

PLEAD my cause, O LORD, with them that strive with me: fight against them that fight against me.
2 Take hold of shield and buckler, and stand up for mine help.
3 Draw out also the spear, and stop the way against them that persecute me: say unto my soul, I am thy salvation.
4 Let them be confounded and put to shame that seek after my soul: let them be turned back and brought to confusion that devise my hurt.
5 Let them be as chaff before the wind: and let the angel of the LORD chase them.
6 Let their way be dark and slippery: and let the angel of the LORD persecute them.
7 For without cause have they hid for me their net in a pit, which without cause they have digged for my soul.
8 Let destruction come upon him at unawares; and let his net that he hath hid catch himself: into that very destruction let him fall.
9 And my soul shall be joyful in the LORD: it shall rejoice in his salvation.
10 All my bones shall say, LORD, who is like unto thee, which deliverest the poor from him that is too strong for him, yea, the poor and the needy from him that spoileth him?
11 False witnesses did rise up: they laid to my charge things that I knew not.
12 They rewarded me evil for good, to the spoiling of my soul.
13 But as for me, when they were sick, my clothing was sackcloth: I humbled my soul with fasting; and my prayer returned into mine own bosom.
14 I behaved myself as though he had been my friend or brother: I bowed down heavily, as one that mourneth for his mother.
15 But in mine adversity they rejoiced, and gathered themselves together: yea, the abjects gathered themselves together against me, and I knew it not; they did tear me, and ceased not:
16 With hypocritical mockers in feasts, they gnashed upon me with their teeth.
17 LORD, how long wilt thou look on? rescue my soul from their destructions, my darling from the lions.
18 I will give thee thanks in the great congregation: I will praise thee among much people.
19 Let not them that are mine enemies wrongfully rejoice over me; neither let them wink with the eye that hate me without a cause.
20 For they speak not peace; but they devise deceitful matters against them that are quiet in the land.

Blessedness of the Righteous. PSALMS XXXIII–XXXV. *An Appeal for Protection.*

Whether, as most likely, the language of David (cf. Ps. 51. 13,), or that of God, this is a promise of divine guidance. **I will ... mine eye**—or, *my* eye shall be on thee, watching and directing thy way. 9. The latter clause, more literally, "*in that they come not near thee*"—*i.e., because* they will not come, &c., unless forced by bit and bridle. 10. The sorrows of the impenitent contrasted with the peace and safety secured by God's mercy. 11. The righteous and upright, or those conforming to the divine teaching for securing the divine blessing, may well rejoice with shouting.

PSALM XXXIII.

Ver. 1-22. A call to lively and joyous praise to God for His glorious attributes and works, as displayed in creation and His general and special providence, in view of which, the Psalmist, for all the pious, professes trust and joy, and invokes God's mercy.

1-3. The sentiment falls in with Ps. 32. 11, (cf. 1 Cor. 14. 15.).The instruments, (Ps. 92. 3; 144. 9,), do not exclude the voice. **a new song**—fresh, adapted to the occasion (Ps. 40. 3; 96. 1.). **play skilfully**—(cf. Ps. 15. 16, 21,). 4-9. Reasons for praise, first, God's truth, faithfulness, and mercy, generally; then, His creative power which all must honour. In **word and breath**—or, *spirit*, there may be an allusion to the Son (John, 1. 1,), and Holy Spirit. **he spake**—*lit., said*, it was—the addition of *done* weakens the sense (cf. Gen. 1. 3-10.). 10, 11. In God's providence He thwarts men's purposes and executes His own. **heathen**—*lit., nations*. 12-19. The inference from the foregoing in *v.* 12, is illustrated by God's special providence, underlying which is His minute knowledge of all men. **looketh**—intently (Isa. 14. 16.). **fashioneth**—or, forms, and hence knows and controls (Pro. 21. 1.). **alike**—*without exception*. **considereth**—or, understands, God knows men's motives. 16, 17. Men's usual reliances in their greatest exigencies are, in themselves, useless. *On the war horse* cf. Job, 39. 19-25.), **a vain thing**—a lie, which deceives us 18, 19. Contrasted is God's guidance and power to save from the greatest earthly evil and its most painful precursor, and hence from all. 20-22. **waiteth**—in earnest expectation **holy name**—(cf. Ps. 5. 12; 22. 22; 30, 4.). Our faith measures mercy (Mat. 9. 29,), and if of grace, it is no more of debt (Rom. 11 6.).

PSALM XXXIV.

Ver. 1-22 On the title cf. 1 Sam. 21. 13. Abimelech was the general name of the sovereign (Gen. 20. 2.). After celebrating God's gracious dealings with him, the Psalmist exhorts others to make trial of His providential care, instructing them how to secure it. He then contrasts God's care of His people and His punitive providence towards the wicked.

1-4. Even in distress, which excites supplication, there is always matter for praising and thanking God (cf. Eph. 5. 20; Phil. 4. 6.), make her boast—glory (Ps. 105. 3; cf. Gal. 6 14.). **humble**—the pious, as Ps. 9. 12; 25. 9. **magnify the Lord**—ascribe greatness to Him, an act of praise. **together**—alike (Ps. 33. 15,), or, equally, without exception. **delivered ... fears**—as well as actual evil (Ps. 64. 1.). 5-7. God's favour to the pious generally, and to him. If specially, is celebrated. **looked**—with desire or help. **lightened**—or, brightened, expressing joy, opposed to the downcast features of those who are ashamed or disappointed (Ps. 25. 2, 3.). This poor man—*lit., humble*, himself as a specimen of such. **angel**—of the covenant (Isa. 63. 9,), of whom as a leader of God's host (Josh. 5. 14; 1 Ki. 22. 19,), the phrase—encampeth, &c.—is appropriate; or *angel*, used collectively for angels (Heb. 1. 14.). 8. **taste and see**—try and experience. 9. Those **fear him**—who are pious—fear and love (Pro. 1. 7; 9. 10.). **saints**—consecrated to His service Isa. 40. 31.) 10. **not want any good**—"Good" is emphatic: they may be afflicted (cf. *v.* 19); but this may be a *good* (2 Cor. 4. 17, 18; Heb. 12. 10, 11.). 11. children—subjects of instruction (Pro. 1. 8, 10.). 12. What man—whoever desires the blessings of piety let him attend. 13, 14. Sins of thought included in those of speech (Luke, 6. 45,), avoiding evil and doing good in our relations to men are based on a right relation to God. 15. **eyes of the Lord are upon**—Ps. 32. 8; 33. 18.). 16. Face ... **against**—*opposed* to them (Lev. 17. 10; 20. 3.). cut off the remembrance—utterly destroy, (Ps. 109. 13.). 17, 18. Humble penitents are objects of God's special tender regard (Ps. 51. 19; Isa. 57. 15.). 20. bones—framework of the body. 21, 22. Contrast in the destiny of righteous and wicked, the former shall be delivered and never come into condemnation (John, 5. 24; Rom. 8. 1.), the latter left under condemnation and desolate.

PSALM XXXV.

Ver. 1-28. The Psalmist invokes God's aid, contrasting the hypocrisy, cunning, and malice of his enemies with his integrity and generosity. The imprecations of the first part including a brief notice of their conduct, the fuller exposition of their hypocrisy and malice in the second, and the earnest prayer for deliverance from their scornful triumph in the last, are each closed (*v* 9, 10, 18, 27, 28,) with promises of praise for the desired relief in which his friends will unite. The historical occasion is probably 1 Sam. 24.

1-3. God is invoked in the character of a warrior (Ex. 15. 3; Deut. 32. 41.). **fight against**—*lit., devour my devourers*. **stop the way against**—*lit., shut up* (the way,), to meet or oppose, &c. **I ... thy salvation**—who saves thee. 4. (Cf. Ps. 9. 17.). **devise my hurt**—purpose for evil to me. 5, 6.—cf. Ps. 1. 4,—a terrible fate; driven by wind on a slippery path in darkness, and hotly pursued by supernatural violence (2 Sam. 24. 16; Acts, 12. 23.). 7, 8. **net in a pit**—or, pit of their net—or, net pit—as holy hill for hill of holiness—(Ps. 2. 6,)—a figure from hunting (Ps. 7. 15.). Their imprecations on impenitent rebels against God need no vindication: His justice and wrath are for such; His mercy for penitents. Cf. Ps. 7. 16; 11. 5, on the peculiar fate of the wicked here noticed. 9, 10. All my **bones**—every part. **him that spoileth him** —(cf. Ps. 10. 2.). 11. False witnesses—*lit., Witnesses of injustice and cruelty* (cf. Ps. 11. 5; 25. 19.) 12-14. Though they rendered evil for good, he showed a tender sympathy in their affliction. **spoiling**—*lit., bereavement*. The usual modes of showing grief are made, as figures, to express his sorrow. **prayer ... bosom**—may denote either the posture—the head bowed—cf. 1 Ki. 18. 42)—or, that the prayer was in secret. Some think there is a reference to the result—the prayer would benefit him if not them. **behaved**—*lit., went on*—denoting his habit. **heavily**—or, *sadly,* **his sorrow occasioning neglect of his**

21 Yea, they opened their mouth wide against me, *and* said, Aha, aha! our eye hath seen it.
22 *This* thou hast *seen*, O LORD: keep not silence: O LORD, be not far from me.
23 Stir up thyself, and awake to my judgment, *even* unto my cause, my God and my Lord.
24 Judge me, O LORD my God, *according to thy righteousness; and let them not rejoice over me.
25 Let them not say in their hearts, Ah! so would we have it: let them not say, We have swallowed him up.
26 Let them be ashamed and brought to confusion together that rejoice at mine hurt: let them be clothed with shame and dishonour that magnify *themselves* against me.
27 Let them shout for joy, and be glad, that favour my righteous cause; yea, let them say continually, Let the LORD be magnified, which hath pleasure in the prosperity of his servant.
28 And my tongue shall speak of thy righteousness *and* of thy praise all the day long.

PSALM XXXVI.

1 Grievous estate of the wicked. 5 Excellency of God's mercy.

To the chief Musician, *A Psalm* of David the servant of the LORD.

THE transgression of the wicked saith within my heart, *that there is* no fear of God before his eyes.
2 For he flattereth himself in his own eyes, until his iniquity be found to be hateful.
3 The words of his mouth *are* iniquity and deceit: he hath left off to be wise, *and* to do good.
4 He deviseth mischief upon his bed; he setteth himself in a way *that is* not good; he abhorreth not evil.
5 Thy mercy, O LORD, *is* in the heavens; *and* thy faithfulness *reacheth* unto the clouds.
6 Thy righteousness *is* like the great mountains; thy judgments *are* a great deep: O LORD, thou preservest man and beast.
7 How excellent *is* thy loving-kindness, O God! therefore the children of men put their trust under the shadow of thy wings.
8 They shall be abundantly satisfied with the fatness of thy house; and thou shalt make them drink of the river of thy pleasures.
9 For with thee *is* the fountain of life: in thy light shall we see light.
10 O continue thy loving-kindness unto them that know thee; and thy righteousness to the upright in heart.
11 Let not the foot of pride come against me, and let not the hand of the wicked remove me.
12 There are the workers of iniquity fallen: they are cast down, and shall not be able to rise.

PSALM XXXVII.

David persuades to patience and humble trust in God, by the happy state of the godly, and the short-lived prosperity of the wicked.

A Psalm of David.

FRET not thyself because of evil-doers, neither be thou envious against the workers of iniquity:
2 For they shall soon be cut down like the grass, and wither as the green herb.

3 Trust in the LORD, and do good; *so* shalt thou dwell in the land, and verily thou shalt be fed.
4 Delight thyself also in the LORD; and he shall give thee the desires of thine heart.
5 Commit thy way unto the LORD; trust also in him, and he shall bring *it* to pass:
6 And he shall bring forth thy righteousness as the light, and thy judgment as the noon-day.
7 Rest in the LORD, and wait patiently for him: fret not thyself because of him who prospereth in his way, because of the man who bringeth wicked devices to pass.
8 Cease from anger, and forsake wrath: fret not thyself in anywise to do evil.
9 For evil-doers shall be cut off: but those that wait upon the LORD, they shall inherit the earth.
10 For yet a little while, and the wicked *shall* not *be:* yea, thou shalt diligently consider his place, and it *shall* not *be.*
11 But the meek shall inherit the earth; and shall delight themselves in the abundance of peace.
12 The wicked plotteth against the just, and gnasheth upon him with his teeth.
13 The Lord shall laugh at him; for he seeth that his day is coming.
14 The wicked have drawn out the sword, and have bent their bow, to cast down the poor and needy, *and* to slay such as be of upright conversation.
15 Their sword shall enter into their own heart, and their bows shall be broken.
16 A little that a righteous man hath *is* better than the riches of many wicked.
17 For the arms of the wicked shall be broken: but the LORD upholdeth the righteous.
18 The LORD knoweth the days of the upright: and their inheritance shall be for ever.
19 They shall not be ashamed in the evil time; and in the days of famine they shall be satisfied.
20 But the wicked shall perish, and the enemies of the LORD *shall be* as the fat of lambs: they shall consume; into smoke shall they consume away.
21 The wicked borroweth, and payeth not again: but the righteous showeth mercy, and giveth.
22 For such as be blessed of him shall inherit the earth; and they that be cursed of him shall be cut off.
23 The steps of a *good* man are ordered by the LORD; and he delighteth in his way.
24 Though he fall, he shall not be utterly cast down: for the LORD upholdeth *him* with his hand.
25 I have been young, and now am old yet have I not seen the righteous forsaken, nor his seed begging bread.
26 *He is* ever merciful, and lendeth; and his seed *is* blessed.
27 Depart from evil, and do good; and dwell for evermore.
28 For the LORD loveth judgment, and forsaketh not his saints; they are preserved for ever: but the seed of the wicked shall be cut off.
29 The righteous shall inherit the land, and dwell therein for ever.
30 The mouth of the righteous speaketh wisdom, and his tongue talketh of judgment.
31 The law of his God *is* in his heart; none of his steps shall slide.

person. Altogether, his grief was that of one for a dearly loved relative. 15, 16. On the contrary, they rejoiced in his affliction. *Halting*, or *lameness*, as Ps. 38, 17, for any distress. *abjects*—either as cripples (cf. 2 Sam. 4. 4; contemptible; or, degraded persons, such as had been beaten (cf. Job, 30, 1-8.). I knew it not—either the persons, or, reasons of such conduct. tear me, and ceased not—*lit*, *were not silent*—showing that the *tearing* meant slandering. mockers—who were hired to make sport at feasts (Pro. 28, 21.). 17. darling—(cf. Ps. 22, 20, 21.). 18. (Cf. Ps. 22, 22.). 19. enemies wrongfully—by false and slanderous imputations. wink with the eye—an insulting gesture (Pro. 6. 13.). without cause—manifests more malice than having a wrong cause. 20. deceitful matters—or, words of deceit. quiet in the land—the pious lovers of peace. 21. On the gesture cf. Ps. 22. 7, and on the expressions of malicious triumph cf. Ps. 10. 13; 28. 3. 23, 24. Cf. Ps. 7. 6; 26. 1; 2 Thes. 1. 6.). God's righteous government is the hope of the pious and terror of the wicked. 25. swallowed him up—utterly destroyed him (Ps. 21. 9; Lam. 2. 16.). 26. clothed—covered wholly (Job, 8. 22.). 27. favour... cause—delight in it, as vindicated by thee. Let the Lord, &c.—Let Him be greatly praised for His care of the just. 28. In this praise of God's equitable government (Ps. 5. 8,), the writer promises ever to engage.

PSALM XXXVI.

Ver. 1-12. On servant of the Lord cf. title Ps. 18. The wickedness of man contrasted with the excellency of God's perfections and dispensations; and the benefit of the latter sought, and the evils of the former depreciated.

1. The general sense of this difficult verse is, "that the wicked have no fear of God." The first clause may be rendered, "Saith transgression in my heart, in respect to the wicked, there is no fear," &c., *i.e.*, such is my reflection on men's transgressions. 2-4. This reflection detailed, until his iniquity, &c.—*lit., for finding his iniquity for hating; i.e.*, he persuades himself God will not so find it—"*for hating*" involving the idea of punishing. Hence his words of *iniquity* and *deceit*, and his bold rejection of all right principles of conduct. The climax is that he deliberately adopts and patronises evil. The negative forms affirm more emphatically their contraries. 5, 6. mercy... aud... faithfulness—as mercy and truth (Ps. 25. 10.). righteousness and judgments—qualities of a good government (Ps. 5. 8; 31. 1.). These all are set forth, by the figures used, as unbounded. 7. shadow of thy wings—(cf. Deut. 32. 11; Ps. 91. 1.). 8. fatness—richness, thy house—residence—for the privileges and blessings of communion with God (Ps. 23. 6; 27. 4.). river of thy pleasures—plenteous supply—may allude to Eden. 9. Light is an emblem of all blessings—given of God as a means to gain more. 10. that know thee—right knowledge of God is the source of right affections and conduct. 11. foot of... hand... wicked—all kinds of violent dealing. 12. There—in the acting of violence, they are overthrown. A signal defeat.

PSALM XXXVII.

Ver. 1-40. A composed and uniform trust in God, and a constant course of integrity, are urged in view of the blessedness of the truly pious, contrasted in various aspects with the final ruin of the wicked. Thus the wisdom and justice of God's providence are vindicated, and its seeming inequalities, which excite the cavils of the wicked and the distrust of the pious, are explained. David's personal history abundantly illustrates the Psalm. 1, 2. The general sentiment of the whole Psalm is expressed. The righteous need not be vexed by the prosperity of the wicked; for it is transient, and their destiny undesirable. 3. Trust—sure of safety. shalt thou dwell—or, dwell thou—repose quietly, verily... fed —or, *feed on truth*—God's promise (Ps. 36, 5, cf. Hos. 12. 1.). 4. desires—(Ps. 20. 5; 21. 2,), what is lawful and right, really good (Ps. 84. 11.). 5. Commit thy way—(Pro. 16. 3.). *Works*—what you have to do and cannot—set forth as a burden. trust... in him—*lit., on Him*. He *will do* what you cannot (cf. Ps. 22. 8; 31. 6.). He will not suffer your character to remain under suspicion. 7, 8. Rest in—*lit., be silent to the Lord*. and wait—be submissive—avoid petulance and murmurings, anger and rash doing. 9. Two reasons. The prosperity of the wicked is short, and the pious, by humble trust, will secure all covenant blessings denoted here, by "inherit the earth" (cf. Ps. 25. 13.). 10, 11. shall not be—*lit., is not*—is not to be found. peace—includes prosperity. 12. gnasheth... teeth—in beastly rage. 13. (Cf. Ps. 2. 4.). seeth—knows certainly. his day—of punishment, long delayed, shall yet come (Heb. 10. 37.). 14, 15. sword, and... bow—for any instruments of violence. slay—*lit., slaughter* (1 Sam. 25. 11.). poor and needy—God's people (Ps. 10, 17; 12. 5.). The punishment of the wicked as drawn on themselves—often mentioned (cf. Ps. 7. 15, 16; 35. 8.) 16. riches—*lit., noise and tumult*, as incidental to much wealth (cf. Ps. 39, 6.). Thus the contrast with the "little" of one man is more vivid. 17. Even the members of the body needed to hold weapons are destroyed. 18, 19. God, who knows his people's changes, provides against evil, and supplies all their need. 20. While the wicked, however mighty, are destroyed, and that utterly, as smoke which vanishes and leaves no trace. 21, 22. payeth not—not able; having grown poor (cf. Deut. 15. 7.). Ability of the one and inability of the other do not exclude moral dispositions. God's blessing or cursing makes the difference. cut of—opposed to "inherit the earth" (cf. Lev. 7. 20, 21.). 23, 24. steps—way, or, course of life; as ordered by God, failures will not be permanent. 25, 26 his seed is blessed—*lit., for a blessing* (Gen. 12. 2; Ps. 21. 6.). This position is still true as the rule of God's economy (1 Tim. 4. 8; 6. 6.). 27-29. The exhortation is sustained by the assurance of God's essential rectitude in that providential government, which provides perpetual blessings for the good, and perpetual misery for the wicked. 30, 31. The righteous described as to the elements of character, thought, word, and action. steps—or, goings —for conduct which is unwavering (Ps. 18.). 32, 33. The devices of the wicked against the good fail, because God acquits them. 34. On the contrary, the good are not only blessed, but made to see the ruin of their foes; 35, 36. of which a picture is given, under the figure of a flourishing tree (cf. *Marg.*), which soon withers. he was not —(cf. *v*. 10.). 37. By the *end* is meant reward (Pro. 23. 18; 24. 14.), or expectation of success,

A prayer in distress. PSALMS XXXVIII–XL. *The shortness of human life.*

32 The wicked watcheth the righteous, and seeketh to slay him.
33 The LORD will not leave him in his hand, nor ᵐ condemn him when he is judged.
34 Wait on the LORD, and keep his way, and he shall exalt thee to inherit the land: when the wicked are cut off, thou shalt see it.
35 I have seen the wicked in great power, and spreading himself like ¹⁰ a green bay tree.
36 Yet he passed away, and, lo, he *was* not; yea, I sought him, but he could not be found.
37 Mark the perfect *man*, and behold the upright: for ⁿ the end of *that* man *is* peace.
38 But the transgressors shall be destroyed together: the end of the wicked shall be cut off.
39 But ᵒ the salvation of the righteous *is* of the LORD; *he is* their strength in the time of trouble.
40 And the LORD shall help them, and deliver them: he shall deliver them from the wicked, and save them, ᵖ because they trust in him.

PSALM XXXVIII.

David moves God to take compassion of his pitiful case, confessing his sins to be the cause thereof.
A Psalm of David, to bring to remembrance.

O LORD, rebuke me not in thy wrath: neither chasten me in thy hot displeasure.
2 For thine arrows stick fast in me, and thy hand presseth me sore.
3 *There is* no soundness in my flesh because of thine anger; neither *is there any* ¹ rest in my bones because of my sin.
4 For mine iniquities are gone over mine head; as an heavy burden they are too heavy for me.
5 My wounds stink *and* are corrupt because of my foolishness.
6 I am ² troubled; I am bowed down greatly; I go mourning all the day long.
7 For my loins are filled with a ᵃ loathsome *disease*; and *there is* no soundness in my flesh.
8 I am feeble and sore broken: I have roared by reason of the disquietness of my heart.
9 Lord, all my desire *is* before thee; and my groaning is not hid from thee.
10 My heart panteth, my strength faileth me: as for the light of mine eyes, it also ³ is gone from me.
11 My lovers and my friends ᵇ stand aloof from my ⁴ sore, and ᵇ my kinsmen stand afar off.
12 They also that seek after my life lay snares *for me;* and they that seek my hurt speak mischievous things, and imagine deceits all the day long.
13 But I, as a deaf *man*, heard not; and *I was* as a dumb man *that* openeth not his mouth.
14 Thus I was as a man that heareth not, and in whose mouth *are* no reproofs.
15 For ⁶ in thee, O LORD, ᶜ do I hope: thou wilt ⁷ hear, O Lord my God.
16 For I said, *Hear me*, lest *otherwise* they should rejoice over me: when my foot slippeth, they magnify *themselves* against me.
17 For I *am* ready ⁸ to halt, and my sorrow *is* continually before me,

18 For I will ᵈ declare mine iniquity; I will be ᵉ sorry for my sin.
19 But mine enemies ⁹ *are* lively, *and* they are strong; and they that hate me wrongfully are multiplied.
20 They also that render evil for good are mine adversaries; ᶠ because I follow the thing that good *is*.
21 Forsake me not, O LORD: O my God, be not far from me.
22 Make haste ¹⁰ to help me, O Lord ᵍ my salvation.

PSALM XXXIX.

1 *David's care of his thoughts:* 4 *his consideration of the brevity and vanity of life:* 8 *he prays for pardon and comfort, etc.*
To the chief Musician, *even* to ᵃ Jeduthun, A Psalm of David.

I SAID, I will ᵇ take heed to my ways, that I sin not with my tongue: I will keep ¹ my mouth with a bridle, ᶜ while the wicked is before me.
2 I was dumb with silence; I held my peace, *even* from good; and my sorrow was ² stirred.
3 My heart was hot within me; while I was musing ᵈ the fire burned: *then* spake I with my tongue,
4 LORD, make me to know mine end, and the measure of my days, what it *is;* that I may know ³ how frail I *am*.
5 Behold, thou hast made my days *as* an handbreadth, and ᵉ mine age *is* as nothing before thee: verily every man ⁴ at his best state *is* altogether vanity. Selah.
6 Surely every man walketh in ⁵ a vain show: surely they are disquieted in vain: he heapeth up *riches*, and knoweth not who shall gather them.
7 And now, Lord, what wait I for? my hope *is* in thee.
8 Deliver me from all my transgressions: make me not the reproach of the foolish.
9 I was dumb, I opened not my mouth; because thou didst *it*.
10 Remove thy stroke away from me: I am consumed by the ⁶ blow of thine hand.
11 When thou with rebukes dost correct man for iniquity, thou makest ⁷ his beauty to consume away like a moth: surely every man *is* vanity. Selah.
12 Hear my prayer, O LORD, and give ear unto my cry; hold not thy peace at my tears: ᶠ for I *am* a stranger with thee, *and* a sojourner, as all my fathers *were*.
13 O spare me, that I may recover strength, before I go hence, and be no more.

PSALM XL.

1 *The benefit of confidence in God.* 6 *Obedience the best sacrifice.*
To the chief Musician, A Psalm of David.

I WAITED patiently for the LORD; and he inclined unto me, and heard my cry.
2 He brought me up also out of ² an horrible pit, out of the miry clay, and set my feet upon a rock, *and* established my goings.
3 And he hath put a new song in my mouth, *even* praise unto our God: many shall see *it*, and fear, and shall trust in the LORD.
4 Blessed ᵃ *is* that man that maketh the LORD his trust, and respecteth not the proud, nor such as turn aside to lies.
5 Many, O LORD my God, *are* thy wonderful works *which* thou hast done, ᵇ and thy thoughts *which* are to us-ward: ³ they cannot be reckoned up in order unto thee:

as *v.* 38, which describes the *end of the wicked* in contrast, and that is *cut off* (cf. Ps. 73. 17.). 38. together—at once—entirely (Ps. 4. 8.). 39, 40. strength—(Ps. 27. 1; 2s. 8.). trouble—straits Ps. 9. 9; 10. 1.). In trust and quietness is the salvation of the pious from all foes and all their devices.

PSALM XXXVIII.

Ver. 1-22. *To bring to remembrance,* or, remind, God of His mercy and himself of his sin. Appealing to God for relief from His heavy chastisement, the Psalmist avows his integrity before men, complains of the detection of friends and persecution of enemies, and in a submissive spirit, casting himself on God, with penitent confession, he pleads God's covenant relation and his innocence of the charges of his enemies, and prays for divine comfort and help.

1-4. He deprecates deserved punishment, which is described (Ps. 6. 1,) under the figure of bodily disease. arrows... and thy hand—the sharp and heavy afflictions he suffered (Deut. 32. 23.). iniquities—afflictions in punishment of sin (2 Sam. 16. 12; Ps. 31. 10; 40. 12.) gone over mine head—as a flood. 5-8. The loathsomeness, corruption, and wasting torture of severe physical disease set forth his mental anguish. It is possible some bodily disease was connected. *The loins* are the seat of strength. His exhaustion left him only the power to groan. 9. That God can hear (Rom. 8. 26.. 10. My heart panteth—as if barely surviving. light... from me—utter exhaustion Ps. 6. 7; 13. 3.). 11, 12. Friends desert but foes increase in malignity. seek after my life—(1 Sam. 20. 1; 22. 23.). 13, 14. He patiently submits, uttering no *reproaches* or replies (John. 19. 9,) to their insulting speeches; 15-17. for he is confident the Lord—*lit., Sovereign* to whom he was a servant', would answer his prayer (Ps. 3. 4; 4. 1,), and not permit their triumph in his *partial halting,* of which he was in danger. 18. Consciousness of sin makes suffering pungent, and suffering, rightly received, leads to confession. 19, 20. Still, while humbled before God, he is the victim of deadly enemies, full of malice and treachery. enemies are lively—*lit., of life,* who would take my life, *i.e.,* deadly. 21, 22. (Cf. Ps. 22. 19; 35. 3.). All terms of frequent use. In this Psalm the language is generally susceptible of application to Christ as a sufferer, David, as such, typifying Him. This does not require us to apply the confessions of sin, but only the pains or penalties which he bore for us.

PSALM XXXIX.

Ver. 1-13. *To Jeduthun* (1 Chr. 16. 41, 42,), one of the chief singers. His name mentioned, perhaps, as a special honour. Under depressing views of his frailty and the prosperity of the wicked, the Psalmist, tempted to murmur, checks the expression of his feelings, till led to regard his case aright, he prays for a proper view of his condition and for the divine compassion.

1. I said—or, resolved. will take heed—watch. ways—conduct, of which the use of the tongue is a part (Jam. 1. 26.). bridle—*lit., muzzle,* (cf. Deut. 25. 4.). while... before me—in beholding their prosperity (Ps. 37. 10, 36.). 2. even from good—(Gen. 31. 24,), everything. 3. His emotions, as a smothered flame, *burst* forth. 4-7. Some take these words as those of fretting, but they are not essentially such. The tinge of discontent arises from the character of his suppressed emotions. But, addressing God, they are softened and subdued. make me to know—experimentally appreciate. how frail I am—*lit., when I shall cease.* 5, 6. His prayer is answered in his obtaining an impressive view of the vanity of the life of all men, and their transient state. Their pomp is a mere *image,* and their wealth is gathered they know not for whom. 7. The interrogation makes the implied negative stronger. Though this world offers nothing to our expectation, God is worthy of all confidence. 8-10. Patiently submissive, he prays for the removal of his chastisement, and that he may not be a reproach. 11. From his own case, he argues to that of all, that the destruction of man's enjoyments is ascribable to sin. 12, 13. Consonant with the tenor of the Psalm, he prays for God's compassionate regard to him as a stranger here, and that, as such was the condition of his fathers, so, like them, he may be cheered instead of being bound under wrath and chastened in displeasure.

PSALM XL.

Ver. 1-17. In this Psalm a celebration of God's deliverance is followed by a profession of devotion to His service. Then follows a prayer for relief from imminent dangers, involving the overthrow of enemies and the rejoicing of sympathising friends. In Heb. 10. 5, &c., Paul quotes *v.* 6-8, as the words of Christ, offering himself as a better sacrifice. Some suppose Paul thus accommodated David's words to express Christ's sentiments. But the value of his quotation would be thus destroyed, as it would have no force in his argument, unless regarded by his readers as the original sense of the passage in the O. T. Others suppose the Psalm describes David's feelings in suffering and joy; but the language quoted by Paul, in the sense given by him, could not apply to David in any of his relations, for as a type the language is not adapted to describe any event or condition of David's career, and as an individual representing the pious generally, neither he nor they could properly use it (cf. on *v.* 7 below.). The Psalm must be taken then, as the sixteenth, to express the feelings of Christ's human nature. The difficulties pertinent to this view will be considered as they occur. 1-3. The figures for deep distress are illustrated in Jeremiah's history (Jer. 38. 6-12.). Patience and trust manifested in distress, deliverance in answer to prayer, and the blessed effect in eliciting praise from God's true worshippers, teach us that Christ's suffering is our example, and His deliverance our encouragement (Heb. 5. 7, 8; 12. 3; 1 Pet. 4. 12-16.). inclined—(the ear, Ps. 17. 6,), as if to catch the faintest sigh. a new song—(Ps. 33. 3.) fear, and... trust—revere with love and faith. 4. Blessed—(Ps. 1. 1; 2. 12.). respecteth—*lit., turns towards,* as an object of confidence. turn aside—from true God and His law to falsehood in worship and conduct. 5. he reckoned up in order—(cf. Ps. 5. 3; 33. 14; Isa. 44. 7,), too many to be set forth regularly. This is but one instance of many. The use of the plural accords with the union of Christ and His people. In suffering and triumph, they are one with Him. 6-8. In Paul's view this passage has more meaning than the mere expression of grateful devotion to God's service. He represents Christ as declaring that the sacrifices, whether vegetable or animal-

Blessedness of the charitable man. PSALMS XLI–XLIV. *Public worship longed for.*

if I would declare and speak of them, they are more than can be numbered.
6 Sacrifice *and offering thou didst not desire; mine ears hast thou opened: burnt offering and sin offering hast thou not required.
7 Then said I, Lo, I come: in the volume of the book it is written of me,
8 I delight to do thy will, O my God: yea, thy law is within my heart.
9 I have preached righteousness in the great congregation: lo, I have not refrained my lips, O LORD, thou knowest.
10 I have not hid thy righteousness within my heart; I have declared thy faithfulness and thy salvation: I have not concealed thy loving-kindness and thy truth from the great congregation.
11 Withhold not thou thy tender mercies from me, O LORD: let thy loving-kindness and thy truth continually preserve me.
12 For innumerable evils have compassed me about: mine iniquities have taken hold upon me, so that I am not able to look up: they are more than the hairs of mine head; therefore my heart faileth me.
13 Be pleased, O LORD, to deliver me: O LORD, make haste to help me.
14 Let them be ashamed and confounded together that seek after my soul to destroy it; let them be driven backward and put to shame that wish me evil.
15 Let them be desolate for a reward of their shame that say unto me, Aha, aha!
16 Let all those that seek thee rejoice and be glad in thee: let such as love thy salvation say continually, The LORD be magnified.
17 But I am poor and needy; yet the Lord thinketh upon me: thou art my help and my deliverer; make no tarrying, O my God.

PSALM XLI.
1 *Blessing of the charitable man.* 4 *David complains of his enemies' treachery;* 11 *he acknowledges God's favour.*
To the chief Musician, A Psalm of David.

BLESSED is he that considereth the poor: the LORD will deliver him in time of trouble.
2 The LORD will preserve him, and keep him alive; and he shall be blessed upon the earth: and thou wilt not deliver him unto the will of his enemies.
3 The LORD will strengthen him upon the bed of languishing: thou wilt make all his bed in his sickness.
4 I said, LORD, be merciful unto me: heal my soul; for I have sinned against thee.
5 Mine enemies speak evil of me, When shall he die, and his name perish?
6 And if he come to see me, he speaketh vanity: his heart gathereth iniquity to itself; when he goeth abroad, he telleth it.
7 All that hate me whisper together against me; against me do they devise my hurt.
8 An evil disease, say they, cleaveth fast unto him: and now that he lieth he shall rise up no more.
9 Yea, mine own familiar friend, in whom I trusted, which did eat of my bread, hath lifted up his heel against me.
10 But thou, O LORD, be merciful unto me, and raise me up, that I may requite them.
11 By this I know that thou favourest me, because mine enemy doth not triumph over me.
12 And as for me, thou upholdest me in

mine integrity, and settest me before thy face for ever.
13 Blessed be the LORD God of Israel from everlasting, and to everlasting. Amen, and Amen.

PSALM XLII.
David's zeal to serve God in the temple.
To the chief Musician, Maschil, for the sons of Korah.

AS the hart panteth after the water brooks, so panteth my soul after thee, O God.
2 My soul thirsteth for God, for the living God: when shall I come and appear before God?
3 My tears have been my meat day and night, while they continually say unto me, Where is thy God?
4 When I remember these things, I pour out my soul in me: for I had gone with the multitude; I went with them to the house of God, with the voice of joy and praise, with a multitude that kept holyday.
5 Why art thou cast down, O my soul? and why art thou disquieted in me? hope thou in God; for I shall yet praise him for the help of his countenance.
6 O my God, my soul is cast down within me: therefore will I remember thee from the land of Jordan, and of the Hermonites, from the hill Mizar.
7 Deep calleth unto deep at the noise of thy water-spouts: all thy waves and thy billows are gone over me.
8 Yet the LORD will command his loving-kindness in the day-time, and in the night his song shall be with me, and my prayer unto the God of my life.
9 I will say unto God my rock, Why hast thou forgotten me? why go I mourning because of the oppression of the enemy?
10 As with a sword in my bones, mine enemies reproach me; while they say daily unto me, Where is thy God?
11 Why art thou cast down, O my soul? and why art thou disquieted within me? hope thou in God; for I shall yet praise him, who is the health of my countenance, and my God.

PSALM XLIII.
David, praying to be restored to the temple, promises to serve God joyfully.

JUDGE me, O God, and plead my cause against an ungodly nation: O deliver me from the deceitful and unjust man.
2 For thou art the God of my strength: why dost thou cast me off? why go I mourning because of the oppression of the enemy?
3 O send out thy light and thy truth: let them lead me; let them bring me unto thy holy hill, and to thy tabernacles.
4 Then will I go unto the altar of God, unto God my exceeding joy: yea, upon the harp will I praise thee, O God, my God.
5 Why art thou cast down, O my soul, and why art thou disquieted within me? hope in God; for I shall yet praise him, who is the health of my countenance, and my God.

PSALM XLIV.
1 *The church, in memory of former favours,* 9 *complains of her present evils;* 17 *professing her integrity,* 23 *she fervently prays for succour.*
To the chief Musician for the sons of Korah, Maschil.

WE have heard with our ears, O God, our fathers have told us, what work general or special expiatory offerings, would not avail to meet the demands of God's law, and that he had come to render the required satisfaction, which he states was effected by "the offering of the body of Christ," for that is the "will of God" which Christ came to fulfil or do, in order to effect man's redemption. We thus see that the contrast to the unsatisfactory character assigned the O. T. offerings in v. 6, is found in the compliance with God's law (cf. v. 7, 8.). Of course, as Paul and other N. T. writers explain Christ's work, it consisted in more than being made under the law or obeying its precepts. It required an "obedience unto death," that is the compliance here chiefly intended, and which makes the contrast with v. 6 clear. mine ears hast thou opened—Whether allusion is made to the custom of boring a servant's ear, in token of voluntary and perpetual enslavement (Ex. 21. 6,), or that *the opening of the ear*, as in Isa. 48. 8; 50. 5, (though by a different word in *Heb.*,) denotes obedience by the common figure of hearing for obeying, it is evident that the clause is designed to express a devotion to God's will as avowed more fully in v. 8, and already explained. Paul however uses the words, "a body hast thou prepared me," which are found in the *Sept.* in the place of the words, "*mine ears* hast thou opened." He does not lay any stress on this clause, and his argument is complete without it. It is, perhaps, to be regarded rather as an interpretation or free translation by the *Sept.*, than either an addition or attempt at verbal translation. The *Sept.* translators may have had reference to Christ's vicarious sufferings as taught in other Scriptures, as Isa. 53; at all events the sense is substantially the same, as a body was essential to the required obedience (cf. Rom. 7. 4; 1 Pet. 2. 24,). 7. Then—in such case, without necessarily referring to order of time. Lo, I come—I am prepared to do, &c., in the volume of the book—*roll of the book*. Such rolls, resembling maps, are still used in the synagogues. written of me—or, on me, prescribed to me (2 Ki. 22. 13.). The first is the sense adopted by Paul. In either case, the Pentateuch, or law of Moses, is meant, and while it contains much respecting Christ directly, as Gen. 3. 15; 49. 10; Deut. 18. 15, and, indirectly, in the Levitical ritual, there is nowhere any allusion to David. 9, 10. Christ's prophetical office is taught. He "preached" the great truths of God's government of sinners. I have preached—*lit.*, announced good tidings. 11. may be rendered as an assertion, that God *will not withhold*, &c. Ps. 16. 1,). 12. evils—inflicted by others. iniquities—or, penal *afflictions*, and sometimes calamities in the wide sense. This meaning of the word is very common (Ps. 31. 11; 38. 4; cf. (Gen. 4. 13, Cain's punishment; (Gen. 19. 15, that of Sodom); (1 Sam. 28. 10. of the witch of Endor); also (2 Sam. 16. 12; Job, 19. 29; Isa, 5. 15; 53. 11.). This meaning of the word is also favoured by the clause, *taken hold of me*, which follows, which can be said appropriately of *sufferings*, but not of *sins* cf. Job, 27. 20; Ps. 69. 24.). Thus, the difficulties, in referring this Psalm to Christ, arising from the usual reading of this verse, are removed. Of the terrible *afflictions*, or sufferings, alluded to and endured for us cf. Luke, 22. 39-44, and the narrative of the scenes of Calvary. my heart faileth me—(Mat. 26. 38,), "My soul is exceeding sorrowful, even unto death." cannot look up—*lit.*, *I cannot see*, not denoting the depression of conscious guilt, as Luke, 18. 13, but exhaustion from suffering, as *dimness* of eyes cf. Ps. 6. 7; 13. 3; 38. 10.). The whole context thus sustains the sense assigned to *iniquities*. 13. (Cf. Ps. 22. 19.). 14, 15. The language is not necessarily imprecatory, but rather a confident expectation Ps. 5. 11,), though the former sense is not inconsistent with Christ's prayer for the forgiveness of His murderers, inasmuch as their confusion and shame might be the very means to prepare them for humbly seeking forgiveness cf. Acts, 2. 37.), for a reward—*lit.*, *in consequence of*. Aha—cf. Ps. 35. 21, 25.). 16. (Cf. Ps. 35. 27., love thy salvation—delight in its bestowal on others as well as themselves. 17. A summary of his condition and hopes. thinketh upon—or, provides for me. "He was heard," "when he had offered up prayers and supplications with strong crying and tears, unto him that was able to save him from death."

PSALM XLI.

Ver. 1-13. The Psalmist celebrates the blessedness of those who compassionate the poor, conduct strongly contrasted with the spite of his enemies and neglect of his friends, in his calamity. He prays for God's mercy in view of his ill desert, and, in confidence of relief, and that God will vindicate his cause, closes with a doxology.
1-3. God rewards kindness to the poor (Pro. 19. 17.). From v. 2 and 11 it may be inferred that the Psalmist describes his own conduct. poor—in person, position, and possessions. shall be blessed—*lit.*, led aright, or, *safely*, prospered (Ps. 23. 3.). up in the earth —or, land of promise (Ps. 25. 13; 27. 3-9, &c.). The figures of v. 3 are drawn from the acts of a kind nurse. 4. I said—I asked the mercy I show. heal my soul—(cf. Ps. 30. 2., "Sin and suffering are united." is one of the great teachings of the Psalms. 5, 6. A graphic picture of the conduct of a malignant enemy. to see me—as if to spy out my case. he speaketh... itself—or, "he speaketh vanity as to his heart"—*i.e.*, does not speak candidly, "he gathereth iniquity to him," collects elements for mischief, and then divulges the gains of his hypocrisy. 7, 8. So of others, *all* act alike. An evil disease—*lit.*, a word of Belial, some slander. cleaveth—*lit.*, poured on him. that he lieth—*who has* now laid down, "he is utterly undone and our victory is sure." 9. mine... friend—*lit.*, man of my peace. eat... bread—who depended on me, or was well treated by me. lifted up his heel—in scornful violence. As David and his fortunes typified Christ and His (cf. *Intr.*), so these words expressed the treatment he received, and also that of his Son and Lord; hence, though not distinctly prophetical, our Saviour John. 13. 18,), applies them to Judas, "that the Scripture may be fulfilled," This last phrase has a wide use in the N. T., and is not restricted to denote special prophecies. 10. A lawful punishment of criminals is not revenge, nor inconsistent with their final good cf. Ps. 40. 14, 15.). 11-13. favonrest—or, tenderly lovest me Gen. 34. 19,), evinced by relief from his enemies; and, farther, God recognises his innocence by upholding him. settest ... before thy face—under thy watch and care, as God *before man's face* Ps. 16. 8,) is an object of trust and love. Blessed—

thou didst in their days, in the times of old.

2 How *a* thou didst drive out the heathen with thy hand, and plantedst them; how thou didst afflict the people, and cast them out.

3 For *b* they got not the land in possession by their own sword, neither did their own arm save them; but thy right hand, and thine arm, and the light of thy countenance, because *c* thou hadst a favour unto them.

4 Thou *d* art my King, O God: command deliverances for Jacob.

5 Through thee *e* will we push down our enemies; through thy name will we tread them under that rise up against us.

6 For *f* I will not trust in my bow, neither shall my sword save me.

7 But thou hast saved us from our enemies, and hast put them to shame that hated us.

8 In *g* God we boast all the day long, and praise thy name for ever. Selah.

9 But thou hast cast off, and put us to shame; and goest not forth with our armies.

10 Thou makest us to *h* turn back from the enemy; and they which hate us spoil for themselves.

11 Thou hast given us [1] like sheep appointed for meat; and hast [i] scattered us among the heathen.

12 Thou *j* sellest thy people [2] for nought, and dost not increase *thy wealth* by their price.

13 Thou makest us a reproach to our neighbours, a scorn and a derision to them that are round about us.

14 Thou makest us a byword among the heathen, a shaking of the head among the people.

15 My confusion *is* continually before me, and the shame of my face hath covered me,

16 For the voice of him that reproacheth and blasphemeth; *k* by reason of the enemy and avenger.

17 All *l* this is come upon us; yet have we not forgotten thee, neither have we dealt falsely in thy covenant.

18 Our heart is not turned back, neither have our [3] steps declined from thy way;

19 Though thou hast sore broken us in the *m* place of dragons, and covered us with the shadow of death.

20 If we have forgotten the name of our God, or stretched out our hands to a strange god;

21 Shall *n* not God search this out? for *o* he knoweth the secrets of the heart.

22 Yea, for thy sake are we killed all the day long; we are counted as sheep for the slaughter.

23 Awake, why sleepest thou, O LORD? arise, cast *us* not off for ever.

24 Wherefore hidest thou thy face, *and* forgettest our affliction and our oppression?

25 For our soul is bowed down to the dust; our belly cleaveth unto the earth.

26 Arise *d* for our help, and redeem us for thy mercies' sake.

PSALM XLV.

1 *Majesty and grace of Christ's kingdom.* 10 *Duty of the church, and benefits thereof.*

To the chief Musician upon Shoshannim, for the sons of Korah, 1 Maschil, A Song of loves.

MY heart [2] is inditing a good matter: I speak of the things which I have made touching the King; my tongue *is* the pen of a ready writer.

2 Thou art fairer than the children of men:

PSALM 44.
a Deu. 7. 1.
b Deu. 8. 17. Josh. 24. 12.
c Deu. 4. 37.
d Ps. 74. 12.
e Dan. 3. 4.
f Ps. 33. 16.
Hos. 1. 7.
g Ps. 34. 2.
Jer. 9. 24.
Rom. 2. 17.
h Lev. 26. 17.
Deu. 28. 25.
Josh. 7. 8, 12.
1 as sheep of meat.
i Deu. 4. 27.
Ps. 60. 1.
j Is. 52. 3, 4.
Jer. 15. 13.
2 without riches.
k Ps. 8. 2.
l Dan. 9. 13.
3 Or, goings.
m Is. 34. 13. Is. 35. 7.
n Job 31. 14.
Ps. 139. 1.
Jer. 17. 10.
o 1 Sa. 16. 7.
1 Chr. 28. 9.
John 2. 25.
Acts 1. 24.
Rev. 2. 23.
4 a help for us.

PSALM 45.
1 Or, of instruction.
2 boileth, or, bubbleth up.
3 prosper thou, ride thou.
a Ps. 93. 2.
Is. 9. 6, 7.
Heb. 1. 1.
b Ps. 33. 5.
Heb. 7. 26.
4 Or, O God.
c Is. 61. 1.
John 20. 17.
d Deu. 31. 13.
e Ps. 95. 6.
Is. 54. 5.
5 thy face.
f Rev. 19. 7, 8.
g 1 Pet. 2. 9.
Rev. 1. 5.
Rev. 5. 10.
Rev. 20. 6.
h Mal. 1. 11.

PSALM 45.
1 Or, of.
a 1 Chr. 15. 20.
2 the heart of the sons.
b Is. 8. 7.
c Ps. 48. 1.
Is. 60. 14.
d Deu. 23. 14.
Is. 12. 6.
Eze. 43. 7.
Hos. 11. 9.
3 when the morning appeareth.
4 an high place for us.

grace is poured into thy lips: therefore God hath blessed thee for ever.

3 Gird thy sword upon *thy* thigh, O *Most* Mighty, with thy glory and thy majesty.

4 And in thy majesty [3] ride prosperously, because of truth and meekness *and* righteousness; and thy right hand shall teach thee terrible things.

5 Thine arrows *are* sharp in the heart of the King's enemies; *whereby* the people fall under thee.

6 Thy *a* throne, O God, *is* for ever and ever: the sceptre of thy kingdom *is* a right sceptre.

7 Thou *b* lovest righteousness, and hatest wickedness: therefore *c* God, *e* thy God, hath anointed thee with the oil of gladness above thy fellows.

8 All thy garments *smell* of myrrh, and aloes, *and* cassia, out of the ivory palaces, whereby they have made thee glad.

9 Kings' daughters *were* among thy honourable women: upon thy right hand did stand the queen in gold of Ophir.

10 Hearken, O daughter, and consider, and incline thine ear; *d* forget also thine own people, and thy father's house;

11 So shall the King greatly desire thy beauty: *e* for he *is* thy Lord; and worship thou him.

12 And the daughter of Tyre *shall be there* with a gift; *even* the rich among the people shall entreat *b* thy favour.

13 The *f* King's daughter *is* all glorious within; her clothing *is* of wrought gold.

14 She shall be brought unto the King in raiment of needlework: the virgins her companions that follow her shall be brought unto thee.

15 With gladness and rejoicing *shall* they be brought: they shall enter into the King's palace.

16 Instead of thy fathers shall be thy children, *g* whom thou mayest make princes in all the earth.

17 I *h* will make thy name to be remembered in all generations: therefore shall the people praise thee for ever and ever.

PSALM XLVI.

1 *Confidence which the church has in God;* 8 *exhortation to contemplate the works of Providence.*

To the chief Musician 1 for the sons of Korah, A Song upon *a* Alamoth.

GOD is our refuge and strength, a very present help in trouble.

2 Therefore will not we fear, though the earth be removed, and though the mountains be carried into [2] the midst of the sea;

3 *Though* the waters thereof roar *and* be troubled, *though* the mountains shake with the swelling thereof. Selah.

4 *There* is *b* a river, the streams whereof shall make glad *c* the city of God, the holy *place* of the tabernacles of the Most High.

5 God is *d* in the midst of her; she shall not be moved: God shall help her, [3] *and that* right early.

6 The heathen raged, the kingdoms were moved: he uttered his voice, the earth melted.

7 The LORD of hosts *is* with us; the God of Jacob *is* [4] our refuge. Selah.

8 Come, behold the works of the LORD, what desolations he hath made in the earth.

9 He maketh wars to cease unto the end of the earth; he breaketh the bow, and

praised, usually applied to God. The word usually applied to men denotes *happiness* (Ps. 1. 1; 32. 1.). With this doxology the first book closes.

PSALM XLII.

Ver. 1-11. *Maschil*—(cf. Ps. 32. title.). *For*, or, *of* cf. *Intr*.) the sons of Korah. The writer, perhaps one of this Levitical family of singers accompanying David in exile, mourns his absence from the sanctuary, a cause of grief aggravated by the taunts of enemies, and is comforted in hopes of relief. This course of thought is repeated with some variety of detail, but closing with the same refrain. 1, 2. Cf. Ps. 63, 1.). panteth—desires, in a state of exhaustion. appear before God—in acts of worship, the terms used in the command for the stated personal appearance of the Jews at the sanctuary. 3. Where is thy God?—implying that He had forsaken him (cf. 2 Sam. 16. 7; Ps. 3. 2; 22. 8.). 4. The verbs are properly rendered as futures, "I will remember," &c., &c.—*i.e.*, the recollection of this season of distress will give greater zest to the privileges of God's worship, when obtained. 5. Hence he chides his despondent soul, assuring himself of a time of joy. help of his countenance—or, face cf. Num. 6, 25; Ps. 4. 6; 10. 11.).6. Dejection again described, therefore —*i.e.*, finding no comfort in myself, I turn to thee, even in this distant "*land of Jordan* and *the* (mountains) *Hermons*," the country east of Jordan. hill M zar—as a name of a small hill contrasted with the mountains round about Jerusalem, perhaps denoted the contempt with which the place of exile was regarded. 7. The roar of successive billows, responding to that of floods of rain, represented the heavy waves of sorrow which overwhelmed him. 8. Still he relies on as constant a flow of divine mercy which will elicit his praise and encourage his prayer to God; 9, 10. in view of which, he dictates to himself a prayer based on his distress, aggravated as it was by the cruel taunts and infidel suggestions of his foes. 11. This brings on a renewed self-chiding, and excites hopes of relief. health [or, help] of my countenance—(cf. v. 5.), who cheers me, driving away clouds of sorrow from my face. my God—It is He of whose existence and favour my foes would have me doubt.

PSALM XLIII.

Ver. 1-5. Excepting the recurrence of the refrain, there is no good reason to suppose this a part of the preceding, though the scope is the same. It has always been placed separate.
1. Judge—or, vindicate (Ps. 10. 18.). plead, &c.—(Ps. 35. 1.). ungodly—neither in character or condition objects of God's favour (cf. Ps. 4, 3.). 2. God of my strength—by covenant relation my stronghold (Ps. 18. 1.). cast me off—in scorn. because—or, in, *i.e.*, in such circumstances of oppression. 3. light—as Ps. 27. 1. truth—or, faithfulness (Ps. 25. 5,), manifest it by fulfilling promises. *Light and truth* are personified as messengers who will bring him to the privileged place of worship. tabernacles—plural, in allusion to the various courts. 4. the altar—as the chief place of worship. The mention of the harp suggests the prominence of praise in his offering.

PSALM XLIV.

Ver. 1-26. In a time of great national distress, probably in David's reign, the Psalmist recounts God's gracious dealings in former times, and the confidence they had learned to repose in him. After a vivid picture of their calamities, he humbly expostulates against God's apparent forgetfulness, reminding Him of their faithfulness and mourning their heavy sorrows.
1-3. This period is that of the settlement of Canaan Josh. 24. 12; Jud. 0. 3.). have told— or, related cf. Ex. 10. 2.). plantedst them—*i.e.*, our fathers, who are also, from the parallel construction of the last clause, to be regarded as the object of "*cast them out*," which means —*lit.*, *send* them out, or, "extend them." *Heathen* and *people* denote the nations who were driven out to make room for the Israelites. 4. Thou art my King—*lit.*, *he who is my King*, sustaining the same covenant relation as to the "fathers." 5. The figure drawn from the habits of the ox. 6-8. God is not only our sole help, but only worthy of praise, thy name—as Ps. 5. 11. put ... to shame— cf. Ps. 6. 10,', disgraced. 9. But—contrasting, *cast off* as abhorrent (Ps. 43. 2.). goest not forth— *lit.*, *will not go* (2 Sam. 5. 23.). In several consecutive verses the leading verb is *future*, and the following one *past* (in Heb.), thus denoting the causes and effects. Thus, (v. 10, 11, 12,), when defeated, spoiling follows, when delivered as sheep, dispersion follows, &c. 11. The Babylonian captivity not necessarily meant. There were others (cf. 1 Ki. 8. 46.). 13, 14. Cf. Deut. 28. 37; Ps. 79. 4.). 15. shame of ... face—blushes in disgrace. 16. Its cause, the taunts and presence of malignant enemies (Ps. 8. 2.). 17-19. They had not apostatised totally—were still God's people. declined—turned aside from God's law. sore broken—crushed. place of dragons—desolate, barren rocky wilderness (Ps. 63. 10; Isa. 13.22. shadow of death— cf. Ps. 23. 4.). 20, 21, A solemn appeal to God to witness their constancy. stretched out ... hands—gesture of worship (Ex. 9. 29; Ps. 88. 9.). 22. Their protracted sufferings as God's people attests the constancy. Paul (Rom. 8. 36,), uses this to describe Christian stedfastness in persecution. 23-26. This style of addressing God, as indifferent, is frequent (Ps. 3. 7; 9. 19; 13. 1, &c.). However low their condition, God is appealed to, on the ground, and for the honour, of His mercy.

PSALM XLV.

Ver. 1-17. *Shoshannim—lit., Lilies*, either descriptive of an instrument so shaped, or denoting some tune or air so called, after which the Psalm was to be sung (cf. Ps. 8. title.). A *song of loves*, or, *of beloved ones* (plural and feminine,)—a conjugal song. *Maschil*—(cf. Ps. 32. and 42.) denotes the didactic character of the Psalm; that it gives *instruction*, the song being of allegorical and not literal import. *The union and glories of Christ and his Church are described*. He is addressed as a king possessed of all essential graces, as a conqueror exalted on the throne of a righteous and eternal government, and as a bridegroom arrayed in nuptial splendour. The Church is pourtrayed in the purity and loveliness of a royally adorned and attended bride, invited to forsake her home and share the honours of her affianced lord. The picture of an oriental wedding thus opened is filled up by representing the complimentary gifts of the wealthy with which the occasion is honoured, the procession of the bride, clothed in splendid raiment, attended by her virgin companions, and the entrance of the joyous throng into the palace of the King. A prediction of a numerous and distinguished progeny, instead of the complimentary wish for it usually expressed (cf. Gen. 24. 60; Ruth, 4. 11, 12,), and an assurance of a perpetual fame, closes the Psalm. All ancient Jewish and Christian interpreters regarded this Psalm as an allegory of the purport above named. In the Song of Songs the allegory is carried out more fully. Hosea (ch. 1-3.) treats the relation of God and His people under the same figure, and its use to set forth the relation of Christ and His Church runs through both parts of the Bible (cf. Isa. 54. 5; 62. 4, 5; Mat. 22. 2; 25. 1; John, 3. 29; Eph. 5, 25-32, &c., &c.). Other methods of exposition have been suggested. Several Jewish monarchs, from Solomon to the wicked Ahab, and various foreign princes, have been named as the hero of the song. But to none of them can the terms here used be shewn to apply, and it is hardly probable that any mere nuptial song, especially of a heathen king, would be permitted a place in the sacred songs of the Jews. The advocates for any other than the Messianic interpretation have generally silenced each other in succession, while the application of the most rigorous rules of a fair system of interpretation has but strengthened the evidences in its favour. The scope of the Psalm above given is easy and sustained by the explication of its details. The quotation of v. 6, 7, by Paul, (Heb. 1, 8, 9,), as applicable to Christ, *ought to be conclusive*, and their special exposition shows the propriety of such an application.

1. An animated preface indicative of strong emotion. Lit., *My heart overflows: a good matter I speak; the things which I have made*, &c. inditing—*lit.*, *boiling up*, as a fountain overflows. my tongue is the pen—a mere instrument of God's use. of a ready writer—*i.e.*, it is fluent. The theme is inspiring and language flows fast. 2. To rich personal attractions is added *grace of the lips*, captivating powers of speech. This is given and becomes a source of power and proves a blessing. Christ is a prophet (Luke, 4. 22,). 3, 4. The king is addressed as ready to go forth to battle. sword—(cf. Rev. 1, 16; 19. 15,). Mighty—(cf. Isa. 9. 6.), glory and ... majesty—generally used as divine attributes (Ps. 96. 6; 104. 1; 111. 3,). or as specially conferred on mortals, (Ps. 21. 5,), perhaps these typically. ride prosperously—or, conduct a successful war. because of—for the interests of truth, &c. meekness ... righteousness—without any connective—*i.e.*, a righteousness, or *equity of government, distinguished by meekness or condescension Ps. 18. 35,). right hand—or, power, as its organ. shall teach thee—point the way to terrible things—*i.e.*, in conquest of enemies. 5. The result. people—whole nations are subdued. 6. No lawful construction can be devised to change the sense here given, and sustained by the ancient versions, and above all, by Paul (Heb. 1. 8.). Of the perpetuity of this government (cf. 2 Sam. 7. 13; Ps. 10. 16; 72. 5; 89. 4; 110. 4; Isa. 9. 7.). 7, As in v. 6, the divine nature is made prominent, here the moral qualities of the human are alleged as the reason or ground of the mediatorial exaltation. Some render "*Oh, God, thy God,*" instead of God, thy God—but the latter is sustained by the same form (Ps. 50. 7,), and it was only of

His human nature that the anointing could be predicated (cf. Isa. 61. 3.). oil of gladness—or, token of gladness, as used in feasts and other times of solemn joy (cf. 1 Ki. 1. 39, 40.). fellows—other kings. 8. The King thus inaugurated is now presented as a bridegroom, who appears in garments richly perfumed, brought out from *ivory palaces*, His royal residence; by which, as indications of the happy bridal occasion, He has been gladdened. 9. In completion of this picture of a marriage festival, female attendants, or bridesmaids of the highest rank, attend Him, while the queen, in rich apparel v. 13, stands ready for the nuptial procession. 10, 11. She is invited to the union, for forming which, she must leave her father's people. She representing, by the form of the allegory, the Church; this address is illustrated by all those scriptures, from Gen. 12. 1, on, which speak of the people of God as a chosen, separate, and peculiar people. The relation of subjection to her spouse at once accords with the law of marriage, as given in Gen. 3. 16; 18. 12; Eph. 5. 22; 1 Pet. 3. 5, 6,), and the relation of the Church to Christ (Eph. 5. 24.). The love of the husband is intimately connected with the entire devotion to which the bride is exhorted. 12. daughter of Tyre—(Ps. 9. 14,), denotes the people. Tyre, celebrated for its great wealth, is selected to represent the richest nations, an idea confirmed by the next clause. These gifts are brought as means to conciliate the royal parties, representing the admitted subjection of the offerers. This well sets forth the exalted position of the Church and her head, whose moral qualities receive the homage of the world. The contribution of material wealth to sustain the institutions of the Church may be included; (cf. "riches of the Gentiles," Ps. 72. 10; Isa. 60. 5-10.). 13. The King's daughter—a term of dignity. It may also intimate, with some allusion to the teaching of the allegory, that the bride of Christ, the Church, is the daughter of the great king, God. within—not only is her outward raiment costly, but all her apparel of the richest texture, wrought gold—gold embroidery, or cloth in which gold is woven. 14, 15. The progress of the procession is described; according to the usual custom the bride and attendants are conducted to the palace. Some, for the words — in raiment of needlework—propose another rendering, *on variegated* (or, embroidered) *cloths*—*i.e.*, in the manner of the East, richly wrought tapestry was spread on the ground, on which the bride walked. As the dress had been already mentioned, this seems to be a probable translation. shall be brought—in solemn form (cf. Job, 10. 19; 21. 22.). The entrance into the palace with great joy closes the scene. So shall the Church be finally brought to her Lord, and united amid the festivities of the holy beings in heaven. 16. As earthly monarchs govern widely extended empires by viceroys, this glorious King is represented as supplying all the principalities of earth with princes of His own numerous progeny. 17. The glories of this empire shall be as wide as the world and lasting as eternity. therefore—because thus glorious, the praise shall be universal and perpetual. Some writers have taxed their ingenuity to find in the history and fortunes of Christ and His Church exact parallels for every part of this splendid allegory, not excepting its gorgeous oriental imagery. Thus, by the dresses of the King and queen, are thought to be meant the eminent endowments and graces of Christ and His people. The attendant women, supposed (though inconsistently it might seem with the inspired character of the work,) to be concubines, are thought to represent the Gentile Churches, and the bride, the Jewish, &c., &c. But it is evident that we cannot pursue such a mode of interpretation. For, following the allegory, we must suspend to the distant future the results of a union, whose consummation as a marriage is still distant (cf. Rev. 21. 9.). In fact the imagery here and elsewhere sets before us the Church in two aspects. As a body, it is yet incomplete, the whole is yet ungathered. As a moral institution, it is yet imperfect. In the final catastrophe, it will be complete and perfect. Thus, as a bride adorned, &c., it will be united with its Lord. Thus the union of Christ and the Church triumphant is set forth. On the other hand, in regard to its component parts, the relation of Christ as head, as husband, &c., already exists, and as these parts form an institution in this world, it is by His union with it, and the gifts and graces with which He endows it, that a spiritual seed arises and spreads in the world. Hence, we must fix our minds only on the *one simple but grand truth, that Christ loves the Church, is Head over all things for it, raises it, in His exaltation, to the highest moral dignity—a dignity of which every, even the meanest, sincere disciple will partake.* As to the *time*, then, in which this allegorical prophecy is to be fulfilled, it may be said, that no periods of time are specially designated. The *characteristics* of the relation of Christ and His Church are indicated, and we may suppose that the whole process of His exaltation from the *declaration* of His Sonship, by His resurrection, to the grand catastrophe of the final judgment, with all the collateral blessings to the Church and the world, lay before the vision of the inspired prophet.

PSALM XLVI.

Ver. 1-11. *Upon Alamoth*—most probably denotes the *treble*, or part sung by female voices, the word meaning *virgins;* and which was sung with some appropriately keyed instrument (cf. 1 Chr. 15. 19-21; Ps. 6. title,). The theme may be stated in Luther's well-known words, "A strong fortress is our God." The great deliverance, (2 Ki. 19. 35; Isa. 37. 36,), may have occasioned its composition.

1. refuge—*lit., a place of trust* (Ps. 2. 12,). strength—(Ps. 18. 2.). present help—*lit., a help he has been found exceedingly.* trouble —as Ps. 18. 7. 2, 3. The most violent civil commotions are illustrated by the greatest physical commotions. swelling—well represents the *pride* and haughtiness of insolent foes. 4. God's favour is denoted by a. river cf. Ps. 36, 8; Zech. 14, 8; Rev. 22. 1,). city of God, the holy place—His earthly residence, Jerusalem and the temple (cf. Ps. 2. 6; 3, 4; 20. 2; 48. 2, &c.). God's favour, like a river whose waters are conducted in channels, is distributed to all parts of His Church. Most High—denoting His supremacy (Ps. 17. 2.). 5. right early—*lit., at the turn of morning,* or, change from night to day, a critical time (Ps. 30. 5; cf. Isa. 37. 36,). 6. (Cf. v. 4,). earth melted—all powers dissolved by His

mere word (Ps. 75. 3; Hos. 2. 22,). 7. with us —on our side, His presence is terror to our enemies, safety to us. refuge—high place (Ps. 9. 9; cf. also Ps. 24. 6, 10.). 8. what desolations—*lit., who hath put desolations,* destroying our enemies. 9. *The usual weapons of war,* (Ps. 7. 12,), as well as those using them, are brought to an end. 10. Be still, &c.—*lit., Leave off to oppose me and vex my people, I am over all for their safety* (cf. Isa. 2. 11; Eph. 1. 22,).

PSALM XLVII.

Ver. 1-9. Praise is given to God for victory, perhaps that recorded (2 Chr. 20.); and His dominion over all people, Jews and Gentiles, is asserted. 1. clap ... hands ... people—*lit., peoples,* or, nations (cf. Deut. 32. 43; Ps. 18. 49; 98. 9.). 2, 3. His universal sovereignty now exists, and will be made known. under us—*i.e.,* His saints; Israel's temporal victories were types of the spiritual conquests of the true Church. 4. He shall ... inheritance—the heathen to be possessed by His Church (Ps. 2. 8,), as Canaan by the Jews. excellency of Jacob—*lit., pride,* or, *that* in which he glories (not necessarily, though often, in a bad sense), the privileges of the chosen people—whom he loved—His love being the sole cause of granting them. 5-7. God, victorious over His enemies, reascends to heaven, amid the triumphant praises of His people, who celebrate His sovereign dominion. This sovereignty is what the Psalm teaches; hence he adds—sing ... praises with understanding—*lit., sing and play an instructive* (Psalm). The whole typifies Christ's ascension (cf. Ps. 68. 18.). 8, 9. The instruction continued. throne of ... holiness —or, holy throne (cf. on Ps. 2, 6; 22. 3.). princes—who represent *peoples.* For—even supply *as,* or, *to—i.e.,* they all become united under covenant with Abraham's God. shields —as Hos. 4. 18, rulers.

PSALM XLVIII.

Ver. 1-14. This is a spirited Psalm and Song (cf. Ps. 30.) having probably been suggested by the same occasion as the foregoing. It sets forth the privileges and blessings of God's spiritual dominion as the terror of the wicked and joy of the righteous.

1. to be praised—always: it is an epithet as Ps. 18. 3. mountain of his holiness—His Church (cf. Isa. 2, 2, 3; 25. 6, 7, 10,); the sanctuary was erected first on *Mount* Zion, then (as the temple) on Moriah; hence the figure. 2, 3. situation—*lit., elevation.* joy of, &c.—source of joy. sides of the north—poetically for eminent, lofty, distinguished, as the ancients believed the *north* to be the highest part of the earth (cf. Isa. 14. 13.). palaces—*lit., citadels.* refuge—(Ps. 9. 10; 18. 3.). He was so known in them, because they enjoyed His presence. 4-6. For—the reason is given. Though the kings (perhaps of Moab and Ammon, cf. Ps. 83. 3-5, combined, a conviction of God's presence with His people, evinced by the unusual courage with which the prophets, (cf. 2 Chr. 20. 12-20,), had inspired them, seized on their minds, and smitten with sudden and intense alarm, they fled astonished. 7. ships of Tarshish—as engaged in a distant and lucrative trade, the most valuable. The phrase may illustrate God's control over all material agencies, whether their literal destruction be meant or not. 8. This present experience assures of that perpetual care which God extends, to His Church. 9. thought of—*lit.,*

cutteth the spear in sunder; he burneth the chariot in the fire.
10 Be still, and know that I *am* God: I will be exalted among the heathen, I will be exalted in the earth.
11 The LORD of hosts *is* with us; the God of Jacob *is* our refuge. Selah.

PSALM XLVII.
The nations are exhorted cheerfully to entertain the kingdom of Christ.
To the chief Musician, A Psalm ¹ for the sons of Korah.

O CLAP your hands, all ye people; shout unto God with the voice of triumph:
2 For the LORD most high *is* ᵃ terrible; *he is* ᵇ a great King over all the earth.
3 He ᶜ shall subdue the people under us, and the nations under our feet.
4 He shall choose our ᵈ inheritance for us, the excellency of Jacob, whom he loved. Selah.
5 God ᵉ is gone up with a shout, the LORD with the sound of a trumpet.
6 Sing praises to God, sing praises; sing praises unto our King, sing praises.
7 For ᶠ God *is* the King of all the earth: sing ᵍ ye praises ² with understanding.
8 God reigneth over the heathen: God sitteth upon the throne of his holiness.
9 ³ The princes of the people are gathered together, *even* the people of the God of Abraham; for the shields of the earth *belong* unto God; he is greatly exalted.

PSALM XLVIII.
Ornaments and privileges of the church.
A Song and Psalm ¹ for the sons of Korah.

GREAT *is* the LORD, and greatly to be praised in the city of our God, *in* the mountain ᵃ of his holiness.
2 Beautiful ᵇ for situation, ᶜ the joy of the whole earth, *is* mount Zion, ᵈ *on* the sides of the north, ᵉ the city of the great King.
3 God is known in her palaces for a refuge.
4 For, lo, ᶠ the kings were assembled, they passed by together.
5 They saw *it, and* so they marvelled; they were troubled, *and* hasted away.
6 Fear took hold upon them there, *and* pain, as of a woman in travail.
7 Thou ᵍ breakest the ships of Tarshish with an east wind.
8 As we have heard, so have we seen in the city of the LORD of hosts, in the city of our God: God ʰ will establish it for ever. Selah.
9 We have thought of thy loving-kindness, O God, in the midst of thy temple.
10 According to ⁱ thy name, O God, so *is* thy praise unto the ends of the earth: thy right hand is full of righteousness.
11 Let mount Zion rejoice, let the daughters of Judah be glad, because of thy judgments.
12 Walk about Zion, and go round about her: tell the towers thereof.
13 ² Mark ye well her bulwarks, ᵍ consider her palaces; that ye may tell *it* to the generation following.
14 For ʲ this God *is* our God for ever and ever: he will be our guide *even* unto death.

PSALM XLIX.
1 *The psalmist calls upon all the earth to join him in his meditations.* 5 *Vanity of trusting in worldly wealth.* 14 *Misery of the wicked, etc.*
To the chief Musician, A Psalm ¹ for the sons of Korah.

HEAR this, all ye people; give ear, all ye inhabitants of the world:

2 Both low and high, rich and poor, together.
3 My mouth shall speak of wisdom; and the meditation of my heart *shall be* of understanding.
4 I will incline mine ear to a parable; I will open my dark saying upon the harp.
5 Wherefore should I fear in the days of evil, *when* the iniquity of my heels shall compass me about?
6 They that ᵃ trust in their wealth, and boast themselves in the multitude of their riches;
7 None *of them* can by any means redeem his brother, nor ᵇ give to God a ransom for him:
8 (For ᶜ the redemption of their soul *is* precious, and it ceaseth for ever;)
9 That he should still ᵈ live for ever, *and* not ᵉ see corruption.
10 For he seeth *that* wise men die, likewise the fool and the brutish person perish, and leave their wealth to others.
11 Their inward thought *is, that* their houses *shall continue* for ever, *and* their dwelling places ² to all generations: they call *their* lands after their own names.
12 Nevertheless man *being* in honour abideth not: he is like the beasts *that* perish.
13 This their way *is* their folly: yet their posterity ³ approve their sayings. Selah.
14 Like sheep they are laid in the grave; death shall feed on them; and ᶠ the upright shall have dominion over them in the morning; and their ⁴ beauty shall consume ⁵ in the grave from their dwelling.
15 But God ᵍ will redeem my soul ᵉ from the power of ⁷ the grave; for he shall receive me. Selah.
16 Be not thou afraid when one is made rich, when the glory of his house is increased;
17 For when he dieth he shall carry nothing away; his glory shall not descend after him:
18 Though ⁸ while he lived he blessed his soul: and *men* will praise thee, when thou doest well to thyself.
19 ⁹ He shall go to the generation of his fathers; they shall never see light.
20 Man *that is* in honour, and understandeth not, is like the beasts *that* perish.

PSALM L.
1 *Majesty of God in the church:* 7 *The pleasure of God is not in ceremonies,* 14 *but in sincerity of obedience.* 16 *The hypocrite rebuked.*
A Psalm ¹ of Asaph.

THE mighty God, *even* the LORD, hath spoken, and called the earth, from the rising of the sun unto the going down thereof.
2 Out of Zion, the perfection of beauty, God hath shined.
3 Our God shall come, and shall not keep silence: a fire shall devour before him, and it shall be very tempestuous round about him.
4 He ᵃ shall call to the heavens from above, and to the earth, that he may judge his people.
5 Gather ᵇ my saints together unto me; those ᶜ that have made a covenant with me by sacrifice.
6 And the heavens shall declare his righteousness: for God *is* judge himself. Selah.
7 Hear, O my people, and I will speak; O Israel, and I will testify against thee: I *am* God, *even* thy God.

compared, or, considered, in respect of former dealings. In the... te ple—in acts of solemn worship cf. 2 Chr. 20. 28.. 10. According... praise—*i.e.*, as thy perfections manifested, cf. Ps. 8. 1; 20. 1-7.), demand praise, it shall be given, everywhere. thy right hand, &c.—thy righteous government is displayed by thy power. 11. the daughters, &c.—*the small towns*, or the people, with the chief city, or rulers of the Church. judgments—decisions and acts of right government. 12-14. The call to survey Zion, or the Church, as a fortified city, is designed to suggest "how well our God secures His fold." This security is perpetual, and its pledge is his guidance through this life.

PSALM XLIX.

Ver. 1-20. This Psalm instructs and consoles. It teaches that earthly advantages are not reliable for permanent happiness, and that, however prosperous worldly men may be for a time, their ultimate destiny is ruin, while the pious are safe in God's care. 1-3. All are called to hear what interests all. world—*lit., duration of life*, the present time. 4. incline—to hear attentively (Ps. 17. 6; 31. 2.). parable—In *Heb.* and *Gr. parable* and *proverb* are translations of the same word. It denotes a *comparison*, or form of speech, which, under one image, includes many, and is expressive of a general truth capable of various illustrations. Hence it may be used for the *illustration* itself. For the former sense, *proverb* (*i.e.*, one word for several is the usual English term, and for the latter, in which comparison is prominent, *parable* (*i.e.*, one thing laid by another). The distinction is not always observed, since here, and Ps. 78. 2, *proverb* would better express the style of the composition (cf. also Pro. 26. 7, 9; Hab. 2. 6; John, 16. 25, 29.). Such forms of speech are often very figurative and also obscure (cf. Mat. 13. 12-15.). Hence the use of the parallel word—dark saying—or, *riddle*, (cf. Ez. 17. 2.). open—is to explain. upon the harp—the accompaniment for a lyric. 5. iniquity—or, calamity (Ps. 40. 12.). of my heels—*lit., my supplanters* (Gen. 27. 36,), or oppressors: "I am surrounded by the evils they inflict." 6. They are vain-glorious, 7-9, yet unable to save themselves or others. It can seta for ever—*i.e.*, the ransom fails, the price is too precious, costly. corruption—*lit. pit*, or, *grave*, thus shewing that *soul* is used for life. 10. For he seeth—*i.e.*, corruption, then follows the illustration. wise ... fool—Ps. 14. 1; Pro. 1. 32; 10. 1]—likewise—alike together—(Ps. 4. 8—die—All meet the same fate. 11. Still infatuated and flattered with hopes of perpetuity, they call their lands, or "celebrate their names on account of (their) lands." 12. Contrasted with this vanity is their frailty. However honoured, man abideth not—*lit., lodgeth not*, remains not till morning, but suddenly perishes as (wild) beasts, whose lives are taken without warning. 13. Though their way is folly, others follow the same course of life. 14. Like sheep—(cf. *v.* 12.), unwittingly, they—are laid—or, put, &c. dea h shall feed on [or, better, *shall rule*] them —as a shepherd (cf. feed Ps. 28. 9, *Marg.*). have dominion over [or, subdue] them in the morning—suddenly, or, in their turn. their beauty—*lit., form*, or, shape, shall consume—*lit., is for the consumption, i.e.*, of the grave, from their dwelling—*lit., from their home* they go) to it, *i.e.*, the grave. 15. The pious, de-

livered from the—power—*lit., the hand*, of death, are taken under God's care. 16-19. applies this instruction. Be not anxious (Ps. 37. 1., &c.) since death cuts off the prosperous wicked whom you dread. Though... lived, &c.—*lit., For in his life he blessed his soul*, or, himself Luke. 12. 19; 16. 25; ; yet (*v.* 19,), he has had his portion. men will praise ... thyself—Flatterers enhance the rich fool's self-complacency; the form of address to him strengthens the emphasis of the sentiment. 20. (Cf. *v.* 12.). The *folly* is more distinctly expressed by *understandeth not* substituted for *abideth not*.

PSALM L.

Ver. 1-23. In the grandeur and solemnity of a divine judgment, God is introduced as instructing men in the nature of true worship, exposing hypocrisy, warning the wicked, and encouraging the pious. 1-4. The description of this majestic appearance of God resembles that of His giving the law (cf. Ex. 19. 16; 20. 18; Deut. 32. 1.). from above—*lit., above* Gen. 1. 7.). heavens ... earth—for all creatures are witnesses (Deut. 4. 26; 30. 19; Isa. 1. 2.). 5. my saints—(Ps. 4. 3]—made [*lit., cut*] a covenant, &c.—alluding to the dividing of a victim of sacrifice, by which covenants were ratified, the parties passing between the divided portions (cf. Gen. 15. 10, 18.). 6. The inhabitants of heaven, who well know God's character, attest His righteousness as a judge. 7. I will testify against—*i.e.*, for failure to worship aright. thy God—and so, by covenant as well as creation, entitled to a pure worship. 8-15. However scrupulous in external worship, it was offered as if they conferred an obligation in giving God His own, and with a degrading view of Him as needing it. Reproving him for such foolish and blasphemous notions, He teaches them to *offer*, or *lit., sacrifice*, thanksgiving, and pay, or perform, their vows —*i.e.*, to bring, with the external symbolical service, the homage of the heart, and faith, penitence, and love. To this is added an invitation to seek, and a promise to afford, all needed help in trouble. 16-20. the wicked—*i.e.*, the formalists, as now exposed, and who lead vicious lives (cf. Rom. 2. 21, 23.). They are unworthy to use even the words of God's law. Their hypocrisy and vice are exposed by illustrations from sins against the seventh, eighth, and ninth commandments. 21, 22. God no longer even in appearance) disregarding such, exposes their sins and threatens a terrible punishment. forget God—This denotes unmindfulness of His true character. 23. offereth praise—(*v.* 14,), so that the external worship is a true index of the heart. ordereth ... aright—acts in a straight, right manner, opposed to turning aside Ps. 25. 5.. In such, pure worship and a pure life evince their true piety, and they will enjoy God's presence and favour.

PSALM LI.

Ver. 1-19. On the occasion cf. 2 Sam. 11, 12. The Psalm illustrates true repentance, in which are comprised conviction, confession, sorrow prayer for mercy, and purposes of amendment, and it is accompanied by a lively faith.

1-4. A plea for mercy is a confession of guilt. blot out—as from a register. transgressions—*lit., rebellions* (Ps. 19. 13; 32. 1.). Wash me—Purity as well as pardon is desired by true penitents. For ... before me—Convic-

8 I will not reprove thee for thy sacrifices or thy burnt offerings, *to have been continually before me.*
9 I *d* will take no bullock out of thy house, nor he-goats out of thy folds:
10 For every beast of the forest *is* mine, and the cattle upon a thousand hills.
11 I know all the fowls of the mountains; and the wild beasts of the field *are* *a* mine.
12 If I were hungry, I would not tell thee: for the world *is* mine, and the fulness thereof.
13 Will I eat the flesh of bulls, or drink the blood of goats?
14 Offer *e* unto God thanksgiving; and pay thy vows unto the Most High:
15 And *f* call upon me in the day of trouble; I will deliver thee, and thou shalt glorify *g* me.
16 But unto the wicked God saith, What hast thou to do to declare my statutes, or that thou shouldest take my covenant in thy mouth?
17 Seeing *h* thou hatest instruction, and castest my words behind thee.
18 When thou sawest a thief, then thou consentedst *i* with him, and *g* hast been partaker with adulterers.
19 *k* Thou givest thy mouth to evil, and thy tongue frameth deceit.
20 Thou sittest *and* speakest against thy brother; thou slanderest thine own mother's son.
21 These *things* hast thou done, *i* and I kept silence; *k* thou thoughtest that I was altogether *such an one* as thyself: but I will reprove thee, and set *them* in order before thine eyes.
22 Now consider this, ye that forget God, lest I tear *you* in pieces, and *there be* none to deliver.
23 Whoso offereth praise glorifieth me: and to him *b* that ordereth *his* conversation *aright* will I show the salvation of God.

PSALM LI.

1 *David prays for remission of sins, whereof he makes a deep confession: 6 he prays for sanctification, etc.*

To *a* the chief Musician, A Psalm of David, when Nathan the prophet came unto him, after he had gone in to Bathsheba.

HAVE mercy upon me, O God, according to thy loving-kindness; according unto the multitude of thy tender mercies *b* blot out my transgressions.
2 Wash *c* me throughly from mine iniquity, and cleanse me from my sin.
3 For *d* I acknowledge my transgressions: and my sin is ever before me.
4 Against *e* thee, thee only, have I sinned, and done *this* evil *f* in thy sight; *g* that thou mightest be justified when thou speakest, *and* be clear when thou judgest.
5 Behold, *h* I was shapen in iniquity; and in sin did my mother *i* conceive me.
6 Behold, thou desirest truth in the inward parts; and in the hidden *part* thou shalt make me to know wisdom.
7 Purge me with hyssop, and I shall be clean; wash me, and I shall be whiter than snow.
8 Make me to hear joy and gladness; *that* the bones *which* thou hast broken may rejoice.
9 Hide thy face from my sins, and blot out all mine iniquities.

10 Create *i* in me a clean heart, O God; and renew *a* a right spirit within me.
11 Cast me not away *f* from thy presence; and take not thy *k* Holy Spirit from me.
12 Restore unto me the joy of thy salvation; and uphold me *with thy i* free Spirit:
13 *Then* will I teach transgressors thy ways; and sinners shall be converted unto thee.
14 Deliver me from *a* blood-guiltiness, O God, thou God of my salvation; *and* my tongue shall sing aloud of thy righteousness.
15 O Lord, open thou my lips: and my mouth shall show forth thy praise.
16 For thou desirest not sacrifice, *c* else would I give *it;* thou delightest not in burnt offering.
17 The sacrifices of God *are* a broken spirit: a broken and a contrite heart, O God, thou wilt not despise.
18 Do good in thy good pleasure unto Zion: build thou the walls of Jerusalem.
19 Then shalt thou be pleased with *m* the sacrifices of righteousness, with burnt offering, and whole burnt offering: then shall they offer bullocks upon thine altar.

PSALM LII.

1 *David, reproving the spitefulness of Doeg, prophesies his destruction: 8 David, in confidence of God's mercy, gives him thanks.*

To the chief Musician, Maschil, A Psalm of David, *a* when Doeg the Edomite came and told Saul, and said unto him, David is come to the house of Ahimelech.

WHY boastest thou thyself in mischief, O *b* mighty man! the goodness of God *endureth* continually.
2 Thy *c* tongue deviseth mischiefs; *d* like a sharp razor, working deceitfully.
3 Thou lovest evil more than good; *and* lying *e* rather than to speak righteousness. Selah.
4 Thou lovest all-devouring words, 1 O thou deceitful tongue.
5 God shall likewise *a* destroy thee for ever: he shall take thee away, and pluck thee out of *thy* dwelling place, and *f* root thee out of the land of the living. Selah.
6 The *g* righteous also shall see, and fear, and *h* shall laugh at him:
7 Lo, *this is* the man *that* made not God his strength; but *i* trusted in the abundance of his riches, *and* strengthened himself in his 3 wickedness.
8 But I *am f* like a green olive tree in the house of God: I trust in the mercy of God for ever and ever.
9 I will praise thee for ever, because thou hast done *it:* and I will wait on thy name; for *k it is* good before thy saints.

PSALM LIII.

1 *The general depravity of mankind; 4 the iniquity of the wicked, and their punishment.*

To the chief Musician upon Mahalath, Maschil, *A Psalm of* David.

THE *a* fool hath said in his heart, There *is* no God. Corrupt are they, and have done abominable iniquity; *b there is* none that doeth good.
2 God *c* looked down from heaven upon the children of men, to see if there were any that did understand, that did *d* seek God.
3 Every *e* one of them is gone back; they are altogether become filthy: *there is* none that doeth good, no, not one.

tion precedes forgiveness, and, as a gift of God, is a plea for it (2 Sam. 12. 13; Ps. 32. 5; 1 John, 1. 9.). Against thee—chiefly, and as sins against others are violations of God's law, in one sense only. that . . . judgest —*i.e.*, all palliation of his crime is excluded; it is the design in making this confession, to recognise God's justice, however severe the sentence. 5, 6. His guilt was aggravated by his essential, native sinfulness, which is as contrary to God's requisitions of inward purity as are outward sins to those for right conduct. thou shalt make, &c.—may be taken to express God's gracious purpose in view of His strict requisition; a purpose of which David might have availed himself as a check to his native love for sin, and, in not doing so, aggravated his guilt. truth . . . and . . . wisdom — are terms often used for piety (cf. Job. 28. 28; Ps. 110. 30.). 7-12. A series of prayers for forgiveness and purifying. Purge . . . hyssop—The use of this plant in the ritual, (Ex. 12. 22; Num. 19, 6, 18,), suggests the idea of atonement as prominent here; *purge* refers to vicarious satisfaction (Num. 19. 17-20.). Make . . . joy—by forgiving me, which will change distress to joy. Hide, &c.—turn from beholding. Create—a work of almighty power. in me—*lit.*, *to*, or, *for me*: bestow as a gift, a heart free from taint of sin Ps. 24. 4; 73. 1.). renew—implies that he had possessed it: the essential principle of a new nature had not been lost, but its influence interrupted, (Luke, 22. 32, ; for *v.* 11 shows that he had not lost God's presence and Spirit. 1 Sam. 16. 13,) though he had lost the "joy of his salvation," (*v.* 12,), for whose return he prays. right spirit—*lit.*, *constant*, firm, not yielding to temptation. free spirit—*thy* ought not to be supplied, for the word *free* is, *lit.*, *willing*, and *spirit* is that of David. "Let a willing spirit uphold me," *i.e.*, with a soul willingly conformed to God's law, he would be preserved in a right course of conduct. 13. Then—such will be the effect of this gracious work. ways—of providence and human duty (Ps. 18. 21, 30; 32. 8; Luke, 22. 32.). 14. Deliver—or, Free me (Ps. 39. 8,) from the *guilt* of murder 2 Sam. 12. 9, 10; Ps. 5 6.. righteousness—as Ps. 7. 17; 31. 1. 15. open, . lips— by removing my sense of guilt. 16. Praise is better than sacrifice Ps. 50. 14,), and implying faith, penitence, and love, glorifies God. In true penitents the joys of pardon mingle with sorrow for sin. 18. Do good, &c. —Visit not my sin on thy Church. build . . walls—is to show favour; cf. Ps. 89. 40, for opposite form and idea. 19. *God reconciled*, material sacrifices will be acceptable (Ps. 4. 5; cf. Isa. 1. 11-17.).

PSALM LII.

Ver. 1-9. Cf. 1 Sam. 21. 1-10; 22. 1-10, for the history of the title. The first verse gives the theme: the boast of the wicked over the righteous is vain; for God constantly cares for His people. This is expanded by describing the malice and deceit, and then the ruin, of the wicked, and the happy state of the pious.

1. mighty man—*lit.*, *hero*. Does may be thus addressed, ironically, in respect of his might in slander. 2. tongue—for self. mischief's—evil to others (Ps. 5. 9; 38. 12.). working deceitfully—(Ps. 10. 7, . as a keen, smoothly moving razor, cutting quietly, but deeply. 3, 4. a l-devouring—*lit.*, *swallowing*, which utterly destroy (cf. Ps. 2. 9; 35. 25.). 5. likewise—or, so, also, as you have done to others God will do to you (Ps. 18. 27.). The following terms describe the most entire ruin. 6. shall . . . fear—regard with religious awe. laugh at him—for his folly; 7. for trusting in riches and being strong in—wickedness—*lit.*, *mischief*, (*v.* 2, , instead of trusting in God, the man—*lit.*, *the mighty man*, or hero, (*v.* 1.). 8. The figure used is common on Ps. 1. 3; Jer. 11. 16). green—fresh. house, &c.—in communion with God .cf. Ps. 27. 4, 5.). for ever and ever—qualifies mercy. 9. hast done—*i.e.*, what the context supplies, preserved in e cf. Ps. 22. 31.. wait . . . name—hope in thy perfections, manifested for my good Ps. 5. 11; 20. 1.). for it is good—*i.e.*, thy name, and the whole method or result of its manifestation (Ps. 54. 6; 69. 16.).

PSALM LIII.

Ver. 1-6. *On Mahalath*—(cf. Ps. 88. title.). Why this repetition of Ps. 14. is given we do not know.

1-4., with few verbal changes, correspond with Ps. 14. 1-4. 5. Instead of assurances of God's presence with the pious, and a complaint of the wicked, Ps. 14. 5, 6, portrays the ruin of the latter, whose "bones" even " are scattered" (cf. Ps. 141. 7,), and who are put to shame as contemptuously rejected of God.

PSALM LIV.

Ver. 1-7. Cf. title of Ps. 4. and 32.; for the history, 1 Sam. 23. 19, 29; 26. 1-25. After an earnest cry for help, the Psalmist promises praise in the assurance of a hearing.

1. by thy name—(Ps. 5. 11.), specially, power. judge me—as Ps. 7. 8; 26. 1. 2. (Cf. Ps. 4. 1; 5. 1.. 3. strangers—perhaps Ziphites. oppressors—*lit.*, *terrible ones*, (Isa. 13. 11; 25. 3.). Such were Saul and his army, not set . . . them—acted as atheists, without God's fear cf. Ps. 16. 8. . 4. Cf. Ps. 30. 10,) with them—on their side, and for me .cf. Ps. 4 11.). 5. He shall . . . evil—or, Evil *shall* return on Ps. 7. 16' my enemies, or watchers, *i.e.*, to do me evil Ps. 6. 7.). in thy truth— thy verified promise. 6. I will freely, &c—or, present a *free will* offering (Lev. 7. 16; Num. 15. 3.). 7. mine eye . . . desire—cf. Ps. 59. 10; 112. 8,), expresses satisfaction in beholding the overthrow of his enemies as those of God, without implying any selfish or unholy feeling (cf. Ps. 52. 6, 7.).

PSALM LV.

Ver. 1-23. In great terror on account of enemies, and grieved by the treachery of a friend, the Psalmist offers an earnest prayer for relief. He mingles confident assurances of divine favour to himself with invocations and predictions of God's avenging judgments on the wicked. The tone suits David's experience, both in the times of Saul and Absalom, though, perhaps, neither was exclusively before his mind.

1. hide not thyself, &c.—'cf. Ps. 13, 1, 27. 9,), withhold not help. 2. The terms of the last clause express full indulgence of grief. 3. oppression—*lit.*, *persecution*. they . . . iniquity —*lit.*, *they make evil doings slide upon me*. 4, 5. express great alarm, come upon—or *lit.*, *into me*, 6. he at res—*lit.*, *dwell*, *i.e.*, permanently. 7, 8. Even a wilderness is a safer place than exposure to such evils, terrible as storm and tempest. 9. Destroy—*lit*, *Swallow* Ps. 21. 9,.. divide their tongues—or, confound their speech, and hence their counsels, (Gen. 11. 7.). the city—perhaps Jerusalem, the scene of anarchy, 10, 11., which is described

Prayers for **PSALMS LIV–LVII.** *deliverance from enemies.*

4 Have the workers of iniquity *f* no knowledge? who eat up my people *as* they eat bread: they have not called upon God.
5 There ¹ were they in great fear, *where* no fear was: for God hath scattered the bones of him that encampeth *against* thee: thou hast put *them* to shame, because God hath despised them.
6 ² Oh that the salvation of Israel *were* come out of Zion! When God bringeth back the captivity of his people, Jacob shall rejoice, *and* Israel shall be glad.

PSALM LIV.

1 *David, complaining of the Ziphims, prays for deliverance:* 4 *in confidence of God's help, he promises sacrifice.*

To the chief Musician on Neginoth, Maschil, *A Psalm* of David, *a* when the Ziphims came and said to Saul, Doth not David hide himself with us?

SAVE me, O God, by thy name, and judge me by thy strength.
2 Hear my prayer, O God; give ear to the words of my mouth.
3 For strangers are risen up against me, and oppressors seek after my soul: they have not set God before them. Selah.
4 Behold, God *is* mine helper: *b* the LORD is with them that uphold my soul.
5 He shall reward evil unto ¹ mine enemies: cut them *c* off in thy truth.
6 I will freely sacrifice unto thee: I will praise thy name, O LORD, for *it is* good.
7 For he hath delivered me out of all trouble; and mine eye hath seen *his desire* upon mine enemies.

PSALM LV.

1 *David complains of his fearful case:* 9 *prays against the wickedness of his enemies:* 16 *comforts himself in God.*

To the chief Musician on Neginoth, Maschil, *A Psalm* of David.

GIVE ear to my prayer, O God; and hide not thyself from my supplication.
2 Attend unto me, and hear me: I mourn in my complaint, and make a noise;
3 Because of the voice of the enemy, because of the oppression of the wicked: for they cast iniquity upon me, and in wrath they hate me.
4 My *a* heart is sore pained within me: and the terrors of death are fallen upon me.
5 Fearfulness and trembling are come upon me, and horror hath ¹ overwhelmed me.
6 And I said, Oh that I had wings like a dove! *for then* would I fly away, and be at rest.
7 Lo, *then* would I wander far off, and remain in the wilderness. Selah.
8 I would hasten my escape from the windy storm *and* tempest.
9 ² Destroy, O Lord, *and* divide their tongues: for I have seen violence and strife in the city.
10 Day and night they go about it upon the walls thereof: mischief also and sorrow *are* in the midst of it.
11 Wickedness *is* in the midst thereof: deceit and guile depart not from her streets.
12 For *it was* not an enemy *that* reproached me; then I could have borne *it:* neither *was it* he that hated me *that* did magnify *himself* against me; then I would have hid myself from him:
13 But *it was* thou, *a* a man mine equal, my *b* guide, and mine acquaintance.
14 ⁴ We took sweet counsel together, *and* walked unto the house of God in company.

PSALM 53.
f Jer. 4. 22.
1 they feared a fear.
Lev. 26. 17.
Ps. 14. 5.
Pro. 28. 1.
2 Who will give salvations, etc.

PSALM 54.
a 1 Sam. 23. 19.
1 Sa. 26. 1.
b Ps. 118. 7.
1 those that observe me.
c Ps. 89. 49.

PSALM 55.
a Ps. 116. 3.
1 covered me.
2 Swallow up.
³ a man according to my rank.
b 2 Sa. 15. 12.
Mic. 7. 6.
4 Who sweetened counsel.
c Nu. 16. 30.
5 Or, the grave.
d Dan. 6. 10.
Lu. 18. 1.
Acts 3. 1.
Acts 10. 3.
1 Thess. 5. 17.
e 2 Chr. 32. 7.
f Deu. 33. 27.
6 Or, With whom also there are no changes, yet they fear not God.
7 he hath profaned.
8 Or, gift.
Mat. 6. 25.
Lu 12. 22.
1 Pet. 5. 7.
g Ps. 37. 24.
8 men of bloods and deceit.
10 shall not half their days.

PSALM 56.
1 Or, A golden Psalm of David.
a 1 Sam. 21. 11.
b Ps. 57. 1.
2 Mine observers.
c Heb. 13. 6.
d Mal. 3. 16.
e Ro. 8. 31.
f Job 33. 30.

PSALM 57.
1 Or, Destroy not, A golden Psalm.
a 1 Sa. 24. 3.

15 Let death seize upon them, *and* let them *e* go down quick into *b* hell: for wickedness *is* in their dwellings, *and* among them.
16 As for me, I will call upon God; and the LORD shall save me.
17 Evening, *d* and morning, and at noon, will I pray, and cry aloud; and he shall hear my voice.
18 He hath delivered my soul in peace from the battle *that was* against me; for there *e* were many with me.
19 God shall hear, and afflict them, *f* even he that abideth of old. Selah. ⁶ Because they have no changes, therefore they fear not God.
20 He hath put forth his hands against such as be at peace with him; ⁷ he hath broken his covenant.
21 *The words* of his mouth were smoother than butter, but war *was* in his heart: his words were softer than oil, yet *were* they drawn swords.
22 Cast thy ⁸ burden upon the LORD, and he shall sustain thee; *g* he shall never suffer the righteous to be moved.
23 But thou, O God, shalt bring them down into the pit of destruction: ⁹ bloody and deceitful men ¹⁰ shall not live out half their days; but I will trust in thee.

PSALM LVI.

1 *David, praying to God in confidence of his word, complains of his enemies:* 9 *he professes his confidence in God's word.*

To the chief Musician upon Jonath-elem-rechokim, ¹ Michtam of David, when *a* the Philistines took him in Gath.

BE *b* merciful unto me, O God; for man would swallow me up: he fighting daily oppresseth me.
2 ² Mine enemies would daily swallow me up: for *they be* many that fight against me, O thou Most High.
3 What time I am afraid, I will trust in thee.
4 In God I will praise his word: in God I have put my trust; *c* I will not fear what flesh can do unto me.
5 Every day they wrest my words: all their thoughts *are* against me for evil.
6 They gather themselves together, they hide themselves, they mark my steps, when they wait for my soul.
7 Shall they escape by iniquity? in *thine* anger cast down the people, O God.
8 Thou tellest my wanderings: put thou my tears into thy bottle: *d are they* not in thy book?
9 When I cry *unto thee*, then shall mine enemies turn back: this I know; for *e* God *is* for me.
10 In God will I praise *his* word; in the LORD will I praise *his* word.
11 In God have I put my trust: I will not be afraid what man can do unto me.
12 Thy vows *are* upon me, O God: I will render praises unto thee.
13 For thou hast delivered my soul from death: *wilt* not *thou deliver* my feet from falling, that I may walk before God in *f* the light of the living?

PSALM LVII.

1 *David complains of his dangerous case:* 7 *he encourages himself to praise God.*

To the chief Musician, ¹ Al-taschith, Michtam of David, *a* when he fled from Saul in the cave.

BE merciful unto me, O God, be merciful unto me; for my soul trusteth in thee: yea, in the shadow of thy wings will I make

David Complains to God. PSALMS LVI–LVIII. *He Comforts Himself in God.*

in detail (cf. Ps. 7. 14-16.). **Wickedness**—*lit., Mischief,* evils resulting from others Ps. 5. 9; 52. 2, 7.'. **streets**—or *lit., wide places,* markets, courts of justice, and any public place. 12-14. This description of treachery does not deny, but aggravates, the injury from enemies. **guide**—*lit., friend,* (Pro. 16. 28; 17. 9.). **acquaintance**—in *Heb.,* a yet more intimate associate. **in company**—*lit., with a crowd,* in a festal procession. 15. Let death, &c.—or, "Desolations are on them." let them go *(lit., they will go:* quick—or, living, in the midst of life, death will come (cf. Num. 16. 33.). among them—or, within them, in their hearts (Ps. 5. 9; 49. 11.). 16-18. God answers his constant and repeated prayers. many with me—*i.e.,* by the context, fighting with me. 19. God hears the wicked in wrath. abideth [or, *sitteth*] of old—enthroned as a sovereign. Because ... no changes—Prosperity hardens them Ps. 73. 5.). 20, 21. The treachery is aggravated by hypocrisy. The changes of number, *v.* 15, 23, and here, enlivens the picture, and implies that the chief traitor and his accomplices are in view together. 22. thy burden—*lit., gift,* what is assigned you. he shall sustain—*lit., supply food,* and so all need (Ps. 37. 25; Mat. 6. 11.). to be moved —from the secure position of his favour (Ps. 10. 6.. 23. bloody ... days—cf. Ps. 5. 6; 61. 14,). deceit and murderous dispositions often united. The threat is directed specially (not as a general truth) against the wicked, then in the writer's view.

PSALM LVI.

Ver. 1-13. *Upon Jonath-elem-rechokim* — *lit., upon the Dove of silence* of distant places; either denoting a melody (cf. on Ps. 9.) of that name, to which this Psalm was to be performed; or it is an enigmatical form of denoting the subject, as given in the history referred to (1 Sam. 21. 11, &c.), David being regarded as an uncomplaining, meek dove, driven from his native home to wander in exile. Beset by domestic and foreign foes, David appeals confidently to God, recites his complaints, and closes with joyful and assured anticipations of God's continued help.

1, 2. would swallow—*lit., pants as a raging beast,* (Acts, 9. 1.). enemies—*watchers* (Ps. 64. 5.). Most High—as it is not elsewhere used absolutely for God, some render the word here, *arrogantly,* or proudly, as qualifying "those who fight," &c. 3. In [or *lit., unto*] thee—to whom he turns in trouble. 4. In God ... his word—By His grace or aid Ps. 60. 12; 108. 13.), or, "I will boast in God as to His word:" in either case His word is the special matter and cause of praise. flesh—for mankind (Ps. 65. 2; Isa. 31. 3.), intimating frailty. 5, 6. A vivid picture of the conduct of malicious enemies. 7. Shall they escape?— or better, " Their escape is by iniquity." cast ... people—humble those who so proudly oppose thy servant. 8. God is mindful of his exile and remembers his tears. The custom of *bottling the tears* of mourners as a memorial, which has existed in some Eastern nations, may explain the figure. 9. God is for me—or, on my side (Ps. 118. 6; 124. 1. 2., hence he is sure of the repulse of his foes. 12. I will ... praises—will pay what I have vowed. 13. The question implies an affirmative answer, drawn from past experience. falling—as from a precipice. before God—in His favour during life

PSALM LVII.

Ver. 1-11. *Al-taschith*—Destroy not. This is perhaps an enigmatical allusion to the critical circumstances connected with the history, for which cf. 1 Sam. 22. 1; 26. 1-3. In Moses' prayer (Deut. 9. 26), it is a prominent petition deprecating God's anger against the people. This explanation suits the 58th and 59th also. Asaph uses it for the 75th, in the scope of which, there is allusion to some emergency. *Michtam*—(cf. Ps. 16.). To an earnest cry for divine aid, the Psalmist adds, as often, the language of praise, in the assured hope of a favourable hearing.

1. my soul—or, self, or life, which is threatened. shadow of thy wings—(Ps. 17. 8; 36. 7.). calamities—*lit., mischiefs,* Ps. 52. 2; 55. 10.). 2. performeth—or, completes what he has begun. 3. from ... swallow me up—that pants in rage after me (Ps. 56. 2.). mercy and ... truth—(Ps. 25. 10; 36. 5,), as messengers (Ps. 43. 3,) sent to deliver him. 4. The mingled figures of wild beasts (Ps. 10. 9; 17. 12, and weapons of war Ps. 11. 2,', heightens the picture of danger. whose ... tongue—or, slanders. 7. This doxology illustrates his view of the connection of his deliverance with God's glory. 6. (Cf. Ps. 7. 15; 9. 15, 16.). 7. I will ... praise—both with voice and instrument. 8. Hence he addresses his *glory,* or *tongue* (Ps. 16. 9; 30. 12,), and his psaltery, or lute and harp. I myself ... early—*lit., I will awaken dawn,* poetically expressing his zeal and diligence. 9, 10. As His mercy and truth, so shall His praise, fill the universe.

PSALM LVIII.

Ver. 1-11. David's critical condition in some period of the Sauline persecution probably occasioned this Psalm, in which the Psalmist teaches that the innate and actual sinfulness of men deserves, and shall receive, God's righteous vengeance, while the pious may be consoled by the evidence of his wise and holy government of men.

1. O congregation—*lit., O dumb*—the word used is never translated "congregation." "Are ye dumb? ye should speak righteousness," may be the translation. In any case, the writer remonstrates with them, perhaps a council, who were assembled to try his cause, and bound to give a right decision. 2. This they did not design; but, weigh ... violence— or, give decisions of violence. *Weigh* is a figure to express the acts of judges. in the earth—publicly. 3-5. describe the wicked generally, who sin naturally, easily, malignantly, and stubbornly. stoppeth her [or *lit., his*] ear—*i.e.,* the wicked man, the singular used collectively,' who thus becomes like the deaf adder which has no ear. 6. He prays for their destruction, under the figure of ravenous beasts (Ps. 3. 7; 7. 2,). 7. which run continually—*lit., they shall go to themselves,* utterly depart, as rapid mountain torrents. he bendeth ... his arrrows—prepares it. The term for preparing a bow applied to arrows (Ps. 64. 3.). let them ... pieces—*lit., as if they cut themselves off—i.e.,* become blunted and of no avail. 8, 9. Other figures of this utter ruin; the last denoting rapidity. In a shorter time than pots feel the heat of thorns on fire —he shall take them away as with a whirlwind —*lit., blow him (them) away,* both living, ... wrath—*lit., as the living or fresh,* as the heated or burning—*i.e.,* thorns—all easily blown away, so easily and quickly the wicked. The figure of the *snail* perhaps alludes to its

Wicked judges reproved. PSALMS LVIII–LX. *Prayer against enemies.*

my refuge, *b* until *these* calamities be overpast.
2 I will cry unto God most high; unto God *c* that performeth all things for me.
3 He *d* shall send from heaven, and save me *2* from the reproach of him that would swallow me up. Selah. God shall *e* send forth his mercy and his truth.
4 My soul *is* among lions; and I lie even among them that are set on fire, even the sons of men, *f* whose teeth are spears and arrows, and *g* their tongue a sharp sword.
5 Be *h* thou exalted, O God, above the heavens; let thy glory be above all the earth.
6 They *i* have prepared a net for my steps; my soul is bowed down: they have digged a pit before me, into the midst whereof they are fallen *themselves*. Selah.
7 My *j* heart is *3* fixed, O God, my heart is fixed; I will sing and give praise.
8 Awake *k* up, my glory; awake, psaltery and harp: I *myself* will awake early.
9 I will praise thee, O LORD, among the people; I will sing unto thee among the nations:
10 For *l* thy mercy *is* great unto the heavens, and thy truth unto the clouds.
11 Be thou exalted, O God, above the heavens: let thy glory be above all the earth.

PSALM LVIII.

1 *David, reproving ungodly judges,* 3 *describes the nature of the wicked,* 6 *and devotes them to God's judgments.*

To the chief Musician, Al-taschith, Michtam of David.

DO ye indeed speak righteousness, O congregation? do ye judge uprightly, O ye sons of men?
2 Yea, in heart ye work wickedness; *a* ye weigh the violence of your hands in the earth.
3 The wicked *b* are estranged from the womb; they go astray *2* as soon as they be born, speaking lies.
4 Their *c* poison is *3* like the poison of a serpent: *they are* like the deaf *4* adder *that* stoppeth her ear;
5 Which will not hearken to the voice of charmers, *5* charming never so wisely.
6 Break *d* their teeth, O God, in their mouth: break out the great teeth of the young lions, O LORD.
7 Let them melt away as waters which run continually: when he bendeth *his bow to shoot* his arrows, let them be as cut in pieces.
8 As a snail which melteth, let *every one of them* pass away; like the untimely birth of a woman, *that* they may not see the sun.
9 Before your pots can feel the thorns, he shall take them away *e* as with a whirlwind, *6* both living, and in *his* wrath.
10 The *f* righteous shall rejoice when he seeth the vengeance: he shall wash his feet in the blood of the wicked.
11 So that a man shall say, *g* Verily *there is 7* a reward for the righteous: verily he is a God that judgeth in the earth.

PSALM LIX.

1 *David prays to be delivered from his enemies;* 6 *complains of their cruelty;* 8 *trusts in God;* 11 *prays against them;* 16 *praises God.*

To the chief Musician, Al-taschith, Michtam of David, *a* when Saul sent, and they watched the house to kill him.

DELIVER me from mine enemies, O my God; *2* defend me from them that rise up against me.

PSALM 57.
b Is. 26. 20.
c Ps. 138. 8.
d Ps. 144. 5.
2 Or, he reproacheth him that would swallow me up.
e Ps. 61. 7.
f Pro. 30. 14.
g Ps. 64. 3.
h Ps. 108. 5.
i Ps. 9. 15.
j Ps. 108. 1.
3 Or, prepared.
k Judg. 5. 12.
l Ps. 108. 4.

PSALM 58.
1 Or, Destroy not, A golden Psalm of David.
a Ps. 94. 20.
Is. 10. 1.
b Ps. 51. 5.
Is. 48. 8.
2 from the belly.
c Ps. 140. 3.
Ecc. 10. 11.
3 according to the likeness.
4 Or, asp.
5 Or, be the charmer never so cunning.
d Job 4. 10.
e Pro. 10. 25.
6 as living as wrath.
f Ps. 52. 6.
Ps. 64. 10.
g Ro. 2. 5–10.
7 fruit of the, etc.

PSALM 59.
1 Or, Destroy not, A golden Psalm of David.

2 Deliver me from the workers of iniquity, and save me from bloody men.
3 For, lo, they lie in wait for my soul: the mighty are gathered against me; not *for* my transgression, nor *for* my sin, O LORD.
4 They run and prepare themselves without *my* fault: awake *3* to help me, and behold.
5 Thou therefore, O LORD God of hosts, the God of Israel, awake to visit all the heathen: be not merciful to any wicked transgressors. Selah.
6 They return at evening: they make a noise like a dog, and go round about the city.
7 Behold, they belch out with their mouth: swords *are* in their lips: for who, *say they,* doth hear?
8 But thou, O LORD, shalt laugh at them; thou shalt have all the heathen in derision.
9 *Because of* his strength will I wait upon thee: for God *is 4* my defence.
10 The God of my mercy shall prevent me: God shall let me see *my desire* upon *5* mine enemies.
11 Slay them not, lest my people forget: scatter them by thy power; and bring them down, O Lord our shield.
12 *For* the sin of their mouth *and* the words of their lips let them even be taken in their pride; and for cursing and lying *which* they speak.
13 Consume *them* in wrath, consume *them,* that they *may* not *be;* and let them know that God ruleth in Jacob unto the ends of the earth. Selah.
14 And at evening let them return; *and* let them make a noise like a dog, and go round about the city.
15 Let them wander up and down *6* for meat, *7* and grudge if they be not satisfied.
16 But I will sing of thy power; yea, I will sing aloud of thy mercy in the morning: for thou hast been my defence and refuge in the day of my trouble.
17 Unto thee, O my strength, will I sing: for God *is* my defence, *and* the God of my mercy.

PSALM LX.

1 *David, complaining to God of former judgments,* 4 *now, upon better hope, prays for deliverance;* 6 *comforting himself in God's promises, he craves that help whereon he trusts.*

To the chief Musician upon Shushan-eduth, 1 Michtam of David, to teach; *a* when he strove with Aram-naharaim, and with Aram-zobah, when Joab returned, and smote of Edom in the valley of Salt twelve thousand.

O GOD, thou hast cast us off, thou hast *2* scattered us, thou hast been displeased; O turn thyself to us again.
2 Thou hast made the earth to tremble; thou hast broken it; heal the breaches thereof; for it shaketh.
3 Thou hast showed thy people hard things: thou hast made us to drink the wine of astonishment.
4 Thou *b* hast given a banner to them that fear thee, that it may be displayed because of the truth. Selah.
5 That *c* thy beloved may be delivered, save *with* thy right hand, and hear me.
6 God hath *d* spoken in his holiness; I will rejoice, I will divide *e* Shechem, and mete out the *f* valley of Succoth.
7 Gilead *is* mine, and Manasseh *is* mine; Ephraim *g* also *is* the strength of mine head; *h* Judah *is* my lawgiver;
8 Moab *is* my washpot; over Edom will I

loss of saliva when moving. Though obscure in its clauses, the general sense of the passage is clear. 10, 11. wash ... wicked—denoting great slaughter. The joy of triumph over the destruction of the wicked is because they are God's enemies, and their overthrow shows that he reigneth (cf. Ps. 52. 5-7; 54. 7.). In this assurance let heaven and earth rejoice (Ps. 96. 10; 97. 1, &c.).

PSALM LIX.
Ver. 1-17. Cf. Ps. 57., and for history, 1 Sam. 19. 11, &c. The scope is very similar to that of the 57th; prayer in view of malicious and violent foes, and joy in prospect of relief. 1. defend—(cf. *Mary.*). rise up ... me—(cf. Ps. 17. 7. . 2. (Cf. Ps. 5. 5; 6. 8. . 4, 5. prepare, &c.—*lit.*, *set themselves as in array*. awake—(cf. Ps. 3.7; 7. 6,)appeals to God in his covenant relation to his people (Ps. 9. 18. . 6, 7. They are as ravening dogs seeking prey, and, as such, *belch out—i.e.,* slanders, their impudent barkings, for who, say they —For the full expression with the supplied words cf. Ps. 64. 5. 8. Cf. Ps. 2, 4; 37. 13. . 9. By judicious expositors, and on good grounds, this is better rendered, "O my strength, on thee will I wait" *v.* 17. , defence—(cf. Ps. 18. 3.) 10. prevent me—(Ps. 21. 3.). see my desire—in their overthrow (Ps. 54. 7.). enemies—as Ps. 5. 8. 11. Slay them not—at once Jud. 2. 21-23); but perpetuate their punishment (Gen. 4. 12; Num. 32. 13,), by scattering or making them wander, and humble them. 12. let them be ... taken in their pride—while evincing it—*i.e.,* to be punished for their lies, &c. 13. Though delayed for wise reasons, the utter destruction of the wicked must come at last, and God's presence and power in and for his Church will be known abroad (1 Sam. 17. 46; Ps. 46. 10, 11. . 14, 15. Meanwhile let the rapacious dogs prowl, they cannot hurt the pious; yea, they shall wander famished and sleepless. grudge if, &c.—*lit., they shall stay all night—i.e.,* obtain nothing. 16, 17. contrast the lot of God's servant, who employs his time in God's praise. sing aloud ... in the morning—when they retire famishing and disappointed, or it may denote delightful diligence in praise, as Ps. 30. 5.

PSALM LX.
Ver. 1-12. *Shushan-eduth*—Lily of testimony. The lily is an emblem of beauty, (ct. Ps. 45. title.). As a description of the Psalm, those terms combined may denote a beautiful poem, witnessing—*i.e.,* for God's faithfulness as evinced in the victories referred to in the history cited. *Aram-naharaim*—Syria of the two rivers, or Mesopotamia beyond *the river* (Euphrates) (2 Sam. 10. 16.). *Aramzobah*—Syria of Zobah (2 Sam. 10. 6,), to whose king the king of the former was tributary. The war with Edom, by Joab and Abishai (2 Chr. 18. 12, 25, , occurred about the same time. Probably, while doubts and fears alternately prevailed respecting the issue of these wars, the writer composed this Psalm, in which he depicts, in the language of God's people, their sorrows under former disasters, offers prayer in present straits, and rejoices in confident hope of triumph by God's aid. 1-3. allude to disasters. cast ... off—in scorn (Ps. 43. 2; 44. 9.). scattered — broken our strength (cf. 2 Sam. 5. 20.). O turn thyself — or, restore to us (prosperity.). The figures of physical, denote great civil, commotions (Ps. 46. 2, 3,). drink ... wine of astonishment—*lit., of staggering—i.e.,* made us weak cf. Ps. 75. 8; Isa. 51. 17, 22.). 4, 5. Yet to God's banner they will rally, and pray that, led and sustained by his power (right hand, Ps. 17. 7; 20. 6,*,* they may be safe. hear me—or, hear us. 6-10. God hath spoken in [or, *by*) his holiness—(Ps. 89. 35; Amos, 4. 2,), on the pledge of his attributes (Ps. 22. 3; 30. 4.). Taking courage from God's promise to give them possession Ex. 23. 31; Deut. 11. 24,), and perhaps renewed to him by special revelation,), with triumphant joy he describes the conquest as already made. Shechem, and ... Succoth—as widely separated points, and —Gilead, ... and Manasseh—as large districts, east and west of Jordan, represent the whole land. divide ... and mete out—means to have entire control over. Ephraim—denotes the military (Deut. 33. 17.); and—Judah— the lawgiver, (Gen. 49. 10,*,* the civil power. Foreign nations are then presented as subdued. Moab—is a washpot—the most ordinary vessel. over [or, at] Edom—(as a slave,), he casts his shoe. Philistia, triumph . . . [or, rather, *shout*] for me—acknowledges subjection (cf. Ps. 108. 9, "over Philistia will I triumph."). 9, 10. He feels assured that, though once angry, God is now ready to favour his people. who will lead me—or, *who has led me,* as if the work were now begun. Wilt not thou—or, Is it not thou? 11, 12. Hence he closes with a prayer for success, and an assurance of a hearing.

PSALM LXI.
Ver. 1-8. *Neginah*—or, Neginoth (cf. Ps. 4. title.). Separated from his usual spiritual privileges, perhaps by Absalom's rebellion, the Psalmist prays for divine aid, and, in view of past mercies, with great confidence of being heard. 1-3. From the end, &c.—*i.e.,* places remote from the sanctuary (Deut. 28. 64.). heart is overwhelmed—*lit., covered over with darkness,* or, distress. to the Rock—(Ps. 18. 2; 40. 2.). higher than I — which otherwise I cannot ascend. shelter ... and strong tower — repeat the same sentiment. 4. I will abide—so I desire to do (cf. Ps. 23. 6.). trust in the covert, &c.—*make* my refuge in the shadow (cf. Ps. 17. 8; 36. 7.). 5. the heritage—or, part in the spiritual blessings of Israel Ps. 21. 2-4,). vows—implies prayers. 6, 7. the king —himself and his royal line ending in Christ. Mercy and truth personified as (Ps. 40. 11; 57. 3. abide before God—*lit., sit as a king in God's presence.* under his protection. 8. Thus for new blessings will new vows of praise ever be paid.

PSALM LXII.
Ver. 1-12. To Jeduthun—(cf. Ps. 39. title.). The general tone of this Psalm is expressive of confidence in God. Occasion is taken to remind the wicked of their sin, their ruin, and their meanness. 1. waiteth—*lit., is silent,* trusts submissively and confidently as a servant. 2. The titles applied to God often occur (Ps. 9. 9; 18. 2,). be greatly moved—(Ps. 10. 6,), no injury shall be permanent, though devised by enemies. 3. Their destruction will come; as a tottering wall they already are feeble and failing. bowing wall shall ye be—better supply *are.* Some propose to apply these phrases to describe the condition of *the man—i.e.,* the pious sufferer: thus, "Will ye slay him," &c,; but the other is a good sense. 4. his excellency—or, elevation, to which God had raised

cast out my shoe: Philistia, ³ triumph thou because of me.
9 Who will bring me *into* the ⁴ strong city? who will lead me into Edom?
10 *Wilt* not thou, O God, *which* hadst cast us off? and *thou*, O God, *which* didst not go out with our armies?
11 Give us help from trouble: for vain *is* the ᵇ help of man.
12 Through God we shall do valiantly: for he *it is that* shall tread down our enemies.

PSALM LXI.

1 *David flees to God upon his former experience:* 4 *he vows perpetual service unto him, because of his promises.*

To the chief Musician upon Neginah, A Psalm of David.

HEAR my cry, O God; attend unto my prayer.
2 From the end of the earth will I cry unto thee, when my heart is overwhelmed: lead me to the Rock *that* is higher than I.
3 For thou hast been a shelter for me, *and* ᵃ a strong tower from the enemy.
4 I will abide in thy tabernacle for ever: I will ¹ trust in the covert of thy wings. Selah.
5 For thou, O God, hast heard my vows: thou hast given *me* the heritage of those that fear thy name.
6 ² Thou wilt prolong the king's life; *and* his years ³ as many generations.
7 He shall abide before God for ever: O prepare mercy and truth, *which* may preserve him.
8 So will I sing praise unto thy name for ever, that I may daily perform my vows.

PSALM LXII.

1 *David, professing his confidence in God, discourages his enemies, and encourages the godly.* 11 *Power and mercy belong to God.*

To the chief Musician, to Jeduthun, A Psalm of David.

TRULY ¹ my soul ² waiteth upon God: from him *cometh* my salvation.
2 He only *is* my rock and my salvation; *he is* my³ defence; I shall not be greatly moved.
3 How long will ye imagine mischief against a man? ye shall be slain all of you: as a bowing wall *shall ye be, and as a* tottering fence.
4 They only consult to cast *him* down from his excellency: they delight in lies: ᵃ they bless with their mouth, but they curse ⁴ inwardly. Selah.
5 My soul, wait thou only upon God; for my expectation *is* from him.
6 He only *is* my rock and my salvation: *he is* my defence; I shall not be moved.
7 In God *is* my salvation and my glory: the rock of my strength, *and* my refuge, *is* in God.
8 Trust in him at all times; *ye* people, pour ᵇ out your heart before him: God *is* a refuge for us. Selah.
9 Surely men of low degree *are* vanity, *and* men of high degree *are* a lie: to be laid in the balance, they *are* ᵇ altogether *lighter* than vanity.
10 Trust not in ᶜ oppression, and become not vain in robbery: ᵈ if riches increase, set not your heart *upon them.*
11 God hath spoken once; twice have I heard this, that ᵉ power *belongeth* unto God.
12 Also unto thee, O Lord, *belongeth* mercy: for ᶠ thou renderest to every man according to his work.

299

PSALM 60.
3 Or, triumph thou over me
4 Or, fenced city
ᵃ city of strength.
2 Sa. 11. 1.
ᵇ salvation.

PSALM 61.
ᵃ Pro. 18. 10.
1 Or, make my refuge.
2 Thou shalt add days to the days of the king.
3 as generation and generation.

PSALM 62.
1 Or, only.
2 is silent.
3 high place.
ᵃ Ps. 28. 3.
4 in their inward parts.
ᵇ 1 Sam. 1. 15.
5 Or, alike.
ᶜ Is. 20. 4.
ᵈ Lu. 12. 15.
6 Or, strength.
ᵉ Jer. 17. 11.
ᶠ 1 Pet. 1. 17.

PSALM 63.
ᵃ 1 Sa. 22. 5.
1 weary land without water.
2 fatness.
3 They shall make him run out like water by the hands of the sword.
ᵇ Zeph. 1. 5.

PSALM 64.
1 Or, speech.
2 to hide snares.
3 Or, we are consumed by that which they have throughly searched.
4 a search searched.
5 their wound shall be.

PSALM 65.
1 is silent.
ᵃ Is. 45. 11.
ᵇ John 12. 32.
² Words, or, Matters of iniquity.
ᶜ Heb. 9. 14. 1 John 1. 7.
ᵈ Ps. 33. 12.

PSALM LXIII.

1 *David's thirst after God's service in his sanctuary.* A Psalm of David, ᵃ when he was in the wilderness of Judah.

O GOD, thou *art* my God; early will I seek thee: my soul thirsteth for thee, my flesh longeth for thee in a dry and ¹ thirsty land, where no water is;
2 To see thy power and thy glory, so *as* I have seen thee in the sanctuary.
3 Because thy loving-kindness *is* better than life, my lips shall praise thee.
4 Thus will I bless thee while I live: I will lift up my hands in thy name.
5 My soul shall be satisfied as *with* ² marrow and fatness; and my mouth shall praise thee with joyful lips;
6 When I remember thee upon my bed, *and* meditate on thee in the *night* watches.
7 Because thou hast been my help, therefore in the shadow of thy wings will I rejoice.
8 My soul followeth hard after thee: thy right hand upholdeth me.
9 But those *that* seek my soul, to destroy *it,* shall go into the lower parts of the earth.
10 ³ They shall fall by the sword: they shall be a portion for foxes.
11 But the king shall rejoice in God; every one ᵇ that sweareth by him shall glory: but the mouth of them that speak lies shall be stopped.

PSALM LXIV.

1 *David prays for deliverance from his enemies.*

To the chief Musician, A Psalm of David.

HEAR my voice, O God, in my prayer: preserve my life from fear of the enemy.
2 Hide me from the secret counsel of the wicked; from the insurrection of the workers of iniquity:
3 Who whet their tongue like a sword, *and* bend *their bows to shoot* their arrows, *even* bitter words;
4 That they may shoot in secret at the perfect: suddenly do they shoot at him, and fear not.
5 They encourage themselves *in* an evil ¹ matter: they commune ² of laying snares privily; they say, Who shall see them?
6 They search out iniquities; ³ they accomplish ⁴ a diligent search: both the inward thought of every one *of them,* and the heart, *is* deep.
7 But God shall shoot at them *with* an arrow; suddenly ⁵ shall they be wounded.
8 So they shall make their own tongue to fall upon themselves: all that see them shall flee away.
9 And all men shall fear, and shall declare the work of God; for they shall wisely consider of his doing.
10 The righteous shall be glad in the LORD, and shall trust in him; and all the upright in heart shall glory.

PSALM LXV.

1 *David praises God for his grace.* 4 *Infinite power and goodness of God.*

To the chief Musician, A Psalm and Song of David.

PRAISE ¹ waiteth for thee, O God, in Zion: and unto thee shall the vow be performed.
2 O thou ᵃ that hearest prayer, ᵇ unto thee shall all flesh come.
3 ² Iniquities prevail against me: *as for* our transgressions, thou shalt ᶜ purge them away.
4 Blessed ᵈ *is the man whom* thou choosest,

him (Ps. 4. 2.). This they try to do by lies and duplicity Ps. 5. 9.). 5, 6, (Cf. Ps. 1. 2.). ' ot be moved—not at all; his confidence has increased. 7. rock of my strength—or, strongest support (Ps. 7. 10; 61. 3.). 8. pour out your heart—give full expression to feeling (1 Sam. 1. 15; Job, 30. 16; Ps. 42. 4.), ye people—God's people. 9. No kind of men are reliable, compared with God Isa. 2. 22; Jer. 17. 5.) altogether—alike, one as the other (Ps. 34. 3.). 10. Not only are oppression and robbery, which are wicked means of wealth, no grounds of boasting, but even wealth, increasing lawfully, ought not to engross the heart. 11. once; twice—(as Job, 33. 14; 40. 5, , are used to give emphasis to the sentiment. God's power is tempered by His mercy, which it also sustains. 12. For thou renderest lit., That thou renderest. &c., connected with "I heard this," as the phrase—"that power," &c.—teaching that by His power he can show both mercy and justice.

PSALM LXIII.

Ver. 1-11. The historical occasion referred to by the title was probably during Absalom's rebellion (cf. 2 Sam. 15. 23, 28; 16. 2.). David expresses an earnest desire for God's favour, and a confident expectation of realising it in his deliverance, and the ruin of his enemies.
1. early... seek thee—earnestly (Isa. 26. 9.). The figurative terms—dry and thirsty—lit., weary, denoting moral destitution, suited his outward circumstances. soul—and—flesh—the whole man (Ps. 16. 9, 10.). 2. The special object of desire was God's perfections as displayed in his worship Ps. 27. 4.). 3. Experiencing God's mercy, which exceeds all the blessings of life, his lips will be opened for his praise Ps. 51. 15. . 4. Thus—lit., Truly, will I bless—praise thee (Ps. 34. 1.). lift up my hands—in worship lit. Ps. 28. 2.). in thy name—in praise of thy perfections. 5-8. Full spiritual blessings satisfy his desires, and acts of praise fill his thoughts and time. night—as well as day. Past favours assure him of future, and hence he presses earnestly near to God, whose power sustains him (Ps. 17. 8; 60. 5.). 9, 10. those..., to destroy it—or lit.. to, or, for ruin—i.e., such as seek to injure me (are) for ruin—appointed to it (cf. Ps. 35. 8.). shall go... earth—into the grave, or, to death; as their bodies are represented as a portion for—foxes—lit., jackals, 11. the king—i.e., David himself, and all who reverence God, "shall share a glorious part," while treacherous foes shall be for ever silenced (Ps. 62. 4.).

PSALM LXIV.

Ver. 1-10. A prayer for deliverance from cunning and malicious enemies, with a confident view of their overthrow, which will honour God and give joy to the righteous.
1. preserve... fear—as well as the danger producing it. 2. insurrection—lit., uproar, noisy assaults, as well as their secret counsels. 3, 4. similar figures for slander (Ps. 57. 4; 59. 7,) bend—lit., tread, or, prepared. The allusion is to the mode of bending a bow by treading on it; here, and Ps. 58. 7, transferred to arrows. the perfect—one innocent of the charges made (Ps. 18. 23,). and fear not—Ps. 55. 10, , not regarding God. 5. A sentiment here more fully presented, by depicting their deliberate malice. 6. This is farther evinced by their diligent efforts and deeply laid schemes. 7. The contrast is heightened by representing God as using weapons like theirs. 8. their... tongue to fail, &c.—i.e., the consequences of their slanders, &c. (cf. Ps. 10. 2; 31. 16.). all that see... away—their partners in evil shall be terrified. 9. 10. Men, generally, will acknowledge God's work, and the righteous, rejoicing in it, shall be encouraged to trust him Ps. 58. 10.).

PSALM LXV.

Ver. 1-13. This is a song of praise for God's spiritual blessings to his people and his kind providence over all the earth.
1. Praise waiteth for thee—lit., To thee silence is praise, or, (cf. Ps. 62. 1.), To thee silence is praise—i.e., Praise is waiting as a servant—it is due to thee. So the last clause expresses the duty of paying vows. These two parts of acceptable worship, mentioned Ps. 50. 14, are rendered in Zion, where God chiefly displays His mercy and receives homage. 2. All are encouraged to pray by God's readiness to hear. 3. God's mercy alone delivers us from the burden of iniquities, by purging or expiating by an atonement the transgressions with which we are charged, and which are denoted by—Iniquities—or lit., Words of iniquities. 4. dwell in thy courts;... [and] satisfied with the goodness... temple — denote communion with God (Ps. 15. 1; 23. 6 ; cf. Ps. 5. 7.). This is a blessing for all God's people, as denoted by the change of number. 5. terrible things—i.e., by the manifestation of justice and wrath to enemies, accompanying that of mercy to his people (Ps. 63. 9-11; 64. 7-9.). the confidence—object of it. of all... earth—the whole world—i.e., deservedly such, whether men think so or not. 6-13. God's great power and goodness are the grounds of this confidence. These are illustrated in His control of the mightiest agencies of nature and nations, affecting men with awe and dread (Ps. 26. 7; 98. 1., &c.,), and in His fertilising showers, causing the earth to produce abundantly for man and beast. outgoings of... rejoice—all people from east to west. visitest—in mercy (cf. Ps. 8. 4.). river of God—His exhaustless resources. thy paths—ways of providence (Ps. 25. 4, 10.). wilderness—places, though not inhabited by men, fit for pasture (Lev. 16. 21, 22; Job, 24. 5.). pastures—(in v. 12,), is lit., folds, or, enclosures for flocks; and in v. 13, it may be lambs—the same word used and so translated (Ps. 37. 20,); so that "the flocks are clothed with lambs," a figure for abundant increase, would be the form of expression.

PSALM LXVI.

Ver. 1-20. The writer invites all men to unite in praise, cites some striking occasions for it, promises special acts of thanksgiving, and celebrates God's great mercy.
1. Make... noise—or, Shout. 2. his name—as Ps. 20. 2. make his praise glorious—lit., make or place honour, His praise, or, as to His praise—i.e., let His praise be such as will glorify Him, or, be honourable to Him. 3, 4. A specimen of the praise. How terrible—(cf. Ps. 65. 8.). submit—(cf. Marg.), show a forced subjection (Ps. 18. 44,), produced by terror. 5, 6. The terrible works illustrated in Israel's history (Ex. 14. 21.). By this example let rebels be admonished. 7. behold the nations—watch their conduct. 8, 9. Here is, perhaps, cited a case of recent deliverance. holdeth ... in life—lit., putteth our soul in life—i.e., out of danger (Ps. 30. 3; 49. 15.). to be moved—(cf. Ps. 10. 6; 55. 22.). 10-12. Out of severe

Infinite goodness of God.   PSALMS LXVI–LXVIII.   *A prayer for God's kingdom.*

and causest to approach *unto thee, that he may dwell in thy courts:* we shall be satisfied with the goodness of thy house, *even* of thy holy temple.

5 *By* terrible things in righteousness wilt thou answer us, O God of our salvation; *who art* the confidence of all the ends of the earth, and of them that are afar off upon the sea:

6 Which by his strength setteth fast the mountains; *being* girded with power:

7 Which *stilleth the noise of the seas, the noise of their waves, and the tumult of the people.

8 They also that dwell in the uttermost parts are afraid at thy tokens: thou makest the outgoings of the morning and evening ³ to rejoice.

9 Thou visitest the earth, and ⁴ waterest it: thou greatly enrichest it with the river of God, *which* is full of water: thou preparest them corn, when thou hast so provided for it.

10 Thou waterest the ridges thereof abundantly; ⁵ thou settlest the furrows thereof; ⁶ thou makest it soft with showers; thou blessest the springing thereof:

11 Thou crownest ⁷ the year with thy goodness; and thy ⁷ paths drop fatness.

12 They drop *upon* the pastures of the wilderness; and the little hills ⁸ rejoice on every side.

13 The pastures are clothed with flocks; the valleys also are covered over with corn; they shout for joy, they also sing.

PSALM LXVI.

1 *David exhorts to praise God, 5 to observe his great works, 8 to bless him for his gracious benefits.*

To the chief Musician, A Song *or* Psalm.

MAKE a joyful noise unto God, ¹ all ye lands;

2 Sing forth the honour of his name; make his praise glorious.

3 Say unto God, How terrible *art thou in* thy works! *ᵃ* through the greatness of thy power shall thine enemies ² submit themselves unto thee.

4 All *ᵇ* the earth shall worship thee, and shall sing unto thee; they shall sing *to* thy name. Selah.

5 Come ᶜ and see the works of God: *he is* terrible *in his* doing toward the children of men.

6 He ᵈ turned the sea into dry *land:* they ᵉ went through the flood on foot: there did we rejoice in him.

7 He ruleth by his power for ever; ƒ his eyes behold the nations: let not the rebellious exalt themselves. Selah.

8 O bless our God, ye people, and make the voice of his praise to be heard:

9 Which ³ holdeth our soul in life, and suffereth not our feet to be moved.

10 For thou, O God, hast proved us: ᵍ thou hast tried us, as silver is tried.

11 Thou broughtest us into the net; thou laidst affliction upon our loins.

12 Thou hast caused men to ride over our heads: we went through fire and through water; but thou broughtest us out into a ⁴ wealthy *place*.

13 I will go into thy house with burnt offerings: ʰ I will pay thee my vows,

14 Which my lips have ⁵ uttered, and my mouth hath spoken, when I was in trouble.

15 I will offer unto thee burnt sacrifices of

PSALM 65.
ᶜ Mat. 8. 26.
3 Or, to sing.
4 Or, after thou hadst made it to desire rain.
5 Or, thou causest rain to descend into the furrows thereof.
6 thou dissolvest it.
7 the year of thy goodness.
ƒ Ps. 104. 3.
8 are girded with joy.

PSALM 66.
1 all the earth.
ᵃ Ps. 18. 44.
2 lie, or, yield feigned obedience.
ᵇ Ps. 67. 3.
ᶜ Ps. 46. 8.
ᵈ Ex. 14. 21.
ᵉ Josh. 3. 14.
ƒ Ps. 11. 4.
3 putteth.
Dan. 5. 23.
Acts 17.28.
ᵍ Zech. 13. 9.
1 Pet. 1. 6.
4 moist.
ʰ Eccl. 5. 4.
5 opened.
6 marrow.
ⁱ Job 27. 9.
Pro. 15. 29.
Pro. 28. 9.
Is. 1. 15.
John 9. 31.
Jam. 4. 3.

PSALM 67.
ᵃ Nu. 6. 25.
1 with us.
ᵇ Acts 13. 25.
ᶜ Luke 2. 30.
Tit. 2. 11.
ᵈ Ps. 96. 10.
ᵉ Ps. 96. 10.
Ps. 98. 9.
2 lead.
ƒ Lev. 26. 4.
Ps. 85. 12.
Ezek. 34. 27.
ᵍ Ps. 22. 27.

PSALM 68.
1 from his face.
2 rejoice with gladness.
3 Or, through the deserts; in JAH is his name.
Ex. 6. 3.
ᵃ 1 Sa. 2. 5.
4 in a house.
ᵇ Judg. 4. 14.
Hab. 3. 13.
5 shake out.
6 confirm it.
ᶜ Deu. 26. 5.
Ps. 74. 19.

fatlings, with the incense of rams: I will offer bullocks with goats. Selah.

16 Come and hear, all ye that fear God, and I will declare what he hath done for my soul.

17 I cried unto him with my mouth, and he was extolled with my tongue.

18 If ⁱ I regard iniquity in my heart, the LORD will not hear *me:*

19 *But* verily God hath heard *me;* he hath attended to the voice of my prayer.

20 Blessed *be* God, which hath not turned away my prayer, nor his mercy from me.

PSALM LXVII.

1 *A prayer for the enlargement of God's kingdom, 3 to the joy of the people, 6 and to the increase of God's blessings.*

To the chief Musician on Neginoth, A Psalm *or* Song.

GOD be merciful unto us, and bless us; and ᵃ cause his face to shine ¹ upon us. Selah.

2 That ᵇ thy way may be known upon earth, ᶜ thy saving health among all nations.

3 Let ᵈ the people praise thee, O God; let all the people praise thee.

4 O let the nations be glad, and sing for joy: for ᵉ thou shalt judge the people righteously, and ² govern the nations upon earth. Selah.

5 Let the people praise thee, O God; let all the people praise thee.

6 *Then* ƒ shall the earth yield her increase; and God, *even* our own God, shall bless us.

7 God shall bless us; and ᵍ all the ends of the earth shall fear him.

PSALM LXVIII.

1 *A prayer at the removing of the ark. 4 An exhortation to praise God for his mercies, 7 and for his care of the church.*

To the chief Musician, A Psalm *or* Song of David.

LET God arise, let his enemies be scattered: let them also that hate him flee ¹ before him.

2 As smoke is driven away, *so* drive them away: as wax melteth before the fire, *so* let the wicked perish at the presence of God.

3 But let the righteous be glad: let them rejoice before God; yea, let them ² exceedingly rejoice.

4 Sing unto God, sing praises to his name : extol him that rideth ³ upon the heavens by his name JAH, and rejoice before him.

5 A father of the fatherless, and a judge of the widows, *is* God in his holy habitation.

6 God ᵃ setteth the solitary ⁴ in families: he bringeth out those which are bound with chains: but the rebellious dwell in a dry land.

7 O God, ᵇ when thou wentest forth before thy people, when thou didst march through the wilderness; Selah:

8 The earth shook, the heavens also dropped at the presence of God: *even* Sinai itself *was moved* at the presence of God, the God of Israel.

9 Thou, O God, didst ⁵ send a plentiful rain, whereby thou didst ⁶ confirm thine inheritance, when it was weary.

10 Thy congregation hath dwelt therein: thou, ᶜ O God, hast prepared of thy goodness for the poor.

trials, God had brought them to safety (cf. Isa. 48. 10; 1 Pet. 1. 7.). affliction—*lit., pressure*, or, as Ps. 55. 3, oppression, which, *laid on the*—loins—the seat of strength (Deut. 33. 11,), enfeebles the frame. men to ride over our heads—*made us to pass*—through fire, &c.— figures describing prostration and critical dangers (cf. Isa. 43. 2; Ez. 36. 12.). wealthy— *lit., overflowing,* or, irrigated, and hence fertile. 13-15. These full and varied offerings constitute the payment of vows (Lev. 22. 18-23.). I will offer—*lit., make to ascend*—alluding to the smoke of burnt-offering, which explains the use of — incense — elsewhere always denoting the fumes of aromatics. 16-20. With these he unites his public thanks, inviting those who fear God (Ps. 60. 4; 61. 5., his true worshippers,), to hear. He vindicates his sincerity, inasmuch as God would not hear hypocrites, but had heard him. he was extolled with my tongue—*lit., exaltation (was) under my tongue,* as a place of deposit, whence it proceeded—*i.e.,* honouring God was habitual. If I regard iniquity— *lit., see iniquity with pleasure.*

PSALM LXVII.

Ver. 1-7. A prayer that, by God's blessing on His people, His salvation and praise may be extended over the earth.

1. cause his face to shine—show us favour (Num. 6. 24, 25; Ps. 31. 16.). 2. thy way—of gracious dealing (Isa. 55. 8,), as explained by — saving health — or *lit., salvation.* 3-5. *Thanks* will be rendered for the blessings of His wise and holy government (cf. Isa. 2. 3, 4; 11. 4.). 6, 7. The blessings of a fruitful harvest are mentioned as types of greater and spiritual blessings, under which all nations shall fear and love God.

PSALM LXVIII.

Ver. 1-35. This is a *Psalm-song* (cf. Ps. 30. title,), perhaps suggested by David's victories, which secured his throne and gave rest to the nation. In general terms, the judgment of God on the wicked, and the equity and goodness of His government to the pious, are celebrated. The sentiment is illustrated by examples of God's dealings, cited from the Jewish history, and related in highly poetical terms. Hence the writer intimates an expectation of equal and even greater triumphs, and summons all nations to unite in praises of the God of Israel. The Psalm is evidently typical of the relation which God, in the person of His Son, sustains to the Church (cf. *v.* 18,).

1-3. Cf. Num. 10. 35; Ps. 1. 4; 22. 14., on the figures here used. before him—as in *v.* 2., *from* His presence, as dreaded; but in *v.* 3., *in* His presence, as under His protection (Ps. 61. 7.). the righteous—all truly pious, whether of Israel or not. 4. extol him . . . heavens—*lit., "cast up for him who rideth in the deserts,* or wilderness" (cf. *v.* 7,), alluding to the poetical representation of His leading His people in the wilderness as a conqueror, before whom a way is to be prepared, or *cast up* cf. Isa. 40. 3; 62. 10.). by his name JAH —or, Jehovah, of which it is a contraction (Ex. 15. 3; Isa. 12. 2,), (*Heb.*). name—or, perfections (Ps. 9. 10; 20. 1,), which 5, 6., are illustrated by the protection to the helpless, vindicat on of the innocent, and punishment of rebels, ascribed to Him. setteth the solitary in families—*lit., settleth the lonely* [or *lit., among*] men—is by Paul "gave gifts wanderers *at home.* Though a general truth, there is perhaps allusion to the wandering and settlement of the Israelites. rebellious dwell in a dry land—removed from all the comforts of home. 7, 8. Cf. Ex. 19. 16-18.). thou wentest—in the pillar of fire. thou didst march—*lit., in thy tread,* thy majestic movement. even Sinai itself—*lit., that Sinai,* as Jud. 5. 5. 9, 10. a plentiful rain—a rain of gifts, as manna and quails. Thy congregation —*lit., troop,* as 2 Sam. 23. 11, 13,—the military aspect of the people being prominent, according to the figures of the context. therein— *i.e.,* in the land of promise. the poor—thy humble people, (*v.* 9. cf. Ps. 10. 17; 12. 5.). 11. gave the word—*i.e.,* of triumph. company— or, choir of females, celebrating victory (Ex. 15. 20,). 12. Kings of armies—*i.e.,* with their armies. she that . . . at home—mostly females so remained, and the ease of victory appears in that such, without danger, quietly enjoyed the spoils. 13. Some translate this, "When ye shall lie between the borders, ye shall," &c., comparing the peaceful rest in the borders or limits of the promised land to the proverbial beauty of a gentle dove. Others understand by the word rendered "pots," the smoked sides of caves, in which the Israelites took refuge from enemies in the times of the judges: or, taking the whole figuratively, the rows of stones on which cooking vessels were hung; and thus that a contrast is drawn between their former low and afflicted state and their succeeding prosperity. In either case, a state of quiet and peace is described by a beautiful figure. 14. Their enemies dispersed, the contrast of their prosperity with their former distress is represented by that of the snow with the dark and sombre shades of Salmon. 15, 16. Mountains are often emblems of nations (Ps. 46. 2; 65. 6.). That of Bashan, N.E of Palestine, denotes a heathen nation, which is described as a *hill of God,* or a great hill. Such are represented as envious of the hill (Zion) on which God resides; 17. and, to the assertion of God's purpose to make it his dwelling, is added evidence of His protecting care. He is described as in the midst of His heavenly armies—thousands of angels—*lit., thousands of repetitions,* or, thousands of thousands—*i.e.,* of chariots. The word—angels— was perhaps introduced in our version, from Deut. 33. 2, and Gal. 3. 19. They are, of course, implied as conductors of the chariots. as . . . Sinai, in the holy place—*i.e.,* He has appeared in Zion as once in Sinai. 18. From the scene of conquest He ascends to His throne, leading—captivity [or, many captives (Jud. 5. 12,)] captive. received gifts for men— accepting their homage, even when forced, as that of rebels. that the Lord God might dwell—or *lit., to dwell, oh Lord God* (cf. *v.* 16,) —*i.e.,* to make this hill, His people or church, His dwelling. This Psalm typifies the conquests of the Church under her divine leader, Christ. He, indeed, "who was with the church in the wilderness" (Acts, 7. 38,), is the *Lord,* described in this ideal ascension. Hence Paul (Eph. 4. 8 applies this language to describe His real ascension, when, having conquered sin, death, and hell, the Lord of glory triumphantly entered heaven, attended by throngs of adoring angels, to sit on the throne and wield the sceptre of an eternal dominion. The phrase — rece ved gifts for [or *lit., among*] men—is by Paul "gave gifts to men." Both describe the acts of a conqueror, who receives and distributes spoils.

11 The LORD gave the word; great *was* the [7] company of those that published it.
12 Kings of armies [8] did flee apace; and she that tarried at home divided the spoil.
13 Though [d] ye have lien among the pots, yet [e] *shall* ye be *as* the wings of a dove covered with silver, and her feathers with yellow gold.
14 When the Almighty scattered kings [9] in it, it was *white* as snow in Salmon.
15 The hill of God *is as* the hill of Bashan; an high hill, *as* the hill of Bashan.
16 Why leap ye, ye high hills? *this is* the hill *which* God desireth to dwell in; yea, the LORD will dwell *in it* for ever.
17 The [f] chariots of God *are* twenty thousand, [10] *even* thousands of angels: the Lord *is* among them, *as* in Sinai, in the holy *place*.
18 Thou [g] hast ascended on high, [h] thou hast led captivity captive; [i] thou hast received gifts [11] for men; yea, *for* [j] the rebellious also, [k] that the LORD God might dwell *among them*.
19 Blessed *be* the Lord, *who* daily loadeth us *with benefits*, *even* the God of our salvation. Selah.
20 *He that is* our God *is* the God of salvation; and [l] unto GOD the Lord *belong* the issues from death.
21 But God shall wound the head of his enemies, *and* the hairy scalp of such an one as goeth on still in his trespasses.
22 The Lord said, I will bring again from Bashan; I will bring *my people* again from the depths of the sea:
23 That thy foot may be [12] dipped in the blood of *thine* enemies, *and* the tongue of thy dogs in the same.
24 They have seen thy goings, O God; *even* the goings of my God, my King, in the sanctuary.
25 The singers went before, the players on instruments *followed* after; among *them were* the damsels playing with timbrels.
26 Bless ye God in the congregations, *even* the LORD, [13] from the fountain of Israel.
27 There *is* little Benjamin *with* their ruler, the princes of Judah [14] *and* their council, the princes of Zebulun, *and* the princes of Naphtali.
28 Thy God hath commanded thy strength: strengthen, O God, that which thou hast wrought for us.
29 Because of thy temple at Jerusalem shall [m] kings bring presents unto thee.
30 Rebuke [15] the company of spearmen, the multitude of the bulls, with the calves of the people, *till every one* submit himself with pieces of silver: [16] scatter thou the people *that* delight in war.
31 Princes [n] shall come out of Egypt; Ethiopia [o] shall soon stretch out her hands unto God.
32 Sing unto God, ye kingdoms of the earth; O sing praises unto the Lord; Selah:
33 To him that rideth upon the heavens of heavens, *which were* of old; lo, he doth [17] send out his voice, *and that* a mighty voice.
34 Ascribe ye strength unto God: his excellency *is* over Israel, and his strength *is* in the [18] clouds.
35 O God, *thou art* terrible out of thy holy *places*: the God of Israel *is* he *p* that giveth strength and power unto *his* people. Blessed *be* God.

PSALM LXIX.

1 David complains of his affliction; 13 prays for deliverance; 31 praises God with thanksgiving.

To the chief Musician upon Shoshannim, *A Psalm of David.*

SAVE me, O God; for the waters are come in unto my soul.
2 I sink in [1] deep mire, where *there is* no standing; I am come into [2] deep waters, where the floods overflow me.
3 I am weary of my crying; my throat is dried: mine eyes fail while I wait for my God.
4 They that [a] hate me without a cause are more than the hairs of mine head: they that would destroy me, *being* mine enemies wrongfully, are mighty: then I restored *that* which I took not away.
5 O God, thou knowest my foolishness; and my [3] sins are not hid from thee.
6 Let not them that wait on thee, O Lord GOD of hosts, be ashamed for my sake; let not those that seek thee be confounded for my sake, O God of Israel.
7 Because for thy sake I have borne reproach; shame hath covered my face.
8 I [b] am become a stranger unto my brethren, and an alien unto my mother's children.
9 For [c] the zeal of thine house hath eaten me up; [d] and the reproaches of them that reproached thee are fallen upon me.
10 When I wept, *and chastened* my soul with fasting, that was to my reproach.
11 I made sackcloth also my garment; and [e] I became a proverb to them.
12 They that sit in the gate speak against me; and I *was* the song of the [4] drunkards.
13 But as for me, my prayer *is* unto thee, O LORD, [f] *in* an acceptable time: O God, in the multitude of thy mercy hear me, in the truth of thy salvation.
14 Deliver me out of the mire, and let me not sink: let me be delivered from them that hate me, and out of the deep waters.
15 Let not the waterflood overflow me, neither let the deep swallow me up, and let not the pit shut her mouth upon me.
16 Hear me, O LORD; for thy loving-kindness *is* good: turn unto me according to the multitude of thy tender mercies.
17 And hide not thy face from thy servant; for I am in trouble: [b] hear me speedily.
18 Draw nigh unto my soul, *and* redeem it: deliver me, because of mine enemies.
19 Thou hast known [h] my reproach, and my shame, and my dishonour: mine adversaries *are* all before thee.
20 Reproach hath broken my heart, and I am full of heaviness: and I looked *for some* [5] to take pity, but *there was* none; and for comforters, but I found none.
21 They gave me also gall for my meat; and [i] in my thirst they gave me vinegar to drink.
22 Let their table become a snare before them; and *that which should have been for* their welfare, *let it become* a trap.
23 Let [j] their eyes be darkened, that they see not: and make their loins continually to shake.
24 Let thou pour out thine indignation upon them, and let thy wrathful anger take hold of them.
25 Let [7] their habitation be desolate; *and* [8] let none dwell in their tents.
26 For they persecute [k] *him* whom thou

God's Care of the Church.   PSALM LXIX.   Prayer in Distress.

The Psalmist uses "*receiving*" as evincing the success. Paul "*gave*" as the act, of the conqueror, who, having subdued his enemies, proceeds to reward his friends. The special application of the passage by Paul was in proof of Christ's exaltation. What the O. T. represents of His descending and ascending corresponds with His history. He who descended is the same who has ascended. As then, ascension was an element of His triumph, so is it now; and He, who, in His humiliation, must be recognised as our vicarious sacrifice and the High Priest of our profession, must also be adored as Head of His Church and author of all her spiritual benefits. 19-21. God daily and fully supplies us. The issues or escapes from death are under His control, who is the God that saves us, and destroys His and our enemies. would the head—or, violently destroy (Num. 24. 8; Ps. 110. 6.). goeth on still in ..., trespasses—perseveringly impenitent. 22. Former examples of God's deliverance are generalised: as He has done so He will do, from Bashan—the farthest region; and—depths of the sea—the severest afflictions. Out of all, God will bring them. The figures of v. 23 denote the completeness of the conquest, not implying any savage cruelty (cf. 2 Ki. 9. 36; Isa. 63. 1-6; Jer. 15. 3.). 24-27. The triumphal procession, after the deliverance, is depicted. They have seen—impersonally, "There have been seen." the goings of my God—as leading the procession, the ark, the symbol of His presence, being in front. The various bands of music (v. 25) follow, and all who are—from [or *lit., of*] the fountain of Israel—*i. e.*, lineal descendants of Jacob, are invited to unite in the doxology. Then by one of the nearest tribes, one of the most eminent, and two of the most remote, are represented the whole nation of Israel, passing forward (Num. 7.). 28, 29. Thanks for the past, and confident prayer for the future, victories of Zion are mingled in a song of praise. thy temple at [or *lit., over*] Jerusalem—His palace or residence (Ps. 5. 7,) symbolised His protecting presence among His people, and hence is the object of homage on the part of others. 30. The strongest nations are represented by the strongest beasts (cf. *Marg.*). 31. Princes—or *lit.*, *Fat ones*, the most eminent from the most wealthy, and the most distant nation, represent the universal subjection. stretch out [or, *make to run*] her hands—denoting haste. 32-36. To Him who is presented as riding in triumph through His ancient heavens and proclaiming His presence—to Him who, in nature, and still more in the wonders of His spiritual government, out of *His holy place* Ps. 43. 3,), is terrible, who rules His Church, and by His Church, rules the world in righteousness—let all nations and kingdoms give honour and power and dominion evermore!

PSALM LXIX.
Ver. 1-36. *Upon Shoshannim*—(cf. Ps. 45. title.). Mingling the language of prayer and complaint, the sufferer, whose condition is here set forth, pleads for God's help as one suffering in His cause, implores the divine retribution on his malicious enemies, and, viewing his deliverance as sure, promises praise by himself, and others, to whom God will extend like blessings. This Psalm is referred to seven times in the N. T. as prophetical of Christ and the gospel times. Although the character, in which the Psalmist appears to some in v. 5, is that of a sinner, yet his *condition* as a *sufferer* innocent of alleged crimes sustains the *typical* character of the composition, and it may be therefore regarded throughout, as the 2.d, as typically expressive of the feelings of our Saviour in the flesh.

1, 2. (Cf. Ps. 40. 2.). come in unto my soul—*lit., come even to my soul*, endanger my life by drowning (Jon. 2. 5.). 3. Cf. Ps. 6. 6.). mine eyes fail—in watching (Ps. 119. 82.). 4. hate me. &c.—(cf. John, 15. 25,). On the number and power of his enemies cf. Ps. 40. 12. then I restored..., away—*i. e.*, he suffered wrongfully under the imputation of robbery. 5. This may be regarded as an appeal, vindicating his innocence, as if he had said, "If sinful, thou knowest," &c. Though *David's* condition as a *sufferer* may *typify* Christ's, without requiring that a parallel be found in *character*. 6. for my sake—*lit., in me*, in my con usion and shame. 7-12. This plea contemplates his relation to God, as a sufferer in his cause. Reproach, domestic estrangement (Mark, 3. 21; John, 7. 5,), exhaustion in God's service (John, 2. 17,), revilings and taunts of base men were the sufferings. wept, (and chastened) my soul—*lit.*, *wept away my soul*, a strongly figurative description of deep grief. sit in the gate—public place (Pro. 31. 31.). 13-15. With increasing reliance on God, he prays for help, describing his distress in the figures of v. 1, 2. 16-18. These earnest terms are often used, and the address to God, as indifferent or averse, is found in Ps. 3. 7; 22. 24; 27. 9, &c. 19, 20. Calling God to witness his distress, he presents its aggravation produced by the want of sympathising friends cf. Isa. 63. 5; Mark, 14. 50,). 21. Instead of such, his enemies increase his pain by giving him most distasteful food and drink. The Psalmist may have thus described by figure what Christ found in reality cf. John, 19. 29, 30.). 22, 23. With unimportant verbal changes, this language is used by Paul to describe the rejection of the Jews who refused to receive the Saviour (Rom. 11. 9, 10.). The purport of the figures used is, that blessings shall become curses, the *table* of joy (as one of food) a *snare*, their *welfare*, *lit., peaceful condition*, or security, a *trap*. Darkened eyes and failing strength complete the picture of the ruin falling on them under the invoked retribution. continually to shake—*lit., to swerve, or, bend*, in weakness. 24, 25. An utter desolation awaits them. They will not only be driven from their homes, but their homes—or *lit., palaces*, indicative of wealth—shall be desolate (cf. Mat. 23. 38.). 26. Though smitten of God (Isa. 53. 4,), men were not less guilty in persecuting the sufferer (Acts, 2. 23.). talk to the grief—in respect to, about it, implying derision and taunts. wounded—or *lit., mortally wounded*. 27, 28. iniquity—or, punishment Ps. 40. 12.). come ...righteousness—partake of its benefits. book of the living—or, *life*, with the next clause, a figurative mode of representing those saved, as having their names in a register (cf. Ex. 32. 32; Isa. 4. 3.). 29. poor and sorrowful—the afflicted pious, often denoted by such terms (cf. Ps. 10. 17; 12. 5.). set me ... high—out of danger. 30, 31. Spiritual are better than mere material

A prayer for deliverance PSALMS LXX–LXXII. *and support in old age.*

hast smitten; and they talk to the grief of those whom thou hast wounded.
27 Add iniquity unto their iniquity; and let them not come into thy righteousness.
28 Let them be blotted out of the book of the living, and not be written with the righteous.
29 But I am poor and sorrowful: let thy salvation, O God, set me up on high.
30 I will praise the name of God with a song, and will magnify him with thanksgiving.
31 *This* also shall please the LORD better than an ox *or* bullock that hath horns and hoofs.
32 The humble shall see *this, and* be glad: and your heart shall live that seek God.
33 For the LORD heareth the poor, and despiseth not his prisoners.
34 Let the heaven and earth praise him, the seas, and every thing that moveth therein.
35 For God will save Zion, and will build the cities of Judah; that they may dwell there, and have it in possession.
36 The seed also of his servants shall inherit it; and they that love his name shall dwell therein.

PSALM LXX.

David solicits God to the speedy destruction of the wicked, and preservation of the godly.

To the chief Musician, *A Psalm* of David, to bring to remembrance.

MAKE haste, O God, to deliver me; make haste to help me, O LORD.
2 Let them be ashamed and confounded that seek after my soul: let them be turned backward, and put to confusion, that desire my hurt.
3 Let them be turned back for a reward of their shame that say, Aha, aha!
4 Let all those that seek thee rejoice and be glad in thee: and let such as love thy salvation say continually, Let God be magnified.
5 But I am poor and needy; make haste unto me, O God: thou *art* my help and my deliverer; O LORD, make no tarrying.

PSALM LXXI.

1 *David, in confidence of God's favour, prays both for himself and against the enemies of his soul;* 14 *he promises constancy;* 17 *prays for support in old age.*

IN thee, O LORD, do I put my trust: let me never be put to confusion.
2 Deliver me in thy righteousness, and cause me to escape: incline thine ear unto me, and save me.
3 Be thou my strong habitation, whereunto I may continually resort: thou hast given commandment to save me; for thou *art* my rock and my fortress.
4 Deliver me, O my God, out of the hand of the wicked, out of the hand of the unrighteous and cruel man.
5 For thou *art* my hope, O Lord GOD: *thou art* my trust from my youth.
6 By thee have I been holden up from the womb: thou art he that took me out of my mother's bowels: my praise *shall be* continually of thee.
7 I am as a wonder unto many: but thou *art* my strong refuge.
8 Let my mouth be filled *with* thy praise *and with* thy honour all the day.
9 Cast me not off in the time of old age; forsake me not when my strength faileth.

10 For mine enemies speak against me; and they that lay wait for my soul take counsel together,
11 Saying, God hath forsaken him: persecute and take him; for *there is* none to deliver *him*.
12 O God, be not far from me: O my God, make haste for my help.
13 Let them be confounded *and* consumed that are adversaries to my soul; let them be covered *with* reproach and dishonour that seek my hurt.
14 But I will hope continually, and will yet praise thee more and more.
15 My mouth shall show forth thy righteousness *and* thy salvation all the day; for I know not the numbers *thereof*.
16 I will go in the strength of the Lord GOD: I will make mention of thy righteousness, *even* of thine only.
17 O God, thou hast taught me from my youth: and hitherto have I declared thy wondrous works.
18 Now also when I am old and greyheaded, O God, forsake me not, until I have showed thy strength unto *this* generation, *and* thy power to every one *that is* to come.
19 Thy righteousness also, O God, *is* very high, who hast done great things: O God, who *is* like unto thee!
20 *Thou,* which hast showed me great and sore troubles, shalt quicken me again, and shalt bring me up again from the depths of the earth.
21 Thou shalt increase my greatness, and comfort me on every side.
22 I will also praise thee with the psaltery, *even* thy truth, O my God: unto thee will I sing with the harp, O thou Holy One of Israel.
23 My lips shall greatly rejoice when I sing unto thee; and my soul, which thou hast redeemed.
24 My tongue also shall talk of thy righteousness all the day long: for they are confounded, for they are brought unto shame, that seek my hurt.

PSALM LXXII.

1 *David, praying for Solomon, shows the goodness and glory of his kingdom in type, and of Christ's in truth;* 18 *he blesses God.*

A Psalm 1 for Solomon.

GIVE the king thy judgments, O God, and thy righteousness unto the king's son.
2 He shall judge thy people with righteousness, and thy poor with judgment.
3 The mountains shall bring peace to the people, and the little hills, by righteousness.
4 He shall judge the poor of the people, he shall save the children of the needy, and shall break in pieces the oppressor.
5 They shall fear thee as long as the sun and moon endure, throughout all generations.
6 He shall come down like rain upon the mown grass, as showers *that* water the earth.
7 In his days shall the righteous flourish; and abundance of peace so long as the moon endureth.
8 He shall have dominion also from sea to sea, and from the river unto the ends of the earth.
9 They that dwell in the wilderness shall bow before him; and his enemies shall lick the dust.

offerings (Ps. 40. 6; 50. 8); hence a promise of the former, and rather contemptuous terms are used of the latter. 32, 33. Others shall rejoice. *Humble* and *poor*, as *v*. 29. your heart, &c.—address to such (cf. Ps. 22. 26.). prisoners—peculiarly liable to be despised. 34-36. The call on the universe for praise is well sustained by the prediction of the perpetual and extended blessings which shall come upon the covenant people of God. Though, as usual, the imagery is taken from terms used of Palestine, the whole tenor of the context indicates that the spiritual privileges and blessings of the Church are meant.

PSALM LXX.
Ver. 1-5. This corresponds with Ps. 40. 13-17 with a very few variations, as "turn back" (*v*. 3 for "desolate," and "make haste unto me" (*v*. 5) for "thinketh upon me." It forms a suitable appendix to the preceding, and is called "a Psalm to bring to remembrance," as the 38th.

PSALM LXXI.
Ver. 1-24. The Psalmist, probably in old age, appeals to God for help from his enemies, pleading his past favours, and stating his present need, and, in confidence of a hearing, promises his grateful thanks and praise. 1-3. Cf. Ps. 30. 1-3.). rock ... fortress—(Ps. 18. 2.). given commandment—*lit., ordained,* as Ps. 44. 4; 68. 28. 4, 5. cruel man—corrupt and ill-natured—*lit., sour.* trust—place of trust. 6-9. His history from early infancy illustrated God's care, and his wonderful deliverances were at once occasions of praise and ground of confidence for the future. my praise ... of thee—*lit.,* in, or, *by thee* Ps. 22. 25.). 10, 11. The craft and malicious taunts of his enemies now led him to call for aid cf. on the terms used, 2 Sam. 17. 12; Ps. 3. 2; 7. 2.). 12. (Cf. Ps. 22. 19; 40. 4.). 13. (Cf. Ps. 35. 4; 40. 14.). 14-16. The ruin of his enemies, as illustrating God's faithfulness, is his deliverance, and a reason for future confidence. for I know ... thereof—innumerable, as he had not time to count them. in the strength, &c.—or, relying on it. thy righteousness—or, faithful performance of promises to the pious (Ps, 7. 17; 31. 1.). 17-21. Past experience again encourages. taught me, &c.—by providential dealings. is very high—distinguished (Ps. 36. 5; Isa. 55. 9.). depths of the earth—debased, low condition. increase, &c.—*i.e.,* the great things done for me (*v*. 19,), (cf. Ps. 40. 5.). 22-24. To the occasions of praise, he now adds the promise to render it. will ... praise—*lit., will thank.* even thy truth—as to thy truth or faithfulness.

PSALM LXXII.
Ver. 1-10. *For,* or *lit., of Solomon.* The closing verse rather relates to the 2d book of Psalms, of which this is the last, and was perhaps added by some collector, to intimate that the collection, to which, as chief author, David's name was appended, was closed. In this view, there may consistently be the productions of others included, as of Asaph, Sons of Korah, and Solomon; and a few of David's may be placed in the latter series. The fact, that here the usual mode of denoting authorship is used, is strongly conclusive that Solomon was the author, especially as no stronger objection appears than what has been now set aside. The Psalm, in highly wrought figurative style, describes the reign of a king, as "righteous, universal, benefi-

cent, and perpetual." By the older Jewish, and most modern Christian interpreters, it has been referred to Christ, whose reign, present and prospective, alone corresponds with its statements. As the imagery of the 2d Psalm was drawn from the martial character of David's reign, that of this is from the peaceful and prosperous state of Solomon's. 1. Give the king, &c.—a prayer which is equivalent to a prediction. judgments—the acts, and (figuratively) the principles, of a right government (John, 5. 22; 9. 39.). righteousness—qualifications for conducting such a government. king's son—same person as king—a very proper title for Christ, as such in both natures. 2, &c. The effects of such a government by one thus endowed are detailed. thy people ... and thy poor—or, *meek,* the pious subjects of his government. 3. As mountains and *hills* are not usually productive, they are here selected to show the abundance of peace, being represented as—bringing—or *lit., bearing* it as a produce. by righteousness—*i.e.,* by means of his eminently just and good methods of ruling. 4. That peace, including prosperity, as an eminent characteristic of Christ's reign (Isa. 2. 4; 9. 6; 11. 9.), will be illustrated in the security provided for the helpless and needy, and the punishment inflicted on oppressors, whose power to injure or mar the peace of others, will be destroyed cf. Isa. 65. 25; Zech. 9. 10.). children of the needy—for the needy cf. sons of strangers, Ps. 18. 45.). 5, as long as ... endure—*lit., with the sun,* coeval with its existence, and *before,* or, *in presence of the moon,* while it lasts (cf. Gen. 11. 28, *before Terah, lit., in presence of,* while he lived.). 6. A beautiful figure expresses the *grateful* nature of His influence; 7., and, carrying out the figure, the results are described in an abundant production. the righteous—*lit., righteousness.* flourish—*lit., sprout,* or, *spring forth.* 8. The foreign nations mentioned (*v*. 9. 10) could not be included in the limits, if designed to indicate the boundaries of Solomon's kingdom. The terms, though derived from those used Ex. 23. 31; Deut. 11. 24) to denote the possessions of Israel, must have a wider sense. Thus, "ends of the earth" is never used of Palestine, but always of the world cf. *Marg.*). 9-11. The extent of the conquests. They that dwell in the wilderness—the wild untutored tribes of the deserts. bow ... dust—in profound submission. The remotest and wealthiest nations shall acknowledge him cf. Ps. 45. 12.). 12-14. These are not the conquests of arms, but the influences of humane and peaceful principles (cf. Isa. 9. 7; 11. 1-9; Zech. 9. 9, 10.). 15. In his prolonged life, he will continue to receive the honourable gifts of the rich, and the prayers of his people shall be made for him, and their praises given to him. 16. The spiritual blessings, as often in Scripture, are set forth by material, the abundance of which is described by a figure, in which a *handful* (or *lit., a piece,* or small portion of corn in the most unpropitious locality, shall produce a crop, waving in the wind in its luxuriant growth, like the forests of Lebanon. they of the city ... earth—This clause denotes the rapid and abundant increase of population—of [or, *from*] the city—Jerusalem, the centre and seat of the typical kingdom. flourish—or, glitter as new grass —*i.e.,* bloom. This increase corresponds

10 The *kings of Tarshish and of the isles shall bring presents: the kings of Sheba and Seba shall offer gifts.
11 Yea, all kings shall fall down before him; all nations shall serve him.
12 For he shall deliver the needy when he crieth; the poor also, and him that hath no helper.
13 He shall spare the poor and needy, and shall save the souls of the needy.
14 He shall redeem their soul from deceit and violence: and precious shall their blood be in his sight.
15 And he shall live, and to him shall be given of the gold of Sheba: prayer also shall be made for him continually; and daily shall he be praised.
16 There shall be an handful of corn in the earth upon the top of the mountains; the fruit thereof shall shake like Lebanon: and they of the city shall flourish like grass of the earth.
17 His name shall endure for ever: his name shall be continued as long as the sun: and men shall be blessed in him: all nations shall call him blessed.
18 Blessed be the LORD God, the God of Israel, who only doeth wondrous things.
19 And blessed be his glorious name for ever: and let the whole earth be filled with his glory. Amen, and Amen.
20 The prayers of David the son of Jesse are ended.

PSALM LXXIII.

1 *The prophet, prevailing in a temptation,* 2 *shows the occasion thereof;* 13 *the victory over it, knowledge of God's purpose.*

A Psalm of Asaph.

TRULY God is good to Israel, even to such as are of a clean heart.
2 But as for me, my feet were almost gone; my steps had well nigh slipped.
3 For I was envious at the foolish, when I saw the prosperity of the wicked.
4 For there are no bands in their death: but their strength is firm.
5 They are not in trouble as other men; neither are they plagued like other men.
6 Therefore pride compasseth them about as a chain; violence covereth them as a garment.
7 Their eyes stand out with fatness: they have more than heart could wish.
8 They are corrupt, and speak wickedly concerning oppression: they speak loftily.
9 They set their mouth against the heavens; and their tongue walketh through the earth.
10 Therefore his people return hither: and waters of a full cup are wrung out to them.
11 And they say, How doth God know? and is there knowledge in the Most High?
12 Behold, these are the ungodly, who prosper in the world; they increase in riches.
13 Verily I have cleansed my heart in vain, and washed my hands in innocency.
14 For all the day long have I been plagued, and chastened every morning.
15 If I say, I will speak thus; behold, I should offend against the generation of thy children.
16 When I thought to know this, it was too painful for me;
17 Until I went into the sanctuary of God; then understood I their end.
18 Surely thou didst set them in slippery places: thou castedst them down into destruction.
19 How are they brought into desolation, as in a moment! they are utterly consumed with terrors.
20 As a dream when one awaketh; so, O Lord, when thou awakest, thou shalt despise their image.
21 Thus my heart was grieved, and I was pricked in my reins.
22 So foolish was I, and ignorant: I was as a beast before thee.
23 Nevertheless I am continually with thee: thou hast holden me by my right hand.
24 Thou shalt guide me with thy counsel, and afterward receive me to glory.
25 Whom have I in heaven but thee? there is none upon earth that I desire besides thee.
26 My flesh and my heart faileth: but God is the strength of my heart, and my portion for ever.
27 For, lo, they that are far from thee shall perish: thou hast destroyed all them that go a whoring from thee.
28 But it is good for me to draw near to God: I have put my trust in the Lord GOD, that I may declare all thy works.

PSALM LXXIV.

1 *The prophet complains of the desolation of the sanctuary;* 10 *he moves God to help, in consideration of his power, and of his covenant.*

Maschil of Asaph.

O GOD, why hast thou cast us off for ever? why doth thine anger smoke against the sheep of thy pasture?
2 Remember thy congregation, which thou hast purchased of old; the rod of thine inheritance, which thou hast redeemed; this mount Zion, wherein thou hast dwelt.
3 Lift up thy feet unto the perpetual desolations, even all that the enemy hath done wickedly in the sanctuary.
4 Thine enemies roar in the midst of thy congregations; they set up their ensigns for signs.
5 A man was famous according as he had lifted up axes upon the thick trees.
6 But now they break down the carved work thereof at once with axes and hammers.
7 They have cast fire into thy sanctuary; they have defiled by casting down the dwelling place of thy name to the ground.
8 They said in their hearts, Let us destroy them together: they have burnt up all the synagogues of God in the land.
9 We see not our signs: there is no more any prophet: neither is there among us any that knoweth how long.
10 O God, how long shall the adversary reproach? shall the enemy blaspheme thy name for ever?
11 Why withdrawest thou thy hand, even thy right hand? pluck it out of thy bosom.
12 For God is my King of old, working salvation in the midst of the earth.
13 Thou didst divide the sea by thy strength: thou brakest the heads of the dragons in the waters.
14 Thou brakest the heads of leviathan in pieces, and gavest him to be meat to the people inhabiting the wilderness.
15 Thou didst cleave the fountain and the flood: thou driedst up mighty rivers.
16 The day is thine, the night also is thine: thou hast prepared the light and the sun.

with the increased productiveness. So, as the gospel blessings are diffused, there shall arise increasing recipients of them, out of the Church in which Christ resides as head. 17. His name—or, glorious perfections, as long as the sun--(cf. v. 5.). men shall be blessed—(Gen. 12. 3; 18. 18.). 18, 19. These words close the Psalm in terms consistent with the style of the context, while 20. is evidently, from its prosaic style, an addition for the purpose above explained. ended—*lit.*, *finished*, or completed; the word never denotes fulfilment, except in a very late usage, as Ezra, 1. 1; Dan. 12. 7.

PSALM LXXIII.

Ver. 1-28. *Of Asaph*—(cf. *Intr.*). *God is good to His people*. For although the prosperity of the wicked, and the afflictions of the righteous, tempted the Psalmist to misgivings of God's government, yet the sudden and fearful ruin of the ungodly, seen in the light of God's revelation, re-assures his heart, and, chiding himself for his folly, he is led to confide renewedly in God, and celebrates His goodness and love. 1. The abrupt announcement of the theme indicates that it is the conclusion of a perplexing mental conflict, which is then detailed (cf. Jer. 12. 1-4.). Truly—or, Surely it is so. clean heart—Ps. 18. 26 describes the true Israel. 2. The figures express his wavering faith, by terms denoting tottering and weakness (cf. Ps. 22. 5; 62. 3,). 3-9. The prosperous wicked are insolently proud (cf. Ps. 5. 5.. They die, as well as live, free from perplexities: pride adorns them, and violence is their clothing; indeed they are inflated with unexpected success. With all this — they are corrupt—or *lit.*, *they deride*, they speak maliciously and arrogantly, and invade even heaven with blasphemy Rev. 13. 6,), and cover earth with slanders (Job, 21. 7-14.). 10-12. Hence God's people are confounded, turned hither (or back and thither, perplexed with doubts of God's knowledge and care, and filled with sorrow. prosper in the world—*lit.*, *secure for ever*. 13, 14. The Psalmist, partaking of these troubles, is especially disturbed in view of his own case, that with all his diligent efforts for a holy life, he is still sorely tried. 15. Freed from idiomatic phrases, this verse expresses a supposition, as, "Had I thus spoken, I should," &c., intimating that he had kept his troubles to himself. generation of thy children—thy people (1 John, 3. 1.). offend—*lit.*, *deceive*, *mislead*. 16, 17. Still he — thought — *lit.*, *studied*. or, pondered this riddle; but in vain: it remained a toil (cf. *Marg.*), till he—went into the sanctuary—to inquire (cf. Ex. 25. 22; Ps. 5. 7; 27. 4.. 18-20. *Their end*, or, *future* Ps. 37. 37, 38,), which is dismal and terribly sudden (Pro. 1. 27; 29. 1,), aggravated and hastened by terror. As one despises an unsubstantial dream, so God, waking up to judgment (Ps. 7. 6; 44. 23,), despises their vain shadow of happiness (Ps. 39. 6; Isa. 29. 7.. They are thrown into ruins as a building falling to pieces (Ps. 74. 3.. 21, 22. He confesses how—to lisu—*lit.*, *stupid*, and—ignorant—*lit.*, *not discerning*, had been his course of thought. before thee—*lit.*, *with thee*, in conduct respecting thee. 23. Still he was *with God*, as a dependent beneficiary, and so kept from falling (v. 2.. 24. All doubts are silenced in confidence of divine guidance and future glory. receive me to glory—*lit.*,

take for (me) glory cf. Ps. 68. 18; Eph. 4. 8.). 25, 26. God is his only satisfying good, strength—*lit.*, *rock* (Ps. 18. 2.). portion—Ps. 16. 5; Lam. 3. 24.). 27, 28. The lot of apostates described by a figure of frequent use (Jer. 3. 1 3; Ez. 23. 35., is contrasted with his, who finds happiness in nearness to God Jam. 4. 8,), and his delightful work the declaration of His praise.

PSALM LXXIV.

Ver. 1-23. If the historical allusions of v. 6-8, &c. be referred, as is probable, to the period of the captivity, the author was probably a descendant and namesake of Asaph, 35. 15; Ezra, 2. 41.). He complains of God's desertion of his church, and appeals for aid, encouraging himself by recounting some of God's mighty deeds, and urges his prayer on the ground of God's covenant relation to His people, and the wickedness of his and their common enemy. 1. cast...off—with abhorence cf. Ps. 43. 2; 44. 9.). There is no disavowal of guilt implied. The figure of fire to denote God's anger is often used; and here, and Deut. 29. 20, by the word "*smoke*," suggests its continuance. sheep...pasture—cf. Ps. 80. 1; 95. 7.. 2. The terms to denote God's relation to His people increase in force: "congregation" —"purchased"—"redeemed" "Zion." His dwelling. 3. Lift...feet—(Gen. 29. 1)—i.e., Come to behold the desolations Ps. 73. 19.. 4. rear—with bestial fury. congregations—*lit.*, *worshipping assemblies*. ensigns—*lit.*, *signs*, substituted their idolatrous objects, or tokens of authority, for those articles of the temple which denoted God's presence. 5, 6. Though some terms and clauses here are very obscure, the general sense is, that the spoilers destroyed the beauties of the temple with the violence of woodmen. was famous —*lit.*, *was known*. carved work—(1 Ki. 6. 29.). thereof—i.e., of the temple. in the writer's mind, though not expressed till v. 7, in which its utter destruction by fire is mentioned (2 Ki. 25. 9; Isa. 64. 11.). defiled—or, profaned, as Ps. 89. 39. 8. together—*at once*, all alike. synagogues — *lit.*, *assemblies*, for places of assembly, whether such as schools of the prophets (2 Ki. 4. 23,), or *synagogues* in the usual sense, there is much doubt. 9. signs —of God's presence, as altar, ark, (cf. v. 4; 2 Chr. 36. 18, 19; Dan. 5. 2.). no more any prophet—(Isn. 3. 2; Jer. 40. 1; 43. 6.). how long—this is to last. Jeremiah's prophecy (25. 11,), if published, may not have been generally known or understood. To the bulk of the people, during the captivity, the occasional and local prophetical services of Jeremiah, Ezekiel, and Daniel, would not make an exception to the clause, "*there is no more any prophet*." 10. Cf. Ps. 31. 1.. how long... reproach—us as deserted of God. blaspheme thy name—or, perfections, as power, goodness, &c. (Ps. 29. 2.. 11. Why cease to help us? (Cf. Ps. 3. 7; 7. 6; 60. 5.. 12. For—*lit.*, *And*, in an adversative sense. 13-15. Examples of the "*salvation wrought*" are cited. divide the sea—*i.e.*, *Red sea*. brakest...waters—Pharaoh and his host cf. Isa. 51. 9, 10; Ez. 29. 3, 4.). heads of leviathan—the word is a collective, and so used for many. the people...wilderness — *i.e.*, wild beasts, as *conies* (Pro. 30. 25, 26,), are called a people. Others take the passages literally, that the sea monsters thrown out on dry land were food for the

17 Thou hast *set all the borders of the earth: thou hast ᵍmade summer and winter.
18 Remember ʰ this, *that* the enemy hath reproached, O LORD, and that the foolish people have blasphemed thy name.
19 O deliver not the soul of thy turtledove unto the multitude *of the wicked:* forget not the congregation of thy poor for ever.
20 Have ᵐ respect unto the covenant: for the dark places of the earth are full of the habitations of cruelty.
21 O let not the ⁿ oppressed return ashamed: let the poor and needy praise thy name.
22 Arise, O God, plead thine own cause: remember how the foolish man ᵒ reproacheth thee daily.
23 Forget not the voice of thine enemies: the tumult of those that rise up against thee ᵍ increaseth continually.

PSALM LXXV.
1 *The prophet praises God,* 4 *and rebukes the proud by the consideration of God's superintending providence.*
To the chief Musician, 1 Al-taschith, A Psalm or Song 2 of Asaph.

UNTO thee, O God, do we give thanks, *unto thee* do we give thanks: for that thy name is near thy wondrous works declare.
2 When I shall ᵃ receive the congregation I will judge uprightly.
3 The earth and all the inhabitants thereof are dissolved: I ᵈ bear up the pillars of it. Selah.
4 I said unto the fools, Deal not foolishly; and to the wicked, Lift not up the horn:
5 Lift not up your horn on high; speak *not* with a stiff neck.
6 For promotion *cometh* neither from the east, nor from the west, nor from the ⁴ south.
7 But God *is* the judge: ᵇ he putteth down one, and setteth up another.
8 For in the hand of the LORD *there is* a cup, and the wine is red; it is full of mixture; and he poureth out of the same: but the dregs thereof, all the wicked of the earth shall wring *them* out, *and drink them*.
9 But I will declare for ever; I will sing praises to the God of Jacob.
10 All the horns of the wicked also will I cut off; *but* the horns of the righteous shall be exalted.

PSALM LXXVI.
1 *A declaration of God's majesty in the church:* 11 *an exhortation to serve him reverently.*
To the chief Musician on Neginoth, A Psalm or Song 1 of Asaph.

IN Judah *is* God known; his name *is* great in Israel.
2 In Salem also is his tabernacle, and his dwelling place in Zion.
3 There ᵃ brake he the arrows of the bow, the shield, and the sword, and the battle. Selah.
4 Thou *art* more glorious *and* excellent than ᵇ the mountains of prey.
5 The ᶜ stout-hearted are spoiled, ᵈ they have slept their sleep; and none of the men of might have found their hands.
6 At ᵉ thy rebuke, O God of Jacob, both the chariot and horse are cast into a dead sleep.
7 Thou, *even* thou, *art* to be feared: and who ᶠ may stand in thy sight when once thou art angry?
8 Thou didst cause judgment to be heard from heaven; the earth feared, and was still.

9 When God arose to judgment, to save all the meek of the earth. Selah.
10 Surely ᵍ the wrath of man shall praise thee; the remainder of wrath shalt thou restrain.
11 Vow, ʰ and pay unto the LORD your God: ⁱ let all that be round about him bring presents ² unto him that ought to be feared.
12 He shall cut off the spirit of princes: he ʲ *is* terrible to the kings of the earth.

PSALM LXXVII.
1 *The psalmist shows what fierce combat he had with diffidence:* 10 *the victory which he had by consideration of God's great and gracious works.*
To the chief Musician, to Jeduthun, A Psalm 1 of Asaph.

I CRIED unto God with my voice, *even* unto God with my voice; and he gave ear unto me.
2 In ᵃ the day of my trouble I ᵇ sought the LORD: ᶜ my sore ran in the night, and ceased not; my soul refused to be comforted.
3 I remembered God, and was troubled: I complained, and my spirit was overwhelmed. Selah.
4 Thou holdest mine eyes waking: I am so troubled that I cannot speak.
5 I ᵉ have considered the days of old, the years of ancient times.
6 I call to remembrance my song in the night: I commune with mine own heart; and my spirit made diligent search.
7 Will the Lord cast off for ever? and will he be favourable no more?
8 Is ᵈ his mercy clean gone for ever? doth his ᵉ promise fail ³ for evermore?
9 Hath God ᶠ forgotten to be gracious? hath he in anger shut up his tender mercies? Selah.
10 And I said, This *is* ᵍ my infirmity: *but I will remember* the years of the right hand of the Most High.
11 I ʰ will remember the works of the LORD: surely I will remember thy wonders of old.
12 I will meditate also of all thy work, and talk of thy doings.
13 Thy ⁱ way, O God, *is* in the sanctuary: who *is* so great a God as our God?
14 Thou *art* the God that doest wonders: thou hast declared thy strength among the people.
15 Thou hast with *thine* arm redeemed thy people, the sons of Jacob and Joseph. Selah.
16 The ʲ waters saw thee, O God, the waters saw thee; they were afraid: the depths also were troubled.
17 ᵏ The clouds poured out water: the skies sent out a sound: thine arrows also went abroad.
18 The voice of thy thunder *was* in the heaven: the lightnings lightened the world: the earth trembled and shook.
19 Thy ᵏ way *is* in the sea, and thy path in the great waters, ˡ and thy footsteps are not known.
20 Thou ᵐ leddest thy people like a flock by the hand of Moses and Aaron.

PSALM LXXVIII.
1 *An exhortation both to learn and to preach the law of God.* 9 *Story of God's wrath against the incredulous and disobedient.*
1 Maschil of Asaph.

GIVE ᵃ ear, O my people, *to* my law: incline your ears to the words of my mouth.

Government of God.   PSALMS LXXV—LXXVIII.   *Great Works of God.*

wandering Arabs. cleave the fountain—*i.e.*, the rocks of *Horeb* and *Kadesh*—for fountains. driest up—Jordan, and, perhaps, Arnon and Jabbok (Num. 21. 14.). 16, 17. The fixed orders of nature and bounds of earth are of God. 18. (Cf. v. 10; Deut. 32. 8.) The contrast is striking—that such a God should be thus insulted! 19. multitude—*lit.*, beast, their flock, or company of men (Ps. 68. 10.). turtle-dove—*i.e.*, the meek and lonely church. congregation—*lit.*, company, as above—thus the Church is represented as the spoiled and defeated remnant of an army, exposed to violence. 20. And the prevalence of injustice in heathen lands is a reason for invoking God's regard to His promise (cf. Num. 14. 21; Ps. 7. 16; 18. 48.). 21. oppressed—broken Ps. 9. 0.;. return—from seeking God, ashamed—(Ps. 35. 4.). 22, 23. Cf. Ps. 3. 7; 7. 6.. God hears the wicked to their own ruin (Gen. 4. 10; 18. 20.).

PSALM LXXV.

Ver. 1-10. *Al-taschith*—cf. Ps. 57. title.). In impending danger, the Psalmist, anticipating relief in view of God's righteous government, takes courage and renders praise.

1. God's name or perfections are set forth by His wondrous works. 2, 3. These verses express the purpose of God to administer a just government, and in a time of anarchy that He sustains the nation. Some apply the words to the Psalmist receive the congregation—*lit.*, take a set time (Ps. 102. 13; Hos. 2. 3,), or an assembly at a set time—*i.e.*, for judging. *Pillars of earth*—1 Sam. 2. 8.). 4-8. Here the writer speaks in view of God's declaration, warning the wicked. Lift . . . up the horn—to exalt power, here, of the wicked himself—*i.e.*, to be arrogant or self-elated. speak . . . neck—insolently. promotion—*lit.*, a lifting up. God is the only right judge of merit. in the hand . . . a cup . . . red —God's wrath often thus represented (cf. Isa. 51. 17; Jer. 25. 15.), but the dregs—*lit.*, surely the dregs, they shall drain it. 9, 10. Contrasted is the lot of the pious who will praise God, and, acting under His direction, will destroy the power of the wicked, and exalt that of the righteous.

PSALM LXXVI.

Ver. 1-12. On *Neginoth*—cf. Ps. 4. title.). This Psalm commemorates what the preceding anticipates: God's deliverance of His people by a signal interposition of power against their enemies. The occasion was probably the events narrated 2 Ki. 19. 35; Isa. 37. Cf. Ps. 46.).

1, 2. These well-known terms denote God's people and Church and His intimate and glorious relations to them. Salem—(Gen. 14. 18) is Jerusalem. 3. brake . . . the arrows—*lit.*, thunderbolts Ps. 78. 48,), from their rapid flight or ignition cf. Ps. 18. 14; Eph. 6. 16.). the battle—for arms (Hos. 2. 18.). 4. Thou—God. mountains of prey—great victorious nations, as Assyria (Isa. 41. 15; Ez. 38. 11, 12; Zech. 4. 7.). 5. slept their sleep—died (Ps. 13. 3.). none . . . found . . . hands—are powerless. 6. chariot and horse—for those fighting on them cf Ps. 68 17.). 7. may . . . sight—contend with thee Deut. 9. 4; Josh. 7. 12.. 8, 9. God's judgment on the wicked is His people's deliverance Ps. 9. 12; 10. 17. 10. Man's wrath praises God by its futility before His power. restrain—or. gird—*i.e.*, thyself, as with as sword, with which to destroy, or as an ornament to thy praise. 11, 12. invite homage to such a God (2 Chr. 32. 23, , who can stop the breath of kings and princes when he will (Dan. 5. 23).

PSALM LXXVII.

Ver. 1-20. To *Jeduthun*—(cf. Ps. 39. title.). In a time of great affliction, when ready to despair, the Psalmist derives relief from calling to mind God's former and wonderful works of delivering power and grace.

1. expresses the purport of the Psalm, 2. his importunacy. my sore ran . . . night—*lit.*, my hand was spread, or, stretched out cf. Ps. 44. 20.). ceased not—*lit.*, grew not numb or, feeble (Gen. 45. 26; Ps. 38. 8.). my soul . . . comforted—cf. Gen. 37. 35; Jer. 31. 15.). 3-9. His sad state contrasted with former joys. was troubled—*lit.*, violently agitated, or, disquieted Ps. 39. 6; 42. 5.). my spirit was overwhelmed—or, fainted (Ps. 107. 5; Jon. 2. 7.). holdest . . . waking—or, fast, that I cannot sleep. Thus he is led to express his anxious feelings in several earnest questions indicative of impatient sorrow. 10. Omitting the supplied words, we may read, "This is my affliction—the years of," &c.—years being taken as parallel to affliction cf. Ps. 90. 15,), as of God's ordering. 11, 12. He finds relief in contrasting God's former deliverances. Shall we receive good at His hands, and not evil? Both are orderings of unerring mercy and unfailing love. 13. Thy way . . . in the sanctuary—God's ways of grace and providence Ps. 22. 3; 67. 2,), ordered on holy principles, as developed in His worship; or implied in His perfections, if *holiness* be used for *sanctuary*, as some prefer translating cf. Ex. 15. 11,). 14-20. Illustrations of God's power in His special interventions for His people (Ex. 14.), and, in the more common, but sublime, control of nature (Ps. 22. 11-14; Hab. 3. 14 which may have attended those miraculous events Ex. 14. 24.). Jacob and Joseph—representing all. footsteps . . . waters—may refer to His actual leading the people through the sea, though also expressing the mysteries of providence.

PSALM LXXVIII.

Ver. 1-72. This Psalm appears to have been occasioned by the removal of the sanctuary from Shiloh in the tribe of Ephraim to Zion in the tribe of Judah, and the co-incident transfer of pre-eminence in Israel from the former to the latter tribe, as clearly evinced by David's settlement as the head of the Church and nation. Though this was the execution of God's purpose. the writer here shows that it also proceeded from the divine judgment on Ephraim, under whose leadership the people had manifested the same sinful and rebellious character which had distinguished their ancestors in Egypt.

1. my people . . my law—the language of a religious teacher (v. 2; Lam. 3. 14. Rom. 2. 16, 27; cf. Ps. 49. 4.). The history which follows was a "dark saying," or riddle, it left unexplained, and its right apprehension required wisdom and attention 3-6. This history had been handed down (Ex. 12. 14; Deut. 6. 20) for God's honour, and that the principles of His law might be known and observed by posterity. The important sentiment is reiterated in v. 7, 8 negative form. testimony—(! s. 19. 7.). stubborn and rebellious —(Deut. 21. 18... set not their heart—on God's service 2 Chr. 12. 14.). 9-11. The privileges of the first-born which belonged to Joseph (1 Chr. 5. 1, 2) were assigned to Ephraim by

Story of God's dealings   PSALM LXXVIII.   *with Israel in the wilderness.*

2 I ^{b} will open my mouth in a parable: I will utter dark sayings of old:
3 Which ^{c} we have heard and known, and our fathers have told us.
4 We ^{d} will not hide *them* from their children, ^{e} showing to the generation to come the praises of the LORD, and his strength, and his wonderful works that he hath done.
5 For he established a testimony in Jacob, and appointed a law in Israel, which he commanded our fathers, that they should make them known to their children;
6 That ^{f} the generation to come might know *them*, *even* the children *which* should be born, *who* should arise and declare *them* to their children;
7 That they might set their hope in God, and not forget the works of God, but keep his commandments:
8 And might not be as their fathers, a stubborn and rebellious generation; a generation ^{2} *that* set not their heart aright, and whose spirit was not stedfast with God.
9 The children of Ephraim, *being* armed, *and* ^{3} carrying bows, turned back in the day of battle.
10 They kept not the covenant of God, and refused to walk in his law;
11 And ^{g} forgat his works, and his wonders that he had shewed them.
12 Marvellous things did he in the sight of their fathers, in the land of Egypt, ^{h} *in* the field of Zoan.
13 He divided the sea, and caused them to pass through; and he made the waters to stand as an heap.
14 In the day-time also he led them with a cloud, and all the night with a light of fire.
15 He ^{i} clave the rocks in the wilderness, and gave *them* drink as *out of* the great depths.
16 He brought ^{j} streams also out of the rock, and caused waters to run down like rivers.
17 And they sinned yet more against him by ^{k} provoking the Most High in the wilderness.
18 And they tempted God in their heart, by asking meat for their lust.
19 Yea, ^{l} they spake against God; they said, Can God ^{4} furnish a table in the wilderness?
20 Behold, ^{m} he smote the rock, that the waters gushed out, and the streams overflowed; can he give bread also? can he provide flesh for his people?
21 Therefore the LORD heard *this*, and was wroth: so a fire was kindled against Jacob, and anger also came up against Israel;
22 Because they ^{n} believed not in God, and trusted not in his salvation.
23 Though he had commanded the clouds from above, ^{o} and opened the doors of heaven,
24 And ^{p} had rained down manna upon them to eat, and had given them of the corn of heaven.
25 ^{5} Man did eat angels' food: he sent them meat to the full.
26 He caused an east wind ^{6} to blow in the heaven, and by his power he brought in the south wind.
27 He rained flesh also upon them as dust, and ^{7} feathered fowls like as the sand of the sea;

28 And he let *it* fall in the midst of their camp, round about their habitations.
29 So they did eat, and were well filled: for he gave them their own desire;
30 They were not estranged from their lust: but while their meat *was* yet in their mouths,
31 The wrath of God came upon them, and slew the fattest of them, and ^{8} smote down the ^{9} chosen *men* of Israel.
32 For all this they sinned still, and believed not for his wondrous works.
33 Therefore their days did he consume in vanity, and their years in trouble.
34 When ^{q} he slew them, then they sought him; and they returned and enquired early after God:
35 And they remembered that God *was* their Rock, and the high God their Redeemer.
36 Nevertheless they did ^{r} flatter him with their mouth, and they lied unto him with their tongues.
37 For their heart was not right with him, neither were they stedfast in his covenant.
38 But he, *being* ^{s} full of compassion, forgave *their* iniquity, and destroyed *them* not: yea, many a time ^{t} turned he his anger away, and did not stir up all his wrath.
39 For he remembered ^{u} that they *were* but flesh; ^{v} a wind that passeth away, and cometh not again.
40 How oft did they ^{10} provoke him in the wilderness, *and* grieve him in the desert!
41 Yea, they turned back, and tempted God, and limited the Holy One of Israel.
42 They remembered not his hand, nor the day when he delivered them ^{11} from the enemy.
43 How he had ^{12} wrought his signs in Egypt, and his wonders in the field of Zoan:
44 And had turned their rivers into blood; and their floods, that they could not drink.
45 He sent divers sorts of flies among them, which devoured them; and frogs, which destroyed them.
46 He gave also their increase unto the caterpillar, and their labour unto the locust.
47 He ^{13} destroyed their vines with hail, and their sycamore trees with ^{14} frost.
48 ^{15} He gave up their cattle also to the hail, and their flocks to ^{16} hot thunderbolts.
49 He cast upon them the ^{17} fierceness of his anger, wrath, and indignation, and trouble, by sending evil angels *among them*.
50 ^{17} He made a way to his anger; he spared not their soul from death, but gave their ^{18} life over to the pestilence;
51 And smote all the first-born in Egypt; the chief of *their* strength in the tabernacles of ^{x} Ham:
52 But made his own people to go forth like sheep, and guided them in the wilderness like a flock.
53 And he led them on safely, so that they feared not: but the sea ^{19} overwhelmed their enemies.
54 And he brought them to the border of his ^{x} sanctuary, *even to* this mountain, *which* his right hand had purchased.
55 He cast out the heathen also before them, and divided them an inheritance by line, and made the tribes of Israel to dwell in their tents.

Jacob (Gen. 48. 1.). The supremacy of the tribe thus intimated was recognised by its position (in the marching of the nation to Canaan, next to the ark Num. 2. 18-24.), by the selection of the first permanent locality for the ark within its borders at Shiloh, and by the extensive and fertile province given for its possession. Traces of this prominence remained after the schism under Rehoboam, in the use, by later writers, of *Ephraim* for *Israel* (cf. Hos. 5. 3-14; 11. 3-12.). Though a strong, well armed tribe, and, from an early period, emulous and haughty (cf. Josh. 17. 14; Jud. 8. 1-3; 2 Sam. 19. 41.), it appears, in this place, that it had rather led the rest in cowardice than courage; and had incurred God's displeasure, because, diffident of His promise, though often heretofore fulfilled, it had failed as a leader to carry out the terms of the covenant, by driving out the heathen (Ex. 23. 24; Deut. 31. 16; 2 Ki. 17. 15.). 12-14. A record of God's dealings and the sins of the people is now made. The writer gives the history from the exode to the retreat from Kadesh; then contrasts their sins with their reasons for confidence, shown by a detail of God's dealings in Egypt, and presents a summary of the subsequent history to David's time. Zoan—for Egypt, as its ancient capital (Num. 13. 22; Isa. 19. 11.). 15, 16. There were two similar miracles (Ex. 17. 6; Num. 20. 11.). great depths—and—rivers —denote abundance. 17-20. yet more — *lit.*, *added to sin*, instead of being led to repentance (Rom. 2. 4.). in their heart—(Mat. 15. 19.). for their lust—*lit.*, *soul*, or, *desire*. provoking—and—tempted — illustrated by their absurd doubts, 19, 20. in the face of His admitted power. 21. fire—the effect of the *anger* (Num. 11. 1.). 22. (Cf. Heb. 8. 8, 9.). 23-29. (Cf. Ex. 16.; Num. 11.). angels' food—*lit.*, *bread of the mighty* (cf. Ps. 105. 40); so called, as it came from heaven. meat—*lit.*, *victuals*, as for a journey. their—*desire*— what they longed for. 30, 31. not estranged ... lust—or, *desire*—*i.e.*, were indulging it. slew ... fattest—or, *among the fattest*; some of them—chosen—the young and strong (Isa. 40. 31.), and so none could resist. 33-39. Though there were partial reformations after chastisement, and God, in pity, withdrew His hand for a time, yet their general conduct was rebellious, and He was thus provoked to waste and destroy them, by long and fruitless wandering in the desert. lied ... tongues—a feigned obedience (Ps. 18. 44.). heart ... not right—or, *firm* (cf. v. 8; Ps. 51. 10.). a wind ... again—*lit.*, *a breath*, thin air (cf. Ps. 103. 16; Jam. 4. 14.). 40, 41. There were ten temptations (Num. 14. 22.). limited—as v. 19, 20. Though some prefer *grieved* or *provoked*. The retreat from Kadesh Deut. 1. 19-23) is meant, whether—turned—be for turning back, or to denote repetition of offence. 43. wrought—set or held forth. 45. The dog-fly or the mosquito. 46. caterpillar —the *Heb.* name, from its voracity, and that of—locust—from its multitude. 47, 48. The additional effects of the storm here mentioned (cf. Ex. 9. 23-34) are consistent with Moses' account. gave ... cattle—*lit.*, *shut up* (cf. Ps. 31. 8.). 49. evil angels—or, *angels of evil*—many were perhaps employed, and other evils inflicted. 50, 51. made a way—removed obstacles, gave it full scope. chief of their strength—*lit.*, *first-fruits*, or, *first-born* (Gen. 49. 3; Deut. 21. 17.). Ham—one of whose sons

gave name *Mizraim*, *Heb.*) to Egypt. 52-54. made his ... forth—or, brought them by periodical journeys (cf. Ex. 15. 1.). border of his sanctuary—or, *holy border*—*i.e.*, region, of which—this mountain—(Zion) was, as the seat of civil and religious government, the representative, used for the whole land, as afterwards for the Church (Isa. 25. 6, 7.). purchased—or, procured by His right hand or power (Ps. 60. 5.). 55. by ... the—or, the portion thus measured, divided them—*i.e.*, the heathen, put for their possessions, so *tents*—*i.e.*, of the heathen cf. Deut. 6. 11.). 56, 57. a deceitful bow—which turns back, and so fails to project the arrow (2 Sam. 1. 22; Hos. 7. 16.). They relapsed. 58. Idolatry resulted from sparing the heathen cf. *v.* 9-11.). 59, 60. heard—perceived (Gen. 11. 7.). abhorred—but not utterly. tent ... placed—*lit.*, *caused to dwell*, set up (Josh. 18. 1.). 61. his strength—the ark, as symbolical of it (Ps. 96. 6.). 62. gave—or, shut up. his people—(v. 48; 1 Sam. 4. 10-17.). 63. fire—either figure of the slaughter (1 Sam. 4. 10.), or a literal burning by the heathen, given to marriage —*lit.*, *praised*—*i.e.*, as brides. 64. Cf. 1 Sam. 4. 17,); and there were, doubtless, others, made no lamentation—either because stupified by grief, or hindered by the enemy. 65. Cf. Ps. 22. 16; Isa. 42. 13.). 66. And he smote ... part—or, struck His enemies' back. The Philistines never regained their position after their defeats by David. 67, 68. tabern. cle of Joseph—or, home, or, tribe, to which—tribe of Ephraim—is parallel cf. Rev. 7. 8.). Its pre-eminence was, like Saul's, only permitted. Judah had been the choice (Gen. 40. 10.). 69. Exalted as—high palaces—or, mountains, and abiding as — the earth. 70-72. God's sovereignty was illustrated in this choice. The contrast is striking—humility and exaltation—and the correspondence is beautiful following ... ewes, &c.—*lit.*, *ewes giving as the* (cf. Isa. 40. 11.). On the pastoral terms cf. Ps. 79. 13.

PSALM LXXIX.

Ver. 1-13. This Psalm, like the 74th, probably depicts the desolations of the Chaldeans (Jer. 52. 12-24.). It comprises the usual complaint, prayer, and promised thanks for relief.

1. (Cf. Ps. 74. 2-7.). 2, 3. (Cf. Jer. 15. 3; 16. 4.). 4. (Cf. Ps. 44. 13; Jer. 42. 18; Lam. 2. 15.). 5. How long—(Ps. 13. 1.). be angry—(Ps. 74. 1-10.). jealousy burn—(Deut. 29. 20.). 6, 7. (Cf. Jer. 10. 25.). Though we deserve much, do not the heathen deserve more for their violence to us Jer. 51. 3-5; Zech. 1. 14 ? The singular denotes the chief power, and the use of the plural indicates the combined confederates, called upon [or, by] thy name—proclaimed thy attributes and professed allegiance (Isa. 12. 4 ; Acts, 2. 21.). 8. former iniquities—*lit.*, *iniquities of former times*. prevent [lit., meet] us—as Ps. 21. 3. 9. for ... glory of thy name [and for] name's sake—both mean for illustrating thy attributes, faithfulness, power, &c. purge ... sius—*lit.*, *make*, or *provide, atonement for us*. Deliverance from sin and suffering, for their good and God's glory, often distinguish the prayers of O.T. saints cf. Eph. 1. 7.). 10. This ground of pleading often used (Ex. 32. 12; Num. 14. 13-16.). blood ... shed—(v. 3.). 11. prisoner—the whole captive people. power—*lit.*, *arm* Ps. 10. 15. . 12. into their bosom—the lap or folds of the dress is used by Eastern people for receiving articles. The

56 Yet they tempted and provoked the most high God, and kept not his testimonies;
57 But *turned back, and dealt unfaithfully like their fathers: they were turned aside *like a deceitful bow.
58 For they provoked him to anger with their *high places, and moved him to jealousy with their graven images.
59 When God *heard this, he was wroth, and greatly abhorred Israel:
60 So *that he forsook the tabernacle of Shiloh, the tent which he placed among men;
61 And *delivered his *strength into captivity, and his glory into the enemy's hand.
62 He gave his people over also unto the sword; and was wroth with his inheritance.
63 The fire consumed their young men; and their maidens were not [20] given to marriage.
64 Their priests fell by the sword; and their *widows made no lamentation.
65 Then the Lord awaked as one out of sleep, and *like a mighty man that shouteth by reason of wine.
66 And he smote his enemies in the hinder part; he put them to a perpetual reproach.
67 Moreover he refused the tabernacle of Joseph, and chose not the tribe of Ephraim;
68 But chose the tribe of Judah, the mount Zion which he loved.
69 And he *built his sanctuary like high palaces, like the earth which he hath [21] established for ever.
70 He chose David also his servant, and took him from the sheepfolds:
71 [22] From following the ewes great with young he brought him *to feed Jacob his people, and Israel his inheritance.
72 So he fed them according to the *integrity of his heart; and guided them by the skilfulness of his hands.

PSALM LXXIX.

1 The psalmist complains of the desolation of Jerusalem: 8 prays for deliverance, 13 and promises thankfulness.

A Psalm 1 of Asaph.

O GOD, the heathen are come into thine inheritance; thy holy temple have they defiled; *they have laid Jerusalem on heaps.
2 The *dead bodies of thy servants have they given to be meat unto the fowls of the heaven, the flesh of thy saints unto the beasts of the earth.
3 Their blood have they shed like water round about Jerusalem; *and there was none to bury them.
4 We are become a reproach to our neighbours, a scorn and derision to them that are round about us.
5 How long, LORD? wilt thou be angry for ever? shall thy *jealousy burn like fire?
6 Pour out thy wrath upon the heathen that have *not known thee, and upon the kingdoms that have *not called upon thy name:
7 For they have devoured Jacob, and laid waste his dwelling place.
8 O*remember not against us 2 former iniquities: let thy tender mercies speedily prevent us; for we are brought very low.
9 Help us, O God of our salvation, for the glory of thy name; and deliver us, and purge away our sins, *for thy name's sake,

406

PSALM 78.
a Exo. 20.27.
* Hos. 7. 16.
b Deu. 12. 2.
c Heb. 4. 18.
d 1 Sa. 4. 11.
Jer. 7. 12.
Jer. 26. 8.
e Judg. 18. 30.
f 1 Sa. 4. 11.
20 praised.
g Job 27. 15.
Eze. 24.23.
h Is. 42. 13.
i 1 Kin. 6. 1.
21 founded.
22 From after.
Gen. 33.13.
j 2 Sa. 5. 2.
1 Chr. 11.2.
k 1 Ki. 9. 4.

PSALM 79.
1 Or, for.
a 2 Ki. 25. 9. Mic. 3. 12.
b Jer. 7. 53.
c Jer. 14. 16. Rev. 11. 9.
d Zeph. 3. 8.
e Is. 45. 4. 2 Thess. 1. 8.
f Ps. 53. 4.
g Is. 43. 25. Is. 44. 22.
Is. 64. 9.
2 Or, the iniquities of them that were before us.
h Jer. 14. 7.
i vengeance.
j Nu. 14. 17.
4 thine arm.
5 reserve the children of death.
6 to generation and generation.

PSALM 80.
1 Or, for.
a Ex. 25. 20. 1 Sa. 4. 4.
b Deu. 33. 2.
2 come for salvation to us.
c Lam. 5. 21.
3 wilt thou smoke.
d 1 Kin. 18. 37.
Jer. 31. 18.
e Is. 5. 1, 7.
Jer. 2. 21.
Eze. 15. 6.
Eze. 17. 6.
Eze. 19. 10.
4 the cedars of God.
f Ex. 23. 31. Ps. 72. 8.
g Is. 5. 5.
Nah. 2. 2.
h Zech. 1. 12, 16, 17.
i Is. 53. 15.
j Is. 49. 6.
k Ps. 80. 21.
l Ex. 4. 22.
m Nu. 6. 25.

10 Wherefore should the heathen say, Where is their God? let him be known among the heathen in our sight by the [3]revenging of the blood of thy servants which is shed.
11 Let the sighing of the prisoner come before thee; *according to the greatness of *thy power *preserve thou those that are appointed to die;
12 And render unto our neighbours sevenfold into their bosom their reproach, wherewith they have reproached thee, O Lord.
13 So we thy people, and sheep of thy pasture, will give thee thanks for ever: *we will show forth thy praise *to all generations.

PSALM LXXX.

1 The psalmist in his prayer complains of the miseries of the church, 14 He prays for deliverance.

To the chief Musician upon Shoshannim-eduth, A Psalm 1 of Asaph.

GIVE ear, O Shepherd of Israel, thou that leadest Joseph like a flock; *thou that dwellest between the cherubim, *shine forth.
2 Before Ephraim and Benjamin and Manasseh stir up thy strength, and 2 come and save us.
3 Turn *us again, O God, and cause thy face to shine; and we shall be saved.
4 O LORD God of hosts, how long 3 wilt thou be angry against the prayer of thy people?
5 Thou feedest them with the bread of tears; and givest them tears to drink in great measure.
6 Thou makest us a strife unto our neighbours; and our enemies laugh among themselves.
7 Turn *us again, O God of hosts, and cause thy face to shine; and we shall be saved.
8 Thou hast brought *a vine out of Egypt: thou hast cast out the heathen, and planted it.
9 Thou preparedst room before it, and didst cause it to take deep root, and it filled the land.
10 The hills were covered with the shadow of it, and the boughs thereof were like *the goodly cedars.
11 She sent out her boughs unto the sea, and her branches *unto the river.
12 Why hast thou then *broken down her hedges, so that all they which pass by the way do pluck her?
13 The boar out of the wood doth waste it, and the wild beast of the field doth devour it.
14 Return, *we beseech thee, O God of hosts; *look down from heaven, and behold, and visit this vine;
15 And the vineyard which thy right hand hath planted, and the branch that thou madest strong *for thyself.
16 It is burnt with fire; it is cut down: they perish at the rebuke of thy countenance.
17 Let *thy hand be upon the *Man of thy right hand, upon the Son of man whom thou madest strong for thyself.
18 So will not we go back from thee: quicken us, and we will call upon thy name.
19 Turn us again, O LORD God of hosts, cause *thy face to shine; and we shall be saved.

Miserable State of the Church. PSALMS LXXX—LXXXIII. *Israel's Confederated Enemies.*

figure denotes retaliation cf. Isa. 65. 6, 7.). They reproached God as well as his people. 13. sheep... pasture— cf. Ps. 74. 1; 78. 70,).

PSALM LXXX.

Ver. 1-19. *Shoshannim*—Lilies Ps. 45. title.). *Eduth*—Testimony, referring to the topic as a testimony of God to his people cf. Ps. 19. 7.). This Psalm probably relates to the captivity of the ten tribes as the former to that of Judah. Its complaint is aggravated by the contrast of former prosperity, and the prayer for relief occurs as a refrain through the Psalm.

1, 2. Joseph—for Ephraim (1 Chr. 7. 20-29; Ps. 78. 67; Rev. 7. 8,, for Israel. Shepherd—(cf. Gen. 49. 24.). leadest, &c.—(Ps. 77. 20. . dwelling... cherubim— Ex. 25. 20.). The place of God's visible glory, whence He communed with the people Heb. 9. 5. shine forth—appear Ps. 50. 2; 94. 1.). Before Ephraim, &c.—These tribes marched next the ark Num. 2. 18-24.). The name of benjamin may be introduced merely in allusion to that fact, and not because that tribe was identified with Israel in the Schism (1 Ki. 12. 16-21; cf. also Num. 10. 24.). 3. turn us—*i.e.*, from captivity. thy f ce to shine—(Num. 6. 25.). 4. be angry— cf. *Marg.*). 5. bread of tears—still an Eastern figure for affliction. 6. strife—object or cause of Isa. 9. 11.. On last clause cf. Ps. 79. 4; Ez. 36. 4. 8-11. brought—or, plucked up. as by roots, to be replanted. a vine— Ps. 78. 47.. The figure Isa. 16. 8 represents the flourishing state of Israel, as predicted Gen. 28. 14, and verified 1 Ki. 4. 20-25. 12. hedges —(Isa. 5. 5.). 13. The boar—may represent the ravaging Assyrian, and the *wild beast* other heathen. 14, 15. visit this vine—favourably (Ps. 8. 4.). And the vineyard—or, "*And* protect or guard what thy right hand," &c. the branch—*lit.*, "*over the Son of Man*," preceding this phrase, with "protect," or "watch," for thyself—a tacit allusion to the plea for help; for 16. it—(the vine) or they—(the people, are suffering from thy displeasure. 17. thy hand... upon—*i.e.*, strengthen Ezra, 7. 6; 8. 22.). Man of... hand—may allude to Benjamin (Gen. 35. 18.). The terms in the latter clause correspond with those of v. 15, from "and the branch," &c., literally, and confirm the exposition given above. 18. We need quickening grace Ps. 71. 20; 119. 25) to persevere in thy right worship (Gen. 4. 26; Rom. 10. 11.). 19. Cf. v. 3, O God; v. 7, O God of hosts.

PSALM LXXXI.

Ver. 1-16. *Gittith* — cf. Ps. 8. title.). A festal Psalm, probably for the passover (cf. Mat. 26. 30,), in which, after an exhortation to praise God, He is introduced, reminding Israel of their obligations, chiding their neglect, and depicting the happy results of obedience.

1. cur strength—(Ps. 38. 7.). 2. unites the most joyful kinds of music, vocal and instrumental. 3. the new moon—or, the month. the time appointed—(cf. Pro. 7. 20.). 5. a testimony — the feasts, especially the passover, attested God's relation to His people. Joseph —for *Israel* Ps. 80. 1.). went out through—or, over, *i.e.*, Israel in the exode. I heard—change of person. The writer speaks for the nation. language—*lit.* lip (Ps. 14. 1.). An aggravation or element of their distress that their oppressors were foreigners (Deut. 28. 49.). 6. God's language alludes to the burdensome slavery of the Israelites. 7. secret

place—the cloud from which He troubled the Egyptians (Ex. 14. 24. proved thee—(Ps. 7. 10; 17. 3., tested their faith by the miracle. 8. (Cf. Ps. 50. 7... The reproof follows to v. 12. if thou wilt hearken—He then propounds the terms of His covenant: they should worship Him alone, who (v. 10) had delivered them, and would still confer all needed blessings. 11, 12. They failed, and He gave them up to their own desires and hardness of heart (Deut. 29. 18; Pro. 1. 30; Rom. 1L 25.). 13-16. Obedience would have secured all promised blessings and the subjection of foes. In this passage, "should have," "would have," &c., are better "should" and "would," expressing God's intention at the time, *i.e.*, when they left Egypt.

PSALM LXXXII.

Ver. 1-8. Before the Great Judge, the judges of the earth are rebuked, exhorted, and threatened.

1. congregation—(cf. Ex. 12. 3; 16. 1.. of the mighty—*i.e.*, of God, of His appointment. gods—or, judges (Ex. 21. 6; 22. 9,), God's representatives. 2. accept the persons—*lit.*, *take*, or, *lift up the faces*, *i.e.*, from dejection, or admit to favour and communion, regardless of merit (Lev. 19. 15; Pro. 18. 5.). 3, 4. So must good judges act (Ps. 10. 14; 29. 12.). poor and needy— cf. Ps. 34. 10; 41. 1.). 5. By the wilful ignorance and negligence of judges, anarchy ensues (Ps. 11. 3; 75. 3.). out of course—(cf. *Marg.*; Ps. 9. 6; 62. 2... 6. 7. Though God admitted them to their official dignity John, 10, 34,), He reminds them of their mortality, fall like, &c.—be cut off suddenly Ps. 20. 8; 91. 7.). 8. As rightful sovereign of earth, God is invoked personally, to correct the evils of His representatives.

PSALM LXXXIII.

Ver. 1-18. *Of Asaph*—(cf. Ps. 74. title.). The historical occasion is probably that of 2 Chr. 20. 1-2 (cf. Ps. 47. and 48.). After a general petition, the craft and rage of the combined enemies are described, God's former dealings recited, and a like summary and speedy destruction on them is invoked.

1. God addressed as indifferent (cf. Ps. 22; 39. 12.). be not still—*lit.*, *not quiet*, as opposed to action. 2. thine enemies—as well as ours Ps. 74. 23; Isa. 37. 23... 3. hidden ones—whom God specially protects (Ps. 27. 5; 91. 1.). 4. from being a nation—utter destruction (Isa. 7. 8; 23. 1.. Israel—here used for Judah, having been the common name. 5. they have consulted—*with heart*, or cordially, together—all alike. 6-8. tabernacles—for people Ps. 78. 67.). Lot, or Ammonites and Moabites (cf. 2 Chr. 20. 1.). 9-11. compare the similar fate of these (2 Chr. 20. 23) with that of the foes mentioned in Jud. 7. 22, here referred to. They destroyed one another (Jud. 4. 6-24; 7. 25.). Human remains form manure (cf. 2 Ki. 9. 37; Jer. 9. 22.). 12. The language of the invaders. houses —*lit.*, *residences*, inclosures, as for flocks (Ps. 65. 12.), of God—as the proprietors of the land (2 Chr. 20. 11; Isa. 14. 25.). 13. like a wheel—or, whirling of any light thing (Isa. 17. 13,), as stubble or chaff (Ps. 1. 4.). 14, 15. pursue them, to an utter destruction. 16. that they may seek—or, as v. 18, supply "men," since v. 17, 18 amplify the sentiment of v. 16, expressing more fully the measure of destruction, and the lesson of God's being and perfections (cf. 2 Chr. 20. 29) taught to all men.

Exhortation to praise God. PSALMS LXXXI–LXXXIV. *Israel's confederated enemies.*

PSALM LXXXI.

1 *An exhortation to a solemn praising of God.* 4 *God challenges that duty by reason of his benefits.*

To the chief Musician upon Gittith, A Psalm of Asaph.

SING aloud unto God our strength: make a joyful noise unto the God of Jacob.
2 Take a psalm, and bring hither the timbrel, the pleasant harp with the psaltery.
3 Blow up the trumpet in the new moon, in the time appointed, on our solemn feast day.
4 For ^{a} this *was* a statute for Israel, *and* a law of the God of Jacob.
5 This he ordained in Joseph *for* a testimony, when he went out ^{2} through the land of Egypt: *where* I heard a language *that* I understood not.
6 I removed his shoulder from the burden: his hands ^{3} were delivered from the ^{4} pots.
7 Thou calledst in trouble, and I delivered thee; I answered thee in the secret place of thunder: I proved thee at the waters of ^{5} Meribah. Selah.
8 Hear, O my people, and I will testify unto thee: O Israel, if thou wilt hearken unto me;
9 There shall no strange god be in thee; neither shalt thou worship any strange god.
10 I am the LORD thy God, which brought thee out of the land of Egypt: ^{b} open thy mouth wide, and I will fill it.
11 But my people would not hearken to my voice; and Israel would none of me.
12 So ^{c} I gave them up ^{6} unto their own hearts' lust: *and* they walked in their own counsels.
13 Oh ^{d} that my people had hearkened unto me, *and* Israel had walked in my ways!
14 I should soon have subdued their enemies, and turned my hand against their adversaries.
15 The haters of the LORD should have ^{7} submitted themselves unto him: but their time should have endured for ever.
16 He should have fed them also ^{8} with the finest of the wheat: and with honey out of the rock should I have satisfied thee.

PSALM LXXXII.

1 *The psalmist, having exhorted the judges,* 5 *and reproved their negligence,* 8 *prays God to judge.*

A Psalm of Asaph.

GOD ^{a} standeth in the congregation of the mighty; he judgeth among ^{b} the gods.
2 How long will ye judge unjustly, and accept ^{c} the persons of the wicked? Selah.
3 ^{2} Defend the poor and fatherless: do justice to the afflicted and needy.
4 Deliver the poor and needy: rid *them* out of the hand of the wicked.
5 They know not, neither will they understand; they walk on in darkness: ^{d} all the foundations of the earth are ^{3} out of course.
6 I ^{e} have said, Ye *are* gods; and all of you *are* children of the Most High:
7 But *f* ye shall die like men, and fall like one of the princes.
8 Arise, O God, judge the earth: ^{g} for thou shalt inherit all nations.

PSALM LXXXIII.

1 *A complaint to God of a powerful confederacy of the enemies of Israel.* 9 *A prayer against those who oppress the church.*

A Song or Psalm of Asaph.

KEEP not thou silence, O God: hold not thy peace, and be not still, O God.
2 For, lo, ^{a} thine enemies make a tumult; and they that hate thee have lifted up the head.
3 They have taken crafty counsel against thy people, and consulted ^{b} against thy hidden ones.
4 They have said, Come, and ^{c} let us cut them off from *being* a nation; that the name of Israel may be no more in remembrance.
5 For they have consulted together with one ^{2} consent: they are confederate against thee:
6 The tabernacles of Edom, and the Ishmaelites; of Moab, and the Hagarenes;
7 Gebal, and Ammon, and Amalek; the Philistines with the inhabitants of Tyre;
8 Assur also is joined with them: ^{3} they have holpen the children of Lot. Selah.
9 Do unto them as *unto* the ^{d} Midianites; as to ^{e} Sisera, as to Jabin, at the brook of Kison;
10 *Which* perished at En-dor: they became *as* dung for the earth.
11 Make their nobles like Oreb and like Zeeb; yea, all their princes as Zebah and as Zalmunna;
12 Who said, Let us take to ourselves the houses of God in possession.
13 O my God, make them like a wheel; as the stubble before the wind.
14 As the fire burneth a wood, and as the flame setteth the mountains on fire;
15 So persecute them with thy tempest, and make them afraid with thy storm.
16 Fill their faces with shame; that they may seek thy name, O LORD.
17 Let them be confounded and troubled for ever; yea, let them be put to shame, and perish:
18 That men may know that thou, whose name alone *is* JEHOVAH, *art* the Most High over all the earth.

PSALM LXXXIV.

1 *The prophet, longing for the communion of the sanctuary,* 4 *shows how blessed they are that dwell therein:* 8 *he prays to be restored unto it.*

To the chief Musician upon Gittith, A Psalm for the sons of Korah.

HOW ^{a} amiable *are* thy tabernacles, O LORD of hosts!
2 My soul longeth, yea, even fainteth for the courts of the LORD: my heart and my flesh crieth out for the living God.
3 ^{2} Yea, the sparrow hath found an house, and the swallow a nest for herself, where she may lay her young, *even* thine altars, O LORD of hosts, my King, and my God.
4 Blessed *are* they that dwell in thy house: they will be still praising thee. Selah.
5 Blessed *is* the man whose strength *is* in thee; in whose heart *are* the ways *of them,*
6 *Who* passing through the valley ^{3} of Baca make it a well; the rain also ^{4} filleth the pools.
7 They go ^{5} from strength to strength; *every one of them* in Zion ^{6} appeareth before God.
8 O LORD God of hosts, hear my prayer: give ear, O God of Jacob. Selah.

PSALM LXXXIV.

Ver. 1-12. Cf. on titles of I's. 8 and 42. The writer describes the desirableness of God's worship, and prays for a restoration to its privileges.

1. amiable—not lovely, but beloved. tabernacles—(Ps. 43. 3.). 2. longeth—most intensely (Gen. 31. 30; Ps. 17. 12.). fainteth—exhausted with desire. courts—as tabernacles (v. 1)—the whole building. crieth out—lit., sings for joy; but here, and Lam. 2. 19, expresses an act of sorrow as the corresponding noun Ps. 17. 1; 61. 2.). heart and ... flesh—as Ps. 63. 1. 3. thine altars—i.e., of burnt-offering and incense, used for the whole tabernacle. Its structure afforded facilities for sparrows and swallows to indulge their known predilections for such places. Some understand the statement as to the birds as a comparison: "as they find homes so do I desire thine altars," &c. 4. This view is favoured by the language here, which, as Ps. 15. 1; 23. 6, recognises the blessing of membership in God's family, by terms denoting a dwelling in His house. 5. (Cf. Ps. 68. 28.). in whose heart ... ways—i.e., who knows and loves the way to God's favour (Pro. 16. 17; Isa. 40. 3, 4.). 6. valley of Baca—or, weeping. Through such, by reason of their dry and barren condition, the worshippers often had to pass to Jerusalem. As they might become wells, or fountains, or pools, supplied by refreshing rain, so the grace of God, by the exercises of His worship, refreshes and revives the hearts of His people, so that for sorrows they have "rivers of delight" (Ps. 36. 8; 46. 4.). 7. The figure of the pilgrim is carried out. As such daily refit their bodily strength till they reach Jerusalem, so the spiritual worshipper is daily supplied with spiritual strength by God's grace, till he appears before God in heaven. appeareth ... God—the terms of the requisition for the attendance on the feasts (cf. Deut. 16. 16.). 9. God is addressed as a shield (cf. v. 11.). thine anointed—David (1 Sam. 16. 12.). 10. I had ... doorkeeper—lit., I choose to sit on the threshold, the meanest place. 11, 12. As a sun, God enlightens (Ps. 27: 1.); as a shield, protects. Grace is God's favour, its fruit—glory the honour He bestows. uprightly—(Ps. 15. 2; 18. 23.). that trusteth—constantly.

PSALM LXXXV.

Ver. 1-13. On the ground of former mercies, the Psalmist prays for renewed blessings, and, confidently expecting them, rejoices.

1. captivity—not necessarily the Babylonian, but any great evil (Ps. 14. 7.). 2, 3. (Cf. Ps. 32. 1-5.). To turn from the fierceness, &c., implies that He was reconcileable, though 4-7. having still occasion for the anger which is deprecated. draw out—or, prolong (Ps. 36.). 8. He is confident God will favour His penitent people Ps. 51. 17; 80. 18.). saints—as Ps. 4. 3, the "godly." 9. They are here termed, "them that fear him," and grace produces glory (Ps. 84. 11.). 10. God's promises of mercy will be verified by His truth (cf. I's. 25. 10; 40. 10; and the "work of righteousness" in His holy government shall be "peace" (Isa. 32. 17.). There is an implied contrast with a dispensation, under which God's truth sustains His threatened wrath, and His righteousness inflicts misery on the wicked. 11. Earth and heaven shall abound with the blessings of this government; 12, 13., and, under this, the deserted land shall be productive, and men be set, or

guided, in God's holy ways. Doubtless, in this description of God's returning favour, the writer had in view that more glorious period, when Christ shall establish His government on God's reconciled justice and abounding mercy.

PSALM LXXXVI.

Ver. 1-17. This is a prayer in which the writer, with deep emotion, mingles petitions and praises, now urgent for help, and now elated with hope, in view of former mercies. The occurrence of many terms and phrases peculiar to David's Psalms clearly intimates its authorship.

1, 2. poor and needy—a suffering child of God as I's. 10. 12, 17; 18. 27. I am holy—or, godly, as Ps. 4. 3; 85. 8. 4. lift up my soul—with strong desire (Ps. 25. 1.). 5-7. unto all ... that call upon thee—or, worship thee Ps. 50. 15; 91. 15) however undeserving (Ex. 34. 6; Lev. 11. 9-13.). 8. neither ... works—lit., nothing like thy works, the gods have none at all. 9, 10. The pious Jews believed that God's common relation to all would be ultimately acknowledged by all men (Ps. 45. 12-16; 47. 9.). 11. Teach—Show, point out. thy way—of providence. walk in thy truth—according to its declarations. unite my heart—fix all my affections Ps. 12. 2; Jam. 4. 8.). so fear thy name — cf. v. 12,), to honour thy perfections. 13, 14. The reason: God had delivered him from death and the power of insolent, violent, and godless persecutors (Ps. 54. 3; Ez. 8. 12.). 15. contrasts God with his enemies cf. v. 5.). 16. son ... handmaid — home-born servant (cf. Luke, 15. 17.). 17. Show me—lit.. Make with me a token, by thy providential care. Thus in and by his prosperity his enemies would be confounded.

PSALM LXXXVII.

Ver. 1-7. This triumphal song was probably occasioned by the same event as the 46th. The writer celebrates the glory of the Church, as the means of spiritual blessing to the nations.

1. His [i.e., God's] foundation—or, what He has founded, i.e., Zion (Isa. 14. 32.). is in the holy mountains—the location of Zion, in the wide sense, for the capital, or Jerusalem, being on several hills. 2. gates—for the enclosures, or city to which they opened Ps. 9. 14; 122. 2; cf. Ps. 132. 13, 14.). 3. spoken of [or, in] thee—i.e., the city of God (Ps. 46. 4; 48. 2.). 4. This is what is spoken by God. to them ... me—lit., for my knowers, they are true worshippers Ps. 36. 10; Isa. 19. 21.). These are mentioned as specimens. This [i.e., nation] ... was born there. Of each it is said, "This was born, or is a native of Zion, spiritually." 5. The writer resumes—This and that man—lit., Man and man, or many (Gen. 14. 10; Ex. 8. 10, 14,), or all (Isa. 44. 5; Gal. 3. 28.). the Highest ... her—God is her protector. 6. The same idea is set forth under the figure of a register made by God (cf. Isa. 4. 3.). 7. As in a great procession of those thus written up, or registered, seeking Zion (Isa. 2. 3; Jer. 50. 5,), the singers and players, or pipers, shall precede. all my springs—so each shall say, "All my sources of spiritual joy are in thee" (Ps. 46. 4; 84. 6.).

PSALM LXXXVIII.

Ver. 1-18. Upon Mahalath—either an instrument, as a lute, to be used as an accompaniment. Leannoth, for singing, or, as others think, an enigmatic title (cf. Ps. 6., 22. and 45. titles) denoting the subject—i.e., "sickness

9 Behold, *O God our shield, and look upon the face of thine anointed.
10 For a day in thy courts is better than a thousand. *I had rather be a doorkeeper in the house of my God, than to dwell in the tents of wickedness.
11 For the LORD God is a sun and shield: the LORD will give grace and glory: no good thing will he withhold from them that walk uprightly.
12 O LORD of hosts, blessed is the man that trusteth in thee.

PSALM LXXXV.

1 *The psalmist, from the experience of former mercies, prays for the continuance thereof: 8 he promises to wait thereon, in confidence of God's goodness.*

To the chief Musician, A Psalm for the sons of Korah.

LORD, thou hast been favourable unto thy land: thou hast brought back the captivity of Jacob.
2 Thou hast forgiven the iniquity of thy people, thou hast covered all their sin. Selah.
3 Thou hast taken away all thy wrath: thou hast turned thyself from the fierceness of thine anger.
4 Turn us, O God of our salvation, and cause thine anger toward us to cease.
5 Wilt thou be angry with us for ever? wilt thou draw out thine anger to all generations?
6 Wilt thou not revive us again, that thy people may rejoice in thee?
7 Show us thy mercy, O LORD, and grant us thy salvation.
8 I will hear what God the LORD will speak: for he will speak peace unto his people, and to his saints: but let them not turn again to folly.
9 Surely his salvation is nigh them that fear him; that glory may dwell in our land.
10 Mercy and truth are met together; righteousness and peace have kissed each other.
11 Truth shall spring out of the earth; and righteousness shall look down from heaven.
12 Yea, the LORD shall give that which is good; and our land shall yield her increase.
13 Righteousness shall go before him, and shall set us in the way of his steps.

PSALM LXXXVI.

1 *David strengthens his prayer by his consciousness of religion: 5 by God's power and goodness: 11 he begs the continuance of his grace.*

A Prayer of David.

BOW down thine ear, O LORD, hear me; for I am poor and needy.
2 Preserve my soul, for I am holy: O thou my God, save thy servant that trusteth in thee.
3 Be merciful unto me, O Lord: for I cry unto thee daily.
4 Rejoice the soul of thy servant: for unto thee, O Lord, do I lift up my soul.
5 For thou, Lord, art good, and ready to forgive; and plenteous in mercy unto all them that call upon thee.
6 Give ear, O LORD, unto my prayer; and attend to the voice of my supplications.
7 In the day of my trouble I will call upon thee: for thou wilt answer me.
8 Among the gods there is none like unto thee, O Lord; neither are there any works like unto thy works.

9 All nations whom thou hast made shall come and worship before thee, O LORD; and shall glorify thy name.
10 For thou art great, and doest wondrous things: thou art God alone.
11 Teach me thy way, O LORD; I will walk in thy truth: unite my heart to fear thy name.
12 I will praise thee, O Lord my God, with all my heart; and I will glorify thy name for evermore.
13 For great is thy mercy toward me; and thou hast delivered my soul from the lowest hell.
14 O God, the proud are risen against me, and the assemblies of violent men have sought after my soul, and have not set thee before them.
15 But thou, O Lord, art a God full of compassion, and gracious, long-suffering, and plenteous in mercy and truth.
16 O turn unto me, and have mercy upon me; give thy strength unto thy servant, and save the son of thine handmaid.
17 Show me a token for good; that they which hate me may see it, and be ashamed: because thou, LORD, hast holpen me, and comforted me.

PSALM LXXXVII.

1 *The seat and glory of the church: 4 the increase and honourable distinction of the members thereof.*

A Psalm or Song for the sons of Korah.

HIS foundation is in the holy mountains.
2 The LORD loveth the gates of Zion more than all the dwellings of Jacob.
3 Glorious things are spoken of thee, O city of God. Selah.
4 I will make mention of Rahab and Babylon to them that know me: behold Philistia, and Tyre, with Ethiopia; this man was born there.
5 And of Zion it shall be said, This and that man was born in her: and the Highest himself shall establish her.
6 The LORD shall count, when he writeth up the people, that this man was born there. Selah.
7 As well the singers as the players on instruments shall be there: all my springs are in thee.

PSALM LXXXVIII.

A prayer containing a grievous complaint.

A Song or Psalm for the sons of Korah, to the chief Musician upon Mahalath Leannoth, Maschil of Heman the Ezrahite.

O LORD God of my salvation, I have cried day and night before thee.
2 Let my prayer come before thee: incline thine ear unto my cry;
3 For my soul is full of troubles, and my life draweth nigh unto the grave.
4 I am counted with them that go down into the pit: I am as a man that hath no strength:
5 Free among the dead, like the slain that lie in the grave, whom thou rememberest no more: and they are cut off from thy hand.
6 Thou hast laid me in the lowest pit, in darkness, in the deeps.
7 Thy wrath lieth hard upon me, and thou hast afflicted me with all thy waves. Selah.
8 Thou hast put away mine acquaintance far from me; thou hast made me an

or disease, for humbling," the idea of spiritual maladies being often represented by disease (cf. Ps. 6. 5, 6; 22. 14, 15, &c.). On the other terms cf. Ps. 42. 32. Heman and Ethan Ps. 89. title) were David's singers (1 Chr. 6. 18, 33; 15. 17,), of the family of Kohath. If the persons alluded to (1 Ki. 4. 31; 1 Chr. 2. 6,), they were probably adopted into the tribe of Judah. Though called a song, which usually implies joy Ps. 83. 1,', both the style and matter of the Psalm are very despondent; yet the appeals to God evince faith, and we may suppose that the word *song* might be extended to such compositions.
1, 2. Cf. on the terms used Ps. 22. 2; 31. 2.
3. grave—*lit.*, *hell* (Ps. 16. 10,', denth in wide sense. 4. go... pit—of destruction Ps. 28. 1,), as a man—*lit.*, *a stout man*, whose strength is utterly gone. 5. Free... dead—Cut off from God's care, as are the slain, who, falling under His wrath, are left, no longer sustained by His hand. 6. Similar figures for distress in Ps. 63. 9; 69. 3. 7. Cf. Ps. 38. 2, on first, and Ps. 42. 7, on last clause. 8. Both cut off from sympathy and made hateful to friends (Ps. 31. 11.). 9. Mine eye mourneth — *lit.*, *decays*, or, *fails*, denoting exhaustion (Ps. 6, 7; 31. 9.). I... called—Ps. 86. 5, 7,). stretched out—for help Ps. 44. 20.). 10. shall the dead [the remains of ghosts] arise—*lit.*, *rise up*, *i.e.*, as dead persons, 11, 12. amplify the foregoing, the whole purport (as Ps. 6. 5) being to contrast death and life as seasons for praising God. 13. prevent—meet—*i.e.*, he will diligently come before God for help (Ps. 18. 41.). 14. On the terms (Ps. 27. 9; 74. 1; 77. 7,. 15. from... youth up—all my life. With 16, 17. the extremes of anguish and despair are depicted. 18. into darkness — better omit "*into*" — nine acquaintances [are darkness, the gloom of death, &c. (Job, 17. 13, 14.).

PSALM LXXXIX.

Ver. 1-52. *Of Ethan*—(see Ps. 88. title.). The Psalm was composed during some season of great national distress, perhaps Absalom's rebellion. It contrasts the promised prosperity and perpetuity of David's throne (with reference to the great promise of 2 Sam. 7,), with a time when God appeared to have forgotten His covenant. The picture thus drawn may typify the promises and the adversities of Christ's kingdom, and the terms of confiding appeal to God provide appropriate prayers for the divine aid and promised blessings.
1. mercies—those promised (Isa. 55. 3; Acts, 13. 34,), and—faithfulness—*i.e.*, in fulfilling them. 2. I have said—expressed, as well as felt, my convictions (2 Cor. 4. 13.). 3, 4. The object of this faith expressed in God's words (2 Sam. 7. 11-16.). with [or *lit.*, *to*] my chosen— as the covenant is in the form of a promise. 6, 7. This is worthy of our belief, for His faithfulness is praised; by the congregation of saints or holy ones, *i.e.*, angels (cf. Deut. 33. 2; Dan. 8. 13.). sons of... mighty (cf. Ps. 29. 1,. So is He to be admired on earth. 8-14. To illustrate His power and faithfulness examples are cited from history. His control of the sea (the most mighty and unstable object in nature), and of Egypt (Ps. 87. 4,), the first great foe of Israel (subjected to utter helplessness from pride and insolence), are specimens. At the same time, the whole frame of nature founded and sustained by Him, Tabor and Hermon for east and west, and "north and south," together represent- ing the whole world, declares the same truth as to His attributes. rejoice in thy name— praise thy perfections by their very existence. 15. His government of righteousness is served by *mercy* and *truth* as ministers (Ps. 85. 10-13.). know the joyful sound—understand and appreciate the spiritual blessings symbolised by the feasts to which the people were called by the *trumpet* (Lev. 25. 9, &c.). walk... countenance—live in His favour Ps. 4. 6; 44. 3.). 16, 17. in [or, *by*] thy righteousness—thy faithful just rule. glory [or, *beauty*] of their strength —they shall be adorned as well as protected. our horn—exalt our power (Ps. 75. 10; Luke, 1. 69.). 18. (Cf. *Marg.*). Thus is introduced the promise to "our shield," "our king," David. 19-37. Then—When the covenant was established, of whose execution the exalted views of God now given furnish assurance. thou... to thy Holy One—or godly, saint, object of favour Ps. 4. 3,'. *Nathan* is meant 2 Sam. 7. 17; 1 Chr. 17. 3-15.). laid help—*lit.*, *given help*. David was chosen and then exalted. 20. I have found — having sought and then selected him 1 Sam. 16. 1-16,'), 21. will protect and sustain (Isa. 41. 10,), 22-25. by restraining and conquering his enemies, and performing my gracious purpose of extending his dominion—hand [and] right hand—power (Ps. 17. 7; 60. 5.). sea, and... rivers—limits of his empire (Ps. 72. 8.). 26, 27. first born—one who is chief, most beloved or distinguished in God's sight and purposes he was the first among all monarchs, and specially so in his typical relation to Christ. 28-37. This relation is perpetual with David's descendants, as a whole typical in official position of his last greatest descendant. Hence, though in personal relations any of them might be faithless and so punished, their typical relation shall continue. His oath confirms his promise, and the most enduring objects of earth and heaven illustrate its perpetual force (Ps. 72. 5, 7, 17.). by my holiness—as a holy God. once—one thing (Ps. 27. 4.). that I will not lie—*lit.*, *if I lie*— part of the form of swearing (1 Sam. 24. 6; 2 Sam. 3. 35.). It shall... moon,... heaven— *lit.*, "*As the moon*, and the witness in the sky is sure, *i.e.*, the moon." 38-52. present a striking contrast to these glowing promises, in mournful evidences of a loss of God's favour. 38. cast off—and *rejected* (cf. Ps. 15. 4; 43. 2; 44. 9.). 39. An insult to the *crown*, as of divine origin, was a profanation. 40-45. The ruin is depicted under several figures— a *vineyard* whose broken hedges, and a *stronghold* whose ruins invite spoilers and the invaders; a warrior, whose enemies are aided by God, and whose sword's *edge*—*lit.*, rock or strength Josh. 5. 2) is useless; and a youth prematurely old. days of his youth—or, youthful vigour, *i.e.*, of the royal line, or promised perpetual kingdom, under the figure of a man. 46. How long? &c.—(cf. Ps. 13. 1; 88. 14; Jer. 4. 4.) 47. These expostulations are excited in view of the identity of the prosperity of this kingdom with the welfare of *all mankind* (Gen. 22. 18; Ps. 72. 17; Isa. 9. 7; 11. 1-10;'; for if such is the fate of this chosen royal line, 48. What man—*lit.*, *strong man*— *shall live?* and, indeed, have not all men been made in vain, as to glorifying God? 49-51. The terms of expostulation are used in view of the actual appearance that God had for-

abomination unto them: *I am* shut up, and I cannot come forth.
9 Mine eye mourneth by reason of affliction: LORD, I have called daily upon thee, I have stretched out my hands unto thee.
10 Wilt thou show wonders to the dead? shall the dead arise *and* praise thee? Selah.
11 Shall thy loving-kindness be declared in the grave? or thy faithfulness in destruction?
12 Shall *b* thy wonders be known in the dark? *c* and thy righteousness in the land of forgetfulness?
13 But unto thee have I cried, O LORD; and in the morning shall my prayer prevent thee.
14 LORD, why castest thou off my soul? *why* hidest thou thy face from me?
15 I *am* afflicted and ready to die from my youth up: *while* I *d* suffer thy terrors I am distracted.
16 Thy *e* fierce wrath goeth over me; thy terrors have cut me off.
17 They came round about me *b* daily like water; they compassed me about together.
18 Lover *e* and friend hast thou put far from me, *and* mine acquaintance into darkness.

PSALM LXXXIX.

1 *The psalmist praises God*, 5 *for his wonderful power*, 15 *for his care of the church*, 19 *and favour to David's kingdom.*

1 Maschil of *a* Ethan the Ezrahite.

I WILL sing of the mercies of the LORD for ever: with my mouth will I make known thy faithfulness to all generations.
2 For I have said, Mercy shall be built up for ever: thy faithfulness shalt thou establish in the very heavens.
3 I have made a covenant with my chosen, I have *b* sworn unto David my servant,
4 Thy seed will I establish for ever, and build up thy throne *c* to all generations. Selah.
5 And the heavens shall praise thy wonders, O LORD; thy faithfulness also in the congregation of the saints.
6 For who in the heaven can be compared unto the LORD? who among the sons of the mighty can be likened unto the LORD?
7 God is greatly to be feared in the assembly of the saints, and to be had in reverence of all *them that are* about him.
8 O LORD God of hosts, who *is* a strong LORD like unto thee? or to thy faithfulness round about thee?
9 Thou *d* rulest the raging of the sea: when the waves thereof arise, thou stillest them.
10 Thou *e* hast broken *g* Rahab in pieces, as one that is slain; thou hast scattered thine enemies *c* with thy strong arm.
11 The heavens *are* thine, the earth also *is* thine: *as for* the world and the fulness thereof, thou hast founded them.
12 The north and the south thou hast created them: *f* Tabor and *g* Hermon shall rejoice in thy name.
13 Thou hast *a* a mighty arm: strong is thy hand, and high is thy right hand.
14 Justice and judgment *are* the *e* habitation of thy throne: mercy and truth shall go before thy face.
15 Blessed *is* the people that know the joyful *h* sound: they shall walk, O LORD, in the light of thy countenance.
16 In thy name shall they rejoice all the day; and in thy righteousness shall they be exalted.
17 For thou *art* the glory of their strength; and in thy favour our horn shall be exalted.
18 For *i* the LORD *is* our defence; and the Holy *(* One of Israel *is* our King.
19 Then thou spakest in vision to thy Holy One, and saidst, I have laid help upon one that *is* mighty; I have exalted one chosen out of the people.
20 I have found David my servant; with my holy oil have I anointed him:
21 With whom my hand shall be established; mine arm also shall strengthen him.
22 The enemy shall not exact upon him; nor the son of wickedness afflict him.
23 And I will beat down his foes before his face, and plague them that hate him.
24 But *j* my faithfulness and my mercy *shall be* with him: and in my name shall his horn be exalted.
25 I will set his hand also in the sea, and his right hand in the rivers.
26 He shall cry unto me, Thou *art* *k* my Father, my God, and the Rock of my salvation.
27 Also I will make him *l* my first-born, higher than the kings of the earth.
28 My *m* mercy will I keep for him for evermore, and my covenant shall stand fast with him.
29 His seed also will I make to endure for ever, *n* and his throne *o* as the days of heaven.
30 If *p* his children forsake *q* my law, and walk not in my judgments;
31 If they *s* break my statutes, and keep not my commandments;
32 Then will I visit their transgression with the rod, and their iniquity with stripes.
33 Nevertheless my loving-kindness *9* will I not utterly take from him, nor suffer my faithfulness *10* to fail.
34 My covenant will I not break, nor alter the thing that *is* gone out of my lips.
35 Once have I sworn *r* by my holiness *11* that I will not lie unto David.
36 His *s* seed shall endure for ever, and his throne as the sun before me.
37 It *t* shall be established for ever as the moon, and *as* a faithful witness in heaven. Selah.
38 But thou hast cast off and abhorred, thou hast been wroth with thine anointed.
39 Thou hast made void the covenant of thy servan' ; *u* thou hast profaned his crown by *casting it* to the ground.
40 Thou hast broken down all his hedges; thou hast brought his strong holds to ruin.
41 All that pass by the way spoil him: he is a reproach to his neighbours.
42 Thou hast set up the right hand of his adversaries; thou hast made all his enemies to rejoice.
43 Thou hast also turned the edge of his sword, and hast not made him to stand in the battle.
44 Thou hast made his *12* glory to cease, and cast his throne down to the ground.
45 The days of his youth hast thou shortened: thou hast covered him with shame. Selah.
46 How long, LORD? wilt thou hide thyself for ever? shall thy wrath burn like fire?
47 Remember *v* how short my time is: wherefore hast thou made all men in vain?

Frailty of Man.   PSALMS XC—XCIII.   *Safety of the Righteous.*

saken His people and forgotten His promise, and the plea for aid is urged in view of the reproaches of His and His people's enemies (cf. Isa. 37. 17-35.). bear in my bosom—as feeling the affliction of the people (Ps. 69. 9.). footsteps—ways (Ps. 56. 6.). Blessed, &c.—denotes returning confidence (Ps. 34. 1-3.). Amen, and Amen—closes the third book of Psalms.

PSALM XC.

Ver. 1-17. Contrasting man's frailty with God's eternity, the writer mourns over it as the punishment of sin, and prays for a return of the divine favour. *A Prayer* (mainly such) *of Moses the man of God*—(Deut. 33. 1; Josh. 14. 6,), as such he wrote this (cf. titles of Ps. 18. and Ps. 36.). 1. dwelling place—home (cf. Ez. 11. 16,), as a refuge (Deut. 33. 27.). 2. brought forth [and] formed—both express the idea of production by birth. 3. to destruction—*lit., even to dust* (Gen. 3. 19,), which is partly quoted in the last clause. 4. Even were our days now 1000 years, as Adam's, they would be but a moment in God's sight 2 Pet. 3. 8.). a watch—or, third part of a night, cf. Ex. 14. 24. . 5, 6. Life is like grass, which, though changing under the influence of the night's dew, and flourishing in the morning, is soon cut down and withereth Ps. 103. 15; 1 Pet. 1. 24.). 7, 8. For—A reason, this is the infliction of God's wrath. troubled—*lit., confounded by terror* (Ps. 2. 5.). Death is by sin (Rom. 5. 12.). Though *secret* the light of God's countenance, as a candle, will bring sin to view Pro. 20. 27; 1 Cor. 4. 5.). 9. are passed —*lit., turn,* as to depart (Jer. 6. 4.). spend—*lit., consume.* as a tale—*lit., a thought,* or, *a sigh* Ez. 2. 10.). Moses' life was an exception (Deut. 34. 7.). it is . . . cut off—or, driven, as is said of the quails in using the same word Num. 11. 31.). In view of this certain and speedy end, life is full of sorrow. 11. The whole verse may be read as a question implying the negative, "No one knows what thy anger can do, and what thy wrath is, estimated by a true piety." 12. This he prays we may know or understand, so as properly to number or appreciate the shortness of our days, that we may be wise. 13. (Cf. Ps. 13. 2.). let it repent—a strong figure, as Ex. 32. 12. imploring a change in His dealings. 14. early—promptly. 15. As have been our sorrows, so let our joys be great and long. 16. thy work—or, providential acts. thy glory—(Ps. 8. 5; 45. 3,), the honour accruing from thy work of mercy to us. 17. let the beauty—or, sum of His gracious acts, in their harmony, be illustrated in us, and favour our enterprises.

PSALM XCI.

Ver. 1-16. David is the most probable author; and the pestilence, mentioned 2 Sam. 24. the most probable of any special occasion, to which the Psalm may refer. The changes of person allowable in poetry are here frequently made.

1. *To dwell in the secret place* (Ps. 27. 5; 31. 20,), denotes nearness to God. Such as do so abide or lodge secure from assaults, and can well use the terms of trust in *v*. 2. 3. snare . . . [and] noisome pestilence—*lit., plagues of mischiefs* Ps. 5. 9; 52. 7,), are expressive figures for various evils. 4. For the first figure cf. Deut. 32. 11; Ps. 3. 37. buckler—*lit., surrounding*—*i.e.,* a kind of shield, covering all over. 5. terror—or, what causes it (Pro. 20. 2.). by night—then aggravated. arrow—*i.e.,* of enemies. 7, 8. The security is more valuable, as being special, and, therefore, evidently of God; and while ten thousands of the wicked fall, the righteous are in such safety, that they only see the calamity. 9-12. This exemption from evil is the result of trust in God, who employs angels as ministering spirits Heb. 1. 14.). 13. Even the fiercest, strongest, and most insidious animals may be trampled on with impunity. 14-16. God Himself speaks (cf. Ps. 46. 10; 75. 2, 3.). All the terms to express safety and peace indicate the most undoubting confidence (cf. Ps. 18. 2; 20. 1; 22. 5., set his love —that of the most ardent kind, show him —*lit., make him see* (Ps. 50. 23; Luke, 2. 30.).

PSALM XCII.

Ver. 1-15. *A Psalm-song*—(cf. Ps. 30. title.). The theme is, that God should be praised for His righteous judgments on the wicked and His care and defence of His people. Such a topic, at all times proper, is specially so for the reflections of the Sabbath-day.

1. sing . . . name—celebrate thy perfections. 2. in the morning . . . every night—diligently and constantly Ps. 42. 8.). loving-kindness—*lit., mercy.* faithfulness—in fulfilling promises Ps. 89. 14.). 3. In such a work all proper aid must be used. with a . . . sound—or, *on Higgaion* cf. Ps. 9. 16.), perhaps an instrument of that name, from its sound resembling the muttered sound of meditation, as expressed also by the word. This is joined with the harp. 4. thy work—*i.e.,* of providence (Ps. 90. 16, 17.). 5. great . . . works—correspond to deep or vast *thoughts* (Ps. 40. 5; Rom. 11. 23.). 6. A brutish man knoweth not —*i.e.,* God's works, so the Psalmist describes himself (Ps. 73. 22) when amazed by the prosperity of the wicked, now understood and explained. 8. This he does in part, by contrasting their ruin with God's exaltation and eternity. most high—as occupying the highest place in heaven (Ps. 7. 7; 18. 16.). 9, 10. A farther contrast with the wicked, in the lot of the righteous, safety and triumph. horn . . . exalt —is to increase power (Ps. 75. 5.). anointed . . . fresh [or, new] oil—(Ps. 23. 5) a figure for refreshment cf. Luke, 7. 46.). Such use of oil is still common in the East. 11. see . . . [and] hear my desire—or *lit., look on* my enemies and hear of the wicked (cf. Ps. 27. 11; 54. 7)—*i.e.,* I shall be gratified by their fall. 12-14. The vigorous growth, longevity, utility, fragrance, and beauty of these noble trees, set forth the life, character, and destiny of the pious; 15. and they thus declare God's glory as their strong and righteous ruler.

PSALM XCIII.

Ver. 1-5. This and the six following Psalms were applied by the Jews to the times of the Messiah. The theme is God's supremacy in creation and providence.

1. God is described as a king entering on his reign, and, for robes of royalty, investing Himself with the glorious attributes of His nature. The result of His thus reigning is the durability of the world. 2-4. His underived power exceeds the most sublime exhibitions of the most powerful objects in nature Ps. 89. 9.). 5. While His power inspires dread, His revealed will should secure our confidence (cf. Ps. 19. 7; 25. 10, , and thus fear and love combined, producing all holy emotions, should distinguish the worship we offer in His house, both earthly and heavenly.

Frailty of man.   PSALMS XC–XCII.   *Safety of the righteous.*

48 What man *is he that* liveth, and shall not see death? shall he deliver his soul from the hand of the grave? Selah.
49 Lord, where *are* thy former lovingkindnesses, *which* thou swarest unto David in thy truth?
50 Remember, Lord, the reproach of thy servants; *how* I do bear in my bosom *the reproach* of all the mighty people;
51 Wherewith thine enemies have reproached, O LORD; wherewith they have reproached the footsteps of thine anointed.
52 Blessed *be* the LORD for evermore. Amen, and Amen.

PSALM XC.

1 *Moses, setting forth God's providence,* 3 *complains of human frailty;* 12 *he prays for the knowledge and sensible experience of God's good providence.*

1 A Prayer of Moses the man of God.

LORD, thou hast been our dwelling place in all generations.
2 Before the *a* mountains were brought forth, or ever thou hadst formed the earth and the world, even from everlasting to everlasting, thou *art* God.
3 Thou turnest man to destruction; and sayest, *b* Return, ye children of men.
4 For *c* a thousand years in thy sight *are but* as yesterday ³ when it is past, and *as a* watch in the night.
5 Thou carriest them away as with a flood; they are as a sleep: in the morning *they* ⁴ *are* like grass *which* ⁴ groweth up.
6 In *e* the morning it flourisheth, and groweth up; in the evening it is cut down, and withereth.
7 For we are consumed by thine anger, and by thy wrath are we troubled.
8 Thou *f* hast set our iniquities before thee, our *g* secret *sins* in the light of thy countenance.
9 For all our days are ⁵ passed away in thy wrath; we spend our years ⁶ as a tale *that is told.*
10 ⁷ The days of our years *are* threescore years and ten; and if by reason of strength *they be* fourscore years, yet *is* their strength labour and sorrow; for it is soon cut off, and we fly away.
11 Who knoweth the power of thine anger? even according to thy fear, *so is* thy wrath.
12 So *h* teach *us* to number our days, that we may ⁸ apply *our* hearts unto wisdom.
13 Return, O LORD, how long? and let it repent *i* thee concerning thy servants.
14 O satisfy us early with thy mercy; that we may rejoice and be glad all our days.
15 Make us glad according to the days *wherein* thou hast afflicted us, *and* the years *wherein* we have seen evil.
16 Let *thy* work appear unto thy servants, and thy glory unto their children.
17 And let the beauty of the LORD our God be upon us: and *k* establish thou the work of our hands upon us; yea, the work of our hands establish thou it.

PSALM XCI.

1 *State of the godly;* 3 *their safety,* 9 *habitation,* 11 *servants,* 14 *and friends; with the effects of them all.*

HE that dwelleth in the secret place of the Most High shall ¹ abide under the shadow of the Almighty.
2 I will say of the LORD, *He is* my refuge and my fortress: my God; in him will I trust.

PSALM 90.
1 Or, A Prayer,
being a Psalm of Moses.
Deu. 33. 1.
² *In generation and generation.*
a Pro. 8. 25.
b Gen. 3. 19. Eccl. 12. 7.
² 2 Pet. 3. 8.
³ Or, *when he hath passed them.*
d Is. 40. 6.
⁴ Or, *is changed.*
e Job 14. 2. Ps. 92. 7.
f Ps. 50. 21. Jer. 16. 17.
g Ps. 19. 12.
⁵ *turned away.*
⁶ Or, *as a meditation.*
⁷ *As for the days of our years, in them are seventy years.*
h Ps. 39. 4. Eph. 5. 15–17.
⁸ *cause to come.*
i Deu. 32. 36.
j Hab. 3. 2.
k Is. 26. 12.

PSALM 91.
¹ *lodge.*
a Ps. 61. 4.
b Job 5. 19. Pro. 3. 23. Is. 43. 2.
c Mal. 1. 5.
d Pro. 1. 33. Pro. 12. 21.
e Ps. 34. 7. Ps. 71. 3.
Mat. 4. 6. Lu. 4. 10. Heb. 1. 14.
f Job 5. 23. Ps. 37. 24.
² Or, *asp.*
g Ps. 50. 15. *h* Ps. 43. 2.
i Is. 2. 30.
³ *length of days.*
Pro. 3. 2.

PSALM 92.
¹ *in the nights.*
² Or, *upon the solemn sound with the harp.*
³ *Higgaion.* Ps. 9. 16.
a Is. 25. 10. Ro. 11. 23.
b Ps. 73. 22. Ps. 94. 8.
c Job 21. 7. Jer. 12. 1. Mal. 3. 15.
d Ps. 37. 7.
e Is. 60. 21.

3 Surely he shall deliver thee from the snare of the fowler, *and* from the noisome pestilence.
4 He *a* shall cover thee with his feathers, and under his wings shalt thou trust: his truth *shall* be thy shield and buckler.
5 Thou *b* shalt not be afraid for the terror by night; *nor* for the arrow *that* flieth by day;
6 *Nor* for the pestilence *that* walketh in darkness; *nor* for the destruction *that* wasteth at noon-day.
7 A thousand shall fall at thy side, and ten thousand at thy right hand; *but* it shall not come nigh thee.
8 Only *c* with thine eyes shalt thou behold and see the reward of the wicked.
9 Because thou hast made the LORD *which is* my refuge, *even* the Most High, thy habitation;
10 There *d* shall no evil befall thee, neither shall any plague come nigh thy dwelling.
11 For *e* he shall give his angels charge over thee, to keep thee in all thy ways.
12 They shall bear thee up in *their* hands, lest *f* thou dash thy foot against a stone.
13 Thou shalt tread upon the lion and ² adder; the young lion and the dragon shalt thou trample under feet.
14 Because he hath set his love upon me, therefore will I deliver him: I will set him on high, because he hath known my name.
15 He *g* shall call upon me, and I will answer him: ³ I *will be* with him in trouble; I will deliver him, and ¹ honour him.
16 With ³ long life will I satisfy him, and show him my salvation.

PSALM XCII.

1 *The prophet exhorts to praise God,* 4 *for his works,* 6 *his judgments on the wicked,* 10 *and goodness to the godly.*

A Psalm *or* Song for the sabbath day.

IT *is* a good thing to give thanks unto the LORD, and to sing praises unto thy name, O Most High:
2 To show forth thy loving-kindness in the morning, and thy faithfulness ¹ every night,
3 Upon an instrument of ten strings, and upon the psaltery; ² upon the harp with ³ a solemn sound.
4 For thou, LORD, hast made me glad through thy work: I will triumph in the works of thy hands.
5 O LORD, how great are thy works! *and* thy ⁴ thoughts are very deep.
6 A *b* brutish man knoweth not; neither doth a fool understand this.
7 When *c* the wicked spring as the grass, and when all the workers of iniquity do flourish; *it is* that they shall be destroyed for ever:
8 But thou, LORD, *art most* high for evermore.
9 For, lo, thine enemies, O LORD, for, lo, thine enemies shall perish; all the workers of iniquity shall be scattered.
10 But my horn shalt thou exalt like *the horn of* an unicorn: I shall be anointed with fresh oil.
11 Mine eye also shall see *my desire* on mine enemies, *and* mine ears shall hear *my desire* of the wicked that rise up against me.
12 The *e* righteous shall flourish like the palm tree: he shall grow like a cedar in Lebanon.
13 Those that be *e* planted in the house of

PSALM XCIV.
Ver. 1-23. The writer, appealing to God in view of the oppression of enemies, rebukes them for their wickedness and folly, and encourages himself, in the confidence that God will punish evil-doers, and favour His people.

1, 2. God's revenge is His judicial infliction of righteous punishment. show thyself—(cf. Marg.). Lift up thyself—or, Arise, both figures representing God as heretofore indifferent (cf. Ps. 3. 7; 22. 16, 20.). 3, 4. In an earnest expostulation he expresses his desire that the insolent triumph of the wicked may be ended. 5, 6. people [and] heritage—are synonymous, the people being often called God's heritage. As justice to the weak is a sign of the best government, their oppression is a sign of the worst (Deut. 10. 18; Isa. 10. 2.). 7. Their cruelty is only exceeded by their wicked and absurd presumption (Ps. 10. 11; 59. 7.). 8. ye brutish—(cf. Ps. 73. 22; 92. 6.). 9-11. The evidence of God's providential government is found in His creative power and omniscience, which also assure us that He can punish the wicked in regard to all their vain purposes. 12, 13. On the other hand, He favours, though He chastens, the pious, and will teach and preserve them till the prosperous wicked are overthrown. 14, 15. This results from His abiding love (Deut. 32. 15.), which is farther evinced by His restoring order in His government, whose right administration will be approved by the good. 16. These questions imply that none other than God will help (Ps. 60. 9.), 17-19., a fact fully confirmed by his past experience. dwelt in silence—as in the grave (Ps. 31. 17.). my thoughts—or, anxious cares. 20. throne—power, rulers. iniquity [and] mischief—both denote evils done to others, as 21. explains. 22, 23. Yet he is safe in God's care. defence—(Ps. 59. 9.). rock cf ... refuge—(Ps. 9. 9; 18. 2.). bring ... iniquity—(cf. Ps. 5. 10; 7. 16.). in their ... wickedness—while they are engaged in evil doing.

PSALM XCV.
Ver. 1-11. David (Heb. 4. 7) exhorts men to praise God for His greatness, and warns them, in God's words, against neglecting His service.

1. The terms used to express the highest kind of joy. Rock—A firm basis, giving certainty of salvation (Ps. 62. 7.). 2. come ... presence—lit., approach, or, meet Him (Ps. 17. 13.). 3. above ... gods—esteemed such by men, though really nothing (Jer. 5. 7; 10. 10-15.). 4, 5. The terms used describe the world in its whole extent, subject to God. 6. come—or, enter, with solemn forms, as well as hearts. 7. This relation illustrates our entire dependence (cf. Ps. 23. 3; 74. 1.). The last clause is united by Paul (Heb. 3. 7) to the following (cf. Ps. 81. 8.), 8-11. warning against neglect; and this is sustained by citing the melancholy fate of their rebellious ancestors, whose provoking insolence is described by quoting the language of God's complaint (Num. 14. 11) of their conduct at Meribah and Massah, names given Ex. 17. 7) to commemorate their strife and contention with Him (Ps. 78. 18, 41.). err in their heart —their wanderings in the desert were but types of their innate ignorance and perverseness. that they should not—lit., if they, &c., part of the form of swearing (cf. Num. 14. 30; Ps. 89. 35.).

PSALM XCVI.
Ver. 1-13. The substance of this Psalm, and portions of the 97th, 98th, and 100th, are found in 1 Chr. 16, which was used by David's directions in the dedication of the tabernacle on mount Zion. The dispensation of the Messiah was typified by that event, involving, as it did, a more permanent seat of worship, and the introduction of additional and more spiritual services. Hence the language of these Psalms may be regarded as having a higher import than that pertinent to the occasion on which it was thus publicly used. 1-3. All nations are invited to unite in this most joyful praise. new song—lit., fresh, for new mercies (Ps. 33. 3; 40. 3.). show forth—lit., declare joyful tidings. The salvation illustrates His glory in its wonders of love and mercy. 4, 5. For He is not a local God, but of universal agency, while idols are nothing. 6. Honour and majesty—are His attendants, declared in His mighty works, while power and grace are specially seen in His spiritual relations to His people. 7-9. Give—or, Ascribe (Ps. 29. 1) due honour to Him, by acts of appointed and solemn worship in His house. offering—of thanks. beauty of holiness—(Ps. 29. 2.). fear ... him— (Ps. 2. 11.). 10. Let all know that the government of the world is ordered in justice, and they shall enjoy firm and lasting peace (cf. Ps. 72. 3, 7; Isa. 9. 6, 7.). 11-13. For which reason the universe is invoked to unite in joy, and even inanimate nature (Rom. 8. 14-22) is poetically represented as capable of joining in the anthem of praise.

PSALM XCVII.
Ver. 1-12. The writer celebrates the Lord's dominion over nations and nature, describes its effect on foes and friends, and exhorts and encourages the latter.

1, 2. This dominion is a cause of joy, because, however our minds are oppressed with terror before the throne of the King of kings (Ex. 19. 16; Deut. 5. 22.), we know it is based on righteous principles and judgments which are according to truth. 3-5. The attending illustrations of God's awful justice on enemies (Ps. 83. 14) are seen in the disclosures of His almighty power on the elements of nature (cf. Ps. 46. 2; 77. 17; Hab. 3. 6, &c.). 6. heavens—or, their inhabitants (Ps. 50. 6., as opposed to nations in the latter clause (cf. Isa. 40. 5; 66. 18.). 7. Idolaters are utterly put to shame, for if angels must worship Him, how much more those who worshipped them. all ye gods—lit., all ye angels (Ps. 8. 5; 1. 8. 1; Heb. 1. 6; 2. 7.). Paul quotes, not as a prophecy, but as language used in regard to the Lord Jehovah, who in the O. T. theophania, is the second person of the Godhead. 8, 9. The exaltation of Zion's king is joy to the righteous and sorrow to the wicked, daughters of Judah—(cf. Ps. 48. 11.). above all gods—(Ps. 95. 3.). 10-13. Let gratitude for the blessings of providence and grace incite saints (Ps. 4. 3) to holy living. Spiritual blessings are in store, represented by light (Ps. 27. 1) and gladness. sown—to spring forth abundantly for such, who alone can and well may rejoice in the holy government of their sovereign Lord (cf. Ps. 30. 4; 32. 11.).

PSALM XCVIII.
Ver. 1-9. In view of the wonders of grace and righteousness displayed in God's salvation, the whole creation is invited to unite in praise.

the LORD shall flourish in the courts of our God.
14 They shall still bring forth fruit in old age; they shall be fat and flourishing;
15 To show that the LORD is upright: *he is* my rock, and *there is* no unrighteousness in him.

PSALM XCIII.
Majesty, stability, power, and holiness of Christ's kingdom.

THE LORD reigneth; he is clothed with majesty; the LORD is clothed with strength, *wherewith* he hath girded himself: the world also is established, that it cannot be moved.
2 Thy throne is established of old: thou art from everlasting.
3 The floods have lifted up, O LORD, the floods have lifted up their voice; the floods lift up their waves.
4 The LORD on high *is* mightier than the noise of many waters, *yea*, *than* the mighty waves of the sea.
5 Thy testimonies are very sure: holiness becometh thine house, O LORD, for ever.

PSALM XCIV.
1 The prophet, calling for justice, complains of the tyranny and impiety of the wicked. 16 God is the defender and avenger of the afflicted.

O LORD God, to whom vengeance belongeth; O God, to whom vengeance belongeth, show thyself.
2 Lift up thyself, thou Judge of the earth: render a reward to the proud.
3 LORD, how long shall the wicked, how long shall the wicked triumph?
4 *How long* shall they utter *and* speak hard things? *and* all the workers of iniquity boast themselves?
5 They break in pieces thy people, O LORD, and afflict thine heritage;
6 They slay the widow and the stranger, and murder the fatherless.
7 Yet they say, The LORD shall not see, neither shall the God of Jacob regard *it*.
8 Understand, ye brutish among the people: and ye fools, when will ye be wise?
9 He that planted the ear, shall he not hear? he that formed the eye, shall he not see?
10 He that chastiseth the heathen, shall not he correct? he that teacheth man knowledge, *shall not he know?*
11 The LORD knoweth the thoughts of man, that they *are* vanity.
12 Blessed *is* the man whom thou chastenest, O LORD, and teachest him out of thy law;
13 That thou mayest give him rest from the days of adversity, until the pit be digged for the wicked.
14 For the LORD will not cast off his people, neither will he forsake his inheritance:
15 But judgment shall return unto righteousness; and all the upright in heart shall follow it.
16 Who will rise up for me against the evil-doers? *or* who will stand up for me against the workers of iniquity?
17 Unless the LORD *had been* my help, my soul had almost dwelt in silence.
18 When I said, My foot slippeth; thy mercy, O LORD, held me up.
19 In the multitude of my thoughts within me thy comforts delight my soul.
20 Shall the throne of iniquity have fellowship with thee, which frameth mischief by a law?

21 They gather themselves together against the soul of the righteous, and condemn the innocent blood.
22 But the LORD is my defence; and my God *is* the rock of my refuge.
23 And he shall bring upon them their own iniquity, and shall cut them off in their own wickedness; *yea*, the LORD our God shall cut them off.

PSALM XCV.
1 Exhortation to praise God, 3 for his greatness. 6 and for his goodness: 8 and not to tempt him.

O COME, let us sing unto the LORD: let us make a joyful noise to the Rock of our salvation.
2 Let us come before his presence with thanksgiving, and make a joyful noise unto him with psalms.
3 For the LORD *is* a great God, and a great King above all gods.
4 In his hand *are* the deep places of the earth: the strength of the hills *is* his also.
5 The sea *is* his, and he made it; and his hands formed the dry *land*.
6 O come, let us worship and bow down: let us kneel before the LORD our Maker.
7 For he *is* our God; and we *are* the people of his pasture, and the sheep of his hand. To-day if ye will hear his voice,
8 Harden not your heart, as in the provocation, *and* as in the day of temptation in the wilderness:
9 When your fathers tempted me, proved me, and saw my work.
10 Forty years long was I grieved with *this* generation, and said, It *is* a people that do err in their heart, and they have not known my ways:
11 Unto whom I sware in my wrath, that they should not enter into my rest.

PSALM XCVI.
1 Exhortation to praise God, 4 for his greatness, 10 for his kingdom, 11 and for his general judgments.

O SING unto the LORD a new song: sing unto the LORD, all the earth.
2 Sing unto the LORD, bless his name; show forth his salvation from day to day.
3 Declare his glory among the heathen, his wonders among all people.
4 For the LORD *is* great, and greatly to be praised: he *is* to be feared above all gods.
5 For all the gods of the nations *are* idols: but the LORD made the heavens.
6 Honour and majesty *are* before him: strength and beauty *are* in his sanctuary.
7 Give unto the LORD, O ye kindreds of the people, give unto the LORD glory and strength.
8 Give unto the LORD the glory due unto his name: bring an offering, and come into his courts.
9 O worship the LORD in the beauty of holiness: fear before him, all the earth.
10 Say among the heathen *that* the LORD reigneth: the world also shall be established that it shall not be moved: he shall judge the people righteously.
11 Let the heavens rejoice, and let the earth be glad; let the sea roar, and the fulness thereof.
12 Let the field be joyful, and all that *is* therein: then shall all the trees of the wood rejoice
13 Before the LORD: for he cometh, for he cometh to judge the earth: he shall judge the world with righteousness, and the people with his truth.

1, gotten ... victory—*lit., made salvation,* enabled Him to save His people. right hand, and ... arm—denote power. holy arm—or, arm of holiness, the power of His united moral perfections (Ps. 22. 3; 32. 11.). 2. The *salvation* is the result of His *righteousness* (Ps. 7. 17; 31. 1.), and both are publicly displayed. 3. The union of *mercy* and *truth* (Ps. 57. 3; 85. 10) secure the blessings of the promise (Gen. 12. 3; 18. 18 to all the world (Isa. 52. 10.). 4-6. make a loui noise—or, burst forth (Isa. 14. 7; 44. 23.). before ... King—hail Him as your sovereign; and while with every aid to demonstrate zeal and joy, intelligent creatures are invited to praise, as in Ps. 96. 11-13, inanimate nature is also summoned to honour Him who triumphs and rules in righteousness and equity.

PSALM XCIX.

Ver. 1-9. God's government is specially exercised in and for His church, which should praise Him for His gracious dealings.

1. sitteth ... cherubim—(cf. 1 Sam. 4. 4; Ps. 80. 1.). tremble ... be moved—inspired with fear by His judgments on the wicked. 2. great in Zion—where He dwells Ps. 9. 11.). 3. thy ... name—perfections of justice, power, &c. great and terrible — producing dread (Deut. 10. 17.), and to be praised by those over whom He is exalted (Ps. 97. 9.), it is holy—or, He is holy (v. 5, 9; Isa. 6. 3.). 4, 5. His wise and righteous government all nations should render honour. king's ... judgment—His power is combined with justice. he is holy—cf. Ps. 22. 3.). 6-8. The experience of these servants of God is cited for encouragement. among ... priests, among ... upon the Lord, [and] He spake ... pillar—may be referred to all three (cf. Ex. 18. 19; Lev. 8, 15; Deut. 5. 5; 1 Sam. 9. 13.). The *cloudy pillar* was the medium of divine intercourse Ex. 33, 9; Num. 12. 5.). Obedience was united with worship. God answered them as intercessors for the people, who, though forgiven, were yet chastened (Ex. 32. 10, 34.).

PSALM C.

Ver. 1-5. As closing this series, (cf. on Ps. 94..), this Psalm is a general call on all the earth to render exalted praise to God, the creator, preserver, and benefactor of men.

1, 2. With thankful praise, unite service as the subjects of a king (Ps. 2. 11, 12.). 3. To the obligations of a creature and subject is added that of a beneficiary (Ps. 95. 7.). 4. Join joyfully in His public worship. The terms are, of course, figurative (cf. Ps. 84. 2; 92. 13; Isa. 66. 23.). Enter—or, Come with solemnity Ps. 95. 6.). 5. The reason: God's eternal mercy and truth (Ps. 25. 8; 89. 7.).

PSALM CI.

Ver. 1-8. In this Psalm the profession of the principles of his domestic and political government testifies, as well as actions in accordance with it, David's appreciation of God's mercy to him, and His judgment on his enemies: and thus he sings or celebrates God's dealings.

2. He avows his sincere purpose, by God's aid, to act uprightly (Gen. 17. 1; Ps. 18. 30.). 3. set ... eyes—as an example to be approved and followed. no wicked thing—*lit., word,* plan or purpose of Belial (Ps. 41. 8.). work of ... aside—apostates. not cleave to me—will not be implicated in it (cf. Ps. 1. 1-3.) 4. A froward [or, *perverse*] heart—(Ps. 18. 26.). Such a temper I will not indulge, nor even know evil or wickedness. 5, 6. The slan-

derers and *haughty persons,* so mischievous in society, I will disown; but—Mine eyes ... upon—or, I will select reliable and honest men for my servants. 7. not dwell—*lit., not sit,* or tarry, or be established. 8. will early —or, diligently. city of the Lord—or, holy place Ps. 48. 2.), where wicked men shall not be tolerated.

PSALM CII.

Ver. 1-28. *A prayer of the afflicted,* &c.— The general terms seem to denote the propriety of regarding the Psalm as suitably expressive of the anxieties of any one of David's descendants, piously concerned for the welfare of the Church It was probably David's composition, and, though specially suggested by some peculiar trials, descriptive of future times. *Overwhelmed*—cf. Ps. 61. 2.). *Complaint*—Ps. 55. 2.). *Pouring out the soul* —Ps. 62. 8.). The tone of complaint predominates, though in view of God's promises and abiding faithfulness, it is sometimes exchanged for that of confidence and hope.

1-3. The terms used occur in Ps. 4. 1; 17. 1, 6; 18. 6; 31. 2, 10; 37. 20. 4. (Ch. Ps. 121. 6.). so that I forget—or, have forgotten, *i.e.,* in my distress (Ps. 107. 18,), and hence strength fails. 5. voice ... groaning—effect put for cause, my agony emaciates me. 6, 7. The figures express extreme loneliness. 8. sworn against me—or, *lit., by me,* wishing others as miserable as I am (Num. 5. 21.). 9. ashes—a figure of grief, my bread; weeping or tears, my drink (Ps. 80. 5.). 10. lifted ... cast me down —or, cast me away as stubble by a whirlwind (Isa. 64. 6.). 11. shadow ... declineth soon to vanish in the darkness of night. 12. Contrast with man's frailty (cf. Ps. 90. 1-7.). thy remembrance—that by which thou art remembered, thy promise. 13, 14. Hence it is here adduced. for [or, *when*] ... the set time &c.—the time promised. the indication of which is the interest felt for Zion by the people of God. 15-17. God's favour to the Church will affect her persecutors with fear. When the Lord shall build—or better, *Because* the Lord hath built, &c., as a reason for the effect on others; for in thus acting and hearing the humble, He is most glorious. 18. people ... created—(cf. Ps. 22. 31), an organised body, as a Church. 19-22. A summary of what shall be written. For—or, That, as introducing the statement of God's condescension. to loose ... appointed—or, deliver them (Ps. 79. 11.). To declare, &c.—or, That God's name may be celebrated in the assemblies of His Church, gathered from all nations (Zech. 8. 20-23,), and devoted to His service. 23-28. The writer, speaking for the Church, finds encouragement in the midst of all his distresses. God's eternal existence is a pledge of faithfulness to His promises, in the way —of providence. weakened — *lit., afflicted,* and made fearful of a premature end, a figure of the apprehensions of the Church, lest God might not perform His promise, drawn from those of a person in view of the dangers of early death (cf. Ps. 89. 47.). Paul (Heb. 1. 10) quotes v. 26-28 as addressed to Christ in His divine nature. The scope of the Psalm, as already seen, so far from opposing, favours this view, especially by the sentiments of v. 12-15 (cf. Isa. 60. 1.). The association of the Messiah with a day of future glory to the Church was very intimate in the minds of O. T. writers, and with correct views of His nature it is very consistent that He should

Exhortations to praise God   PSALMS XCVII–CII.   *for his greatness and majesty.*

PSALM XCVII.

1 *Majesty of God's kingdom.* 8 *The church rejoices at God's judgments upon idolaters.*

THE LORD reigneth; let the earth rejoice; let the *f* multitude of isles be glad thereof.
2 Clouds and darkness *are* round about him: righteousness and judgment *are* the habitation of his throne.
3 A *a* fire goeth before him, and burneth up his enemies round about.
4 His lightnings enlightened the world: the earth saw, and trembled.
5 The hills melted like wax at the presence of the LORD, at the presence of the Lord of the whole earth.
6 The heavens declare his righteousness, and all the people see his glory.
7 Confounded *b* he all they that serve graven images, that boast themselves of idols: *c* worship him, all ye gods.
8 Zion heard, and was glad; and the daughters of Judah rejoiced because of thy judgments, O LORD.
9 For thou, LORD, *art d* high above all the earth: thou art exalted far above all gods.
10 Ye that love the LORD, *e* hate evil: he *f* preserveth the souls of his saints; *g* he delivereth them out of the hand of the wicked.
11 Light *is* sown for the righteous, and gladness for the upright in heart.
12 Rejoice in the LORD, ye righteous; and give thanks *h* at the remembrance of his holiness.

PSALM XCVIII.

1 *The psalmist exhorts the Jews,* 4 *the Gentiles,* 7 *and all the creatures, to praise God.*

A Psalm.

O SING unto the LORD a new song; for he hath done marvellous things: *a* his right hand, and his holy arm, hath gotten him the victory.
2 The *b* LORD hath made known his salvation: *c* his righteousness hath he 1 openly shewed in the sight of the heathen.
3 He hath *d* remembered his mercy and his truth toward the house of Israel: *e* all the ends of the earth have seen the salvation of our God.
4 Make a joyful noise unto the LORD, all the earth: make a loud noise, and rejoice, and sing praise.
5 Sing unto the LORD with the harp; with the harp, and the voice of a psalm.
6 With trumpets and sound of cornet make a joyful noise before the LORD, the King.
7 Let the sea roar, and the fulness thereof; the world, and they that dwell therein.
8 Let the floods clap *their* hands: let the hills be joyful together
9 Before the LORD: for he cometh to judge the earth: with righteousness shall he judge the world, and the people with equity.

PSALM XCIX.

1 *The prophet, setting forth God's kingdom in Zion,* 5 *exhorts all, by the example of their forefathers, to worship God at his holy hill.*

THE LORD reigneth; let the people tremble: he sitteth *between* the cherubim; let the earth be moved.
2 The LORD *is* great in Zion; and he *is* high above all people.
3 Let them praise *a* thy great and terrible name; for it *is* holy.

4 The *b* king's strength also loveth judgment: thou dost *c* establish equity, thou executest judgment and righteousness in Jacob.
5 Exalt ye the LORD our God, and worship at *d* his footstool; *for* 2 he *is* holy.
6 Moses and Aaron among his priests, and Samuel among them that call upon his name; they called upon the LORD, and he answered them.
7 He *e* spake unto them in the cloudy pillar: they kept his testimonies, and the ordinance *that* he gave them.
8 Thou answeredst them. O LORD our God: *f* thou wast a God that forgavest them, though *g* thou tookest vengeance of their inventions.
9 Exalt the LORD our God, and worship at his holy hill; for the LORD our God *is* holy.

PSALM C.

1 *Exhortation to praise God cheerfully,* 3 *for his greatness,* 4 *and for his power.*

A Psalm of 1 praise.

MAKE a joyful noise unto the LORD, *a* all ye lands.
2 Serve the LORD with gladness; come before his presence with singing.
3 Know ye that the LORD he *is* God: *it* *is* he *that* hath made us, 2 and not we ourselves: *b* *we are* his people, and the sheep of his pasture.
4 Enter into his gates with thanksgiving, *and* into his courts with praise: be thankful unto him, *and* bless his name.
5 For the LORD *is* good; his mercy *is* everlasting; and his truth endureth *c* to all generations.

PSALM CI.

David makes a vow and profession of godliness.

A Psalm of David.

I WILL sing of mercy and judgment: unto thee, O LORD, will I sing.
2 I will *a* behave myself wisely in a perfect way. O when wilt thou come unto me? I will *b* walk within my house with a perfect heart.
3 I will set no 1 wicked thing before mine eyes: I hate the work of them *c* that turn aside; *it* shall not cleave to me.
4 A froward heart shall depart from me: I will not *d* know a wicked *person*.
5 Whoso privily slandereth his neighbour, him will I cut off: *e* him that hath an high look and a proud heart will not I suffer.
6 Mine *f* eyes *shall be* upon the faithful of the land, that they may dwell with me: he that walketh 2 in a perfect way, he shall serve me.
7 He that worketh deceit shall not dwell within my house; he that telleth lies 3 shall not tarry in my sight.
8 I will *g* early destroy all the wicked of the land; that I may cut off all *h* wicked doers from the city of the LORD.

PSALM CII.

1 *The prophet in his prayer makes a grievous complaint:* 12 *he takes comfort in the eternity and mercy of God.* 18 *The mercies of God to be recorded.*

A Prayer of the afflicted, when he is overwhelmed, and poureth out his complaint before the LORD.

HEAR my prayer, O LORD, and let my cry come unto thee.
2 Hide not thy face from me in the day when I am in trouble; incline thine ear

be addressed as the Lord and Head of His Church, who would bring about that glorious future on which they ever dwelt with fond and delightful anticipations.

PSALM CIII.

Ver. 1-22. A Psalm of joyous praise, in which the writer rises from a thankful acknowledgment of personal blessings to a lively celebration of God's gracious attributes, as not only intrinsically worthy of praise, but as specially suited to man's frailty, and concludes by invoking all creatures to unite in his song.

1. Bless, &c. — when God is the object, praise. my soul — myself Ps. 3. 3; 25. 1,', with allusion to the act, as one of intelligence. all ... with in me—(Deut. 6. 5,). his holy name — Ps. 5. 11,), His complete moral perfections. 2. forget not all—not any, none of His benefits. 3. diseases. as penal inflictions (Deut. 39. 2; 2 Chr. 21. 19.). 4. redeemeth—cost is implied. destruction—lit., pit of corruption (Ps. 16. 10.). crowneth—or, adorneth (Ps. 65. 11.). tender mercies—compassions (cf. Ps. 25. 6; 40. 11.. 5. By God's provision, the saint retains a youthful vigour like the eagles' Ps. 92. 14; cf. Isa. 40. 31.'. 6. Lit., righteousnesses and judgments, denoting various acts of God's government. 7. ways—of providence, &c., as usual (Ps. 25. 4; 67. 2.). acts—lit., wonders Ps. 9. 11; 78. 17.). 8-10. God's benevolence implies no merit. He shows it to sinners, who also are chastened for a time (Ex. 34. 6,). bear anger —in Lev. 19. 18, bear a grudge (Jer. 3. 5, 12.). 11. great—efficient. 12. removed ... from us —so as no longer to affect our relations to Him. 13. pitieth—lit., has compassion on. 14. he [who formed, Ps. 94. 9,] knoweth our frame—lit., our form. we are dust—made of and tending to it (Gen. 2. 7.). 15, 16. So short and frail is life that a breath may destroy it. it is gone—lit, it is not. know it no more—no more recognise him (Ps. 90. 6; Isa. 40. 6-8.). 17, 18. For similar contrast cf. Ps. 90. 2-6; 102. 27, 28. such ... covenant — limits the general terms preceding. righteousness—as usual Ps. 7. 17; 31. 1.'. 19. God's firm and universal dominion is a pledge that He will keep His promise Ps. 11. 4; 47. 8.). 20-22. do his commandments, ... word—or lit.. so as to hearken, &c., i.e., their acts of obedience are prompt, so that they are ever ready to hear, and know, and follow implicitly His declared will cf. Deut. 26. 17; Luke, 1. 19.). ye his hosts—myriads, or armies, as corresponding to angels of great power; denoting multitude also. all his works—creatures of every sort, every where.

PSALM CIV.

Ver. 1-35. The Psalmist celebrates God's glory in His works of creation and providence, teaching the dependence of all living creatures; and contrasts the happiness of those who praise him with the awful end of the wicked.

1. God's essential glory, and also that displayed by His mighty works, afford ground for praise. 2. light—is a figurative representation of the glory of the invisible God (Mat. 17. 2; 1. Tim. 6. 16.). Its use in this connection may refer to the first work of creation (Gen. 1. 3.). stretchest out the heavens—the visible heavens or sky which cover the earth as a curtain Isa. 40. 12.). 3. in the waters—or, it may be with; using this fluid for the beams, or frames, of His residence accords with the figure of clouds for chariots,

and winds as means of conveyance. walketh - or, moveth (cf. Ps. 18. 10, 11; Amos. 9. 6.). 4. This is quoted by Paul Heb. 1. 7 to denote the subordinate position of angels, i.e., they are only messengers as other and material agencies, spirits—lit., winds, flaming fire — Ps. 105. 32,), being here so called. 5. The earth is firmly fixed by His power. 6-'. These verses rather describe the wonders of the flood than the creation (Gen. 7. 19, 20; 2 Pet 3. 5, 6.'. God's method of arresting the flood and making its waters subside is poetically called a rebuke (Ps. 76. 6: Isa. 50. 2,), and the process of their subsiding by undulations among the hills and valleys is vividly described. 10-13. Once destructive, these waters are subjected to the service of God's creatures. In rain and dew from His chambers (cf. v. 3., and fountains and streams, they give drink to thirsting animals, and fertalise the soil. Trees thus nourished supply homes to singing birds, and the earth teems with the productions of God's wise agencies, 14, 15. so that men and beasts are abundantly provided with food. for the service— lit., for the culture, &c., by which he secures the results. oil ... shine—lit., makes his face to shine more than oil, i.e., so cheers and invigorates him, that outwardly he appears better than if anointed. strengtheneth ... heart—gives vigour to man (cf. Jud. 19. 5.). 16-19. God's care of even wild animals and uncultivated parts of the earth. 20-23. He provides and adapts to man's wants the appointed times and seasons. 24-26. From a view of the earth thus full of God's blessings, the writer passes to the sea, which, in its immensity, and as a scene and means of man's activity in commerce, and the home of countless multitudes of creatures, also displays divine power and beneficence. The mention of leviathan—(Job, 40, 20) heightens the estimate of the sea's greatness, and of His power who gives such a place for sport to one of His creatures. 27-30. The entire dependence of this immense family on God is set forth. With Him, to kill or make alive is equally easy; To hide His face is to withdraw favour Ps. 13. 1.'. By His spirit, or breath, or mere word, He gives life. It is His constant providence which repairs the wastes of time and disease. 31-34. While God could equally glorify His power in destruction, that He does it in preservation is that we may well spend our lives in grateful praise, honouring to Him, and delightful to pious hearts Ps. 147. 1.'. 35. Those who refuse such a protector and withhold such a service mar the beauty of His works, and must perish from His presence. The Psalm closes with an invocation of praise, the translation of a Heb. phrase, which is used as an English word, "Hallelujah," and may have served the purpose of a chorus as often as in our psalmody, or to give fuller expression to the writer's emotions. It is peculiar to Psalms composed after the captivity, as Selah is to those of an earlier date.

PSALM CV.

Ver. 1-45. After an exhortation to praise God, addressed especially to the chosen people, the writer presents the special reasons for praise, in a summary of their history from the calling of Abraham to their settlement in Canaan, and reminds them that their obedience was the end of all God's gracious dealings.

unto me; in the day when I call answer me speedily.
3 For *my days are consumed ¹ like smoke, and ᵇ my bones are burned as an hearth.
4 My heart is smitten, and withered like grass; so that I forget to eat my bread.
5 By reason of the voice of my groaning my bones cleave to my ² skin.
6 I am like ᶜ a pelican of the wilderness; I am like an owl of the desert.
7 I watch, and am as a sparrow alone upon the house-top.
8 Mine enemies reproach me all the day; and they that are mad against me ᵈ are sworn against me.
9 For I have eaten ashes like bread, and mingled my drink with weeping,
10 Because of thine indignation and thy wrath: for ᵉ thou hast lifted me up, and cast me down.
11 My days are like a shadow that declineth; and ᶠ I am withered like grass.
12 But thou, O LORD, shalt ᵍ endure for ever, and thy remembrance unto all generations.
13 Thou shalt arise, and have mercy upon Zion: for the time to favour her, yea, the set ʰ time, is come.
14 For thy ⁱ servants take pleasure in her stones, and favour the dust thereof.
15 So the heathen shall ʲ fear the name of the LORD, and all the kings of the earth thy glory.
16 When the LORD shall build up Zion, he ᵏ shall appear in his glory.
17 He ˡ will regard the prayer of the destitute, and not despise their prayer.
18 This shall be ᵐ written for the generation to come: and ⁿ the people which shall be created shall praise the LORD.
19 For he hath ᵒ looked down from the height of his sanctuary; from heaven did the LORD behold the earth;
20 To hear the groaning of the prisoner; to loose ᵖ those that are appointed to death;
21 To declare the name of the LORD in Zion, and his praise in Jerusalem;
22 When ᵖ the people are gathered together, and the kingdoms, to serve the LORD.
23 He ⁴ weakened my strength in the way; he shortened my days.
24 I said, O my God, take me not away in the midst of my days: ᵠ thy years are throughout all generations.
25 Of ʳ old hast thou laid the foundation of the earth; and the heavens are the work of thy hands.
26 They ˢ shall perish, but thou shalt ᵗ endure; yea, all of them shall wax old like a garment; as a vesture shalt thou change them, and they shall be changed:
27 But ᵘ thou art the same, and thy years shall have no end.
28 The children of thy servants shall continue, and their seed shall be established before thee.

PSALM CIII.
Exhortation to bless God for his mercy.
A Psalm of David.

BLESS the LORD, O my soul; and all that is within me, bless his holy name.
2 Bless the LORD, O my soul, and forget not all his benefits:
3 Who ᵃ forgiveth all thine iniquities; who healeth ᵇ all thy diseases;

PSALM 102.
a Jam. 4, 14.
1 Or. into smoke.
b Lam 1. 13.
2 Or, flesh.
c Is. 34. 11.
Zeph. 2. 14.
d Acts 23. 12.
e Ps. 30. 7.
f Jam. 1. 10.
g 1 Tim. 6. 16.
h Is. 40. 2.
i Dan. 9. 2.
j 1 Ki. 8. 43.
k Is. 60. 1.
l Neh. 2. 8.
m Ro. 15. 4.
1 Cor. 10. 11.
n Is. 43. 21.
o Deu. 26. 15.
8 the children of death.
p Hos. 1. 11.
Hos. 3. 5.
4 afflicted.
q Hab. 1. 12.
r Heb. 1. 10.
s Is. 65. 22.
Rom. 8. 20.
2 Pet. 3. 7.
5 stand.
t Mal. 3. 6.
Heb. 13. 8.
Jam. 1. 17.

PSALM 103.
a Is. 33. 24.
Mat. 9. 2.
Mark 2. 5.
Lu. 7. 47.
b Ex. 15. 26.
Jer. 17. 14.
c Ex. 34. 6.
Nu. 14. 18.
Deu. 5. 10.
Neh. 9. 17.
Jer. 32. 18.
1 great of mercy.
d Is. 57. 16.
Jer. 3. 5.
e Ezra 9. 13.
2 according to the height of the heaven.
f Is. 43. 25.
Eph. 1. 7.
g Mal. 3. 17.
3 it is not.
h Ex. 20. 6.
i Deu. 7. 9.
j Ps. 47. 2.
4 mighty in strength.
k Mat. 6. 10.
l Gen. 32. 2.
m Dan. 7. 9.

PSALM 104.
a Amos 9. 6.
b Is. 19. 1.
c Heb. 1. 7.
1 He hath founded the earth upon her bases.
2 Or, The mountains ascend, the valleys descend.
d Job 38. 10.
e Job 26. 10.

4 Who redeemeth thy life from destruction; who crowneth thee with loving-kindness and tender mercies;
5 Who satisfieth thy mouth with good things; so that thy youth is renewed like the eagle's.
6 The LORD executeth righteousness and judgment for all that are oppressed.
7 He made known his ways unto Moses, his acts unto the children of Israel.
8 The ᶜ LORD is merciful and gracious, slow to anger, and ¹ plenteous in mercy.
9 He ᵈ will not always chide; neither will he keep his anger for ever.
10 He ᵉ hath not dealt with us after our sins, nor rewarded us according to our iniquities.
11 For ² as the heaven is high above the earth, so great is his mercy toward them that fear him.
12 As far as the east is from the west, so far hath he ᶠ removed our transgressions from us.
13 Like ᵍ as a father pitieth his children, so the LORD pitieth them that fear him.
14 For he knoweth our frame; he remembereth that we are dust.
15 As for man, his days are as grass; as a flower of the field, so he flourisheth:
16 For the wind passeth over it, and ³ it is gone; and the place thereof shall know it no more.
17 But the mercy of the LORD is from everlasting to everlasting upon them that fear him, and his righteousness ʰ unto children's children;
18 To ⁱ such as keep his covenant, and to those that remember his commandments to do them.
19 The LORD hath prepared his throne in the heavens; and ʲ his kingdom ruleth over all.
20 Bless the LORD, ye his angels, ⁴ that excel in strength, that ᵏ do his commandments, hearkening unto the voice of his word.
21 Bless ye the LORD, all ye ˡ his hosts; ye ᵐ ministers of his, that do his pleasure.
22 Bless the LORD, all his works in all places of his dominion: bless the LORD, O my soul.

PSALM CIV.
1 *A meditation upon the majesty, power, and wonderful providence of God.* 31 *God's glory is eternal.* 33 *Praise ascribed to God.*

BLESS the LORD, O my soul, O LORD my God, thou art very great; thou art clothed with honour and majesty.
2 Who coverest thyself with light as with a garment; who stretchest out the heavens like a curtain;
3 Who ᵃ layeth the beams of his chambers in the waters; ᵇ who maketh the clouds his chariot; who walketh upon the wings of the wind;
4 Who ᶜ maketh his angels spirits; his ministers a flaming fire:
5 ¹ Who laid the foundations of the earth, that it should not be removed for ever.
6 Thou coveredst it with the deep as with a garment: the waters stood above the mountains.
7 At thy rebuke they fled; at the voice of thy thunder they hasted away.
8 ² They go up by the mountains; they go down by the valleys ᵈ unto the place which thou hast founded for them.
9 Thou ᵉ hast set a bound that they may

God's Providence over Abraham. PSALM CV. God's Providence over Joseph.

1. call ... name—(Ps 79. 6; Rom. 10. 13.). Call on Him, according to His historically manifested glory. After the example of Abraham, who, as often as God acquired for Himself a name in guiding him, *called in solemn worship upon the name of the Lord* (Gen. 12. 8; 13. 4.). **among the people**—or, peoples (Ps. 18. 49.). **deeds**—or, wonders (Ps. 103. 7.). **3, 4.** Seeking God's favour is the only true mode of getting true happiness, and *His strength* is the only true source of protection (cf. Ps. 32. 11; 40. 16.). **Glory ... name**—Boast in His perfections. The world glories in its horses and chariots against the Church of God lying in the dust; but *our* hope is in the name, i.e., the power and love of God to His people, manifested in past deliverances. **5, 6. judgments ... mouth** — His judicial decisions for the good and against the wicked. **chosen**—rather qualifies *children* than *Jacob*, as a plural. **7. Rather, "He, Jehovah, is our God."** His title, JEHOVAH, implies that He, the unchangeable, self-existing Being, makes things to be, i.e., fulfils His promises, and therefore will not forsake His people. Though specially of His people, He is God over all. **8-11.** The covenant was often ratified. **commanded**—or, ordained (Ps. 68. 28.). **word**—answering to "covenant" in the parallel clause, viz., the word of promise, which, according to v. 10, He set forth for an inviolable law. **to a ... generations**—perpetually. A verbal allusion to Deut. 7. 9 (cf. Ex. 20. 6.). **9. Which covenant**—or, "Word" (v. 8.). **10, 11.** Alluding to God's promise to Jacob Gen. 28. 13.). Out of the whole storehouse of the promises of God, only one is prominently brought forward, namely, that concerning the possession of Canaan. Every thing revolves round this. The wonders and judgments have all for their ultimate design the fulfilment of this promise. **12-15. few ... in number**—alluding to Jacob's words (Gen. 34. 30,), "I being *few in number.*" yea, **very few**—lit., "*as a few,*" *i.e.*, like fewness itself (cf. Isa. 1. 9.). **strangers**—sojourners in the land of their future inheritance, as in a strange country (Heb. 11. 9.). **13. from one nation to another**—and so from danger to danger: now in Egypt, now in the wilderness, and lastly in Canaan. Though a few strangers, wandering among various nations, God protected them. **reproved kings** — Pharaoh of Egypt and Abimelech of Gerar (Gen. 12. 17; 20. 3.). **Touch not**—Referring to Gen. 26. 11, where Abimelech says of Isaac, "He that *toucheth* this man or his wife, shall surely be put to death." **mine anointed**—as specially consecrated to me (Ps. 2. 2.). The patriarch was the prophet, priest, and king of his family. **my prophets**—in a similar sense (cf. Gen. 20. 7.). The "anointed" are those vessels of God, consecrated to His service, "in whom (as Pharaoh said of Joseph, Gen. 41. 38) the Spirit of God is." The term is applied in a somewhat wider sense to Cyrus, as the instrument of God's will (Isa. 45. 1.); in the stricter sense (Zech. 4. 14.). The *Heb.* for "prophets" means *God-spoken* men not as commonly explained, an *orator*, or mouthpiece of God's will); even as Abraham, in Gen. 15., received divine communications both by *vision* and *dream*. So Isaac, at Beersheba; Jacob, at Bethel, Mahanaim, and Jabbok. [HENGST.] **16.** God ordered the famine. God "*called for* famine," as if it were a servant, ready to come at God's bidding. Cf. the centurion's words, as to disease being God's servant (Mat. 8. 8, 9.). **staff of bread**—what supports life (Lev. 26. 26; Ps. 104. 15; Isa. 3. 1.). **upon the land**—*viz.*, Canaan (Gen. 41. 54.). **17-21.** Joseph was sent of God (Gen. 45. 5.). **hurt with fetters**—(Gen. 40. 3.). **was laid in iron**—*lit.*, *his soul*, or, he (Ps. 16. 10) came into iron, or, he was bound to his grief (cf. Ps. 3. 2; 11. 1.). Joseph is referred to, as being an appropriate type of those "bound in affliction and iron" (Ps. 107. 10.). The "soul" is put for the whole person, because the soul of the captive suffers still more than the body. **his word came**—His prophecy (Gen. 41. 11-20) to the officers came to pass, or was fulfilled (Jud. 13. 12, 17; 1 Sam. 9. 6, explain the form of speech.). **the word [or, saying, or, decree] of the Lord tried [or, proved] him**—by the afflictions it appointed him to endure before his elevation (cf. Gen. 41. 40-43.). HENGST. *transl.*, "cleared," or "purified" him; in reference to (Ps. 18. 30.), "The word of the Lord is tried," or "purified," leading to the peculiar expression: he explains the "word of the Lord" (distinct from Joseph's word, v. 19.), as "the promise of the possession of Canaan, the accomplishment of which demanded the preceding residence in Egypt" (v. 11, 42.). Probably the "word of the Lord" includes both *the decree for Joseph's afflictions* which *proved* and *tested* him (he not failing under the test as Hezekiah failed, 2 Chr. 32.), and the ultimate purpose of making all this instrumental towards *the final establishment of Israel in Canaan.* HENGST. remarks, The copiousness of detail as to Joseph, probably was with an eye to Daniel, the second Joseph. He too had been a captive, when his interpretation of a dream procured for him a high position, which enabled him to promote the welfare of his captive brethren. **22. To bind**—Not literally *bind;* but, *exercise over them absolute control;* as the parallel in the second clause shows; also Gen. 41. 40, 44, in which not literal *fettering*, but *commanding obedience* is spoken of. It refers to v. 18. The soul that was once *bound* itself now *binds* others, even princes. The same moral *binding* is assigned to the saints (Ps. 149. 8.). **teach ... senators wisdom**:—the ground of his exaltation by Pharaoh was his *wisdom* (Gen. 41. 39,), *viz.*, in state policy, and ordering well a kingdom. **23-25. Israel ... and Jacob**—*i.e.*, Jacob himself is meant, as v. 24 speaks of *his people*. Still he came with his whole house (Gen. 46. 6, 7.). **sojourned**—(Gen. 47. 4.). **land of Ham**—or, Egypt (Ps. 78. 51.). turned their heart — God controls men's free acts (cf. 1 Sam. 10. 9.). "When Saul had turned his back to go from (God's prophet) Samuel, God *turned* (*Marg.*) him to another heart" (see Ex. 1. 8, &c.). Whatever evil the wicked man plots against God's people, God holds bound even his heart, so as not to lay a single plan except what God permits. Thus Isaiah (43. 17) saith it was *God* who *brought forth* the army of Pharaoh to pursue Israel to their own destruction (Ex. 4. 21; 7. 3.). Moses ... chosen — both what they were by divine choice (Ps. 78. 70.). **27. signs** — *lit.*, *words of signs*, or rather, as *words* in *Heb.* mean *things*, "things of His signs," *i.e.*, His marvellous tokens of power (Ps. 145. 5, *Marg.*). Cf. the same Hebraism (Ps. 65. 3, *Marg.*). **28-36.** The ninth plague is made prominent as peculiarly wonderful. they rebelled not—Moses and Aaron promptly obeyed God (Heb.

not pass over; *f* that they turn not again
to cover the earth.
10 ⁸ He sendeth the springs into the valleys, *which* ⁴ run among the hills.
11 They give drink to every beast of the field; the wild asses ⁵ quench their thirst.
12 By them shall the fowls of the heaven have their habitation, *which* ⁶ sing among the branches.
13 He watereth the hills from his chambers: the earth is satisfied with the fruit of thy works.
14 He ⁷ causeth the grass to grow for the cattle, and herb for the service of man: that he may bring forth ʰ food out of the earth;
15 And ⁴ wine *that* maketh glad the heart of man, *and* ⁷ oil to make *his* face to shine, and bread *which* strengtheneth man's heart.
16 The ⁸ trees of the LORD are full *of sap;* the cedars of Lebanon, *j* which he hath planted;
17 Where the birds make their nests: *as for* the stork, the fir trees *are* her house.
18 The high hills *are* a refuge for the wild goats, *and* the rocks for ᵏ the conies.
19 He ᶦ appointed the moon for seasons: the sun ᵐ knoweth his going down.
20 Thou ⁿ makest darkness, and it is night: wherein ⁹ all the beasts of the forest do creep *forth.*
21 The ᵒ young lions roar after their prey, and seek their meat from God.
22 The sun ariseth, they gather themselves together, and lay them down in their dens.
23 Man goeth forth unto ᵖ his work and to his labour until the evening.
24 O ᵠ LORD, how manifold are thy works! in wisdom hast thou made them all: the earth is full of thy riches;
25 *So is* this great and wide sea, wherein are things creeping innumerable, both small and great beasts.
26 There go the ships; *there is* that ʳ leviathan, *whom* thou hast ¹⁰ made to play therein.
27 These wait ˢ all upon thee, that thou mayest give *them* their meat in due season.
28 *That* thou givest them they gather: thou openest thine hand, they are filled with good.
29 Thou hidest thy face, they are troubled: thou ᵗ takest away their breath, they die, and return to their dust.
30 Thou ᵘ sendest forth thy spirit, they are created; and thou renewest the face of the earth.
31 The glory of the LORD ¹¹ shall endure for ever: the LORD shall rejoice in his works.
32 He looketh on the earth, and it ᵛ trembleth; he toucheth the hills, and they smoke.
33 I will sing unto the LORD as long as I live; I will sing praise to my God while I have my being.
34 My meditation of him shall be sweet: I will be glad in the LORD.
35 Let ʷ the sinners be consumed out of the earth, and let the wicked be no more. Bless thou the LORD, O my soul. ¹² Praise ye the LORD.

PSALM CV.

1 Exhortation to praise God, to seek him, and remember his works. 8 God's providence and care of his people described.

O ᵃ GIVE thanks unto the LORD; call upon his name: make known his deeds among the people.

414

PSALM 104.
f Gen. 9. 11.
³ Who sendeth.
⁴ walk.
⁵ break.
⁶ give a voice.
g Gen. 1. 29, 30.
Gen. 8. 18.
Gen. 9. 8.
Ps. 147. 8.
ʰ Ps. 136.25.
Ps. 147. 9.
Job 28. 5.
i Judg. 9, 13.
Ps. 23. 5.
Pro. 31.6,7.
⁷ to make his face shine with oil, or, more than oil.
⁸ That is, large trees.
j Nu. 24. 6.
ᵏ Pro. 30.26.
ᶦ Gen. 1. 14.
ᵐ Job 38. 12.
ⁿ Is. 45. 7.
⁹ all the beasts thereof do trample on the forest.
ᵒ Job 38. 39.
Joel 1. 20.
ᵖ Gen. 3. 19.
ᵠ Pro. 3. 19.
Job 41. 1.
10 formed.
ʳ Rom. 11.36.
ˢ Eccl. 12. 7.
ᵗ Is. 32. 15.
Ezek 37.9.
11 shall be.
ᵘ Hab. 3. 10.
ᵛ Pro. 2. 22.
12 Hallelujah.

PSALM 105.
ᵃ Is. 12. 4.
ᵇ Ps. 27. 8.
ᶜ Ps. 77. 11.
ᵈ Is. 26. 8.
ᵉ Lu. 1. 72.
f Gen. 17. 2.
Heb. 6. 17.
g Gen. 15.18.
¹ the cord.
ʰ Gen. 34. 30.
i Heb. 11. 9.
j Gen. 35. 5.
ᵏ Gen. 12.17.
l Gen. 41. 54.
ᵐ Lev. 26. 26.
ⁿ Gen. 45. 5.
ᵒ Gen. 37. 28.
ᵖ Gen. 40. 15.
² his soul came into iron.
³ possession.
q Gen. 46. 6.
r Ex. 1. 7.
s Num. 16. 5.
⁴ words of his signs.
Jer. 22. 30.
t Ps. 99. 7.
ᵘ He gave their rain hail.
ᵛ Gen. 49. 3.

2 Sing unto him, sing psalms unto him: talk ye of all his wondrous works.
3 Glory ye in his holy name: let the heart of them rejoice that seek the LORD.
4 Seek the LORD, and his strength; ᵇ seek his face evermore.
5 Remember ᶜ his marvellous works that he hath done; his wonders, and the judgments of his mouth;
6 O ye seed of Abraham his servant, ye children of Jacob his chosen.
7 He *is* the LORD our God: ᵈ his judgments *are* in all the earth.
8 He hath ᵉ remembered his covenant for ever, the word *which* he commanded to a thousand generations:
9 Which *f* covenant he made with Abraham, and his oath unto Isaac;
10 And confirmed the same unto Jacob for a law, *and* to Israel *for* an everlasting covenant;
11 Saying, *g* Unto thee will I give the land of Canaan, ¹ the lot of your inheritance:
12 When ʰ they were *but* a few men in number; yea, very few, *i* and strangers in it.
13 When they went from one nation to another, from *one* kingdom to another people,
14 He *j* suffered no man to do them wrong; yea, ᵏ he reproved kings for their sakes;
15 *Saying,* Touch not mine anointed, and do my prophets no harm.
16 Moreover *l* he called for a famine upon the land: he brake the whole ᵐ staff of bread.
17 He ⁿ sent a man before them, *even* Joseph, *who* ᵒ was sold for a servant;
18 Whose ᵖ feet they hurt with fetters: ² he was laid in iron:
19 Until the time that his word came: the word of the LORD tried him.
20 The king sent and loosed him; *even* the ruler of the people, and let him go free.
21 He made him lord of his house, and ruler of all his ³ substance;
22 To bind his princes at his pleasure, and teach his senators wisdom.
23 Israel ᵠ also came into Egypt; and Jacob sojourned in the land of Ham.
24 And ʳ he increased his people greatly, and made them stronger than their enemies.
25 He turned their heart to hate his people, to deal subtilly with his servants.
26 He sent Moses his servant, *and* Aaron whom ˢ he had chosen.
27 They showed ⁴ his signs among them, and wonders in the land of Ham.
28 He sent darkness, and made it dark; and *t* they rebelled not against his word.
29 He turned their waters into blood, and slew their fish.
30 Their land brought forth frogs in abundance in the chambers of their kings.
31 He spake, and there came divers sorts of flies, *and* lice in all their coasts.
32 ᵘ He gave them hail for rain, *and* flaming fire in their land.
33 He smote their vines also and their fig trees, and brake the trees of their coasts.
34 He spake, and the locusts came, and caterpillars, and that without number,
35 And did eat up all the herbs in their land, and devoured the fruit of their ground.
36 He smote also all the first-born in their land, ᵛ the chief of all their strength.

11. 27.', cf. Ex. 7-11. and Ps. 78. 44-51, with which this summary substantially agrees.,. Or rather, the "darkness" here is figurative (Jer. 13. 16,', the literal plague of darkness (Ex. 10. 22. 23) being only *alluded* to as the symbol of God's wrath which overhung Egypt as a dark cloud during all the plagues. Hence it is placed first, out of the historical order. Thus, "They rebelled not (*i.e.*, no longer against His word," refers to the *Egyptians*. Whenever God sent a plague on them, *they were ready to let Israel go*, though refusing when the plague ceased. "His word" is His command to let Israel go. [HENGST.] Of the ten plagues, only eight are mentioned, the fifth, the murrain of beasts, and the sixth, the boils, being omitted. 29, 30. He deprived them of their favourite *fish*, and gave them instead out of the water. loathsome *frogs*, and (*v.* 31) upon their land tormenting flies *the dog-fly*, according to MAUR.) and lice *gnats*, HENGST.). 32. hail for rain —instead of fertilising showers, hail destructive to trees. This forms the transition to the vegetable kingdom. The locusts in *v.* 34, similarly are destructive to plants. gave them—referring to Lev. 26. 4, "I give you rain in due season." His "gift" to Israel's foes is one of a very different kind from that bestowed on His people. 33. their coasts— all their land (Ps. 75. 54.). 34. caterpillars— lit., *the lickers up*, devouring insects; probably, *the hairy winged locust*. 36. the chief— lit., *the firstlings*, &c. The ascending climax passes from the food of man to man himself. The language here is quoted from I's. 78. 51. 37. wi h silver and gold—*presented* them by the Egyptians, as an acknowledgment due for their labours in their bondage cf. Ex. 12. 35.. one feeble person—or, stumbler, unfit for the line of march. Cf. "harnessed," *i.e.*, accoutred and marshalled as an army on march Ex. 13. 18; Isa. 5. 27.). 38. Cf. Ex. 12. 33; Deut. 11. 25.). 39. covering — in sense of protection (cf. Ex. 13. 21; Num. 10. 34.). In the burning sands of the desert the cloud protected the congregation from the heat of the sun; an emblem of God's protecting favour over His people, as interpreted by Isaiah (Isa. 4. 5, 6; cf. Num. 9. 16.). 42-45. The reasons for these dealings: (1) God's faithfulness to His covenant, "His holy promise" of Canaan is the fountain whence flowed so many acts of marvellous kindness to His people cf. *v.* 8. 11.). Ex. 2. 24, is the fundamental passage. [HENGST.] (2) that they might be obedient. The observance of God's commands by Abraham was the object of the covenant with him (Gen. 18. 19.); as it was also the object of the covenant with Israel, that they might observe God's statutes. remembered ... and Abraham — or, "remembered His holy word (*i.e.*, covenant confirmed) *with Abraham*." inherited the labour — i.e., the fruits of their labour; their corn and vineyards (Josh. 21. 43-45.)

PSALM CVI.

Ver. 1-48. This Psalm gives a detailed confession of the sins of Israel in all periods of their history, with special reference to the terms of the covenant as intimated (l's. 105. 45.). It is introduced by praise to God for the wonders of His mercy, and concluded by a supplication for His favour to His afflicted people, and a doxology.

1. Praise, &c.—(Ps. 104. 24.), begins and ends the Psalm, intimating the obligations of praise however we sin and suffer. 1 Chr. 16. 34-36, is the source from which the beginning and end of this Psalm are derived. 2. His acts exceed our comprehension, as His praise our powers of expression (Rom. 11. 33.). Their unutterable greatness is not to keep us back, but to urge us the more, to try to praise Him as best we can (Ps. 40. 5: 71. 15.). 3. The blessing is limited to those whose principles and acts are right. How "blessed" Israel would be now, if he had "observed God's statutes" (Ps. 105. 45.). This sense of having not fulfilled the condition suggests the transition to the Church's cry for mercy, as being God's "chosen" people, accompanied with the confession of sin so condemning as to leave no hope but God's compassion. So in Dan. 9. 4, the confession of not having fulfilled the condition, follows the statement of it, "God keeping the covenant, to them that love Him." 4. 5. In view of the desert of sins to be confessed, the writer invokes God's covenant mercy to himself and the Church, in whose welfare he rejoices. The speaker, *me, I*, is not the Psalmist himself, but the people, the present generation (cf. *v.* 6,). visit—(cf. Ps. 8. 4.,. see the good—participate in it I s. 37. 13.). thy chosen—*viz.*, Israel, God's elect (Isa. 43. 20; 45. 4.). As God seems to have *forgotten* them, they pray that He would "remember" them with the favour which *belongs* to His own people, and which once they had enjoyed. thine inheritance— Deut. 9. 29; 32. 9.). 6. Cf. 1 Ki. 8. 47; Dan. 9. 5, where the same three verbs occur in the same order and connection, the original of the two later passages being the first one, the prayer of Solomon in dedicating the temple. sinned ... fathers — like them, and so partaking of their guilt. The terms denote a rising gradation of sinning (cf. Ps. 1. 1.). with our fathers—we and they together forming one mass of corruption. 7-12. Special confession. Their rebellion at the sea Ex. 14. 11) was because they had not remembered nor understood God's miracles on their behalf. That God saved them in their unbelief was of His mere mercy, and for His own glory. the sea ... the Red sea—the very words in which Moses' song celebrated the scene of Israel's deliverance (Ex. 15. 4.). Israel began to rebel against God at the very moment and scene of his deliverance by God! 8. for his name's sake—(Ez. 20. 14.). 9. rebuked—(Ps. 104. 7.). as through the wilderness— Isa. 63. 11-14.). 12. believed ... his words—this is said not to praise the Israelites, but God, who constrained even so unbelieving a people momentarily to "believe", whilst in lume diate view of His wonders, a faith which they immediately after lost *v.* 13; Ex. 14. 31; 15. 1.). 13-15. The faith induced by God's display of power in their behalf was short-lived, and their new rebellion and temptation was visited by God with fresh punishment, inflicted by leaving them to the result of their own gratified appetites, and sending on them spiritual poverty (Num. 11. 18.). They soon forgat—*lit., They hasted, they forgat* (cf. Ex. 32. 8.). They have turned aside *quickly* (or *hastily*) out of the way." The haste of our desires is such that we can scarcely allow God one day. Unless He immediately answer our call, instantly then arise impatience, and at length despair. his works—(Deut. 11. 3, 4; Dan. 9. 14.). his counsel — they waited not for the development of God's counsel, or

37 He brought them forth also with silver and gold: and *there was* not one feeble person among their tribes.
38 Egypt was glad when they departed; for the fear of them fell upon them.
39 He *spread a cloud for a covering, and fire to give light in the night.
40 *The* people asked, and he brought quails, and satisfied them with the bread of heaven.
41 He *opened the rock, and the waters gushed out; they ran in the dry places like a river.
42 For he remembered *his holy promise, and Abraham his servant.
43 And he brought forth his people with joy, *and* his chosen with gladness:
44 And *gave them the lands of the heathen: and they inherited the labour of the people;
45 That *they might observe his statutes, and keep his laws. *Praise ye the LORD.

PSALM CVI.

1 *The psalmist exhorts to praise God: 4 he prays to share in his people's joy: 6 history of the people's rebellion, and God's mercy.

PRAISE ¹ ye the LORD. O give thanks unto the LORD; for *he is* good: for his mercy *endureth* for ever.
2 Who can utter the mighty acts of the LORD? who can show forth all his praise?
3 Blessed *are* they that keep judgment, *and* he that doeth righteousness at *all times.
4 Remember me, O LORD, with the favour *that thou bearest unto* thy people: O visit me with thy salvation;
5 That I may see the good of thy chosen, that I may rejoice in the gladness of thy nation, that I may glory with thine inheritance.
6 We have sinned with our fathers, we have committed iniquity, we have done wickedly.
7 Our fathers understood not thy wonders in Egypt; they remembered not the multitude of thy mercies; but provoked *him* at the sea, *even* at the Red sea.
8 Nevertheless he saved them for his name's sake, that he might make his mighty power to be known.
9 He rebuked the Red sea also, and it was dried up: so he led them through the depths, as through the wilderness.
10 And he saved them from the hand of him that hated *them*, and redeemed them from the hand of the enemy.
11 And the waters covered their enemies; there was not one of them left.
12 Then believed they his words; they sang his praise.
13 *They soon forgat his works; they waited not for his counsel:
14 But ³ lusted exceedingly in the wilderness, and tempted God in the desert.
15 And he gave them their request; but sent leanness into their soul.
16 They envied Moses also in the camp, *and* Aaron the saint of the LORD.
17 The earth opened and swallowed up Dathan, and covered the company of Abiram.
18 And a fire was kindled in their company; the flame burned up the wicked.
19 They made a calf in Horeb, and worshipped the molten image.
20 Thus they changed their glory into the similitude of an ox that eateth grass.

21 They forgat God their Saviour, which had done great things in Egypt;
22 Wondrous works in the land of Ham, *and* terrible things by the Red sea.
23 Therefore he said that he would destroy them, had not Moses his chosen stood before him in the breach, to turn away his wrath, lest he should destroy them.
24 Yea, they despised the pleasant land; they believed not his word:
25 But murmured in their tents, *and* hearkened not unto the voice of the LORD.
26 Therefore he lifted up his hand against them, to overthrow them in the wilderness:
27 To overthrow their seed also among the nations, and to scatter them in the lands.
28 They joined themselves also unto Baal-peor, and ate the sacrifices of the dead.
29 Thus they provoked *him* to anger with their inventions; and the plague brake in upon them.
30 Then stood up Phinehas, and executed judgment: and so the plague was stayed.
31 And that was counted unto him for righteousness unto all generations for evermore.
32 They angered *him* also at the waters of strife, so that it went ill with Moses for their sakes:
33 Because they provoked his spirit, so that he spake unadvisedly with his lips.
34 They did not destroy the nations, concerning whom the LORD commanded them:
35 But were mingled among the heathen, and learned their works.
36 And they served their idols: which were a snare unto them.
37 Yea, they sacrificed their sons and their daughters unto devils,
38 And shed innocent blood, *even* the blood of their sons and of their daughters, whom they sacrificed unto the idols of Canaan: and the land was polluted with blood.
39 Thus were they defiled with their own works, and went a whoring with their own inventions.
40 Therefore was the wrath of the LORD kindled against his people, insomuch that he abhorred his own inheritance.
41 And he gave them into the hand of the heathen; and they that hated them ruled over them.
42 Their enemies also oppressed them, and they were brought into subjection under their hand.
43 Many times did he deliver them; but they provoked *him* with their counsel, and were brought low for their iniquity.
44 Nevertheless he regarded their affliction, when he heard their cry:
45 And he remembered for them his covenant, and repented according to the multitude of his mercies.
46 He made them also to be pitied of all those that carried them captives.
47 Save us, O LORD our God, and gather us from among the heathen, to give thanks unto thy holy name, *and* to triumph in thy praise.
48 Blessed be the LORD God of Israel from everlasting to everlasting: and let all the people say, Amen. ⁷ Praise ye the LORD.

plan for their deliverance, at His own time, and in His own way. 14. Lit., lusted a lust (quoted from Num. 11. 4, Marg.). Previously, there had been impatience as to necessaries of life; here it is lusting (Ps. 78. 18.). 15. but sent leanness—rather, "and sent," i.e., and thus, even in doing so, the punishment was inflicted at the very time their request was granted. So Ps. 78. 30, "While their meat was yet in their mouths, the wrath of God came upon them." soul—the animal soul, which craves for food (Num. 11. 6; Ps. 107. 18.). This soul got its wish, and with it and in it its own punishment. The place was therefore called Kibroth-Hattaavah, "the graves of lust," because there they buried the people who had lusted. Animal desires when gratified mostly give only a hungry craving for more (Jer. 2. 13.). 16-19. All the congregation took part with Dathan, Korah, &c., and their accomplices (Num. 16. 41.). Aaron the saint—lit., the holy one, as consecrated priest; not a moral attribute, but one designating his office as holy to the Lord. The rebellion was followed by a double punishment: 1) (v. 17) of the non-Levitical rebels, the Reubenites, Dathan and Abiram, &c. (Deut. 11. 6; Num. 26. 10,), these were swallowed up by the earth. covered—"closed upon them" (Num. 16. 33.). 2) Of the Levitical rebels, with Korah at their head (v. 18: Num. 16. 35; 26. 10.), these had sinned by fire, and were punished by fire, as Aaron's (being high priest) sons had been Lev. 10. 2; Num. 16. 1-35.), 19-23. From indirect setting God at nought, they pass to direct. made—though prohibited in Ex. 20. 4, 5, to make a likeness, even of the true God. calf—called so in contempt. They would have made an ox or bull, but their idol turned out but a calf; an imitation of the divine symbols, the cherubim; or of the sacred bull of Egyptian idolatry. This idolatry was more sinful in view of their recent experience of God's power in Egypt and His wonders at Sinai (Ex. 32. 1-6.). On v. 20 cf. Jer. 2. 10-13; Rom. 1. 23. "Their glory" is Jehovah, who, being peculiarly their God, was their distinguishing glory above other nations (Deut. 4. 7; 10. 21.). "Thy praise," i.e., glory. God signified His presence with Israel by the Shechinah, cloud of glory (1 Ki. 8. 11; Rom. 9. 4.). Though intending to worship Jehovah under the symbol of the calf, yet as this was incompatible with His nature (Deut. 4. 15-17,), they in reality gave up Him, and so were given up by Him. Instead of the Lord of heaven, they had as their glory the image of an ox that does nothing but eat grass. 23. he said—viz., to Moses (Deut. 9. 13.). With God, saying is as certain as doing; but His purpose, whilst full of wrath against sin, takes into account the mediation of Him of whom Moses was the type (Ex. 32. 11-14; Deut. 9. 18, 19.). Moses his chosen—i.e., to be His servant (cf. Ps. 105. 26.). in the breach—as a warrior covers with his body the broken part of a wall or fortress besieged, a perilous place (Ez. 13. 5; 22. 30.). to turn away [or, prevent] his wrath—(Num. 25. 11; Ps. 78. 38.). 24-27. The sin of refusing to invade Canaan "the pleasant land" (Jer. 3. 19; Ez. 20. 6; Dan. 8. 9) "the land of beauty," was punished by the destruction of that generation (Num. 14. 28,), and the threat of dispersion Deut. 4. 25; 28. 33 afterwards made to their posterity, and fulfilled in the great calamities now bewailed, may have also been then added. despised—(Num. 14. 31.). Seven transgressions are enumerated, one in Egypt, six in the wilderness; to which are opposed the seven miracles of God for His people cf. Num. 14. 22; Deut. 32. 6,). b h ved not his word—by which He promised He would give them the land; but rather the word of the faithless spies (cf. Ps. 78. 22.). lifted up his hand — or, swore, the usual form of swearing (cf. Num. 14. 30, Marg.). 27. To overthrow—lit., "To make them fall;" alluding to the words Num. 14. 29.). among...nations lands—the "wilderness" was not more destructive to the fathers (v. 26,), than residence among the heathen ("nations") shall be to the children. Lev. 26. 33, 38, is here before the Psalmist's mind, the determination against the "seed," when rebellious, being not expressed in Num. 14. 31-33, but implied in the determination against the fathers. 23-30. sacrifices of the dead — i.e., of lifeless idols, contrasted with "the living God" (Jer. 10. 3-10; cf. Ps. 115. 4-7; 1 Cor. 12. 2.). On the words, "joined themselves to Baal Peor," see Num. 25. 2, 3, 5. Baal-Peor, i.e., the possessor of Peor, the mountain on which Chemosh, the idol of Moab, was worshipped, and at the foot of which Israel at the time lay encamped (Num. 23. 28.). The name never occurs except in connection with that locality and that circumstance. provoked — excited grief and indignation (Ps. 6. 7; 78. 58.). stood—as Aaron "stood between the living and the dead, and the plague was stayed" Num. 16. 48.). executed judgment — lit., judged, including sentence and act. 31. counted... righteousness —"a just and rewardable action." for—or, unto, to the procuring of righteousness, as in Rom. 4. 2; 10. 4. Here it was a particular act, not faith, nor its object Christ; and what was procured was not justifying righteousness or what was to be rewarded with eternal life; for no one act of man's can be taken for complete obedience, but it was that which God approved and rewarded with a perpetual priesthood to him and his descendants (Num. 25. 13; 1 Chr. 6. 4, &c.). 32, 33. (Cf. Num. 20. 3-12; Deut. 1. 37; 3. 26.). went ill with [lit., was bad for] Moses—his conduct, though under great provocation, was punished by exclusion from Canaan. 34-39. They not only failed to expel the heathen, as God "commanded" (Ex. 23. 32, 33,), lit., said, (they should.), but conformed to their idolatries, and thus became spiritual adulterers (Ps. 73. 27.). unto devils—Sept., demons (cf. 1 Cor. 10. 20,), or evil spirits. polluted with blood—lit., blood, or murder Ps. 5. 6; 26. 9,). 40-43. Those nations first seduced and then oppressed them (cf. Jud. 1. 34; 2. 14; 3. 30.). Their apostasies ungratefully repaid God's many mercies till He finally abandoned them to punishment (Lev. 26. 39.). 44-46. If, as is probable, this Psalm was written at the time of the captivity, the writer now intimates the tokens of God's returning favour. repented—(cf. Ps. 90. 13.). made . . . pitied — (1 Ki. 8. 50; Dan. 1. 9.). These tokens encourage the prayer and the promise of praise (Ps. 30. 4.), which is well closed by a doxology.

PSALM CVII.

Ver. 1-43. Although the general theme of this Psalm may have been suggested by God's special favour to the Israelites in their restoration from captivity, it must be regarded as an instructive celebration of God's praise

PSALM CVII.

The psalmist exhorts God's redeemed to praise his goodness, and to observe his manifold providence, in many varieties of life.

O GIVE thanks unto the LORD, for *he is good*; for his mercy *endureth* for ever.

2 Let the redeemed of the LORD say so, whom he hath redeemed from the hand of the enemy;

3 And gathered them out of the lands, from the east, and from the west, from the north, and from the south.

4 They wandered in the wilderness in a solitary way; they found no city to dwell in.

5 Hungry and thirsty, their soul fainted in them.

6 Then they cried unto the LORD in their trouble, *and* he delivered them out of their distresses.

7 And he led them forth by the right way, that they might go to a city of habitation.

8 Oh that *men* would praise the LORD *for* his goodness, and *for* his wonderful works to the children of men!

9 For he satisfieth the longing soul, and filleth the hungry soul with goodness.

10 Such as sit in darkness, and in the shadow of death, *being* bound in affliction and iron;

11 Because they rebelled against the words of God, and contemned the counsel of the Most High:

12 Therefore he brought down their heart with labour: they fell down, and *there was* none to help.

13 Then they cried unto the LORD in their trouble, *and* he saved them out of their distresses.

14 He brought them out of darkness and the shadow of death, and brake their bands in sunder.

15 Oh that *men* would praise the LORD for his goodness, and *for* his wonderful works to the children of men!

16 For he hath broken the gates of brass, and cut the bars of iron in sunder.

17 Fools, because of their transgression and because of their iniquities, are afflicted;

18 Their soul abhorreth all manner of meat; and they draw near unto the gates of death.

19 Then they cry unto the LORD in their trouble, *and* he saveth them out of their distresses.

20 He sent his word, and healed them, and delivered *them* from their destructions.

21 Oh that *men* would praise the LORD for his goodness, and *for* his wonderful works to the children of men!

22 And let them sacrifice the sacrifices of thanksgiving, and declare his works with rejoicing.

23 They that go down to the sea in ships, that do business in great waters;

24 These see the works of the LORD, and his wonders in the deep.

25 For he commandeth, and raiseth the stormy wind, which lifteth up the waves thereof.

26 They mount up to the heaven, they go down again to the depths: their soul is melted because of trouble.

27 They reel to and fro, and stagger like a drunken man, and are at their wit's end.

28 Then they cry unto the LORD in their trouble, and he bringeth them out of their distresses.

29 He maketh the storm a calm, so that the waves thereof are still.

30 Then are they glad because they be quiet; so he bringeth them unto their desired haven.

31 Oh that *men* would praise the LORD *for* his goodness, and *for* his wonderful works to the children of men!

32 Let them exalt him also in the congregation of the people, and praise him in the assembly of the elders.

33 He turneth rivers into a wilderness, and the water-springs into dry ground;

34 A fruitful land into barrenness, for the wickedness of them that dwell therein.

35 He turneth the wilderness into a standing water, and dry ground into watersprings.

36 And there he maketh the hungry to dwell, that they may prepare a city for habitation;

37 And sow the fields, and plant vineyards, which may yield fruits of increase.

38 He blesseth them also, so that they are multiplied greatly, and suffereth not their cattle to decrease.

39 Again, they are minished and brought low through oppression, affliction, and sorrow.

40 He poureth contempt upon princes, and causeth them to wander in the wilderness, *where there is* no way.

41 Yet setteth he the poor on high *from* affliction, and maketh *him* families like a flock.

42 The righteous shall see *it*, and rejoice; and all iniquity shall stop her mouth.

43 Whoso *is* wise, and will observe these things, even they shall understand the loving-kindness of the LORD.

PSALM CVIII.

1 David encourages himself to praise God; 5 he prays for God's assistance according to his promise: 11 his confidence in God's help.

A Song or Psalm of David.

O GOD, my heart is fixed; I will sing and give praise, even with my glory.

2 Awake, psaltery and harp; I *myself* will awake early.

3 I will praise thee, O LORD, among the people: and I will sing praises unto thee among the nations.

4 For thy mercy *is* great above the heavens, and thy truth *reacheth* unto the clouds.

5 Be thou exalted, O God, above the heavens; and thy glory above all the earth;

6 That thy beloved may be delivered: save with thy right hand, and answer me.

7 God hath spoken in his holiness; I will rejoice, I will divide Shechem, and mete out the valley of Succoth.

8 Gilead *is* mine; Manasseh *is* mine; Ephraim also *is* the strength of mine head; Judah *is* my lawgiver;

9 Moab *is* my washpot; over Edom will I cast out my shoe; over Philistia will I triumph.

10 Who will bring me into the strong city? who will lead me into Edom?

11 *Wilt* not thou, O God, *who* hast cast us off? and wilt not thou, O God, go forth with our hosts?

12 Give us help from trouble: for vain *is* the help of man.

13 Through God we shall do valiantly: for he *it is that* shall tread down our enemies.

for His merciful providence to men in their various emergencies. Of these several are given; captivity and bondage, wandering by land and sea, and famine; some as evidences of God's displeasure, and all the deliverances as evidences of His goodness and mercy to them who humbly seek Him.

1, 2. This call for thankful praise is the burden or chorus (cf. v. 8, 15, &c.). redeemed of the Lord—cf. Isa. 35. 9, 10.). say—i.e., that His mercy, &c. hand of—or, power of enemy. 3. gathered—all ding to the dispersion of captives throughout the Babylonian empire. from the south—lit., the sea, or, Red sea Ps. 114. 3,), which was on the south. 4-7. A graphic picture is given of the sufferings of those who from distant lands returned to Jerusalem ; or, as city of habitation may mean the land of Palestine. fainted—was overwhelmed Ps. 61. 3; 77. 3,). 8, 9. To the chorus is added, as a reason for praise, an example of the extreme distress from which they had been delivered—extreme hunger, the severest privation of a journey in the desert. 10-16. Their sufferings were for their rebellion against (Ps. 105. 28) the words, or purposes, or promises, of God for their benefit. When humbled they cry to God, who delivers them from bondage, described as a dark dungeon with doors and bars of metal, in which they are bound in iron—i.e., chains and fetters. shadow of death—darkness with danger Ps. 23. 4.); broken—lit., shivered (Isa. 45. 2.). 17-22. Whether the same or not, this exigency illustrates that dispensation of God, according to which sin brings its own punishment. are afflicted—lit., afflict themselves, i.e., bring on disease, denoted by loathing of food, and drawing near unto [lit., even to] the gates [or, domains, Ps. 9. 16.] of death. sent his word—i.e., put forth His power. their destructions—i.e., that which threatened them. To the chorus is added the mode of giving thanks, by a sacrifice and joyful singing Ps. 50. 14.). 23-32. Here are set forth the perils of sea-faring, futility of man's and efficiency of God's help. go ... sea—alluding to the elevation of the land at the coast. These see ... deep—illustrated both by the storm He raises and the calm He makes with a word (Ps. 33. 9.). waves thereof—lit., His waves (God's) (Ps. 42. 7.). are ... end—lit., all their wisdom swallows up itself, destroys itself by vain and contradictory devices, such as despair induces. He maketh ... calm—or, to stand to stillness, or in quiet. Instead of acts of temple worship, those of the synagogue are here described, where the people with the assembly, or session of elders, convened for reading, singing, prayer, and teaching. The coincidence as to persons and routine of service with those of Presbyterian Churches is not forced.). 33-41. God's providence is illustriously displayed in His influence on two great elements of human prosperity, the earth's productiveness, and the powers of government. He punishes the wicked by destroying the sources of fertility, or, in mercy, gives fruitfulness to deserts, which become the homes of a busy and successful agricultural population. By a permitted misrule and tyranny, this scene of prosperity is changed to one of adversity. He rules rulers, setting up one and putting down another. wander ... wilderness—reduced to misery (Job. 12. 24.). 42, 43. In this providential government, good men will rejoice, and the cavils of the wicked will be stopped (Job. 5. 16; Isa. 52. 15,), and all who take right views will appreciate God's unfailing mercy and unbounded love.

PSALM CVIII.

Ver. 1-13. This Psalm is composed, v. 1-5 of Ps. 57. 7-11, and v. 6-12 of Ps. 60. 5-12. The varieties are verbal and trivial, except that in v. 9, "over Philistia will I triumph," differs from Ps. 60. 8, the interpretation of which it confirms. Its altogether triumphant tone may intimate that it was prepared by David, omitting the plaintive portions of the other Psalms, as commemorative of God's favour in the victories of His people.

PSALM CIX.

Ver. 1-31. The writer complains of his virulent enemies, on whom he imprecates God's righteous punishment, and to a prayer for a divine interposition in his behalf appends the expression of his confidence and a promise of his praises. This Psalm is remarkable for the number and severity of its imprecations. Its evident typical character (cf. v. 8) justifies the explanation of these already given, that as the language of David respecting his own enemies, or those of Christ, it has respect not to the penitent, but to the impenitent and implacable foes of good men, and of God and His cause, whose inevitable fate is thus indicated by inspired authority.

1. God of my praise—its object, thus recognising God as a certain helper. Be not silent (cf. Ps. 17. 13; 28. 1.). 2. For the mouth ... opened [or, They have opened a wicked mouth] against me—lit., with me, i.e., Their intercourse is lying, or, They slander me to my face (Mat. 26. 59.). 3. (Cf. Ps. 35. 7; 69. 4.). 4, 5. They return evil for good (cf. Ps. 27. 12; Pro. 17. 13.). I give myself unto prayer—or, lit., I [am] prayer, or, as for me, prayer, i.e., it is my resource for comfort in distress. 6. over him—one of his enemies prominent in malignity (Ps. 55. 12.). let Satan stand—as an accuser, whose place was the right hand of the accused (Zech. 3. 1, 2.). 7. The condemnation is aggravated, when prayer for relief is treated as a sin. 8. The opposite blessing is long life (Ps. 91. 16; Pro. 3. 2.). The last clause is quoted as to Judas by Peter (Acts. 1. 20.). office—lit., charge, Sept., and Peter, oversight. 9, 10. Let his family share the punishment, his children be as wandering beggars to prowl in their desolate homes, a greedy and relentless creditor grasp his substance, his labour, or the fruit of it, enure to strangers and not his heirs, and his unprotected, fatherless children fall in want, so that his posterity shall utterly fail. 13. posterity—lit., end, as Ps. 37. 38, or what comes after, i.e., reward, or success, or its expectation, of which posterity was to a Jew a prominent part. 14, 15. Added to the terrible overthrow following his own sin, let there be the imputation of his parents' guilt, that it may now come before God, for His meting out its full consequences, in cutting off the memory of them (i.e., the parents) from the earth (Ps. 34. 16.). 16. Let God remember guilt, because he (the wicked) did not remember mercy. poor and needy ... broken in heart—i.e., pious sufferer (Ps. 34. 18; 35. 10; 40. 17.). 17-19. Let his loved sin, cursing, come upon him in punishment (Ps. 35. 8,), thoroughly fill him as water and oil, permeating to every part of his system (cf. Num. 5. 22-27.), and become a garment

Imprecations on the wicked. PSALMS CIX–CXII. *The Messiah's kingdom.*

PSALM CIX.

1 *David complains of his enemies;* 16 *he shows their sin;* 21 *complaining of his own misery, he prays for help.*

To the chief Musician, A Psalm of David.

HOLD *a* not thy peace, O God of my praise;
2 For the mouth of the wicked and the mouth of the deceitful *b* are opened against me: they have spoken against me with a lying tongue.
3 They compassed me about also with words of hatred; and fought against me without *c* a cause.
4 For my love they are my adversaries: but I *give myself unto* prayer.
5 And *c* they have rewarded me evil for good, and hatred for my love.
6 Set thou a wicked man over him; and let *d* Satan stand at his right hand.
7 When he shall be judged, let him *e* be condemned; and *d* let his prayer become sin.
8 Let his days be few; and *e* let another take his *f* office.
9 Let *f* his children be fatherless, and his wife a widow.
10 Let his children be continually *g* vagabonds, and beg: let them seek *their* bread also out of their desolate places.
11 Let *h* the extortioner catch all that he hath; and let the stranger spoil his labour.
12 Let there be none to extend mercy unto him; neither let there be any to favour his fatherless children.
13 Let *i* his posterity be cut off; *and* in the generation following let their *j* name be blotted out.
14 Let *k* the iniquity of his fathers be remembered with the LORD: and let not the sin of his mother *l* be blotted out.
15 Let them be before the LORD continually, that he may *m* cut off the memory of them from the earth.
16 Because that he remembered not to show mercy, but persecuted the poor and needy man, that he might even slay the broken in heart.
17 As he loved cursing, so let it come unto him; as he delighted not in blessing, so let it be far from him.
18 As he clothed himself with cursing like as with his garment, so let it come *o* into his bowels like water, and like oil into his bones.
19 Let it be unto him as the garment *which* covereth him, and for a girdle wherewith he is girded continually.
20 *Let* this be the reward of mine adversaries from the LORD, and of them that speak evil against my soul.
21 But do thou for me, O GOD the Lord, for thy name's sake: because thy mercy *is* good, deliver thou me.
22 For I am poor and needy, and my heart is wounded within me.
23 I am gone like the shadow when it declineth: I am tossed up and down as the locust.
24 My *n* knees are weak through fasting; and my flesh faileth of fatness.
25 I became also a reproach unto them: *when* they looked upon me *o* they shaked their heads.
26 Help me, O LORD my God: O save me according to thy mercy;
27 That *p* they may know that this *is* thy hand; *that* thou, LORD, hast done it.

PSALM 109.
a Ps. 83. 1.
1 mouth of deceit.
2 have opened themselves.
b John 15. 25.
c Ps. 38. 20.
3 Or. an adversary.
Zech. 3. 1.
4 gone out guilty, or, wicked.
d Pro. 28. 9.
e Acts 1. 20.
5 Or. charge.
f Ex. 22. 24.
g Gen. 4. 12.
h Job 18. 9.
i Ps. 37. 28.
j Pro. 10. 7.
k Ex. 20. 5.
l Neh. 4. 5.
Jer. 18. 23.
m Job 18. 17.
6 within him.
Nu. 6. 22.
n Heb. 12. 12.
o Mat. 27. 39.
p Job 37. 7.
7 Is. 65. 14.
7 from the judges of his soul.

PSALM 110.
a Ps. 45. 6.
Mat. 22. 44.
Mar. 12. 36.
Lu. 20. 42.
Acts 2. 34.
1 Cor. 15. 25.
Heb. 1. 13.
1 Pe. 3. 22.
b Judg. 5.
c Acts 2. 41.
1 Or. more than the womb of the morning thou shalt have, etc.
d Nu. 23. 19.
e Zech. 6. 13.
Heb. 5. 6.
Heb. 6. 20.
Heb. 7. 17.
f Ps. 16. 8.
g Ps. 2. 6.
Rom. 2. 5.
Rev. 11. 18.
h Hab. 3. 13.
2 Or. great.
i Is. 61. 1.
John 3. 34.
j Is. 58. 12.

PSALM 111.
1 Hallelujah.
a Job 38. 1.
2 prey.
b Ps. 19. 7.
3 are established.
c Rev. 15. 3.
d Deut. 4. 6
Job 23. 28.
Ecc. 12. 13.
4 Or. good success.
5 that do them.

28 Let them curse, but bless thou: when they arise, let them be ashamed; but let thy *q* servant rejoice.
29 Let mine adversaries be clothed with shame, and let them cover themselves with their own confusion, as with a mantle.
30 I will greatly praise the LORD with my mouth; yea, I will praise him among the multitude.
31 For he shall stand at the right hand of the poor, to save *him* *r* from those that condemn his soul.

PSALM CX.

1 *The kingdom,* 4 *the priesthood,* 5 *the conquest,* 7 *and the passion of Christ.*

A Psalm of David.

THE *a* LORD said unto my Lord, Sit thou at my right hand, until I make thine enemies thy footstool.
2 The LORD shall send the rod of thy strength out of Zion: rule thou in the midst of thine enemies.
3 Thy *b* people *shall be* willing in the day of thy power, *c* in the beauties of holiness 1 from the womb of the morning; thou hast the dew of thy youth.
4 The LORD hath sworn, and *d* will not repent, *e* Thou *art* a priest for ever after the order of Melchizedek,
5 The Lord *f* at thy right hand shall strike through kings *g* in the day of his wrath.
6 He shall judge among the heathen, he shall fill *the places* with the dead bodies; he *h* shall wound the heads over 2 many countries.
7 He *i* shall drink of the brook in the way: therefore *j* shall he lift up the head.

PSALM CXI.

1 *The psalmist by his example incites others to praise God for his glorious and gracious works.*

The fear of God the source of true wisdom.

PRAISE 1 ye the LORD. I will praise the LORD with *my* whole heart, in the assembly of the upright, and in the congregation.
2 The *a* works of the LORD *are* great, sought out of all them that have pleasure therein.
3 His work *is* honourable and glorious; and his righteousness endureth for ever.
4 He hath made his wonderful works to be remembered: the LORD *is* gracious, and full of compassion.
5 He hath given 2 meat unto them that fear him: he will ever be mindful of his covenant.
6 He hath showed his people the power of his works, that he may give them the heritage of the heathen.
7 The works of his hands *are* verity and judgment; *b* all his commandments *are* sure.
8 They *c* stand fast for ever and ever, *and are* *c* done in truth and uprightness.
9 He sent redemption unto his people: he hath commanded his covenant for ever: holy and reverend *is* his name.
10 The *d* fear of the LORD *is* the beginning of wisdom; *a* good understanding have all they 3 that do *his commandments:* his praise endureth for ever.

PSALM CXII.

1 *Godliness hath the promises of this life,* 4 *and of the life to come.*

PRAISE ye the LORD. Blessed *is* the man *that* feareth the LORD, *that* delighteth greatly in his commandments.
2 His seed shall be mighty upon earth:

and a girdle for a perpetual dress. 20. Let this... reward—or, wages, pay for labour, the fruit of the enemy's wickedness. from the Lord—as His judicial act. 21, 22. do... for me—i.e., kindness, wounded—lit., pierced (Ps. 69. 26, 29.). 23. like the shadow—cf. Ps. 102. 11.). tossed up and down—or, driven (Ex. 10. 19.). 24, 25. Taunts and reproaches aggravate his afflicted and feeble state (Ps. 22. 6, 7.). 26, 27. Let my deliverance glorify thee (cf. Ps. 59. 13.). 28-31. In confidence that God's blessing would come on him, and confusion and shame on his enemies (Ps. 73. 13.), he ceases to regard their curses, and anticipates a season of joyful and public thanksgiving; for God is near to protect (Ps. 10. 8; 34. 6) the poor from all unrighteous judges who may condemn him.

PSALM CX.

Ver. 1-7. The explicit application of this Psalm to our Saviour, by Him (Mat. 22. 42-45.), and by the apostles (Acts, 2. 34; 1 Cor. 15. 25; Heb. 1. 13,), and their frequent reference to its language and purport (Eph. 1. 20-22; Phil. 2. 9-11; Heb. 10. 12, 13.), leave no doubt of its purely prophetic character. Not only was there nothing in the position or character, personal or official, of David or any other descendant, to justify a reference to either, but the utter severance from the royal office of all priestly functions (so clearly assigned the subject of this Psalm) positively forbids such a reference. The Psalm celebrates the exaltation of Christ to the throne of an eternal and increasing kingdom, and a perpetual priesthood (Zech. 6. 13.), involving the subjugation of His enemies and the multiplication of His subjects, and rendered infallibly certain by the word and oath of Almighty God.

1. The Lord said—lit., A saying of the Lord (cf. Ps. 36. 1.), a formula, used in prophetic or other solemn or express declarations. my Lord—That the Jews understood this term to denote the Messiah their traditions show, and Christ's mode of arguing on such an assumption (Mat. 22. 44) also proves. To sit at the right hand was not only a mark of honour (1 Ki. 2. 19.), but also implied participation of power (Ps. 45. 9; Mark, 16. 19; Eph. 1. 20.). Sit—as a king (Ps. 29. 10.), though the position rather than posture is intimated cf. Acts, 7. 55, 56.). until I make, &c.—The dominion of Christ over His enemies, as commissioned by God, and intrusted with all power (Mat. 28. 18) for their subjugation, will assuredly be established (1 Cor. 15. 24-28.). This is neither His government as God, nor that which, as the incarnate Saviour, He exercises over His people, of whom He will ever be Head. thine enemies thy footstool—an expression taken from the custom of Eastern conquerors (cf. Josh. 10. 24; Judg. 1. 7.), to signify a complete subjection. 2. the rod of thy strength—the rod of correction (Isa. 9. 4; 10. 15; Jer. 48. 12.), by which thy strength will be known. This is His Word of truth (Isa. 2. 3; 11. 4,), converting some and confounding others (cf. 2 Thes. 2. 8.). out of Zion—or, the Church, in which God dwells by His Spirit, as once by a visible symbol in the tabernacle on Zion (cf. Ps. 2. 6.). rule thou, &c.—over enemies now conquered. in their midst—once set upon, as by ferocious beasts (Ps. 22. 16.), now humbly, though reluctantly, confessed as Lord (Phil. 2. 10. 11.). 3. Thy people...willing —lit., Thy people (are) free-will-offerings; for such is the proper rendering of the word "willing," which is a plural noun, and not an adjective (cf. Ex. 25. 2; Ps. 54. 6.), also a similar form (Jud. 5. 2-9.). in the day of thy power— thy people freely offer themselves (Rom. 12. 1) in Thy service, enlisting under thy banner. in the beauties of holiness—either as Ps. 29. 2, the loveliness of a spiritual worship, of which the temple service, in all its material splendours, was but a type; or more probably, the appearance of the worshippers, who, in this spiritual kingdom, are a nation of kings and priests (1 Pet. 2. 9; Rev. 1. 5) attending this Priest and King, clothed in those eminent graces which the beautiful vestments of the Aaronic priests (Lev. 16. 4 typified. The last very obscure clause—from the womb... youth—may, according to this view, be thus explained: The word youth denotes a period of life distinguished for strength and activity (cf. Eccl. 11. 9,),—the dew is a constant emblem of whatever is refreshing and strengthening (Pro. 19. 12; Hos. 14. 5.). The Messiah, then, as leading His people, is represented as continually in the vigour of youth, refreshed and strengthened by the early dew of God's grace and Spirit. Thus the phrase corresponds as a member of a parallelism with "the day of thy power" in the first clause. "In the beauties of holiness" belongs to this latter clause, corresponding to "Thy people" in the first, and the colon after "morning" is omitted. Others prefer: Thy youth, or youthful vigour, or body, shall be constantly refreshed by successive accessions of people, as dew from the early morning; and this accords with the N. T. idea that the Church is Christ's body (cf. Mic. 5. 7.). 4. The perpetuity of the priesthood, here asserted on God's oath, corresponds with that of the kingly office just explained. after the order—(Heb. 7. 15,), after the similitude of Melchisedec, is fully expounded by Paul, to denote not only perpetuity, appointment of God, and a royal priesthood, but also the absence of priestly descent and succession, and superiority to the Aaronic order. 5. at thy right hand—as Ps. 109. 31, upholding and aiding, which is not inconsistent with v. 1, where the figure denotes participation of power, for here He is presented in another aspect, as a warrior going against enemies, and sustained by God, strike through—smite or crush. kings—not common men, but their rulers, and so all under them (Ps. 2. 2, 10.). 6. The person is again changed. The Messiah's conquests are described, though His work and God's are the same. As after a battle, whose field is strewn with corpses, the conqueror ascends the seat of empire, so shall He judge or rule among many nations, and subdue the head (or (as used collectively for many) the heads] over many lands. wound—lit., smite, or, crush (cf. v. 5.). 7. As a conqueror, "faint, yet pursuing," He shall be refreshed by "the brook in the way," and pursue to completion His divine and glorious triumphs.

PSALM CXI.

Ver. 1-10. The Psalmist celebrates God's gracious dealings with His people, of which a summary statement is given.

1. Praise ye the Lord—or, Hallelujah (Ps. 104. 35.). This seems to serve as a title to those of the later Psalms, which, like this, set forth God's gracious government and its blessed fruits. This praise claims the whole

the generation of the upright shall be blessed.
3 Wealth *and riches shall be in his house; and his righteousness endureth for ever.
4 Unto the upright there ariseth light in the darkness: he is gracious, and full of compassion, and righteous.
5 A b good man showeth favour, and lendeth: he will guide his affairs with 1 discretion.
6 Surely he shall not be moved for ever: the righteous shall be in everlasting remembrance.
7 He shall not be afraid of evil tidings: his heart is fixed, trusting in the LORD.
8 His heart is established, he shall not be afraid, until he see his desire upon his enemies.
9 He c hath dispersed, he hath given to the poor; his righteousness endureth for ever; his horn shall be exalted with honour.
10 The d wicked shall see it, and be grieved; he shall gnash with his teeth, and melt away: the desire of the wicked shall perish.

PSALM CXIII.

1 *Exhortation to praise God for his excellency,* 7 *and for his mercy.*

PRAISE 1 ye the LORD. Praise, O ye servants of the LORD, praise the name of the LORD.
2 Blessed *a be the name of the LORD from this time forth and for evermore.
3 From b the rising of the sun unto the going down of the same the LORD's name is to be praised.
4 The LORD is high above all nations, and his glory above the heavens.
5 Who is like unto the LORD our God, who 2 dwelleth on high,
6 Who c humbleth himself to behold the things that are in heaven, and in the earth!
7 He d raiseth up the poor out of the dust, and lifteth the needy out of the dunghill;
8 That he may e set him with princes, even with the princes of his people.
9 He f maketh the barren woman 3 to keep house, and to be a joyful mother of children. Praise ye the LORD.

PSALM CXIV.

Exhortation, by the example of inanimate creation, to fear God in his church.

WHEN Israel went out of Egypt, the house of Jacob from a people of strange language;
2 Judah was his sanctuary, and Israel his dominion.
3 The sea saw it, and fled: Jordan was driven back.
4 The a mountains skipped like rams, and the little hills like lambs.
5 What ailed thee, O thou sea, that thou fleddest? thou Jordan, that thou wast driven back?
6 Ye mountains, that ye skipped like rams, and ye little hills, like lambs?
7 Tremble, thou earth, at the presence of the Lord, at the presence of the God of Jacob;
8 Which b turned the rock into a standing water, the flint into a fountain of waters.

PSALM CXV.

1 *God entreated to assert his honour against the reproaches of the heathen.* 4 *Idols are vanity:* 9 *Exhortation to trust in God.*

NOT a unto us, O LORD, not unto us, but unto thy name give glory, for thy mercy, and for thy truth's sake.

2 Wherefore should the heathen say, Where b is now their God?
3 But c our God is in the heavens: he hath done whatsoever he hath pleased.
4 Their d idols are silver and gold, the work of men's hands.
5 They have mouths, but they speak not; eyes have they, but they see not;
6 They have ears, but they hear not; noses have they, but they smell not;
7 They have hands, but they handle not; feet have they, but they walk not; neither speak they through their throat.
8 They e that make them are like unto them; so is every one that trusteth in them.
9 O Israel, trust thou in the LORD: f he is their help and their shield.
10 O g house of Aaron, trust in the LORD: he is their help and their shield.
11 Ye that fear the LORD, trust in the LORD: he is their help and their shield.
12 The LORD hath been mindful of us: he will h bless us; he will bless the house of Israel; he will bless the house of Aaron.
13 He i will bless them that fear the LORD, both small 1 and great.
14 The LORD shall increase you more and more, you and your children.
15 Ye are j blessed of the LORD k which made heaven and earth.
16 The heaven, even the heavens, are the LORD's; but the earth hath he given to the children of men.
17 The dead praise not the LORD, neither any that go down into silence.
18 But l we will bless the LORD from this time forth and for evermore. Praise the LORD.

PSALM CXVI.

1 *The psalmist professes his love and duty to God for his deliverance;* 12 *he studies to be thankful.*

I LOVE the LORD, because he hath heard my voice and my supplications.
2 Because he hath inclined his ear unto me, therefore will I call upon him 1 as long as I live.
3 The sorrows of death compassed me, and the pains of hell 2 gat hold upon me: I found trouble and sorrow.
4 Then called I upon the name of the LORD; O LORD, I beseech thee, deliver my soul.
5 Gracious is the LORD, and a righteous; yea, our God is merciful.
6 The LORD preserveth the simple: I was brought low, and he helped me.
7 Return unto thy b rest, O my soul; for the LORD hath dealt bountifully with thee.
8 For thou hast delivered my soul from death, mine eyes from tears, and my feet from falling.
9 I will walk before the LORD in the land of the living.
10 I c believed, therefore have I spoken: I was greatly afflicted.
11 I said in my haste, d All men are liars.
12 What shall I render unto the LORD for all his benefits toward me?
13 I will take the cup of salvation, and call upon the name of the LORD.
14 I e will pay my vows unto the LORD now in the presence of all his people.
15 Precious f in the sight of the LORD is the death of his saints.
16 O LORD, truly I am thy servant; I am thy servant, and the son of thine handmaid: thou hast loosed my bonds.

heart (Ps. 86. 12,), and is rendered publicly. **upright**—a title of the true Israel (Ps. 32. 11.). 2. His *works*, i.e., of providence and grace, are sought—or, carefully studied, by all desiring to know them. 3, 4. honourable and glorious — *lit.*, *honour and majesty*, which illustrate His glorious perfections. righteousness—(Ps. 7. 17; 31. 1,', which He has made memorab'e by wonders of love and mercy, in supplying the wants of His people according to covenant engagements. 6-8. His power was shown especially in giving them the promised land, and His faithfulness and justice thus displayed are, like His precepts, reliable and of permanent obligation. 9. The deliverance He provided accorded to His established covenant. Thus He manifested Himself in the sum of His perfections (Ps. 20. 1, 7; 22. 3) worthy of reverence. 10. And hence, love and fear of such a God is the chief element of true wisdom (cf. Pro. 1. 7; 9. 10.).

PSALM CXII.

Ver. 1-10. This Psalm may be regarded as an exposition of Ps. 111. 10, presenting the happiness of those who fear and obey God, and contrasting the fate of the ungodly. 1. True fear produces obedience and this happiness. 2, 3. Temporal blessings follow the service of God, exceptions occurring only as they are seen by God to be inconsistent with those spiritual blessings which are better. 4. light—*fig.*, for relief (Ps. 27. 1; 97. 11.). The *upright* are like God (Lev. 6. 30; Ps. 111. 4.). 5-9. Generosity, sound judgment in business, and confidence in God, form a character which preserves from fear of evil and insures success against enemies. While a man thus truly pious is liberal, he increases in substance. not be moved—(cf. Ps. 13. 4; 15. 5.). heart is established—or, firm in right principles. see his desire—(Ps. 50, 23; 54. 7.). 10. Disappointed in their malevolent wishes by the prosperity of the pious, the wicked are punished by the working of their evil passions, and come to nought.

PSALM CXIII.

Ver. 1-9. God's majesty contrasted with His condescension and gracious dealings towards the humble furnish matter and a call for praise. The Jews, it is said, used this and Ps. 114-118. on their great festivals, and called them the *Greater Hallel*, or *Hymn*. 1-3. Earnestness and zeal are denoted by the emphatic repetitions. servants—or, all the people of God. name of the Lord—perfections (Ps. 5. 11; 111. 9.). From the rising, &c. —All the world. 4-6. God's exaltation enhances His condescension; 7, 8., which is illustrated as often in raising the worthy poor and needy to honour (cf. 1 Sam. 2. 8; Ps. 44. 25.). 9. On this special case, cf. 1 Sam. 2. 21. Barrenness was regarded as a disgrace, and is a type of a deserted Church (Isa. 54. 1.). the barren woman ... house—*lit., the barren of the house*, so that the supplied words may be omitted.

PSALM CXIV.

Ver. 1-8. The writer briefly and beautifully celebrates God's former care of His people, to whose benefit nature was miraculously made to contribute. 1-4. cf strange language—(cf. Ps. 81, 5.). skipped ... rams—(Ps. 29. 6,), describes the waving of mountain forests, poetically representing *the motion* of the mountains. The poetical description of the effect of God's presence on the sea and Jordan alludes to the history

(Ex. 14. 21; Josh. 3. 14-17.). *Judah* is put as a parallel to *Israel*, because of the destined as well as real prominence of that tribe. 5-8. The questions place the implied answers in a more striking form. at the presence of—*lit., from before*, as if affrighted by the wonderful display of God's power. Well may such a God be trusted, and great should be His praise.

PSALM CXV.

Ver. 1-18. The Psalmist prays that God would vindicate His glory, which is contrasted with the vanity of idols, while the folly of their worshippers is contrasted with the trust of God's people, who are encouraged to its exercise and to unite in the praise which it will occasion. 1-3. The vindication of God's mercy and faithfulness (Ps. 25. 10; 36. 6) is the *glory* of His *name*, which is desired to be illustrated in the deliverance of His people, as the implied mode of its manifestation. In view of the taunts of the heathen, faith in His dominion as enthroned in the heaven (Ps. 2. 4; 11. 4) is avowed. Where is now, &c.—now is "not a particle of time, but of entreaty," as in our forms of speech, "Come now," "See now," &c. 4-7. (Cf. Isa. 40. 18-20; 44. 9-20.). speak ... throat—*lit., mutter*, not even utter articulate sounds. 8. every one that trusteth —they who trust, whether makers or not. 9-13. The repetitions imply earnestness. 14. Opposed to the decrease pending and during the captivity. 15-17. They were not only God's peculiar people, but as living inhabitants of earth, assigned the work of His praise as monuments of divine power, wisdom, and goodness. 18. Hence let us fulfil the purpose of our creation, and evermore show forth His praise.

PSALM CXVI.

Ver. 1-19. The writer celebrates the deliverance from extreme perils by which he was favoured, and pledges grateful and pious public acknowledgments. 1, 2. A truly grateful love will be evinced by acts of worship, which *calling on God* expresses (v. 13, Ps. 55. 16; 86. 7; cf. Ps. 17. 6; 31. 2,). 3, 4. For similar figures for distress Ps. 18. 4, 5,). gat hold upon me—another sense (" found") of the same word follows, as we speak of disease *finding* us, and of our finding or catching disease. 5-8. The relief which he asked is the result not of his merit, but of God's known pity and tenderness, which is acknowledged in assuring himself his soul, Ps. 11. 1; 16. 10) of rest and peace. All calamities are represented by *death, tears*, and *falling of the feet* Ps. 56. 13.). 9. walk before the Lord—act, or live under His favour and guidance (Gen. 17. 1; Ps. 61. 7.). land of the living — (Ps. 27. 13.). 10, 11. Confidence in God opposed to distrust of men, as not reliable Ps. 68. 8, 9.). He speaks from an experience of the result of his faith, in my haste—*lit., terror*, or *agitation*, produced by his affliction (cf. Ps. 31. 22.). 12-14. These are modes of expressing acts of worship (cf. v. 4; Ps. 50. 14; Jon. 2. 9.). the cup of salvation—the drink-offering which was part of the thank-offering (Num. 15. 3-5.). now—(cf. Ps. 115. 2) "oh! that (I may do it," in the presence, &c. 15, 16. By the plea of being a home-born servant, he intimates his claim on God's covenant love to His people. 17-19. An ampler declaration of his purpose, designating the place the Lord's house, or earthly residence in Jerusalem

17 I will offer to thee the sacrifice of thanksgiving, and will call upon the name of the LORD.
18 I will pay my vows unto the LORD now in the presence of all his people,
19 In the courts of the LORD's house, in the midst of thee, O Jerusalem. Praise ye the LORD.

PSALM CXVII.
Exhortation to all nations to praise God for his mercy and truth.

O PRAISE the LORD, all ye nations: praise him, all ye people.
2 For his merciful kindness is great toward us: and the truth of the LORD endureth for ever. Praise ye the LORD.

PSALM CXVIII.
1 *Exhortation to praise God for his mercy.* 19 *By the psalmist in type, the coming of Christ's kingdom is expressed.*

O GIVE thanks unto the LORD; for he is good: because his mercy endureth for ever.
2 Let Israel now say, that his mercy endureth for ever.
3 Let the house of Aaron now say, that his mercy endureth for ever.
4 Let them now that fear the LORD say, that his mercy endureth for ever.
5 I called upon the LORD in distress: the LORD answered me, and set me in a large place.
6 The LORD is on my side; I will not fear: what can man do unto me?
7 The LORD taketh my part with them that help me: therefore shall I see my desire upon them that hate me.
8 It is better to trust in the LORD than to put confidence in man.
9 It is better to trust in the LORD than to put confidence in princes.
10 All nations compassed me about: but in the name of the LORD will I destroy them.
11 They compassed me about; yea, they compassed me about: but in the name of the LORD I will destroy them.
12 They compassed me about like bees: they are quenched as the fire of thorns: for in the name of the LORD I will destroy them.
13 Thou hast thrust sore at me, that I might fall: but the LORD helped me.
14 The LORD is my strength and song, and is become my salvation.
15 The voice of rejoicing and salvation is in the tabernacles of the righteous: the right hand of the LORD doeth valiantly.
16 The right hand of the LORD is exalted: the right hand of the LORD doeth valiantly.
17 I shall not die, but live, and declare the works of the LORD.
18 The LORD hath chastened me sore: but he hath not given me over unto death.
19 Open to me the gates of righteousness: I will go in to them, and I will praise the LORD:
20 This gate of the LORD, into which the righteous shall enter.
21 I will praise thee: for thou hast heard me, and art become my salvation.
22 The stone which the builders refused is become the head stone of the corner.
23 This is the LORD's doing; it is marvellous in our eyes.
24 This is the day which the LORD hath made; we will rejoice and be glad in it.

25 Save now, I beseech thee, O LORD: O LORD, I beseech thee, send now prosperity.
26 Blessed be he that cometh in the name of the LORD: we have blessed you out of the house of the LORD.
27 God is the LORD, which hath showed us light: bind the sacrifice with cords, even unto the horns of the altar.
28 Thou art my God, and I will praise thee: thou art my God, I will exalt thee.
29 O give thanks unto the LORD; for he is good: for his mercy endureth for ever.

PSALM CXIX.
Sundry prayers, praises, and professions of obedience.

ALEPH.

BLESSED are the undefiled in the way, who walk in the law of the LORD.
2 Blessed are they that keep his testimonies, and that seek him with the whole heart.
3 They also do no iniquity: they walk in his ways.
4 Thou hast commanded us to keep thy precepts diligently.
5 O that my ways were directed to keep thy statutes!
6 Then shall I not be ashamed, when I have respect unto all thy commandments.
7 I will praise thee with uprightness of heart, when I shall have learned thy righteous judgments.
8 I will keep thy statutes: O forsake me not utterly.

BETH.

9 Wherewithal shall a young man cleanse his way? By taking heed thereto according to thy word.
10 With my whole heart have I sought thee: O let me not wander from thy commandments.
11 Thy word have I hid in mine heart, that I might not sin against thee.
12 Blessed art thou, O LORD: teach me thy statutes.
13 With my lips have I declared all the judgments of thy mouth.
14 I have rejoiced in the way of thy testimonies, as much as in all riches.
15 I will meditate in thy precepts, and have respect unto thy ways.
16 I will delight myself in thy statutes: I will not forget thy word.

GIMEL.

17 Deal bountifully with thy servant, that I may live, and keep thy word.
18 Open thou mine eyes, that I may behold wondrous things out of thy law.
19 I am a stranger in the earth: hide not thy commandments from me.
20 My soul breaketh for the longing that it hath unto thy judgments at all times.
21 Thou hast rebuked the proud that are cursed, which do err from thy commandments.
22 Remove from me reproach and contempt; for I have kept thy testimonies.
23 Princes also did sit and speak against me: but thy servant did meditate in thy statutes.
24 Thy testimonies also are my delight, and my counsellors.

DALETH.

25 My soul cleaveth unto the dust: quicken thou me according to thy word.
26 I have declared my ways, and thou heardest me: teach me thy statutes.

PSALM CXVII.

Ver. 1, 2. This may be regarded as a doxology, suitable to be appended to any Psalm of similar character, and prophetical of the prevalence of God's grace in the world, in which aspect Paul quotes it, (Rom. 15. 11) (cf. Ps. 47. 2; 66. 8.). **2. is great toward us**—*lit.,* prevailed over, or, protected us.

PSALM CXVIII.

Ver. 1-29 After invoking others to unite in praise, the writer celebrates God's protecting and delivering care towards him, and then represents himself and the people of God as entering the sanctuary and uniting in solemn praise, with prayer for a continued blessing. Whether composed by David on his accession to power, or by some later writer in memory of the restoration from Babylon, its tone is joyful and trusting, and, in describing the fortune and destiny of the Jewish Church and its visible head, it is typically prophetical of the Christian Church and her greater and invisible Head. **1-4.** The trine repetitions are emphatic (cf. v. 10-12, 15, 16; Ps. 115. 12, 13.). Let ... say—as Ps. 115. 2; so in v. 3, 4. After "*now say*" supply "*give thanks.*" that his mercy—or, *for* his mercy. **5.** distress—*lit.,* straits, to which "large place" corresponds, as Ps. 4. 1; 31. 8. **6, 7.** Men are helpless to hurt him, if God be with him Ps. 56. 9,), and, if enemies, will be vanquished (Ps. 54. 7.. **8, 9.** Even the most powerful men are less to be trusted than God. **10-12.** Though as numerous and irritating as bees, by God's help his enemies would be destroyed, as the fire of thorns—suddenly. in the name, &c.—by the power Ps. 20. 5; 124. 8.). **13-16.** The enemy is triumphantly addressed as if present. rejoicing and salvation—the latter as cause of the former. right hand ... is exalted —His power greatly exerted. **17, 18.** He would live, because confident his life would be for God's glory. **19-21.** Whether an actual or figurative entrance into God's house be meant, the purpose of solemn praise is intimated, in which only the righteous would or could engage. **22, 23.** These words are applied by Christ (Mat. 21. 42) to Himself, as the foundation of the Church cf. Acts. 4. 11; Eph. 2. 20; 1 Pet. 2. 4, 7.). It may here denote God's wondrous exaltation to power and influence of him whom the rulers of the nation despised, whether (see above) David or Zerubbabel cf. Hag. 2. 2; Zech. 4. 7-10 be primarily meant, there is here typically represented God's more wonderful doings in exalting Christ, crucified as an impostor, to be the Prince and Saviour and Head of His Church. **24.** This is the day—or, period distinguished by God's favour of all others. **25.** Save now—Heb., Hosannah (cf. Ps. 115. 2, &c. as to *now*) a form of prayer (Ps. 20. 9 since, in our use, of praise. **26.** he that cometh ... Lord—As above intimated, this may be applied to the visible head of the Jewish Church entering the sanctuary, as leading the procession; typically it belongs to Him of whom the phrase became an epithet Mal. 3. 1; Mat. 21. 9.). **27-29.** showed us light—or, favour (Ps. 27. 1; 97. 11.). With the sacrificial victim brought bound to the altar is united the more spiritual offering of praise Ps. 50. 14, 23,), expressed in the terms with which the Psalm opened.

PSALM CXIX.

Ver. 1-176. This celebrated Psalm has several peculiarities. It is divided into twenty-two parts, or stanzas, denoted by the twenty-two letters of the Hebrew alphabet. Each stanza contains eight verses, and the first letter of each verse is that which gives name to the stanza. Its contents are mainly praises of God's word, exhortations to its perusal, and reverence for it, prayers for its proper influence, and complaints of the wicked for despising it. There are but two verses (122, 132) which do not contain some term or description of God's word. These terms are of various derivations, but here used, for the most part, synonymously, though the use of a variety of terms seems designed, in order to express better the several aspects in which our relations to the revealed word of God are presented. The Psalm does not appear to have any relation to any special occasion or interest of the Jewish Church or nation, but was evidently "intended as a manual of pious thoughts, especially for instructing the young, and its peculiar artificial structure was probably adopted to aid the memory in retaining the language."
1. undefiled—*lit.,* complete, perfect, or sincere (cf. Ps. 37. 37., in [or, *of*] the way—course of life. walk [act] in the law—according to it (cf. Luke, 1. 6.). Law, from a word meaning to teach, is a term of rather general purport, denoting the instruction of God's word. **2.** testimonies—The word of God is so called, because in it He *testifies* for truth and against sin. seek him—*i.e.*, a knowledge of Him, with desire for conformity to His will. **3.** his ways —the course He reveals as right. **4-6.** precepts —are those directions which relate to special conduct, from a word meaning to inspect. statutes—or, ordinances, positive laws of permanent nature. Both words originally denote rather positive than moral laws, such as derive force from the divine appointment whether their nature or the reasons for them are apprehended by us or not. commandments—or, institutions. The term is comprehensive, but rather denotes fundamental directions for conduct, both enjoining and forbidding. have respect unto—or, regard carefully as to their whole purport. **7.** judgments — rules of conduct formed by God's judicial decisions. Hence the wide sense of the word in the Psalms, so that it includes decisions of approval as well as condemnation. **8.** recognises the need of divine grace. **9.** The whole verse may be read as a question: for, By taking heed—is better, *For* taking heed, *i.e.,* so as to do it. The answer is implied, and inferable from v. 5, 10, 18, &c., *i.e.*, by God's grace. **10-16.** We must carefully treasure up the word of God, declare it to others, meditate on it, and heartily delight in it, and then by His grace we shall act according to it.
17-20. Life is desirable in order to serve God; that we may do so aright we should seek to have our eyes opened to behold His truth, and earnestly desire fully to understand it. **21-24.** God will rebuke those who despise His word, and deliver His servants from their reproach, giving them boldness in and by His truth, even before the greatest men. **25-27.** Submitting ourselves in depression to God, He will revive us by His promises, and lead us to declare His mercy to others. **28-32.** In order to adhere to His word we

Prayers, praises,   PSALM CXIX.   *and professions of obedience.*

27 Make me to understand the way of thy precepts: so shall I talk of thy wondrous works.
28 My soul melteth for heaviness: strengthen thou me according unto thy word.
29 Remove from me the way of lying; and grant me thy law graciously.
30 I have chosen the way of truth; thy judgments have I laid before me.
31 I have stuck unto thy testimonies: O LORD, put me not to shame.
32 I will run the way of thy commandments, when thou shalt enlarge my heart.

HE.

33 Teach me, O LORD, the way of thy statutes; and I shall keep it unto the end.
34 Give me understanding, and I shall keep thy law; yea, I shall observe it with my whole heart.
35 Make me to go in the path of thy commandments; for therein do I delight.
36 Incline my heart unto thy testimonies, and not to covetousness.
37 Turn away mine eyes from beholding vanity; *and* quicken thou me in thy way.
38 Stablish thy word unto thy servant, who *is devoted* to thy fear.
39 Turn away my reproach which I fear; for thy judgments *are* good.
40 Behold, I have longed after thy precepts: quicken me in thy righteousness.

VAU.

41 Let thy mercies come also unto me, O LORD, *even* thy salvation, according to thy word.
42 So shall I have wherewith to answer him that reproacheth me: for I trust in thy word.
43 And take not the word of truth utterly out of my mouth; for I have hoped in thy judgments.
44 So shall I keep thy law continually for ever and ever.
45 And I will walk at liberty: for I seek thy precepts.
46 I will speak of thy testimonies also before kings, and will not be ashamed.
47 And I will delight myself in thy commandments, which I have loved.
48 My hands also will I lift up unto thy commandments, which I have loved; and I will meditate in thy statutes.

ZAIN.

49 Remember the word unto thy servant, upon which thou hast caused me to hope.
50 This *is* my comfort in my affliction: for thy word hath quickened me.
51 The proud have had me greatly in derision; *yet* have I not declined from thy law.
52 I remembered thy judgments of old, O LORD; and have comforted myself.
53 Horror hath taken hold upon me because of the wicked that forsake thy law.
54 Thy statutes have been my songs in the house of my pilgrimage.
55 I have remembered thy name, O LORD, in the night, and have kept thy law.
56 This I had, because I kept thy precepts.

CHETH.

57 Thou *art* my portion, O LORD: I have said that I would keep thy words.
58 I entreated thy favour with *my* whole heart: be merciful unto me according to thy word.
59 I thought on my ways, and turned my feet unto thy testimonies.

60 I made haste, and delayed not to keep thy commandments.
61 The bands of the wicked have robbed me: *but* I have not forgotten thy law.
62 At midnight I will rise to give thanks unto thee because of thy righteous judgments.
63 I *am* a companion of all *them* that fear thee, and of them that keep thy precepts.
64 The earth, O LORD, is full of thy mercy: teach me thy statutes.

TETH.

65 Thou hast dealt well with thy servant, O LORD, according unto thy word.
66 Teach me good judgment and knowledge: for I have believed thy commandments.
67 Before I was afflicted I went astray; but now have I kept thy word.
68 Thou *art* good, and doest good: teach me thy statutes.
69 The proud have forged a lie against me: *but* I will keep thy precepts with *my* whole heart.
70 Their heart is as fat as grease; *but* I delight in thy law.
71 *It is* good for me that I have been afflicted; that I might learn thy statutes.
72 The law of thy mouth *is* better unto me than thousands of gold and silver.

JOD.

73 Thy hands have made me and fashioned me: give me understanding, that I may learn thy commandments.
74 They that fear thee will be glad when they see me; because I have hoped in thy word.
75 I know, O LORD, that thy judgments *are* right, and *that* thou in faithfulness hast afflicted me.
76 Let, I pray thee, thy merciful kindness be for my comfort, according to thy word unto thy servant.
77 Let thy tender mercies come unto me, that I may live: for thy law *is* my delight.
78 Let the proud be ashamed; for they dealt perversely with me without a cause: *but* I will meditate in thy precepts.
79 Let those that fear thee turn unto me, and those that have known thy testimonies.
80 Let my heart be sound in thy statutes, that I be not ashamed.

CAPH.

81 My soul fainteth for thy salvation; *but* I hope in thy word.
82 Mine eyes fail for thy word, saying, When wilt thou comfort me?
83 For I am become like a bottle in the smoke; *yet* do I not forget thy statutes.
84 How many are the days of thy servant? when wilt thou execute judgment on them that persecute me?
85 The proud have digged pits for me, which *are* not after thy law.
86 All thy commandments *are* faithful: they persecute me wrongfully; help thou me.
87 They had almost consumed me upon earth; but I forsook not thy precepts.
88 Quicken me after thy lovingkindness; so shall I keep the testimony of thy mouth.

LAMED.

89 For ever, O LORD, thy word is settled in heaven.
90 Thy faithfulness *is* unto all generations: thou hast established the earth, and it abideth.

Prayers, Praises, PSALM CXIX. *and Professions of Obedience.*

must seek deliverance from temptations to sin as well as from despondency. enlarge [or, expand] my heart—with gracious affections.

33-38. To encourage us in prayer for divine aid in adhering to His truth, we are permitted to believe that by His help we shall succeed, the way of thy statutes—*i.e.*, the way or manner of life prescribed by them. The help we hope to obtain by *prayer* is to be the basis on which our *resolutions* should rest. Turn away mine eyes—*lit.*, *Make my eyes to pass, not noticing evil.* vanity—*lit.*, *falsehood*, all other objects of trust than God; idols, human power, &c. (Ps. 31. 6; 40. 4; 60. 11; 62. 9.). quicken ... in thy way—make me with *living* energy to pursue the way marked out by thee. *Revive* me from the *death* of spiritual helplessness (v. 17, 25, 40, 50; Ps. 116. 3. . who is devoted to thy fear—or better, *which (i.e.,* thy word) *is for thy fear,* for producing it. "Which is to those who fear thee." God's word of promise belongs peculiarly to such (cf. Gen. 18. 19; 1 Ki. 2. 4; 8. 25.). [HENGST.] 39, 40. Our hope of freedom from the *reproach of inconsistency* is in God's power, quickening us to live according to His word, which He leads us to love. for thy judgments are good—the time must therefore be at hand when thy justice will turn the "reproach" from thy Church upon the world (Isa. 25. 8; 66. 5; Zeph. 2. 8-10.).

41-44. The sentiment more fully carried out. God's mercies and salvation, as revealed in His Word, provide hope of forgiveness for the past and security in a righteous course for the future. 42. The possession of God's gift of "salvation" v. 41 will be the Psalmist's answer to the foe's "reproach," that his hope was a fallacious one. 45-48. To freedom from reproach, when imbued with God's truth, there is added "great boldness in the faith," accompanied with increasing delight in the holy law itself, which becomes an element of happiness. 48. My hands...lift up unto ...commandments—*i.e.*, I will *prayerfully* (Ps. 28. 2) direct my heart to keep thy commandments.

49-51. Resting on the promises consoles under affliction and the tauntings of the insolent. 49. upon which—rather, "Remember thy word unto thy servant, *because,*" &c. So the Heb. requires. [HENGST.] 50. for—rather, "This is my comfort...*that,*" &c. [MAUR.] hath quickened—what the word *has already done* is to faith a pledge of what *it shall yet do.* 52-56. The pious take comfort, when harassed and distressed by wickedness of men who forsake God's law, in remembering that the great principles of God's truth will still abide; and also God's "judgments of old" v. 52, *i.e.*, His past interpositions in behalf of His people are a pledge that He will again interpose to deliver them; and they become the theme of constant and delightful meditation. The more we keep the more we love the law of God. 53. Horror—rather, "Vehement wrath." [HENGST.] 54. songs—the exile sings songs of his home (Ps. 137. 3.), so the child of God, "a stranger on earth," sings the songs of heaven, his true home (Ps. 39. 12.). In ancient times. laws were put in verse, to imprint them the more on the memory of the people. So God's laws are the believer's songs. house of my pilgrimage — present life (Gen. 17. 8; 47. 9; Heb. 11. 13.). 56. Rather, "This is peculiarly mine (*lit., to me,), that* I keep thy precepts." [HENGST. and MAUR.]

57-60. Sincere desires for God's favour, penitence, and activity in a new of edience, truly evince the sincerity of those who profess to find God a portion (Num. 18. 20; Ps. 16. 5; Lam. 3. 24.). 58. favour—*Heb.*, "face" (Ps. 45. 12.). 59. So the prodigal son, when reduced to straits of misery (Luke, 15. 17, 18.). 61, 62. This the more, if opposition of enemies, or love of ease, is overcome in thus honouring God's law. have robbed me—better, *surrounded* me, either as forcible constraints like fetters, or as the cords of their nets. HENGST. *transl.*, "snares." 62. At midnight—HENGST. supposes a reference to the time when the Lord went forth to slay the Egyptian first-born (Ex. 11. 4; 12. 29; cf. Job, 34. 20.). But it rather refers to the Psalmist's own praises and prayers in the night time. Cf. Paul and Silas (Acts, 16. 25; cf. Ps. 63. 6.). 63. The communion of the saints. Delight in their company is an evidence of belonging to them (Ps. 16. 3; Amos, 3. 3; Mal. 3. 16.). 64. While opposed by the wicked, and opposing them, the pious delight in those who fear God, but, alter all, rely for favour and guidance not on merit but mercy.

65-67. The reliance on promises (v. 49) is strengthened by experience of past dealings according with promises, and a prayer for guidance, encouraged by sanctified affliction. 66. Teach me good judgment and knowledge—viz., *in thy word* so as to fathom its deep spirituality; for the corresponding expression v. 12, 64, 68,), is "Teach me thy statutes." 67. Referred by HENGST. to the chastening effect produced on the Jews' minds by the captivity (Jer. 31. 18, 19.). The truth is a general one (Job, 5. 6; John, 15. 2; Feb. 12. 11.). 68. Cf. also to the Lord Jesus Acts, 10. 38.). 69, 70. The crafty malice of the wicked, in slandering him, so far from turning him away, but binds him closer to God's word, which they are too stupid in sin to appreciate, HENGST. refers the "lie" (v. 69) to such slanders against the Jews during the captivity, as that in Ezra, 4. of sedition. fat as grease—spiritually insensible (Is. 17. 10; 73. 7; Isa. 6. 10.). 71, 72. So also affliction of any kind acts as a wholesome discipline in leading the pious more highly to value the truth and promises of God.

73. As God made, so He can best control, us. So as to Israel, He owed to God his whole internal and external existence Deut. 32. 6.). 74. So when He has led us to rely on His truth, He will "make us to the praise of His grace" by others. "Those who fear thee will be glad at my prosperity, as they consider my cause their cause" (Ps. 34. 2; 142. 7.). 75-78. In faithfulness — *i.e.*, without in the least violating thy faithfulness; because my sins deserved and needed fatherly chastisement. Enduring chastisement with a filial temper (Heb. 12. 6-11.), God's promises of mercy Rom. 8. 28 will be fulfilled, and He will give comfort in sorrow (Lam. 3. 22; 2 Cor. 1. 3, 4.). 77. Let thy tender mercies come unto me—As I am not able to come unto them. But the wicked will be confounded. 78. but I ... meditate in thy precepts—and so shall not be "ashamed," *i.e.*, put to shame (v. 80.). 79, 80. These who may have thought his afflictions an evidence of God's rejection will then be led to return to Him; as the friends of Job did on his restoration, having been previously led through his afflictions to doubt the reality of his religion. Let my ...

Prayers, praises, PSALM CXIX. *and professions of obedience.*

91 They continue this day according to thine ordinances: for all *are* thy servants.
92 Unless thy law had been my delights, I should then have perished in mine affliction.
93 I will never forget thy precepts: for with them thou hast quickened me.
94 I *am* thine, save me; for I have sought thy precepts.
95 The wicked have waited for me to destroy me: *but* I will consider thy testimonies.
96 I have seen an end of all perfection: *but* thy commandment is exceeding broad.

MEM.

97 O how love I thy law! it is my meditation all the day.
98 Thou through thy commandments hast made me wiser than mine enemies; for they are ever with me.
99 I have more understanding than all my teachers: for thy testimonies *are* my meditation.
100 I understand more than the ancients, because I keep thy precepts.
101 I have refrained my feet from every evil way, that I might keep thy word.
102 I have not departed from thy judgments: for thou hast taught me.
103 How sweet are thy words unto my taste! *yea, sweeter* than honey to my mouth!
104 Through thy precepts I get understanding: therefore I hate every false way.

NUN.

105 Thy word *is* a lamp unto my feet, and a light unto my path.
106 I have sworn, and I will perform *it,* that I will keep thy righteous judgments.
107 I am afflicted very much: quicken me, O LORD, according unto thy word.
108 Accept, I beseech thee, the free-will offerings of my mouth, O LORD, and teach me thy judgments.
109 My soul *is* continually in my hand: yet do I not forget thy law.
110 The wicked have laid a snare for me: yet I erred not from thy precepts.
111 Thy testimonies have I taken as an heritage for ever: for they *are* the rejoicing of my heart.
112 I have inclined mine heart to perform thy statutes alway, *even* unto the end.

SAMECH.

113 I hate vain thoughts: but thy law do I love.
114 Thou *art* my hiding place and my shield: I hope in thy word.
115 Depart from me, ye evil-doers: for I will keep the commandments of my God.
116 Uphold me according unto thy word, that I may live: and let me not be ashamed of my hope.
117 Hold thou me up, and I shall be safe: and I will have respect unto thy statutes continually.
118 Thou hast trodden down all them that err from thy statutes: for their deceit *is* falsehood.
119 Thou puttest away all the wicked of the earth like dross: therefore I love thy testimonies.
120 My flesh trembleth for fear of thee; and I am afraid of thy judgments.

AIN.

121 I have done judgment and justice: leave me not to mine oppressors.

122 Be surety for thy servant for good: let not the proud oppress me.
123 Mine eyes fail for thy salvation, and for the word of thy righteousness.
124 Deal with thy servant according unto thy mercy, and teach me thy statutes.
125 I *am* thy servant; give me understanding, that I may know thy testimonies.
126 *It is* time for *thee,* LORD, to work; *for* they have made void thy law.
127 Therefore I love thy commandments above gold, yea, above fine gold.
128 Therefore I esteem all thy precepts concerning all *things to be* right; *and* I hate every false way.

PE.

129 Thy testimonies *are* wonderful: therefore doth my soul keep them.
130 The entrance of thy words giveth light; it giveth understanding unto the simple.
131 I opened my mouth, and panted: for I longed for thy commandments.
132 Look thou upon me, and be merciful unto me, as thou usest to do unto those that love thy name.
133 Order my steps in thy word: and let not any iniquity have dominion over me.
134 Deliver me from the oppression of man: so will I keep thy precepts.
135 Make thy face to shine upon thy servant; and teach me thy statutes.
136 Rivers of waters run down mine eyes, because they keep not thy law.

TZADDI.

137 Righteous *art* thou, O LORD, and upright *are* thy judgments.
138 Thy testimonies that thou hast commanded *are* righteous and very faithful.
139 My zeal hath consumed me; because mine enemies have forgotten thy words.
140 Thy word *is* very pure: therefore thy servant loveth it.
141 I *am* small and despised; *yet* do not I forget thy precepts.
142 Thy righteousness *is* an everlasting righteousness, and thy law is the truth.
143 Trouble and anguish have taken hold on me; yet thy commandments *are* my delights.
144 The righteousness of thy testimonies *is* everlasting: give me understanding, and I shall live.

KOPH.

145 I cried with *my* whole heart; hear me, O LORD: I will keep thy statutes.
146 I cried unto thee; save me, and I shall keep thy testimonies.
147 I prevented the dawning of the morning, and cried: I hoped in thy word.
148 Mine eyes prevent the *night* watches, that I might meditate in thy word.
149 Hear my voice, according unto thy lovingkindness: O LORD, quicken me according to thy judgment.
150 They draw nigh that follow after mischief: they are far from thy law.
151 Thou *art* near, O LORD; and all thy commandments *are* truth.
152 Concerning thy testimonies, I have known of old that thou hast founded them for ever.

RESH.

153 Consider mine affliction, and deliver me; for I do not forget thy law.

be sound—*i.e.*, *perfect, sincere.* ashamed—disappointed in my hope of salvation.
81-83. In sorrow the pious heart yearns for the comforts of God's promises (Ps. 73. 26; 84. 2.). 82. Mine eyes fail for thy word—*i.e.*, with yearning desire for thy word. When the eyes fail, yet faith must not. 83. bottle in the smoke —as a skin bottle dried and shrivelled up, in smoke, so is he withered by sorrow. Wine bottles of skin used to be hung up in smoke to dry them, before the wine was put in them. [MAUR.] 84-87. The shortness of my life requires that the relief afforded to me from mine enemies should be speedy. 85. pits—plots for my destruction. which—rather. "who," *i.e.*, *the proud:* "pits" is not the antecedent. 67. consumed me upon earth—HENGST. *transl.*, "in the land," understanding "me" of the *nation* Israel, of which but a small remnant was left. But E. V. is simpler; either "They have consumed me so as to leave almost nothing, of me on earth;" or, "They have almost destroyed and prostrated me on the earth." [MAUR.] 87. I forsook not—Whatever else I am forsaken of, I forsake not thy precepts, and so am not forsaken of thee (Ps. 59. 5, 13; 2 Cor. 4. 8, 9.), and the injuries and insults of the wicked increase the need for it. But, however they act regardless of God's law, the pious, adhering to its teaching, receive quickening grace, and are sustained stedfast.
88-91. In all changes God's word remains firm 1 Pet. 1. 25.). Like the heavens, it continually attests God's unfailing power and unchanging care (Ps. 89. 2.). is settled in— *i.e.*, stands as firmly as the heaven in which it dwells, whence it emanated. 90. 1 s. 33. 9.). 91. They—The heaven (*v.* 89) and the earth *v.* 90,). HENGST. *transl.*, "They stand *for* thy *judgments,*" *i.e.* ready, as obedient servants, to execute them. The usage of this Psalm favours this view. But see Jer. 33. 25. 92-94. Hence the pious are encouraged and inclined to seek a knowledge of it, and persevere amidst the efforts of those planning and *waiting* to destroy him. 92. my delights—*plur.*, not merely *delight,* but equal to all other delights. 93. The bounds of created perfection may be defined, but those of God's law in its nature, application, and influence, are infinite. There is no human thing so perfect, but that something is wanting to it; its limits are narrow, whereas God's law is of infinite breadth, reaching to all cases, perfectly meeting what each requires, and to all times (Ps. 19. 3, 6, 7-11; Eccl. 3. 11.). It cannot be cramped within any definitions of man's dogmatical systems. Man never outgrows the word. It does not shock the ignorant man with declared anticipations of discoveries which he had not yet made; whilst in it the man of science finds his newest discoveries by tacit anticipation provided for.
97. This characteristic love for God's law (cf. Ps. 1. 2) insures increase, 98-100., of knowledge, both of the matter of all useful, moral truth, and an experience of its application. 98. wiser than mine enemies—with all their carnal cunning (Deut. 4. 6, 8.). they are ever with me—The *Heb.* is, rather, *sing.*, "it is ever with me;" the commandments forming ONE *complete whole,* thy law. 100. more than the ancients—antiquity is no help against stupidity, where it does not accord with God's word [LUTHER] Job, 32. 7-9.). The Bible is the key of all knowledge, the history of the world, past, present, and to come Ps. 111. 10.). He who does the will of God shall know of the doctrine (John, 7. 17.). understanding—is practical skill (Ps. 2. 10; 32. 8.). 101-104. Avoidance of sinful courses is both the effect and means of increasing in divine knowledge (cf. Ps. 19. 10.. 105. Not only does the word of God inform us of His will, but, as a light on a path in darkness, shows us how to follow the right and avoid the wrong way. The lamp of the word is not the sun. He would blind our eyes in our present fallen state; but we may bless God for the light shining as in a dark place, to guide us until the Sun of Righteousness shall come, and we shall be made capable of seeing Him 2. Pet. 1. 19; Rev. 22. 4.). The lamp is fed with the oil of the Spirit. The allusion is to the lamps and torches carried at night before an Eastern caravan. 106-108. Such was the national covenant at Sinai and in the fields of Moab. 108. freewill offerings—the spontaneous expressions of his gratitude, as contrasted with the *appointed* "offerings" of the temple Hos. 14. 2; Heb. 13. 15.. He determines to pursue this way, relying on God's quickening power (*v.* 50) in affliction, and a gracious acceptance of his "spiritual sacrifices of prayer and praise" Ps. 50. 5, 14, 23.). 109, 110 In the midst of deadly perils (the phrase is drawn from the fact that what we carry in our hands may easily slip from them, Jud. 12. 3; 1 S. m. 28. 21; Job, 13. 14; cf. 1 Sam. 19. 5.), and exposed to crafty enemies, his safety and guidance is in the truth and promises of God, 111, 112. These he joyfully takes as his perpetual heritage, to perform the duties and receive the comforts they teach, evermore. 113. vain thoughts—better, unstable persons, *lit., divided men,* those of a *divided,* doubting mind (Jam. 1. 8, "a double minded man, [HENGST.], sceptics, or, sceptical notions as opposed to the certainty of God's word. 114. hiding place—(cf. Ps. 27. 5.). shield—Ps. 3. 3; 7. 10.). hope in thy word—confidently rest on its teachings and promises. 115-117. Hence he fears not wicked men, nor dreads disappointment, sustained by God in making His law the rule of life. Depart from me—Ye can do nothing with me; *for,* &c. (Ps. 6. 8.). 118-120. But the disobedient and rebellious will be visited by God's wrath, which impresses the pious with wholesome fear and awe. their deceit is falsehood—*i.e.*, all their cunning deceit, wherewith they seek to entrap the godly, *is in vain.* 120. The "judgments" are those on the wicked (*v.* 119.). Joyful hope goes hand in hand with fear Hab. 3. 16-18..
121-126. On the grounds of his integrity, desire for God's word, and covenant relation to Him, the servant of God may plead for His protecting care against the wicked, gracious guidance to the knowledge of truth, and His effective vindication of the righteous and their cause, which is also His own. Be surety—Stand for me against my oppressors (Gen. 43. 9; Isa. 38. 14.). 127, 128. Therefore (*i.e.*, In view of these benefits, or, Because of the glory of thy law, so much praised in the previous parts of the Psalm) I love, &c. [and] Therefore repented.—All its precepts, on all subjects, are estimable for their purity, and lead one imbued with their spirit to hate all evil (Ps. 19. 10.). The word of God admits of no eclecticism; its least tittle is perfect Ps 12. 6; Mat. 5. 17-19.).

Prayers and praises.   PSALMS CXX–CXXIV.   *Safety of God's people.*

154 Plead *h* my cause, and deliver me: quicken me according to thy word.
155 Salvation *i* is far from the wicked: for they seek not thy statutes.
156 [20] Great *are* thy tender mercies, O LORD: quicken me according to thy judgments.
157 Many *are* my persecutors and mine enemies; *yet* do I not decline from thy testimonies.
158 I beheld the transgressors, and was grieved; because they kept not thy word.
159 Consider how I love thy precepts: quicken me, O LORD, according to thy lovingkindness.
160 [21] Thy word *is* true *from* the beginning: and every one of thy righteous judgments *endureth* for ever.

SCHIN.

161 Princes *j* have persecuted me without a cause: but my heart standeth in awe of thy word.
162 I rejoice at thy word, as one that findeth great spoil.
163 I hate and abhor lying: *but* thy law do I love.
164 Seven times a day do I praise thee because of thy righteous judgments.
165 Great *k* peace have they which love thy law: and [22] nothing shall offend them.
166 LORD, I have hoped for thy salvation, and done thy commandments.
167 My soul hath kept thy testimonies; and I love them exceedingly.
168 I have kept thy precepts and thy testimonies: *l* for all my ways *are* before thee.

TAU.

169 Let my cry come near before thee, O LORD: give me understanding according to thy word.
170 Let my supplication come before thee: deliver me according to thy word.
171 My lips shall utter praise, when thou hast taught me thy statutes.
172 My tongue shall speak of thy word: for all thy commandments *are* righteousness.
173 Let thine hand help me: for *m* I have chosen thy precepts.
174 I have longed for thy salvation, O LORD; and thy law *is* my delight.
175 Let my soul live, and it shall praise thee; and let thy judgments help me.
176 I *n* have gone astray like a lost sheep: seek thy servant; for I do not forget thy commandments.

PSALM CXX.

David prays against Doeg, whose calumnies had driven him among strangers.

A Song of degrees.

IN my distress I cried unto the LORD, and he heard me.
2 Deliver my soul, O LORD, from lying lips, *and* from a deceitful tongue.
3 What shall be given unto thee? or what shall be [z] done unto thee, thou false tongue?
4 Sharp arrows of the mighty, with coals of juniper.
5 Woe is me, that I sojourn in *a* Mesech, *that b* I dwell in the tents of Kedar!
6 My soul hath long dwelt with him that hateth peace.
7 I am *[?]* for peace: but when I speak, they are for war.

PSALM 119.
h 1 Sa. 24.15.
Ps. 35. 1.
Mic. 7. 9.
i Job 5. 4.
28 Or, Many.
29 The beginning of thy word is true.
j 1 Sa. 24. 11.
k Pro. 3. 2.
Is. 32. 17.
30 they shall have no stumblingblock.
l Job 34. 22.
Pro. 5. 21.
m Lu. 10.42.
n Is. 53. 6.
Lu. 15. 4.
1 Pet. 2.25.

PSALM 120.
1 Or, What shall the deceitful tongue give unto thee? or, what shall it profit thee?
2 added.
3 Or, It is as the sharp arrows of the mighty man, with coals of juniper.
a Gen. 10. 2.
b Eze. 27.13.
b Gen. 25. 13.
1 Sa. 25. 1.
Jer. 49. 28.
4 Or, a man of peace.

PSALM 121.
1 Or, Shall I lift up mine eyes to the hills? whence should my help come?
a 1 Sa. 2. 9.
Pro. 3. 23.
b Is. 27. 3.
c Is. 49. 10.
Rev. 7. 16.
d Job 5. 19.
e Deu. 28. 6.
Pro. 2. 8.
Pro. 3. 6.

PSALM 122.
a Is. 2. 3.
Zech. 8.21.
b 2 Sam. 5.9.
Eph. 2. 21.
c Deu. 16. 16.
d Ex. 16. 36.
1 do sit.
Deu. 17. 8.
2 Chr.19 8.
e Is. 62. 6.
Jer. 51. 50.

PSALM 123.
a Heb. 13. 6.
Rom. 8.31.
b Ps. 57. 6.
Pro. 1. 11.

PSALM CXXI.
The great safety of the godly, who put their trust in God's protection.

A Song of degrees.

I [1] WILL lift up mine eyes unto the hills, from whence cometh my help.
2 My help *cometh* from the LORD, which made heaven and earth.
3 He *a* will not suffer thy foot to be moved: he *b* that keepeth thee will not slumber.
4 Behold, he that keepeth Israel shall neither slumber nor sleep.
5 The LORD *is* thy keeper: the LORD *is* thy shade upon thy right hand.
6 The *c* sun shall not smite thee by day, nor the moon by night.
7 The LORD shall *d* preserve thee from all evil: he shall preserve thy soul.
8 The LORD shall *e* preserve thy going out, and thy coming in, from this time forth, and even for evermore.

PSALM CXXII.

1 *David professes his joy for the church, and for placing the ark in Zion:* 6 *he prays for the peace thereof.*

A Song of degrees of David.

I WAS glad when they said unto me, *a* Let us go into the house of the LORD.
2 Our feet shall stand within thy gates, O Jerusalem.
3 Jerusalem is builded as a city that is compact *b* together:
4 Whither *c* the tribes go up, the tribes of the LORD, unto *d* the testimony of Israel, to give thanks unto the name of the LORD.
5 For there *l* are set thrones of judgment, the thrones of the house of David.
6 Pray *e* for the peace of Jerusalem: they shall prosper that love thee.
7 Peace be within thy walls, *and* prosperity within thy palaces.
8 For my brethren and companions' sakes, I will now say, Peace *be* within thee.
9 Because of the house of the LORD our God I will seek thy good.

PSALM CXXIII.

1 *The godly profess their confidence in God,* 3 *and pray to be delivered from contempt.*

A Song of degrees.

UNTO thee lift I up mine eyes, O thou that dwellest in the heavens.
2 Behold, as the eyes of servants *look* unto the hand of their masters, *and* as the eyes of a maiden unto the hand of her mistress; so our eyes *wait* upon the LORD our God, until that he have mercy upon us.
3 Have mercy upon us, O LORD, have mercy upon us: for we are exceedingly filled with contempt.
4 Our soul is exceedingly filled with the scorning of those that are at ease, *and* with the contempt of the proud.

PSALM CXXIV.

The godly bless God for a miraculous deliverance.

A Song of degrees of David.

IF it had not been the LORD who was *a* on our side, now may Israel say;
2 If it had not been the LORD who was on our side, when men rose up against us:
3 Then they had *b* swallowed us up quick, when their wrath was kindled against us:
4 Then the waters had overwhelmed us, the stream had gone over our soul:
5 Then the proud waters had gone over our soul.
6 Blessed *be* the LORD, who hath not given us *as* a prey to their teeth.

129. wonder'ul—*lit.*, *wonders*, *i.e.*, of moral excellence. 130. The entrance—*lit.*, *opening*; God's words, as an open door, let in light, or knowledge. Rather, as HENGST. explains it, "*The opening up*," or "*explanation* of thy word." To the natural man the doors of God's word are shut. Luke, 24. 27, 31; Acts, 17. 3; Eph. 1. 18, confirms this view, "*Opening* (*i.e.*, explaining) and alleging," &c. unto the simple—those needing or desiring it (cf. Ps. 19. 7.). 131-135. An ardent desire (cf. Ps. 56. 1, 2) for spiritual enlightening, establishment in a right course, deliverance from the wicked, and evidence of God's favour is expressed. I opened my mouth, and panted—as a traveller in a hot desert pants for the cooling breeze (Ps. 63. 1; 84. 2.). Look . . . upon me—or—posed to hiding or averting the face cf. Ps. 80. 15; 86. 6; 102. 17.). as thou usest to do—or, "as it is *right* in regard to those who love thy name." Such have a *right* to the manifestations of God's grace, resting on the nature of God as faithful to his promises to such, not on their own merits. Order my steps—*Make firm*, so that there be no halting Ps. 40. 2., any iniquity—v. 34 favours HENGST., "any iniquitous man," any "oppressor." But the parallel first clause in this (*v.* 33.), favours E V. (Ps. 19. 13.). His hope of deliverance from *external* oppression of man (*v.* 34. is founded on his deliverance from the *internal* "dominion of iniquity," in answer to his prayer (*v.* 33.). 136. Zealous himself to keep God's law, he is deeply afflicted when others violate it cf. *v.* 53.). *Lit.*, *Mine eyes come down* dissolved) *like water brooks* (Lam. 3. 48; Jer. 9. 1.), because, &c.— cf. Ez. 9. 4; Jer. 13. 17. 137-139. God's justice and faithfulness in His government aggravate the neglect of the wicked, and more excite the lively zeal of His people. 139. (Ps. 69. 9.) 140. very pure—*lit.*, *refined*, shown pure by trial. 141. The pious, however despised of men, are distinguished in God's sight by a regard for His law. 142-144. The principles of God's government are permanent and reliable, and in the deepest distress His people find them a theme of delightful meditation and a source of reviving power (*v.* 17, 116.). everlasting—Ps. 111. 3., though to outward appearance seeming dead. law is truth—it therefore can not deceive as to its promises. 145-149. An intelligent devotion is led by divine promises, and is directed to an increase of gracious affections, arising from a contemplation of revealed truth. prevented —*lit.*, *came before*, anticipated, not only the *dawn*, but even the usual periods of *the night;* when the night watches, which might be expected to find me asleep, come, they find me awake (Ps. 63. 6; 77. 4; Lam. 2. 19.). Such is the earnestness of the desire and love for God's truth. quicken me—revive my heart according to those principles of justice, founded on thine own nature, and revealed in thy law, which specially set forth thy mercy to the humble as well as justice to the wicked (cf. *v.* 30.. 150-152. Though the wicked are *near* to injure, because *far* from God's law. He is *near* to help, and faithful to His word. which abides for ever. 153-155. Though the remembering of God's law is not meritorious, yet it evinces a filial temper, and provides the pious with promises to plead, while the wicked, in neglecting His law, reject God and despise His promises (cf. Ps. 9. 13; 43. 1; 69. 18.). 154. Plead, &c.—

HENGST. *transl.*, "Fight my fight." (See Ps. 35. 1; 43. 1; Mic. 7. 9.. 156. Cf. *v.* 149.. 157 (Cf. *v.* 86, 87, 95.). 158. Cf. *v.* 1. 6.. transgressors—or, *lit.*, *traitors*, who are faithless to a righteous sovereign, and side with His enemies (cf. Ps. 25. 3. 8.. 159. Cf. *v.* 121-126;153-155.). quicken, &c.— *v.*88.. This prayer occurs here for the ninth time, showing a deep sense of frailty. 160. God has been ever faithful, and the principles of His government will ever continue worthy of confidence. from the beginning—*i.e.*, "every word *from Genesis* called by the Jews from its first words, 'In the beginning') to the end of the Scriptures is true." HENGST. *transl.* more *lit.*, "The *sum* of thy words is truth." The sense is substantially the same. The whole body of revelation is truth. "Thy word is nothing but truth." [LUTHER.] 161-165. (Cf, *v.* 46, 86.. 161. awe—reverential, not slavish fear, which could not co-exist with love (*v.* 163; 1 John, 4. 8.). Instead of fearing his persecutors, he fears God's word alone Luke, 12, 4, 5.). the Jews inscribe in the first page of the great Bible (Gen. 28.), "How dreadful is this place! This is none other but the house of God, and this is the gate of heaven" 162. (Cf. Mat. 13. 44, 45.). Though persecuted by the mighty, the pious are not turned from revering God's authority to seek their favour, but rejoice in the possession of this "pearl of great price," as great victors in spoils. Hating falsehood and loving truth, often, every day, praising God for it, they find peace and freedom from temptation. 163. lying—*i.e.*, as in *v.* 29, unfaithfulness to the covenant of God with His people; apostasy.)othing shall offend them—or, *cause them* to offend cf. *Marg.*). 166-168. As they keep God's law from motives of love for it, and are free from slavish fear, they are ready to subject their lives to His inspection. 168. all my ways are before thee—I wish to order my ways as before thee, rather than in reference to man (Gen. 17. 1; Ps. 73. 23.). All men's ways are under God's eye Pro. 5. 21;; the godly alone realise the fact and live accordingly. 169, 170. The prayer for *understanding* of the truth precedes that for *deliverance*. The fulfilment of the first is the basis of the fulfilment of the second (Ps. 90. 11-17.). On the terms "cry" and "supplication" (cf. Ps. 6. 9;17. 1.). 171, 172. shall utter—or, *pour* out praise (cf. Ps. 19. 2;); shall cause thy praises to stream forth as from a bubbling, overflowing fountain. My tongue shall speak thy word—*lit.*, *answer thy word*, *i.e.*, with praise, *respond to thy word*. Every expression in which we praise God and His word is a response. An acknowledgement, corresponding to the perfections of Him whom we praise. 173, 174. (Cf. *v.* 77, 81, 92.. I have chosen—in preference to all other objects of delight. 175. Save me that I may praise thee. thy judgments—as *v.* 149, 156. 176. Though a wanderer from God, the truly pious ever desires to be drawn back to Him, and though for a time negligent of duty, never forgets the commandments by which it is taught. lost:—therefore utterly helpless as to recovering itself (Jer. 50. 6; Luke, 15. 4.). Not only the sinner before conversion, but the believer after conversion, is unable to recover himself; but the latter, after temporary wandering, knows to whom to look for restoration. These last two verses seem to sum up the petitions.

Grateful acknowledgments   PSALMS CXXV–CXXXII.   *of deliverance.*

7 Our soul is escaped as a bird out of the snare of the fowlers: the snare is broken, and we are escaped.
8 Our help *is* in the name of the LORD, who made heaven and earth.

PSALM CXXV.

1 *Safety of such as trust in God.* 4 *Prayer for the godly, and against the wicked.*

A Song of degrees.

THEY that trust in the LORD *shall be* as mount Zion, *which* cannot be removed, *but* abideth for ever.
2 *As* the mountains *are* round about Jerusalem, so the LORD *is* round about his people from henceforth, even for ever.
3 For the rod of *the* wicked shall not rest upon the lot of the righteous; lest the righteous put forth their hands unto iniquity.
4 Do good, O LORD, unto *those that be* good, and to *them that are* upright in their hearts.
5 As for such as turn aside unto their crooked *ways*, the LORD shall lead them forth with the workers of iniquity: *but* peace *shall be* upon Israel.

PSALM CXXVI.

1 *The church, celebrating her incredible return out of captivity,* 4 *prays for, and prophesies the good success thereof.*

A Song of degrees.

WHEN the LORD turned again the captivity of Zion, we were like them that dream.
2 Then *was* our mouth filled with laughter, and our tongue with singing: then said they among the heathen, The LORD hath done great things for them.
3 The LORD hath done great things for us; *whereof* we are glad.
4 Turn again our captivity, O LORD, as the streams in the south.
5 They that sow in tears shall reap in joy.
6 He that goeth forth and weepeth, bearing precious seed, shall doubtless come again with rejoicing, bringing his sheaves *with him.*

PSALM CXXVII.

1 *The vanity of human endeavours without God's blessing.* 3 *Children are his gift.*

A Song of degrees for Solomon.

EXCEPT the LORD build the house, they labour in vain that build it: except the LORD keep the city, the watchman waketh *but* in vain.
2 *It is* vain for you to rise up early, to sit up late, to eat the bread of sorrows: for so he giveth his beloved sleep.
3 Lo, children *are* an heritage of the LORD: *and* the fruit of the womb *is* his reward.
4 As arrows *are* in the hand of a mighty man; so *are* children of the youth.
5 Happy *is* the man that hath his quiver full of them: they shall not be ashamed, but they shall speak with the enemies in the gate.

PSALM CXXVIII.

Sundry blessings which follow those who fear God.

A Song of degrees.

BLESSED *is* every one that feareth the LORD; that walketh in his ways.
2 For thou shalt eat the labour of thine hands: happy *shalt* thou *be*, and *it shall be* well with thee.
3 Thy wife *shall be* as a fruitful vine by the sides of thine house: thy children like olive plants round about thy table.
4 Behold, that thus shall the man be blessed that feareth the LORD.
5 The LORD shall bless thee out of Zion: and thou shalt see the good of Jerusalem all the days of thy life.
6 Yea, thou shalt see thy children's children, *and* peace upon Israel.

PSALM CXXIX.

1 *God's goodness in saving Israel out of their great afflictions.* 5 *Prayer against the haters of the church.*

A Song of degrees.

MANY a time have they afflicted me from my youth, may Israel now say:
2 Many a time have they afflicted me from my youth: yet they have not prevailed against me.
3 The plowers plowed upon my back; they made long their furrows.
4 The LORD *is* righteous: he hath cut asunder the cords of the wicked.
5 Let them all be confounded and turned back that hate Zion.
6 Let them be as the grass upon the house-tops, which withereth afore it groweth up:
7 Wherewith the mower filleth not his hand, nor he that bindeth sheaves his bosom.
8 Neither do they which go by say, The blessing of the LORD *be* upon you: we bless you in the name of the LORD.

PSALM CXXX.

The psalmist in distress professes his hope in God; 5 *his patience in hope;* 7 *exhorts Israel to hope in God.*

A Song of degrees.

OUT of the depths have I cried unto thee, O LORD.
2 Lord, hear my voice: let thine ears be attentive to the voice of my supplications.
3 If thou, LORD, shouldest mark iniquities, O Lord, who shall stand?
4 But *there is* forgiveness with thee, that thou mayest be feared.
5 I wait for the LORD, my soul doth wait, and in his word do I hope.
6 My soul *waiteth* for the Lord more than they that watch for the morning; *I say,* more *than* they that watch for the morning.
7 Let Israel hope in the LORD: for with the LORD *there is* mercy, and with him *is* plenteous redemption.
8 And he shall redeem Israel from all his iniquities.

PSALM CXXXI.

1 *David, professing his humility,* 3 *exhorts Israel to hope in God.*

A Song of degrees of David.

LORD, my heart is not haughty, nor mine eyes lofty: neither do I exercise myself in great matters, or in things too high for me.
2 Surely I have behaved and quieted myself, as a child that is weaned of his mother: my soul *is* even as a weaned child.
3 Let Israel hope in the LORD from henceforth and for ever.

PSALM CXXXII.

1 *David's prayer at the removing of the ark,* 11 *with a repetition of God's promises.*

A Song of degrees.

LORD, remember David, *and* all his afflictions;
2 How he sware unto the LORD, *and* vowed unto the mighty God of Jacob;

Safety of the Godly.   PSALMS CXX—CXXVII.   *Their Confidence in God.*

confessions, and professions of the Psalm. The writer desires God's favour, that he may praise Him for His truth, confesses that he has erred, but, in the midst of his wanderings and adversities, professes an abiding attachment to the revealed word of God, the theme of such repeated eulogies, and the recognised source of such great and unnumbered blessings. Thus the Psalm, though more than usually didactic, is made the medium of both parts of devotion—prayer and praise.

PSALM CXX.

Ver. 1-7. This is the first of fifteen Psalms, (120-134,), entitled, "A Song of degrees" 121st—*lit.,* A Song *for* the degrees, , or *ascents.* It seems most probable they were designed for the use of the people, when *going up* cf. 1 Ki. 12. 27, 28; to Jerusalem on the festival occasions (Deut. 16. 16,), three times a-year. David appears as the author of four, Solomon of one (127.) and the other ten are anonymous, probably composed after the captivity. In this Psalm the writer acknowledges God's mercy, prays for relief from a malicious foe, whose punishment he anticipates, and then repeats his complaint.

2, 3. Slander and deceit charged on his foes implies his innocence. tongue—as Ps. 52, 2, 4. 4. coals of juniper—which retain heat long. Sharp arrows of the mighty—Destructive inflictions. This verse may be read as a description of the wicked, but better as their punishment, in reply to the question of *v.* 3. 5. A residence in these remote lands pictures his miserable condition. 6, 7. While those who surrounded him were maliciously hostile, he was disposed to peace. This Psalm may well begin such a series as this, as a contrast to the promised joys of God's worship.

PSALM CXXI.

Ver. 1-8. God's guardian care of His people celebrated.

1. To *lift up the eyes* expresses desire 'cf. Ps. 25. 1.,' mingled with expectation. The last clause, read as a question, is answered. 2. by avowing God to be the helper, of whose ability His creative power is a pledge (Ps. 115. 16,), to which, 3, 4., His sleepless vigilance is added. to be moved—(cf. 1 s. 38. 16; 66. 9.). 5. upon thy right hand—a protector's place (Ps. 109. 31; 110. 5.). 6-8. God keeps His people at all times and in all perils. nor the moon by night—poetically represents the dangers of the night, over which the moon presides Gen. 1. 16.. thy going out, &c.—All thy ways (Deut. 28. 19; Ps. 104. 23,). evermore—includes a future state.

PSALM CXXII.

Ver. 1-8. This Psalm might well express the sacred joy of the pilgrims on entering the holy city, where praise, as the religious as well as civil metropolis, is celebrated, and for whose prosperity, as representing the Church, prayer is offered.

1, 2. Our feet shall stand—*lit., are standing.* gates—(cf. Ps. 9. 14; 87. 2.). 3-5. compact together —All parts united, as in David's time. testimony—If *unto* is supplied, this may denote the ark Ex. 25. 10-21;'; otherwise the *act of going* is denoted, called a *testimony* in allusion to the requisition Deut. 16. 16,), with which it was a compliance. there are set thrones—or, *do sit, thrones* used for the occupants, David's sons 2 Sam. 8. 18.). 6, 7. Let peace, including prosperity, every where prevail. 8, 9. As the welfare of the city, in

its civil, and especially the religious relations, was involved that of Israel. now—as Ps. 115 2. Let me say—house of . . . God—in wider sense, the Church, whose welfare would be promoted by the good of Jerusalem.

PSALM CXXIII.

Ver. 1-4. An earnest and expecting prayer for divine aid in distress.
1. (Cf. Ps. 121. 1.). thou that dwellest—*lit., sittest as enthroned* cf. Ps. 2. 4; 113. 4, 5.. 2. Deference, submission, and trust, are all expressed by the figure. 3. *The contempt* was that of the heathen, and, perhaps, Samaritans (Neh. 1. 3; 2. 19.). 4. of these that are at ease—self-complacently, disregarding God's law, and despising His people.

PSALM CXXIV.

Ver. 1-8. The writer, for the Church praises God for past, and expresses trust for future, deliverance from foes.
1, 2. on our side—for us (Ps. 56. 9.). now—or, *oh!* let Israel, &c. rose . . . against, &c.— Ps. 3. 1; 56. 11.'. Then—*i.e.* The time of our danger. quick—*lit., living* (Num. 16. 32, 33,), description of ferocity. 4, 5. Cf. Ps. 18. 4, 16.. The epithet *proud* added to *waters* denotes insolent enemies. 6, 7. The figure is changed to that of a rapacious wild beast (Ps. 3. 7,), and then of a fowler (Ps. 91. 3,), and complete escape is denoted by breaking the net. 8. (Cf. Ps. 121. 2.). name—in the usual sense Ps. 5. 11; 20. 1.).

PSALM CXXV.

Ver. 1-5. God honours the confidence of His people, by protection and deliverance, and leaves hypocrites to the doom of the wicked.

1, 2. mount Zion—as an emblem of permanence, and the locality of Jerusalem as one of security, represent the firm and protected condition of God's people (cf. Ps. 46. 5,). They that trust—(v. 1.), are "His people," v. 2.). 3. *Though* God may leave them for a time under the *rod,* or, *power* Ps. 2. 9,) and oppression of the wicked as a chastisement, He will not suffer them to be tempted so as to fall into sin 1 Cor. 10. 13.'. 4. Cf. Ps. 7. 10; 84. 11.;. 5. Those who turn aside under temptation) permanently, show that they are hypocrites, and their lot or portion shall be with the wicked (Ps. 28. 3.). crooked ways—(cf. Deut. 9. 16; Mal. 2. 8, 9,). The byeways of sin from the way of life.

PSALM CXXVI.

Ver. 1-6. To praise for God's favour to His people is added a prayer for its continued manifestation.

1-3. The joy of those returned from Babylon was ecstatic, and elicited the admiration even of the heathen, as illustrating God's great power and goodness. turned again the captivity—*i.e.* restored from it Job, 9. 12.; Ps. 14. 7; Pro. 12. 14.). 4. All did not return at once; hence the prayer for repeated favours. as the streams in the south—or, the torrents reappearing after dry seasons. 5, 6. As in husbandry, the sower may cast his seed in a dry and parched soil, with desponding fears, so those shall reap abundant fruit who toil in tears with the prayer of faith. Cf. the history (Ezra, 6. 16, 22.).

PSALM CXXVII.

Ver. 1-5. The theme of this Psalm, *that human enterprises only succeed by the divine blessing,* was probably associated with the building of the temple by Solomon, its author. It may have been adopted in this

3 Surely I will not come into the tabernacle of my house, nor go up into my bed;
4 I will ᵃ not give sleep to mine eyes, or slumber to mine eyelids,
5 Until I find out a place for the LORD, ¹ an habitation for the mighty God of Jacob.
6 Lo, we heard of it ᵇ at Ephratah; ᶜ we found it ᵈ in the fields of the wood.
7 We will go into his tabernacles; we will worship at his footstool.
8 Arise, ᵉ O LORD, into thy rest; thou, and the ark of thy strength.
9 Let thy priests ᶠ be clothed with righteousness; and let thy saints shout for joy.
10 For thy servant David's sake turn not away the face of thine anointed.
11 The LORD hath sworn in truth unto David; he will not turn from it; ᵍ Of the fruit of ² thy body will I set upon thy throne.
12 If thy children will keep my covenant and my testimony that I shall teach them, their children shall also sit upon thy throne for evermore.
13 For the LORD hath chosen Zion; he hath desired it for his habitation.
14 This is my rest for ever: here will I dwell; for I have desired it.
15 I will ʰ abundantly bless her provision: I will satisfy her poor with bread.
16 I ʰ will also clothe her priests with salvation; ⁱ and her saints shall shout aloud for joy.
17 There ʲ will I make the horn of David to bud: I have ordained a ᵏ lamp for mine anointed.
18 His enemies will I clothe with shame: but upon himself shall his crown flourish.

PSALM CXXXIII.
Benefit of the communion of saints.
A Song of degrees of David.

BEHOLD, how good and how pleasant it is for ᵃ brethren to dwell ¹ together in unity!
2 It is like ᵇ the precious ointment upon the head, that ran down upon the beard, even Aaron's beard; that went down to the skirts of his garments;
3 As the dew of ᶜ Hermon, and as the dew that descended upon the mountains of Zion: for ᵈ there the LORD commanded the blessing, even life for evermore.

PSALM CXXXIV.
An exhortation to bless God.
A Song of degrees.

BEHOLD, bless ye the LORD, all ye servants of the LORD, ᵃ which by night stand in the house of the LORD.
2 Lift ᵇ up your hands ¹ in the sanctuary, and bless the LORD.
3 The ᶜ LORD that made heaven and earth bless ᵈ thee out of Zion.

PSALM CXXXV.
1 *Exhortation to God's servants to praise him for his mercy, 5 power, 8 and judgments. 15 Vanity of idols. 19 Exhortation to bless God.*

PRAISE ye the LORD. Praise ye the name of the LORD; praise him, O ye servants of the LORD.
2 Ye ᵃ that stand in the house of the LORD, in the courts of the house of our God,
3 Praise the LORD; for the LORD is good: sing praises unto his name; for it is pleasant.
4 For ᵇ the LORD hath chosen Jacob unto himself, and Israel for his peculiar treasure.

PSALM 132.
ᵃ Pro. 6. 4.
1 habitations.
ᵇ Josh. 18. 1.
1 Sam. 17. 12.
ᶜ 1 Sa. 7. 1.
ᵈ 1 Chr. 13 5.
ᵉ Nu. 10. 36.
2 Chr. 6. 41.
ᶠ Job 29. 14. Is. 61. 10.
ᵍ 2 Sa. 7. 12. Lu. 1. 69.
Acts 2. 30.
2 thy belly.
3 Or, surely.
ʰ 2 Chr. 6.41.
ⁱ Hos. 11.12.
ʲ Ezek. 29. 21.
Lu. 1. 69.
4 Or, candle.

PSALM 133.
ᵃ Gen. 13. 8.
1 Cor. 1. 10.
Heb. 13. 1.
1 even together.
ᵇ Ex. 30. 30.
ᶜ Deu. 4. 48.
ᵈ Lev. 25 21.
Deu. 28. 8.
Ps. 42. 8.

PSALM 134.
ᵃ 1 Chr. 9. 33.
ᵇ 1 Tim. 2. 8.
1 Or, in holiness.
ᶜ Ps. 124. 8.
ᵈ Ps. 128. 5.

PSALM 135.
ᵃ Deut. 10. 17.
ᵇ 1 Tim. 6. 15.
Rev. 17.14.
ᶜ Pro. 3. 19.
Jer. 51. 15.
ᵈ Job 26. 7.
Jer. 10. 12.
ᵉ Deu. 4. 19.
1 for the ruling of day.
ᶠ Ex. 12. 51.
ᵍ Ex. 14. 21.
Ps. 75. 13.
2 shaked off.
ʰ Deu. 6. 15.

5 For I know that the LORD is great, and that our Lord is above all gods.
6 Whatsoever the LORD pleased, that did he in heaven, and in earth, in the seas, and all deep places.
7 He ᶜ causeth the vapours to ascend from the ends of the earth; ᵈ he maketh lightnings for the rain: he bringeth the wind out of his ᵉ treasuries.
8 Who smote the first-born of Egypt, ¹ both of man and beast.
9 Who sent tokens and wonders into the midst of thee, O Egypt, upon Pharaoh, and upon all his servants.
10 Who ᶠ smote great nations, and slew mighty kings;
11 Sihon king of the Amorites, and Og king of Bashan, and ᵍ all the kingdoms of Canaan:
12 And gave their land for an heritage, an heritage ʰ unto Israel his people.
13 Thy ⁱ name, O LORD, endureth for ever; and thy memorial, O LORD, ² throughout all generations.
14 For ʲ the LORD will judge his people, and he will repent himself concerning his servants.
15 The idols of the heathen are silver and gold, the work of men's hands.
16 They have mouths, but they speak not; eyes have they, but they see not;
17 They have ears, but they hear not; neither is there any breath in their mouths.
18 They that make them are like unto them; so is every one that trusteth in them.
19 Bless the LORD, O house of Israel: bless the LORD, O house of Aaron.
20 Bless the LORD, O house of Levi: ye that fear the LORD, bless the LORD.
21 Blessed be the LORD out of Zion, which dwelleth at Jerusalem. Praise ye the LORD.

PSALM CXXXVI.
Exhortation to praise God for particular mercies.

O GIVE thanks unto the LORD; for he is good: for his mercy endureth for ever.
2 O give thanks unto ᵃ the God of gods: for his mercy endureth for ever.
3 O give thanks to the ᵇ Lord of lords: for his mercy endureth for ever.
4 To him who alone doeth great wonders: for his mercy endureth for ever.
5 To ᶜ him that by wisdom made the heavens: for his mercy endureth for ever.
6 To ᵈ him that stretched out the earth above the waters: for his mercy endureth for ever.
7 To ᵉ him that made great lights: for his mercy endureth for ever:
8 The sun ¹ to rule by day: for his mercy endureth for ever:
9 The moon and stars to rule by night: for his mercy endureth for ever.
10 To him that smote Egypt in their firstborn: for his mercy endureth for ever:
11 And ᶠ brought out Israel from among them: for his mercy endureth for ever:
12 With a strong hand, and with a stretched-out arm: for his mercy endureth for ever.
13 To ᵍ him which divided the Red sea into parts: for his mercy endureth for ever:
14 And made Israel to pass through the midst of it: for his mercy endureth for ever:
15 But ² overthrew Pharaoh and his host in the Red sea: for his mercy endureth for ever.
16 To ʰ him which led his people through

Blessings of the Godly. PSALMS CXXVIII–CXXXIV. *David's Care for the Ark.*

view, as suited to this series especially, as appropriately expressing the sentiments of God's worshippers in relation to the erection of the second temple.

1, 2. suggest the view of the theme given, so he giveth his beloved sleep—*i.e.*, His providential care gives sleep which no efforts of ours can otherwise procure, and this is a reason for trust as to other things (cf. Mat. 6. 26-32.). 3-5. Posterity is often represented as a blessing from God Gen. 30. 2, 18; 1 Sam. 1. 19, 20.). Children are represented as the defenders *(arrows)* of their parents in war, and in litigation, *adversaries in the gate*, or place of public business (cf. Job, 5. 4; Ps. 69. 12.).

PSALM CXXVIII.

Ver. 1-6. The temporal blessings of true piety.

1. (Cf. Ps. 1. 1.). 2. For thou shalt eat—*i.e.*, It is a blessing to live on the fruits of one's own industry. 3. by the sides—or, within (Ps. 48. 2.). olive plants are peculiarly luxuriant (Ps. 52. 8.). 5. In temporal blessings the pious do not forget the richer blessings of God's grace, which they shall ever enjoy. 6. Long life crowns all other temporal favours. As Ps. 125. 5, this Psalm closes with a prayer for peace, with prosperity for God's people.

PSALM CXXIX.

Ver. 1-8. The people of God, often delivered from enemies, are confident of His favour, by their overthrow in future.

1, 2. may Israel now say—or, oh! let Israel say (Ps. 124. 1.). Israel's youth was the sojourn in Egypt (Jer. 2. 2; Hos. 2. 15.). prevailed—*lit., been able, i.e.*, to accomplish their purpose against me (Ps. 13. 4.). 3, 4. The *ploughing* is a figure of scourging, which most severe physical infliction aptly represents all kinds. the cords—*i.e.*, which fasten the plough to the ox; and *cutting*, this denotes God's arresting the persecution. 5, 6. The ill-rooted roof grass, which withers before it grows up, and procures for those gathering it no harvest blessing (Ruth, 2, 4,), sets forth the utter uselessness, and the rejection of the wicked.

PSALM CXXX.

Ver. 1-8. The penitent sinner's hope is in God's mercy only.

1, 2. depths—for great distress (Ps. 40. 2; 69. 3.). 3. shouldest mark—or, take notice, implying a confession of the existence of sin, who shall stand—(Ps. 1. 6.). The question implies a negative, which is thus more strongly stated. 4. Pardon produces filial fear. 5, 6. wait for the Lord—in expectation (Ps. 27. 14.). watch for, &c.—in earnestness and anxiety. 7, 8. Let Israel, &c.—*i.e.*, All are invited to seek and share divine forgiveness, from all his iniquities—or, punishments of them (Ps. 40. 12. &c.).

PSALM CXXXI.

Ver. 1-3. This Psalm, while expressive of David's pious feelings on assuming the royal office, teaches the humble submissive temper of a true child of God.

1. eyes l.fty—a sign of pride (Ps. 18. 27.). exercise myself—*lit., walk about*, or *meddle with*. 2. Surely, &c.—The form is that of an oath, or strongest assertion. Submission is denoted by the figure of a weaned child. Soul may be taken for desire, which gives a more definite sense, though one included in the idea conveyed by the usual meaning, *myself*.

PSALM CXXXII.

Ver. 1-18. The writer, perhaps Solomon (cf. *v.* 8, 9,), after relating David's pious zeal for God's service, pleads for the fulfilment of the promise (2 Sam. 7. 16,), which, providing for a perpetuation of David's kingdom, involved that of God's right worship and the establishment of the greater and spiritual kingdom of David's greater son. Of Him and His kingdom both the temple and its worship, and the kings and kingdom of Judah, were types. The congruity of such a topic, with the tenor of this series of Psalms, is obvious.

1-5. This vow is not elsewhere recorded. It expresses, in strong language, David's intense desire to see the establishment of God's worship as well as of His kingdom. remember David—*lit., remember for David, i.e.*, all his troubles and anxieties on the matter. habitation—*lit., dwellings*, generally used to denote the sanctuary. 6. These may be the "words of David" and his pious friends, who, at Ephratah, or Bethlehem Gen. 48. 7,), where he once lived, may have heard of the ark, which he found for the first time, in the fields of the wood—or, *Jair*, or *Kirjath-jearim* City of woods (1 Sam. 7. 1; 2 Sam. 6. 3, 4.), whence it was brought to Zion. 7. The purpose of engaging in God's worship is avowed. 8, 9. The solemn entry of the ark, symbolical of God's presence and power, with the attending priests, into the sanctuary, is proclaimed in the words used by Solomon (2 Chr. 6. 41.). 10-12. For thy servant David's sake [*i.e.*, On account of the promise made to him] urn ... anointed—Repulse not him who, as David's descendant, pleads the promise to perpetuate his royal line. After reciting the promise, substantially from 2 Sam. 7. 12-16, cf. Acts, 2. 30. &c.), an additional plea, 13., is made on the ground of God's choice of Zion there used for Jerusalem as His dwelling, inasmuch as the prosperity of the kingdom was connected with that of the Church Ps. 122. 8, 9. 14-18. That choice is expressed in God's words, *I will sit or dwell*, or sit enthroned. The joy of the people springs from the blessings of His grace, conferred through the medium of the priesthood. make the horn ... to bud—enlarge his power. a lamp—the figure of prosperity Ps. 18. 10, 28; 89. 17.). With the confounding of his enemies is united his prosperity and the unceasing splendour of his crown.

PSALM CXXXIII.

Ver. 1-3. The blessings of fraternal unity.

1, 2. As the fragrant oil is refreshing, so this affords delight. As the copious dew, such as fell on *Hermon*, falls in fertalising power on the mountains of Zion, so this unity is fruitful in good works. 3. there—*i.e.*, in Zion, the Church; the material Zion, blessed with enriching dews, suggests this allusion to the source of the influence enjoyed by the spiritual Zion, commanded the blessing—(cf. Ps. 68. 28.).

PSALM CXXXIV.

Ver. 1-3. 1, 2. The people arriving at the sanctuary call on the priests, who *stand in the house of the Lord*, to unite in praising God, using appropriate gestures, to which the priests reply. 3. After the manner directed (Num. 6. 23.). by night—as opposed to *morning* (Ps. 92. 2.). Lift up your hands—(cf. Ps. 28. 2.). out of Zion—the Church, as His residence, and thus seat of blessings. Thus closes the songs of degrees.

Distress in captivity. PSALMS CXXXVII–CXXXIX. *God's all-seeing providence.*

the wilderness: for his mercy *endureth* for ever.
17 To him which smote great kings: for his mercy *endureth* for ever:
18 And *slew famous kings: for his mercy *endureth* for ever:
19 Sihon *king of the Amorites: for his mercy *endureth* for ever:
20 And Og the king of Bashan: for his mercy *endureth* for ever:
21 And *gave their land for an heritage: for his mercy *endureth* for ever:
22 *Even* an heritage unto Israel his servant: for his mercy *endureth* for ever.
23 Who *remembered us in our low estate: for his mercy *endureth* for ever:
24 And hath redeemed us from our enemies: for his mercy *endureth* for ever.
25 Who *giveth food to all flesh: for his mercy *endureth* for ever.
26 O give thanks unto the God of heaven: for his mercy *endureth* for ever.

PSALM CXXXVII.

1 *Constancy of the Jews in captivity.* 7 *The prophet curses Edom and Babel.*

BY *the rivers of Babylon, there we sat down; yea, we wept, when we remembered Zion.
2 We hanged our *harps upon the willows in the midst thereof.
3 For there they that carried us away captive required of us *a song; and they that *wasted us *required of us* mirth, saying, Sing us one of the songs of Zion.
4 How shall we sing the LORD's song in a *strange land?
5 If I forget thee, O Jerusalem, let my right hand forget *her cunning*.
6 If I do not remember thee, let *my tongue cleave to the roof of my mouth; if I prefer not Jerusalem above *my chief joy.
7 Remember, O LORD, *the children of Edom in the day of Jerusalem; who said, *Rase *it*, rase *it*, even to the foundation thereof.
8 O daughter of Babylon, *who art to be *destroyed; happy *shall he be* 7 that rewardeth thee as thou hast served us.
9 Happy *shall he be* that taketh and dasheth thy little ones against *the stones.

PSALM CXXXVIII.

1 *David praises God for the truth of his word;* 4 *he prophesies that the kings of the earth shall praise God.*

A Psalm of David.

I WILL praise thee with my whole heart: before *the gods will I sing praise unto thee.
2 I will worship *toward thy holy temple, and praise thy name for thy loving-kindness and for thy truth: for thou hast magnified *thy word above all thy name.
3 In the day when I cried thou answeredst me, *and *strengthenedst me *with* strength in my soul.
4 All the kings of the earth shall praise thee, O LORD, when they hear the words of thy mouth.
5 Yea, they shall sing in the ways of the LORD: for great *is* the glory of the LORD.
6 Though the LORD be high, yet *hath he respect unto the lowly: but the proud he knoweth afar off.
7 Though *I walk in the midst of trouble, thou wilt revive me; thou shalt stretch forth thine hand against the wrath of mine enemies, and thy right hand shall save me.
8 The *LORD will perfect *that which* concerneth me: thy mercy, O LORD, *endureth* for ever: forsake not the works of thine own hands.

PSALM CXXXIX.

1 *David praises God for his all-seeing providence;* 21 *his hatred of the wicked.*

To the chief Musician, A Psalm of David.

O LORD, *thou hast searched me, and known me.
2 Thou *knowest my down-sitting and mine up-rising, thou *understandest my thought afar off.
3 Thou *compassest my path and my lying down, and art acquainted *with* all my ways.
4 For *there is* not a word in my tongue, but, lo, O LORD, *thou knowest it altogether.
5 Thou hast beset me behind and before, and laid thine hand upon me.
6 Such knowledge *is* too wonderful for me; it is high, I cannot *attain* unto it.
7 Whither shall I go from thy Spirit? or whither shall I flee from thy presence?
8 If I ascend up into heaven, thou *art* there: *if I make my bed in hell, behold, thou *art* there.
9 *If* I take the wings of the morning, *and* dwell in the uttermost parts of the sea;
10 Even there shall thy hand lead me, and thy right hand shall hold me.
11 If I say, Surely the darkness shall cover me; even the night shall be light about me.
12 Yea, the darkness *hideth not from thee; but the night shineth as the day: *the darkness and the light *are* both alike to *thee*.
13 For thou hast possessed my reins: thou hast covered me in my mother's womb.
14 I will praise thee; for I am fearfully *and* wonderfully made: marvellous *are* thy works; and that my soul knoweth *right well.
15 My *substance was not hid from thee, when I was made in secret, *and* curiously wrought in the lowest parts of the earth.
16 Thine eyes did see my substance, yet being unperfect; and in thy book *all my members were written, 7 *which* in continuance were fashioned, when *as yet there was* none of them.
17 How precious also are thy thoughts unto me, O God! how great is the sum of them!
18 *If* I should count them, they are more in number than the sand: when I awake, I am still with thee.
19 Surely thou wilt *slay the wicked, O God: depart from me therefore, ye bloody men.
20 For they *speak against thee wickedly, *and* thine enemies take *thy* name in vain.
21 Do not I hate them, O LORD, that hate thee? and am not I grieved with those that rise up against thee?
22 I hate them with perfect hatred; I count them mine enemies.
23 Search *me, O God, and know my heart: try me, and know my thoughts;
24 And see *if there be any* *wicked way in me, and *lead me in the way everlasting.

PSALM CXXXV.

Ver. 1-21. A Psalm of praise, in which God's relations to His Church, His power in the natural world, and in delivering His people, are contrasted with the vanity of idols and idol worship.

1-3. In the general call for praise, the priests, *that stand in the house of the Lord*, are specially mentioned. 4-7. God's choice of Israel is the first reason assigned for rendering praise; the next His manifested greatness in creation and providence, heaven, and . . . seas, and all . . . ends of the earth—denote universality. 8, 9. The last plague is cited to illustrate His "tokens and wonders." 10-12. The conquest of Canaan was by God's power, not that of the people, heritage—or, possession. 13. name [and] memorial—Each denote that by which God is made known. 14. will judge—do justice Ps. 72, 2.). repent himself—change his dealings Ps. 90, 13.). 15-18. Cf. Ps. 115. 4-8.). are like unto them—or, shall be like, &c. Idolaters become spiritually stupid, and perish with their idols (Isa. 1. 31.). 19-21. Cf. Ps. 115. 9-11.). There we have *trust* for *bless* here. out of Zion—(cf. Ps. 110. 2; 134. 3.). From the Church, as a centre, His praise is diffused throughout the earth.

PSALM CXXXVI.

Ver. 1-26. The theme is the same as that of 135th. God should be praised for His works of creation and providence, His deliverance and care of His people, and judgments on their enemies, and His goodness to all. The chorus to every verse is in the terms of that of Ps. 106. 1; 118. 1-4, and was perhaps used at the *Amen* by the people, in worship cf. 1 Chr. 16. 36; Ps. 105. 45.).

1-3. The divine titles denote supremacy. 4. alone—excluding all help. 5, 6. by [or, in] wisdom—Ps. 104. 24.). made—*lit., maker of.* above [or, higher than] the waters—(Ps. 24, 2.). 12. Cf. similar expressions, Ex. 3. 20; Deut. 4. 34, &c.). 15. overthrew—*lit., shook off,* as Ex. 14. 27, as a contemptuous rejection of a reptile. 23. remembered us—or, for us (Ps. 132. 1.). our low estate—*i.e.,* captivity. 24. And hath redeemed [or *lit., snatched*] us—alluding to the sudden deliverance effected by the overthrow of Babylon. 25. To the special favours to His people is added the record of God's goodness to all His creatures cf. Mat. 6. 30.. 26. God of heaven—occurs but once (Jon. 1. 9 before the captivity. It is used by the later writers as specially distinguishing God from idols.

PSALM CXXXVII.

Ver. 1-9. This Psalm records the mourning of the captive Israelites, and a prayer and prediction respecting the destruction of their enemies.

1. rivers of Babylon—The name of the city used for the whole country, remembered Zion —or, Jerusalem, as Ps. 132. 13. 2. upon the willows—which may have grown there then, if not now; as the palm, which was once common, is now rare in Palestine. 3, 4. Whether the request was in curiosity or derision, the answer intimates that a compliance was incongruous with their mournful feelings Pro. 25. 20.). 5, 6. For joyful songs would imply forgetfulness of their desolated homes and fallen Church. The solemn imprecations on the "hand" and "tongue," if thus forgetful, relate to the cunning or skill in playing, and the power of singing. 7-9. Remember . . . the children of Edom— cf. Ps. 132. 1,), *i.e.,* to punish, the day of Jerusalem—its downfall Lam. 4. 21, 22; Obad. 11-13.). daughter of Babylon—the people Ps. 9. 13.). Their destruction had been abundantly foretold (Isa. 13. 14; Jer. 51. 23.). For the terribleness of that destruction, God's righteous judgment, and not the passions of the chafed Israelites, was responsible.

PSALM CXXXVIII.

Ver. 1-8. David thanks God for His benefits, and, anticipating a wider extension of God's glory, by His means, assures himself of His continued presence and faithfulness.

1. Cf. Ps. 9. 1.). before the gods—whether *angels* Ps. 8. 5;); or *princes* (Ex. 21. 6; Ps. 82. 6;); or *idols* Ps. 97. 7;); denotes a readiness to worship the true God alone, and a contempt of all other objects of worship. 2, (Cf. Ps. 5. 7.). thy word above all thy name—*i.e.,* God's promise (2 Sam, 7,), sustained by His mercy and truth, exceeded all other manifestations of Himself as subject of praise. 3-5. That promise, as an answer to his prayers in distress, revived and strengthened his faith, and, as the basis of other revelations of the Messiah, will be the occasion of praise by all who hear and receive it Ps. 68. 29, 31; Isa. 4. 3.). for great (is) the glory—or, when the glory shall be great, in God's fulfilling His purposes of redemption. 6, 7. On this general principle of God's government (Isa. 2. 11; 57. 15; 66. 2,) he relies for God's favour in saving him, and overthrowing his enemies. knoweth afar off —their ways and deserts (Ps. 1. 6,). 8. God will fulfil His promise.

PSALM CXXXIX.

Ver. 1-24. After presenting the sublime doctrines of God's omnipresence and omniscience, the Psalmist appeals to Him, avowing his innocence, his abhorrence of the wicked, and his ready submission to the closest scrutiny. Admonition to the wicked and comfort to the pious are alike implied inferences from these doctrines.

1, 2. searched me—as one searches, or digs for ore Job, 28. 3.). knowest—all my conditions and acts. understandest my thought [or, in respect to my thought, its origin and purport] afar off—not hindered by distance. 3. compassest [explorest] my path—track, or course. lying down—*lit., lair,* the terms all suiting the figure of a hunter seeking game. 4, 5. The accuracy and fulness of this knowledge strikingly expressed. 6. We must believe, though we cannot comprehend, God's omniscience. 7-10. The questions involve a most positive denial. All parts of the universe are denoted by the examples. The terms of *v.* 10 imply friendship Ps. 18. 16; 55. 6.). 11, 12. We are under His eye by day and night. 13. For—As a reason, implies that these attributes are evinced in God's creative agency, now unfolded, since He must know His own work, with whose hidden origin He is familiar. 14-16. The sentiment of *v.* 13 more fully unfolded, as ground for praising God. My substance—or, Frame work Ps. 6. 2.). lowest parts of the earth—the most inscrutably secret place, open only to God's eyes. In Job, 1. 21, the figure is inverted, and the grave is used for the womb. curiously wrought—*lit., embroidered, as needle work,* intricate and wonderfully adjusted (cf. Ps. 26. 30.). my substance . . . unperfect—*lit., unformed substance,* or *embryo.* The rest of this obscure verse may be translated: "and in thy book are written all of them: days are

PSALM CXL.

1 David prays to be delivered from Saul and Doeg: 8 he prays against them: 12 he comforts himself by confidence in God.

To the chief Musician, A Psalm of David.

DELIVER me, O LORD, from the evil man: preserve me from the [1] violent man;
2 Which imagine mischiefs in *their* heart: continually are they gathered together *for* war.
3 They have sharpened their tongues like a serpent; adders' poison *is* under their lips. Selah.
4 Keep me, O LORD, from the hands of the wicked; preserve me from the violent man; who have purposed to overthrow my goings.
5 The *a* proud have hid a snare for me, and cords; they have spread a net by the way-side; they have set gins for me. Selah.
6 I said unto the LORD, Thou *art* my God: hear the voice of my supplications, O LORD.
7 O GOD the Lord, the strength of my salvation, thou hast covered my head in the day of battle.
8 Grant not, O LORD, the desires of the wicked: further not his wicked device, 2 *lest* they exalt themselves. Selah.
9 *As for* the head of those that compass me about, let the mischief of their own lips cover them.
10 Let burning coals fall upon them: let them be cast into the fire; into deep pits, that they rise not up again.
11 Let not [3] an evil speaker be established in the earth: evil shall hunt the violent man to overthrow *him*.
12 I know that the LORD will maintain the cause of the afflicted, *and* the right of the poor.
13 Surely the righteous shall give thanks unto thy name: the upright shall dwell in thy presence.

PSALM CXLI.

1 David prays that his suit may be acceptable, 3 his conscience sincere, 9 and his life safe from snares.

A Psalm of David.

LORD, I cry unto thee: make haste unto me; give ear unto my voice, when I cry unto thee.
2 Let my prayer be [1] set forth before thee as *a* incense, *and* *b* the lifting up of my hands as the evening sacrifice.
3 Set a watch, O LORD, before my mouth; keep the door of my lips.
4 Incline *c* not my heart to any evil thing, to practise wicked works with men that work iniquity: *d* and let me not eat of their dainties.
5 [2] Let the righteous smite me; *it shall be* a kindness; and let him reprove me; *it shall be* an excellent oil, *which* shall not break my head: for yet my prayer also *shall be* in their calamities.
6 When their judges are overthrown in stony places, they shall hear my words; for they are sweet.
7 Our bones are scattered *e* at the grave's mouth, as when one cutteth and cleaveth *wood* upon the earth.
8 But *f* mine eyes *are* unto thee, O GOD the Lord: in thee is my trust; *g* leave not my soul destitute.
9 Keep me from the snares *which* they have laid for me, and the gins of the workers of iniquity.

PSALM 140.
1 man of violences.
a Jer. 18. 22.
2 Or, let them not be exalted. Deu. 32. 27.
3 a man of tongue, or, an evil speaker, a wicked man of violence, be established in the earth: let him be hunted to his overthrow.

PSALM 141.
1 directed.
a Rev. 8. 3.
b 1 Tim. 2. 8.
c Mat. 6. 13. Jam. 1. 13.
d Pro. 23. 6.
2 Or, Let the righteous smite me kindly, and reprove me; let not their precious oil break my head, etc.
e 2 Cor. 1. 9.
f Ps. 25. 15.
3 make not my soul bare.
g Ps. 35. 8.
4 pass over.

PSALM 142
1 Or, A Psalm of David, giving instruction.
a 1 Sa. 22. 1.
2 Or, Look on the right hand.
3 perished from me.
4 no man sought after my soul.
b Lam. 3. 24.

PSALM 143.
c Job 14. 3.
d Ex. 34. 7.
1 Or, for I am become like, etc.
2 hide me with thee.
e Ps. 25. 4.
d John 14. 26. 2 Tim. 1. 14.

PSALM 144.
1 my rock.
a 2 Sa. 22. 35.
2 to the war, etc.

10 Let *g* the wicked fall into their own nets, whilst that I withal [4] escape.

PSALM CXLII.

David shows that in his trouble all his comfort was in prayer unto God.

1 Maschil of David; A Prayer *a* when he was in the cave.

I CRIED unto the LORD with my voice; with my voice unto the LORD did I make my supplication.
2 I poured out my complaint before him; I showed before him my trouble.
3 When my spirit was overwhelmed within me, then thou knewest my path. In the way wherein I walked have they privily laid a snare for me.
4 [2] I looked on *my* right hand, and beheld, but *there was* no man that would know me: refuge [3] failed me; [4] no man cared for my soul.
5 I cried unto thee, O LORD: I said, Thou *art* my refuge *and* *b* my portion in the land of the living.
6 Attend unto my cry; for I am brought very low: deliver me from my persecutors; for they are stronger than I.
7 Bring my soul out of prison, that I may praise thy name: the righteous shall compass me about; for thou shalt deal bountifully with me.

PSALM CXLIII.

1 David prays for favour in judgment; 7 prays for grace, 9 deliverance, 10 God's guidance and support.

A Psalm of David.

HEAR my prayer, O LORD, give ear to my supplications: in thy faithfulness answer me, *and* in thy righteousness.
2 And *a* enter not into judgment with thy servant: for *b* in thy sight shall no man living be justified.
3 For the enemy hath persecuted my soul; he hath smitten my life down to the ground; he hath made me to dwell in darkness, as those that have been long dead.
4 Therefore is my spirit overwhelmed within me; my heart within me is desolate.
5 I remember the days of old; I meditate on all thy works; I muse on the work of thy hands.
6 I stretch forth my hands unto thee: my soul *thirsteth* after thee, as a thirsty land. Selah.
7 Hear me speedily, O LORD; my spirit faileth: hide not thy face from me, lest I be like unto them that go down into the pit.
8 Cause me to hear thy loving-kindness in the morning; for in thee do I trust: cause me to know the way wherein I should walk; for I lift up my soul unto thee.
9 Deliver me, O LORD, from mine enemies: I [2] flee unto thee to hide me.
10 Teach *c* me to do thy will; for thou *art* my God: *d* thy spirit *is* good; lead me into the land of uprightness.
11 Quicken me, O LORD, for thy name's sake: for thy righteousness' sake bring my soul out of trouble.
12 And of thy mercy cut off mine enemies, and destroy all them that afflict my soul: for I *am* thy servant.

PSALM CXLIV.

1 David blesses God for his mercy; 5 he prays that God would deliver him from his enemies.

A Psalm of David.

BLESSED *be* the LORD [1] my strength, which *a* teacheth my hands [2] to war, *and* my fingers to fight;

formed and not one among them (yet was,", i.e., all our days Job. 14. 5,, or our lives, with their changes and events, were written, or planned by God, not one yet ex'sting. 17. How precious ... sum of them—Thy thoughts or purposes concerning me are many and most valuable. It is a privilege to be governed by such a God. 18. still with thee—to meditate on these wonders. 19. Utter rejection of all society with the wicked is denoted by recognising them as deserving destruction from God, and addressing them in terms of rebuke. bloody men—cf. l's. 5. 6; 26. 9. They are hated as God's enemies. 20. take ... in vain—either as Ps. 24. 4, or we may translate, *lift up to vanity*, i.e., exalting themselves against God. 23, 24. Only an innocent man, or one resting on God's mercy, can properly use this appeal. wicked way—*lit., way of pain*, i.e., which leads to it. way everlasting—which will not perish (Ps. 1. 6,), or leads to life everlasting.

PSALM CXL.

Ver. 1-13. The style of this Psalm resembles those of David in the former part of the book, presenting the usual complaint, prayer, and confident hope of relief.

1. evil man—which of David's enemies is meant is not important. 2-5. This character of the wicked, and the devices planned against the pious, correspond to Ps. 10. 7; 31. 13; 58. 4, &c. sharpened ... like a serpent—not like a serpent does, but they are thus like a serpent in cunning and venom, snare [and] net—for threatening dangers (cf. Ps. 38. 12; 57. 6. Cf. Ps. 5. 1-12; 10. 2.. 7. day of battle—*lit., of armour*, i.e., when using it. 8. (Cf. Ps. 57. 12; 66. 7,). lest they exalt themselves—or, they will be exalted if permitted to prosper. 9. contrasts his head covered by God, (v. 7), with theirs, or as head may be used for persons with them, covered with the results of their wicked deeds Ps. 7. 16,). 10. (Cf. Ps. 11. 6; 120. 4.). To *cast into fire* and *deep pits*, figures for utter destruction. 11. an evil speaker—or, slanderer, will not be tolerated Ps. 101.7.). The last clause may be translated: "*an evil* (man) *He* (God) *shall hunt*," &c. 12. (Cf. Ps. 9. 4.). 13. After all changes, the righteous shall have cause for praise. Such *shall dwell*, or sit securely, under God's protection (Ps. 21. 6; 41. 12.).

PSALM CXLI.

Ver. 1-10. This psalm evinces its authorship as the preceding, by its structure and the character of its contents. It is a prayer for deliverance from sins to which affliction tempted him, and from the enemies who caused it.

1. (Cf. Ps. 17. 6; 64. 1.). 2. be set forth—or, established, constantly accepted, as incense. lifting up of ... hands—a gesture in prayer (cf. Ps. 28. 2,). The *sacrifice* meant was the meat-offering. 3, 4. A prayer to be kept from the sins of speech, and the influence of evil associations, especially by means of the luxuries of the rich Pro. 23. 1-3.). 5. Though in details obscure, the verse seems to teach that he prefers the rebukes of the righteous to the allurements of the wicked; and, returning to speak of the latter, illustrates the benefits of the chastisements alluded to, by avowing a continued prayerful temper as to the wicked, when in affliction. not break my head—or *lit., my head shall not refuse*. 6. their judges — or, leading men, i.e., of the wicked in distress, shall appreciate my words

of prayer, or assurance of innocence and integrity, or both cf. 1 Sam. 24. 8-17; 2 Sam. 1. 19-22. . overthrown in stony places—a mode of punishment (2 Chr. 25. 12, here used to denote any grievous calamity. 7. The desperate condition of his party is stated. Some of them were left unburied and uncared for as scattered chips. 8. But—or, *For*, implying an avowal of his hope in this desperate state. The expressions of confidence are such as Ps. 2. 12; 25. 15; 31. 1. 9. (Cf. Ps. 140. 5.), from the snares—*lit., from the hand*, or *power of the snare*. 10. Cf. Ps. 7. 15,). witha:—*lit., at once*, or same time. Their destruction, and the deliverance of the pious, come together.

PSALM CXLII.

Ver. 1-7. *Maschil*—(cf. l's. 32. title.). *When he was in the cave*, either of Adullam 1 Sam. 22. 1,), or En-gedi 1 Sam. 24. 3. . This does not mean that the Psalm was composed *in the cave*, but that the precarious mode of life, of which his refuge in caves was a striking illustration, occasioned the complaint, which constitutes the first part of the Psalm, and furnishes the reason for the prayer with which it concludes, and which, as the prominent characteristic, gives its name.

1. with my voice — audibly, because earnestly. 2. (Cf. Ps. 63. 8.). comp.ai̇nt—or, a sad musing. 3. thou knewest ... path—the appeal is indicative of conscious innocence: knowest it to be right, and that my affliction is owing to the snares of enemies, and is not deserved cf. Ps. 42. 4; 61. 2. . 4. Utter desolation is meant. right hand—the place of a protector Ps. 110. 5.). cared for—*lit., sought after*, to do good. 5. (Cf. Ps. 31. 14; 62. 7. . 6. (Cf. l's. 17. 1.). 7. (Cf. Ps. 25. 17.). that I may praise — *lit., for praising*, or that thy name may be praised, i.e., by the righteous, who shall surround me with sympathising joy (Ps. 55. 27.).

PSALM CXLIII.

Ver. 1-12. In structure and style, like the preceding (Ps. 140-142.,), this Psalm is clearly evinced to be David's. It is a prayer for pardon, and for relief from enemies; afflictions, as usual, producing confession and penitence.

1. in thy faithfulness ... and ... righteousness—or, God's regard to the claims which He has permitted His people to make in His covenant. 2. enter ... judgment—deal not in strict justice. shall no ... justified—or, is no man justified, or innocent (Job, 14. 3; Rom. 3. 20.). 3, 4. The exciting reason for his prayer—his afflictions—led to confession as just made: he now makes the complaint. as these that have been long dead—(deprived of life's comforts cf. Ps. 40. 15; 88. 3-6. . 5, 6. The distress is aggravated by the contrast of former comfort (Ps. 22. 3-5,), for whose return he longs. a thirsty land—which needs rain, as did his spirit God's gracious vi ts (Ps. 28. 1; 69. 17.). 7. spirit faileth—is exhausted. 8. (Cf. Ps. 25. 1-4; 50. 16.). the way ... walk—i.e., the way of safety and righteousness Ps. 142. 3-6.). 9. (Cf. Ps. 31. 15-20. 10. (Cf. Ps. 5. 8; 27. 11.). laud of uprightness—*lit., an even land* Ps. 26. 12. . 11. (Cf. Ps. 23. 3; 119. 156. . 12. God's mercy to his people is often wrath to His and their enemies cf. Ps. 31 17.). thy servant—as chosen to be such, entitled to divine regard.

PSALM CXLIV.

Ver. 1-15. David's praise of God as his all-sufficient help is enhanced by a recognition of the intrinsic worthlessness of man.

2 ³ My goodness, and my fortress; my high tower, and my deliverer; my shield, and he in whom I trust; who subdueth my people under me.
3 LORD, ᵇwhat *is* man, that thou takest knowledge of him! *or* the son of man, that thou makest account of him!
4 Man is like to vanity: his days *are* as a shadow that passeth away.
5 Bow ᶜthy heavens, O LORD, and come down: touch the mountains, and they shall smoke.
6 Cast forth lightning, and scatter them: shoot out thine arrows, and destroy them.
7 Send thine ᵈ hand from above; ᵈ rid me, and deliver me out of great waters, from the hand of ᵉ strange children;
8 Whose mouth speaketh vanity, and their right hand *is* a right hand of falsehood.
9 I will ᶠsing a new song unto thee, O God: upon a psaltery *and* an instrument of ten strings will I sing praises unto thee.
10 *It is* he that giveth ᵇ salvation unto kings: who delivereth David his servant from the hurtful sword.
11 Rid me, and deliver me from the hand of strange children, whose mouth speaketh vanity, and their right hand *is* a right hand of falsehood.
12 That our sons may be as plants grown up in their youth; *that* our daughters *may be* as corner-stones, ⁶ polished *after* the similitude of a palace;
13 *That* our garners *may be* full, affording ⁷ all manner of store; *that* our sheep may bring forth thousands and ten thousands in our streets;
14 *That* our oxen *may be* ⁸ strong to labour; *that there be* ⁹ no breaking in, nor going out; that *there be* no complaining in our streets.
15 Happy ʰ *is that* people that is in such a case; *yea*, happy *is that* people whose God *is* the LORD.

PSALM CXLV.

1 *David praiseth God for his fame, 7 goodness, 11 the glory of his kingdom, 18 and for his special favour for the righteous.*

David's Psalm of praise.

I WILL extol thee, my God, O King; and I will bless thy name for ever and ever.
2 Every day will I bless thee; and I will praise thy name for ever and ever.
3 Great *is* the LORD, and greatly to be praised: ¹ and his greatness *is* unsearchable.
4 One generation shall praise thy works to another, and shall declare thy mighty acts.
5 I will speak of the glorious honour of thy majesty, and of thy wondrous ² works.
6 And *men* shall speak of the might of thy terrible acts: and I will ³ declare thy greatness.
7 They shall abundantly ⁴ utter the memory of thy great goodness, and shall sing of thy righteousness.
8 The ᵃ LORD *is* gracious, and full of compassion; slow to anger, and ⁵ of great mercy.
9 The LORD ᵇ *is* good to all; and his tender mercies *are* over all his works.
10 All ᶜ thy works shall praise thee, O LORD; and thy saints shall bless thee.
11 They shall speak of the glory of thy kingdom, and talk of thy power;
12 To make known to the sons of men his

PSALM 144.
ᵃ Or, My mercy.
ᵇ Heb. 2. 6.
ᶜ Is. 64. 1.
ᵈ hands.
ᵉ Ps. C9. 1.
ᶠ Mal. 2. 11.
ᵍ Ps. 33. 2.
⁵ Or, victory.
⁶ cut.
⁷ from kind to kind.
⁸ able to bear burdens, or, loaden with flesh.
ᵍ Lev. 20. 17.
ʰ Deu. 33. 29.

PSALM 145.
¹ and of his greatness there is no search.
Ro. 11. 33.
² things, or, words.
³ declare it.
⁴ boil up.
ᵃ Ps. 45. 1.
ᵇ Ex 34. 6. Nu. 14. 18.
⁵ great in mercy.
ᵇ Ps. 100. 5. Nah. 1. 7. Mat. 5. 45. Acts 14. 17.
ᶜ Ps. 19. 1.
⁶ a kingdom of all ages.
Is. 9. 7.
Dan. 7. 14.
⁷ Or, look unto thee.
⁸ Or, merciful, or, bountiful.
ᵈ John 14. 23. Jam. 4. 8.
ᵉ John 4. 24.
ᶠ 1 John 5. 14.
ᵍ 1 Pet. 1. 5.

PSALM 146.
¹ Hallelujah.
ᵃ Is. 2. 22.
² Or, salvation.
ᵇ Eccl. 12. 7.
ᶜ 1 Cor. 2. 6.
ᵈ Jer. 17. 7.
ᵉ Rev. 14. 7.
ᶠ Mic. 7. 20.

PSALM 147.
ᵃ Deu. 30. 3.
ᵇ Is. 61. 1. Luke 4. 18.
¹ grief.
ᶜ Gen. 15. 5. Is. 40. 26.
ᵈ 1 Chr. 16. 25.
ᵉ Nah. 1. 3.
² of his understanding there is no number.
ᶠ Ps. 146. 8.
ᵍ Eph. 5. 20.
³ answer.
Ex. 15. 21.
ʰ Job 38. 26.

mighty acts, and the glorious majesty of his kingdom.
13 Thy kingdom *is* ⁶ an everlasting kingdom, and thy dominion *endureth* throughout all generations.
14 The LORD upholdeth all that fall, and raiseth up all *those* that be bowed down.
15 The eyes of all ⁷ wait upon thee; and thou givest them their meat in due season.
16 Thou openest thine hand, and satisfiest the desire of every living thing.
17 The LORD *is* righteous in all his ways, and ⁸ holy in all his works.
18 The ᵈ LORD *is* nigh unto all them that call upon him, to all that call upon him ᵉ in truth.
19 He will ᶠ fulfil the desire of them that fear him: he also will hear their cry, and will save them.
20 The LORD ᵍ preserveth all them that love him: but all the wicked will he destroy.
21 My mouth shall speak the praise of the LORD: and let all flesh bless his holy name for ever and ever.

PSALM CXLVI.

1 *The psalmist vows perpetual praises to God: 3 he exhorts not to trust in man. 5 God is only worthy to be trusted.*

PRAISE ¹ ye the LORD. Praise the LORD, O my soul.
2 While I live will I praise the LORD; I will sing praises unto my God while I have any being.
3 Put ᵃ not your trust in princes, *nor* in the son of man, in whom *there is* no ² help.
4 His ᵇ breath goeth forth, he returneth to his earth; in that very day ᶜ his thoughts perish.
5 Happy ᵈ *is he* that hath the God of Jacob for his help, whose hope *is* in the LORD his God:
6 Which ᵉ made heaven and earth, the sea, and all that therein is; which ᶠ keepeth truth for ever;
7 Which executeth judgment for the oppressed; which giveth food to the hungry. The LORD looseth the prisoners:
8 The LORD openeth the *eyes of* the blind: the LORD raiseth them *that are* bowed down: the LORD loveth the righteous:
9 The LORD preserveth the strangers; he relieveth the fatherless and widow: but the way of the wicked he turneth upside down.
10 The LORD shall reign for ever, *even* thy God, O Zion, unto all generations. Praise ye the LORD.

PSALM CXLVII.

1 *The prophet exhorts to praise God for his care of the church, 15 his power over the elements, 19 and his ordinances given to Israel.*

PRAISE ye the LORD: for *it is* good to sing praises unto our God; for *it is* pleasant; *and* praise is comely.
2 The LORD doth build up Jerusalem: ᵃ he gathereth together the outcasts of Israel.
3 He ᵇ healeth the broken in heart, and bindeth up their ¹ wounds.
4 He ᶜ telleth the number of the stars; he calleth them all by *their* names.
5 Great ᵈ *is* our Lord, and of great ᵉ power: ² his understanding *is* infinite.
6 The ᶠ LORD lifteth up the meek: he casteth the wicked down to the ground.
7 Sing unto the LORD with ᵍ thanksgiving; ³ sing praise upon the harp unto our God:
8 Who ʰ covereth the heaven with clouds,

God's Goodness Extolled. **PSALMS CXLV—CXLVIII.** *Exhortations to Praise God.*

Confidently imploring God's interposition against his enemies he breaks forth into praise and joyful anticipations of the prosperity of his kingdom, when freed from vain and wicked men.

1, 2. Cf. Ps. 18. 2, 34, 43, &c., in which most of these terms descriptive of God occur. My goodness—or, mercy, *i.e.*, who shows it to me (Ps. 59. 17.). my people—subjects. All his success, and that of his descendants, including Christ, over Jews and Gentiles, in the typical and real kingdom, is solely of God (cf. Mat. 28. 18.). 3, 4. Cf. 2 Sam. 7. 18; Ps. 8. 4.). Of himself, man presents no reason for being an object of God's favour. 5. (Cf. Ps. 18. 9; 104. 32.). 6. Cast forth [*lit.*, *Lighten*] lightnings,...arrows, &c.— cf. Ps. 18. 14.). then: —the enemies, 7., who are now mentioned (cf. Ps. 18. 16, 44, 45.). waters—calamities, as Ps. 18. 1 ; 124. 3, 4. 8. right ... falsehood—alluding to its use in swearing or bargaining. False subjects Ps. 18. 44 may be meant. 9. (Cf. Ps. 33. 2, 3.). 10. salvation unto kings—much more then to people. David is servant —cf. Ps. 143. 2, 12.). 12. That our sons, &c.— The result of answered prayer. grown up... youth—or, large, early developing a vigorous constitution. corner-stones ... palace — or, temple cf. Heb. Ps. 5. 7; 11. 4,), which were specially polished, 13 all manner — divers kinds (2 Chr. 16. 14) in succession (cf. Ps. 84. 7.). streets—*lit.*, *out places*, roads, and even fields Job, 5. 10. . 14. ur oxen ... to labour—*lit.*, *our oxen burdened, i.e.*, with loads of produce. breaking in, &c.— no invasion, exile, or oppression. 15. As much as to say, those are in such a state of prosperity whose God is the Lord.

PSALM CXLV.

Ver. 1-21. A Psalm of praise to God for His mighty, righteous, and gracious government of all men, and of His humble and suffering people in particular.

1, 2. (Cf. Ps. 30. 1.). bless thy name—celebrate thy perfections Ps. 5. 11.). God is addressed as king, alluding to His government of men. 3. Cf. Ps. 18. 3; 48. 1.). greatness—as (is) layed in his works. 4. shall declare—*lit.*, *they shall declare, i.e.,* all generations. 5. I will speak—or, muse Ps. 77. 12; 119. 15.). thy w ndrous works—or,words of thy wonders,*i.e.*, which describe them (Ps. 105. 27.), (*Marg.*). 6. terrible acts—which produce dread or fear. 7. memory— Ps. 6. 5., remembrance, or what causes to be remembered. righteousness—as Ps. 143. 1, goodness according to covenant engagement. 9, 9. (Cf. Ps. 103. 8; 111. 4. . over all, &c.—rests on all His works. 10. bless—as *v.* 1, to praise with reverence, more than merely to praise. 11, 12, The declaration of God's glory is for the extension of his knowledge and perceptions in the world. 13. (Cf. Dan. 4. 3, 34.). 14. (Cf. Ps. 37. 17; 54. 4.. 15, 16. eyes of ... thee—or, look with expecting faith (Ps. 104. 27, 28.). 17. holy ... works —*lit.*, *merciful or kind, goodness* (Ps. 144. 2 is the corresponding noun. righteous—in a similar relation of meaning to *righteousness* (*v.* 7.). 18, 19. Cf. Ps. 34. 7, 10.). 20. Those who fear him (*v.* 19! are those who are here said to love him. 21. Cf. Ps. 33. 21.). all flesh — Ps. 65. 2.). The Psalm ends, as it began, with ascriptions of praise, in which the pious will ever delight to join.

PSALM CXLVI.

Ver. 1-10. An exhortation to praise God, who, by the gracious and faithful exercise of His power in goodness to the needy, is alone worthy of implicit trust.

1. Cf. Ps. 104. 3 . 3. in whom ... help—for themselves or others Ps. 118. 8. 9. . 4. His breath—or, *spirit*, the element of life, the gifts —*lit.*, *schemes*, or plans of life Ps. 1 6. . 5. for his help—*lit.*, *in his help*, engaged in it. whose hope—or, reliance Ps. 51. 4.). 6. God's combined power in creation, and faithfulness to His promise, are good grounds for such confidence. 7. executath judgment—or, gives a right decision in the cause of the afflicted. of whom examples are given cf. Ps. 68. 5, 6.i. 8. openeth ... blind—the verb is used almost solely of the eyes. Blindness, both bodily and mental, may be meant . The three classes of sufferers here named are specially provided for in the law cf. Ex. 22. 22; Lev. 19. 33.). turneth ... down- or, makes crooked, denoting the infliction of calamity, as "making the way straight," denotes giving prosperity. 10. This God is our God, the God of his Church, Zion. Let our delight be in celebrating His eternal kingdom. Hallelujah.

PSALM CXLVII.

Ver. 1-20. This and the remaining Psalms have been represented as specially designed to celebrate the rebuilding of Jerusalem (cf. Neh. 6. 16; 12. 27.). They all open and close with the stirring call for praise. This specially declares God's providential care towards all creatures, and particularly His people.

1. (Cf. Ps. 92. 1; 135 3.). 2. (Cf. Ps. 107. 3; Isa. 11. 12.). 3. Though applicable to the captive Israelites,this is a general and precious truth. wounds—(cf. *Marg*.). 4, 5. God's power in nature (Isa. 40. 26-28, and often is presented as a pledge of His power to help His people. tel'eth...stars—what no man can do Gen.15.5.. 6. That power is put forth for the good of the meek and suffering pious, and confusion of the wicked Ps. 146. 8, 9.). 7-9. His providence supplies bountifully the wild animals in their mountain homes. Sing ... Lord—*lit.*, *Answer the Lord*, *i.e.*, in grateful praise to His goodness, thus declared in His acts. 10, 11. The advantages afforded, as in war, by the strength of the horse or the agility of man, do not incline God to favour any; but those who fear and, of course, trust Him, will obtain His approbation and aid. 12-14. strengthened ... gates—or, means of defence against invaders. maketh ... borders— or, territories (Gen. 23. 17; Isa. 54. 12). filleth thee, &c.—cf. *Mary*.). 15-18. God's word, as a swift messenger, executes His purpose, for with Him to command is to perform (Gen. 1. 3; Ps. 33. 9,), and He brings about the wonders of providence as easily as men cast crumbs, morsels—used as to food (Gen. 18. 5,), perhaps here denotes hail. 19, 20. This mighty ruler and benefactor of heaven and earth is such especially to His chosen people, to whom alone (Deut. 4. 32-34) He has made known His will, while others have been left in darkness. Therefore unite in the great hallelujah.

PSALM CXLVIII.

Ver. 1-14. The scope of this Psalm is the same as of the preceding.

1. heavens [and] heights—are synonymous. 2. hosts—(cf. Ps. 103. 21. . 4. heavens of heavens—the very highest. waters—clouds, resting above the visible heavens (cf. Gen. 1. 7.). 5. praise the name—as representing His perfections. he commanded —*He* is emphatic, ascribing creation to God alone. 6. The

who prepareth rain for the earth, who maketh grass to grow upon the mountains.
9 He giveth to the beast his food, and to the young ravens which cry.
10 He delighteth not in the strength of the horse: he taketh not pleasure in the legs of a man.
11 The LORD taketh pleasure in them that fear him, in those that hope in his mercy.
12 Praise the LORD, O Jerusalem; praise thy God, O Zion:
13 For he hath strengthened the bars of thy gates; he hath blessed thy children within thee.
14 He maketh peace in thy borders, and filleth thee with the finest of the wheat.
15 He sendeth forth his commandment upon earth: his word runneth very swiftly.
16 He giveth snow like wool: he scattereth the hoar-frost like ashes.
17 He casteth forth his ice like morsels: who can stand before his cold?
18 He sendeth out his word, and melteth them: he causeth his wind to blow, and the waters flow.
19 He showeth his word unto Jacob, his statutes and his judgments unto Israel.
20 He hath not dealt so with any nation: and as for his judgments, they have not known them. Praise ye the LORD.

PSALM CXLVIII.
1 The psalmist calls upon the celestial, 7 terrestrial, 11 and rational creatures, to praise God.

PRAISE ye the LORD. Praise ye the LORD from the heavens: praise him in the heights.
2 Praise ye him, all his angels: praise ye him, all his hosts.
3 Praise ye him, sun and moon: praise him, all ye stars of light.
4 Praise him, ye heavens of heavens, and ye waters that be above the heavens.
5 Let them praise the name of the LORD: for he commanded, and they were created.
6 He hath also stablished them for ever and ever: he hath made a decree which shall not pass.
7 Praise the LORD from the earth, ye dragons, and all deeps:
8 Fire, and hail; snow, and vapour; stormy wind fulfilling his word:
9 Mountains, and all hills; fruitful trees, and all cedars:
10 Beasts, and all cattle; creeping things, and flying fowl:

11 Kings of the earth, and all people; princes, and all judges of the earth;
12 Both young men and maidens; old men, and children:
13 Let them praise the name of the LORD: for his name alone is excellent; his glory is above the earth and heaven.
14 He also exalteth the horn of his people, the praise of all his saints; even of the children of Israel, a people near unto him. Praise ye the LORD.

PSALM CXLIX.
1 The prophet exhorts to praise God for his love to the church, 5 and the power he has given to his saints.

PRAISE ye the LORD. Sing unto the LORD a new song, and his praise in the congregation of saints.
2 Let Israel rejoice in him that made him; let the children of Zion be joyful in their King.
3 Let them praise his name in the dance: let them sing praises unto him with the timbrel and harp.
4 For the LORD taketh pleasure in his people: he will beautify the meek with salvation.
5 Let the saints be joyful in glory: let them sing aloud upon their beds.
6 Let the high praises of God be in their mouth, and a two-edged sword in their hand;
7 To execute vengeance upon the heathen, and punishments upon the people;
8 To bind their kings with chains, and their nobles with fetters of iron;
9 To execute upon them the judgment written: this honour have all his saints. Praise ye the LORD.

PSALM CL.
An exhortation to praise God.

PRAISE ye the LORD. Praise God in his sanctuary: praise him in the firmament of his power.
2 Praise him for his mighty acts: praise him according to his excellent greatness.
3 Praise him with the sound of the trumpet: praise him with the psaltery and harp.
4 Praise him with the timbrel and dance: praise him with stringed instruments and organs.
5 Praise him upon the loud cymbals: praise him upon the high-sounding cymbals.
6 Let every thing that hath breath praise the LORD. Praise ye the LORD.

THE

BOOK OF PROVERBS.

CHAPTER I.

1 Use of the Proverbs. 7 Exhortation to fear God, and regard parents; 10 to avoid the enticings of sinners. 20 Wisdom complains of contempt of scorners.

THE Proverbs of Solomon the son of David, king of Israel;
2 To know wisdom and instruction; to perceive the words of understanding;
3 To receive the instruction of wisdom, justice, and judgment, and equity;
4 To give subtilty to the simple, to the young man knowledge and discretion.

5 A wise man will hear, and will increase learning; and a man of understanding shall attain unto wise counsels:
6 To understand a proverb, and the interpretation; the words of the wise, and their dark sayings.
7 The fear of the LORD is the beginning of knowledge: but fools despise wisdom and instruction.
8 My son, hear the instruction of thy father, and forsake not the law of thy mother:
9 For they shall be an ornament of grace

perpetuity of the frame of nature is, of course, subject to Him who formed it, a decree... His ordinances respecting them shall not change Jer. 36, 31,), or perish (Job, 34. 20; Ps. 37. 36.). 7-10. The call on the earth, as opposed to heaven, includes seas or depths, whose inhabitants, the dragon, as one of the largest (cf. on leviathan, Ps. 104. 26,), is selected to represent. The most destructive and ungovernable agents of inanimate nature are introduced, fulfilling his word—or, law, may be understood of each. Next the most distinguished productions of the vegetable world, fruitful trees—or, trees of fruit, as opposed to forest trees. Wild and domestic, large and small, animals are comprehended, 11, 12. Next all rational beings, from the highest in rank to little children. princes—or, military leaders. 13. Let them—all mentioned, excellent — or, exalted (Isa. 12. 4.). his g.ory—majesty (Ps. 45. 3.), above ... heaven —their united splendours fail to match His. 14. exalteth the horn—established power (Ps. 75. 5. 6.). praise of [or lit., for] his saints—i.e., occasions for them to praise Him. They are further described as His people, and near Him, sustaining by covenanted care a peculiarly intimate relation.

PSALM CXLIX.

Ver. 1-9. This Psalm sustains a close connection with the foregoing. The chosen people are exhorted to praise God, in view of past favours, and also future victories over enemies, of which they are impliedly assured.

1. cf. Ps. 96. 1.). 2. God had signalised His relation as a sovereign, in restoring them to their land. 3. in the dance—(Ps. 30. 11.). The dance is connected with other terms, expressive of the great joy of the occasion. The word may be rendered lute, to which the other instruments are joined. sing praises—or, sing and play. 4. taketh pleasure—lit., accepts, alluding to acceptance of propitiatory offerings (cf. Ps. 7. 18.). beautify, &c.—adorn the humble with faith, hope, joy, and peace. 5. in g.ory—the honourable condition to which they are raised, upon their beds—once a place of mourning (Ps. 6. 6.). 6. high (praises)—or, deeds. They shall go forth as religious warriors, as once religious labourers (Neh. 4. 17.). 7. The destruction of the incorrigibly wicked attends the propagation of God's truth, so that the military successes of the Jews, after the captivity, typified the triumphs of the gospel. 9. the judgment written—either in God's decrees, or perhaps as Deut. 32. 41-43. this honour—i.e., to be thus employed, will be an honourable service, to be assigned his saints—or, godly ones (Ps. 16. 3..

PSALM CL.

Ver. 1-6. This is a suitable doxology for the whole book, reciting the "place, theme, mode, and extent" of God's high praise.

1. in his sanctuary—on earth, firmament, &c. —which illustrates His power. 2. mighty acts—(Ps. 145. 4.). excellent greatness — or, abundance of greatness. 3, 4. The trumpet was used to call religious assemblies; the organ, or pipe, a wind instrument, and the others were used in worship. 5. cymbals —suited to loud praise (Neh. 12. 27.). 6. LIVING VOICES SHALL TAKE UP THE FAILING SOUNDS OF DEAD INSTRUMENTS, AND AS THEY CEASE ON EARTH, THOSE OF INTELLIGENT RANSOMED SPIRITS AND HOLY ANGELS, AS WITH THE SOUND OF MIGHTY THUNDERS, WILL PROLONG, ETERNALLY, THE PRAISE, SAYING: "ALLELUIA! SALVATION, AND GLORY, AND HONOUR, AND POWER, UNTO THE LORD OUR GOD;" "ALLELUIA! FOR THE LORD GOD OMNIPOTENT REIGNETH." AMEN!

THE BOOK OF PROVERBS.

INTRODUCTION.

I.—THE NATURE AND USE OF PROVERBS.—A proverb is a pithy sentence, concisely expressing some well-established truth, susceptible of various illustrations and applications. The word is of Latin derivation, literally meaning for a word, speech, or discourse, i.e., one expression for many. The Heb. word for proverb, (mashal) means a comparison. Many suppose it was used, because the form or matter of the proverb, or both, involved the idea of comparison. Most of the proverbs are in couplets or triplets, or some modifications of them, the members of which correspond in structure and length, as if arranged to be compared one with another. They illustrate the varieties of parallelism, a distinguishing feature of Heb. poetry, cf. Intr. to Poetical Books. Many also clearly involve the idea of comparison in the sentiments express'd, (cf. ch. 12. 1-10; 25. 10-15; 26. 1-9.). Sometimes, however, the designed omission of one member of the comparison, exercising the reader's sagacity or study for its supply, presents the proverb as a "riddle" or "dark saying," (cf. ch. 30. 15-33; 1. 6; Ps. 49. 4.). The sententious form of expression, which thus became a marked feature of the proverbial style, was also adopted for continuous discourse, even when not always preserving traces of comparison, either in form or matter, (cf. chs 1-9.). In Ez. 17. 1; 24. 3, we find the same word properly translated parable, to designate an illustrative discourse. Then the Gr. translators have used a word, paraboa'a, (parable), which the gospel writers (except John) employ for our Lord's discourses of the same character, and which also seems to involve the idea of comparison, though that may not be its primary meaning. It might seem, therefore, that the proverbial and parabolic styles of writing were originally and essentially the same. The proverb is a "concentrated parable, and the parable an extension of the proverb by a full illustration." The proverb is thus the moral, or theme of a parable, which sometimes precedes it as Mat. 19. 30; (cf. ch. 20. 1): or succeeds it, as Mat. 22. 1-16; Luke, 15. 1-10. This style being poetical, and adapted to the expression of a high order of poetical sentiment, such as prophecy, we find the same term used to designate such compositions, (cf. Num. 23. 7; Mic. 2. 4; Hab. 2. 6.).

unto thy head, and chains about thy neck.

10 ¶ My son, if sinners entice thee, *consent thou not.

11 If they say, Come with us, let us *lay wait for blood, let us lurk privily for the innocent without cause:

12 Let us swallow them up alive as the grave; and whole, *as those that go down into the pit:

13 We shall find all precious substance, we shall fill our houses with spoil:

14 Cast in thy lot among us; let us all have one purse;

15 My son, *walk not thou in the way with them; refrain thy foot from their path:

16 For *their feet run to evil, and make haste to shed blood:

17 (Surely in vain the net is spread *in the sight of any bird:)

18 And they lay wait for their own blood; they lurk privily for their own lives.

19 So *are the ways of every one that is greedy of gain; which taketh away the life of the owners thereof.

20 ¶ *Wisdom crieth without; she uttereth her voice in the streets:

21 She crieth in the chief place of concourse, in the openings of the gates: in the city she uttereth her words, *saying*,

22 How long, ye simple ones, will ye love simplicity? and the scorners delight in their scorning, and fools hate knowledge?

23 Turn you at my reproof: behold, *I will pour out my Spirit unto you, I will make known my words unto you.

24 ¶ Because *I have called, and ye refused; I have stretched out my hand, and no man regarded;

25 But ye *have set at nought all my counsel, and would none of my reproof:

26 I also will laugh at your calamity; I will mock when your fear cometh;

27 When your fear cometh as desolation, and your destruction cometh as a whirlwind; when distress and anguish cometh upon you.

28 Then *shall they call upon me, but I will not answer; they shall seek me early, but they shall not find me:

29 For that they *hated knowledge, and did not choose the fear of the LORD:

30 They would none of my counsel; they despised all my reproof:

31 Therefore *shall they eat of the fruit of their own way, and be filled with their own devices.

32 For the *turning away of the simple shall slay them, and the prosperity of fools shall destroy them.

33 But whoso hearkeneth unto me shall dwell safely, and shall be quiet from fear of evil.

CHAPTER II.

1 *Wisdom promises godliness to her children*, 10 *protection from evil company*, 20 *and direction in good ways.*

MY son, if thou wilt receive my words, and hide my commandments with thee;

2 So that thou incline thine ear unto wisdom, *and* apply thine heart to understanding;

3 Yea, if thou criest after knowledge, *and* liftest up thy voice for understanding;

4 If *thou seekest her as silver, and searchest for her as *for* hid treasures;

5 Then shalt thou understand the fear of the LORD, and find the knowledge of God.

6 For *the LORD giveth wisdom: out of his mouth cometh knowledge and understanding.

7 He layeth up sound wisdom for the righteous: *he is* a buckler to them that walk uprightly.

8 He keepeth the paths of judgment, and preserveth *the way of his saints.

9 Then shalt thou understand righteousness, and judgment, and equity; *yea,* every good path.

10 ¶ When wisdom entereth into thine heart, and knowledge is pleasant unto thy soul;

11 Discretion shall preserve thee, *understanding shall keep thee:

12 To deliver thee from the way of the evil man, from the man that speaketh froward things;

13 Who leave the paths of uprightness, to walk *in the ways of darkness;

14 Who rejoice to do evil, *and* delight in the frowardness of the wicked;

15 Whose ways *are* crooked, and *they* froward in their paths:

16 To deliver thee from the strange woman, *even* from the stranger *which* flattereth with her words;

17 Which *forsaketh the guide of her youth, and forgetteth the *covenant of her God.

18 For her house inclineth unto death, and her paths unto the dead.

19 None *that go unto her return again, neither take they hold of the paths of life.

20 That thou mayest *walk in the way of good men, and keep the paths of the righteous.

21 For the upright shall dwell in the land, and the perfect shall remain in it.

22 But the wicked shall be cut off from the earth, and the transgressors shall be rooted out of it.

CHAPTER III.

1 *Exhortation to obedience*, 6 *faith*, 7 *mortification*, 9 *devotion*, 11 *patience*. 13 *Happy gain of wisdom.*

MY son, forget not my law; *but let thine heart keep my commandments:

2 For length of days, and *long life, and peace, shall they add to thee.

3 Let not mercy and truth forsake thee: bind *them about thy neck; *write them upon the table of thine heart:

4 So *shalt thou find favour and *good understanding in the sight of God and man.

5 ¶ Trust in the LORD with all thine heart; and *lean not unto thine own understanding.

6 In *all thy ways acknowledge him, and he shall *direct thy paths.

7 Be *not wise in thine own eyes: fear the LORD, and depart from evil.

8 It shall be *health to thy navel, and *marrow to thy bones.

9 Honour *the LORD with thy substance, and with the first-fruits of all thine increase:

10 So *shall thy barns be filled with plenty, and thy presses shall burst out with new wine.

11 ¶ My son, *despise not the chastening of the LORD; neither be weary of his correction:

INTRODUCTION—PROVERBS.

Though the *Heb.* used the same term for proverb and parable, the *Gr.* employs two, though the sacred writers have not always appeared to recognise a distinction. The term for proverb is, *paroimia*, which the *Gr.* translators employ for the title of this book, evidently with special reference to the later definition of a proverb, as a trite sententious form of speech, which appears to be the best meaning of the term. John uses the same term to designate our Saviour's instructions, in view of their characteristic obscurity, (cf. ch. 16. 25-29, *Gr.*), and even for his illustrative discourses, (ch. 10. 6,), whose sense was not at once obvious to all his hearers. This form of instruction was well adapted to aid the learner. The parallel structure of sentences, the repetition, contrast, or comparison of thought, were all calculated to facilitate the efforts of memory; and precepts of practical wisdom, which extended into logical discourses, might have failed to make abiding impressions, by reason of their length or complicated character, were thus compressed into pithy, and, for the most part, very plain statements. Such a mode of instruction has distinguished the written or traditional literature of all nations, and was, and still is, peculiarly current in the East.

In this book, however, we are supplied with a proverbial wisdom commended by the seal of divine inspiration. God has condescended to become our teacher on the practical affairs belonging to all the relations of life. He has adapted His instruction to the plain and unlettered, and presented, in this striking and impressive method, the great principles of duty to Him and to our fellow-men. To the prime motive of all right conduct, the fear of God, are added all lawful and subordinate incentives, such as honour, interest, love, fear, and natural affection. Besides the terror excited by an apprehension of God's justly provoked judgments, we are warned against evil-doing by the exhibition of the inevitable temporal results of impiety, injustice, profligacy, idleness, laziness, indolence, drunkenness, and debauchery. To the rewards of true piety which follow in eternity, are promised the peace, security, love, and approbation of the good, and the comforts of a clear conscience, which render this life truly happy.

II.—INSPIRATION AND AUTHORSHIP.—With no important exception, Jewish and Christian writers have received this book as the inspired production of Solomon. It is the first book of the Bible prefaced by the name of the author. The N. T. abounds with citations from the Proverbs. Its intrinsic excellence commends it to us as the production of a higher authority than the apocryphal writings, such as Wisdom or Ecclesiasticus. Solomon lived 500 years before the "seven wise men" of Greece, and 700 before the age of Socrates, Plato, and Aristotle. It is thus very evident, whatever theory of his sources of knowledge be adopted, that he did no draw upon any heathen repositories with which we are acquainted. It is far more probable, that by the various migrations, captivities, and dispersions of the Jews, heathen philosophers drew from this inspired fountain many of those streams, which continue to refresh mankind amidst the otherwise barren and parched deserts of profane literature.

As, however, the Psalms are ascribed to David, because he was the leading author, so the ascription of this book to Solomon, is entirely consistent with the titles of chs. 30 and 31, which assign those chapters to Agur and Lemuel respectively. Of these persons we know nothing. This is not the place for discussing the various speculations respecting them. By a slight change of reading some propose to translate ch. 30. 1: "The words of Agur, the son of her, who was obeyed, (*i.e.* the Queen of) Massa; and ch. 31. 1: "The words of Lemuel, king of Massa;" but to this the earliest versions are contradictory, and nothing other than the strongest exegetical necessity ought to be allowed to justify a departure from a well established reading and version, when nothing useful to our knowledge is gained. It is better to confess ignorance than indulge in useless conjectures.

It is probable that out of the "three thousand proverbs" (1 Ki. 4. 32,), which Solomon spoke, he selected and edited chs. 1-24, during his life. Chs. 25-29. were also of his production, and copied out in the days of Hezekiah, by his "men," perhaps, the prophets Isaiah, Hosea, and Micah. Such a work was evidently in the spirit of this pious monarch, who set his heart so fully on a reformation of God's worship. Learned men have endeavoured to establish the theory that Solomon himself was only a collector; or that the other parts of the book, as these chapters, were also selections by later hands; but the reasons adduced to maintain these views have never appeared so satisfactory as to change the usual opinions on the subject, which have the sanction of the most ancient and reliable authorities.

III.—DIVISIONS OF THE BOOK.—Such a work is, of course, not susceptible of any logical analysis. There are, however, some well-defined marks of division, so that very generally, the book is divided into five or six parts.

1. The first contains nine chapters, in which are discussed and enforced by illustration, admonition, and encouragement, the principles and blessings of wisdom, and the pernicious schemes and practices of sinful persons. These chapters are introductory. With few specimens of the proper proverb, they are distinguished by its conciseness and terseness. The sentences follow very strictly the form of parallelism; and generally of the synonymous species, only forty of the synthetic, and four (ch. 3. 32-35) of the antithetic appearing. The style is ornate, the figures bolder and fuller, and the illustrations more striking and extended.

2. The antithetic and synthetic parallelism, to the exclusion of the synonymous, distinguish chs. 10-22. 16, and the verses are entirely unconnected, each containing a complete sense in itself.

3. Chs. 22. 16,-24., present a series of admonitions as if addressed to a pupil, and generally each topic occupies two or more verses.

4. Chs. 25-29. are entitled to be regarded as a distinct portion, for the reason above given, as to its origin. The style is very much mixed; of the peculiarities of, parts 2 and 3.

5. Ch. 30. is peculiar, not only for its authorship, but as a specimen of the kind of proverb, which has been described as "dark sayings" or "riddles."

6. To a few pregnant, but concise admonitions, suitable for a king, is added a most inimitable portraiture of female character. In both parts, 5 and 6, the distinctive peculiarity of the original proverbial style gives place to the modifications already mentioned, as marking a later composition, though both retain the concise and nervous method of stating truth, equally valuable for its deep impression, and permanent retention by the memory.

12 For whom the LORD loveth he correcteth, 'even as a father the son *in whom* he delighteth.
13 ¶ Happy *is* the man *that* findeth wisdom, and *the* man *that* getteth understanding.
14 For ᵐ the merchandise of it *is* better than the merchandise of silver, and the gain thereof than fine gold.
15 She *is* more precious than rubies: and all ⁿ the things thou canst desire are not to be compared unto her.
16 Length ᵒ of days *is* in her right hand; *and* in her left hand riches and honour.
17 Her ᵖ ways *are* ways of pleasantness, and all her paths *are* peace.
18 She is ᑫ a tree of life to them that lay hold upon her; and happy *is every one* that retaineth her.
19 The ʳ LORD by wisdom hath founded the earth; by understanding hath he ⁶ established the heavens.
20 By his knowledge the depths are broken up, and ˢ the clouds drop down the dew.
21 ¶ My son, let not them depart from thine eyes: keep sound wisdom and discretion:
22 So shall they be life unto thy soul, and grace to thy neck.
23 Then shalt thou walk in thy way safely, and thy foot shall not stumble.
24 When ᵗ thou liest down, thou shalt not be afraid; yea, thou shalt lie down, and thy sleep shall be sweet.
25 Be not afraid of sudden fear, neither of the desolation of the wicked, when it cometh.
26 For the LORD shall be thy confidence, and shall keep thy foot from being taken.
27 ¶ Withhold ᵘ not good from ⁷ them to whom it is due, when it is in the power of thine hand to do *it*.
28 Say ᵛ not unto thy neighbour, Go, and come again, and to-morrow I will give; when thou hast it by thee.
29 ⁶ Devise not evil against thy neighbour, seeing he dwelleth securely by thee.
30 Strive ʷ not with a man without cause, if he have done thee no harm.
31 ¶ Envy thou not ⁹ the oppressor, and choose none of his ways.
32 For the froward *is* abomination to the LORD: but his secret *is* with the righteous.
33 The ˣ curse of the LORD *is* in the house of the wicked: but ʸ he blesseth the habitation of the just.
34 Surely ᶻ he scorneth the scorners: but he giveth grace unto the lowly.
35 The ᵃ wise shall inherit glory: but shame ¹⁰ shall be the promotion of fools.

CHAPTER IV.

1 *Solomon, to persuade obedience,* 3 *shows what instruction he had of his parents.*

HEAR, ᵃ ye children, the instruction of a father, and attend to know understanding.
2 For I give you good doctrine, forsake ye not my law.
3 For I was my father's son, ᵇ tender and only *beloved* in the sight of my mother.
4 He ᶜ taught me also, and said unto me, Let thine heart retain my words: keep my commandments, and live.
5 Get wisdom, get understanding: forget *it* not; neither decline from the words of my mouth.

6 Forsake her not, and she shall preserve thee; ᵈ love her, and she shall keep thee.
7 Wisdom ᵉ *is* the principal thing; *therefore* get wisdom: and with all thy getting get understanding.
8 Exalt ᶠ her, and she shall promote thee; she shall bring thee to honour, when thou dost embrace her.
9 She shall give to thine head an ornament of grace: ¹ a crown of glory shall she deliver to thee.
10 Hear, O my son, and receive my sayings; and the years of thy life shall be many.
11 I have taught thee in the way of wisdom; I have led thee in right paths.
12 When thou goest, ᵍ thy steps shall not be straitened; ʰ and when thou runnest, thou shalt not stumble.
13 Take fast hold of instruction; let *her* not go; keep her; for she *is* thy life.
14 ¶ Enter not into the path of the wicked, and go not in the way of evil *men.*
15 Avoid it, pass not by it, turn from it, and pass away.
16 For they sleep not, except they have done mischief; and their sleep is taken away, unless they cause *some* to fall.
17 For they eat the bread of wickedness, and drink the wine of violence.
18 But ⁱ the path of the just ʲ *is* as the shining light, that shineth more and more unto the perfect day.
19 The ᵏ way of the wicked *is* as darkness; they know not at what they stumble.
20 ¶ My son, attend to my words; incline thine ear unto my sayings:
21 Let them not depart from thine eyes; keep them in the midst of thine heart:
22 For they *are* life unto those that find them, and ² health to all their flesh.
23 ¶ Keep thy heart ³ with all diligence; for out of it *are* the issues of life.
24 Put away from thee ⁴ a froward mouth, and perverse lips put far from thee.
25 Let thine eyes look right on, and let thine eyelids look straight before thee.
26 Ponder the path of thy feet, and ⁵ let all thy ways be established.
27 Turn not to the right hand nor to the left: ˡ remove thy foot from evil.

CHAPTER V.

1 *Solomon exhorts to study wisdom:* 3 *mischief of whoredom and riot:* 15 *he exhorts to contentedness, liberality, and chastity.*

MY son, attend unto my wisdom, *and* bow thine ear to my understanding;
2 That thou mayest regard discretion, and *that* thy lips may ᵃ keep knowledge.
3 ¶ For the lips of a strange woman drop *as* an honey-comb, and her ¹ mouth *is* smoother than oil:
4 But her end is ᵇ bitter as wormwood, sharp ᶜ as a two-edged sword.
5 Her feet go down ᵈ to death; her steps take hold on hell.
6 Lest thou shouldest ponder the path of life, her ways are moveable, *that* thou canst not know *them.*
7 Hear me now therefore, O ye children, and depart not from the words of my mouth.
8 Remove thy way far from her, and come not nigh the door of her house;
9 Lest thou give thine honour unto others, and thy years unto the cruel;
10 Lest strangers be filled with ² thy

CHAPTER I.

Ver. 1-33. After the title the writer defines the design and nature of the instructions of the book. He paternally invites attention to those instructions, and warns his readers against the enticements of the wicked. In a beautiful personification, Wisdom is then introduced, in a most solemn and impressive manner, publicly inviting men to receive its teachings, warning those who reject, and encouraging those who accept, the proffered instructions.

1-4. (Cf. *Intr.* I.). To know... instruction—lit., *For knowing*, i.e., such is the design of these writings. wisdom—or, the use of the best means for the best ends, is generally employed in this book for true piety. instruction — discipline, by which men are trained. to perceive [lit., *for perceiving*, the meaning. design as above] ... understanding — i.e., words which enable one to discern good and evil. To receive ... of wisdom—For receiving that discipline which *discretion* imparts. The Heb. for wisdom differs from that of v. 2, and denotes rather discreet counsel. Cf. the opposite traits of the fool (ch. 16. 22.). justice... equity—all the attributes of one, upright in all his relations to God and man. simple—one easily led to good or evil; so the parallel young man—one inexperienced. subtilty — or, prudence, (ch. 3. 21; 5. 2.). discretion—*lit., device*, both qualities, either good or bad, according to their use. Here good, as they imply wariness by which to escape evil and find good. 5, 6. Such writings, the wise, who pursue right ends by right means, will value. learning—not the act, but matter of it. wise counsels—or, the art and principles of governing. To understand—so as to ... such will be the result. interpretation—(cf. *Marg.*). words of the wise—(cf. v. 2.). dark sayings—(cf. Ps. 49. 4; John, 16. 25; and *Intr.* I.). 7. The fear of the Lord—The principle of true piety (cf. ch. 2. 5; 14. 26, 27; Job. 28 28; Ps. 34. 11; 111. 10; Acts, 9. 31.). beginning—first part, foundation. fools—the stupid and indifferent to God's character and government; hence the wicked. 8. My son—This paternal form denotes a tender regard for the reader. Filial sentiments rank next to piety towards God, and insure most distinguished rewards (cf. ch. 6. 20; Eph. 6. 2, 3.). On the figures of v. 9. cf. Gen. 41. 42; Sol. Song, 1. 10; 4. 9. 10-19. A solemn warning against temptation. 10. entice—*lit., open the way.* consent ... not—sin is in consenting or yielding to temptation, not in being tempted. 11-14. Murder and robbery are given as specific illustrations. lay wait ... lurk privily—express an effort and hope for successful concealment. swallow ... grave—utterly destroy the victim and traces of the crime (Num. 16. 33; Ps. 55. 15.). Abundant rewards of villany are promised as the fruits of this easy and safe course. 15, 16. The society of the wicked (way, or path) is dangerous. Avoid the beginnings of sin (ch. 4. 14; Ps. 1. 1; 119. 101.). 17-19. Men warned ought to escape danger, as birds instinctively avoid visibly spread nets. But stupid sinners rush to their own ruin (Ps. 9. 16.), and, greedy of gain, succeed in the very schemes which destroy them (1 Tim. 6. 10,), not only failing to catch others, but procuring their own destruction. 20-33. Some interpreters regard this address as the language of the Son of God under the name of Wisdom (cf. Luke,

11. 49.). Others think that wisdom, as the divine attribute specially employed in acts of counsel and admonition, is here personified, and represents God. In either case, the address is a most solemn and divine admonition, whose matter and spirit is eminently evangelical and impressive cf. note on ch. 8.). 20. Wisdom—*lit., Wisdoms*, the plural used either because of the unusual sense, or as indicative of the great excellency of wisdom (cf. ch. 9. 1.). streets—or, most public places, not secretly. 21. The publicity further indicated by terms designating places of most common resort. 22. simple ones—(cf. v. 4.). simplicity—implying ignorance. scorners—(Ps. 1. 1.), who despise, as well as reject, truth. fools—though a different word is used from that of v. 7, yet it is of the same meaning. 23. reproof—implying conviction, deserving it (cf. John, 16. 8, *Marg.*). pour out—abundantly impart. my Spirit—whether of Wisdom personified, or of Christ, a divine agent. 24. stretched ... hand — earnestness, especially in beseeching, is denoted by the figure (cf. Job, 11. 13; Ps. 68, 31; 88. 9.) 25. set at nought—rejected as of no value. would none of—*lit., were not willing or inclined to it.* 26, 27. In their extreme distress, He will not only refuse help, but aggravate it by derision. fear—the object of it. desolation—*lit., a tumultuous noise*, denoting their utter confusion. destruction—or, calamity (v. 26,). compared to a whirlwind, as to fatal rapidity. distress—(Ps. 4. 1; 44. 11.) anguish—a state of inextricable oppression, the deepest despair. 28. Now, no prayers or most diligent seeking will avail (ch. 8. 17.). 29, 30. The sinner's infatuated rejection brings his ruin. 31. fruit ... way—result of conduct (Isa. 3. 10; Ez. 11. 21; Rom. 6. 21; Gal. 6. 7, 8.). be filled—even to repletion (Ps. 123. 4.). 32. turning away—i.e., from the call of v. 23. simple—as v. 22. prosperity—quiet, implying indifference. 33. dwell safely — *lit., in confidence* (Deut. 12. 10.). be quiet—or, at ease, in real prosperity. from fear—without fear.

CHAPTER II.

Ver. 1-22. Men are invited to seek wisdom, because it teaches those principles by which they may obtain God's guidance, and avoid the society and influence of the wicked, whose pernicious courses are described.

1-5. Diligence in hearing and praying for instruction must be used to secure the great principle of godliness, the fear of God. 1. hide ... with thee—*lay up in store* (cf. ch. 7. 1.). 2. Listen attentively and reflect seriously (ch. 1. 24; Ps. 130. 2.). understanding—right perception of truth. 3. Yea, if—*lit., When if*, i.e., in such a case. knowledge—or, discrimination. understanding—as v. 2. 4. There must be earnest prayer and effort. 5. understand—or, perceive intelligently. find — obtain. 6. For—God is ready (Jam. 1. 5: 4. 8.). out of his mouth—by revelation from Him. 7. sound wisdom—*lit., substance*, opposed to what is fictitious. According to the context, this may be assistance, as here corresponding with *buckler*, or safety, or wisdom, which procures it (cf. ch. 3. 21; 8. 14; 18. 1; Job, 6. 13; 12. 13.). layeth up—provides, ever ready. 8. keepeth ... way—God defends the right way, and those in it. saints — objects of favour cf. Ps. 4. 3; &c.). He guides and guards them. 9. Then—emphatic, in such a case. righteousness, ... path—all parts of duty to God and man. 10, 11. idea of v. 9.

wealth, and thy labours be in the house of a stranger;

11 And thou mourn at the last, when thy flesh and thy body are consumed,

12 And say, How have I hated instruction, and my heart despised reproof;

13 And have not obeyed the voice of my teachers, nor inclined mine ear to them that instructed me!

14 I was almost in all evil in the midst of the congregation and assembly.

15 ¶ Drink waters out of thine own cistern, and running waters out of thine own well.

16 Let thy fountains be dispersed abroad, and rivers of waters in the streets.

17 Let them be only thine own, and not strangers' with thee.

18 Let thy fountain be blessed: and rejoice with the wife of thy youth.

19 Let her be as the loving hind and pleasant roe; let her breasts satisfy thee at all times; and be thou ravished always with her love.

20 And why wilt thou, my son, be ravished with a strange woman, and embrace the bosom of a stranger?

21 For the ways of man are before the eyes of the LORD, and he pondereth all his goings.

22 His own iniquities shall take the wicked himself, and he shall be holden with the cords of his sins.

23 He shall die without instruction; and in the greatness of his folly he shall go astray.

CHAPTER VI.

1 *Against suretiship, 6 and idleness. 16 Seven things hateful to God. 20 Blessings of obedience. 25 Mischiefs of whoredom.*

MY son, if thou be surety for thy friend, if thou hast stricken thy hand with a stranger,

2 Thou art snared with the words of thy mouth, thou art taken with the words of thy mouth.

3 Do this now, my son, and deliver thyself, when thou art come into the hand of thy friend; go, humble thyself, and make sure thy friend.

4 Give not sleep to thine eyes, nor slumber to thine eyelids.

5 Deliver thyself as a roe from the hand of the hunter, and as a bird from the hand of the fowler.

6 ¶ Go to the ant, thou sluggard; consider her ways, and be wise:

7 Which having no guide, overseer, or ruler,

8 Provideth her meat in the summer, and gathereth her food in the harvest.

9 How long wilt thou sleep, O sluggard? when wilt thou arise out of thy sleep?

10 Yet a little sleep, a little slumber, a little folding of the hands to sleep:

11 So shall thy poverty come as one that travelleth, and thy want as an armed man.

12 ¶ A naughty person, a wicked man, walketh with a froward mouth.

13 He winketh with his eyes, he speaketh with his feet, he teacheth with his fingers;

14 Frowardness is in his heart, he deviseth mischief continually; he soweth discord.

15 Therefore shall his calamity come suddenly; suddenly shall he be broken without remedy.

16 ¶ These six *things* doth the LORD hate; yea, seven are an abomination unto him:

17 A proud look, a lying tongue, and hands that shed innocent blood,

18 An heart that deviseth wicked imaginations, feet that be swift in running to mischief,

19 A false witness *that* speaketh lies, and he that soweth discord among brethren.

20 ¶ My son, keep thy father's commandment, and forsake not the law of thy mother:

21 Bind them continually upon thine heart, *and* tie them about thy neck.

22 When thou goest, it shall lead thee; when thou sleepest, it shall keep thee; and *when* thou awakest, it shall talk with thee.

23 For the commandment *is* a lamp; and the law *is* light; and reproofs of instruction *are* the way of life:

24 To keep thee from the evil woman, from the flattery of the tongue of a strange woman.

25 Lust not after her beauty in thine heart; neither let her take thee with her eyelids.

26 For by means of a whorish woman *a man is brought* to a piece of bread; and the adulteress will hunt for the precious life.

27 Can a man take fire in his bosom, and his clothes not be burnt?

28 Can one go upon hot coals, and his feet not be burnt?

29 So he that goeth in to his neighbour's wife; whosoever toucheth her shall not be innocent.

30 *Men* do not despise a thief, if he steal to satisfy his soul when he is hungry;

31 But *if* he be found, he shall restore sevenfold; he shall give all the substance of his house.

32 *But* whoso committeth adultery with a woman lacketh understanding: he *that* doeth it destroyeth his own soul.

33 A wound and dishonour shall he get; and his reproach shall not be wiped away.

34 For jealousy *is* the rage of a man; therefore he will not spare in the day of vengeance.

35 ¶ He will not regard any ransom; neither will he rest content, though thou givest many gifts.

CHAPTER VII.

1 *Solomon persuades to obedience, and to a sincere and kind familiarity with wisdom. 6 Cunning of a lewd woman, etc.*

MY son, keep my words, and lay up my commandments with thee.

2 Keep my commandments, and live; and my law as the apple of thine eye.

3 Bind them upon thy fingers, write them upon the table of thine heart.

4 Say unto wisdom, Thou *art* my sister; and call understanding *thy* kinswoman:

5 That they may keep thee from the strange woman, from the stranger *which* flattereth with her words.

6 ¶ For at the window of my house I looked through my casement,

7 And beheld among the simple ones, I discerned among the youths, a young man void of understanding,

8 Passing through the street near her corner; and he went the way to her house,

9 In the twilight, in the evening, in the black and dark night;

10 And, behold, there met him a woman

amplified; on terms, cf. v. 4, and v. 2. 12-15. To deliver—as from great danger (ch. 6. 5.). way... man—(Ps. 1. 1.. froward things—perversity (ch. 6. 14; 23. 23,), what is opposed to truth. paths of uprightness—or, plainness, walk — habitually act; 14. and that with pleasure, in ignorance of good and pursuit of evil. frowardness—not only their own perversity, but that of others is their delight. They love most the worst things. 15. crooked —tortuous, unprincipled. fr. ward—*lit.*, (they) are going back, not only aside from right, but opposite to it. 16-19. Deliverance from another danger. the s'range woman—this term is often used for harlot, or loose woman (Jud. 11. 1, 2,), married (ch. 7. 5, 19, or not, 1 Ki. 11. 1,), so called, because such were, perhaps at first, foreigners, though *strange* may also denote whatever is opposed to right or proper, as *strange fire* Num. 3. 4; ; *strange incense* Ex. 30. 9,). flattereth—*lit.*, *smooths*. her words—(Ps. 5, 9.). 17. guide... youthlawful husband (Jer. 3. 4,). covenant... God —of marriage made in God's name. 18. inclineth—sinks down (cf. Num. 13. 31.). the dead—or, shades of the departed (I's. 88. 10.). 19. *i.e.*, such as remain impenitent (cf. Eccl. 7. 26.). paths of life—(l's. 16. 11, , opposed to paths unto the dead. 20. That ... way of g. d —*i.e.*. Such is the object of these warnings. 21, 22. (Cf. Ps. 37, 3, 9, 22, 27.). transgressors —or, impious rebels (cf. Jer. 9. 2.. rooted out—utterly destroyed, as trees plucked up by the roots.

CHAPTER III.

Ver. 1-35. The study of truth commended. God must be feared, honoured, and trusted, and filial submission, under chastisement, exhibited. The excellence of wisdom urged and illustrated by its place in the divine counsels. Piety enforced by a contrast of the destiny of the righteous and the wicked. 1. law and commandments—all divine instructions (cf. Ps. 119.'. let thine heart keep —or, sincerely observe (ch. 4. 13; 5. 2.). 2. length... life—often promised as blessings (Ps. 21. 4; 91. 10.). peace—includes prosperity (Ps. 125. 5.). add—abound to thee. 3. mercy and truth—God's faithfulness to his promises is often expressed by these terms (Ps. 25. 10; 67. 3.). As attributes of men, they express integrity in a wide sense (ch. 16. 6; 20. 28.). bind... write... heart — outwardly adorn and inwardly govern motives. 4. favourgrace, amiability (ch. 22. 11; Ps. 45. 2; ; united with this, a good understanding—(cf. *Marg.*,), a discrimination, which secures success. in the sight ... man—such as God and man approve. 5. Trust ... heart — This is the centre and marrow of true wisdom (ch. 22. 19; 28. 25.). The positive duty has its corresponding negation in the admonition against self-confidence. 6. ways—(Ps. 1. 1.). acknowledge—by seeking His wise aid (ch. 16. 3; Ps. 37. 5; Jer. 9. 23, 24.). direct—*lit.*, *make plain* (cf. Heb. 12. 13.). 7. (Cf. ch. 27. 2; Rom. 12. 16.. fear .. evil — reverentially regarding His law. 8. It—This conduct. health—(cf. *Marg.*). to thy navel—for all the organs of nourishment. marrow — (cf. *Marg.*). bones —frame of body. True piety promotes bodily health. 9, 10. (Cf. ch. 11. 25; Ex. 23. 19; Deut. 18. 4; Isa. 32. 8; 2 Cor. 9. 13.). presses— or, wine fats (Joel, 2. 24; 3. 13.). 11, 12. The true intent of afflictions considered; they do not contradict the assertion of the blessed state of the pious (Job, 5. 17; Heb. 12. 5, 6.).

he delighteth — or, receiveth as denoting reconciliation regarding the offence which produced chastisement. 13. findeth — *lit.*, *reaches*, or, *obtains by seeking.* getteth—*lit.*, *draws out*, as n.etals by digging. 14, 15. The figure of v. 13 carried out. it—*i.e.*, wisdom. merchandise — acquisition by trading. fine gold—dug gold, solid as a *nugget*. rubiesgems, or pearls. 16, 17. Wisdom personified as bringing the best blessings cf. Mat. 6. 33; 1 Tim, 4. 8.). Her ways—Such as she directs us to take. 18. Wisdom allegorised as a tree of life—(Gen. 2. 9; 3. 22,), whose fruit preserves life, gives all that makes living a blessing. 19, 20. The place of wisdom in the economy of creation and providence commends it to men, who, in proportion to their finite powers, may possess this invaluable attribute, and are thus encouraged by the divine example of its use, to seek its possession. 21. sound wisdom—(cf. ch. 2. 7.). let ... eyes—*i.e.*, these words of instruction. 22-24. assign reasons in their value for happiness and ornament, guidance and support in dangers, both when waking and sleeping. 25. Be not—or, You shall not be. sudden fear —what causes it (ch. 1. 27.), any unlooked for evil (Ps. 46. 3; 91. 12; 1 Pet. 3. 14.). desolation—(ch. 1. 27.). 26. The reason; such are objects of God's favour. be thy confidence— *lit., in thy confidence*, in the source of thy strength (cf. Nah. 3. 9, for same construction, Heb.). 27, 28. Promptly fu.fil all obligations both of justice and charity (cf. Jam. 2. 15, 16.). 29, 30. Do not abuse confidence, and avoid litigation. 31. oppressor—or, man of mischief. The destiny of successful evil-doers warns against desiring their lot (Ps. 37. 1, 2, 35, 36.). 32-35. Reasons for the warning. froward— (ch. 2. 15.) secret ... righteous—in their communion (Amos, 3. 7.). 33. curse ... wicked —it abides with them, and will be manifested. 34. The retribution of sinners, as Ps. 18. 26. 35. inherit—as a portion. shame—or, disgrace, as opposed to honour. promotion—(cf. *Marg.*), as honour for well doing makes men conspicuous, so fools are signalised by disgrace.

CHAPTER IV.

Ver. 1-27. To an earnest call for attention to his teachings, the writer adds a commendation of wisdom, preceded and enforced by the counsels of his father and teacher. To this he adds a caution against the devices of the wicked, and a series of exhortations to docility, integrity, and uprightness. 1, 2. (Cf. ch. 1. 8.). to know—in order to know. doctrine—the matter of learning (ch. 1. 5,), such as he had received, (Lam. 3. 1.). 3. father's son—emphatic, a son specially regarded, and so called *tender*, as an object of special care (cf. 1 Chr. 22. 7; 29. 1); an idea further expressed by only beloved (or, as an only son, (Gen. 22. 2,), though he had brothers (1 Chr. 3. 5.). 4. He taught—or, directed me. retain—as well as receive. keep ... and live—observe, that you may live (ch. 7. 2.). 5. Get—As a possession, not to be given up. neither decline—*i.e.*, from obeying my word. 6. Not only accept but love wisdom, who will keep thee from evil, and evil from thee. 7. (Cf. Job, 28. 28.). getting—or, possession, a desire for wisdom is wise. 8. As you highly esteem her, she will raise you to honour. embrace her—with fond affection. 9. ornament—such as the chaplet or wreath of conquerors. deliver — (cf. Gen. 14. 20.). The allusion to a shield, contained in the

with the *f* attire of an harlot, and subtil of heart.
11 (She *is* loud and stubborn; *g* her feet abide not in her house:
12 Now *is* she without, now in the streets, and lieth in wait at every corner.)
13 So she caught him, and kissed him, *and* ³ with an impudent face said unto him,
14 ⁴ *I have* peace offerings with me; this day have I paid my vows:
15 Therefore came I forth to meet thee, diligently to seek thy face, and I have found thee.
16 I have decked my bed with coverings of tapestry, with carved *works*, with *h* fine linen of Egypt.
17 I have perfumed my bed with myrrh, aloes, and cinnamon.
18 Come, let us take our fill of love until the morning; let us solace ourselves with loves.
19 For the goodman *is* not at home, he is gone a long journey:
20 He hath taken a bag of money ⁵ with him, *and* will come home at ⁶ the day appointed.
21 With her much fair speech she caused him to yield, with the flattering of her lips she forced him.
22 He goeth after her ⁷ straightway, as an ox goeth to the slaughter, or as a fool to the correction of the stocks;
23 Till a dart strike through his liver; as a bird hasteth to the snare, and knoweth not that it *is* for his life.
24 ¶ Hearken unto me now therefore, O ye children, and attend to the words of my mouth.
25 Let not thine heart decline to her ways, go not astray in her paths:
26 For she hath cast down many wounded, yea, *i* many strong men have been slain by her.
27 Her house *is* the way to hell, going down to the chambers of death.

CHAPTER VIII.

1 *Fame, 6 and evidence of wisdom*: 10 *its excellency*, 12 *nature*, 15 *power*, 18 *riches*, 22 *eternity*, 32 *and desirableness*.

DOTH not *a* wisdom cry? and understanding put forth her voice?
2 She standeth in the top of high places, by the way in the places of the paths;
3 She crieth at the gates, at the entry of the city, at the coming in at the doors:
4 Unto you, O men, I call; and my voice is to the sons of man.
5 O ye simple, understand wisdom: and, ye fools, be ye of an understanding heart.
6 Hear; for I will speak of *b* excellent things; and the opening of my lips *shall be* right things.
7 For my mouth shall speak *c* truth; and wickedness *is* ¹ an abomination to my lips.
8 All the words of my mouth *are* in righteousness; *there is* nothing ² froward or perverse in them.
9 They *are* all plain to him that understandeth, and right to them that find knowledge.
10 Receive my instruction, and not silver; and knowledge rather than choice gold.
11 For *d* wisdom *is* better than rubies; and all the things that may be desired are not to be compared to it.
12 I wisdom dwell with ³ prudence, and find out knowledge of witty inventions.
13 The *e* fear of the LORD *is* to hate evil:

pride, *f* and arrogancy, and the evil way, and *g* the froward mouth, do I hate.
14 Counsel *is* mine, and sound wisdom: I *am* understanding; *h* I have strength.
15 By *i* me kings reign, and princes decree justice.
16 By me princes rule, and nobles, *even* all the judges of the earth.
17 I *j* love them that love me; and *k* those that seek me early shall find me.
18 Riches *l* and honour *are* with me; *yea*, durable riches and righteousness.
19 My *m* fruit *is* better than gold, yea, than fine gold; and my revenue than choice silver.
20 I ⁴ lead in the way of righteousness, in the midst of the paths of judgment;
21 That I may cause those that love me to inherit substance; and I will fill their treasures.
22 The *n* LORD possessed me in the beginning of his way, before his works of old.
23 I ⁵ was set up from everlasting, from the beginning, or ever the earth was.
24 When *there were* no depths, I was brought forth; when *there were* no fountains abounding with water.
25 Before *p* the mountains were settled, before the hills was I brought forth:
26 While as yet he had not made the earth, nor the ⁵ fields, nor ⁶ the highest part of the dust of the world.
27 When he prepared the heavens, I *was* there: when he set ⁷ a compass upon the face of the depth:
28 When he established the clouds above; when he strengthened the fountains of the deep:
29 When *q* he gave to the sea his decree, that the waters should not pass his commandment: when *r* he appointed the foundations of the earth:
30 Then *s* I was by him, *as* one brought up *with him:* *t* and I was daily *his* delight, rejoicing always before him;
31 Rejoicing ⁴ in the habitable part of his earth; and *u* my delights *were* with the sons of men.
32 Now therefore hearken unto me, O ye children; *v* for *w* blessed *are they that* keep my ways.
33 Hear instruction, and be wise, and refuse it not.
34 Blessed *is* the man that heareth me, watching daily at my gates, waiting at the posts of my doors.
35 For *x* whoso findeth me findeth life, and shall *y* obtain favour of the LORD.
36 But he that sinneth against me ³ wrongeth his own soul: all they that hate me love death.

CHAPTER IX.

1 *Discipline and doctrine of wisdom*. 13 *Custom*, 16 *and* ⁴ *error of folly*.

WISDOM hath *a* builded her house, she hath hewn out her seven pillars:
2 She hath killed ¹ her beasts; she hath mingled her wine; she hath also furnished her table:
3 She hath *b* sent forth her maidens: she crieth upon the highest places of the city,
4 Whoso *c* is simple, let him turn in hither: *as for* him that wanteth understanding, she saith to him,
5 Come, *d* eat of my bread, and drink of the wine *which* I have mingled.
6 Forsake the foolish, and live; and go in the way of understanding.

Heb., suggests protection as well as honour (cf. v. 6.). 10. (Cf. ch. 2. 1; 3. 2.). 11, 12. way of wisdom—which it prescribes, led thee —lit., caused thee to tread, as a path (Ps. 107. 7.). not be straitened—have ample room (Ps. 18. 36.). 13. Cf. ch. 3. 18.. The figure of laying hold with the hand suggests earnest effort. 14. (Cf. I's. 1. 1.). Avoid all temptations to the beginning of evil. 16, 17. The reason is found in the character of sinners, whose zeal to do evil is forcibly depicted (ch. 6. 4; Ps. 36. 5.). They live by flagrant vices (ch. 1. 13.). Some prefer to render, "Their bread is wickedness, their drink violence" (cf. Job, 15. 16; 34. 7.). 18, 19. As shining light increases from twilight to noonday splendour, so the course of the just increases in purity, but that of the wicked is as thickest darkness, in which one knows not on what he stumbles. 20-22. (Cf. v. 10, 13; ch. 3. 8, &c.). 22. health... flesh—by preserving from vices destructive of health. 23. with all diligence—or, above, or more than all custody (cf. Marg.), all that is kept (cf. Ez. 38. 7.), because the heart is the depository of all wisdom and the source of whatever affects life and character (Mat. 12. 35; 15. 19.). 24. a froward mouth—i.e., a mouth, or words of ill nature. The Heb. word differs from that used (ch. 2. 15; 3. 32.). perverse—or, quarrelling, lips—or, words. 25. Let... before thee—i.e., Pursue a sincere and direct purpose, avoiding temptations. 26. Ponder—Well consider; a wise course results from wise forethought. 27. (Cf. v. 25.). Avoid all byepaths of evil (Deut. 2, 27; 17. 11.). A life of integrity requires attention to heart, speech, eyes, and conduct.

CHAPTER V.

Ver. 1-23. A warning against the seductive arts of wicked women, enforced by considering the advantages of chastity, and the miserable end of the wicked.
1. This connection of *wisdom* and *understanding* is frequent (ch. 2. 2; 3. 7.); the first denotes the use of wise means for wise ends; the other, the exercise of a proper discrimination in their discovery. 2. regard —or, observe. keep—preserve constantly. 3. (Cf. ch. 2. 16.). Her enticing promises are deceitful. 4. her end—*lit., her future*, in sense of reward, what follows (cf. Ps. 37. 37; 73. 17.). Its nature is evinced by the use of figures, opposite those of v. 3. The physical and moral suffering of the deluded profligate are notoriously terrible. 5. feet,... steps—i.e., course of life ends in death. 6. her ways ... know—Some prefer, "that she may not ponder the path of life," &c.; but perhaps a better sense is, "her ways are varied, so as to prevent your knowledge of her true character, and so of true happiness." 8, 9. Avoid the slightest temptation. thine honour — in whatever consisting, strength (ch. 3. 13.), or wealth. thy years—by cutting them off in dissipation. to the cruel—for such the sensual are apt to become. 10. wealth—*lit., strength*, or the result of it. labours—the fruit of thy painful exertions (Ps. 127. 2.). There may be a reference to slavery, a commuted punishment for death due the adulterer (Deut. 22. 22.). 11. at the last—the end, or reward (cf. v. 4.). mourn—roar in pain. flesh and ... body—the whole person under incurable disease. 12-14. The ruined sinner vainly laments his neglect of warning and his sad fate in being brought to public disgrace. evil—for affliction, as Gen. 19. 20; 49. 15. 15-20. By figures, in which well, cistern, and fountain represent the *wife*, and rivers of waters, the children. men are exhorted to constancy and satisfaction in lawful conjugal enjoyments. In v. 16, *fountains* in the plural rather denote the produce or waters of a spring, *lit.*, *what is from a spring*, and corresponds with *rivers of waters*. only thine own—harlots' children have no known father. wife... youth — married in youth. loving... roe—other figures for a wife from the well known beauty of these animals. breasts — cf. Sol. Song, 1. 13; Ez. 23. 3, 8.). ravished—*lit., intoxicated*, i.e., fully satisfied. 21. The reason, God's eye is on you; 22, 23., and He will cause sin to bring its punishment, without instruction—*lit., in want of instruction*, having refused it (cf. Job, 13. 18; Heb. 11. 24.). go astray—*lit., be drunken*. The word is *ravished* (v. 19) here denotes fulness of punishment.

CHAPTER VI.

Ver. 1-35. After admonitions against suretiship and sloth (cf. v. 6-8,), the character and fa·e of the wicked generally are set forth, and the writer (v. 20-35) resumes the warnings against incontinence, pointing out its certain and terrible results. This train of thought seems to intimate the kindred of these vices 1, 2. if—the condition extends through both verses. be surety—art pledged. stricken... hand—bargained (cf. Job, 17. 3.). with a stranger —i.e., for a friend (cf. ch. 11. 15; 17. 18.). 3. come... friend—in his power. humble... sure thy friend—urge as a suppliant, i.e., induce the triend to provide otherwise for his debt, or secure the surety. 4, 5. The danger requires promptness. 6-8. The improvident sluggards usually want sureties. Hence such are advised to industry by the ant's example. 9, 10. Their conduct graphically described; 11., and the fruits of their self-indulgence and indolence presented. as... travelleth—*lit., one who walks backwards and forwards*, i.e., a highwayman. armed man—i.e., one prepared to destroy. 12. A naughty person—*lit., A man of Belial*, or of worthlessness, i.e., for good, and so depraved, or wicked (cf. 1 Sam. 25. 25; 30. 22, &c.). Idleness and vice are allied. Though indolent in acts, he actively and habitually (*walketh*) is illnatured in speech (ch. 4. 24.). 13, 14. If, for fear of detection, he does not speak, he uses signs to carry on his intrigues. These signs are still so used in the East. deviseth—*lit., constructs, as an artisan*. mischief—evil to others. Frowardness—As ch. 2. 14. discord—especially litigation. Cunning is the talent of the weak and lazy. 15. Suddenness aggravates evil (cf. v. 11; ch. 29. 1.). calamity—*lit., a crushing weight*. broken — shivered as a potter's vessel; utterly destroyed (Ps. 2. 9.). 16-19. six... seven—a mode of speaking to arrest attention (ch. 30. 15, 18; Job, 5. 19.). proud look—*lit., eyes of loftiness* (Ps. 131. 1.). Eyes, tongue, &c. for persons. speaketh—*lit., breathes out*, habitually speaks (Ps. 27. 12; Acts, 9. 1.). 20-23. (Cf. ch. 1. 8; 3. 3, &c.). it—cf. v. 23.), denotes the instruction of parents (v. 20.), to which all the qualities of a safe guide and guard and ready teacher are ascribed. It prevents the ingress of evil by supplying good thoughts, even in dreams (ch. 3. 21-23; Ps. 19. 9; 2 Pet. 1. 19.). reproofs —(ch. 1. 23.), the convictions of error produced by instruction. 24. A specimen of

Moral virtues   PROVERBS, X, XI.   *and contrary vices.*

7 He that reproveth a scorner getteth to himself shame; and he that rebuketh a wicked man getteth himself a blot.
8 Reprove *not a scorner, lest he hate thee: *rebuke a wise man, and he will love thee.
9 Give *instruction* to a wise man, and he will be yet wiser: teach a just man, *and he will increase in learning.
10 The *fear of the LORD is the beginning of wisdom; and the knowledge of the Holy *is* understanding:
11 For *by me thy days shall be multiplied, and the years of thy life shall be increased.
12 If *thou be wise, thou shalt be wise for thyself: but if thou scornest, thou alone shalt bear it.
13 ¶ A foolish woman *is* clamorous; *she is* simple, and knoweth nothing.
14 For she sitteth at the door of her house, on a seat in the high places of the city,
15 To call passengers who go right on their ways:
16 Whoso *is* simple, let him turn in hither: and *us for* him that wanteth understanding, she saith to him,
17 Stolen *waters are sweet, and bread *eaten* in secret is pleasant.
18 But he knoweth not that the dead *are* there; *and that* her guests *are* in the depths of hell.

CHAPTER X.

From this chapter to the five and twentieth are sundry observations of moral virtues, and their contrary vices.

THE Proverbs of Solomon. A wise son maketh a glad father: but a foolish son *is* the heaviness of his mother.
2 Treasures *a* of wickedness profit nothing: *but righteousness delivereth from death.
3 The *LORD will not suffer the soul of the righteous to famish: but he casteth away *the substance of the wicked.
4 He becometh poor that dealeth *with* a slack hand; but *d* the hand of the diligent maketh rich.
5 He that gathereth in summer *is* a wise son: but he that sleepeth in harvest is a son that causeth shame.
6 Blessings *are* upon the head of the just: but *violence covereth the mouth of the wicked.
7 The *memory of the just *is* blessed: but the name of the wicked shall rot.
8 The wise in heart will receive commandments: but *a prating fool *shall fall.
9 He *that walketh uprightly walketh surely: but he that perverteth his ways shall be known.
10 He that winketh with the eye causeth sorrow: but a prating fool *shall fall.
11 The *mouth of a righteous man *is* a well of life: but *violence covereth the mouth of the wicked.
12 Hatred stirreth up strifes: but *love covereth all sins.
13 In the *lips of him that hath understanding wisdom is found: but a rod *is* for the back of him that is void of understanding.
14 Wise men lay up knowledge: but the mouth of the foolish *is* near destruction.
15 The *rich man's wealth *is* his strong city: the destruction of the poor *is* their poverty.

16 The labour of the righteous *tendeth* to life: the fruit of the wicked to sin.
17 He *is in* the way of life that keepeth instruction: but he that refuseth reproof *erreth.
18 He that hideth hatred *with* lying lips, and he that uttereth a slander, *is a fool.
19 In *the multitude of words there wanteth not sin: but *he that refraineth his lips *is* wise.
20 The tongue of the just *is as* choice silver: the heart of the wicked *is* little worth.
21 The lips of the righteous feed many: but fools die for want *of wisdom.
22 The *blessing of the LORD, it maketh rich, and he addeth no sorrow with it.
23 *It is* as sport to a fool to do mischief: but a man of understanding hath wisdom.
24 The *fear of the wicked, it shall come upon him: but *the desire of the righteous shall be granted.
25 As the whirlwind passeth, so *is* the wicked no *more:* but *the righteous *is* an everlasting foundation.
26 As vinegar to the teeth, and as smoke to the eyes, so *is* the sluggard to them that send him.
27 The fear of the LORD *prolongeth days: but *the years of the wicked shall be shortened.
28 The *hope of the righteous *shall be* gladness: but the *expectation of the wicked shall perish.
29 The way of the LORD *is* *strength to the upright: *but destruction *shall be* to the workers of iniquity.
30 The righteous shall never be removed: but the wicked shall not inhabit the earth.
31 The mouth of the just bringeth forth wisdom: but the froward tongue shall be cut out.
32 The lips of the righteous know what is acceptable: but the mouth of the wicked *speaketh* frowardness.

CHAPTER XI.

A FALSE balance *is* abomination to the LORD: but *a just weight *is* his delight.
2 When *pride cometh, then cometh shame: but with the lowly *is* wisdom.
3 The integrity of the upright shall guide them: but the perverseness of transgressors shall destroy them.
4 Riches *profit not in the day of wrath: but *righteousness delivereth from death.
5 The righteousness of the perfect shall *direct his way: but the wicked shall fall by his own wickedness.
6 The *righteousness of the upright shall deliver them: but *transgressors shall be taken in *their own* naughtiness.
7 When a wicked man dieth, *his* expectation shall perish; and the hope of unjust men perisheth.
8 The righteous is delivered out of trouble, and the wicked cometh in his stead.
9 An *hypocrite with *his* mouth destroyeth his neighbour: but through knowledge shall the just be delivered.
10 When *it goeth well with the righteous, the city rejoiceth; and when the wicked perish, *there is* shouting.
11 By the blessing of the upright the city is exalted: but it is overthrown by the mouth of the wicked.
12 He that is *void of wisdom despiseth

2 E*

its benefit. By appreciating truth, men are not affected by lying flattery. 25. One of the cautions of this instruction, avoid alluring beauty. take [or, ensnare] ... eyelids—by painting the lashes, females enhanced beauty. 26. The supplied words give a better sense than the old version: "The price of a whore is a piece of bread" adulteress—(cf. *Marg.*,),which the parallel and context (:9-35) sustains. Of similar results of this sin, cf. ch. 5. 9-12. will hunt—alluding to the snares spread by harlots (cr. ch. 7. 6-8.). precious life—more valuable than all else. 27-29. The guilt and danger most obvious. 30, 31. Such a thief is pitied, though heavily punished. sevenfold—(cf. Ex. 22. 1-4,), for many, ample (cf. Gen. 4. 24; Mat. 18. 21,), even if all his wealth is taken. 32. lacketh understanding—or, heart; destitute of moral principle and prudence. 33. dishonour—or, shame, as well as hurt of body (ch. 3. 35,). reproach... away—no restitution will suffice; 34, 35., nor any terms of reconciliation be admitted. regard [or, accept] any ransom.

CHAPTER VII.

Ver. 1-27. The subject continued, by a delineation of the arts of strange women, as a caution to the unwary.

1-4. Similar calls (ch. 3. 1-3; 4. 10, &c.). apple ... eye—pupil of eye, a custody (ch. 4. 23) of special value. Bind ... fingers—as inscriptions on rings. 5. The design of the teaching (cf. ch. 2. 16; 6. 24,). 6. For — or, Since, introducing an example to illustrate the warning, which, whether a narrative or a parable, is equally pertinent. window [or, opening of the] casement—or, lattice. looked —*lit., watched earnestly* (Jud. 5. 28.). 7. simple—as ch. 1. 4. void of, &c.—(cf. ch. 6. 32,). 8. her corner—where she was usually found. went... house—implying, perhaps, confidence in himself by his manner, as denoted in the word "went"—*lit., tread pompously.* 9. The time, *twilight*, ending in darkness. black ... night—*lit., pupil, or, eye, i.e.,* middle of night. 10. attire—that of harlots was sometimes peculiar. subtil—or, wary, cunning. 11, 12. loud—or, noisy, bustling. stubborn—not submissive. without,...streets, ... corner—(cf. 1 Tim. 5. 13; Tit. 2. 5,). 13-15. The preparations for a feast do not necessarily imply peculiar religious professions. The offerer retained part of the victim for a feast (Lev. 3. 9, &c.). This feast she professes was prepared for him whom she boldly addresses as one sought specially to partake of it. 16, 17. my bed—or, couch, adorned in the costliest manner. bed—in v. 17, a place for sleeping. 18-20. There is no fear of discovery. the day appointed—perhaps *lit., a full moon*, i.e., a fortnight's time (cf. v. 19.). 21. caused ... yield—or, inclines. flattering—(cf. ch. 5. 3.). forced him—by persuasion overcoming his scruples. 22. straightway — quickly, either as ignorant of danger, or incapable of resistance. 23. Till—He is now caught (ch. 6. 26.). 24. The inferential admonition is followed, 26, 27., by a more general allegation of the evils of this vice. Even the mightiest fail to resist her deathly allurements.

CHAPTER VIII.

Ver. 1-36. Contrasted with sensual allurements are the advantages of divine wisdom, which publicly invites men, offers the best principles of life, and the most valuable benefits resulting from receiving her counsels. Her relations to the divine plans and acts is introduced, as in ch. 3. 19, 20, though more fully, to commend her desirableness for men, and the whole is closed by an assurance that those finding her find God's favour, and those neglecting ruin themselves. Many regard the passage as a description of the Son of God by the title, Wisdom, which the older Jews used and by which He is called, Luke. 11. 49,), as John. 1. 1, &c., describes Him by that of *Logos*, the Word. But the passage may be taken as a personification of wisdom: for, 1. Though described as with God, wisdom is not asserted to be God. 2. The use of personal attributes is equally consistent with a *personification*, as with the description of a real person. 3. The personal pronouns used accord with the gender (fem.) of wisdom constantly, and are never changed to that of the person meant, as sometimes occurs in a corresponding use of *spirit*, which is neuter in Greek, but to which masculine pronouns are often applied John, 16, 14, . when the acts of the Holy Spirit are described. 4. Such a personification is agreeable to the style of this book (cf. chs. 1. 20; 3. 16, 17; 4. 8; 6. 20 22; 9. 1-4,), whereas no prophetical or other allusions to the Saviour or the new dispensation are found among the quotations of this book in the N. T., and unless this be such, none exist. 5. Nothing is lost as to the importance of the passage, which still remains a most ornate and also solemn and impressive teaching of inspiration on the value of wisdom.

1-4. The publicity and universality of the call contrast with the secrecy and intrigues of the wicked (ch. 7. 8, &c.). 5. wisdom—*lit., subtilty in a good sense*, or, prudence. fools —as ch. 1. 22. 6. excellent things—or, plain, manifest. opening ... things—upright words. 7. For ... truth—*lit., My palate shall meditate*, or (as orientals did) *mutter*, my thoughts expressed only to myself are truth. wickedness — specially falsehood, as opposed to truth. 8. in righteousness—or, righteous (Ps. 9. 8; 11. 7,). froward—*lit., twisted*, or contradictory, i.e., to truth. 9. plain ... understandeth— easily seen by those who apply their minds. that find—implying search. 10. not silver—preferable to it, so last clause implies comparison. 11. (Cf. ch. 3. 14, 15,). 12. prudence—as v. 5. The connection of *wisdom* and *prudence* is that of the dictates of sound wisdom and its application. find... inventions —or, devices, discreet ways ch. 1, 4,). 13. For such is the effect of the fear of God, by which hatred to evil preserves from it. froward mouth—or, speech (ch. 2. 12; 6. 14,). 14. It also gives the elements of good character in counsel. sound wisdom—(ch. 2. 7,). I ... strength—or, "As for me, understanding is strength to me," the source of power (Eccl. 9. 16;;) good judgment gives more efficiency to actions; 15, 16. of which a wisely conducted government is an example. 17. early—or, diligently, which may include the usual sense of early in life. 18. durable ... righteousness —such are the *riches*, enduring sources of happiness in moral possessions (cf. ch. 3. 16,). 19. (Cf. v. 11; 3. 16.). 20, 21. The courses in which wisdom leads conduct to a true present prosperity (ch. 23. 5.). 22-31. Strictly, God's attributes are part of Himself. Yet, to the poetical structure of the whole passage, this commendation of wisdom is entirely consonant. In order of time all His attributes

his neighbour: but a man of understanding holdeth his peace.
13 ⁵ A talebearer revealeth secrets: but he that is of a faithful spirit concealeth the matter.
14 Where ʰ no counsel is, the people fall: but in the multitude of counsellors there is safety.
15 He that is surety for a stranger ⁶ shall smart for it; and he that hateth ⁷ suretiship is sure.
16 A gracious woman retaineth honour; and strong men retain riches.
17 The ⁱ merciful man doeth good to his own soul: but he that is cruel troubleth his own flesh.
18 The wicked worketh a deceitful work: but ʲ to him that soweth righteousness shall be a sure reward.
19 As righteousness tendeth to life; so he that pursueth evil pursueth it to his own death.
20 They that are of a froward heart are abomination to the LORD: but such as are upright in their way are his delight.
21 Though hand join in hand, the wicked shall not be unpunished: but the seed of the righteous shall be delivered.
22 As a jewel of gold in a swine's snout, so is a fair woman which ⁸ is without discretion.
23 The desire of the righteous is only good: but the expectation of the wicked is ᵏ wrath.
24 There is that scattereth, and yet increaseth; and there is that withholdeth more than is meet, but it tendeth to poverty.
25 ⁹ The liberal soul shall be made fat; and ˡ he that watereth shall be watered also himself.
26 He ᵐ that withholdeth corn, the people shall curse him: but ⁿ blessing shall be upon the head of him that selleth it.
27 He that diligently seeketh good procureth favour; ᵒ but he that seeketh mischief, it shall come unto him.
28 He ᵖ that trusteth in his riches shall fall: but ᵠ the righteous shall flourish as a branch.
29 He that troubleth his own house ʳ shall inherit the wind; and the fool shall be servant to the wise of heart.
30 The fruit of the righteous is a tree of life; and he that ¹⁰ winneth souls is wise.
31 Behold, ˢ the righteous shall be recompensed in the earth: much more the wicked and the sinner.

CHAPTER XII.

WHOSO loveth instruction loveth knowledge: but he that hateth reproof is brutish.
2 A good man obtaineth favour of the LORD: but a man of wicked devices will he condemn.
3 A man shall not be established by wickedness: but the root of the righteous shall not be moved.
4 A ᵃ virtuous woman is a crown to her husband: but she that maketh ashamed is as ᵇ rottenness in his bones.
5 The thoughts of the righteous are right: but the counsels of the wicked are deceit.
6 The words of the wicked are to lie in wait for blood: but the mouth of the upright shall deliver them.
7 The ᶜ wicked are overthrown, and are not: but the house of the righteous shall stand.

B. C. 1000.

CHAP. 11.
5 He that walketh, being a talebearer. Lev. 19.16.
ʰ 1 Ki. 12. 1.
6 shall bo sore broken.
7 those that strike hands.
ⁱ Mat. 25. 34.
ʲ Hos. 10.12. Gal. 6. 8, 9. Jam. 3. 18.
⁸ departeth from.
ᵏ Rom. 2. 8.
9 The soul of blessing.
2 Cor. 9. 6.
ˡ Mat. 5. 7.
ᵐ Amos 8.5.
ⁿ Job 29. 13.
ᵒ Esth. 7. 10.
ᵖ Job 31. 24. Mar.10.24. Lu. 12 21.
ᵠ 1 Ti. 6. 17.
ʳ Jer. 17. 8.
ˢ Eccl. 5. 16.
10 taketh. Dan. 12.3. 1 Cor. 9. 19.
Jam. 5.20.
ᵗ Jer. 25. 29. 1 Pet. 4. 17.

CHAP. 12.
ᵃ 1 Cor.11.7.
ᵇ ch. 14. 30.
ᶜ Mat. 7. 24.
ᵈ 1 Sa. 25.17.
1 perverse of heart.
ᵉ Deu. 25. 4.
2 Or, bowels.
ᶠ Gen. 3. 19.
3 Or, the fortress.
ᵍ Jer. 17. 8.
4 The snare of the wicked is
in the transgression of lips.
ʰ 2 Pet. 2. 9.
ⁱ Ia. 3. 10.
ʲ Lu. 18. 11.
ᵇ in that day.
ᵏ Zech.1.5,6.
ˡ 2 Thess.1.6.
ᵐ Rev.22.15.
ⁿ 1 Ki.11.28. ch. 10. 4.
5 Or, deceitful.
ᵒ Is. 50. 4.
7 Or, abundant.
ᵖ Rom. 6. 21. 2 Cor. 4. 17.

CHAP. 13.
ᵃ 1 Sa. 2. 25.
ᵇ Ps. 39. 1. Jam. 3. 2.
ᶜ Col. 3. 9.
Rom. 12. 9.

8 A man shall be commended according to his wisdom: ᵈ but he that is ¹ of a perverse heart shall be despised.
9 He that is despised, and hath a servant, is better than he that honoureth himself, and lacketh bread.
10 A ᵉ righteous man regardeth the life of his beast: but the ² tender mercies of the wicked are cruel.
11 He ᶠ that tilleth his land shall be satisfied with bread: but he that followeth vain persons is void of understanding.
12 The wicked desireth ³ the net of evil men: but the ⁴ root of the righteous yieldeth fruit.
13 ⁴ The wicked is snared by the transgression of his lips: ʰ but the just shall come out of trouble.
14 A man shall be satisfied with good by the fruit of his mouth; ⁱ and the recompence of a man's hands shall be rendered unto him.
15 The ʲ way of a fool is right in his own eyes: but he that hearkeneth unto counsel is wise.
16 A fool's wrath is ⁵ presently known: but a prudent man covereth shame.
17 He that speaketh truth showeth forth righteousness: but a false witness deceit.
18 There is that speaketh like the piercings of a sword: but the tongue of the wise is health.
19 The ʰ lip of truth shall be established for ever: but a lying tongue is but for a moment.
20 Deceit is in the heart of them that imagine evil: but to the counsellors of peace is joy.
21 There ⁱ shall no evil happen to the just: but the wicked shall be filled with mischief.
22 Lying ᵐ lips are abomination to the LORD: but they that deal truly are his delight.
23 A prudent man concealeth knowledge: but the heart of fools proclaimeth foolishness.
24 The ⁿ hand of the diligent shall bear rule: but the ⁶ slothful shall be under tribute.
25 Heaviness in the heart of man maketh it stoop: but ᵒ a good word maketh it glad.
26 The righteous is more ⁷ excellent than his neighbour; but the way of the wicked seduceth them.
27 The slothful man roasteth not that which he took in hunting: but the substance of a diligent man is precious.
28 In the way of righteousness ᵖ is life; and in the pathway thereof there is no death.

CHAPTER XIII.

A WISE son heareth his father's instruction: ᵃ but a scorner heareth not rebuke.
2 A man shall eat good by the fruit of his mouth: but the soul of the transgressors shall eat violence.
3 He ᵇ that keepeth his mouth keepeth his life: but he that openeth wide his lips shall have destruction.
4 The soul of the sluggard desireth, and hath nothing: but the soul of the diligent shall be made fat.
5 A righteous man hateth ᶜ lying: but a wicked man is loathsome, and cometh to shame.

Commendation of Wisdom. PROVERBS, IX, X. *Moral Virtues.*

are coincident and eternal as Himself. But to set forth the importance of wisdom as devising the products of benevolence and power, it is here assigned a precedence. As it has such in divine, so should it be desired in human affairs (cf. ch. 3, 19.). 22. possessed —or, created, in either sense, the idea of precedence. in the beginning—or simply, beginning, in apposition with *me*. before … of old—preceding the most ancient deeds. 23. I was set up—ordained, or inaugurated (Ps. 2. 6.. The other terms carry out the idea of the earliest antiquity, and 24-29. illustrate it by the details of creation. brought forth— (cf. Ps. 90. 2.). abounding—or, laden with water. settled — *i.e.*, sunk in foundations. fields—or, *out places*, deserts, as opposed to (habitable *world*. highest part—or, sum, all particles together. when he set … cepth— marked out the circle, according to the popular idea of the earth, as circular, surrounded by depths on which the visible concave heavens rested. established … deep— *i.e.*, so as to sustain the waters above and repress those below the firmament (Gen. 1, 7-11; Job, 26, 8.). commandment—better, the shore, *i.e.*, of the sea. foundations—figuratively denotes the solid structure (Job, 38, 4; Ps. 24, 2.). 30, 31. one brought up—an object of special and pleasing regard. The bestowal of wisdom on men is represented by its finding a delightful residence and pleasing God. 32-36. Such an attribute men are urged to seek. watching … waiting — *lit.*, *so as to watch;* wait, denoting a most sedulous attention. sinneth … me—or better, missing me, as opposed to finding. 35. (Cf. Luke, 13, 23, 24.). love death—act as if they did (cf. ch. 17. 9.).

CHAPTER IX.

Ver. 1-18. The commendation of wisdom continued, under the figure of a liberal host, and its provisions under that of a feast (cf. Luke, 14. 16-24.. The character of those who are invited is followed by a contrasted description of the rejectors of good counsel; and with the invitations of wisdom are contrasted the allurement of the wicked woman. 1. house—(cf. ch. 8. 34.). her—or, *its* (the house.). seven pillars—the number seven for many, or a sufficiency (ch. 6. 31.). 2. mingled —to enhance the flavour (ch. 23. 30; Isa. 5. 22.. furnished—*lit.*, *set out*, *arranged.* 3. maidens —servants to invite (cf. Ps. 68. 11; Isa. 40. 9.). highest places—ridges or heights, conspicuous places. 4-6. (Cf. ch. 1. 4; 6. 32.. Wisdom not only supplies right but forbids wrong principles. 7, 8. shame—(cf. ch. 3. 35.). a blot—or, stain on character. Both terms denote the evil done by others to one whose faithfulness secures a wise man's love. 9. The more a wise man learns, the more he loves wisdom. 10. (Cf. ch. 1. 7.). of the Holy —*lit.*, *holies*, persons or things, or both. This knowledge gives right perception. 11. (Cf. ch. 3. 16-18; 4 10.). 12. You are mainly concerned in your own conduct. 13. foolish woman — or *lit.*, *woman of folly*, specially manifested by such as are described. clamorous—or, noisy ch. 7. 11.. knoweth nothing —*lit.*, *knoweth not what*, *i.e.*, is right and proper. 14. on a seat — *lit.*, *throne*, takes a prominent place, impudently and haughtily. 15, 16., to allure those who are right minded, and who are addressed as in v. 4, as simple—*i.e.*, easily led (ch. 1. 4 and unsettled, though willing to do right. 17. The language

of a proverb, meaning that forbidden delights are sweet and pleasant, as fruits of risk and danger. 18. (Cf. ch. 2, 18, 19; 7. 27.).

CHAPTER X.

Ver. 1-32. Here begins the second part of the book, ch. 10-22. 16, which, with the third, ch. 22. 16,-ch. 25.. contains series of proverbs whose sense is complete in one or two verses, and which, having no logical connection, admit of no analysis. The parallelism of chs. 10-15. are mostly antithetic; and those of chs. 16-22. 16. synthetic. The evidences of art in the structure are very clear, and indicate, probably, a purpose of facilitating the labour of memorising.

1. wise [and] foolish—as they follow or reject the precepts of wisdom. maketh … father—or, gladdens a father. heaviness—or, grief. 2. Treasures … nothing—*i.e.*, Ill-gotten gains give no true happiness (cf. ch. 4. 17: Mat. 6. 19.. righteousness—especially *beneficence* (Ps. 112. 9.). death—the greatest of all evils. 3. (Cf. Ps. 37. 16-20.). The last clause is better: "He will repel the greedy desires of the wicked." 4. maketh rich—cf. v. 22.). slack—*lit.*, *deceitful*, failing of its purpose (cf. Hos. 7. 16.). 5. son—as ch. 1. 8, 10, and often. sleepeth — in indolence, and not for rest. causeth shame—*lit.*, *is base* (cf. ch. 14. 35; 17. 2.). 6. Blessings—*lit.*, *Praises*. The last clause is better: "The mouth of the wicked covereth, or concealeth, violence, or mischievous devices," to be executed in due time (Ps. 5. 9; 10, 7; Rom. 3. 14,), and hence has no praises (cf. *v*. 11.). 7. blessed—*lit.*, *for a blessing*, or praise. shall rot—*lit.*, *be worm-eaten*, useless and disgusting. 8. wise, &c.—(cf. ch. 9, 8, 9, 16,). opposed to prating fool—or, fool of lips of wicked language. fall — headlong, suddenly. 9. perverteth his way—acts deceitfully. known—discovered and punished. 10. Two vices contrasted; hypocrisy, or insinuating evil against one (ch. 6. 13; Ps. 35. 19,). and rashness of speech. In each case, the results are on the evil doers. 11. a well—or, source of good to himself and others (John, 7. 37, 38.. On last clause cf. *v*. 6. 12. strifes—or, litigations. covereth—by forgiveness and forbearance. 13. In the lips … found—hence, not beaten, as the wicked-speaking fool. void of understanding—(ch. 6. 32; 7. 7.). 14. lay up knowledge—*i.e.*, as treasures for good use. mouth … destruction—or, as to the mouth, &c., destruction is near; they expose themselves to evil by prating. 15. Both by trusting in "uncertain riches" (1 Tim. 6. 17,), or by the evils of poverty (ch. 30, 9,), men, not fearing God, fall into dangers. 16. The industry of the righteous is alone truly successful, while the earnings of the wicked tempt and lead to sin. 17. keepeth—observes reproof, which might direct him aright. 18. Both vices must one day be known and punished, and hence their folly. 19. Much speech involves risk of sin; hence the wisdom of restraining the tongue Ps. 39. 1; Jam. 1. 26.). 20. Right speech is the fruit of a good heart, but the wicked show theirs to be useless. 21. The fool not only fails to benefit others, as do the righteous, but procure their own ruin (cf. *v*. 11, 17; Hos. 4. 6.. 22. it maketh, &c.— *it* is emphatic. Riches from God are without the sorrow of ill-gotten wealth (cf. Eccl. 2. 21-23; 1 Tim. 6. 9, 10, 17.). 23. Sin is the pleasure of the wicked; wisdom that of the good. 24. it—the very thing. The wicked

6 Righteousness *keepeth him that is upright in the way: but wickedness overthroweth ¹ the sinner.
7 There is that maketh himself rich, yet hath nothing: there is that maketh himself poor, yet hath great riches.
8 The ransom of a man's life are his riches: but the poor heareth not rebuke.
9 The light of the righteous rejoiceth: but the ²lamp of the wicked shall be put out.
10 Only by pride cometh contention: but with the well-advised is wisdom.
11 Wealth *gotten by vanity shall be diminished: but he that gathereth ³ by labour shall increase.
12 Hope deferred maketh the heart sick: but when the desire cometh, it is a tree of life.
13 Whoso ⁄despiseth the word shall be destroyed: but he that feareth the commandment ⁴ shall be rewarded.
14 The ᵍ law of the wise is a fountain of life, to depart from ʰ the snares of death.
15 Good understanding giveth favour: but the way of transgressors is hard.
16 Every ⁱ prudent man dealeth with knowledge: but a fool ⁵ layeth open his folly.
17 A wicked messenger falleth into mischief: but ⁶ a faithful ambassador is health.
18 Poverty and shame shall be to him that refuseth instruction: but ⱼ he that regardeth reproof shall be honoured.
19 The desire accomplished is sweet to the soul: but it is abomination to fools to depart from evil.
20 He that walketh with wise men shall be wise: but a companion of fools ⁷ shall be destroyed.
21 Evil ᵏ pursueth sinners: but to the righteous good shall be repaid.
22 A good man leaveth an inheritance to his children's children: and ⁱ the wealth of the sinner is laid up for the just.
23 Much ᵐ food is in the tillage of the poor: but there is that is destroyed for want of judgment.
24 He ⁿ that spareth his rod hateth his son: but he that loveth him chasteneth him betimes.
25 The righteous eateth to the satisfying of his soul: but the belly of the wicked shall want.

CHAPTER XIV.

EVERY ᵃwise woman buildeth her house: but the foolish plucketh it down with her hands.
2 He that walketh in his uprightness feareth the LORD: ᵇ but he that is perverse in his ways despiseth him.
3 In the mouth of the foolish is a rod of pride: ᶜ but the lips of the wise shall preserve them.
4 Where no oxen are, the crib is clean: but much increase is by the strength of the ox.
5 A ᵈ faithful witness will not lie: but a false witness will utter lies.
6 A scorner seeketh wisdom, and findeth it not: but ᵉ knowledge is easy unto him that understandeth.
7 Go from the presence of a foolish man, when thou perceivest not in him the lips of knowledge.
8 The wisdom of the prudent is to understand his way: but the ⁄folly of fools is deceit.

B. C. 1000.

CHAP. 13.
ᵈ ch. 11. 3.
1 sin.
2 Or, candle.
ᵉ ch. 20. 20.
3 with the hand.
ⱼ 2 Chr. 86. 16.
4 Or, shall be in peace.
Is. 66. 2.
Mal. 3. 16.
ᵍ ch. 16. 22.
ʰ 2 Sa. 22. 6.
ⁱ ch. 12. 23.
5 spreadeth.
6 an ambassador of faithfulness.
ⱼ ch. 15. 5.
7 shall be broken.
ᵏ Ps. 32. 10.
ⁱ Job 27. 16.
Eccl. 2. 26.
ᵐ ch. 12. 11.
ⁿ ch. 23. 13.

CHAP. 14.
ᵃ Ruth 4. 11.
ᵇ Job 12. 4.
ᶜ ch. 12. 6.
ᵈ Ex. 20. 16.
Ex. 23. 1.
ᵉ ch. 17. 24.
⁄ Lu. 12. 20.
1 Cor. 3. 19.
ᵍ ch. 10. 23.
1 the bitterness of his soul.
ʰ Job 8. 15.
ⁱ ch. 16. 25.
ⱼ Rom. 6. 21.
ᵏ Eccl. 2. 2.
ⁱ ch. 12. 14.
ᵐ 2 Cor. 1. 12.
Phil. 4. 7.
ⁿ ch. 22. 3.
ᵒ ch. 19. 7.
2 many are the lovers of the rich.
ᵖ Ps. 41. 1.
ᵠ ch. 13. 14.
ʳ Jam. 1. 19.
3 short of spirit
ˢ Ps. 112. 10.
ᵗ Mat. 25. 40.
1 John 3. 17.
ᵘ Job 31. 15.
ᵛ Job 12. 15.
Job 19. 26.
Ps. 23. 4.
Ps. 87. 37.
2 Cor. 1. 9.
2 Cor. 5. 8.
2 Ti. 4. 18.
4 to nations.

CHAP. 15.
1 boisterous, or, bubbleth.
ᵃ Job 34. 21.
Jer. 16. 17.
Jer. 32. 19.
Heb. 4. 13.
2 The healing of the tongue.

9 Fools ᵉ make a mock at sin: but among the righteous there is favour.
10 The heart knoweth ¹ his own bitterness; and a stranger doth not intermeddle with his joy.
11 The ʰ house of the wicked shall be overthrown: but the tabernacle of the upright shall flourish.
12 There ⁱ is a way which seemeth right unto a man; but ⱼ the end thereof are the ways of death.
13 Even in laughter the heart is sorrowful; and ᵏ the end of that mirth is heaviness.
14 The backslider in heart shall be ⁱ filled with his own ways; and ᵐ a good man shall be satisfied from himself.
15 The simple believeth every word: but the prudent man looketh well to his going.
16 A ⁿ wise man feareth, and departeth from evil: but the fool rageth, and is confident.
17 He that is soon angry dealeth foolishly; and a man of wicked devices is hated.
18 The simple inherit folly: but the prudent are crowned with knowledge.
19 The evil bow before the good; and the wicked at the gates of the righteous.
20 The ᵒ poor is hated even of his own neighbour: but ² the rich hath many friends.
21 He that despiseth his neighbour sinneth: ᵖ but he that hath mercy on the poor, happy is he.
22 Do they not err that devise evil? but mercy and truth shall be to them that devise good.
23 In all labour there is profit: but the talk of the lips tendeth only to penury.
24 The crown of the wise is their riches; but the foolishness of fools is folly.
25 A true witness delivereth souls: but a deceitful witness speaketh lies.
26 In the fear of the LORD is strong confidence; and his children shall have a place of refuge.
27 The ᵠ fear of the LORD is a fountain of life, to depart from the snares of death.
28 In the multitude of people is the king's honour: but in the want of people is the destruction of the prince.
29 He ʳ that is slow to wrath is of great understanding: but he that is ³ hasty of spirit exalteth folly.
30 A sound heart is the life of the flesh: but ᵗ envy the rottenness of the bones.
31 He ᵗ that oppresseth the poor reproacheth ᵘ his Maker: but he that honoureth him hath mercy on the poor.
32 The wicked is driven away in his wickedness: but ᵛ the righteous hath hope in his death.
33 Wisdom resteth in the heart of him that hath understanding: but that which is in the midst of fools is made known.
34 Righteousness exalteth a nation: but sin is a reproach ⁴ to any people.
35 The king's favour is toward a wise servant: but his wrath is against him that causeth shame.

CHAPTER XV.

A SOFT answer turneth away wrath: but grievous words stir up anger.
2 The tongue of the wise useth knowledge aright: but the mouth of fools ¹ poureth out foolishness.
3 The ᵃ eyes of the LORD are in every place, beholding the evil and the good.
4 ² A wholesome tongue is a tree of life:

get dreaded evil; the righteous, desired good. 25. (Cf. Ps. 1. 4; 37. 9, 10, 36., righteous ... foundation—well laid and firm (Mat. 7. 24, 25.). 26. *i.e.*, causes vexation. 27. Cf. ch. 9. 11; Ps. 55. 23.). 28. glauness—in confidence of realising it. expectation ... perish—in disappointment. 29. The way, &c.—*i.e.*, God's providence sustains the righteous, and overthrows the wicked (Hos. 14. 9.). 30. Cf. ch. 12. 3; Ps. 37. 9-11; 102. 2s.). earth—or, land of promise. 31. bringeth forth—*lit.*, *germinates as a plant*. froward—(cf. ch. 2. 12, 14., cut off—as an unproductive plant. 32. known—regard and provide for Ps. 1. 6.). frowardness—all kinds of deceit and illnature. The word is plural.

CHAPTER XI.

Ver. 1-31. 1. (Cf. *Marg.*). The Hebrews used *stones* for weights, just—complete in measure. 2. Self-conceit is unteachable; the humble grow wise (cf. ch. 16. 18; 18. 12.). 3. guide—to lead, as a shepherd ch. 6. 37; Ps. 78. 52.). perverseness — illnature. destroy—with violence. 4. (Cf. ch. 10. 2., wrath—*i.e.*, of God. 5. direct—or, make plain; wicked ways are not plain (ch. 13. 17.). 6. deliver them—*i.e.*, from evil, which the wicked suffer by their own doings (ch. 5. 22. Ps. 9. 16.). 7. expectation ... perish—for death cuts short all his plans (Luke, 16. 25.). hope of unjust—better, "hope of wealth," or power cf. Isa. 40. 29, *Heb.*). This gives an advance on the sentiment of the first clause. Even hopes of gain die with him. 8. Perhaps the *trouble* prepared by the wicked, and which he inherits cf. *v*. 6.). 9. (Cf. Ps. 35. 16; Dan. 11. 32.). The just is saved by superior discernment. 10, 11. The last may be a reason for the first. Together, they set forth the relative moral worth of good and bad men. By the blessing—implying active benevolence. despise—or, reviles, a course contrasted with the prudent silence of the wise. holdeth his peace—as if neither hearing nor telling. 13. talebearer—(cf. *Marg.*), one trading as a pedlar in scandal, whose propensity to talk leads him to betray confidence. 14. counsel—the art of governing (ch. 1. 5.). counsellors—*lit.*, *one giving counsel*; the participle used as a collective. 15. Cf. ch. 6. 1.). suretiship—cf. *Marg.*), the actors put for the action, which may be lawfully hated. 16. retain—or *lit.*, *lay hold of as a support*. Honour is to a feeble woman thus as valuable as riches to men. 17. merciful—kind to others; opposed to cruel. Such benefit themselves by doing good to others (cf. ch. 24. 5, while the cruel injure themselves as well as others. flesh — *i.e.*, his body, by penuriousness Col. 2. 23.). 18. a deceitful work—or, wages, which fail to satisfy, or flee away (ch. 10. 2; 23. 5.). sure rew rd—or, gain, as from trading Hos. 10. 12; Gal. 6. 8, 9.). 19. Inference from *v*. 18, (cf. *v*. 5, 6; ch. 10. 16.). 20. (Cf. *v*. 5.). froward—as ch. 2. 15, opposed to the simplicity and purity of the *upright*, in their way—or, conduct. 21. The combined power of the wicked cannot free them from just punishment, while the unaided children of the righteous find deliverance by reason of their pious relationship Ps. 37. 25, 26.). 22. Jewels were often suspended from the nose Gen. 24. 47; Isa. 3. 21.). Thus adorned, a hog disgusts less than a fair and indiscreet woman. 23. (Cf. ch. 10. 28. . The wrath is that of God. 24-31. The scope of the whole is a comment on *v*. 23. Thus liberality (*v*. 24,), by God's blessing, secures increase, while penuriousness, instead of expected gain, procures poverty. 25. liberal soul—(cf. *Marg.*, made fat—prospers (ch. 28. 25; Deut. 32. 15; Luke, 6. 38.). wa ere h ... watered—a comm n figure for blessing. 26. Another example of the truth of *v*. 23; the miser loses reputation, though he saves corn, selleth it—*i.e.*, at a fair price. 27. good [and] mischief—*i.e.*, of others. procureth ... seeketh—implying success. 28. Cf. ch. 10. 15; Ps. 49. 6; 1 Tim. 6. 17.). righteous ...branch- Ps. 1. 3; Jer. 17. 8,\. 29. troubleth—as ch. 15. 27, explains, by greediness for gain cf. *v*. 17.). inherit ... wind—even successful, his gains are of no real value. So the fool, thus acting, either comes to poverty, or heaps up for others. 30. a tree of life—blessings to others proceed from the works of the righteous ch. 3. 18.). winneth souls—(cf. *Marg.*), to do them good as opposed to ch. 6. 25; Ez. 13. 18 c'. Luke, 5, 10.). 31. Behold—Thus calling attention to the illustrations (cf. *v*. 23,\, the sentiment of which is confirmed even in time, not excluding future rewards and punishments.

CHAPTER XII.

Ver. 1-28. 1. loveth know edge—as the fruit of instruction or training ch. 1. 2.). hateth reproof—(ch. 10. 17.). brutish—stupid, regardless of his own welfare (Ps. 49. 10; 73. 22.). 3. Wickedness cannot give permanent prosperity. root ... not be moved — firm as a flourishing tree—(Ps. 1. 3; 15. 5; Jer. 17. 8.). 4. a virtuous woman—in the wide sense of well disposed to all moral duties ch. 31. 10.). maketh asham ed—*i.e.*, by misconduct. rottenness—an incurable evil. 5. thoughts—or, purposes. are right—*lit.*, *are judgment, i.e.*, true decisions. counsels—(cf. ch. 11. 14.). deceit—contrary to truth and honesty. 6. words—or, expressed designs of the wicked are for evil purposes. the mouth—or, words of the righteous delivering instead of ensnaring men. 7. Such conduct brings a proper return, by the destruction of the wicked and wellbeing of the righteous and his family. 8. despised—as opposed to commended (ch. 11. 12.). perverse heart—or, wicked principles, as opposed to one of wisdom. 9. Despised—held in little repute, obscure (1 Sam. 18. 23; Isa. 3. 5.). hath a servant—implying some means of honest living. honoureth himself:—is self-conceited. 10. regardeth—*lit.*, *knoweth* Ps. 1. 6.). mercies ... cruel—as acts of compassion ungraciously rendered to the needy. The righteous more regards a beast than the wicked a man. 11. The idler's fate is the result of indolence and want of principle ch. 6. 32; 7. 7. 12. The wicked ... evil—They love the crafty arts of deception. the root ... fruit—their own resources supply them; or, it may be rendered: "He (God) giveth, or sets (Ez. 17. 22,), the root of the righteous," and hence it is firm: or, the verb is impersonal: "As to the root, &c., it is firm" ch. 17. 19.). 13, 14. The sentiment expanded. While the wicked, such as liars, flatterers, &c., fall by their own words, the righteous are unhurt. Their good conduct makes friends, and God rewards them. 15. The way ... eyes—The fool is self-conceited cf. *v*. 1; ch. 1. 32; 16. 17; Jam. 3. 17.). 16. prudent ... shame—he is slow to denounce his insulters Jam. 1. 19.). 18. speaketh—*lit.*, *speaketh hastily*, or indiscreetly (Ps. 106. 33.), as an angry man retorts harsh and provoking invectives. tongue ... health

PROVERBS, XVI.

but perverseness therein is a breach in the spirit.

5 A fool despiseth his father's instruction: but he that regardeth reproof is prudent.

6 In the house of the righteous is much treasure: but in the revenues of the wicked is trouble.

7 The lips of the wise disperse knowledge: but the heart of the foolish doeth not so.

8 The sacrifice of the wicked is an abomination to the LORD: but the prayer of the upright is his delight.

9 The way of the wicked is an abomination unto the LORD: but he loveth him that followeth after righteousness.

10 Correction is grievous unto him that forsaketh the way: and he that hateth reproof shall die.

11 Hell and destruction are before the LORD: how much more then the hearts of the children of men?

12 A scorner loveth not one that reproveth him: neither will he go unto the wise.

13 A merry heart maketh a cheerful countenance: but by sorrow of the heart the spirit is broken.

14 The heart of him that hath understanding seeketh knowledge: but the mouth of fools feedeth on foolishness.

15 All the days of the afflicted are evil: but he that is of a merry heart hath a continual feast.

16 Better is little with the fear of the LORD, than great treasure, and trouble therewith.

17 Better is a dinner of herbs where love is, than a stalled ox and hatred therewith.

18 A wrathful man stireth up strife: but he that is slow to anger appeaseth strife.

19 The way of the slothful man is as an hedge of thorns: but the way of the righteous is made plain.

20 A wise son maketh a glad father: but a foolish man despiseth his mother.

21 Folly is joy to him that is destitute of wisdom: but a man of understanding walketh uprightly.

22 Without counsel purposes are disappointed: but in the multitude of counsellors they are established.

23 A man hath joy by the answer of his mouth; and a word spoken in due season, how good is it!

24 The way of life is above to the wise, that he may depart from hell beneath.

25 The LORD will destroy the house of the proud: but he will establish the border of the widow.

26 The thoughts of the wicked are an abomination to the LORD: but the words of the pure are pleasant words.

27 He that is greedy of gain troubleth his own house: but he that hateth gifts shall live.

28 The heart of the righteous studieth to answer: but the mouth of the wicked poureth out evil things.

29 The LORD is far from the wicked: but he heareth the prayer of the righteous.

30 The light of the eyes rejoiceth the heart; and a good report maketh the bones fat.

31 The ear that heareth the reproof of life abideth among the wise.

32 He that refuseth instruction despiseth his own soul: but he that heareth reproof getteth understanding.

33 The fear of the LORD is the instruction of wisdom; and before honour is humility.

CHAPTER XVI.

THE preparations of the heart in man, and the answer of the tongue, is from the LORD.

2 All the ways of a man are clean in his own eyes: but the LORD weigheth the spirits.

3 Commit thy works unto the LORD, and thy thoughts shall be established.

4 The LORD hath made all things for himself; yea, even the wicked for the day of evil.

5 Every one that is proud in heart is an abomination to the LORD: though hand join in hand, he shall not be unpunished.

6 By mercy and truth iniquity is purged: and by the fear of the LORD men depart from evil.

7 When a man's ways please the LORD, he maketh even his enemies to be at peace with him.

8 Better is a little with righteousness, than great revenues without right.

9 A man's heart deviseth his way: but the LORD directeth his steps.

10 A divine sentence is in the lips of the king: his mouth transgresseth not in judgment.

11 A just weight and balance are the LORD's; all the weights of the bag are his work.

12 It is an abomination to kings to commit wickedness: for the throne is established by righteousness.

13 Righteous lips are the delight of kings; and they love him that speaketh right.

14 The wrath of a king is as messengers of death: but a wise man will pacify it.

15 In the light of the king's countenance is life; and his favour is as a cloud of the latter rain.

16 How much better is it to get wisdom than gold? and to get understanding rather to be chosen than silver?

17 The highway of the upright is to depart from evil: he that keepeth his way preserveth his soul.

18 Pride goeth before destruction, and an haughty spirit before a fall.

19 Better it is to be of an humble spirit with the lowly, than to divide the spoil with the proud.

20 He that handleth a matter wisely shall find good; and whoso trusteth in the LORD, happy is he.

21 The wise in heart shall be called prudent; and the sweetness of the lips increaseth learning.

22 Understanding is a well-spring of life unto him that hath it: but the instruction of fools is folly.

23 The heart of the wise teacheth his mouth, and addeth learning to his lips.

24 Pleasant words are as an honeycomb, sweet to the soul, and health to the bones.

25 There is a way that seemeth right unto a man; but the end thereof are the ways of death.

26 He that laboureth, laboureth for himself; for his mouth craveth it of him.

27 An ungodly man diggeth up evil; and in his lips there is as a burning fire.

28 A froward man soweth strife; and a whisperer separateth chief friends.

29 A violent man enticeth his neighbour,

Moral Virtues, and   PROVERBS, XIII, XIV.   their Contrary Vices.

—by soothing and gentle language. 19. Words of truth are consistent and stand all tests, while lies are soon discovered and exposed. 20. that intrigue—or, plan (ch. 3. 29.). They design a deceitful course, to which, with all its evils and dangers to others and themselves, the happiness of peace-makers is opposed (cf. Mat. 5. 9; Rom. 12. 18.). 21. no evil—(as Ps. 91. 10,), under God's wise limitations (Rom. 8. 28.). mischief—as penal evil. 22. deal truly—or, faithfully, i.e., according to promises (cf. John. 3. 21.). 23. concealeth—by his modesty (ch. 10. 14; 11. 13.). heart ... proclaimeth—as his lips speak his thoughts (cf. Eccl. 10. 3.). 24. slothful—cf. Marg.,), so called because he fails to meet his promises, under tribute—not denoting legal taxes, but the obligation of dependence. 25. a good word—one of comfort. 26. more excellent—(cf. Marg.,), or, more successful, while the wicked fail; or, we may read it: "The righteous guides his friend, but," &c., i.e., The ability of the righteous to aid others is contrasted with the ruin to which the way of the wicked leads themselves. 27. (Cf. v. 24.). took in hunting—or, his venison. He does not improve his advantages, the substance ... precious — or, the wealth of a man of honour is being diligent, or diligence. precious—lit., honour (Eccl. 10. 1.). 28. (Cf. ch. 8. 8, 20, &c.). A sentiment often stated; here first affirmatively, then negatively.

CHAPTER XIII.

Ver. 1-25. 1. (Cf. ch. 6. 1-5; 10. 1, 17.). 2. shall eat—i.e., obtain (ch. 12. 14.). transgressors—as ch. 2. 22. violence—or, mischief to themselves. 3. He ... mouth ... life — Because evil speeches may provoke violence from others. On last clause cf. ch. 10. 14. 4. (Cf. ch. 12. 11, 27.). 5. loathsome ... shame—better, causeth shame and reproach (cf. ch. 19. 26,), by slander, &c., which the righteous hates. 6. A sentiment of frequent recurrence, that piety benefits, and sin injures. 7. In opposite ways men act hypocritically for gain of honour, or wealth. 8. Riches save some from punishment, while others suffer because they will not heed the rebuke of sloth, which makes and keeps them poor. 9. light [and] lamp—prosperity; the first, the greater, and it rejoiceth—or, burns brightly, or continues, while the other, at best, small, soon fails. 10. The obstinacy which attends self-conceit, produces contention, which, the well advised, thus evincing modesty, avoid. 11. by vanity—or, nothingness, i.e., which is vain or useless to the public as card playing and similar vices. . gathereth . . . labour—(cf. Marg.,), little by little, laboriously. 12. desire cometh—is realised, a tree of life—or, cause of happiness. 13. the word—i.e., of advice, or instruction (cf. ch. 10. 27; 11. 31.). 14. Cf. ch. 10. 11.. fountain—or, source of life, to depart—,cf. ch. 1. 2-4,), or, for departing, &c., and so gives live. 15. Right perception and action secures good-will, while evil ways are difficult as a stony road. The wicked left of God find punishment of sin in sinning. hard—or, harsh (cf. (Heb.) Deut. 21. 4; Jer. 5. 15.). 16. dealeth—acts with foresight. a fool ... folly—for want of caution. 17. A wicked—[or, untaithful] messenger falleth into—or, by mischief, or evil, and so his errand fails. Contrasted is the character of the faithful, whose faithfulness benefits others. 18. Cf. ch. 10. 17; 12. 1.). 19. Self-denial, which fools will not endure, is essential to success. 20.

The benefits of good and evils of bad society are contrasted. 21. (Cf. ch. 11. 31.). good ... repaid—or, He (God) will repay good. 22. wealth ... just — while good men's estates remain in their families, God so orders that the gains of sinners enure to the just (cf. ch. 28. 8; Ps. 37. 18, 22, 26, &c.. 23. The labouring poor prosper more than those who injudiciously or wickedly strive, by fraud and violence, to supersede the necessity of lawful labour. 24. spareth—or, withholds. rod—of correction. hateth—or, acts as if he hated him cf. ch. 3. 12; 8. 36.). chasteneth ... betimes—or, diligently seeks for him all useful discipline. 25. The comparative temporal prosperity of the righteous and wicked, rather than contentment and discontent, is noted.

CHAPTER XIV.

Ver. 1-35. 1. Every wise, &c.—lit., The wisdoms (cf. ch. 9. 1) of women, plural, a distributive form of speech. buildeth ... house—increases wealth, which the foolish, by mismanagement, lessens. 2. uprightness—is the fruit of fearing God, as falsehood and ill-nature (ch. 2. 15; 3. 32) of despising Him and His law. 3. rod of pride—i.e., the punishment of pride, which they evince by their words. The words of the wise procure good to them. 4. crib is clean—or, empty; so "cleanness of teeth" denotes want of food (cf. Amos. 4. 6.). Men get the proper fruit of their doings (Gal. 6. 7,.. 5. A faithful witness, &c.—One tested to be such. utter [or, breathe out] lies—i.e., habitually lies (ch. 6. 19; cf. Acts, 9. 1.). Or the sense is, that habitual truthfulness, or lying, will be evinced in witness-bearing. 6. An humble, teachable spirit succeeds in seeking (ch. 8. 9; John, 7. 17; Jam. 1. 5, 6.). 7. Avoid the society of those who cannot teach you. 8. Appearances deceive the thoughtless, but the prudent discriminate. 9. Fools ... sin—or, Sin deludes fools. righteous ... favour—i.e., of God, instead of the punishment of sin. 10. Each one best knows his own sorrows or joys. 11. (Cf. ch. 12. 7.). The contrast of the whole is enhanced by that of house and tabernacle, a permanent and a temporary dwelling. 12. (nd thereof—or, reward, what results (cf. ch. 5. 4.). ways of death—leading to it. 13. The preceding sentiment illustrated by the disappointments of a wicked or untimely joy. 14. filled ... ways—receive retribution (ch. 1. 31.). a good man ... his self—lit., is away from such, will not associate with him. 15. The simple ... word—He is credulous, not from love, but heedlessness (ch. 13. 16.). 16. (Cf. ch. 3. 7; 28. 14.). rageth—acts proudly and conceitedly. 17. He ... angry — lit., short of anger cf. v. 29, opposite idea.). man ... hated—i.e., the deliberate evil-doer is more hated than the rash. 18. inherit—as a portion (ch. 3. 35.. are crowned—lit., are surrounded with it, abound in it. 19. describes the humbling of the wicked by the punishment their sins incur. 20. This sad but true picture of human nature is not given approvingly, but only as a fact. 21. For such contempt of the poor is contrasted as sinful with the virtuous compassion of the good. 22. As usual, the interrogative negative strengthens the affirmative. mercy and truth—i.e., God's v. 57. 23; (1. 7.). 23. labour—or, painful diligence. talk ... penury—Idle and vain promises and plans. 24. (Cf. ch. 3. 16.). foolishness ... folly—folly remains, or produces folly, has no benefit. 25. Life often depends on truth

and leadeth him into the way *that is* not good.
30 He shutteth his eyes to devise froward things: moving his lips he bringeth evil to pass.
31 The hoary head *is* a crown of glory, *if* it be found in the way of righteousness.
32 *He that is* slow to anger *is* better than the mighty; and he that ruleth his spirit than he that taketh a city.
33 The lot is cast into the lap; but the whole disposing thereof *is* of the LORD.

CHAPTER XVII.

BETTER *is* a dry morsel, and quietness therewith, than an house full of ¹ sacrifices *with* strife.
2 A wise servant shall have rule over a son that causeth shame, and shall have part of the inheritance among the brethren.
3 The *a* fining pot *is* for silver, and the furnace for gold: but the LORD trieth the hearts.
4 A wicked doer giveth heed to false lips; *and* a liar giveth ear to a naughty tongue.
5 Whoso mocketh the poor reproacheth his Maker; *and* ᵇ he that is glad at calamities shall not be ² unpunished.
6 Children's children *are* the crown of old men; and the glory of children *are* their fathers.
7 ³ Excellent speech becometh not a fool; much less do ⁴ lying lips a prince.
8 A gift *is as* ⁵ a precious stone in the eyes of him that hath it: whithersoever it turneth, it *ᶜ* prospereth.
9 He that covereth a transgression ⁶ seeketh love; but he that repeateth a matter separateth *very* friends.
10 ⁷ A reproof entereth more into a wise man than a hundred stripes into a fool.
11 An evil man seeketh only rebellion; therefore a cruel messenger shall be sent against him.
12 Let a bear robbed of her whelps meet a man, rather than a fool in his folly.
13 Whoso *ᵈ* rewardeth evil for good, evil shall not depart from his house.
14 The beginning of strife *is as* when one letteth out water; therefore ⁶ leave off contention, before it be meddled with.
15 He that *ᶠ* justifieth the wicked, and he that condemneth the just, even they both *are* abomination to the LORD.
16 Wherefore *is there* a price in the hand of a fool to get wisdom, seeing he hath no heart *to it?*
17 A friend loveth at all times, and a brother is born for adversity.
18 A man void of ⁸ understanding striketh hands, *and* becometh surety in the presence of his friend.
19 He loveth transgression that loveth strife: *and* he that exalteth his gate seeketh destruction.
20 ⁹ He that hath a froward heart findeth no good; and he that hath a perverse tongue falleth into mischief.
21 He that begetteth a fool *doeth it* to his sorrow: and the father of a fool hath no joy.
22 A merry heart doeth good ¹⁰ *like* a medicine: but a broken spirit drieth the bones.
23 A wicked *man* taketh a gift out of the bosom *ᵍ* to pervert the ways of judgment.
24 Wisdom ʰ *is* before him that hath understanding: but the eyes of a fool *are* in the ends of the earth.
25 A foolish son *is* a grief to his father, and bitterness to her that bare him.

26 Also to punish the just *is* not good, *nor* to strike princes for equity.
27 He *ⁱ* that hath knowledge spareth his words: *and* a man of understanding is of ¹¹ an excellent spirit.
28 Even a fool, when he holdeth his peace, is counted wise; *and* he that shutteth his lips *is esteemed* a man of understanding.

CHAPTER XVIII.

THROUGH ¹ desire a man, having separated himself, seeketh *and* intermeddleth with all wisdom.
2 A fool hath no delight in understanding, but that his heart may discover itself.
3 When the wicked cometh, *then* cometh also contempt, and with ignominy reproach.
4 The words of a man's mouth *are as* deep waters, *ᵃ and* the well-spring of wisdom *as* a flowing brook.
5 *It* ᵇ *is* not good to accept the person of the wicked, to overthrow the righteous in judgment.
6 A fool's lips enter into contention, and his mouth calleth for strokes.
7 A fool's mouth *is* his destruction, and his lips *are* the snare of his soul.
8 The words of a ² talebearer *are* ³ as wounds, and they go down into the ⁴ innermost parts of the belly.
9 He also that is slothful in his work is brother to him that is a great waster.
10 The *ᵉ* name of the LORD *is* a strong tower: the righteous runneth into it, and ⁵ is safe.
11 The rich man's wealth *is* his strong city, and as an high wall in his own conceit.
12 Before destruction the heart of man is haughty, and before honour *is* humility.
13 He that ⁶ answereth a matter before he heareth *it*, it *is* folly and shame unto him.
14 The spirit of a man will sustain his infirmity: but a wounded spirit who can bear;
15 The *ᵈ* heart of the prudent getteth knowledge; and the ear of the wise seeketh knowledge.
16 A *ᵉ* man's gift maketh room for him, and bringeth him before great men.
17 *He that is* first in his own cause *seemeth* just; but his neighbour cometh and searcheth him.
18 The lot causeth contentions to cease, and parteth between the mighty.
19 A brother offended *is harder to be won* than a strong city; and *their* contentions *are* like the bars of a castle.
20 A man's belly shall be satisfied with the fruit of his mouth; *and* with the increase of his lips shall he be filled.
21 Death *ᶠ* and life *are* in the power of the tongue: and they that love it shall eat the fruit thereof.
22 *ᵍ* Whoso findeth a wife findeth a good *thing*, and obtaineth favour of the LORD.
23 The poor useth entreaties; but the rich answereth *ᵍ* roughly.
24 A man *that hath* friends must show himself friendly: and there is a friend *that* sticketh closer than a brother.

CHAPTER XIX.

BETTER *ᵃ is* the poor that walketh in his integrity, than *he that is* perverse in his lips, and is a fool.
2 Also, that the ᵇ soul *be* without knowledge, *it is* not good; and he that hasteth with *his* feet sinneth.
3 The foolishness of man perverteth his way: *ᶜ and* his heart fretteth against the LORD.

Moral Virtues, and   PROVERBS, XV, XVI.   *their Contrary Vices.*

telling. a deceitful ... lies—he that breathes out lies is deceit, not to be trusted (v. 5.). 26. The blessings of piety descend to children (ch. 13. 22; 20. 7; Ex. 20. 6.). 27. (Cf. ch. 15. 14.). fear of the Lord—or, *law of the wise*, is wisdom (Ps. 111. 10.). 28. The teaching of a true political economy. 29. slow ... understanding —cf. v. 17.). hasty—(cf. v. 17.). exalteth folly —makes it conspicuous, as if delighting to honour it. 30. A sound heart—Both literally and figuratively, a source of health; in the latter sense, opposed to the known effect of evil passions on health. 31. reproacheth his Maker—who is the God of such, as well as of the rich (ch. 22. 2; Job, 31. 15; and specially 1 Sam. 2. 8; Ps. 113. 7.). 32. driven—or, thrust out violently (cf. Ps. 35. 5, 6.). hath hope—or, trusteth (ch. 10. 2; 11. 4; Ps. 2. 12.), implying assurance of help. 33. resteth—preserved in quietness for use, while fools blazon their folly (ch. 12. 23; 13. 16.). 34. Righteousness—Just principles and actions. exalteth—raises to honour. is a reproach—or, brings on them the ill-will of others (cf. ch. 13. 6.). 35. wise —discreet, or prudent. causeth shame—(ch. 10. 5; 12. 4) acts basely.

CHAPTER XV.

Ver. 1-33. 1. soft — tender, or gentle. turneth ... wrath—from any one. stir up—as a smouldering fire is excited. 2. useth ... aright—commends knowledge by its proper use. poureth out—utters abundantly (ch. 12. 23,), and so disgusts others. 3. beholding—watching (cf. ch. 5. 21; Ps. 66. 7.). 4. A wholesome tongue — (cf. *Marg.*), pacifying and soothing language. tree of life—ch. 3. 18; 11. 30.). p rverseness therein—cross ill-natured language. breach ... spirit—cf. Isa. 65. 14, Heb.,., grieves, instead of appeasing. 5. (Cf. ch. 4. 1; 10. 17; 13. 1-18.). is prudent—acts discreetly. 6. treasure—implying utility, trouble —vexation and affliction. 7. (Cf. ch. 10. 20, 21.). heart ... not so—not right, or vain. 8, 9. The sacrifice [and] prayer—are acts of worship. way [and] followeth ... righteousness—denote conduct. God's regard for the worship and deeds of the righteous and wicked respectively, so stated Ps. 50. 17; Isa. 1. 11. 10. (Cf. ch. 10. 17.). the way—that in which God would have him to go (ch. 2. 13; Ps. 119. 1.). 11. Hell—(Ps. 16. 10.). destruction—or, abaddon, the place of the destroyer. All the unseen world is open to God, much more men's hearts. 12. (Cf. ch. 9. 8,). go unto the wise—to be instructed. 13. m.keth ... countenance—or, benefits the countenance. spirit is broken—and so the countenance is sad. 14. (Cf. ch. 10. 21. 22.). The wise grow wiser, the fools more foolish (ch. 9. 9,). 15. The state of the heart governs the outward condition. evil—*sad*, contrasted with the cheerfulness of a feast. 16. trouble—agitation, implying the anxieties and perplexities attending wealth held by worldlings (ch. 16. 18; 1 Tim. 6. 6.). 17. dinner [or, allowance (2 Ki. 25. 30.) of herbs]—and that the plainest, and hatred — cf. ch. 10. 12, 18.). 18. (Cf. ch. 14. 29; 16. 32.). 19. The difficulties of the slothful result from want of energy; the righteous find a plain [and open] way—*lit.*, *a highway*, by diligence (1 Sam. 10. 7; Ps. 1. 3. 20. Cf. ch. 10. 1.). 21. walketh uprightly — and so finds his joy (ch. 3. 6; 10. 23,). 22. Without counsel — or, deliberation, implying a wise deference to the opinions of the wise and good, contrasted with rashness. 23. Good advice blesses the giver and receiver. 24. (Cf. Col. 3. 2.). Holy purposes prevent sinning, and so its evils. 25. The most desolate who have God's aid have more permanent good than the self-reliant sinner ch. 2. 22; 12. 7.). border—or, boundary for possessions (Ps. 78. 54.. 26. are pleasant words—*i.e.*, pleasing to God (ch. 8. 8, 9.. 27. (Cf. ch. 11. 17... Avarice brings trouble to him and his. hateth gifts—or, bribes Ex. 23. 8; Ps. 15. 5,, and is not avaricious. 28. Cf. v. 14; ch. 10. 11.,. Caution is the fruit of wisdom; rashness of folly. 29. far ... wicked—in His love and favour (Ps. 2. 11; 119. 155.. 30. Light of the eyes—(ch. 13. 9.: What gives light rejoiceth the heart, by relieving from anxiety as to our course, so good report—or, doctrine (Isa. 28. 9; 53. 1.;. maketh ... fat—or, gives prosperity (ch. 3. 13-17; 9. 11). The last clause is illustrated by the first. 31, 32. Cf. ch. 10. 17.. reproof of life—which leads to life. abideth ... wise—is numbered among them. re useth — or, neglects, passes by (ch. 1. 25; 4. 15.). despiseth ... soul—so acts as it esteeming its interests of no value. 33. The .ear ... wisdom — Wisdom instructs in true piety. before ... humility—cf. Luke, 24. 26; 1 Pet. 1. 11;; opposite cf. ch. 16. 18.,.

CHAPTER XVI.

Ver. 1-33. 1. prepaiations — or, schemes. in man—or *lit., to man*, belonging, or pertaining to him. the answer ... Lord—the efficient ordering is from God: "Man proposes; God disposes." 2. clean—or, faultless. weigheth —or, tries, judges, implying that they are faulty (ch. 21. 2; 24. 12.). 3. Cf. *Marg.*). Rely on God for success to your lawful purposes. 4. for himself—or, "for its answer, or purpose," *i.e.*, according to God's plan; the wicked are for the day of evil (Ps. 49. 5; Jer. 17. 18); sinning and suffering answer to each other, are indissolubly united. 5. (Cf. ch. 3. 32.). 6. By mercy and truth — *i.e.*, God's (Ps. 85. 10,), He effects the atonement, or covering of sin; and the principles of true piety incline men to depart from evil; or, *mercy* and *truth* may be man's, indicative of the gracious tempers which work instrumentally in procuring pardon. purged—expiated. as Lev. 16. 33; Isa. 27. 9, *Heb.*,. 7. Persecutions, of course, excepted. 8. (Cf. ch. 15. 6, 16, 17... 9. (Cf. v. 3.). directeth—establisheth. 10. The last clause depends on the first, expressing the importance of equity in decisions, so authoritative. 11. are the Lord's ... his work—*i.e.*, what He has ordered, and hence should be observed by men. 12. Rulers are rightly expected, by their position, to hate evil; for their power is sustained by righteousness. 13. A specification of the general sentiment of v. 12. 14, 15. This wrath, so terrible and certain, like messengers of death (1 Ki. 2. 25,), can be appeased by the wise. light of ... countenance—favour Ps. 4. 6,). life —preserves it, or gives blessings which make it valuable. the latter rain—fell just before harvest, and matured the crop; hence specially valuable (Deut. 11. 14,). 16. Cf. ch. 3. 16; 4. 5.). 17. The highway—A common, plain road, represents the habitual course of the righteous in departing from evil. keepeth — or, observes. 18, 19. (Cf. ch. 15. 33.). Haughtiness and pride imply self-confidence, which produces carelessness, and hence the fall—*lit., sliding*. divide the spoil—*i.e.*, conquer. Avoid the society of the proud (Jam. 4...). 20. handleth a matter—or, wisely considers *the word, i.e.*, of God (cf. ch. 13. 13.).

4 Wealth maketh many friends: but the poor is separated from his neighbour.
5 A false witness shall not be unpunished, and he that speaketh lies shall not escape.
6 Many will entreat the favour of the prince: and every man is a friend to him that giveth gifts.
7 All the brethren of the poor do hate him; how much more do his friends go far from him? he pursueth them with words, yet they are wanting to him.
8 He that getteth wisdom loveth his own soul: he that keepeth understanding shall find good.
9 A false witness shall not be unpunished, and he that speaketh lies shall perish.
10 Delight is not seemly for a fool; much less for a servant to have rule over princes.
11 The discretion of a man deferreth his anger; and it is his glory to pass over a transgression.
12 The king's wrath is as the roaring of a lion; but his favour is as dew upon the grass.
13 A foolish son is the calamity of his father: and the contentions of a wife are a continual dropping.
14 House and riches are the inheritance of fathers: and a prudent wife is from the LORD.
15 Slothfulness casteth into a deep sleep; and an idle soul shall suffer hunger.
16 He that keepeth the commandment keepeth his own soul; but he that despiseth his ways shall die.
17 He that hath pity upon the poor lendeth unto the LORD; and that which he hath given will he pay him again.
18 Chasten thy son while there is hope, and let not thy soul spare for his crying.
19 A man of great wrath shall suffer punishment: for if thou deliver him, yet thou must do it again.
20 Hear counsel, and receive instruction, that thou mayest be wise in thy latter end.
21 There are many devices in a man's heart; nevertheless the counsel of the LORD, that shall stand.
22 The desire of a man is his kindness: and a poor man is better than a liar.
23 The fear of the LORD tendeth to life; and he that hath it shall abide satisfied; he shall not be visited with evil.
24 A slothful man hideth his hand in his bosom, and will not so much as bring it to his mouth again.
25 Smite a scorner, and the simple will beware: and reprove one that hath understanding, and he will understand knowledge.
26 He that wasteth his father, and chaseth away his mother, is a son that causeth shame, and bringeth reproach.
27 Cease, my son, to hear the instruction that causeth to err from the words of knowledge.
28 An ungodly witness scorneth judgment; and the mouth of the wicked devoureth iniquity.
29 Judgments are prepared for scorners, and stripes for the back of fools.

CHAPTER XX.

WINE is a mocker, strong drink is raging: and whosoever is deceived thereby is not wise.
2 The fear of a king is as the roaring of a lion: whoso provoketh him to anger sinneth against his own soul.
3 It is an honour for a man to cease from strife: but every fool will be meddling.
4 The sluggard will not plow by reason of the cold; therefore shall he beg in harvest, and have nothing.
5 Counsel in the heart of man is like deep water: but a man of understanding will draw it out.
6 Most men will proclaim every one his own goodness: but a faithful man who can find?
7 The just man walketh in his integrity: his children are blessed after him.
8 A king that sitteth in the throne of judgment scattereth away all evil with his eyes.
9 Who can say, I have made my heart clean, I am pure from my sin?
10 Divers weights, and divers measures, both of them are alike abomination to the LORD.
11 Even a child is known by his doings, whether his work be pure, and whether it be right.
12 The hearing ear, and the seeing eye, the LORD hath made even both of them.
13 Love not sleep, lest thou come to poverty: open thine eyes, and thou shalt be satisfied with bread.
14 It is naught, it is naught, saith the buyer: but when he is gone his way, then he boasteth.
15 There is gold, and a multitude of rubies: but the lips of knowledge are a precious jewel.
16 Take his garment that is surety for a stranger: and take a pledge of him for a strange woman.
17 Bread of deceit is sweet to a man; but afterwards his mouth shall be filled with gravel.
18 Every purpose is established by counsel: and with good advice make war.
19 He that goeth about as a talebearer revealeth secrets: therefore meddle not with him that flattereth with his lips.
20 Whoso curseth his father or his mother, his lamp shall be put out in obscure darkness.
21 An inheritance may be gotten hastily at the beginning; but the end thereof shall not be blessed.
22 Say not thou, I will recompense evil; but wait on the LORD, and he shall save thee.
23 Divers weights are an abomination unto the LORD; and a false balance is not good.
24 Man's goings are of the LORD; how can a man then understand his own way?
25 It is a snare to the man who devoureth that which is holy, and after vows to make enquiry.
26 A wise king scattereth the wicked, and bringeth the wheel over them.
27 The spirit of man is the candle of the LORD, searching all the inward parts of the belly.
28 Mercy and truth preserve the king; and his throne is upholden by mercy.
29 The glory of young men is their strength: and the beauty of old men is the grey head.
30 The blueness of a wound cleanseth away evil: so do stripes the inward parts of the belly.

,rusteth— cf. Ps. 2. 12; 118. 8, 9.). 21. wise n heart—who rightly consider duty. sweetness of the lips—eloquent discourse, persuades and instructs others. 22. Understanding—or, discretion, is a constant source of blessing, ch. 13. 14,), benefiting others; but fools' best efforts are folly. 23. The heart is the source of wisdom flowing from the mouth. 24. (Cf. ch. 15. 26.). Gentle, kind words, by soothing the mind, give the body health. 25. (Cf. ch. 14. 2.. 26. Diligence is a duty due to one's self, for his wants require labour. 27. ungodly man—(cf. ch. 6. 12.). diggeth up evil—labours for it. in his lips ... fire—his words are calumniating (Jam. 3, 6.). 28. Cf. ch. 6. 14; 10. 31.). whisperer—prater, tale-bearer ch. 18. 8; 26. 20.). 29. violent man—or, man of mischief (ch. 3. 31.). enticeth—(ch. 1. 10.). 30. He shutteth his eyes—denoting deep thought (Ps. 64. 6.). moving [or, biting] his lips—a determined purpose (ch. 6. 13.). 31. (Cf. ch. 20. 29.). if—or, *which* may be supplied properly, or without it; the sense is as ch. 3. 16; 4. 10, that piety is blessed with long life. 32. Cf. ch. 14. 29. . taketh a city—*i.e.*, by fighting. 33. Seemingly the most fortuitous events are ordered by God.

CHAPTER XVII.
Ver. 1-28. 1. sacrifices—or, feasts made with part of them (ch. 7. 14; Lev. 2. 3; 7. 31. . with—or, *lit., of.* strife—its product, or attendant. 2. (Cf. ch. 14. 35.). causeth shame —(ch. 10. 5.). shall ... inheritance—*i.e.*, share a brother's part (cf. Num. 27. 4, 7.). 3. God only knows, as He tries (Ps. 12. 6; 66. 10.), the heart. 4. Wicked doers and speakers alike delight in calumny. 5. (Cf. ch. 14. 31. . glad at calamities—rejoicing in others' evil. Fools are rightly punished by God who knows their hearts. 6. Prolonged posterity is a blessing, its cutting off, a curse ch. 13. 22; Ps. 109. 13-15.), hence children may glory in a virtuous ancestry. 7. Excellent speech — (Cf. *Marg.*). Such language as ill suits a fool, as lying (ought to suit) a prince (ch. 16. 12, 13.). 8. One so corrupt as to take a bribe evinces his high estimate of it by subjection to its influence (ch. 18. 16; 19. 6.). 9. seeketh love—(cf. *Marg.*). The contrast is between the peace-maker and tale-bearer. 10. Reproof more affects the wise, than severe scourging fools. 11. Such meet just retribution 1 Ki. 2. 25.). a cruel messenger—one to inflict it. 12. They are less rational in anger than wild beasts. 13. (Cf. Ps. 7. 4; 35. 12.). evil—injury to another ch. 13. 21.). 14. letteth ... water—as a breach in a dam. before ... meddled with —before strife has become sharp, or by an explanation better suiting the figure, before it *rolls on*, or increases. 15. abomination ... Lord—as reversing His method of acting ch. 3. 32; 12. 2.). 16. Though wealth cannot buy wisdom for those who do not love it, yet wisdom procures wealth (ch. 3. 16; 14. 24.). 17. To the second of these parallel clauses, there is an accession of meaning, *i.e.*, that a brother's love is specially seen in adversity. 18. (Cf. ch. 6. 1-5; 11. 15. . in the presence, &c. —*i.e.*, he either fails to consult his friend, or to follow his advice. 19. strife—or, contention is, and leads to, sin. he that exalteth his gate—gratifies a vain love of costly building. seeketh — or, findeth, as if he sought it. "loveth death," ch. 8. 36.). 20. The second clause advances on the first. The ill-natured fail of good, and the cavilling and fault-finding incur evil. 21. (Cf. ch. 23. 24.) Different words are rendered by *fool*, both denoting stupidity and impiety. 22. (Cf. ch. 14. 30; 15. 13. . The effect of the mind on the body is well known. drieth—as if the marrow were exhausted. medicine—or, *body*, which better corresponds with bone. 23. a gift ... bosom —money and other valuables were borne in a fold of the garment, called the bosom. to pervert—*i.e.*, by bribery. 24. Wisdom ... him —ever an object of regard, while a fool's affections are unsettled. 25. a grief—or, cross, vexation cf. v. 21; ch. 10. 1.). 26. Also—*i.e.*, Equally to be avoided are other sins, punishing good subjects, or resisting good rulers. 27, 28. Prudence of speech is commended, an excellent, or calm spirit, not excited to vain conversation.

CHAPTER XVIII.
Ver. 1-24. 1. Through desire ... seeketh—*i.e.*, seeks selfish gratification. intermeddleth ... wisdom—or, rushes on (ch. 17. 14) against all *wisdom*, or what is valuable (ch. 2. 7.). 2. that his heart ... itself—*i.e.*, takes pleasure in revealing his folly cf. ch. 12. 23; 15. 2. . 3. So surely are sin and punishment connected (ch. 16. 4.). *Wicked*, for *wickedness*, answers to *ignominy*, or the state of such; and contempt, the feeling of others to them; and to *reproach*, a manifestation of contempt. 4. Wise speech is like an exhaustless stream of benefit. 5. accept the person—(cf. Ps. 82. 2.). "It is not good" is to be supplied before *to overthrow*. 6, 7. The quarrelsome bring trouble on themselves. Their rash language ensnares them (ch. 6. 2.). 8. (Cf. ch. 16. 28.). as wounds—not sustained by the *Heb.*; better, as "*sweet morsels*," which men gladly swallow. innermost ... belly—or, the mind, or heart (cf. ch. 20. 27-30; Ps. 22. 14.). 9. One by failing to get, the other by wasting wealth, grows poor. waster—*lit., master of wasting*, a prodigal. 10. name of the Lord—manifested perfections (Ps. 8. 1; 20. 2.), as faithfulness, power, mercy, &c., on which men rely. is safe —*lit., set on high, out of danger* (Ps. 18. 2; 91. 4.). 11. contrasts with v. 10 (cf. ch. 10. 15.). Such is a vain trust (cf. Ps. 73. 6.). 12. (Cf. ch. 15. 33; 16. 18.). 13. Hasty speech evinces self-conceit, and insures shame (ch. 26. 12.). 14. infirmity—bodily sickness, or outward evil. The *spirit*, which sustains, being *wounded*, no support is left, except, as implied, in God. 15. (Cf. ch. 1. 5, 15, 31.). 16. (Cf. ch. 17. 8, 23.). Disapproval of the fact stated is implied. 17. One-sided statements are not reliable. searcheth — thoroughly (ch. 17. 9, 19.). 18. The lot—whose disposal is of God (ch. 16. 33.), may, properly used, be a right mode of settling disputes. 19. No feuds so difficult of adjustment as those of relatives; hence great care should be used to avoid them. 20. (Cf. ch. 12. 14; 13. 2.). Men's words are the *fruit*, or *increase of lips*, and when good, benefit them. satisfied with— Cf. ch, 1. 31; 14. 14.). 21. Death and life—or, The greatest evil and good. that love it—*i.e.*, the tongue, or its use for good or evil. — fruit—cf. v. 19; Jam. 1. 19.). 22. The old versions supply "good" before the "wife," as the last clause, and ch. 19. 14, imply (cf. ch. 31. 10. . 23. The rich ... roughly —he is tolerated because rich, implying that the estimate of men by wealth is wrong. 24. A man ... friendly—better, "A man ... is) to, or may triumph (Ps. 108. 9.), or shout for joy Ps. 5. 11. , *i.e.*, may congratulate himself. Indeed, there is a friend who is better than

CHAPTER XXI.

THE king's heart *is* in the hand of the LORD, *as* the rivers of water: he turneth it whithersoever he will.

2 Every way of a man *is* right in his own eyes: *a* but the LORD pondereth the hearts.

3 To *b* do justice and judgment *is* more acceptable to the LORD than sacrifice.

4 ¹ An high look, and a proud heart, *and* ² the plowing of the wicked, *is* sin.

5 The thoughts of the diligent *tend* only to plenteousness; but of every one *that is* hasty, only to want.

6 The getting of treasures by a lying tongue *is* a vanity tossed to and fro of them that seek death.

7 The robbery of the wicked shall ³ destroy them; because they refuse to do judgment.

8 The way of man *is* froward and strange: but *as for* the pure, his work *is* right.

9 *It is* better to dwell in a corner of the house-top, than with ⁴ a brawling woman in ⁵ a wide house.

10 The ᶜ soul of the wicked desireth evil: his neighbour ⁶ findeth no favour in his eyes.

11 When the scorner is punished, the simple is made wise: and when the wise is instructed, he receiveth knowledge.

12 The ᵈ righteous *man* wisely considereth the house of the wicked: *but* God overthroweth ᵉ the wicked for *their* wickedness.

13 Whoso *f* stoppeth his ears at the cry of the poor, he also shall cry himself, but shall not be heard.

14 A gift in secret pacifieth anger, and a reward in the bosom strong wrath.

15 *It is* joy to the just to do judgment: but destruction *shall be* to the workers of iniquity.

16 The man that wandereth out of the way of understanding shall remain in the congregation of the dead.

17 He that loveth *g* pleasure *shall be* a poor man; he that loveth wine and oil shall not be rich.

18 The *g* wicked *shall be* a ransom for the righteous, and the transgressor for the upright.

19 *It is* better to dwell *g* in the wilderness, than with a contentious and an angry woman.

20 *There* *h* *is* treasure to be desired and oil in the dwelling of the wise: but a foolish man spendeth it up.

21 He *i* that followeth after righteousness and mercy findeth life, righteousness, and honour.

22 A wise *man* scaleth the city of the mighty, and casteth down the strength of the confidence thereof.

23 Whoso keepeth his mouth and his tongue keepeth his soul from troubles.

24 Proud *and* haughty scorner *is* his name who dealeth ⁹ in proud wrath.

25 The desire of the slothful killeth him; for his hands refuse to labour.

26 He coveteth greedily all the day long: but the righteous giveth and spareth not.

27 The sacrifice of the wicked *is* abomination; how much more *when* he bringeth it ¹⁰ with a wicked mind?

28 ¹¹ A false witness shall perish: but the man that heareth speaketh constantly.

29 A wicked man hardeneth his face: but, *as for* the upright, he ¹² directeth his way.

30 *There is* no wisdom nor understanding nor counsel against the LORD.

31 The horse *is* prepared against the day of battle: but ¹³ safety *is* of the LORD.

CHAPTER XXII.

A GOOD name *is* rather to be chosen than great riches, *and* ¹ loving favour rather than silver and gold.

2 The rich and poor meet together: the LORD *is* the maker of them all.

3 A prudent *man* foreseeth the evil, and hideth himself: but the simple pass on, and are punished.

4 By ² humility, *and* the fear of the LORD, *are* riches, honour, and life.

5 Thorns *and* snares *are* in the way of the froward: *a* he that doth keep his soul shall be far from them.

6 ³ Train up a child ⁴ in the way he should go; and when he is old, he will not depart from it.

7 The rich ruleth over the poor, and the borrower *is* servant ⁵ to the lender.

8 He that soweth iniquity shall reap vanity: ⁶ and the rod of his anger shall fail.

9 ⁷ He that hath a bountiful eye shall be blessed; for he giveth of his bread to the poor.

10 Cast out the scorner, and contention shall go out; yea, strife and reproach shall cease.

11 He that loveth pureness of heart, ⁸ *for* the grace of his lips the king *shall be* his friend.

12 The eyes of the LORD preserve knowledge; and he overthroweth ⁹ the words of the transgressor.

13 The slothful *man* saith, *There is* a lion without, I shall be slain in the streets.

14 The mouth of strange women *is* a deep pit: he that is abhorred of the LORD shall fall therein.

15 Foolishness *is* bound in the heart of a child; *but* the rod of correction shall drive it far from him.

16 He *b* that oppresseth the poor to increase his *riches, and* he that giveth to the rich, *shall* surely *come* to want.

17 ¶ Bow down thine ear, and hear the words of the wise, and apply thine heart unto my knowledge:

18 For *it is* a pleasant thing if thou keep them ¹⁰ within thee; they shall withal be fitted in thy lips.

19 That thy trust may be in the LORD, I have made known to thee this day, ¹¹ even to thee.

20 Have not I written to thee excellent things in counsels and knowledge;

21 That I might make thee know the certainty of the words of truth; *c* that thou mightest answer the words of truth ¹² to them that send unto thee?

22 Rob not the poor, because he *is* poor; neither *d* oppress the afflicted in the gate:

23 For the LORD will plead their cause, and spoil the soul of those that spoiled them.

24 Make no friendship with an angry man; and with a furious man thou shalt not go;

25 Lest thou learn his ways, and get a snare to thy soul.

26 Be not thou *one* of them that strike hands, *or* of them that are sureties for debts.

27 If thou hast nothing to pay, why should he take away thy bed from under thee?

28 Remove not the ancient ¹³ landmark, which thy fathers have set.

Moral Virtues, and   PROVERBS, XIX—XXI.   *their Contrary Vices.*

a brother; such is the "Friend of sinners," who may have been before the writer's mind.

CHAPTER XIX.

Ver. 1-29. **1.** Cf. ch, 28. 6. "**Rich**" for "*fool*" here. . Integrity is better than riches (ch. 15. 16, 17; 16. 8.). **2.** The last illustrates the first clause. Rashness, the result of ignorance, brings trouble. **3.** pe. verteth . . . w.y—turns him back from right ch. 13. 6; Jam. 1. 13; ; and he blames God for his failures. **4.** Cf. ch. 14. 20,). Such facts are often adduced with implied disapprobation. **5.** Cf. v. 9, where "*perish*" explains "*not escape*" here (cf. Ps. 88. 9, 10.), **8.** Cf. *Marg.*; ch. 15. 32.), loveth . . . soul—or, himself, which he evinces by regarding his best interests. keepeth—or, regards. **10.** (Cf. ch. 17. 7.). The fool is as incapable of properly using pleasure as knowledge, yet for him to have it is less incongruous than the undue elevation of servants. Let each abide in his calling 1 Cor. 7. 20,). **11.** (Cf. ch. 14. 29; 16. 32.). This inculcation of a forgiving spirit shows that true religion is always the same (Mat. 5. 22-24.) 12. (Cf. ch. 16. 14, 15; 20. 2.). A motive to submission to lawful authority. **13.** calamity—*lit.*, *calamities*, varied and many. continual dropping—a perpetual annoyance, wearing out patience. **14.** A contrast of men's gifts and God's, who, though author of both blessings, confers the latter by His more special providence. and —or, but, implying that the evils of v. 13 are only avoided by His care. **15.** a deep sleep—a state of utter indifference. idle soul—or person (cf. ch. 10. 4; 12. 24.). **16.** (Cf. ch. 10. 17; 13. 13.). despiseth . . . way—opposed to keeping or observing, neglects ,ch. 16. 17, (as 17. or easily obtained. mouth . . . gravel—unworthy of regard; his moral conduct. **17.** (Cf. ch. 14. 21; 1 s. 37. 26. . hath pity—shown by acts (cf. *Marg.*). **18.** (Cf. ch. 13. 24; 23. 13.). let not . . . spare—*lit.*, *do not lift up thy soul* (Ps. 24. 4; 25. 1,), *i.e.*, do not desire to his death; a caution to passionate parents against angry chastisement. **19.** Repeated efforts of kindness are lost on ill-natured persons. 20. Cf. ch. 13. 18-20.). latter end—(ch. 5. 11.). In youth prepare for age. **21.** (Cf. ch, 16. 1, 9; Ps. 33. 10, 11.). The failure of man's devices is implied. **22.** desire—*i.e.*, to do good, indicates a kind disposition ch. 11. 23;; and the poor thus affected are better than liars, who say and do not. **23.** The fear . . . life—cf. ch. 3. 2.). abide—or, remain contented 1 Tim. 4. 8.). not visited . . . evil—ch. 10. 3; Ps. 37. 25,), as a judgment, in which sense visit is often used (Ps. 89. 32; Jer. 6. 15.). **24.** bosom—*lit.*, *a wide dish in which the hand was plunged in eating* Mat. 26. 23,). Cf. ch. 26. 15, the sentiment expressed with equal irony and less exaggeration. **25.** Such is the benefit of reproof, even the simple profit, much more the wise. **26.** Unfilial conduct often condemned (ch. 17. 21 25; 20. 20; Deut. 21. 18. 21.). **27.** Avoid whatever leads from truth. **28.** ungodly witness—(cf. *Marg.*,), one false by bad principles (cf. ch. 6. 12.). scorneth judgment—sets at nought the dictates of justice. devoureth—*lit.*, swalloweth, as something delightful. **29.** Their punishment is sure, fixed, and ready cf. ch. 3. 34; 10. 13.).

CHAPTER XX.

Ver. 1-30. **1.** mocker—or, scorner. Such men are made by wine. raging—or, boisterous, as a drunkard. strong drink—made by spicing wine (cf. Isa. 5. 11, 22.; and it may include wine. deceived—*lit.*, *erring*, or reeling. **2.** (Cf. ch. 19. 12. . Men who resist authority injure themselves (Rom. 13. 2.. **3.** to cease . . . strife—or better, " to dwell from or without stri e," denoting the habit of life. tool . . . meddling—ch. 17. 14. . **4.** shall . . . beg —*lit.*, *ask* (in this sense, Ps. 109. 10,). **5.** Counsel . . . water—*i.e.*, deeply hidden ch. 18. 4; Ps. 13. 2.). The wise can discern well. **6.** Boasters are unreliable. goodness—or, kind disposition. **7.** The conduct of good men proclaims their sound principles. God's covenant and their good example secure blessing to their children (ch. 4. 26; Ps. 112. 1, 2,). **8.** As ch. 14. 35; 16. 10, 15, this is the character of a good king, not of all kings. **9.** The interrogation in the affirmative strengthens the implied negation cf. Job, 15. 14; Eccl. 7. 20,). **10.** Various measures . . . implying that some are wrong cf. ch, 11. 1; 16. 11.. **11.** The conduct of children even is the best test of principle cf. Mat. 7. 16.). **12.** Hence, of course, God will know all you do (Ps. 94, 9. . **13.** Activity and diligence contrasted with sloth (ch. 6. 9; 10.; 11.,, lest . . . poverty—*lit.*, *be deprived of inheritance.* **14.** when . . . his way—implying that he goes about boasting of his bargains. **15.** The contrast denotes the greater value of knowledge (cf. ch. 3. 14-16.). **16.** *To take the garment* implies severe exaction, justified by the surety's rashness. a strange woman—by some readings, *strangers*, but the former here, and ch. 27. 13, is allowable, and strengthens the sense. The debauchee is less reliable than the merely careless. **17.** Bread . . . sweet—either as unlawfully ch. 9. 17,', or easily obtained. mouth . . . gravel—well expresses the pain and grief given at last. **18.** (Cf. ch. 15. 22.). Be careful and considerate in important plans. **19.** Those who love to tell news will hardly keep secrets. flattereth . . . lips—cf. *Marg.*; ch. 1. 10.). meddle . . . him—*lit.*, *join, or associate with.* **20.** his lamp—(cf. ch. 13. 9; 24. 20.). **21.** gotten hastily—contrary to God's providence ch. 28. 20,), implying its unjust or easy attainment; hence the man is punished, or spends freely what he got easily cf. v. 17. . **22.** (Cf. Ps. 27. 14; Rom. 12. 17-19.). **23.** (Cf. v. 10: ch. 11. 1.). **24.** Man's goings—*lit.*, *Stately steppings of a strong man.* a man—any common man. understand—[or, perceive] his . . . way. **25.** devoureth . . . holy—or, better, who rashly speaks promises, or devotes what is holy, consecrating any thing. This suits better the last clause, which expresses a similar view of the results of rashly vowing. **26.** (Cf. v. 8.). bringeth . . . over them—the wheel was used for threshing grain. The figure denotes severity (cf. Amos, 1. 3.). **27.** The spirit . . . Lord—men's minds are God's gifts, and thus able to search one another (cf. v. 5; ch. 18. 8, 17; 1 Cor. 2. 11.). **28.** (Cf. ch. 3. 3; 16. 6, 12... **29.** Age has its peculiar excellence ch. 16. 31.). **30.** blueness—*lit.*, joining, the process of uniting the edges of a wound throws off purulent matter. stripes . . . belly—so punishment provides healing of soul (ch. 18. 8,), by deterring from evil courses.

CHAPTER XXI.

Ver. 1-31. **1.** rivers—irrigating channels (Ps. 1. 3,), whose course was easily turned (cf. Deut. 11. 10.). God disposes even kings as He pleases ,ch. 16. 9; Ps. 33. 15.). **2.** (Cf. ch.

29 Seest thou a man *diligent in his business? he shall stand before kings; he shall not stand before mean men.

CHAPTER XXIII.

WHEN thou sittest to eat with a ruler, consider diligently what is before thee;

2 And put a knife to thy throat, if thou be a man given to appetite.

3 Be not desirous of his dainties; for they are deceitful meat.

4 Labour ^{a} not to be rich; ^{b} cease from thine own wisdom.

5 ^{1} Wilt thou set thine eyes upon that which is not? for riches certainly make themselves wings; they fly away as an eagle toward heaven.

6 Eat ^{c} thou not the bread of him that hath ^{d} an evil eye, neither desire thou his dainty meats;

7 For as he thinketh in his heart, so is he: Eat and drink, saith he to thee; but his heart is not with thee.

8 The morsel which thou hast eaten shalt thou vomit up, and lose thy sweet words.

9 Speak ^{e} not in the ears of a fool; for he will despise the wisdom of thy words.

10 Remove not the old ^{2} landmark; and enter not into the fields of the fatherless;

11 For ^{f} their Redeemer is mighty; he shall plead their cause with thee.

12 Apply thine heart unto instruction, and thine ears to the words of knowledge.

13 Withhold not correction from the child; for if thou beatest him with the rod, he shall not die.

14 Thou shalt beat him with the rod, and shalt ^{g} deliver his soul from hell.

15 My son, if thine heart be wise, my heart shall rejoice, ^{3} even mine ;

16 Yea, my reins shall rejoice when thy lips speak right things.

17 Let not thine heart envy sinners: but be thou in the fear of the LORD all the day long.

18 For ^{h} surely there is an ^{4} end; and thine expectation shall not be cut off.

19 Hear thou, my son, and be wise, and guide thine heart in the way.

20 Be ^{i} not among wine-bibbers; among riotous eaters of ^{5} flesh:

21 For the drunkard and the glutton shall come to poverty; and drowsiness shall clothe a man with rags.

22 Hearken ^{j} unto thy father that begat thee, and despise not thy mother when she is old.

23 Buy ^{k} the truth, and sell it not; also wisdom, and instruction, and understanding.

24 The father of the righteous shall greatly rejoice: and he that begetteth a wise child shall have joy of him.

25 Thy father and thy mother shall be glad, and she that bare thee shall rejoice.

26 My son, give me thine heart, and let thine eyes observe my ways.

27 For a whore is a deep ditch; and a strange woman is a narrow pit.

28 She also lieth in wait ^{6} as for a prey, and increaseth the transgressors among men.

29 Who ^{l} hath woe? who hath sorrow? who hath contentions? who hath babbling? who hath wounds without cause? who hath redness of eyes?

30 They that tarry long at the wine; they that go to seek mixed wine.

31 Look not thou upon the wine when it

B. C. 1000.

CHAP. 22.
^{e} 1 Kin. 11.
23.
$^{ch.}$ 12. 24.
Rom. 12.11.
14 obscure men.

CHAP. 23.
^{a} 1 Tim. 6.9.
^{b} Ro. 12. 15.
1 Wilt thou cause thine eyes to fly upon.
^{c} Ps. 141. 4.
^{d} Deu. 15. 9.
^{e} Mat. 7. 6.
2 Or, bound.
^{f} Job 31. 21. Jer. 51. 36.
^{g} 1 Cor. 5. 5.
3 Or, even I will rejoice.
^{h} Lu. 10. 25.
4 Or, reward.
^{i} Is. 5. 22.
Mat. 24. 49.
Lu. 21. 34.
Rom. 13.13.
Eph. 5. 18.
5 of their flesh.
^{j} Eph. 6. 1.
^{k} Mat. 13.44.
6 Or, as a robber.
^{l} Is. 5. 11.
7 Or, a cockatrice.
8 in the heart of the son.
^{m} Jer. 5. 3.
9 I knew it not.
Eph. 4. 19.
^{n} Deu.29.19.
Is. 50. 13.
2 Pe. 2. 22.

CHAP. 24.
1 is in strength.
2 strengtheneth might.
^{a} Mat. 15.19.
Acts 8. 22.
3 narrow.
^{b} Is. 58. 6, 7.
1 John 3.16.
^{c} Rom. 2. 6.
Rev. 2. 23.
4 upon thy palate.
^{d} Ps. 34. 19.
Mic. 7. 8.
5 it be evil in his eyes.
6 Or, Keep not company with the wicked.
^{e} Ps. 11. 6.
Is. 3. 11.
7 Or, lamp.
^{f} Rom. 13. 7.
1 Pet. 2.17.
8 changers.
^{g} Deu. 11.12. John 7. 24.
^{h} Is. 5. 23.

is red, when it giveth his colour in the cup, when it moveth itself aright:

32 At the last it biteth like a serpent, and stingeth like ^{7} an adder.

33 Thine eyes shall behold strange women, and thine heart shall utter perverse things.

34 Yea, thou shalt be as he that lieth down ^{8} in the midst of the sea, or as he that lieth upon the top of a mast.

35 They ^{m} have stricken me, shalt thou say, and I was not sick; they have beaten me, and ^{9} I felt it not: ^{n} when shall I awake? I will seek it yet again.

CHAPTER XXIV.

BE not thou envious against evil men, neither desire to be with them;

2 For their heart studieth destruction, and their lips talk of mischief.

3 Through wisdom is an house builded, and by understanding it is established.

4 And by knowledge shall the chambers be filled with all precious and pleasant riches.

5 A wise man ^{1} is strong; yea, a man of knowledge ^{2} increaseth strength.

6 For by wise counsel thou shalt make thy war: and in multitude of counsellors there is safety.

7 Wisdom is too high for a fool: he openeth not his mouth in the gate.

8 He that deviseth to do evil shall be called a mischievous person.

9 The ^{a} thought of foolishness is sin: and the scorner is an abomination to men.

10 If thou faint in the day of adversity, thy strength is ^{3} small.

11 If ^{b} thou forbear to deliver them that are drawn unto death, and those that are ready to be slain;

12 If thou sayest, Behold, we knew it not; doth not he that pondereth the heart consider it? and he that keepeth thy soul, doth not he know it? and shall not he render to every man ^{c} according to his works?

13 My son, eat thou honey, because it is good; and the honey-comb, which is sweet ^{4} to thy taste:

14 So shall the knowledge of wisdom be unto thy soul: when thou hast found it, then there shall be a reward, and thy expectation shall not be cut off.

15 Lay not wait, O wicked man, against the dwelling of the righteous; spoil not his resting place:

16 For ^{d} a just man falleth seven times, and riseth up again: but the wicked shall fall into mischief.

17 Rejoice not when thine enemy falleth, and let not thine heart be glad when he stumbleth;

18 Lest the LORD see it, and ^{5} it displease him, and he turn away his wrath from him.

19 ^{e} Fret not thyself because of evil men, neither be thou envious at the wicked;

20 For ^{e} there shall be no reward to the evil man; the ^{7} candle of the wicked shall be put out.

21 My son, ^{f} fear thou the LORD and the king; and meddle not with ^{6} them that are given to change:

22 For their calamity shall rise suddenly; and who knoweth the ruin of them both?

23 These things also belong to the wise. It ^{g} is not good to have respect of persons in judgment.

24 He ^{h} that saith unto the wicked, Thou art righteous; him shall the people curse, nations shall abhor him;

25 But to them that rebuke him shall be

14. 2; 16. 2 25.). 3. (Cf. Ps. 50. 7-15; Isa. 1. 11, 17.). 4. high look — (cf. *Marg.*; Ps. 131. 1.); proud heart—or, heart of breadth, one that is swollen (cf. Ps. 101. 5.). plowing —better *lamp*, a frequent figure for prosperity (ch. 20. 20.), hence joy or delight. 5. The contrast is between steady industry and rashness (cf. ch. 19. 2.). 6. The getting —or, what is obtained (cf. Job. 7. 2; Jer. 22. 13, *Heb.*). vanity... to and fro—as fleeting as chaff or stubble in the wind (cf. ch. 20. 17-21; Ps. 62. 10.). Such getting as are unsatisfactory. them... death—act as if they did (ch. 8. 36; 17. 19.). 7. robbery—or, destruction, especially oppression, of which they are authors. shall destroy—*lit.*, *cut with a saw* (1 Ki. 7. 9.), *i.e.*, utterly ruin them. Their sins shall be visited on them in kind. to do judgment—what is just and right. 8. of man—any one, his way is opposed to truth and also estranged from it. The pure proves himself such by his right conduct. 9. corner —a turret, or arbour on the roof. brawling—or, contentious. wide house—*lit.*, *house of fellowship, or large enough for several families.* 10. So strongly does he desire to do evil (Ps. 10. 3; Eccl. 8. 11.), that he will not even spare his friend if in his way. 11. (Cf. ch. 19. 25.). That which the simple learn by the terrors of punishment, the wise learn by teaching. 12. (Cf. Ps. 37. 35-38; 73. 17, 20.). house — family, or interests. overthroweth—either supply God (cf. ch. 10. 24.), or the word is used impersonally. 13. The principles of retribution, often taught (cf. Ps. 18. 26; Mat. 7. 1-12.). 14. The effect of bribery (ch. 17. 23) is enhanced by secrecy, as the bribed person does not wish his motives made known. 15. But the just love right, and need no bribes. The wicked, at last, meet destruction, though for a time happy in concealing corruption. 16. the way of understanding—(cf. ch. 12. 26; 14. 22.). remain—*i.e.*, rest as at a journey's end ; death will be his unchanging home. 17. Costly luxuries impoverish. 18. (Cf. ch. 11. 8.). By suffering what they had devised for the righteous, or brought on them, the wicked became their ransom, in the usual sense of substitutes (cf. Josh. 7. 26; Esth. 7. 9.). 19. (Cf. *v.* 9.). wilderness—pasture, though uninhabitable ground (Ps. 65. 12.). 20. The wise, by diligence and care, lay up and increase wealth, while fools spend, *lit.*, *swallow it up*, greedily. 21. He who tries to act justly and kindly (Ps. 34. 14) will prosper and obtain justice and honour. 22. " Wisdom is better than strength" (Eccl. 7. 19; 9. 15.). strength... thereof—that in which they confide. 23. (Cf. ch. 13. 2, 3; Jam. 3. 6-10.). 24. The reproachful name is deserved by those who treat others with anger and contempt. 25. desire—*i.e.*, of ease and idleness, brings him to starvation. 26. The sin of covetousness marks the sluggard, as the virtue of benevolence the righteous. 27. God regards the heart, and hypocrisy is more odious than open inconsistency. mind—or, design (ch. 1. 4.). 28. (Cf. ch. 19. 5.). that heareth — or, heeds instruction, and so grows wise. speaketh constantly— or, sincerely (cf. Hab. 1. 5.), and hence is believed (ch. 12. 19; Jam. 1. 19.). 29. hardeneth his face—is obstinate. directeth... way—considers it, and acts advisedly. 30, 31. Men's best devices and reliances are vain, compared with God's, or without His aid (ch. 19. 21; Ps. 20. 7; 33. 17.).

CHAPTER XXII.

Ver. 1-29. 1. A good name — (Job, 30. 8, *Heb.*). Good is supplied here from Eccl. 7. 1. loving favour—kind regard, *i.e.*, of the wise and good. 2. Before God all are on the same footing (ch. 14. 31; 17. 5.). 3. are punished— *i.e.*, for their temerity; for the *evil* is not necessarily punitive, as the prudent might otherwise be its objects. 4. humility and the fear of the Lord—are in apposition; one produces the other. On the results cf. ch. 3. 16; 8. 18. 5. he that ... them—those who properly watch over their own souls are thus preserved from the dangers which attend the way of perverse men (ch. 16. 17.). 6. Train—Initiate, or early instruct, the way— *lit.*, *his way*, that selected for him, in which he should go; for early training secures habitual walking in it. 7. The influence of wealth sets aside moral distinctions is implied, and, of course, disapproved (cf. ch. 19. 6; 21. 14, &c.). 8. (Cf. ch. 11. 18; Ps. 109. 16-20; Gal. 6. 7, 8.). the rod ... fail—his power to do evil will be destroyed. 9. a bountiful eye—*i.e.*, a beneficent disposition. for he giveth...poor —his acts prove it. 10. Cast out—or, Drive away. Scorners foster strife by taunts and revilings. 11. (Cf. ch. *Marg.*). pureness of heart —and gentle, kind words win favour, even from kings. 12. preserve—or, guard. knowledge—its principles and possessors. overthroweth—utterly confounds and destroys the wicked. 13. Frivolous excuses satisfy the indolent man's conscience. 14. The mouth— or, flattering speeches (ch. 5. 3; 7. 5) ensnare man, *as pits*, beasts. God makes their own sin their punishment. 15. is bound—or, firmly fixed. Chastisement deters from crime, and so leads to reformation of principle. 16. These two vices pertain to the same selfish feeling, and are both deservedly odious to God, and incur punishment. 17. Here begins another division of the book, marked by those encouragements to the pursuit of wisdom, which are found in the earlier chapters. It will be observed, that from *v.* 22, to ch. 24. 12, the proverbs are generally expressed in two verses instead of one (cf. *Intr.*). 18. These lessons must be laid up in the mind, and *jitted*, or better, fixed in the lips, so as to be ever ready. 19. That ... Lord— This is the design of the instruction. 20. counsels and knowledge—both advice and instruction. 21. Specially, he desires to secure accuracy, so that his pupil may teach others. 22, 23. Here follow ten precepts of two verses each. Though men fail to defend the poor, God will (ch. 17. 5; Ps. 12. 5.). in the gate— place of public gathering (Job, 5. 4; Ps. 69. 12.). 24, 25. (Cf. ch. 2. 12-15; 4. 14.). a snare... soul —the unsuspecting are often misled by bad company. 26. 27. (Cf. ch. 6. 1; 17. 18.). should he take, &c.—*i.e.*, the creditor. 28. (Cf. ch. 23. 10.). Do not entrench on others (Deut. 19. 14; 27. 17.). 29. Success rewards diligence (ch. 10. 4; 21. 5.).

CHAPTER XXIII.

Ver. 1-35. 1-3. Avoid the dangers of gluttony. put a knife—an Eastern figure for putting restraint on the appetite. are deceitful meat—though well tasted, injurious. 4, 5. (Cf. 1 Tim. 6. 9, 10.). thine own wisdom— which regards riches intrinsically a blessing. Wilt ... *eyes*—As the eyes fly after, or seek, riches, they are not, *i.e.*, either become transitory, or, unsatisfying; fully expressed by

delight, and a good blessing shall come upon them.
26 Every man shall kiss his lips that giveth a right answer.
27 Prepare thy work without, and make it fit for thyself in the field; and afterwards build thine house.
28 He not a witness against thy neighbour without cause; and deceive not with thy lips.
29 Say not, I will do so to him as he hath done to me; I will render to the man according to his work.
30 I went by the field of the slothful, and by the vineyard of the man void of understanding;
31 And, lo, it was all grown over with thorns, and nettles had covered the face thereof, and the stone wall thereof was broken down.
32 Then I saw, and considered it well; I looked upon it, and received instruction.
33 Yet a little sleep, a little slumber, a little folding of the hands to sleep:
34 So shall thy poverty come as one that travelleth; and thy want as an armed man.

CHAPTER XXV.

1 Of kings, 8 of avoiding quarrels, and sundry causes thereof.

THESE are also proverbs of Solomon, which the men of Hezekiah king of Judah copied out.
2 It is the glory of God to conceal a thing: but the honour of kings is to search out a matter.
3 The heaven for height, and the earth for depth, and the heart of kings is unsearchable.
4 Take away the dross from the silver, and there shall come forth a vessel for the finer.
5 Take away the wicked from before the king, and his throne shall be established in righteousness.
6 Put not forth thyself in the presence of the king, and stand not in the place of great men:
7 For better it is that it be said unto thee, Come up hither, than that thou shouldest be put lower in the presence of the prince whom thine eyes have seen.
8 Go not forth hastily to strive, lest thou know not what to do in the end thereof, when thy neighbour hath put thee to shame.
9 Debate thy cause with thy neighbour himself, and discover not a secret to another;
10 Lest he that heareth it put thee to shame, and thine infamy turn not away.
11 A word fitly spoken is like apples of gold in pictures of silver.
12 As an earring of gold, and an ornament of fine gold, so is a wise reprover upon an obedient ear.
13 As the cold of snow in the time of harvest, so is a faithful messenger to them that send him; for he refresheth the soul of his masters.
14 Whoso boasteth himself of a false gift is like clouds and wind without rain.
15 By long forbearing is a prince persuaded, and a soft tongue breaketh the bone.
16 Hast thou found honey? eat so much as is sufficient for thee, lest thou be filled therewith, and vomit it.
17 Withdraw thy foot from thy neighbour's house; lest he be weary of thee, and so hate thee.

18 A man that beareth false witness against his neighbour is a maul, and a sword, and a sharp arrow.
19 Confidence in an unfaithful man in time of trouble is like a broken tooth, and a foot out of joint.
20 As he that taketh away a garment in cold weather, and as vinegar upon nitre, so is he that singeth songs to an heavy heart.
21 If thine enemy be hungry, give him bread to eat; and if he be thirsty, give him water to drink:
22 For thou shalt heap coals of fire upon his head, and the LORD shall reward thee.
23 The north wind driveth away rain; so doth an angry countenance a backbiting tongue.
24 It is better to dwell in a corner of the house-top, than with a brawling woman and in a wide house.
25 As cold waters to a thirsty soul, so is good news from a far country.
26 A righteous man falling down before the wicked is as a troubled fountain, and a corrupt spring.
27 It is not good to eat much honey; so for men to search their own glory is not glory.
28 He that hath no rule over his own spirit is like a city that is broken down, and without walls.

CHAPTER XXVI.

1 Of fools, 13 sluggards, 17 and busybodies.

AS snow in summer, and as rain in harvest; so honour is not seemly for a fool.
2 As the bird by wandering, as the swallow by flying, so the curse causeless shall not come.
3 A whip for the horse, a bridle for the ass, and a rod for the fool's back.
4 Answer not a fool according to his folly, lest thou also be like unto him.
5 Answer a fool according to his folly, lest he be wise in his own conceit.
6 He that sendeth a message by the hand of a fool cutteth off the feet, and drinketh damage.
7 The legs of the lame are not equal; so is a parable in the mouth of fools.
8 As he that bindeth a stone in a sling, so is he that giveth honour to a fool.
9 As a thorn goeth up into the hand of a drunkard, so is a parable in the mouth of fools.
10 The great God, that formed all things, both rewardeth the fool, and rewardeth transgressors.
11 As a dog returneth to his vomit, so a fool returneth to his folly.
12 Seest thou a man wise in his own conceit? there is more hope of a fool than of him.
13 The slothful man saith, There is a lion in the way; a lion is in the streets.
14 As the door turneth upon his hinges, so doth the slothful upon his bed.
15 The slothful hideth his hand in his bosom; it grieveth him to bring it again to his mouth.
16 The sluggard is wiser in his own conceit than seven men that can render a reason.
17 He that passeth by, and meddleth with strife belonging not to him, is like one that taketh a dog by the ears.
18 As a mad man, who casteth firebrands, arrows, and death,
19 So is the man that deceiveth his neighbour, and saith, Am not I in sport?

Moral Virtues, and   PROVERBS, XXIV, XXV.   *their Contrary Vices.*

their flying away. 6-8. Beware of deceitful men, whose courtesies even you will repent of having accepted. evil eye—or, purpose (ch. 22. 9; Deut. 15. 9; Mat. 6. 23.). The morsel ...words—*i.e.*, disgusted with his true character, all pleasant intercourse will be destroyed. 9. (Cf. ch. 9. 8.). "Cast not your pearls," &c. (Mat. 7. 6.). 10, 11. (Cf. ch. 22. 22, 23.). Redeemer—or, Avenger (Lev. 25. 25, 26; Num. 35. 12,), hence Advocate (Job, 19. 25.). plead...thee—(cf. Job, 31. 21; Ps. 35. 1; 68. 5.). 12. Here begins another series of precepts, 13, 14. While there is little danger that the use of the "divine ordinance of the rod" will produce bodily harm, there is great hope of spiritual good. 15, 16. The pleasure afforded the teacher by the pupil's progress is a motive to diligence. my reins—(cf. Ps. 7. 9.). 17, 18. (Cf. *Marg.*). The prosperity of the wicked is short, an end — or, hereafter, another time, when apparent inequalities shall be adjusted (cf. Ps. 37. 28-38. . 19-21. guide...way—or, direct thy thoughts to a right course of conduct (cf. ch. 4. 4; 9. 6.). riotous...flesh — prodigal, or eating more than necessary. Instead of *their flesh*, (cf. *Marg.*), better, "flesh to them." *i.e.* used for pleasure. drowsiness—the dreamy sleep of the slothful. 22. Hearken—*i.e.*, Obey (ch. 1. 8; Eph. 6. 1.). despise...old—adults revere the parents whom, as children, they once obeyed. 23. Buy—*lit.*, *Get* (ch. 4. 5.). truth —generally and specially as opposed to errors of all kinds. 24, 25. (Cf. ch. 10. 1; 17. 21, 25.). 26-35. A solemn warning against whoredom and drunkenness (Hos. 4. 11.). 26. give... heart—This is the address of that divine Wisdom so often presented (ch. 8. 1; 9. 3, &c.). heart — confidence. observe — or, keep, my ways—such as I teach you (ch. 3. 17; 9. 6.). 27, 28. deep ditch—a narrow pit, out of which it is hard to climb. lieth in wait—to ensnare men into the pit, as hunters entrap game (cf. ch. 22. 14.). increaseth...transgressors—(ch. 5. 6-10.). The vice alluded to is peculiarly hardening to the heart. 29, 30. This picture is often sadly realised now. mixed wine— (cf. ch. 9, 2; Isa. 5. 11.). 31. when...red—the colour denoting greater strength (cf. Gen. 49. 11; Deut. 32. 14.). giveth...cup—*lit.*, *gives its eye*, *i.e.*, sparkles. moveth...aright—perhaps its foaming is meant. 32. The acute miseries resulting from drunkenness contrasted with the temptations. 33, 34. The moral effect: it inflames passion (Gen. 19. 31, 35.), lays open the heart, produces insensibility to the greatest dangers, and debars from reformation, under the severest sufferings. 35. awake — *i.e.*, from drunkenness (Gen. 9. 24.). This is the language rather of acts than of the tongue.

retributive justice cannot be avoided by professed ignorance. 13, 14. As delicious food whets the appetite, so should the rewards of wisdom excite us to seek it. reward—*lit.*, *after part*, the proper result (cf. ch. 23. 18; Ps. 37. 37, 38.). 15, 16. The plots of the wicked against the good, though partially, shall not be fully successful (Ps. 37. 24); while the wicked, falling under penal evil, find no help. even times—often, or many (ch. 6. 16, 31; 9. 1.). 17, 18. Yet let none rejoice over the fate of evil doers, lest God punish their wrong spirit by relieving the sufferer (cf. ch. 17. 5; Job, 31. 29.). 19, 20. (Ps. 37. 1, 38; 18. 28.). candle—or, prosperity, it shall come to an end (ch. 13. 9; 20. 20.). 21, 22. A warning against impiety and resistance to lawful rule (Rom. 13. 1-7; 1 Pet. 2. 17.). meddle...change —(cf. *Marg.*), *lit.*, *mingle yourself*, avoid the society of restless persons, their calamity, &c.—either what God and the king inflict, or what *changers* and their company suffer: better the first. 23. These...wise— *lit.*, *are of the wise*, as authors (cf. "Psalms of David," Heb.). *These* are the verses following, to ch. 25. to have respect—*lit.*, *to discern faces*, show partiality. 24, 25., of which an example is justifying the wicked, to which is opposed, rebuking him, which has a blessing. 26. kiss his lips—love and obey. do homage (Ps. 2. 12; Sol. Song 8. 1.). right answer—*lit.*, *plain* (ch. 8. 9) *words*, opposed to deceptive, or obscure. 27. Prepare in the field—*i.e.*, Secure, by diligence, a proper support, and then build; provide necessaries, then comforts, to which a house rather pertained, in a mild climate, permitting the use of tents. 28. Do not speak even truth needlessly against any, and never falsehood. 29. Especially avoid retaliation (Mat. 5. 43-45; Rom. 12. 17.). 30, 31. A striking picture of the effects of sloth. 32-34. From the folly of the sluggard learn wisdom (ch. 6. 10, 11.).

CHAPTER XXV.

Ver. 1-28. 1. The character of these proverbs sustains the title (cf. *Intr.*). also—refers to the former part of the book. copied out— *lit.*, *transferred*, *i.e.*, from some other book to this; not given from memory. 2. God's unsearchableness impresses us with awe (cf. Isa. 45. 15; Rom. 11. 33.). But kings, being finite, should confer with wise counsellors; 3. Yet wisely keeping state secrets, which to common men are as inaccessible heights and depths. 4, 5. As separating impurities from ore leaves pure silver, so taking from a king wicked counsellors leaves a wise and beneficent government. before—or, in presence of, as courtiers stood about a king. 6, 7. Do not intrude into the presence of the king, for the elevation of the humble is honourable, but the humbling of the proud, disgraceful (Luke, 14. 8-10.). 8. (Cf. ch. 3. 30.). let... shame—lest you do what you ought not, when shamed by defeat, or "lest thou art shut out from doing any thing." 9, 10. (Cf. Mat. 5. 25; *Marg.*). secret—*i.e.*, of your opponent, for his disadvantage, and so you be disgraced, not having discussed your difficulties with him. 11. a word fitly—*lit.*, *quickly*, as wheels roll, just in time. The comparison "*as apples* ...*silver*" gives a like sense, apples, &c.—either real apples of golden colour, in a silver net-work basket, or imitations on silver embroidery. 12. Those who desire to know, and do rightly, most highly esteem good counsel (ch. 9. 9; 15. 31.). The listening ear

CHAPTER XXIV.

Ver. 1-34. 1, 2. (Cf. ch. 23. 3, 17; Ps. 37. 1.). studieth—meditateth. talk...mischief—their expressed purposes are to do evil. 3, 4. (Cf. ch. 14. 1; Isa. 54. 14.). house—including the family. by knowledge...riches—(ch. 8. 18; 21. 20.). 5, 6. The general statement (Eccl. 9. 16, 18) is specially illustrated (cf. ch. 21. 22; Ps. 144. 1.). 7. (Cf. ch. 14. 16.). in the gate— (Cf. ch. 22. 22.). 8. So called even if he fails to *do evil*. 9. Same thought varied. 10. *Lit.*, *If thou fail in the day of straits* [adversity], strait (or small) is thy strength," which is then truly tested. 11, 12. Neglect of known duty is sin (Jam. 4. 17.). ready [*lit.*, *bowing down*] *to be slain—i.e.*, unjustly. God's

Maxims and observations　PROVERBS, XXVII, XXVIII.　of Solomon.

20 ¹⁰ Where no wood is, *there* the fire goeth out; so where *there is* no ¹¹ talebearer, the strife ¹² ceaseth.
21 *As* coals *are* to burning coals, and wood to fire; so *is* a contentious man to kindle strife.
22 The words of a talebearer *are* as wounds, and they go down into the ¹³ innermost parts of the belly.
23 Burning lips and a wicked heart *are like* a potsherd covered with silver dross.
24 He that hateth ¹⁴ dissembleth with his lips, and layeth up deceit within him;
25 When he ¹⁵ speaketh fair, believe him not: for *there are* seven abominations in his heart.
26 ¹⁶ *Whose* hatred is covered by deceit, his wickedness shall be showed before the *whole* congregation.
27 Whoso diggeth a pit shall fall therein; and he that rolleth a stone, it will return upon him.
28 A lying tongue ᵃ hateth *those that are* afflicted by it; and a flattering mouth worketh ruin.

CHAPTER XXVII.

1 Self-love, 5 true love, 11 care to avoid offences, 23 and the household care.

BOAST ᵃ not thyself of 1 to-morrow; for thou knowest not what a day may bring forth.
2 Let another man praise thee, and not thine own mouth; a stranger, and not thine own lips.
3 A stone *is* ² heavy, and the sand weighty; but a fool's wrath *is* heavier than them both.
4 ³ Wrath *is* cruel, and anger *is* outrageous; but ᵇ who *is* able to stand before ⁴ envy?
5 Open ᶜ rebuke *is* better than secret love.
6 Faithful *are* the wounds of a friend: but the kisses of an enemy *are* ⁵ deceitful.
7 The full soul ⁶ loatheth an honey-comb: but to the hungry soul every bitter thing is sweet.
8 As a bird that wandereth from her nest, so *is* a man that wandereth from his place.
9 Ointment and perfume rejoice the heart; so *doth* the sweetness of a man's friend ⁷ by hearty counsel.
10 Thine own friend, and thy father's friend, forsake not; neither go into thy brother's house in the day of thy calamity: *for* better *is* a neighbour *that is* near, than a brother far off.
11 My son, be wise, and make my heart glad, ᵈ that I may answer him that reproacheth me.
12 A prudent *man* foreseeth the evil, *and* hideth himself: *but* the simple pass on, *and* are punished.
13 Take his garment that is surety for a stranger, and take a pledge of him for a strange woman.
14 He that blesseth his friend with a loud voice, rising early in the morning, it shall be counted a curse to him.
15 A continual dropping in a very rainy day and a contentious woman are alike.
16 Whosoever hideth her hideth the wind, and the ointment of his right hand, *which* bewrayeth *itself.*
17 Iron sharpeneth iron; so a man sharpeneth the countenance of his friend.
18 Whoso ᵉ keepeth the fig tree shall eat the fruit thereof; so he that waiteth on his master shall be honoured.

19 As in water face *answereth* to face, so the heart of man to man.
20 Hell ᶠ and destruction are ⁸ never full; so the eyes of man are never satisfied.
21 *As* the fining pot for silver, and the furnace for gold; so *is* a man to his praise.
22 Though thou shouldest bray a fool in a mortar among wheat with a pestle, *yet* will not his foolishness depart from him.
23 Be thou diligent to know the state of thy flocks, *and* ⁹ look well to thy herds:
24 For ¹⁰ riches *are* not for ever: and doth the crown endure ¹¹ to every generation?
25 The hay appeareth, and the tender grass showeth itself, and herbs of the mountains are gathered.
26 The lambs *are* for thy clothing, and the goats *are* the price of the field.
27 And thou shalt have goats' milk enough for thy food, for the food of thy household, and *for* the ¹² maintenance for thy maidens.

CHAPTER XXVIII.

Of impiety and religious integrity.

THE wicked flee when no man pursueth: but the righteous are bold as a lion.
2 For the transgression of a land many are the princes thereof: but ¹ by a man of understanding *and* knowledge the state *thereof* shall be prolonged.
3 A ᶜ poor man that oppresseth the poor *is* like a sweeping rain ² which leaveth no food.
4 They that forsake the law praise the wicked: ᵇ but such as keep the law contend with them.
5 Evil men understand not judgment: but they ᶜ that seek the LORD understand all *things.*
6 Better *is* the poor that walketh in his uprightness, than *he that is* perverse *in his* ways, though he *be* rich.
7 Whoso keepeth the law *is* a wise son: but he that ᶜ is a companion of riotous *men* shameth his father.
8 He that by usury and ⁴ unjust gain increaseth his substance, he shall gather it for him that will pity the poor.
9 He ᵈ that turneth away his ear from hearing the law, ᵉ even his prayer *shall be* abomination.
10 Whoso causeth the righteous to go astray in an evil way, he shall fall himself into his own pit: ᶠ but the upright shall have good *things* in possession.
11 The rich man *is* wise ᵇ in his own conceit; but the poor that hath understanding searcheth him out.
12 When righteous *men* do rejoice, *there* is great glory: but when the wicked rise, a man is ⁶ hidden.
13 He that covereth his sins shall not prosper: but whoso confesseth and forsaketh *them* shall have mercy.
14 Happy *is* the man that feareth alway: but he that hardeneth his heart shall fall into mischief.
15 *As* a roaring lion, and a ranging bear; *so* ᵍ *is* a wicked ruler over the poor people.
16 The prince that wanteth understanding *is* also a great oppressor: *but* he that hateth covetousness shall prolong *his* days.
17 A man that doeth violence to the blood of *any* person shall flee to the pit; let no man stay him.
18 Whoso walketh uprightly shall be saved: but *he that is* perverse *in his* ways shall fall at once.
19 He that tilleth his land shall have

Maxims and Observations PROVERBS, XXVI, XXVII. *of Solomon.*

is better than one hung with gold. 13. Snow from mountains was used to cool drinks; so refreshing is a faithful messenger (ch. 13. 17.). 14. clouds—*lit.*, *vapours* (Jer. 10. 13,), clouds only in appearance, a false gift—promised, but not given. 15. Gentleness and kindness overcome the most powerful and obstinate. long forbearing—or, slowness to anger (ch. 14. 29; 15. 18.). 16, 17. A comparison, as a surfeit of honey produces physical disgust, so your company, however agreeable in moderation, may, if excessive, lead your friend to hate you. 18. *A false witness* is as destructive to reputation, as such weapons to the body (ch. 24. 28.). beareth ... witness—*lit.*, *answereth questions*, as before a judge, against his neighbour. 19. *Treachery* annoys as well as deceives. 20. Not only is the incongruity of songs (*i.e.*, joyful) and sadness meant, but an accession of sadness, by want of sympathy, is implied. 21, 22. (Cf. Mat. 5. 44; Rom. 12. 20.). As metals are melted by heaping coals upon them, so is the heart softened by kindness. 23. Better, "As the north wind bringeth forth (Ps. 90. 2) or produces rain, so does a concealed, or slandering, tongue produce anger. 24. (Cf. ch. 21. 9, 19.). 25. (Cf. *v.* 13.). good news—*i.e.*, of some loved interest or absent friend, the more grateful as coming from afar. 26. From troubled fountains and corrupt springs, no healthy water is to be had, so when the righteous are oppressed by the wicked, their power for good is lessened, or destroyed. 27. Satiety surfeits (*v.* 16, , so men who are self-glorious find shame. is not glory—*not* is supplied from the first clause, or *is grievous*, in which sense a similar word is used (ch. 27. 2.*j.* 28. Such are exposed to the incursions of evil thoughts and successful temptations.

CHAPTER XXVI.

Ver. 1-28. 1. The incongruities of nature illustrate also those of the moral world. The fool's unworthiness is also implied (ch. 17. 7; 19. 10.). 2. Though not obvious to us, the bird—*lit. sparrow*—and swallow—have an object in their motions, so penal evil falls on none without a reason. 3. The rod is as much needed by fools and as well suited to them, as whips and bridles are for beasts. 4, 5. Answer not—*i.e.* approvingly by like folly. Answer—by reproof. 6. A fool fails by folly as surely as if he were maimed. drinketh damage—*i.e.*, gets it abundantly (Job, 15. 16; 34. 7.). 7. legs ... equal—or, "take away the legs," or the legs ... are weak. In any case the idea is that they are the occasion of an awkwardness, such as the fool shows in using a parable or proverb cf. *Intr.*; ch. 17. 7.). 8. A stone, bound in a sling, is useless, so honour, conferred on a fool, is thrown away. 9. As vexatious and unmanageable as a thorn in a drunkard's hand is a parable to a fool. He will be as apt to misuse it as to use it rightly. 10. Various versions of this are proposed (cf. *Marg.*). Better perhaps—"Much He injures (or *lit.*, *wounds*) all who reward," &c., *i.e.*, Society is injured by encouraging evil men, transgressors—may be rendered vagrants. The word God is improperly supplied. 11. returneth ... folly—Though disgusting to others, the fool delights in his folly. 12. The self-conceited are taught with more difficulty than the stupid. 13. (Cf. ch. 22. 13.'. 14. (Cf. ch. 6. 10 ; 24. 33.). He moves but does not leave his place. 15. (Cf. ch. 19. 24.). 16. The thoughtless being ignorant of their ignorance are conceited. 17. meddleth—as ch. 20. 19 ; 24. 21, as either holding a dog by the ears or letting him go involves danger, so success in another man's strife or failure involves a useless risk of reputation, does no good, and may do us harm. 18, 19. Such are reckless of results. 20, 21. The tale-bearers foster (ch. 16. 28,), and the contentious excite, strife. 22. (Cf. ch. 18. 8.). 23. *Warm professions* can no more give value to insincerity than silver coating to rude earthenware. 24. dissembleth—though an unusual sense of the word 'cf. *Marg.*), is allowable, and better suits the context, which sets forth hypocrisy. 25. Sentiment of *v.* 24 carried out. seven ... heart—*i.e.*, very many cf. ch. 24. 16.). 26, 27. Deceit will at last be exposed, and the wicked by their own arts often bring on retribution (cf. ch. 12. 13 ; Ps. 7. 16 ; 9. 17. &c.. 28. Men hate those they injure. lying tongue —*lips* for the persons (cf. ch. 4. 24 ; Ps. 12. 3.).

CHAPTER XXVII.

Ver. 1-27. 1. Do not confide implicitly in your plans (ch. 16. 9 ; 19. 21; Jam. 4. 13-15.). 2. Avoid self-praise. 3. The literal sense of *heavy*, applied to material subjects, illustrates its figurative, *grievous*, applied to moral. a fool's wrath—is unreasonable and excessive. 4. envy—or, jealousy, (cf. *Marg.*; ch. 6. 34,), is more unappeasable than the simpler bad passions. 5, 6. love—not manifested in acts is useless ; and even, if its exhibition by rebukes wounds us, such love is preferable to the frequent (cf. *Marg.*), and hence deceitful, kisses of an enemy. 7. The luxury of wealth confers less happiness, than the healthy appetite of labour. 8. Such are not only out of place, but out of duty and in danger. 9. rejoice the heart—the organ of perceiving what pleases the senses. sweetness ... counsel—or, wise counsel is also pleasing. 10. Adhere to tried friends. The ties of blood may be less reliable than those of genuine friendship. 11. The wisdom of children both reflects credit on parents and contributes to their aid in difficulties. 12, 13. (Cf. ch. 20, 16; 22. 3.'. 14. Excessive zeal in praising raises suspicions of selfishness. 15. (Cf. ch. 19. 13.). very ... day—*lit.*, *a day of showers*. 16. hideth—or, restrains (*i.e.*, tries to do it , is as fruitless an effort, as that of holding the wind. the ointment ... right hand—the organ of power (Ps. 17. 7 ; 18. 35.). His right hand endeavours to repress perfume, but vainly. Some prefer: "His right hand comes on oil, *i.e.*, cannot take hold." Such a woman cannot be tamed. 17. a man sharpeneth ... friend, *i.e.*, conversation promotes intelligence, which the face exhibits. 18. Diligence secures a reward, even for the humble servant. 19. We may see our characters in the developed tempers of others. 20. Men's cupidity is as insatiable as the grave. 21. Praise tests character. a man to his praise—according to his praise, as he bears it. Thus vain men seek it, weak men are inflated by it, wise men disregard it, &c. 22. The obstinate wickedness of such is incurable by the heaviest inflictions. 23, 24. flocks—constituted the staple of wealth. It is only by care and diligence that the most solid possessions can be perpetuated (ch. 23. 5.). 25-27. The fact that providential arrangements furnish the means of competence to those who properly use them is another motive to diligence cf. Ps. 65. 9-13.). household—*lit.*, *house*, the

Maxims of Solomon. PROVERBS, XXIX, XXX. *Agur's confession and prayer.*

plenty of bread: but he that followeth after vain *persons* shall have poverty enough.
20 A faithful man shall abound with blessings: but he that maketh haste to be rich shall not be innocent.
21 To have respect of persons *is* not good; for, for a piece of bread *that* man will transgress.
22 He that hasteth to be rich *hath* an evil eye, and considereth not that poverty shall come upon him.
23 He that rebuketh a man, afterwards shall find more favour than he that flattereth with the tongue.
24 Whoso robbeth his father or his mother, and saith, *It is* no transgression; the same *is* the companion of a destroyer.
25 He that is of a proud heart stirreth up strife: but he that putteth his trust in the LORD shall be made fat.
26 He that trusteth in his own heart is a fool: but whoso walketh wisely, he shall be delivered.
27 He that giveth unto the poor shall not lack: but he that hideth his eyes shall have many a curse.
28 When the wicked rise, men hide themselves: but when they perish, the righteous increase.

CHAPTER XXIX.

1 *Of public government, 15 and of private.* 22 *Of anger, pride, theft, cowardice, and corruption.*

HE that, being often reproved, hardeneth his neck, shall suddenly be destroyed, and that without remedy.
2 When the righteous are in authority, the people rejoice: but when the wicked beareth rule, the people mourn.
3 Whoso loveth wisdom rejoiceth his father: but he that keepeth company with harlots spendeth his substance.
4 The king by judgment establisheth the land: but he that receiveth gifts overthroweth it.
5 A man that flattereth his neighbour spreadeth a net for his feet.
6 In the transgression of an evil man *there is* a snare: but the righteous doth sing and rejoice.
7 The righteous considereth the cause of the poor: *but* the wicked regardeth not to know *it*.
8 Scornful men bring a city into a snare: but wise men turn away wrath.
9 *If* a wise man contendeth with a foolish man, whether he rage or laugh, *there is* no rest.
10 The blood-thirsty hate the upright: but the just seek his soul.
11 A fool uttereth all his mind: but a wise man keepeth it in till afterwards.
12 If a ruler hearken to lies, all his servants *are* wicked.
13 The poor and the deceitful man meet together; the LORD lighteneth both their eyes.
14 The king that faithfully judgeth the poor, his throne shall be established for ever.
15 The rod and reproof give wisdom: but a child left *to himself* bringeth his mother to shame.
16 When the wicked are multiplied, transgression increaseth: but the righteous shall see their fall.
17 Correct thy son, and he shall give thee rest; yea, he shall give delight unto thy soul.

18 Where *there is* no vision, the people perish: but he that keepeth the law, happy *is* he.
19 A servant will not be corrected by words; for though he understand he will not answer.
20 Seest thou a man *that is* hasty in his words? *there is* more hope of a fool than of him.
21 He that delicately bringeth up his servant from a child shall have him become his son at the length.
22 An angry man stirreth up strife, and a furious man aboundeth in transgression.
23 A man's pride shall bring him low: but honour shall uphold the humble in spirit.
24 Whoso is partner with a thief hateth his own soul: he heareth cursing, and bewrayeth *it* not.
25 The fear of man bringeth a snare: but whoso putteth his trust in the LORD shall be safe.
26 Many seek the ruler's favour: but every man's judgment *cometh* from the LORD.
27 An unjust man *is* an abomination to the just; and *he that is* upright in the way *is* abomination to the wicked.

CHAPTER XXX.

The confession and instructions of Agur.

THE words of Agur the son of Jakeh, *even* the prophecy: the man spake unto Ithiel, even unto Ithiel and Ucal,
2 Surely I *am* more brutish than *any* man, and have not the understanding of a man.
3 I neither learned wisdom, nor have the knowledge of the holy.
4 Who hath ascended up into heaven, or descended? who hath gathered the wind in his fists? who hath bound the waters in a garment? who hath established all the ends of the earth? what *is* his name, and what *is* his son's name, if thou canst tell?
5 Every word of God *is* pure: he *is* a shield unto them that put their trust in him.
6 Add thou not unto his words, lest he reprove thee, and thou be found a liar.
7 Two things have I required of thee; deny me *them* not before I die:
8 Remove far from me vanity and lies; give me neither poverty nor riches; feed me with food convenient for me:
9 Lest I be full, and deny *thee*, and say, Who *is* the LORD? or lest I be poor, and steal, and take the name of my God *in* vain.
10 Accuse not a servant unto his master, lest he curse thee, and thou be found guilty.
11 *There is* a generation *that* curseth their father, and doth not bless their mother.
12 *There is* a generation *that are* pure in their own eyes, and *yet* is not washed from their filthiness.
13 *There is* a generation, O how lofty are their eyes! and their eyelids are lifted up.
14 *There is* a generation whose teeth *are as* swords, and their jaw-teeth *as* knives, to devour the poor from off the earth, and the needy from *among* men.
15 The horse-leach hath two daughters, *crying*, Give, give. There are three *things that* are never satisfied, *yea*, four *things* say not, *It is* enough:

Maxims and Observations PROVERBS, XXVIII—XXX. *of Solomon.*

family (Acts, 10. 15; 1 Cor. 1. 16.). The **hay appeareth**—*lit., Grass appeareth* (Job, 40. 15; Ps. 104. 14.).

CHAPTER XXVIII.

Ver. 1-28. **1. A bad conscience makes men** timid; the righteous are alone truly bold (ch. 14. 26; Ps. 27. 1.). **2.** Anarchy producing contending rulers shortens the reign of each, but by a man ... prolonged—or, "by a man of understanding—*i.e.*, a good ruler,—he who knows or regards the right, *i.e.*, a good citizen, shall prolong (his days)." Good rulers are a blessing to the people. Bad government as a punishment for evil is equated with good as blessing to the good. **3. A poor man** ... &c.—Such, in power, exact more severely, and so leave subjects bare. **4.** They that forsake ... wicked—Wrong doers encourage one another. **5.** (Cf. John, 7. 17.). Ignorance of moral truth is due to unwillingness to know it. **6.** (Cf. ch. 10. 6.). Riches cannot compensate for sin, nor the want of them affect integrity. **7.** (Cf. ch. 17. 25.). riotous men—or, gluttons (ch. 23. 20, 21.). **8.** usury ... unjust gain—cf. *Marg.*, the two terms, meaning nearly the same, may denote excessive interest. God's providence directs the proper use of wealth. **9.** (Cf. ch. 15. 8; 21. 27.). hearing—*i.e., obeying.* God requires sincere worshippers (Ps. 66. 18; John, 4. 24.). **10.** Cf. ch. 26. 27.). **11. A poor but wise man can** discover and expose) the rich and self-conceited. **12. great glory—or,** cause for it to a people, for the righteous rejoice in good, and righteousness exalts a nation ch. 14. 34.). a man ... hidden—*i.e.*, the good retire, or all kinds try to escape a wicked rule. **13.** (Cf. Ps. 32. 3-5.). Concealment of sin delivers none from God's wrath, but He shows mercy to the humble penitent (Ps. 51. 4.). **14.** feareth—*i.e.*, God, and so repents. hardeneth his heart—makes himself insensible to sin, and so will not repent ch. 14. 16; 29. 1.). **15. The** rapacity and cruelty of such beasts well represents some wicked men (cf. Ps. 7. 2; 17. 12.). **16. The prince** ... understanding, *i.e.*, He does not perceive that oppression jeopards his success. Covetousness often produces oppression, hence the contrast. **17.** doeth violence ... blood, &c.—or, "that is oppressed by the blood or *life* (Gen. 9. 6,), which he has taken—pit—*to* or even to the pit, the grave or destruction (ch. 1. 12; Job, 33. 18-24; Ps. 143. 7.). stay him—sustain or deliver him. **18.** (Cf. ch. 10. 9; 17. 20.). Double dealing is eventually fatal. **19.** (Cf. ch. 10. 4; 20. 4.). vain persons—idle, useless drones, implying that they are also wicked (ch. 12. 11; Ps. 26. 14.). **20.** maketh haste ... rich—implying deceit or fraud (ch. 20. 21,), and so opposed to *faithful* or reliable. **21.** respect of persons—(ch. 24. 23., Such are led to evil by the slightest motive. **22.** Cf. v. 20.). evil eye—in the general sense of ch. 23. 6, here more specific for covetousness (cf. ch. 22. 9; Mat. 20. 15.). poverty ... him —by God's providence. **23.** (Cf. 9. 8, 9; 27. 5.). Those benefited by reproof will love their monitors. **24.** (Cf. Mat. 15. 4-6.). Such, though heirs, are virtually thieves, to be ranked with highwaymen. **25.** of a proud he r—*lit., or puffed up of soul—i.e., self-confident*, and hence overbearing and litigious, in de la—or, prosperous ch. 11. 25; 16. 20. **26.** Cf. ch. 3. 6-8.). walketh wise.y—*i.e.*, trusting in God (ch. 22. 17-19. **27.** Cf. ch. 11. 24-26. . hideth his eyes—as the face Ps. 27. 9; 69. 17,). denotes inattention. **28.** The elevation

of the wicked to power drives men to seek refuge from tyranny (cf. v. 12; ch. 11. 10; Ps. 12. 8.).

CHAPTER XXIX.

Ver. 1-27. **1. hardeneth ... neck—obsti**nately refuses counsel (2 Ki. 17. 14; Neh. 9. 16.). destroyed—*lit., shivered or utterly broken to pieces. without remedy—lit., without healing or repairing.* **2.** (Cf. ch. 11. 10; 28. 28.). in authority—(cf. *Marg.*,), increased in power. **3.** Cf. ch. 5. 6, 7; 10. 1, &c.). **4.** by judgment—*i.e.*, righteous decisions, opposed to those procured by gifts (cf. ch. 28. 21,), by which good government is perverted. land—for nation. **5.** Cf. ch. 26. 28.). spreadeth ... feet—by misleading him as to his real character, the flatterer brings him to evil, prepared by himself or others. **6.** In (or. By) the transgression—he is brought into difficulty (ch. 12. 13,), but the righteous go on prospering, and so sing or rejoice. **7.** considereth—*lit., knows*, as Ps. 1. 6. the cause—*i.e.*, in courts of justice (cf. v. 14.). The voluntary neglect of it by the wicked (ch. 28. 27) occasions oppression. **8.** Scornful men—Those who contemptuously disregard God's law. bring—(cf. *Marg.*), kindle strife. turn away [*i.e.*, abate] wrath. **9.** contendeth—*i.e.*, in law. whether ... laugh —The fool, whether angry or good humoured, is unsettled, or referring the words to the wise man, the sense is, that, all his efforts, severe or gentle, are unavailing to pacify the fool. **10.** blood-thirsty—(cf. *Marg.*,), murderers (Ps. 5. 6; 26. 9.). hate, &c.—ch. 1. 11; Gen. 3. 4.). seek ... soul—*i.e.*, to preserve it. **11.** Cf. ch. 12. 16; 16. 32.). mind—or, spirit, for anger or any ill passion which the righteous restrain. **12.** His servants imitate him. **13.** (Cf. ch. 22. 2.). deceitful man—*lit., man of vexations*, an exactor. the Lord ... their eyes—sustains their lives (1 Sam. 14. 27; Ps. 13. 3,), *i.e.*, Both depend on Him, and He will do justice. **14.** (Cf. ch. 20. 28; 25. 5.). Such is the character of the King of kings Ps. 72. 4, 12.). **15.** Cf. ch. 13. 24; 23. 13.). **16.** (Cf. v. 2, 12; Ps. 12. 1-8.). shall see ... fall —and triumph in it (Ps. 37. 34-38; 58. 10, 11.). **17.** Cf. v. 3, 15; ch. 19. 18.). give thee rest—peace, and quiet cf. v. 9. **18.** no vision—instruction in God's truth, which was by prophets, through visions (1 Sam. 3. 1.). people perish—(cf. *Marg.*), are deprived of moral restraints. keepeth the law—has, and observes, instruction (ch. 14. 11, 34; Ps. 19. 11.). **19. A servant—who lacks good principle,** corrected—or, discovered. will not answer—*i.e.*, obey. **20.** (Cf. ch. 21. 5.). hasty in ... words—implying self-conceit (ch. 26. 12.). **21.** become his son—assume the place and privileges of one. **22.** Cf. ch. 15. 18.). Such are delighted by discord and violence. **23.** (Cf. ch. 16. 19; 18. 12.). honour ... spirit—or, such shall lay hold on honour (ch. 11. 16. **24.** hateth ... soul—(cf. ch. 8. 36,). heareth cursing—(Lev. 5. 1,). risks the punishment, rather than reveal truth. **25.** The fear ... snare—involves men in difficulty (cf. v. 6.). shall be safe—(cf. *Marg.*; ch. 18. 10.). **26.** (Cf. *Marg.*; Ps. 27. 8.). God alone will and can do exact justice. **27.** (Cf. ch. 3. 32.). On last clause cf. v. 10; Ps. 37. 12.

CHAPTER XXX.

Ver. 1-33. **1.** This is the title of this chapter (cf. *Intr.*). the prophecy—(cf. *Marg.*; cf. Isa. 13. 1; Zech. 9. 1,], used for any divine instruction; not necessarily a prediction, which was only a kind of prophecy (1 Chr. 15. 27, *a song.*).

443

The sayings of Agur.   PROVERBS, XXXI.   *A virtuous woman described.*

16 The *l* grave; and the barren womb; the earth *that* is not filled with water; and the fire *that* saith not, *It is* enough.
17 The *m* eye *that* mocketh at *his* father, and despiseth to obey *his* mother, the ravens of *δ* the valley shall pick it out, and the young eagles shall eat it.
18 There be three *things which* are too wonderful for me, yea, four which I know not:
19 The way of an eagle in the air, the way of a serpent upon a rock, the way of a ship in the *9* midst of the sea, and the way of a man with a maid.
20 Such *is* the way of an adulterous woman; she eateth, and wipeth her mouth, and saith, I have done no wickedness.
21 For three *things* the earth is disquieted, and for four *which* it cannot bear:
22 For *n* a servant when he reigneth; and a fool when he is filled with meat;
23 For an odious *woman* when she is married; and an handmaid that is heir to her mistress.
24 There be four *things which are* little upon the earth, but they *are* 10 exceeding wise;
25 The *o* ants *are* a people not strong, yet they prepare their meat in the summer;
26 The *p* conies *are but* a feeble folk, yet make they their houses in the rocks;
27 The locusts have no king, yet go they forth all of them 11 by bands;
28 The spider taketh hold with her hands, and is in kings' palaces.
29 There be three *things* which go well, yea, four are comely in going:
30 A 12 lion, *which is* strongest among beasts, and turneth not away for any;
31 A 13 greyhound; an he-goat also; and a king, against whom *there is* no rising up.
32 If thou hast done foolishly in lifting up thyself, or if thou hast thought evil, *q lay* thine hand upon thy mouth.
33 Surely the churning of milk bringeth forth butter, and the wringing of the nose bringeth forth blood; so the forcing of wrath bringeth forth strife.

CHAPTER XXXI.

1 *Lemuel's lesson of chastity and temperance.* 6 *The afflicted to be comforted and defended.* 10 *Praise and properties of a good wife.*

THE words of king Lemuel, the 1 prophecy that his mother taught him.
2 What, my son? and what, the son of my womb? and what, the son of my vows?
3 Give not thy strength unto women, nor thy ways *a* to that which destroyeth kings.
4 *It b is* not for kings, O Lemuel, *it is* not for kings to drink wine, nor for princes strong drink;
5 Lest *c* they drink, and forget the law, and *2* pervert the judgment *3* of any of the afflicted.

B. C. 700.

CHAP. 30.
l Hab. 2. 5.
m Gen. 9.22.
Lev. 20. 9.
8 Or, the brook.
p heart.
n ch. 19. 10.
Eccl. 10. 7.
10 wise,
made wise.
o ch. 6. 6.
p Ps. 104. 18.
11 gathered together.
12 mighty old lion.
13 girt in the loins, *or*, horse.
q Eccl. 8. 2.
Mic. 7. 16.

CHAP. 31.
1 burden.
ch. 30. 1.
Is. 13. 1.
a Deu. 17.17.
Neh. 13.26.
ch. 7. 26.
b Eccl. 10.17.
c Hos. 4. 11.
2 alter.
3 of all the sons of affliction.
d Ps. 104. 15.
4 bitter of soul.
1 Sa. 1. 10.
5 the sons of destruction.
e Lev. 19. 15.
Deu. 1. 16.
f Job 29. 12.
Is. 1. 17.
Jer. 22. 16.
g Rom.12.11.
h Lu. 12. 42.
6 taketh.
8 She tasteth.
8 She spreadeth.
Ps. 41. 1.
ch. 19. 17.
Eph. 4. 28.
Heb.13.16.
9 Or, double garments.
i Deu. 15.15.
ch. 12. 4.
j 1 Tim. 5. 14.
k 1 Ki. 2. 19.
10 Or, have gotten riches.
l Ps. 112. 1.

6 Give *d* strong drink unto him that is ready to perish, and wine unto those that be *4* of heavy hearts.
7 Let him drink, and forget his poverty, and remember his misery no more.
8 Open thy mouth for the dumb in the cause of all *5* such as are appointed to destruction.
9 Open thy mouth, *e* judge righteously, and *f* plead the cause of the poor and needy.
10 ¶ Who can find a virtuous woman? for her price *is* far above rubies.
11 The heart of her husband doth safely trust in her, so that he shall have no need of spoil.
12 She will do him good and not evil all the days of her life.
13 She seeketh wool and flax, and worketh willingly with her hands.
14 She is like the merchants' ships; she bringeth her food from afar.
15 She *g* riseth also while it is yet night, and *h* giveth meat to her household, and a portion to her maidens.
16 She considereth a field, and *6* buyeth it: with the fruit of her hands she planteth a vineyard.
17 She girdeth her loins with strength, and strengtheneth her arms.
18 She perceiveth that her merchandise *is* good: her candle goeth not out by night.
19 She layeth her hands to the spindle, and her hands hold the distaff.
20 *8* She stretcheth out her hand to the poor; yea, she reacheth forth her hands to the needy.
21 She is not afraid of the snow for her household: for all her household *are* clothed with *9* scarlet.
22 She maketh herself coverings of tapestry; her clothing *is* silk and purple.
23 Her husband is known *i* in the gates, when he sitteth among the elders of the land.
24 She maketh fine linen, and selleth *it*, and delivereth girdles unto the merchant.
25 Strength and honour *are* her clothing; and she shall rejoice in time to come.
26 She openeth her mouth with wisdom; and in her tongue is the law of kindness.
27 She *j* looketh well to the ways of her household, and eateth not the bread of idleness.
28 Her *k* children arise up, and call her blessed; her husband *also*, and he praiseth her.
29 Many daughters 10 have done virtuously, but thou excellest them all.
30 Favour *is* deceitful, and beauty *is* vain: but a woman that *l* feareth the LORD, she shall be praised.
31 Give her of the fruit of her hands; and let her own works praise her in the gates.

ECCLESIASTES;

OR, THE PREACHER.

CHAPTER I.

1 *The Preacher shows that all things here below are vain.*

THE words of the Preacher, the son of David, king of Jerusalem.

B. C. 977.

CHAP. 1.
a Ps. 39. 5.
b Rom. 8. 20.
c ch. 3. 9.

2 Vanity *a* of vanities, saith the Preacher, vanity of vanities; *b* all is vanity.
3 What *c* profit hath a man of all his labour which he taketh under the sun?
4 *One* generation passeth away, and

Prophets were inspired men, who spoke for God to man, or man to God (Gen. 20. 7; Ex. 7.; 14. 15, 16.). Such, also, were the N. T. prophets. In a general sense, Gad, Nathan, and others were such, who were divine teachers, though we do not learn they ever predicted. the man spake—*lit., the saying of the man;* an expression used to denote any solemn and important announcement (cf. 2 Sam. 23. 1; Ps. 36. 1; 110. 1; Isa. 1. 24, &c.). Ithiel and Ucal were perhaps pupils. 2-4. brutish—stupid, a strong term to denote his lowly self-estimation; or he may speak of such as his natural condition, as contrasted with God's all-seeing comprehensive knowledge and almighty power. The questions of the last clause emphatically deny the attributes mentioned to be those of any creature, thus impressively strengthening the implied reference of the former to God (cf. Deut. 30. 12-14; Isa. 40. 12; Eph. 4. 8.). 5. (Cf. Ps. 12. 6; 119. 140.). 6. Add... words—Implying that his sole reliance was on God's all-sufficient teaching. reprove [convict] thee—and so the falsehood will appear. 7-9. A prayer for exemption from wickedness, and the extremes of poverty and riches, the *two things* mentioned. Contentment is implied as desired. vanity—all sorts of sinful acts (Job, 11. 11; Isa. 5. 18.). be full... deny—*i.e.,* puffed up by the pride of prosperity. take the name... vain—this is not (*Heb.*) the form (cf. Ex. 20. 7,) but *take* rather denotes laying violent hold on any thing, *i.e.,* lest I assail God's name, or attributes, as justice, mercy, &c., which the poor are tempted to do. 10. Accuse not —Slander not (Ps. 10. 7.). curse... guilty— lest, however lowly, he be exasperated to turn on thee, and your guilt be made to appear. 11-14. Four kinds of hateful persons— (1) graceless children, (2) hypocrites, (3) the proud, (4) cruel oppressors (cf. on v. 14, 1's. 14. 4; 52. 2,),—are now illustrated, (1) v. 15, 16, the insatiability of prodigal children and their fate; v. 17, (2) hypocrisy, or the concealment of real character; v. 18-20, (3 and 4) various examples of pride and oppression. 15, 16. horse-leech—supposed by some to be the vampire (a fabulous creature,), as being literally insatiable; but the other subjects mentioned must be taken as this, comparatively insatiable. The use of a fabulous creature agreeably to popular notions is not inconsistent with inspiration cf. Isa. 14.; 31.). There are three... yea, four—(cf. ch. 6. 16.). 17. The eye—for the person, with reference to the use of the organ to express mockery and contempt, and also as that by which punishment is received. the ravens... eagles... eat—either as dying unnaturally, or being left unburied, or both. 18-20. Hypocrisy is illustrated by four examples of the concealment of all methods, or traces of action, and a pertinent example of double dealing in actual vice, is added, *i.e.,* the *adulterous woman.* she eateth... mouth— *i.e.,* she hides the evidences of her shame, and professes innocence. 21-23. Pride and cruelty, the undue exaltation of those unfit to hold power, produce those vices which disquiet society (cf. ch. 19. 10; 28. 3.). heir ... mistress—*i.e.,* takes her place as a wife (Gen. 16. 4.). 24-31. These verses provide two classes of apt illustrations of various aspects of the moral world, which the reader is left to apply. By the first, diligence and providence are commended; the success of these insignificant animals, being due to their instinctive sagacity and activity, rather than strength. conies—mountain mice, or rabbits. spider—tolerated, even in palaces, to destroy flies. taketh... hands—or, uses with activity the limbs provided for taking prey. The other class provides similes for whatever is majestic or comely, uniting efficiency with gracefulness. 32. As none can hope, successfully, to resist such a king, suppress even the thought of the attempt. lay... hand upon thy mouth—*lay* is well supplied (Jud. 18. 19; Job, 20. 9; 40. 4.). 33. *i.e.,* strife—or, other ills, as surely arise from devising evil, as natural effects from natural causes.

CHAPTER XXXI.

Ver. 1-31. 1. Of the title of this, the 6th part of the book, cf. *Intr.* prophecy—as ch. 30. 1. 2. What, my son?—*i.e.,* What shall I say? repetitions denote earnestness. son... womb—as our phrase, "my own son," a term of special affection. son... vows—as one dedicated to God; so the word *Lemuel* may mean. 3-9. Succinct but solemn warnings against vices to which kings are peculiarly tempted, as carnal pleasures and oppressive and unrighteous government are used to sustain sensual indulgence. 3. strength — mental and bodily resources for health and comfort. thy ways—or, course of life. to that ... kings—*lit., to the destroying of kings,* avoid destructive pleasures cf. ch. 5. 9; 7. 22, 27; Hos. 4. 11.). 4, 5. Stimulants enfeeble reason, and pervert the heart, and do not suit rulers, who need clear and steady minds, and well-governed affections (cf. ch. 20. 1; 22. 29.). pervert... afflicted—they give unrighteous decisions against the poor. 6, 7. The proper use of such drinks is to restore tone to feeble bodies and depressed minds (cf. Ps. 104. 15.). 8, 9. Open... cause—Plead for those who cannot plead for themselves, as the orphan, stranger, &c. (cf. Ps. 72, 12; Isa. 1. 17.). appointed to destruction—who are otherwise ruined by their oppressors (cf. ch. 20. 14, 16.). 10-31. This exquisite picture of a truly lovely wife is conceived and drawn in accordance with the customs of Eastern nations, but its moral teachings suit all climes. In *Heb.* the verses begin with the letters of the *Hcb.* alphabet in order (cf. *Intr.* to Poetical Books.). 10. Who... woman?—The question implies that such are rare, though not entirely wanting (cf. ch. 18. 22; 19. 14.). virtuous—*lit., of strength, i.e.,* moral courage (cf. ch. 12. 4; Ruth, 3. 11.). her price, &c.—(cf. ch. 3. 15.). 11. heart... trust in her—he relies on her prudence and skill. no need of spoil—does not lack profit or gain, especially that obtained by the risk of war. 12. do... good—contribute good to him. 13, 14. Ancient women of rank thus wrought with their hands, and such, indeed, were the customs of Western women a few centuries since. In the East also, the fabrics were articles of merchandise. 15. She diligently attends to expending as well as gathering wealth; 16., and hence has means to purchase property. 17, 18. To energy she adds a watchfulness in bargains, and a protracted and painful industry. The last clause may figuratively denote that her prosperity (cf. ch. 24. 20) is not short lived. 19. No work, however mean, if honest, is disdained. 20. Industry enables her to be charitable. 21. scarlet—or, *purple,* by reason of the dyes used, the best fabrics, as a another generation cometh: but the earth abideth for ever.

5 The sun also ariseth, and the sun goeth down, and hasteth to his place where he arose.

6 The wind goeth toward the south, and turneth about unto the north; it whirleth about continually; and the wind returneth again according to his circuits.

7 All the rivers run into the sea; yet the sea is not full: unto the place from whence the rivers come, thither they return again.

8 All things are full of labour; man cannot utter it: the eye is not satisfied with seeing, nor the ear filled with hearing.

9 The thing that hath been, it is that which shall be; and that which is done is that which shall be done: and there is no new thing under the sun.

10 Is there any thing whereof it may be said, See, this is new? it hath been already of old time, which was before us.

11 There is no remembrance of former things; neither shall there be any remembrance of things that are to come with those that shall come after.

12 ¶ I the Preacher was king over Israel in Jerusalem;

13 And I gave my heart to seek and search out by wisdom concerning all things that are done under heaven: this sore travail hath God given to the sons of man, to be exercised therewith.

14 I have seen all the works that are done under the sun; and, behold, all is vanity and vexation of spirit.

15 That which is crooked cannot be made straight: and that which is wanting cannot be numbered.

16 I communed with mine own heart, saying, Lo, I am come to great estate, and have gotten more wisdom than all they that have been before me in Jerusalem; yea, my heart had great experience of wisdom and knowledge.

17 And I gave my heart to know wisdom, and to know madness and folly: I perceived that this also is vexation of spirit.

18 For in much wisdom is much grief: and he that increaseth knowledge increaseth sorrow.

CHAPTER II.

1 *Vanity of human courses in the works of pleasure.* 18 *Vanity of human labour, the fruit of which must soon be left to others.* 24 *Of the cheerful use of what a man hath.*

I SAID in mine heart, Go to now, I will prove thee with mirth; therefore enjoy pleasure: and, behold, this also is vanity.

2 I said of laughter, It is mad: and of mirth, What doeth it?

3 I sought in mine heart to give myself unto wine, yet acquainting mine heart with wisdom, and to lay hold on folly, till I might see what was that good for the sons of men which they should do under the heaven all the days of their life.

4 I made me great works; I builded me houses; I planted me vineyards;

5 I made me gardens and orchards, and I planted trees in them of all kind of fruits;

6 I made me pools of water, to water therewith the wood that bringeth forth trees;

7 I got me servants and maidens, and had servants born in my house; also I had great possessions of great and small cattle above all that were in Jerusalem before me;

8 I gathered me also silver and gold, and the peculiar treasure of kings and of the provinces; I gat me men singers and women singers, and the delights of the sons of men, as musical instruments, and that of all sorts.

9 So ¶ I was great, and increased more than all that were before me in Jerusalem: also my wisdom remained with me.

10 And whatsoever mine eyes desired I kept not from them, I withheld not my heart from any joy; for my heart rejoiced in all my labour: and this was my portion of all my labour.

11 Then I looked on all the works that my hands had wrought, and on the labour that I had laboured to do; and, behold, all was vanity and vexation of spirit, and there was no profit under the sun.

12 ¶ And I turned myself to behold wisdom, and madness, and folly: for what can the man do that cometh after the king? even that which hath been already done.

13 Then I saw that wisdom excelleth folly, as far as light excelleth darkness.

14 The wise man's eyes are in his head; but the fool walketh in darkness: and I myself perceived also that one event happeneth to them all.

15 Then said I in my heart, As it happeneth to the fool, so it happeneth even to me; and why was I then more wise? Then I said in my heart, that this also is vanity.

16 For there is no remembrance of the wise more than of the fool for ever; seeing that which now is, in the days to come shall all be forgotten. And how dieth the wise man? as the fool.

17 Therefore I hated life; because the work that is wrought under the sun is grievous unto me: for all is vanity and vexation of spirit.

18 ¶ Yea, I hated all my labour which I had taken under the sun; because I should leave it unto the man that shall be after me.

19 And who knoweth whether he shall be a wise man or a fool? yet shall he have rule over all my labour wherein I have laboured, and wherein I have shewed myself wise under the sun. This is also vanity.

20 Therefore I went about to cause my heart to despair of all the labour which I took under the sun.

21 For there is a man whose labour is in wisdom, and in knowledge, and in equity; yet to a man that hath not laboured therein shall he leave it for his portion. This also is vanity and a great evil.

22 For what hath man of all his labour, and of the vexation of his heart, wherein he hath laboured under the sun?

23 For all his days are sorrows, and his travail grief; yea, his heart taketh not rest in the night. This is also vanity.

24 ¶ There is nothing better for a man, than that he should eat and drink, and that he should make his soul enjoy good in his labour. This also I saw, that it was from the hand of God.

25 For who can eat, or who else can hasten hereunto, more than I?

26 For God giveth to a man that is good in his sight wisdom, and knowledge,

matter of taste also, the colour suits cold, coverings of tapestry—or, *coverlets*, *i.e.*, for beds. silk [or, linen (cf. Ex. 26. 1; 27. 9)] and purple—*i.e.*, the most costly goods. 23. in the gates—(cf. ch. 22. 22.). His domestic comfort promotes his advancement in public dignity. 24. fine linen—or, linen shirts, or the material for them. girdles—were often costly and highly valued (2 Sam. 18. 11.). delivereth—or, giveth as a present, or to sell. 25. Strength and honour—or, *Strong* and *beautiful*, is her clothing: or, figuratively, for moral character, vigorous and honourable. shall rejoice ... come—in confidence of certain maintenance. 26. Her conversation is wise and gentle. 27. (Cf. 1 Tim. 5. 14; Tit. 2. 5.). She adds to her example a wise management of those under her control. 28. She is honoured by those who best know her. 29. The words are those of her husband, praising her, virtuously—(cf. *v.* 10.). 30. Favour—or, Grace of personal manner. beauty—of face, or form (cf. ch. 11. 22.). True piety alone commands permanent respect and affection (1 Pet. 3. 3.). 31. The result of her labours is her best eulogy. Nothing can add to the simple beauty of this admirable portrait. On the measure of its realisation in the daughters of our own day rest untold issues, in the domestic, and, therefore, the civil and religious, welfare of the people.

ECCLESIASTES;

OR, THE PREACHER,) THE GREEK TITLE IN THE LXX.

INTRODUCTION

THE Hebrew *title* is Koheleth, which the speaker in it applies to himself (ch. 1. 12.), "I, Koheleth, was king over Israel." It means *an Assembler* or *Convener of a meeting*, and a *Preacher* (to such a meeting. The feminine form of the Hebrew noun, and its construction once (ch. 7. 27) with a feminine verb, show that it not only signifies *Solomon*, the Preacher to assemblies (in which case it is construed with the verb or noun masculine,), but also *Divine Wisdom* (feminine in Hebrew) speaking by the mouth of the inspired king. In six cases out of seven it is construed with the masculine. Solomon was endowed with inspired wisdom (1 Ki. 3. 5-14; 6. 11, 12; 9. 1, &c.; 11. 9-11,), specially fitting him for the task. The Orientals delight in such meetings for grave discourse. Thus the Arabs formerly had an assembly yearly, at Ocadh, for hearing and reciting poems. Cf. "Masters of assemblies" (note, ch. 12. 11, also 12. 9.). "The Preacher taught the people knowledge," probably *viva voce*: 1 Ki. 4. 34; 10. 2, 8, 24; 2 Chr. 9. 1, 7, 23, plainly refer to a somewhat public divan met for literary discussion. So "spake," thrice repeated (1 Ki. 4. 32, 33,), refers, not to *written* compositions, but to addresses *spoken* in assemblies convened for the purpose. The Holy Ghost, no doubt, signifies also by the term, that Solomon's doctrine is intended for the "great congregation," the Church of all places and ages (Ps. 22. 25; 49. 2-4.).

Solomon was plainly *the author* (ch. 1. 12, 16; 2. 15; 12. 9.). That the Rabbins attribute it to Isaiah or Hezekiah, is explicable, by supposing that one or the other inserted it *in the canon*. The difference of its style, as compared with Proverbs and Song of Solomon, is due to the difference of subjects, and the different period of his life in which each was written; the Song, in the fervour of his first love to God; Proverbs, about the same time, or somewhat later; but Ecclesiastes in an older age, as the seal and testimony of repentance of his apostasy in the intervening period: (Ps. 89. 30, 33,), proves his penitence. The substitution of the title Koheleth for Solomon (that is, *peace*,), may imply that, having *troubled* Israel, meantime he forfeited his name of *peace* (1 Ki. 11. 14, 23;); but now, having repented, he wishes to be henceforth a *Preacher* of righteousness. The alleged foreign expressions in the Hebrew may have been easily imported, through the great intercourse there was with other nations during his long reign. Moreover, supposed Chaldaisms may be fragments preserved from the common tongue, of which Hebrew, Syriac, Chaldee, and Arabic, were offshoots.

THE SCOPE of Ecclesiastes is *to contrast the vanity of all mere human pursuits, when made the chief end, as contrasted with the real blessedness of true wisdom, i.e., religion*. The immortality of the soul is dwelt on incidentally, as subsidiary to the main scope. Moses' law took this truth for granted, but drew its sanctions of rewards and punishments in accordance with the theocracy, which was under a special providence of God as the *temporal* King of Israel, from *the present life*, rather than the future. But after that Israel chose an earthly king, God withdrew, in part, his extraordinary providence, so that under Solomon, temporal rewards did not invariably follow virtue, and punishments vice (cf. ch. 2. 16; 3. 19; 4. 1; 5. 8; 7. 15; 8. 14; 9. 2, 11.). Hence the need arises to show that these anomalies will be rectified hereafter, and this is the grand "conclusion," therefore, of the "whole" book, that, seeing there is a coming judgment, and seeing that present goods do not satisfy the soul, "man's whole duty is to fear God and keep his commandments" (ch. 12. 13, 14,), and meanwhile, to use, in joyful and serene sobriety, and not abuse the present life (ch. 3. 12, 13.).

It is objected that sensual epicurism seems to be inculcated (ch. 3. 12, 13, 22, &c.;); but it is a contented thankful enjoyment of God's present gifts that is taught, as opposed to a murmuring, anxious, avaricious spirit, as is proved by ch. 5. 18, cf. with 11-15, not making them the *chief end* of life; not the joy of levity and folly: a misunderstanding which he guards against in ch. 7. 2-6; 11. 9; 12. 1. Again, ch. 7. 16; 9. 2-10, might seem to teach fatalism and scepticism. But these are words put in the mouth of an objector; or rather, were the language of Solomon himself during his apostasy, finding an echo in the heart of every sensualist, who *wishes* to be an unbeliever, and who, therefore, sees difficulties enough in the world around, wherewith to prop up his wilful unbelief. The answer is given (ch. 7. 17, 18; 9. 11, &c.; 11. 1, 6; 12. 13.). Even if these passages be taken as words of Solomon, they are to be understood as forbidding a self-made "righteousness" which tries to constrain God to grant salvation to imaginary good works and external strictness with which it wearies itself; also, that speculation which tries to fathom all God's inscrutable counsels (ch. 8. 17.), and that carefulness about the future, forbidden in Mat. 6. 25.

Vanity of all ECCLESIASTES, I. *Human Courses.*

THE CHIEF GOOD is that, the possession of which makes us happy, to be sought as the *end*, for its own sake; whereas, all other things are but *means* towards it. Philosophers, who made it the great subject of inquiry, restricted it to the present life, treating the eternal as unreal, and only useful to awe the multitude with. But Solomon shows the vanity of all human things (so-called philosophy included) to satisfy the soul, and that heavenly wisdom alone is the chief good. He had taught so when young (Pro. 1. 20; 8. 1, &c.;); so also, in Song of Solomon, he had spiritualised the subject in an allegory; and now, after having long personally tried the manifold ways in which the worldly seek to reach happiness, he gives the fruit of his experience in old age.

It is divided into two parts, chs. 1-6. 10, showing the vanity of earthly things, ch. 6. 10, to ch. 12, the excellence of heavenly wisdom. Deviations from strict logical method occur in these divisions, but in the main they are observed. The deviations make it the less stiff and artificial, and the more suited to all capacities. It is in poetry; the hemistichal division is mostly observed, but occasionally not so. The choice of epithets, imagery, inverted order of words, ellipses, parallelism, or in its absence, similarity of diction, mark versification.

CHAPTER I.

Ver. 1-18.—INTRODUCTION. 1. the Preacher—and *Convener of assemblies* for the purpose. See my Preface. "Koheleth" in *Heb.*, a symbolical name for *Solomon*, and of *Heavenly Wisdom* speaking through and identified with him. Verse 12, shows that "king of Jerusalem" is in apposition, not with "David," but "Preacher," of Jerusalem—rather, *in* Jerusalem, for it was merely his metropolis, not his whole kingdom. 2. The theme proposed of the first part of his discourse. Vanity of vanities—Hebraism for the most utter vanity. So "holy of holies" (Ex. 26.: "servant of servants" (Gen. 9. 25.). The repetition increases the force. all—*Heb.* "*the* all;" all without exception, *viz.*, earthly things. vanity—not in themselves, for God maketh nothing in vain (1 Tim. 4. 4, 5.), but vain when put in the place of God and made the *end*, instead of the *means* (Ps. 39. 5, 6; 62. 9; Mat. 6. 33;); vain, also, because of the "vanity" to which they are "subjected" by the fall (Rom. 8. 20.). 3. What profit...labour—*i.e.*, "What profit" as to the chief good (Mat. 16. 26.). Labour is profitable *in its proper place* (Gen. 2. 15; 3. 19; Pro. 14. 23.). under the sun—*i.e.*, *in this life*, as opposed to the future world. The phrase often recurs, but only in Eccl. 4. earth...for ever—(Ps. 104. 5.). While the *earth* remains the same, the generations of men are ever changing; what lasting profit, then, can there be from the toils of one whose sojourn on earth, as an individual, is so brief? The "for ever" is comparative, not absolute (Ps. 102. 26.). 5. (Ps. 19. 5, 6.). *Panting* is the *Heb.* for "hasteth," metaphor, from a runner (Ps. 19. 5, "a strong man") in a "race." It applies rather to the *rising* sun which seems *laboriously* to mount up to the meridian, than to the setting sun; the accents too, favour MAUR., "And (that too, returning) to his place, where panting he riseth." 6. according to his circuits—*i.e.*, it returns afresh to its former circuits, however many be its previous veerings about. The N. and S. winds are the two prevailing winds in Palestine and Egypt. 7. By subterraneous cavities, and by evaporation forming rain-clouds, the fountains and rivers are supplied from the sea, into which they then flow back. The connection is: *Individual* men are continually changing, whilst the *succession of the race* continues: just as the sun, wind, and rivers are ever shifting about, whilst the cycle in which they move is invariable; they return to the point whence they set out. Hence in man, as in these objects of nature which are his analogue, with all the seeming changes "there is no new thing" (v. 9.). 8. MAUR. *transl.*, "All words are wearied out," *i.e.*, are

inadequate, as also, "man cannot express" all the things in the world which undergo this ceaseless, changeless cycle of vicissitudes: "The eye is not satisfied with seeing them," &c. But it is plainly a return to the idea (v. 3.), as to *man's* "labour," which is only wearisome and profitless; "no new" good can accrue from it. v. 9; ; for as the sun, &c., so man's laborious works move in a changeless cycle. The "eye" and "ear" are two of the taskmasters for which man toils. But these are never "satisfied" (ch. 6. 7; Pro. 27. 20.). Nor can they be so hereafter, for there will be nothing "new." Not so the chief good, Jesus Christ (John, 4. 13, 14; Rev. 21. 5.). 9. Rather, "no new thing *at all*;" as Num. 11. 6. This is not meant in a general sense; but there is no new source of happiness (the subject in question) which can be devised; the same round of petty pleasures, cares, business, study, wars, &c., being repeated over and over again [HOL.] 10. old time [*Heb.* ages,] which was—The *Heb. plur.* cannot be joined to the verb *sing.* Therefore *transl.*, "It hath been in the ages before; certainly it hath been before us." [HOL.] Or, as MAUR., "That which has been (done) before us (in our presence, 1 Chr. 16. 33,) has been (done) already in the old times." 11. The reason why some things are thought "new," which are not really so, is the imperfect record that exists of preceding ages among their successors. these that ... come after—*i.e.*, those that live *still later* than the "things rather *the persons* or 'generations,'" v. 4, with which this verse is connected, the six intermediate verses being merely illustrations of v. 4. [WEISS]) that are to come" ch. 2. 16; 9. 5.). 12. Resumption of v. 1. the statement of his thesis. Therefore, "the Preacher" (Koheleth) is repeated. was king—instead of "am," because he is about to give the results of his *past* experience during his long reign. in Jerusalem—specified, as opposed to David, who reigned both in Hebron and Jerusalem; whereas Solomon reigned only in Jerusalem. "King of Israel in Jerusalem," implies that he reigned over *Israel and Judah combined*; whereas David, at Hebron, reigned only over *Judah*, and not until he was settled in Jerusalem, over both Israel and Judah. 13. this sore travail—*viz.*, that of "searching out all things done under heaven." Not human wisdom in general, which comes afterwards (ch. 2. 12, &c.,; but laborious inquiries into, and speculations about, the works of men, *ex. gr.*, political science. As man is doomed to get his bread, so his knowledge, by the sweat of his brow (Gen. 3. 19.). [GILL.] exercised—*i.e., disciplined; lit.*, "that they may thereby *chastise* or *humble* themselves." 14. The reason is here given why investigation into man's "works" is only "sore travail" (v. 13,), viz., because all man's ways are vain (v. 18,). and cannot be mended (v. 15.). vexation of (a *preying* upon the) spirit—MAUR. *transl.*, "the pursuit of wind," as ch. 6. 16; Hos. 12. 1. "Ephraim feedeth on wind." But old versions support the *E. V.* 15. Investigation (v. 13) into human ways is vain labour, for they are hopelessly "crooked" and "cannot be made straight" by it (ch. 7. 13.). God, the chief good, alone can do this (Isa. 40. 4; 45. 2.). wanting—(Dan. 5. 27.). numbered—so as to make a complete number: so equivalent to, *supplied.* [MAUR.] Or rather, man's state is *utterly wanting*; and that which is wholly defective cannot be numbered or calculated. The investigator thinks he can draw up, in accurate *numbers*, statistics of man's wants; but these, including the defects in the investigator's labour, are not partial, but total. 16. communed with ... heart—(Gen. 24. 45.). come to great estate—Rather, "I have *magnified* and gotten," (*lit.*, added, increased), &c. all ... before me in Jerusalem—*viz.*, the priests, judges, and two kings that preceded Solomon. His wisdom exceeded that of all before Jesus Christ, the anti typical Koheleth, or "*Gatherer* of men" (Luke, 13. 34,), and "Wisdom" incarnate Mat. 11. 19; 12. 42.). had ... experience—*lit.*, had *seen* (Jer. 2. 31.). Contrast with this glorying in worldly wisdom Jer. 9. 23, 24. 17. wisdom ... madness—i.e., their effects, the works of human wisdom and folly respectively. "Madness," *lit.*, *vaunting extravagance*; ch. 2. 12; 7. 25, &c. support *E. V.* rather than DATHE," "splendid matters." "Folly" is read by *E. V.* with some MSS., instead of the present *Heb.* text. "prudence." If *Heb.* be retained, understand "prudence," *falsely so called* (1 Tim. 6. 20,). "craft" (Dan. 8. 25.). 18. wisdom ... knowledge—not in general; for wisdom, &c., are most excellent in their place; but *speculative knowledge of man's ways* (v. 13, 17.), which, the farther it goes, gives one the more pain to find how "crooked" and "wanting" they are (v. 15; ch. 12. 12.).

CHAPTER II.

Ver. 1-26. He next tries pleasure and luxury, retaining, however, his worldly "wisdom" (ch. 3. 9,), but all proves "vanity" in respect to the chief good. 1. I said ... heart—(Luke, 12. 19.). thee—my heart, I will test whether thou canst find that solid good in pleasure which was not in "worldly wisdom." But this also proves to be "vanity" (Isa. 50. 11.). 2. laughter—including *prosperity* and *joy* in general (Job, 8. 21.). mad—*i.e.*, *when made the chief good*; it is harmless in its proper place. What doeth it?—Of what avail is it in giving solid good? (ch. 7. 6; Pro. 14. 13.). 3-11. Illustration more at large of v. 1, 2. 3. sought—I resolved, after search into many plans, give myself unto—*lit.*, *to draw my flesh* (body) *to wine* (including all banquetings.). Image from a captive drawn after a chariot in triumph (Rom. 6. 16, 19; 1 Cor. 12. 2.); or, one "allured" (2 Pet. 2. 18, 19.). yet acquainting ... wisdom—*lit.*, "and my heart (still) *was behaving*, or *guiding itself*, with wisdom." [GES.] MAUR. *transl.*, "*was weary of* (worldly) wisdom." But the end of v. 9 confirms *E. V.* folly—*viz.*, pleasures of the flesh, termed "mad," v. 2. all the days, &c.—(see *Marg.* and ch. 6. 12; Job, 15. 20.). 4. (1 Ki. 7. 1-8; 9. 1, 19; 10. 18, &c.). vineyards—(Sol. Song 8. 11.). 5. gardens—*Heb.*, *paradises*, a foreign word; *Sanscrit*, "a place enclosed with a wall;" *Armen.* and *Arab.*, "a pleasure-ground with flowers and shrubs near the king's house, or castle." An earthly paradise can never make up for the want of the heavenly Rev. 2. 7.). 6. pools—artificial, for irrigating the soil (Gen. 2. 10; Neh. 2. 14; Isa. 1. 30.). Three such reservoirs are still found, called Solomon's cisterns, a mile and a-half from Jerusalem. wood that bringeth forth—rather, "the grove that *flourisheth with* trees." [LOWTH.] born in my house — these were esteemed more trustworthy servants than those bought (Gen. 14. 14; 15. 2, 3; 17. 12, 13, 27; Jer. 2. 14,), called *sons of* one's *handmaid* (Ex. 23. 12; cf. Gen. 12. 16; Job, 1. 3.). 8. (1 Ki. 10. 27; 2 Chr. 1. 15; 9. 20.). peculiar treasure of kings and ... provinces — contributed by them, as tributary to him (1 Ki. 4. 21, 24;); a poor substitute for the wisdom whose "gain is better than fine gold" (Pro. 3. 14, 15.). singers — so David (2 Sam. 19. 35.), musical instruments ... of all sorts—introduced at banquets (Isa. 5. 12; Amos, 6. 5. 6;); rather, *a princess and princesses*, from an Arabic root. One regular wife, or queen (Esth. 1. 9;); Pharaoh's daughter 1 Ki. 3. 1;); other secondary wives, "princesses," distinct from the "concubines" (1 Ki. 11. 3; Ps. 45. 10; Sol. Song 6. 8,). [WEISS; GES.] Had these been omitted, the enumeration would be incomplete. 9. great—opulent (Gen. 24. 35; Job, 1. 3; see 1 Ki. 10. 23.). remained—(v. 3.). 10. my labour—in procuring pleasures. this—evanescent "joy" was my only "portion out of all my labour" (ch. 3. 22; 5. 18: 9. 9; 1 Ki. 10. 5.). 11. But all these I felt were only "vanity," and of no "profit" as to the chief good. "Wisdom" (worldly *common-sense*, sagacity,), which still "remained with me" (v. 9,), showed me that these could not give solid happiness. 12. He had tried (worldly) wisdom (ch. 1. 12-18.), and folly (foolish pleasure) (v. 1-11;;); he now compares them (v. 12,), and finds that whilst (worldly) wisdom excelleth folly (v. 13, 14,), yet the one event, death, befalls both (v. 14-16,), and that thus the wealth acquired by the wise man's "labour" may descend to a "fool." that hath not laboured (v. 18, 19, 21;); therefore all his labour is vanity (v. 22, 23,). what can the man do ... already done—(ch. 1. 9.). Parenthetical. A future investigator can strike nothing out "new," so as to draw a different conclusion from what I draw by comparing "wisdom and madness." HOL., with less ellipsis, *transl.*, "What, O man, shall come after the king?" &c. Better, GROT., "What man can come after completely the king in the things which are done?" None ever can have the same means of testing what all earthly things can do towards satisfying the soul; namely, worldly wisdom, science, riches, power, longevity, all combined. 13, 14. (Pro. 17. 24.). The worldly "wise" man has *good sense* in managing his affairs, *skill* and *taste* in building and planting, and keeps within *safe* and *respectable* bounds in pleasure, whilst the "fool" is wanting in these respects: ("darkness," equivalent to *fatal error, blind infatuation*,), yet one event, death, happeneth to both (Job, 21. 26.). 15. why was I—so anxious to become, &c. (2 Chr. 1. 10.). Then—Since such is the case, this—*viz.*, pursuit of (worldly) wisdom. It can never fill the place of the true wisdom

A season for every thing. ECCLESIASTES, III–V. *Vanity through oppression.*

and joy; but to the sinner he giveth travail, to gather and to heap up, that he may give to *him that is* good before God. This also *is* vanity and vexation of spirit.

CHAPTER III.
1 *By the necessary change of times, vanity is added to human travail.* 16 *Men and beasts equally subject to mortality;* 21 *their spirits which go different ways are unknown.*

TO every thing there is a season, and a time to every purpose under the heaven:
2 A time ¹ to be born, and ᵇ a time to die; a time to plant, and a time to pluck up *that which is* planted;
3 A ᶜ time to kill, and a time to heal; a time to break down, and a time to build up;
4 A time to weep, and a time to laugh; a time to mourn, and a time ᵈ to dance;
5 A time to cast away stones, and a time to gather stones together; a time to embrace, and a time ᵉ to refrain from embracing;
6 A time to ᶠ get, and a time to lose; a time to keep, and a time to cast away;
7 A time to rend, and a time to sew; ᵍ a time to keep silence, and a time to speak;
8 A time to love, and a time ʰ to hate; a time of war, and a time of peace.
9 What ⁱ profit hath he that worketh in that wherein he laboureth?
10 I ʲ have seen the travail which God hath given to the sons of men to be exercised in it.
11 He ᵏ hath made every *thing* beautiful in his time: also he hath set the world in their heart; so that ˡ no man can find out the work that God maketh from the beginning to the end.
12 I know that *there is* no good in them, but for *a man* to rejoice, and to do good in his life.
13 And also ᵐ that every man should eat and drink, and enjoy the good of all his labour, it *is* the gift of God.
14 I know that whatsoever God doeth, it shall be for ever: ⁿ nothing can be put to it, nor any thing taken from it: and God doeth *it,* that *men* should fear before him.
15 That ᵒ which hath been is now; and that which is to be hath already been; and God requireth ᵖ that which is past.
16 And moreover ᵠ I saw under the sun the place of judgment, *that* wickedness *was* there; and the place of righteousness, *that* iniquity *was* there.
17 I said in mine heart, ʳ God shall judge the righteous and the wicked: for *there is* a time there for every purpose and for every work.
18 I said in mine heart concerning the estate of the sons of men, ˢ that God might manifest them, and that they might see that they themselves are beasts.
19 For ᵗ that which befalleth the sons of men befalleth beasts; even one thing befalleth them: as the one dieth, so dieth the other; yea, they have all one breath: so that a man hath no pre-eminence above a beast: for all *is* vanity.
20 All go unto one place; ᵘ all *are* of the dust, and all turn to dust again.
21 Who knoweth the spirit ᵛ of man that ʷ goeth upward, and the spirit of the beast that goeth downward to the earth?
22 Wherefore I perceive that *there is* nothing better, than that a man should

B. C. 977.
—
CHAP. 3.
a ch. 2. 6.
1 to bear.
b Heb. 9. 27.
c Gen. 9. 6.
d Ps. 149. 3.
2 to be far from.
Joel 2. 16.
1 Cor. 7. 5.
3 Or, seek.
e Amos 5.13.
f Lu. 14. 26.
g ch. 1. 3.
h ch. 1. 13.
i Deu. 32. 4.
j ch. 8. 17.
Ro. 11. 33.
k ch. 2. 24.
l Jam. 1. 17.
m ch. 1. 9.
4 that which is driven away.
n ch. 5. 8.
o Job 34. 11.
Ps. 62. 12.
Jer. 17. 10.
Mat. 16.27.
Rom. 2. 6.
2 Cor. 5.10.
2 Thes. 1.6.
5 Or, that they might clear God, and see, etc.
p Ps. 49. 12.
q Gen. 3, 19.
6 of the sons of man.
7 la ascending.
ch. 12. 7.
Heb. 9.27.
r ch. 2. 10.
—
CHAP. 4.
a Job 3. 17.
b Job 3, 11.
ch. 6. 3.
2 all the rightness of work.
3 this is the envy of a man from his neighbour.
c Pro. 6. 10.
Pro. 24. 33.
d Pro. 27.20.
1 John 2. 16.
e Ps. 39. 6.
4 who knoweth not to be admonished.
Pro. 29.12.
—
CHAP. 5.
a Ex. 3. 5.
Jos. 5. 15.
Ps. 89, 7.
Ps. 93. 5.
Is. 1. 12.
5 1 Sam. 15. 22.
Ps. 50. 8.
Pro. 15. 8.
Pro. 21. 27.
Hos. 6. 6.
1 Or, word.
c Pro. 10.19.
Mat. 5, 7.

rejoice in his own works; for ʳ that *is* his portion: for who shall bring him to see what shall be after him?

CHAPTER IV.
1 *Vanity increased unto men by oppression,* 4 *by envy,* 5 *by idleness,* 7 *by covetousness,* 9 *by solitariness,* 13 *and by wilfulness.*

SO I returned, and considered all the oppressions that are done under the sun: and behold the tears of *such as were* oppressed, and they had no comforter; and on the ⁱ side of their oppressors *there was* power; but they had no comforter.
2 Wherefore ᵈ I praised the dead which are already dead, more than the living which are yet alive.
3 Yea, ᵇ better *is* he than both they which hath not yet been, who hath not seen the evil work that is done under the sun.
4 ¶ Again, I considered all travail, and ² every right work, that ³ for this a man is envied of his neighbour. This *is* also vanity and vexation of spirit.
5 ¶ The ᶜ fool foldeth his hands together, and eateth his own flesh.
6 Better *is* an handful *with* quietness, than both the hands full *with* travail and vexation of spirit.
7 ¶ Then I returned, and I saw vanity under the sun.
8 There is one *alone,* and *there is* not a second; yea, he hath neither child nor brother: yet *is there* no end of all his labour; neither is his ᵈ eye satisfied with riches; ᵉ neither *saith he,* For whom do I labour, and bereave my soul of good? This *is* also vanity, yea, it *is* a sore travail.
9 ¶ Two *are* better than one; because they have a good reward for their labour.
10 For if they fall, the one will lift up his fellow: but woe to him *that is* alone when he falleth; for *he hath* not another to help him up.
11 Again, if two lie together, then they have heat: but how can one be warm *alone?*
12 And if one prevail against him, two shall withstand him; and a threefold cord is not quickly broken.
13 ¶ Better *is* a poor and a wise child than an old and foolish king, ⁴ who will no more be admonished.
14 For out of prison he cometh to reign; whereas also *he that is* born in his kingdom becometh poor.
15 I considered all the living which walk under the sun, with the second child that shall stand up in his stead.
16 *There is* no end of all the people, *even* of all that have been before them; they also that come after shall not rejoice in him. Surely this also *is* vanity and vexation of spirit.

CHAPTER V.
1 *Vanities in divine service,* 8 *in murmuring against oppression,* 9 *and in riches.* 18 *To live contentedly is the gift of God.*

KEEP ᵃ thy foot when thou goest to the house of God, and be more ready to hear ᵇ than to give the sacrifice of fools: for they consider not that they do evil.
2 Be not rash with thy mouth, and let not thine heart be hasty to utter *any* ¹ thing before God: for God *is* in heaven, and thou upon earth; therefore let thy ᶜ words be few.
3 For a dream cometh through the multitude of business; and a fool's voice *is* known by multitude of words.

(Job. 28. 28; Jer. 8. 9.). 16. remembrance—a great aim of the worldly (Gen. 11. 4.). The righteous alone attain it (Ps. 112. 6; Pro. 10. 7.). for ever—no *perpetual* memorial. that which now is—MAUR., "In the days to come all things shall be *now long ago* forgotten." 17. Disappointed in one experiment after another he is weary of life. The backslider ought to have rather reasoned as the prodigal (Hos. 2. 6, 7; Luke, 15. 17, 18.). grievous unto me —(Job, 10. 1.). 18, 19. One hope alone was left to the disappointed worldling, the perpetuation of his name and riches, laboriously gathered, through his successor. For selfishness is mostly at the root of worldly parents' alleged providence for their children. But now the remembrance of how he himself, the piously reared child of David, had disregarded his father's dying charge (1 Chr. 28. 9,), suggested the sad misgiving as to what Rehoboam, his son by an idolatrous Ammonitess, Naamah, should prove to be; a foreboding too fully realised (1 Ki. 12.; 14. 21-31.). 20. *I gave up as desperate all* hope of solid fruit from *my* labour. 21. Suppose "there is a man," &c. equity—rather, "with success," as the Hebrew is rendered (ch. 11. 6,), "prosper," though *Marg.* gives "right." [HOL. and MAUR.] evil—not in itself, for this is the ordinary course of things, but "evil," as regards the chief good, that one should have toiled so fruitlessly. 22. Same sentiment as *v.* 21, interrogatively. 23. The only fruit he has is, not only sorrows *in* his days, but *all* his days are sorrows, and his travail (not only *has* griefs connected with it, but *is* itself, grief. 24. *E. V.* gives a seemingly Epicurean sense, contrary to the general scope. The *Heb., lit.*, is, "It is *not good* for man that he should eat," &c., "and should make his soul see good" (or "*show* his soul, *i.e.*, *himself*, happy,"), &c. [WEISS.] According to HOL. and WEISS, ch. 3. 12, 22, differ from this verse in the text and meaning: here he means, "It is not good that a man should feast himself, and falsely make as though his soul were happy;" he thus refers to a false *pretending* of happiness *acquired by and for one's self;* in ch. 3. 12, 22, and 5. 18, 19, to *real seeing*, or *finding* pleasure *when God gives it.* There it is said to be *good* for a man to enjoy with satisfaction and thankfulness the blessings which God gives; here it is said *not* to be *good* to take an unreal pleasure to one's self by feasting, &c. This also I saw—I perceived by experience that good (real pleasure) is not to be taken at will, but comes only from the hand of God [WEISS] (Ps. 4. 6; Isa. 57. 19-21.). Or as HOL., "It is the appointment from the hand of God, that the sensualist has no solid satisfaction" (good.). 25. hasten—after indulgences (Pro. 7. 23; 19. 2.), *eagerly pursue* such enjoyments. None can compete with me in this. If I, then, with all my opportunities of enjoyment, failed utterly to obtain solid pleasure of my own making, apart from God, who else can? God mercifully spares His children the sad experiment which Solomon made, by denying them the goods which they often desire. He gives them the fruits of Solomon's experience, without their paying the dear price at which Solomon bought it. 26. True, literally, in the Jewish theocracy; and in some measure in all ages Job, 27. 16, 17; Pro. 13. 22; 28. 8.). Though the retribution be not so visible and immediate now as then, it is no less real. Happiness even here is more truly the portion of the godly (Ps. 84. 11; Mat. 5, 6; Mark, 10. 29, 30; Rom. 8. 28; 1 Tim. 4. 8.). that he [the sinner] may give — *i.e.*, unconsciously and in spite of himself. The godly Solomon had satisfaction in his riches and wisdom, when God gave them (2 Chr. 1.). The backsliding Solomon had no happiness, when he sought it in them apart from God; and the riches which he heaped up became the prey of Shishak (2 Chr. 12.).

CHAPTER III.

Ver. 1-22. Earthly pursuits are no doubt lawful in their proper time and order (*v.* 1-8,), but unprofitable when out of time and place, as for instance, when pursued as the solid and chief good *v.* 9, 10;; whereas God makes every thing beautiful in its season, which man obscurely comprehends (*v.* 11.). God allows man to enjoy moderately and virtuously His earthly gifts (*v.* 12, 13.). What contrasts us amidst the instability of earthly blessings is, (God's counsels are immutable *v.* 14.). 1. Man has his appointed cycle of seasons and vicissitudes, as the sun, wind, and water, ch. 1. 5-7.). purpose—as there is a fixed "season" in God's "purposes" (*ex. gr.*, He has fixed the "time" when man is "to be born," and "to die," *v.* 2,', so there is a lawful "time" for man to carry out his "purposes" and inclinations. God does not condemn, but approves of, the "use" of earthly blessings (*v.* 12;); it is the "abuse" that He condemns, the making them the chief end (1 Cor. 7. 31.). The earth, without human desires, love, taste, joy, sorrow, would be a dreary waste, without water; but, on the other hand, the misplacing and excess of them, as of a flood, need control. Reason and revelation are given to control them. 2. time to die—(Ps. 31. 15; Heb. 9. 27.). plant—A man can no more reverse the times and order of "planting," and of "digging up," and transplanting, than he can alter the times fixed for his "birth" and "death." To try to "plant" *out of season* is vanity, however good *in season;* so to make earthly things *the chief end* is vanity, however good they be in order and season, GILL takes it, not so well, *fig.*, (Jer. 18. 7, 9; Amos, 9. 15; Mat. 15. 13.). 3. time to kill— *viz.*, judicially, criminals; or, in wars of self-defence; not in malice. Out of this time and order, killing is murder. to heal—God hastes His times for "healing," (*lit.*, Isa. 38. 5, 21; *fig.*, Deut. 32. 39; Hos. 6. 1; spiritually, Ps. 147. 3; Isa. 57. 19.). To *heal* spiritually, before the sinner feels his *wound*, would be out of time, and so injurious. time to break down— cities, as Jerusalem, by Nebuchadnezzar, build up—as Jerusalem, in the time of Zerubbabel; spiritually (Amos, 9. 11,), "the set time" (Ps. 102. 13-16.). 4. mourn—*viz.*, for the dead (Gen. 23. 2.). dance—as David before the ark (2 Sam. 6. 12-14; Ps. 30. 11,); spiritually (Mat. 9. 15; Luke, 6. 21; 15. 25.). The Pharisees, by requiring sadness out of *time*, erred seriously. 5. cast away stones—as out of a garden or vineyard (Isa. 5. 2.). gather—for building, *fig.*, the Gentiles, once cast-away stones, were in due time made parts of the spiritual building (Eph. 2. 19, 20,', and children of Abraham (Mat. 3. 9;); so the restored Jews hereafter (Ps. 102. 13, 14; Zech. 9. 16.). refrain . . . embracing—(Joel, 2. 16; 1 Cor. 7. 5, 6.). 6. time to get —*ex. gr.*, to gain honestly a livelihood (Eph. 4. 28.). lose—when God wills•losses to us, then is our time to be content. keep—not to give to the idle beggar (2 Thes. 3. 10.), cast away—in charity (Pro. 11. 24,); or to part with the dearest object, rather than the soul (Mark, 9. 43.). To be careful is right in its place, but not when it comes between us and Jesus Christ (Luke, 10. 40-42.). 7. rend—garments, in mourning (Joel, 2. 13.). *Fig.*, lamentations, as Israel from Judah, already foretold, in Solomon's time (1 Ki. 11. 30, 31,), to be "sewed" together hereafter (Ez. 37. 15, 22.). silence—(Amos, 5. 13,), in a national calamity, or that of a friend (Job, 2. 13; ; also not to murmur under God's visitation (Lev. 10. 3; Ps. 39. 1, 2, 9.). 8. hate—*ex. gr.*, sin, lusts (Luke, 14. 26); *i.e.*, to love God so much more, as to seem in comparison to *hate* "father or mother," when coming between us and God. time of war... peace—(Luke, 14. 31.). 9. But these earthly pursuits, whilst lawful in their season, are "unprofitable" when made by man, what God never intended them to be, the chief good. Solomon had tried to create an artificial forced joy, at times when he ought rather to have been serious; the result, therefore, of his labour to be happy, out of God's order, was disappointment. "A time to plant" v. 2, refers to his *planting* (ch. 2. 5;); "laugh" (v. 4,), to ch. 2. 1, 2, "his mirth;" "laughter;" to build up," "gather stones" (v. 3, 5,), to his "building" (ch. 2. 4;); "embrace," "love," to his "princess" (note, ch. 2. 8;); "get" (perhaps also "gather," v. 5, 6,), to his "gathering" (ch. 2. 6.). All these were of no "profit," because not in God's time and order of bestowing happiness. 10. (Ch. 1. 13.). 11. his time—*i.e.*, *in its proper season* (Ps. 1. 3,), opposed to worldlings putting earthly pursuits *out of their proper time and place* (note, v. 9.). set the world in their heart—given them capacities to understand *the world* of nature as reflecting God's wisdom in its beautiful order and times (Rom. 1. 19, 20.). "Everything" answers to "world," in the parallelism. so that—*i.e.*, but in such a manner that man only sees a portion, not the whole "from beginning to end" (ch. 8. 17; Job, 26. 14; Rom. 11. 33; Rev. 15. 4.). PARKH., for "world," *transl.* "Yet He hath put *obscurity in the midst of them," lit., a secret*; so man's mental *dimness of sight* as to the full mystery of God's works. So HOL. and WEISS. This incapacity for "finding out" comprehending) God's work is chiefly the fruit of the fall. The worldling ever since, not knowing God's time and order, labours in vain, because out of time and place. 12. in them—in God's works (v. 11,), as far as relates to man's duty. Man cannot fully comprehend them, but he ought joyfully to receive ("rejoice in") God's gifts, and "do good" with them to himself and to others. This is never out of season (Gal. 6. 9. 10.). Not sensual joy and self-indulgence (Phil. 4. 4; Jam. 4. 10, 17.). 13. *Lit.*, "And also as to every man who eats," &c., "this is the gift of God" v. 22; ch. 5. 18.). When received as God's gifts, and to God's glory, the good things of life are enjoyed in their due time and order (Acts, 2. 46; 1 Cor. 10. 31; 1 Tim. 4. 3, 4. . 14. (1 Sam. 3. 12; 2 Sam. 23. 5; Ps. 89. 34; Mat. 24. 35; Jam. 1. 17.), for ever—as opposed to man's perishing labours (ch. 2. 15-18.), any thing taken from it — opposed to man's "crooked and wanting" works (ch. 1. 15; 7. 13.). The event of man's labours depends wholly on God's immutable purpose. Man's part, therefore, is to do and enjoy every earthly thing *in its proper season* v. 12, 13,), not setting aside God's order, but observing deep reverence towards God; for the mysteriousness and unchangeableness of God's purposes are designed to lead "man to fear before Him." Man knows not the event of each act, otherwise he would think himself independent of God. 15. Resumption of ch. 1. 9. Whatever changes there be, the succession of events is ordered by God's "everlasting" laws (v. 14,), and returns in a fixed cycle, requireth that... past—after many changes, God's law *requires* the return of the same cycle of events, as in *the past, lit., that which is driven on*. LXX. and *Syr. transl.*, "God requireth (*i.e.*, avengeth) the *persecuted* man;" a transition to v. 16. 17. The parallel clauses of the verse support E. V. 16. Here a difficulty is suggested. If God "requires" events to move in their perpetual cycle, why are the wicked allowed to deal unrighteously in the place where injustice ought least of all to be, *viz.*, "the place of judgment" (Jer. 12. 1.). 17. Solution of it. There is a coming judgment in which God will vindicate His righteous ways. The sinner's "time" of his unrighteous "work" is short. God also has his "time" and "work" of judgment; and, meanwhile, is overruling, for good at last, what seems now dark. Man cannot now "find out" the plan of God's ways (v. 11; Ps. 97. 2.). If judgment instantly followed every sin, there would be no scope for free will, faith, and perseverance of saints in spite of difficulties. The previous darkness will make the light at last the more glorious. there—(Job, 3. 17-19,), in eternity, in the presence of the divine Judge, opposed to the "there," in the human place of judgment (v. 16;); so "from *thence*" (Gen. 49. 24.). 18. estate—the estate of fallen man is so ordered (these wrongs are permitted), that God might "manifest," *i.e.*, thereby *prove* them, and that they might themselves see their mortal frailty, like that of the beasts. sons of men—rather, *sons of Adam*, a phrase used for *fallen men*. The toleration of injustice until the judgment is designed to "manifest" men's characters in their fallen state, to see whether the oppressed will bear themselves aright amidst their wrongs, knowing that the time is short, and there is a coming judgment. The oppressed share in death, but the comparison to "beasts" applies especially to *the ungodly oppressors* (Ps. 49. 12. 20;); they too need to be "manifested" (proved,), whether, considering that they must soon die as the "beasts," and fearing the judgment to come, they will repent (Dan. 4. 27.). 19. *Lit.*, "For the sons of men (Adam) *are a mere chance*, as also the beast is a mere chance." These words can only be the sentiments of the sceptical oppressors. God's delay in judgment gives scope for the "manifestation" of their infidelity (ch. 8. 11; Ps. 55. 19; 2 Pet. 3, 4.). They *are* "brute *beasts*," morally v. 18; Jude, 10;); and they end by maintaining that man, physically, has no pre-eminence over the beast, both alike being "fortuities." Probably this was the language of Solomon himself in his apostasy. He answers it in *v.* 21. If *v.* 19, 20, be *his* words, they express only that *as regards liability to death*, excluding the future judgment, as the sceptic oppressors do, man is on a level with the beast. Life is "vanity," if regarded independently of religion. But *v.* 21 points out the vast

Vanity through Oppression. ECCLESIASTES, IV, V. *Vanity of Kingly Power.*

difference between them in respect to the future destiny; also (*v.* 17,), beasts have no "judgment" to come. breath—vitality. 21. Who knoweth—Not *doubt* of the destination of man's spirit (ch. 12. 7;); but "*how few*, by reason of the outward mortality to which man is as liable as the beast, and which is the ground of the sceptic's argument, comprehend the wide difference between man and the beast" (Isa. 53. 1.). The Hebrew expresses the difference strongly. "The spirit of man that ascends, it belongeth to on high; but the spirit of the beast that descends, it belongeth to below, even to the earth." Their destinations and proper element differ utterly. [WEISS.] 22. (Cf. *v*. 12; ch. 5. 18.). Inculcating a thankful enjoyment of God's gifts, and a cheerful discharge of man's duties, founded on fear of God; not as the sensualist (ch. 11. 9;); not as the anxious money-seeker (ch. 2. 23; 5. 10-17.). his portion—in the present life. If it were made his *main* portion, it would be "vanity" (ch. 2. 1; Luke, 16. 25.). for who, &c.—our ignorance as to the future, which is God's "time" (*v*. 11,). should lead us to use the present time in the best sense, and leave the future to His infinite wisdom (Mat. 6. 20, 25, 31-34.).

CHAPTER IV.

Ver. 1-16. 1. returned—*viz*., to the thought set forth (ch. 3. 16; Job. 35, 9.). power—MAUR., not so well, "*violence*." no comforter—twice said to express *continued* suffering without any to give comfort (Isa. 53. 7.). 2. A profane sentiment if severed from its connection; but just in its bearing on Solomon's scope. If religion were not taken into account (ch. 3. 17, 19,), to die as soon as possible would be desirable, so as not to suffer or witness "oppressions;" and still more so, not to be born at all (ch. 7. 1.). Job (3. 13; 21. 7, , David (Ps. 73. 3, &c.,), Jeremiah (12. 1,), Habakkuk (1. 13.), all passed through the same perplexity, until they went into the sanctuary, and looked beyond the present to the "judgment" (Ps. 73. 17; Hab. 2. 20; 3. 17, 18.). Then they saw the need of delay, before completely punishing the wicked, to give space for repentance, or else for accumulation of wrath (Rom. 2. 15;); and before completely rewarding the godly, to give room for faith and perseverance in tribulation Ps. 92. 7-12.). Earnests, however, are often even now given, by partial judgments, of the future complete one, to assure us, in spite of difficulties, that God governs the earth. 3. seen — nor *experienced.* 4. right—rather 'as ch. 2. 21, note,). *prosperous.* Prosperity, which men so much covet, is the very source of provoking oppression (*v.* 1) and "envy," so far is it from constituting the chief good. 5. Still the "fool" (the *wicked* oppressor) is not to be envied even in this life, who "folds his hands together" *in idleness* (Pro. 6. 10; 24. 33.). living on the means he wrongfully wrests from others: for such a one "eateth his own flesh," *i.e.*, is a *self-tormentor*, never satisfied, his spirit preying on itself (Isa. 9. 20; 49. 26.). 6. *Heb.*. "One *open hand palm) full of* quietness, than both *closed hands full of* travail". "Quietness," (mental tranquillity flowing from honest labour,), opposed to "eating one's own flesh" (*v.* 5,), also opposed to anxious labour to gain (*v.* 8; Pro. 15. 16, 17; 16. 8. . 7. *A* vanity, described in *v*. 8. 8. not a second—no partner. child—"son or brother," put for any heir Deut. 25. 5-10.). eye—(ch. 1. 8.). The miser would not be able to give an account of his infatuation. 9. Two—opposed to "one" (*v.* 8.). Ties of union, marriage, friendship, religious communion, are better than the selfish solitariness of the miser (Gen. 2. 18.). reward—advantage accrues from their efforts being conjoined. TALM says, "A man without a companion is like a left hand without the right." 10. if they fall—if *the one or other* fall, as may happen to *both*, *viz.*, into any distress of body, mind, or soul. 11. 1 Ki. 1. 1.). The image is taken from man and wife, but applies universally to the *warm* sympathy derived from social ties. So Christian ties Luke, 24. 32; Acts, 28. 15. , 12. one—enemy. threefold cord — proverbial for a *combination of many*, *ex. gr.*, husband, wife, and children (Pro. 11. 14,); so Christians, (Luke, 10. 1; Col. 2. 2, 19.). Untwist the cord, and the separate threads are easily "broken." 13. The "threefold cord" of social ties suggests the subject of *civil government*. In this case too, he concludes that kingly power confers no lasting happiness. The "wise" child, though a supposed case of Solomon, answers, in the event foreseen by the Holy Ghost, to Jeroboam, then a poor but valiant youth, once a "servant" of Solomon, and (1 Ki. 11. 26-40) appointed by God through the prophet Ahijah to be heir of the kingdom of the ten tribes about to be rent from Rehoboam. The "old and foolish king" answers to Solomon himself, who had lost his wisdom, when, in defiance of two warnings of God (1 Ki. 3. 14; 9. 2-9,), he forsook God, will no more be admonished—knows not yet how to take warning (see *Marg.*). God had by Ahijah already intimated the judgment coming on Solomon (1 Ki. 11. 11-13.). 14. out of p ison—Solomon uses this phrase of a supposed case, *ex. gr.*, Joseph raised from a dungeon to be lord of Egypt. His words are at the same time so framed by the Holy Ghost that they answer virtually to Jeroboam who fled to escape a "prison" and death from Solomon, to Shishak of Egypt (1 Ki. 11. 40.). This unconscious presaging of his own doom, and that of Rehoboam, constitutes the irony. David's elevation from poverty and exile, under Saul (which may have been before Solomon's mind,), had so far their counterpart in that of Jeroboam, whereas... becometh poor—rather, "though he (the youth) was born poor in his kingdom" (in the land where afterwards he was to reign.). 15. "I considered all the living," the present generation, in relation to ("with") the "*second* youth" (the *legitimate successor* of "the old king," as opposed to the "poor youth," the one *first* spoken of, about to be raised from poverty to a throne.). *i.e.*, Rehoboam. in his stead—the old king's. 16. Notwithstanding their now worshipping the rising sun, the heir-apparent, I reflected that "there were no bounds no stability (2 Sam. 15. 6; 20. 1,), no check on the love of innovation) of all that have been before them," *i.e.*, the past generation: so "also they that come after," *i.e.*, the next generation, "shall not rejoice in him," *viz.*, Rehoboam. The parallel, "shall not rejoice," fixes the sense of "no bounds," *no permanent adherence*, though now men *rejoice in him*.

CHAPTER V.

Ver. 1-20. 1. From vanity connected with kings, he passes to vanities (*v.* 7 which may be fallen into in serving the King of kings, even by those who, convinced of the vanity

The vanity of riches. ECCLESIASTES, VI, VII. *Remedies against vanity.*

4 When ^d thou vowest a vow unto God, defer not to pay it; for *he hath* no pleasure in fools: ^e pay that which thou hast vowed.
5 Better *f is it* that thou shouldest not vow, than that thou shouldest vow and not pay.
6 Suffer not thy mouth to cause thy flesh to sin; ^g neither say thou before the angel, that it *was* an error; wherefore should God be angry at thy voice, and destroy the work of thine hands?
7 For in the multitude of dreams and many words *there are* also *divers* vanities: but ^h fear thou God.
8 ¶ If thou ⁱ seest the oppression of the poor, and violent perverting of judgment and justice in a province, marvel not ² at the matter: for *j he that is* higher than the highest regardeth; and *there be* higher than they.
9 ¶ Moreover the profit of the earth is for all: the king *himself* is served by the field.
10 He that loveth silver shall not be satisfied with silver; nor he that loveth abundance with increase. This *is* also vanity.
11 When goods increase, they are increased that eat them: and what good *is there* to the owners thereof, saving the beholding *of them* with their eyes?
12 The sleep of a labouring man *is* sweet, whether he eat little or much: but the abundance of the rich will not suffer him to sleep.
13 There ^k is a sore evil *which* I have seen under the sun, *namely*, riches kept for the owners thereof to their hurt.
14 But those riches perish by evil travail; and he begetteth a son, and *there is* nothing in his hand.
15 As ^l he came forth of his mother's womb, naked shall he return to go as he came, and shall take nothing of his labour, which he may carry away in his hand.
16 And this also *is* a sore evil, *that* in all points as he came, so shall he go: and ^m what profit hath he that ⁿ hath laboured for the wind?
17 All his days also he ^o eateth in darkness, and *he hath* much sorrow and wrath with his sickness.
18 ¶ Behold *that* which I have seen: ³ *it is* good and comely *for one* to eat and to drink, and to enjoy the good of all his labour that he taketh under the sun ⁴ all the days of his life, which God giveth him; for it *is* his portion.
19 Every man also to whom God hath given riches and wealth, and hath given him power to eat thereof, and to take his portion, and to rejoice in his labour; this *is* the gift of God.
20 ⁵ For he shall not much remember the days of his life; because ^p God answereth him in the joy of his heart.

CHAPTER VI.

1 *Vanity of riches without use;* 3 *of many children, and long life, without good;* 7 *of insatiable desires, etc.*

THERE is an evil which I have seen under the sun, and it *is* common among men:
2 A man to whom God hath given riches, wealth, and honour, ^a so that he wanteth nothing for his soul of all that he desireth, yet ^b God giveth him not power to eat thereof, but a stranger eateth it: this *is* vanity, and it *is* an evil disease.

3 ¶ If a man beget an hundred *children*, and live many years, so that the days of his years be many, and his soul be not filled with good, and ^c also *that* he have no burial; I say, ^d *that* an untimely birth *is* better than he:
4 For he cometh in with vanity, and departeth in darkness, and his name shall be covered with darkness.
5 Moreover he hath not seen the sun, nor known any thing: this hath more rest than the other.
6 Yea, though he live a thousand years twice *told*, yet hath he seen no good: do not all go to one place?
7 All ^e the labour of man *is* for his mouth, and yet the ¹ appetite is not filled.
8 For what hath the wise more than the fool? what hath the poor, that knoweth to walk before the living?
9 Better *is* the sight of the eyes ² than the wandering of the desire: this *is* also vanity and vexation of spirit.
10 ¶ That which hath been is named already, and it is known that it *is* man: neither *f* may he contend with him that is mightier than he.
11 Seeing there be many things that increase vanity, what *is* man the better?
12 For who knoweth what *is* good for man in *this* life, ³ all the days of his vain life which he spendeth as ^g a shadow? for ^h who can tell a man what shall be after him under the sun?

CHAPTER VII.

1 *Remedies against vanity are a good name,* 2 *mortification,* 7 *patience,* 11 *wisdom.* 23 *Difficulty of getting wisdom.*

A GOOD name is better than precious ointment; and ^a the day of death than the day of one's birth.
2 ¶ *It is* better to go to the ^b house of mourning than to go to the house of feasting: for that *is* the end of all men; and the living will lay *it* to his heart.
3 ¹ Sorrow *is* better than laughter: ^c for by the sadness of the countenance the heart is made better.
4 The heart of the wise *is* in the house of mourning: but the heart of fools *is* in the house of mirth.
5 *It* is better to hear the rebuke of the wise, than for a man to hear the song of fools.
6 For as the ² crackling of thorns under a pot, so *is* the laughter of the fool. This also *is* vanity.
7 ¶ Surely oppression maketh a wise man mad; ^d and a gift destroyeth the heart.
8 Better *is* the end of a thing than the beginning thereof; *and* ^e the patient in spirit *is* better than the proud in spirit.
9 Be *f* not hasty in thy spirit to be angry: for anger resteth in the bosom of fools.
10 Say not thou, What is *the cause* that the former days were better than these? for thou dost not enquire ^g wisely concerning this.
11 ¶ Wisdom ⁴ *is* good with an inheritance; and *by it there is* profit to them that see the sun.
12 For wisdom *is* a ⁵ defence, *and* money *is* a defence: but the excellency of knowledge *is, that* wisdom giveth life to them that have it.
13 Consider the work of God: ^h for who can make *that* straight which he hath made crooked?

Vanities in Divine Service. ECCLESIASTES, V. *Vanities in Riches.*

of the creature, wish to worship the Creator. Keep thy foot—In going to worship, go with considerate circumspect, reverent feeling. The allusion is to the taking off of the shoes, or sandals, in entering a temple (Ex. 3. 5; Josh. 5. 15, which passages perhaps gave rise to the custom.). WEISS needlessly reads, "Keep thy *feast days*" (Ex. 23. 14, 17; the three great feasts.. hear—rather, "To be ready (to draw nigh with the desire to hear obey) is a better sacrifice than the offering of fools." [HOL.] (*Vulg.*; *Syr.*) [Ps. 51. 16, 17; Pro. 21. 3; Jer. 6. 20; 7. 21-23; 14. 12; Amos. 5. 21-24.). The warning is against mere ceremonial self-righteousness, as in ch. 7. 12. *Obedience* is the spirit of the law's requirements (Deut. 10. 12.. Solomon sorrowfully looks back on his own neglect of this (cf. 1 Ki. 8. 63, with 11. 4, 6.. *Positive* precepts of God must be kept, but will not stand instead of obedience to His *moral* precepts. The last provided no sacrifice for *wilful* sin (Num. 15. 30, 31; Heb. 10. 26-29.). 2. rash—opposed to the *considerate* *reverence* ("keep thy foot," v. 1.). This verse illustrates v. 1, as to *prayer* in the house of God ("before God," Isa. 1. 12;); so v. 4-6, as to *vows.* The remedy to such vanities is stated (v. 6.). "Fear thou God." God is in heaven—Therefore He ought to be approached with carefully-weighed words, by thee a frail creature of earth. .. *As* much "business," engrossing the mind, gives birth to incoherent "dreams," so many words, uttered inconsiderately in prayer, give birth to and betray "a fool's speech" (ch. 10. 14.). [HOL. and WEISS.] But v. 7 implies that the "dream" is not a comparison, but the *vain thoughts of the fool* (sinner) (Ps. 73. 20,), arising from multiplicity of (worldly) "business." His "dream" is, that God hears him for his much speaking (Mat. 6. 7,), independently of the frame of mind. [E. V. and MAUR.] "Fool's voice" answers to "dream" in the parallel; it comes by the many "words" flowing from the fool's "dream." 4. Hasty words in *prayer* (v. 2, 3) suggest the subject of hasty *vows.* A vow should not be hastily made (Jud. 11. 35; 1 Sam. 14. 24.). When made, it must be kept (Ps. 76. 11,), even as God keeps His word to us (Ex. 12. 41, 51; Josh. 21. 45.). 5. (Deut. 23. 21, 23.). 6. thy flesh—vow not with "thy mouth" a vow (ex. gr. fasting,), which the lusts of thy flesh (body, *Marg.*, ch. 2. 3) may tempt thee to break (Pro. 20. 25.). angel—the "messenger" of God (Job, 33. 23;); minister (Rev. 1. 20;); *i.e.*, the priest (Mal. 2. 7,). "Before" whom a breach of a vow was to be confessed (Lev. 5. 4, 5.). We, Christians, in our vows (ex. gr., at baptism, the Lord's supper, &c.) vow in the presence of Jesus Christ, "the angel of the covenant" (Mal. 3. 1,), and of ministering angels as witnesses (1 Cor. 11. 10; 1 Tim. 5. 21.). Extenuate not any breach of them as a slight error. 7. (Note, v. 3,). God's service, which ought to be our chief good, becomes by "dreams" (foolish fancies as to God's requirements of us in worship,), and random "words," positive "vanity." The remedy is, whatever fools may do, "Fear *thou* God" (ch. 12. 13.). 8. As in ch. 3. 16. so here the difficulty suggests itself. If God is so exact in even punishing hasty words (v. 1-6,), why does He allow gross injustice? In the remote "provinces," the "poor" often had to put themselves for protection from the inroads of Philistines, &c., under chieftains, who oppressed them even

in Solomon's reign (1 Ki. 12. 4). the matter—*lit.*, the *pleasure*, or *purpose* (Isa. 53. 10.). Marvel not at this *dispensation of God's will*, as if He had abandoned the world. Nay, there is coming a capital judgment at last, and an earnest of it in partial punishments of sinners meanwhile. higher than the highest—(Dan. 7. 18.). regardeth—(2 Chr. 16. 9.). there be higher—*plur., i.e.*, the three persons of the Godhead, or else, "regardeth not only the 'highest' kings, than whom He 'is higher,' but even the petty tyrants of the provinces, *viz.*) the high ones who are above them" (the poor.). [WEISS.] 9. "The profit (produce) of the earth is (ordained) for the common good of) all: even the king himself is served by (the fruits of) the field" (2 Chr. 26. 10.). Therefore the common Lord of all, high and low, will punish at last those who rob the "poor" of their share in it (Pro. 22. 22, 23; Amos, 8. 4-7.). 10. Not only will God punish at last, but meanwhile the oppressive gainers of "silver" find no solid "satisfaction" in it. shall not be satisfied—so the oppressor "eateth his own flesh" (ch. 4. 1, 5, note,). with increase—is not satisfied with the gain that he makes. 11. they ... that eat them—the rich man's dependents (Ps. 23. 5.). 12. Another argument against anxiety to gain riches. "Sleep ... sweet." answers to "quietness" (ch. 4. 6;); "not suffer ... sleep," to "vexation of spirit." Fears for his wealth, and an over-loaded stomach without "labouring," (cf. ch. 4. 5,), will not suffer the rich oppressor to sleep. 13, 14. Proofs of God's judgments even in this world (Pro. 11. 31.). The rich oppressor's wealth provokes enemies, robbers, &c. Then, after having kept it for an expected son, he loses it beforehand, by misfortune ("by evil travail,"), and the son is born to be heir of poverty. Ch. 2. 19, 23, gives another aspect of the same subject. 16. Even supposing that he loses not his wealth before death, *then* at least he must go stripped of it all (Ps. 49. 17.). laboured for ... wind — (Hos. 12. 1; 1 Cor. 9. 26.). 17. eateth — appropriately put for "liveth" in general, as connected with v. 11, 12, 18. darkness—opposed to "light (joy) of countenance" (ch. 8. 1; Pro. 16. 15.). wrath—fretfulness, *lit.*, "His sorrow is much, and his infirmity (of body) and wrath." 18. returns to the sentiment (ch. 3. 12, 13, 22,), *transl.*, "Behold the good which I have seen, and which is becoming" (in a man,). which God giveth—*viz.*, both the good of his labour, and his life. his portion — legitimately. It is God's gift that makes it so, when regarded as such. Such a one will use, not abuse, earthly things (1 Cor. 7. 31.). Opposed to the anxious life of the covetous (v. 10, 17.). 19. As v. 18 refers to the "labouring" man (v. 12,), so v. 19. to the "rich" man, who gets wealth, not by "oppression" (v. 8,), but by "God's gift." He is distinguished also from the "rich" man (ch. 6. 2,), in having received by God's gift, not only "wealth," but also "power to eat thereof," which that one has not. "To take his portion," limits him to the lawful use of wealth, not keeping back from God *His* portion, while enjoying *his own*. 20. He will not remember much (looking back with disappointment, as the ungodly do (ch. 2. 11) on) the days of his life. answereth ... in the joy—God *answers* his prayers in giving him "power" to *enjoy* his blessings. GES. and *Vulg., transl.*, "For God (so) *occupies* him with joy," &c.,

447

that he thinks not much of the shortness and sorrows of life. HoL., "Though (God) gives not much (as to real enjoyment,), yet he remembers (with thankfulness) the days; for (he knows) God *exercises* him by the joy," &c. (tries him by prosperity,), so *Marg.*, but *E. V.* is simplest.

CHAPTER VI.

Ver. 1-12. 1. common—or, else more *lit.*, *great upon man*, falls heavily upon man. 2. for his soul—*i.e.*, his enjoyment. God giveth him not power to eat—this distinguishes him from the "rich" man in ch. 5. 19. "God hath given," distinguishes him also from the man who got his wealth by "oppression" (ch. 5. 8. 10.). stranger — those not akin, nay, even hostile to him (Jer. 51. 51; Lam. 5. 2; Hos. 7. 9.). He seems to have it in his "power" to do as he will with his wealth, but an unseen power gives him up to his own avarice; God wills that he should toil for "a stranger" (ch. 2. 26.), who has found favour in God's sight. 3. Even if a man (of this character) have very many (equivalent to "a hundred," 2 Ki. 10. 1) children, and not have a "stranger" as his heir *v.* 2,), and live long , "days of years" express the *brevity* of life *at its best*, Gen. 47. 9. , yet enjoy no real "good" in life, and lie unhonoured, without "burial," at death ,2 Ki. 9. 26, 35.), the embryo is better than he. In the East, to be without burial is the greatest degradation. "Better the fruit that drops from the tree before it is ripe, than that left to hang on till later." [HENRY.] 4. be—rather, *it*, "the untimely birth." So "its" not "*his* name," with vanity—to no purpose; a type of the driftless existence of him who makes riches the chief good. darkness—of the abortive: a type of the unhonoured death and dark future beyond the grave, of the avaricious. 5. this—*yet* "it has more rest, than" the toiling gloomy miser. 6. If the miser's length of "life" be thought to raise him above the abortive, Solomon answers, long life, without enjoying real good, is but lengthened misery, and riches cannot exempt him from going whether "all go." He is fit neither for life, nor death, nor eternity. 7. man—rather, "the man," *viz.*, the miser (*v.* 3-6.). For not *all* men labour for the month, *i.e.*, for selfish gratification. appetite—*Heb.*, *the soul*. The insatiability of the desire prevents that which is the only end proposed in toils, *viz.*, self-gratification; "the man" thus gets no "good" out of his wealth (*v.* 3.). 8. For—However. [MAUR.] The "for" means (in contrast to the insatiability of the miser), *For what* else is the advantage which *the wise man hath above the fool? What* (advantage, *i.e.*, superiority, above him who knows not how to walk upright) *hath the poor who knoweth to walk before the living?* *i.e.*, to use and enjoy life aright (ch. 5. 18, 19,), a cheerful, thankful, godly "walk" (Ps. 116. 9.), 9. Answer to the question in *v.* 8. This is the advantage: "Better is the sight of the eyes (the wise man's godly enjoyment of present *seen* blessings,), than the (fool's) wandering (*lit.*, *walking*, Ps. 73. 9) of the desire," *i.e.*, vague, insatiable desires for what he has not (*v.* 7; Heb. 13. 5.). this—restless wandering of desire, and not enjoying contentedly the present (1 Tim. 6. 6, 8.).

10. Part II. here begins. Since man's toils are vain, what is the chief good ! (*v.* 12.). The answer is contained in the rest of the book. "That which hath been

(man's various circumstances) is named already (not only has existed (ch. 1. 9; 3. 15.), but has received its just *name* 'vanity,' long ago,), and it is known that it (vanity) is man" (*Heb.*, *Adam*, equivalent to man " of *red* dust," as his Creator appropriately named him from his frailty.). neither may he contend, &c.—(Rom. 9. 20.). 11. "Seeing" that man cannot escape from the "vanity," which by God's "mighty" will is inherent in earthly things, and cannot *call in question* God's wisdom in these dispensations (equivalent to, "contend," &c.,), "what is man the better" of these vain things, as regards the chief good ? None whatever. 12. For who knoweth, &c.—The ungodly know not what is really "good" during life, nor "what shall be after them," *i.e.*, what will be the event of their undertakings (ch. 3. 22; 8. 7.). The godly might be tempted to "contend with God" (*v.* 10.), as to His dispensations; but they cannot fully know the wise purposes served by them now and hereafter. Their sufferings from the oppressors are more really good for them than cloudless prosperity; sinners are being allowed to fill up their measure of guilt. Retribution in part vindicates God's ways even now. The judgment shall make all clear. In ch. 7. he states what is good, in answer to this verse.

CHAPTER VII.

Ver. 1-29. 1. (See note, ch. 6. 12.). name—character; a godly mind and life; not mere *reputation* with man, but what a man *is* in the eyes of God, with whom the *name* and *reality* are one thing (Isa. 9. 6.). This alone is "good," whilst all else is "vanity," when made the chief end. ointment—used lavishly at costly banquets, and peculiarly refreshing in the sultry East. The *Heb.* for *name* and for *ointment*, have a happy paronomasia, *Shem*, *Shemen*. "Ointment" is fragrant only in the place where the person is whose head and garment are scented, and only for a time. The " name" given by God to His child (Rev. 3. 12) is for ever, and in all lands. So in the case of the woman who received an everlasting name from Jesus Christ, in reward for her precious ointment Isa. 56. 5; Mark, 14. 3-9.). Jesus Christ Himself hath such a name, as the Messiah, equivalent to Anointed ,Sol. Song 1. 3., and the day of [his]death, &c.—but, connected with the previous clause, death is to him, who hath a godly name, "better" than the day of his birth: "far better," as Phil. 1. 23, hath it. 2. Proving that it is not a *sensual* enjoyment of earthly goods, which is meant in ch. 3. 13; 5. 18. A thankful use of these is right, but frequent feasting Solomon had found dangerous to piety in his own case. So Job's fear ,ch. 1. 4, 5.). The house of feasting often shuts out thoughts of God and eternity. The sight of the dead in the "house of mourning" causes "the living" to think of their own "end." 3. Sorrow—Such as arises from serious thoughts of eternity. laughter—reckless mirth ;ch. 2. 2.). by the sadness . . . better—(Ps. 126. 5, 6; 2 Cor. 4. 17; Heb. 12. 10, 11.). MAUR. *transl.*, "In sadness of countenance there is (may be) a good (*cheerful* heart." So *Heb.*, for "good," equivalent to cheerful (ch. 11. 9,); but the parallel clause supports *E. V.* 5. (Ps. 141. 4, 5.). Godly reproof offends the flesh, but benefits the spirit. Fools' songs in the house of mirth please the flesh, but injure the soul.

447 [1]

6. The "crackling" answers to the loud merriment of fools. It is the very fire consuming them, which produces the seeming merry noise (Joel, 2. 5.). Their light soon goes out in the black darkness. There is a paronomasia in the Heb., *Sirim* (thorns,), *Sir* pot. The wicked are often compared to "thorns" (2 Sam. 23. 6; Nah. 1. 10.). Dried cow dung was the common fuel in Palestine; its slowness in burning makes the quickness of a fire of thorns the more graphic, as an image of the sudden end of fools (Ps. 118. 12,). 7. oppression—recurring to the idea (ch. 3. 16; 5. 8.). Its connection with v. 4-6 is, the sight of "oppression" perpetrated by "fools" might tempt the "wise" to call in question God's dispensations, and imitate the folly (equivalent to "madness") described (v. 5. 6.). WEISS, for "oppression," transl., "distraction," produced by merriment. But ch. 5. 8, favours E. V. a gift—i.e., the sight of *bribery* in "places of judgment" (ch. 3. 16, might cause the wise to lose their wisdom (equivalent to "heart,") (Job, 12. 6; 21. 6, 7; 24. 1, &c.). This suits the parallelism better than "a heart of gifts," a benevolent heart, as WEISS. 8. connected with v. 7. Let the "wise" wait for "the end," and the "oppressions," which now (in "the beginning") perplex their faith, will be found by God's working to be overruled to their good. "Tribulation worketh *patience*" (Rom. 5. 3,), which is infinitely better than "the proud spirit," that prosperity might have generated in them, as it has in fools (Ps. 73. 2, 3, 12-14, 17-20; Jam. 5. 11.). 9. angry—impatient at adversity befalling thee, as Job was (ch. 5. 2; Pro. 12. 16.). 10. Do not call in question God's ways in making thy former days better than thy present, as Job did (ch. 29. 2-5.). The very putting of the question argues that heavenly "wisdom" (Marg.) is not as much as it ought made the chief good with thee. 11. Rather, "Wisdom, as compared with an inheritance, is good," i.e., is as good as an inheritance; "yea, better (lit., *and a profit*) to them that see the sun" (i.e., *the living*, ch. 11. 7; Job, 3. 16; Ps. 49. 19.). 12. Lit., (To be) in (i.e., under) the *shadow* (Isa. 30. 2) of wisdom (is the same as to be) in (under) the *shadow* of money: wisdom no less *shields* one from the ills of life, than money does. is, that—rather, "the excellency of the knowledge *of* wisdom giveth life," i.e., life in the highest sense, here and hereafter (Pro. 3. 18; John, 17. 3; 2 Pet. 1. 3.). Wisdom (religion) cannot be lost, as money can. It *shields* one in adversity, as well as prosperity; money, only in prosperity. The question in v. 10 implies a want of it. 13. *Consider* as to *God's work*, that it is impossible to alter His dispensations: *for who can*, &c. straight ... crooked—man cannot amend what God wills to be "wanting" and "adverse" (ch. 1. 15; Job, 12. 14,). 14. consider—resumed from v. 13. "Consider," i.e., regard it as "the work of God," for "God has made (Heb., for 'set') this (adversity) also as well as the other" (prosperity,). "Adversity" is one of the things which "God has made crooked," and which man cannot "make straight." He ought therefore to be "patient" (v. 8.), after him—equivalent to, "that man may not find anything (to blame) after God" i.e., *after* "considering God's work," v. 13.). *Vulg.* and *Syr.*, "against Him" (cf. v. 10; Rom. 3. 4.). 15. An objection entertained by Solomon "in the days of his vanity" (apostasy) (ch. 8. 14; Job, 21. 7.). Just ... perisheth—(1 Ki. 21. 13.). *Temporal* not eternal death (John, 10. 28.). But see note, v. 16; "*just*" is probably a *self-justiciary*. wicked ... prolongeth—see the antidote to the abuse of this statement, in ch. 8. 12. 16. HOL. makes v. 16 the scoffing inference of the objector, and v. 17 the answer of Solomon now repentant. So (1 Cor. 15. 32) the sceptic's objection; (v. 33) the answer. However, "Be not righteous over much," may be taken as Solomon's words, forbidding a *self-made* righteousness of outward performances, which would wrest salvation from God, instead of receiving it as the gift of His *grace*. It is a fanatical, Pharisaical righteousness separated from God; for the "fear of God" is in antithesis to it (v. 18; ch. 5. 3, 7; Mat. 6. 1-7; 9. 14; 23. 23, 24; Rom. 10. 3; 1 Tim. 4. 3.). over wise—Job, 11. 12; Rom. 12. 3, 16,), presumptuously self-sufficient, as if acquainted with the whole of divine truth. destroy thyself—expose thyself to needless persecution, austerities, and the wrath of God; hence to an untimely death. "Destroy thyself" answers to "perisheth" (v. 15, "righteous over much," to "a just man." Therefore, in v. 15, it is a *self-justiciary*, not a truly righteous man, that is meant. 17. over much wicked—so worded, to answer to "righteous *over* much." For if not taken thus, it would seem to imply, that we *may* be wicked *a little*. "Wicked" refers to "wicked man" (v. 15;; "die before thy time," to "prolongeth·his life," antithetically. There may be a wicked man spared to "live long," owing to his avoiding gross excesses (v. 15.). Solomon says, therefore, Be not so foolish (answering antithetically to "over wise" (v. 16,), as to run to such excess of riot, that God will be provoked to cut off prematurely thy day of grace (Rom. 2. 5.). The precept is addressed to *a sinner*. Beware of aggravating thy sin, so as to make thy case desperate. It refers to the days of Solomon's "vanity" (apostasy, v. 15,), when only such a precept would be applicable. By LITOTES it includes, "Be not wicked *at all*." 18. this, ... this—the two opposite excesses v. 16, 17,), fanatical, self-wise righteousness, and presumptuous foolhardy wickedness: he that feareth God shall come forth of them all —shall escape all such extremes (Pro. 3. 7,). 19. *Heb.*, "*The wisdom*," i.e., the true wisdom, religion (2 Tim. 3. 15.). than ten mighty —i.e., able and valiant generals v. 12; ch. 9. 13-18; Pro. 21. 22, 24. 5.). These "watchmen" wake in vain, except the Lord keep the city" (Ps. 127. 1.). 20. Referring to v. 16. Be not self-righteous, seek not to make thyself "*just*" before God, by a superabundance of self-imposed performances; "for (true 'wisdom, or 'righteousness,' shows that there is not a *just* man," &c. 21. As therefore thou being far from perfectly "just" thyself, hast much to be forgiven by God, do not take too strict account, as the *self-righteous* do (v. 16; Luke, 18. 9, 11.,), and thereby shorten their lives, (v. 15, 16,), of words spoken against thee by others, ex. gr., thy servant: Thou art then "fellow-servant" before God (Mat. 15. 32-35,). 22. (1 Ki. 2. 44.). 23. All this—Resuming the "all" in v. 15; v. 15-22, is, therefore, the fruit of his dearly-bought experience in the days of his "vanity." I will be wise—I tried to "be wise," independently of God. But true wisdom was then "far from him," in spite of his human wisdom, which he retained by God's gift. So "over wise" (v. 16.). 24. That ... far

ECCLESIASTES, VIII, IX.

14 In the day of prosperity be joyful, but in the day of adversity consider: God also hath set the one over against the other, to the end that man should find nothing after him.
15 All things have I seen in the days of my vanity: there is a just man that perisheth in his righteousness, and there is a wicked man that prolongeth his life in his wickedness.
16 Be not righteous over much; neither make thyself over wise: why shouldest thou destroy thyself?
17 Be not over much wicked, neither be thou foolish: why shouldest thou die before thy time?
18 It is good that thou shouldest take hold of this; yea, also from this withdraw not thine hand: for he that feareth God shall come forth of them all.
19 Wisdom strengtheneth the wise more than ten mighty men which are in the city.
20 For there is not a just man upon earth, that doeth good, and sinneth not.
21 Also take no heed unto all words that are spoken; lest thou hear thy servant curse thee:
22 For oftentimes also thine own heart knoweth that thou thyself likewise hast cursed others.
23 All this have I proved by wisdom: I said, I will be wise; but it was far from me.
24 That which is far off, and exceeding deep, who can find it out?
25 I applied mine heart to know, and to search, and to seek out wisdom, and the reason of things, and to know the wickedness of folly, even of foolishness and madness:
26 And I find more bitter than death the woman whose heart is snares and nets, and her hands as bands: whoso pleaseth God shall escape from her; but the sinner shall be taken by her.
27 Behold, this have I found, saith the Preacher, counting one by one, to find out the account;
28 Which yet my soul seeketh, but I find not: one man among a thousand have I found; but a woman among all those have I not found.
29 Lo, this only have I found, that God hath made man upright; but they have sought out many inventions.

CHAPTER VIII.

2 Kings greatly to be respected. 6 Divine providence to be observed. 12 It is better with the godly in adversity than with the wicked in prosperity. 16 Work of God unsearchable.

WHO is as the wise man? and who knoweth the interpretation of a thing? a man's wisdom maketh his face to shine, and the boldness of his face shall be changed.
2 I counsel thee to keep the king's commandment, and that in regard of the oath of God.
3 Be not hasty to go out of his sight: stand not in an evil thing; for he doeth whatsoever pleaseth him.
4 Where the word of a king is, there is power: and who may say unto him, What doest thou?
5 Whoso keepeth the commandment shall feel no evil thing: and a wise man's heart discerneth both time and judgment.
6 Because to every purpose there is time and judgment, therefore the misery of man is great upon him.
7 For he knoweth not that which shall be: for who can tell him when it shall be?
8 There is no man that hath power over the spirit, to retain the spirit; neither hath he power in the day of death: and there is no discharge in that war; neither shall wickedness deliver those that are given to it.
9 All this have I seen, and applied my heart unto every work that is done under the sun: there is a time wherein one man ruleth over another to his own hurt.
10 And so I saw the wicked buried, who had come and gone from the place of the holy, and they were forgotten in the city where they had so done. This is also vanity.
11 Because sentence against an evil work is not executed speedily, therefore the heart of the sons of men is fully set in them to do evil.
12 Though a sinner do evil an hundred times, and his days be prolonged, yet surely I know that it shall be well with them that fear God, which fear before him:
13 But it shall not be well with the wicked, neither shall he prolong his days, which are as a shadow; because he feareth not before God.
14 There is a vanity which is done upon the earth; that there be just men, unto whom it happeneth according to the work of the wicked; again, there be wicked men, to whom it happeneth according to the work of the righteous. I said, that this also is vanity.
15 Then I commended mirth, because a man hath no better thing under the sun, than to eat, and to drink, and to be merry; for that shall abide with him of his labour the days of his life, which God giveth him under the sun.
16 ¶ When I applied mine heart to know wisdom, and to see the business that is done upon the earth: (for also there is that neither day nor night seeth sleep with his eyes:)
17 Then I beheld all the work of God, that a man cannot find out the work that is done under the sun: because though a man labour to seek it out, yet he shall not find it; yea farther, though a wise man think to know it, yet shall he not be able to find it.

CHAPTER IX.

1 Like things happen to good and bad. 7 How to enjoy the good of this life. 11 Human probabilities uncertain. 13 Wisdom is better than strength.

FOR all this I considered in my heart, even to declare all this, that the righteous, and the wise, and their works, are in the hand of God: no man knoweth either love or hatred by all that is before them.
2 All things come alike to all: there is one event to the righteous, and to the wicked; to the good and to the clean, and to the unclean; to him that sacrificeth, and to him that sacrificeth not: as is the good, so is the sinner; and he that sweareth, as he that feareth an oath.
3 This is an evil among all things that are done under the sun, that there is one event unto all: yea, also the heart of the sons of men is full of evil, and madness is

off... deep—True wisdom is so when sought independently of "fear of God" (v. 18; Deut. 30. 1:, 13; Job, 11. 7, 8; 28. 12-20, 2S; Ps. 64. 6; Rom. 10. 6, 7.). **25.** *Lit., I turned myself and mine heart to.* A phrase peculiar to Ecclesiastes, and appropriate to the penitent *turning* back to *commune with his heart* on his past life. wickedness of folly—he is now a step further on the path of penitence, than ch. 1. 17; 2. 12, where "folly" is put without "wickedness" prefixed. reason—rather, *the right estimation* of things. HOL. *transl.,* also "foolishness" *i.e.,* sinful folly, answering to 'wickedness' in the parallel) of madness," *i.e.,* of man's mad pursuits.). **26.** " I find" that, of all my sinful follies, none has been so ruinous a snare in seducing me from God, as idolatrous women (1 Ki. 11. 3, 4; Pro. 5. 3, 4; 22. 14.). As "God's favour is better than life," she who seduces from God is "more bitter than death." whoso pleaseth God—as Joseph (Gen. 39. 2, 3. 9.). It is God's *grace* alone that keeps any from falling. **27.** this—*viz.,* what follows in *v.* 28. counting one by one—by comparing one thing with another. [HOL. and MAUR.] account—a right estimate. But *v.* 28 more favours GES., "Considering *women one by one."* **28.** Rather, referring to his *past* experience, "Which my soul *sought* further, but I *found* not.", one man—*i.e.,* worthy of the name, "man," "upright:" not more than one in a thousand of my courtiers Job, 33. 23; Ps. 12. 1.). Jesus Christ alone of men fully realises the perfect ideal of "man." "Chiefest among ten thousand" (Sol. Song 5. 10.). No *perfect* "woman" has ever existed, not even the Virgin Mary. Solomon, in the word "thousand," alludes to his 300 wives and 700 concubines. Among these it was not likely that he should find the fidelity which *one* true wife pays to *one* husband. Connected with *v.* 26, not an unqualified condemnation of the sex, as Pro. 12. 4; 31. 10, &c., prove. **29.** The "only" way of accounting for the scarcity of even comparatively upright men and women is that, whereas God made man upright, they (men) have, &c. The only account to be "found" of the origin of evil, the great mystery of theology, is that given in Holy Writ (Gen. 2.; 3.). Among man's "inventions" was the one especially referred to in *v.* 26, the bitter fruits of which Solomon experienced, the breaking of God's primeval marriage law, joining one man to *one* woman (Mat. 19. 4, 5, 6.). "Man" is *sing., viz.,* Adam: "they," *plur.,* Adam, Eve, and their posterity.

CHAPTER VIII.

Ver. 1-17. **1.** Praise of true wisdom continued ch. 7. 11, &c.). "Who" is to be accounted "equal to the wise man?" "Who (like him) knoweth the interpretation" of God's providences (*ex. gr.,* ch. 7. 8, 13, 14,), and God's word (*ex. gr.,* ch. 7. 29, note; Pro. 1. 6.). face to shine—(ch. 7. 14; Acts, 6. 15.). *A sunny countenance,* the reflection of a tranquil conscience and serene mind. Communion with God gives it (Ex. 34. 29, 30.). boldness—austerity, changed—into a benign expression by true wisdom religion (Jam. 3. 17.). MAUR. *transl.,* "The *shining* (brightness) of his face is *doubled,*" arguing that the *Heb.* noun for "boldness" is never used in a bad sense Pro. 4. 18.). Or as *Marg., strength* (ch. 7. 19; Isa. 40. 31; 2 Cor. 3. 18.). But the adjective is used in a bad sense (Deut. 28. 50,). **2.** the king's—Jehovah, peculiarly the king of Israel in the theocracy; *v.* 3, 4 prove it is not the earthly king who is meant. the oath of God—the covenant which God made with Abraham and renewed with David; Solomon remembered Ps. 89. 35, "I have *sworn,"* &c. *v.* 36,). and the penalties if David's children should forsake it (*v.* 30-32;); inflicted on Solomon himself; yet God not "utterly" forsaking him (*v.* 33, 34.). **3.** hasty—rather, "Be not *terror-struck* so as to go out of His sight." Slavishly "terror-struck" is characteristic of the sinner's feeling toward God; he vainly tries to flee out of His sight (Ps. 139. 7.); opposed to the "shining face" of filial confidence *v.* 1; John, 8. 33-36; Rom. 8. 2; 1 John, 4. 18.). stand not—persist not. for he doeth—God inflicts what punishment He pleases on persisting sinners (Job, 23. 13; Ps. 115. 3.). True of none save God. **4.** God's very "word" is "power." So the gospel word (Rom. 1. 16; Heb. 4. 12.). who may say, &c.—(Job, 9. 12; 33. 13; Isa. 45. 9; Dan. 4. 35. . Scripture does not ascribe such arbitrary power to earthly kings. **5.** fee — experience. time—the neglect of the right "times" causes much of the sinful folly of the spiritually unwise ch. 3. 1-11.). judgment—the right manner. [HOL.] But as God's future "judgment" is connected with the "time for every purpose" in ch. 3. 17, so it is here. The punishment of persisting sinners (*v.* 3) suggests it. The wise man realises the fact, that as there is a fit "time" for every purpose, so for the "judgment." This thought cheers him in adversity ch. 7. 14; 8. 1. . therefore the misery, &c.—because the foolish sinner does not think of the right "times" and the "judgment." **7.** re—the sinner, by neglecting times *ex. gr.,* "the accepted *time,* and the day of salvation," 2 Cor. 6. 2.), is taken by surprise by the judgment (ch. 3. 22 6. 12; 9. 12). The godly wise observe the due times of things (ch. 3. 1,), and so, looking for the judgment, are not taken by surprise, though not knowing the precise "when" (1 Thes. 5. 2-4;); they "know the time" to all saving purposes (Rom. 13. 11.). **8.** spirit—*breath of life* (ch. 3. 19,), as the words following require. Not "wind," as WEISS thinks (Pro. 30. 4.). This verse naturally follows the subject of "times" and "judgment" *v.* 6, 7.). discharge—alluding to the liability to military service of all above twenty years old Num. 1. 3,), yet many were exempted (Deut. 20. 5-8.). But in *that* war (death) there is no exemption. those ... given to it—*lit.,* the *master* of it. Wickedness can get money for the sinner, but cannot deliver him from the death temporal and eternal, which is its penalty (Isa. 28. 15, 18.). **9.** his own hurt—the tyrannical "ruler hurts" not merely his subjects, but *himself;* so Rehoboam (1 Ki. 12;); but the "time" of "hurt" chiefly refers to eternal ruin, incurred by "wickedness," at "the *day* of death" *v.* 8,), and the "*time"* of "judgment" (*v.* 6; Pro. 8. 36.). **10.** the wicked—*viz.,* rulers (*v.* 9.). buried—with funereal pomp by man, though little meriting it (Jer. 22. 19.); but this only formed the more awful contrast to their death temporal and eternal inflicted by God (Luke, 16. 22, 23.). come and gone from the place of the holy—went to and came from *the place of judicature,* where they sat as *God's representatives* (Ps. 82. 1-6,), with pomp. HOL. WEISS *transl.,* "Buried and *gone* (utterly,), even from the holy place they departed." As Joab, by Solomon's command, was sent to the grave from the "holy place" *in the temple,* which was not a sanctuary to murderers (Ex.

21. 14; 1 Ki. 2, 28, 31,). The use of the very word "bury" there makes this view l.kely; still "who had come and gone" may be retained. Joab came to the altar, but had to go from it: so the "wicked rulers" (v. 9, ,including High Priests) came to , and went from, the temple, on occasions of solemn worship, but did not thereby escape their doom. forg: ten— Pro. 10, 7. 11. The reason why the wicked persevere in sin: God's delay in judgment (Mat. 24. 48-51; 2 Pet. 3. 8, 9.). "They see not the smoke of the pit, therefore they dread not the fire." [SOUTH.] (Ps. 55. 19.). Joab's escape from the punishment of his murder of Abner, so far from "leading him to repentance," as it ought (Rom. 2. 4.), led him to the additional murder of Amasa. 12. He says this, lest the sinner should abuse the statement (ch. 7. 15,), "A wicked man prolongeth his life." before him—&c. at His presence; reverently serve Him, realising His continual presence. 13. neither shall he prolong—not a contradiction to v. 12. The "prolonging" of his days there is only seeming, not real. Taking into account his eternal existence, his present days, however seemingly long, are really short. God's delay (v. 11) exists only in man's shortsighted view. It gives scope to the sinner to repent, or else to fill up his full measure of guilt; and so, in either case, tends to the final vindication of God's ways. It gives exercise to the faith, patience, and perseverance of saints. shadow— ch. 6. 12; Job, 8, 9.). 14. An objection is here started entertained by Solomon in his apostasy, , as in ch. 3. 16; 7. 15, to the truth of retributive justice. from the fact of the just and the wicked not now receiving always according to their respective deserts; a cavil, which would seem the more weighty to men living under the Mosaic covenant of temporal sanctions. The objector adds, as Solomon had said, that the worldling's pursuits are "vanity" (v. 10,). "I say (not 'said' this also is vanity. Then I commend mirth," &c. [HoL.] V. 14,15, may, however, be explained as teaching a cheerful, thankful use of God's gifts "under the sun," i.e., not making them the chief good, as sensualists do, which ch. 2. 2; 7. 2, forbid; but in "the fear of God," as ch. 3. 12; 5. 18; 7. 18; 9. 7, opposed to the abstinence of the self-righteous ascetic ch. 7. 16,, and of the miser (ch. 5. 17. 15. no better thing, &c.—viz., to the "just" man, whose cheng good is religion, not for the worldly. abide—Heb., adhere; not for ever, but it is the only sure good to be enjoyed from earthly labours equivalent to "of his labour the days of his life.". Still, the language resembles the sceptical precept (1 Cor. 15. 32, introduced only to be refuted: and "abide" is too strong language, perhaps, for a religious man to apply to "eating" and "mirth." 16. Reply to v. 14, 15. When I applied myself to observe man's toils after happiness (some of them so incessant as not to allow sufficient time for "sleep,"), then (v. 17, the apodosis) I saw that "man cannot find out the reason of) God's inscrutable dealings with the "just" and with the "wicked" here (v. 14; ch. 3. 11; Job, 5, 9; Rom. 11. 33.); his duty is to acquiesce in them a good, because they are God's, though he sees not all the reasons for them Ps. 73. 16.). It is error in to know "the righteous are in God's hand" ch. 9. 1.). "Over wise" (ch. 7. 16,), i.e., speculations above what is written are vain.

CHAPTER IX.

1. declare—rather, explore, the result of my exploring is this, that "the righteous, &c., are in the hand of God. No man knoweth either the love or hatred (of God to them) by all that is before them," i.e., by what is outwardly seen in His present dealings (ch. 8. 14, 17. However, from the sense of the same words, in v. 6, "love and hatred" seem to be the feelings of the wicked towards the righteous, whereby they caused to the latter comfort or sorrow. Transl., "Even the love and hatred" (exhibited towards the righteous, are in God's hand) (Ps. 76. 10; Pro. 16. 7). man knoweth all that is before them." 2. All things, alike—not universally; but as to death. V. 2-10 are made by HoL. the objection of a sceptical sensualist. However, they may be explained as Solomon's language. He repeats the sentiment already implied in ch. 2. 14; 3. 20; 8. 14. one event—not eternally; but death is common to all. good morally. clean— ceremonially. sacrificet.— alike to Josiah who sacrificed to God, and to Ahab who made sacrifice to Him ceas. sweareth— rashly and falsely. 3. Transl., "There is an evil above all (evils) that are done," &c., viz., that not only "there is one event to all," but "also the heart of the sons of men" makes this fact a reason for "madly" persisting in "evil while they live, and after that," &c., sin is "madness." the dead—(Pro. 2. 18; 9. 18.). 4. For—rather, Nevertheless. E. V. rightly reads as the Marg., Heb., "that is joined," instead of the text, "who is to be chosen?" hope—not of mere temporal good (Job, 14. 7;); but of yet repenting and being saved. dog—metaphor for the vilest persons 1 Sam. 24. 14.). lion—as to nobility of animals (Pro. 30. 30.). better—as to hope of salvation: the noblest who die unconverted have no hope; the vilest, so long as they have life, have hope. 5. know that they shall die—and may thereby be led "so to number their days, that they may apply their hearts to wisdom" (ch. 7. 1-4; Ps. 90. 12.). dead know not anything—i.e., so far as their bodily senses and worldly affairs are concerned (Job, 14. 21: Isa. 63. 16;); also, they know no door of repentance open to them, such as is to all on earth. neither... reward—no advantage from their worldly labours (ch. 2. 18-22; 4. 9.). memory—not of the righteous (Ps. 112. 6; Mal. 3. 16,), but the wicked, who with all the pains to perpetuate their names (Ps. 49. 11 are soon "forgotten" (ch. 8. 10.). 6. love, and...hatred, &c. —referring to v. 1, where see the note.). Not that these cease in a future world absolutely (Ez. 32. 27; Rev. 22. 11;); but as the end of this verse shows, relatively to persons and things in this world. Man's love and hatred can no longer be exercised for good or evil in the same way as here; but the fruits of them remain. What he is found at death, he remains for ever. "Envy," too, marks the wicked as referred to, since it was therewith that they assailed the righteous (v. 1, note.). portion— their "portion" was "in this life" (Ps. 17. 14,), that they now "cannot have any more." 7. Addressed to the "righteous wise," spoken of in v. 1. Being "in the hand of God," who now accepteth "thy works" in His service, as He has previously accepted thy person (Gen. 4. 4.), thou mayest "eat, &c., with a cheerful (not sensually 'merry') heart" ch. 3. 13; 5. 18; Acts, 2. 46.). 8. white—in token of joy (Isa. 61. 3,). Solomon was clad in white

(JOSEPH. *Antiq.* viii. 7, 3;); hence his attire is compared to the "*lilies*" Mat. 6. 28,), typical of the spotless righteousness of Jesus Christ, which the redeemed shall wear (Rev. 3. 18; 7. 14.). ointment—Ps. 23. 5,), opposed to a gloomy exterior (2 Sam. 14. 2; Ps. 45. 7; Mat. 6. 17;); typical, also (ch. 7. 1; Sol. Song. 1. 3.). 9. wif.... oves'—godly and true love, opposed to the "snares" of the "thousand" concubines ch. 7. 26, 28,). "among" whom Solomon could not find the true love which joins one man to *one* woman (Pro. 5. 15, 18, 19; 18. 22; 19. 13.). 10. "Whatsoever," *viz.*, in the service of God. This and last verse plainly is the language of Solomon, not of a sceptic, as HOL. would explain it. hand, &c.—(*Marg.* Lev. 12. 8; *Marg.* 1 Sam. 10. 7.). thy might—diligence (Deut. 6. 5; *Marg.* Jer. 48. 10.). no work... in the grave—(John. 9. 4; Rev. 14. 13.). "The soul's play-day is Satan's workday; the idler the man the busier the tempter." [SOUTH.] 11. This verse qualifies the sentiment, *v.* 7-9. Earthly "enjoyments," however lawful in their place (ch. 3. 1.), are to give way, when any work, to be done for God, requires it. Reverting to the sentiment ch. 8. 17,), we ought, therefore, not only to work God's work "with might" (*v.* 10,), but also with the feeling that the event is wholly "in God's hand" (*v.* 1.). race... not to the swift—(2 Sam. 18. 23;); spiritually Zeph. 3. 19; Rom. 9. 16,), nor... battle to... strong —(1 Sam. 17. 47; 2 Chr. 14. 9, 11, 15; Ps. 33. 16..). bread — livelihood. favour — of the great. chance—seemingly, really Providence. But as man cannot "find it out" (ch. ?. 11,), he needs "with all might" to use opportunities. Duties are ours; events, God's. 12. his time—*viz.*, of death (ch. 7. 15; Isa. 13. 22,). Hence the danger of delay in doing the work of God, as one knows not when his opportunity will end (*v.* 10.). evil net—fatal to them. The unexpected suddenness of the capture is the point of comparison. So the second coming of Jesus Christ, "as a snare" (Luke, 21. 35.). evil time—as an "evil net," fatal to them. 13. Rather, "I have seen wisdom of this kind also," *i.e.*, exhibited in the way which is described in what follows. [MAUR.] 14, 15. (2 Sam. 20. 16-22.). bulwarks —military works of besiegers. 15. poor—as to the temporal advantages of true wisdom, though it often saves others, it receives little reward from the world, which admires none save the rich and great. no man remembered— (Gen. 40. 23.). 16. Resuming the sentiment (ch. 7. 19; Pro. 21. 22; 24. 5.). poor man's wisdom is despised—not the poor man mentioned in *v.* 15; for *his* wisdom could not have saved the city, had "his words not been heard;" but poor men in general. So Paul (Acts, 27. 11.). 17. Though generally the poor wise man is not heard *v.* 16,), yet "the words of" wise men, when heard in quiet (when calmly given heed to, as in *v.* 15,), are more serviceable than," &c. ruleth—as the "great king" (*v.* 14.). Solomon reverts to "the rulers to their own hurt" ch. 8. 9.). 18. one sinner, &c. —(Josh. 7. 1, 11, 12.). Though wisdom excels folly (*v.* 16; ch. 7. 19,), yet **a** "little folly (equivalent to *sin*) can destroy much good." both in himself (ch. 10. 1; Jam. 2. 10) and in others. "Wisdom" must, from the antithesis to "sinner," mean religion. Thus typically, the "little city" may be applied to *the church* (Luke, 12. 32; Heb. 12. 22;); the great king to Satan (John, 12. 31;); the despised poor wise

man, Jesus Christ (Isa. 53. 2, 3; Mark, 6. 3; 2 Cor. 8. 9; Eph. 1, 7, 8; Col. 2. 3,).

CHAPTER X.

Ver. 1-20. 1. Following up ch. 9. 18. him that is in reputation—*ex. gr.*, David (2 Sam. 12. 14;); Solomon 1 Kl. 11. ;); Jehoshaphat (2 Chr. 18.; 19. 2;; Josiah (2 Chr. 35. 22.. The more delicate the perfume, the more easily spoiled is the ointment. Common oil is not so liable to injury. So the higher a man's religious character is, the more hurt is caused by a sinful folly in him. Bad savour is endurable in oil, but not in what professes to be, and is compounded by the perfumer ("apothecary") for, fragrance. "Flies" answer to "a little folly" (sin,), appropriately, being small (1 Cor. 5. 6;); also, "Beelzebub" means *prince of flies*. "Ointment" answers to "reputation" (ch. 7. 1; Gen. 34. 30. , The verbs are *plur.*, the noun *plur.*, implying that *each* of the flies causes the stinking savour. 2. Ch. 2. 14.). right—the right hand is more expert than the left. The godly wise is more on his guard than the foolish sinner, though at times he slip. Better a diamond with a flaw, than a pebble without one. 3. by the way—in his ordinary *course*; in his simplest acts (Pro. 6. 12-14.). That he "saith," *virtually*, "that he" himself, &c. (LXX.). But *Vulg.*, "He thinks that *every one* (*else* whom he meets) is a fool." 4. spirit—anger. yielding pacifieth—(Pro. 15. 1.). This explains "leave not thy place;" do not in a *resisting* spirit withdraw from thy post of duty (ch. 8. 3.). 5. as—rather, "*by reason of* an error." [MAUR. and HOL.] 6. rich—not in mere wealth, but in *wisdom*, as the antithesis to "folly" (for "foolish men") shows. So Heb. *rich*, equivalent to "liberal," in a good sense (Isa. 32. 5.). Mordecai and Haman (Esth. 3. 1, 2; 6. 6-11.). 7. servants upon horses — the worthless exalted to *dignity* (Jer. 17. 25;); and *vice versâ* (2 Sam. 15. 30.). 8. The fatal results to kings of such an unwise policy; the wrong done to others recoils on themselves (ch. 8. 9; ; they fall into the pit which they dug for others (Esth. 7. 10; Ps. 7. 15; Pro. 26. 27.). Breaking through the wise fences of their throne, they suffer unexpectedly themselves; as when one is stung by a serpent lurking in the stones of his neighbour's garden wall (Ps. 80. 12,), which he maliciously pulls down (Amos, 5. 19.). 9. removeth stones—*viz.*, of an ancient building. [WEISS.] His neighbour's landmarks. [HOL.] *Cuts out* from the quarry. [MAUR.] endangered—by the splinters, or by the head of the hatchet, flying back on himself. Pithy aphorisms are common in the East. The sense is: Violations of true wisdom recoil on the perpetrators. 10. iron ... blunt—in "cleaving wood" *v.* 9,), answering to the "fool set in dignity" (*v.* 6, , who wants sharpness. More force has then to be used in both cases ; but force without judgment "endangers" one's self. *Transl.*, "If one hath blunted his iron." [MAUR.] The preference of rash to judicious counsellors, which entailed the pushing of matters by *force*, proved to be the "hurt" of Rehoboam (1 Ki. 12.). wisdom is profitable to direct—to a prosperous issue. Instead of forcing matters by main "strength" to one's own hurt (ch. 9. 16, 18.). 11. A "serpent will bite" if "enchantment" is not used; "and a babbling calumniator is no better." Therefore, as one may escape a serpent by charms (Ps. 58. 4, 5,), in their heart while they live, and after that *they* go to the dead.

4 For to him that is joined to all the living there is hope: for a living dog is better than a dead lion.

5 For the living know that they shall die: but *the dead know not any thing, neither have they any more a reward; for the memory of them is forgotten.

6 Also their love, and their hatred, and their envy, is now perished; neither have they any more a portion for ever in any thing that is done under the sun.

7 ¶ Go thy way, eat thy bread with joy, and drink thy wine with a merry heart; for God now accepteth thy works.

8 Let thy garments be always white; and let thy head lack no ointment.

9 ² Live joyfully with the wife whom thou lovest all the days of the life of thy vanity, which he hath given thee under the sun, all the days of thy vanity: for that *is* thy portion in *this* life, and in thy labour which thou takest under the sun.

10 Whatsoever thy hand findeth to do, do *it* with thy might; for *there is* no work, nor device, nor knowledge, nor wisdom, in the grave, whither thou goest.

11 ¶ I returned, and saw under the sun, that the race *is* not to the swift, nor the battle to the strong, neither yet bread to the wise, nor yet riches to men of understanding, nor yet favour to men of skill; but time and chance happeneth to them all.

12 For ʰ man also knoweth not his time: as the fishes that are taken in an evil net, and as the birds that are caught in the snare; so *are* the sons of men ˢ snared in an evil time, when it falleth suddenly upon them.

13 ¶ This wisdom have I seen also under the sun, and it *seemed* great unto me:

14 *There* ʲ *was* a little city, and few men within it; and there came a great king against it, and besieged it, and built great bulwarks against it.

15 Now there was found in it a poor wise man, and he by his wisdom delivered the city; yet no man remembered that same poor man.

16 Then ʰ said I, Wisdom *is* better than strength: nevertheless ˡ the poor man's wisdom *is* despised, and his words are not heard.

17 The ᵐ words of wise *men are* heard in quiet more than the cry of him that ruleth among fools.

18 Wisdom *is* better than weapons of war: but ⁿ one sinner destroyeth much good.

CHAPTER X.

1 *Of wisdom and folly.* 16 *of riot,* 18 *slothfulness,* 19 *and money.* 20 *Men's thoughts of kings ought to be reverent.*

DEAD ¹ flies cause the ointment of the apothecary to send forth a stinking savour: *so doth* a little folly him that is in reputation for wisdom *and* honour.

2 A wise ᵃ man's heart *is* at his right hand; but a fool's heart at his left.

3 Yea also, when he that is a fool walketh by the way, ² his wisdom faileth *him,* ᵇ and he saith to every one *that* he *is* a fool.

4 If the spirit of the ruler rise up against thee, ᶜ leave not thy place; for ᵈ yielding pacifieth great offences.

5 There is an evil *which* I have seen under the sun, as an error *which* proceedeth ³ from the ruler:

6 ⁶ ⁱ⁵ ˡ ʸ is set ⁴ in great dignity, and the rich sit in low place.

7 I have seen servants ᵉ upon horses, and princes walking as servants upon the earth.

8 He that diggeth a pit shall fall into it; and whoso breaketh an hedge, a serpent shall bite him.

9 Whoso removeth stones shall be hurt therewith; *and* he that cleaveth wood shall be endangered thereby.

10 If the iron be blunt, and he do not whet the edge, then must he put to more strength: but wisdom *is* profitable to direct.

11 Surely the serpent will bite *f* without enchantment; and ᵍ a babbler is no better.

12 The words of a wise man's mouth *are* ᵍ gracious; but the lips of a fool will swallow up himself.

13 The beginning of the words of his mouth *is* foolishness; and the end of ⁷ his talk *is* mischievous madness.

14 A fool also ⁸ is full of words: a man cannot tell what shall be; and what shall be ᶠ after him, who can tell him?

15 The labour of the foolish wearieth every one of them, because he knoweth not how to go to the city.

16 ¶ Woe ʰ to thee, O land, when thy king *is* a child, and thy princes eat in the morning!

17 Blessed *art* thou, O land, when thy king *is* the son of nobles, and ⁱ thy princes eat in due season, for strength, and not for drunkenness!

18 ¶ By much slothfulness the building decayeth; and through idleness of the hands the house droppeth through.

19 ¶ A feast is made for laughter, and wine ᵒ maketh merry: but money answereth all *things.*

20 ¶ Curse *f* not the king, no not in thy ¹⁰ thought; and curse not the rich in thy bed-chamber; for ¹¹ a bird of the air shall carry the voice, and that which hath wings shall tell the matter.

CHAPTER XI.

1 *Directions for charity.* 7 *Death ought to be remembered in life,* 9 *and the day of judgment in the days of youth.*

CAST thy bread ¹ upon the waters: ᵃ for thou shalt find it after many days.

2 Give ᵇ a portion ᶜ to seven, and also to eight; ᵈ for thou knowest not what evil shall be upon the earth.

3 If the clouds be full of rain, they empty themselves upon the earth; and if the tree fall toward the south, or toward the north, in the place where the tree falleth, there it shall be.

4 He that observeth the wind shall not sow; and he that regardeth the clouds shall not reap.

5 As ᵉ thou knowest not what *is* the way of the spirit, *nor* how the bones *do grow* in the womb of her that is with child; even so thou knowest not the works of God who maketh all.

6 In the morning sow thy seed, and in the evening withhold not thine hand; for thou knowest not whether ² shall prosper, either this or that, or whether they both *shall be* alike good.

7 ¶ Truly the light *is* sweet, and a pleasant *thing it is* for the eyes to behold the sun;

8 But if a man live many years, *and* rejoice in them all, yet let him remember

so one may escape the sting of a calumniator by discretion (v. 12.). (HOL.] Thus, "without enchantment" answers to "not whet the edge" (v. 10.), both expressing, figuratively, want of judgment. MAUR. transl., "There is no gain to the enchanter" (Marg., "master of the tongue") from his enchantments, because the serpent bites before he can use them; hence the need of continual caution. Ver. 8-10, caution in acting; v. 11, and following verses, caution in speaking. 12. gracious--thereby he takes precaution against sudden injury (v. 11.). swallow up himself—Pro. 10. 8, 14, 21, 32; 12. 13; 15. 2; 22. 11.). 13. Illustrating the folly and injuriousness of the fool's words; last clause of v. 12. 14. full of words—(ch. 5. 2.). a man cannot tell what shall be—(ch. 3. 22; 6. 12; 8. 7; 11. 2; Pro. 27. 1.). If man, universally (including the wise man,), cannot foresee the future, much less can the fool; his "many words" are therefore futile. 15. labour...wearieth—(Isa. 55. 2; Hab. 2. 13.). knoweth not how to go to the city—proverb for ignorance of the most ordinary matters (v. 3;); spiritually, the heavenly city (Ps. 107. 7; Mat. 7. 13, 14.). MAUR. connects v. 15 with the following verses. The labour (vexation) caused by the foolish (injurious princes, v. 4-7,), harasses him who "knows not how to go to the city," to ingratiate himself with them there. E. V. is simpler. 16. a child — given to pleasures; behaves with childish levity. Not in years; for a nation may be happy under a young prince, as Josiah. eat in the morning—the usual time for dispensing justice in the East (Jer. 21. 12;); here, given to feasting (Isa. 5. 11; Acts. 2. 15.). 17. son of nobles—not merely in blood, but in virtue, the true nobility (Sol. Song 7. 1; Isa. 32. 5, 8.). in due season—(ch. 3. 1,), not until day has first been attended to. for strength—to refresh the body, not for revelry (included in "drunkenness."). 18. building—lit., the joining of the rafters, viz., the kingdom v. 16; Isa. 3. 6; Amos, 9. 11.). hands—(ch. 4. 5; Pro. 6. 10.). droppeth—by neglect to repair the roof in time, the rain gets through. 19. Referring to v. 18. Instead of repairing the breaches in the commonwealth (equivalent to "building,"), the princes "make a feast for laughter (ch. 10,), and wine maketh their life glad (Ps. 104. 15,), and (but) money supplieth (answereth their wishes by supplying) all things," i.e., they take bribes to support their extravagance; and hence arise the wrongs that are perpetrated (v. 5, 6; ch. 3. 16; Isa. 1. 23; 5. 23,). MAUR. takes "all things" of the wrongs to which princes are instigated by "money;" ex. gr., the heavy taxes, which were the occasion of Rehoboam losing ten tribes (1 Ki. 12. 4, &c.). 20. thought—lit., consciousness. rich—the great. The language, as applied to earthly princes knowing the "thought" is figurative. But it literally holds good of the King of kings (Ps. 139.,), whose consciousness of every evil thought we should ever realise. bed-chamber—the most secret place (2 Ki. 6. 12.). bird of the air, &c.—proverbial (cf. Hab. 2. 11; Luke, 19. 40;); in a way as marvellous and rapid, as if birds or some winged messenger carried to the king information of the curse so uttered. In the East superhuman sagacity was attributed to birds (see my note, Job 28. 21; hence the proverb.).

CHAPTER XI.

Ver. 1-10. 1. Ver. 2 shows that charity is here inculcated. bread—bread-corn. As in the Lord's prayer, all things needful for the body and soul. Solomon reverts to the sentiment ch. 9. 10.. waters—image from the custom of sowing seed by casting it from boats into the overflowing waters of the Nile, or in any marshy ground. When the waters receded, the grain in the alluvial soil sprang up (Isa. 32. 20.). "Waters" express multitudes, so v. 2; Rev. 17. 15; also the seemingly hopeless character of the recipients of the charity; but it shall prove at last to have been not thrown away (Isa. 40. 4.). 2. portion —of thy bread. seven—the perfect number. eight—even to more than seven, i.e., to many (so "waters," v. 1.), nay, even to very many in need (Job, 5. 19; Mic. 5. 5,). evil—the day may be near, when you will need the help of those whom you have bound to you by kindnesses (Luke, 16. 9.). The very argument which covetous men use against liberality, viz., that bad times may come, the wise man uses for it. 3. clouds—answering to "evil" (v. 2,, meaning, When the times of evil are fully ripe, evil must come; and speculations about it before hand, so as to prevent one sowing seed of liberality, are vain v. 4.). tree—once that the storm uproots it, it lies either northward, or southward, according as it fell. So man's character is unchangeable, whether for hell or heaven, once that death overtakes him (Rev. 22. 11, 14, 15.). Now is his time for liberality, before the evil days come (ch. 12. 1,). 4. Therefore sow thy charity in faith, without hesitancy or speculation as to results, because they may not seem promising (ch. 9. 10.). So in v. 1, man is told to "cast his bread-corn" on the seemingly unpromising "waters" (Ps. 126. 5. 6.). The farmer would get on badly, who, instead of sowing and reaping, spent his time in watching the wind and clouds. 5. spirit—how the soul animates the body. Thus the transition to the formation of the body "in the womb" is more natural, than if with MAUR. we transl. it "wind" (ch. 1. 6; John, 3. 8.). bones ...grow —(Job, 10. 8, 9; Ps. 139. 15. 16.). knowest not the works of God—(ch. 3. 11; 8. 17; 9. 12.). 6. morning...evening—early and late; when young and when old; in sunshine and under clouds. seed — of godly works (Hos. 10. 12; 2 Cor. 9. 10; Gal. 6. 7.). prosper—(Isa. 55. 10, 11.). both...alike—both the unpromising and the promising sowing may bear good fruit in others: certainly they shall to the faithful sower. 7. light—of life (ch. 7. 11; Ps. 49. 19.). Life is enjoyable, especially to the godly. 8. But whilst man thankfully enjoys life, "let him remember" it will not last for ever. The "many days of darkness," i.e., the unseen world (Job, 10. 21, 22; Ps. 88. 12,). also days of "evil" in this world (v. 2) are coming; therefore sow the good seed whilst life and good days last, which are not too long for accomplishing life's duties. All that cometh—i.e., All that followeth in the evil and dark days is vain, as far as work for God is concerned (ch. 9. 10.). 9. Rejoice—Not advice, but warning. So 1 Ki. 22. 15, is irony; if thou dost rejoice (carnally, ch. 2. 2; 7. 2, not moderately, as ch. 5. 18,), &c., then "know" that ...God will bring thee into judgment" ch. 3. 17; 12. 14.). youth ... youth—distinct Heb. words. adolescence or boyhood (before v. 13,), and full-grown youth. It marks the gradual progress in self-indulgence, to which the young especially are prone; they see the roses, but do not discover the thorns, until the days of darkness; for they shall be many. All that cometh is vanity.

9 ¶ Rejoice, O young man, in thy youth, and let thy heart cheer thee in the days of thy youth, and walk in the ways of thine heart, and in the sight of thine eyes: but know thou, that for all these things God will bring thee into judgment.

10 Therefore remove sorrow from thy heart, and put away evil from thy flesh: for childhood and youth are vanity.

CHAPTER XII.

1 *The Creator to be remembered in the days of youth, and must not be deferred.* 8 *The Preacher's care to edify.* 13 *The fear of God the chief concern of man.*

REMEMBER now thy Creator in the days of thy youth, while the evil days come not, nor the years draw nigh, when thou shalt say, I have no pleasure in them;

2 While the sun, or the light, or the moon, or the stars, be not darkened, nor the clouds return after the rain:

3 In the day when the keepers of the house shall tremble, and the strong men shall bow themselves, and the grinders cease, because they are few, and those that look out of the windows be darkened,

4 And the doors shall be shut in the streets, when the sound of the grinding is low, and he shall rise up at the voice of the bird, and all the daughters of music shall be brought low;

5 Also when they shall be afraid of that which is high, and fears shall be in the

way, and the almond tree shall flourish, and the grasshopper shall be a burden, and desire shall fail; because man goeth to his long home; and the mourners go about the streets:

6 Or ever the silver cord be loosed, or the golden bowl be broken, or the pitcher be broken at the fountain, or the wheel broken at the cistern.

7 Then shall the dust return to the earth as it was; and the spirit shall return unto God who gave it.

8 ¶ Vanity of vanities, saith the Preacher; all is vanity.

9 And moreover, because the Preacher was wise, he still taught the people knowledge; yea, he gave good heed, and sought out, and set in order many proverbs.

10 The Preacher sought to find out acceptable words; and that which was written was upright, even words of truth.

11 The words of the wise are as goads, and as nails fastened by the masters of assemblies, which are given from one shepherd.

12 And further, by these, my son, be admonished: of making many books there is no end; and much study is a weariness of the flesh.

13 ¶ Let us hear the conclusion of the whole matter: Fear God, and keep his commandments: for this is the whole duty of man.

14 For God shall bring every work into judgment, with every secret thing, whether it be good, or whether it be evil.

THE
SONG OF SOLOMON.

CHAPTER I.

1 *The church's love to Christ:* 5 *she confesses her deformity.* 7 *and prays to be directed to his flock.* 8 *Christ directs her to the shepherds' tents;* 9 *and showing his love to her,* 11 *gives her gracious promises.* 12 *The church and Christ congratulate each other.*

THE Song of songs, which is Solomon's.

2 Let him kiss me with the kisses of his mouth: for thy love is better than wine.

3 Because of the savour of thy good ointments thy name is as ointment poured forth, therefore do the virgins love thee.

4 Draw me, we will run after thee. The King hath brought me into his chambers: we will be glad and rejoice in thee: we will remember thy love more than wine: the upright love thee.

5 ¶ I am black, but comely, O ye daughters of Jerusalem, as the tents of Kedar, as the curtains of Solomon.

6 Look not upon me, because I am black, because the sun hath looked upon me: my mother's children were angry with me; they made me the keeper of the vineyards; but mine own vineyard have I not kept.

7 Tell me, O thou whom my soul loveth, where thou feedest, where thou makest thy flock to rest at noon: for why should I be as one that turneth aside by the flocks of thy companions?

8 ¶ If thou know not, O thou fairest

among women, go thy way forth by the footsteps of the flock, and feed thy kids beside the shepherds' tents.

9 I have compared thee, O my love, to a company of horses in Pharaoh's chariots.

10 Thy cheeks are comely with rows of jewels, thy neck with chains of gold.

11 We will make thee borders of gold, with studs of silver.

12 ¶ While the King sitteth at his table, my spikenard sendeth forth the smell thereof.

13 A bundle of myrrh is my well-beloved unto me; he shall lie all night betwixt my breasts.

14 My beloved is unto me as a cluster of camphire in the vineyards of En-gedi.

15 Behold, thou art fair, my love; behold, thou art fair; thou hast doves' eyes.

16 Behold, thou art fair, my beloved, yea, pleasant: also our bed is green.

17 The beams of our house are cedar, and our rafters of fir.

CHAPTER II.

1 *Mutual love of Christ and his church.* 8 *Her hope,* 10 *and calling.* 14 *Christ's care of her.* 16 *Her profession, faith, and hope.*

I AM the rose of Sharon, and the lily of the valleys.

2 As the lily among thorns, so is my love among the daughters.

3 As the apple tree among the trees of the

pierced by them. Religion will cost self-denial, but the want of it infinitely more (Luke, 14. 28.). 10. sorrow—*i.e., the lusts* that end in "sorrow," opposed to "rejoice," and "heart cheer thee" *v.* 9;); *Marg.*, "anger," *i.e.*, all "ways of thine heart:" "remove," &c. is thus opposed to "walk in." &c. (*v.* 9.). flesh—the bodily organ by which the sensual *thoughts* of the "heart" are embodied in *acts.* can da ot—rather, *boyhood;* the same *Heb.* word as the first, "youth" in *v.* 9. A motive for self-restraint; the time is coming when the vigour of youth, on which thou reliest, will seem vain, except in so far as it has been given to God ch. 12. 1.). youth—*lit., the dawn* of thy days.

CHAPTER XII.

Ver. 1-14. 1. As ch. 11. 9, 10, showed what youths are to shun, so this verse shows what they are to follow. Creator—" Remember" that thou art not thine own, but God's property; for He has *created* thee (Ps. 100. 3.). Therefore serve him with thy "all" ;Mark, 12. 30), and with thy *best* days, not with the dregs of them (Pro. 8. 17; 22. 6; Jer. 3. 4; Lam. 3. 27.). The *Heb.* is *Creators*, *plur.*, implying the plurality of persons, as in Gen. 1. 26; so *Heb., Makers* Isa. 54. 5.). while ... no:—*i.e.*, *before* that Pro. 8. 26; the evil days come, *viz.*, calamity and old age, when one can no longer serve God, as in youth (ch. 11. 2, 8.). no pleasure—of a sensual kind 2 Sam. 19. 35; Ps. 90. 10.). Pleasure in God continues to the godly old (Isa. 46. 4.). 2. illustrating "the evil days" (Jer. 13. 16.). "Light," "sun," &c., express *prosperity;* "darkness," *pain* and *calamity* (Isa. 13. 10; 30. 26.). clouds ... after ... rain—after rain sunshine comfort might be looked for, but only a brief glimpse of it is given, and the gloomy clouds pains return. 3. keep rs of tne house—*viz., the hands and arms* which *protected* the body, as guards do a palace Gen. 49. 24; Job, 4. 19; 2 Cor. 5, 1.), are now palsied. s rong men ... bow—(Jud. 16. 25, 30.). Like supporting pillars, *the feet and knees* (Sol. Song 5. 15;); the *strongest* members (Ps. 147. 10.;. grinders—the molar teeth. cease—are idle. those that look out of tne windows—the eyes; the powers of vision, looking out from beneath the eyelids, which open and shut like the casement of a window. 4. doors—*the lips,* which are closely *shut* together as *doors*, by old men in eating; for, if they did not do so, the food would drop out (Job, 41. 14; Ps. 141. 3; Mic. 7. 5.). in the streets—*i.e.*, toward the street, "the *outer* doors." [MAUR. and WEISS.] sound of ... grinding—the teeth being almost gone, and the lips "shut" in eating, the sound of mastication is scarcely heard. tne bird—the cock. In the East all mostly rise with the dawn. But the old are glad to rise from their sleepless couch, or painful slumbers still earlier, *viz.*, when the cock crows, before dawn (Job, 7. 4.). [HOL.] The least noise awakens them. [WEISS.] daughters of music—the organs that produce and that enjoy music; *the voice* and *ear.* 5. that which is high—the old a. e afraid of ascending a *hill.* fears ... in the way—even on the level *highway* they are full of fears of falling, &c. almond ... flourish—in the East the hair is mostly dark. The *white head* of the old among the dark haired is like *an almond tree*, with its white blossoms, among the dark trees around. [HOL.]· The almond tree *flowers* on a leafless stock in *winter*

(answering to *old age*, in which all the powers are dormant,), whilst the other trees are flowerless. GES. takes the *Heb* for *flourishes* fro n a different root, *cast off;* when the old man *loses* his gray hairs, as the almond tree *casts* its white flowers. grasshopper—the dry, shrivelled, old man, his backbone sticking out, his knees projecting forwards, his arms backwards, his head down, and the apophyses enlarged, is like that insect. Hence arose the fable, that Tithonus in very old age was changed into a grasshopper. [PARKH.] "The locust *raises itself* to fly:" the old man about to leave the body is like a locust when it is assuming its winged form, and is about to fly. [MAUR.] a burden—*viz.*, to himself. desire shall fail—satisfaction shall be abolished. For *desire*, *Vulg.* has "the caper tree," provocative of lust; not so well. long home—(Job, 16. 22; 17. 13.). mourners—Jer. 9. 17-20,), hired for the occasion (Mat. 9. 23.). 6. A double image to represent *death*, as *v.* 1-5, *old age.* (1.) A *lamp* of frail material, but *gilded* over, often in the East hung from roofs by a *cord* of silk and *silver* interwoven; as the lamp is dashed down and broken, when the cord breaks, so man at death: "the golden bowl" of the lamp answers to *the skull,* which, from the vital preciousness of its contents, may be called "golden;" "the silver cord" is *the spinal marrow*, which is white and precious as silver, and is attached to the brain. 2.) A *fountain*, from which water is drawn by *a pitcher* let down by a rope wound round *a wheel;* as, when the pitcher and wheel are broken, water can no more be drawn, so life ceases when the vital energies are gone. The "fountain" *may* mean the right ventricle of the heart; the "cistern," the left; the pitcher, the veins; the wheel, the aorta, or great artery. [SMITH.] The circulation of the blood, whether known or not to Solomon, seems to be implied in the language put by the Holy Ghost into his mouth. This gloomy picture of old age applies to those who have not "remembered their Creator in youth." They have none of the consolations of God, which they might have obtained in youth; it is now too late to seek them. A good old age is a blessing to the godly (Gen. 15. 15; Job, 5. 26; Pro. 16. 31; 20. 29.). 7. dust—the dust-formed body. spirit—surviving the body; implying its immortality (ch. 3, 11.). 8-12. A summ ary of the first part. 13, 14. A summary of the second. Vanity, &c.—Resumption of the sentiment with which the book began (ch. 1. 2; 1 John, 2. 17.). 9. g ve good heed—*lit.*, *he weighed.* The "teaching the people" seems to have been *oral;* the "proverbs," *in writing.* There must then have been auditories *assembled to hear* the inspired *wisdom of the Preacher.* See the explanation of "Koheleth" in the *Intr.* and ch. 1. 1 Ki. 4. 34.). that which was written, &c.—rather, (he sought) "*to write down* uprightly (or 'aright)' words of truth." [HOL. and WEISS.] "Acceptable" means an agreeable style; "uprightly,.. truth," correct sentiment. 11. goads—piercing deeply into the mind (Acts, 2. 37; 9. 5; Heb. 4. 12;); evidently *inspired words*, as the end of the verse proves. fas ened—rather, on account of the *Heb.* genders, (The words) "are fastened (in the memory, like nails. [HOL.] masters f assemb.ies—rather, "the masters of collections (*i.e.*, collectors of inspired sayings, Pro, 25. 1) are given ('have published them as proceeding' [Hol.]) from one Shepherd," viz., the Spirit of Jesus Christ [Weiss] Fz. 37. 24.). However, the mention of "goads" favours the E. V., "masters of assemblies," viz., under-shepherds, inspired by the Chief Shepherd (1 Pet. 5. 2-4.). SCHMIDT transl., "The masters of assemblies are fastened (made sure) as nails," so Isa. 22. 23. 12. (Note, ch. 1, 18,). many books—of mere human composition, opposed to "by these;" these inspired writings are the only sure source of "admonition." (ever much) study—in mere human books, wearies the body, without solidly profiting the soul. 13. The grand inference of the whole book. Fear God—The antidote to following creature-idols, and "vanities,' whether self-righteous:c; (ch. 7. 16, 18,), or wicked oppression and other evils (ch. 8. 12, 13,), or mad mirth (ch. 2. 2; 7. 2-5,), or self mortifying avarice (ch. 8. 13, 17,), or youth spent without God (ch. 11. 9; 12. 1,). t. is is the whole duty of man—lit., this is the whole man, the full ideal of man, as originally contemplated, realised wholly by Jesus Christ alone; and, through Him, by saints now in part, hereafter perfectly 1 John. 3. 22-24; Rev. 22. 14.). 14. The future judgment is the test of what is "vanity,' what solid, as regards the chief good, the grand subject of the book.

THE SONG OF SOLOMON.

INTRODUCTION.

THE Song of Solomon, called in the Vulgate and LXX., "The Song of songs," from the opening words. This title denotes its superior excellence, according to the Hebrew idiom: so holy of holies, equivalent to most holy (Ex. 29. 37;); the heaven of heavens, equivalent to the highest heaven (Deut. 10, 14,). It is one of the five volumes (megilloth,) placed immediately after the Pentateuch in MSS. of the Jewish scriptures. It is also fourth of the Hagiographa ("Cetubim" writings,), or the third division of the O. T., the other two being the Law and the Prophets. The Jewish enumeration of the Cetubim is Psalms, Proverbs, Job, Canticles, Ruth, Lamentations, Ecclesiastes, Esther, Daniel, Ezra (including Nehemiah,), and Chronicles. Its canonicity is certain; it is found in all Hebrew MSS. of scripture; also in the Greek LXX.; in the catalogues of Melito, bishop of Sardis, A.D. 170 (Euseb., H.E. iv. 26,), and of others of the ancient Church.

Origen and Jerome tell us, that the Jews forbade it to be read by any until he was thirty years old. It certainly needs a degree of spiritual maturity to enter aright into the holy mystery of love which it allegorically sets forth. To such as have attained this maturity, of whatever age they be, the Song of songs is one of the most edifying of the sacred writings. Rosenmuller justly says, The sudden transitions of the bride from the court to the grove are inexplicable, on the supposition that it describes merely human love. Had it been the latter, it would have been positively objectionable, and never would have been inserted in the holy canon. The allusion to "Pharaoh's chariots" (ch. 1. 9,), has been made a ground for conjecturing, that the love of Solomon and Pharaoh's daughter is the subject of the Song. But this passage alludes to a remarkable event in the history of the O. T. Church, the deliverance from the hosts and chariots of Pharaoh at the Red Sea. (See however note there.) The other allusions are quite opposed to the notion; the bride is represented at times as a shepherdess (ch. 1. 7,), "an abomination to the Egyptians" (Gen. 46. 34; so also ch. 1. 6; 3. 4; 4. 8; 5. 7,), are at variance with it. The Christian fathers, Origen and Theodoret, compared the teaching of Solomon to a ladder with three steps; Ecclesiastes, natural (the nature of sensible things, vain;); Proverbs, moral; Canticles, mystical (figuring the union of Christ and the Church.). The Jews compared Proverbs to the outer court of Solomon's temple, Ecclesiastes to the holy place, and Canticles to the holy of holies. Understood allegorically, the Song is cleared of all difficulty. "Shulamith' (ch. 6. 13,), the bride is thus an appropriate name, Daughter of Peace, being the feminine of Solomon, equivalent to the Prince of Peace. She by turns is a vinedresser, shepherdess, midnight inquirer, and prince's consort and daughter, and He a suppliant drenched with night-dews, and a king in His palace, in harmony with the various relations of the Church and Christ. As Ecclesiastes set forth the vanity of love of the creature, Canticles sets forth the fulness of the love which joins believers and the Saviour. The entire economy of salvation, says Harris, aims at restoring to the world the lost spirit of love. God is love, and Christ is the embodiment of the love of God. As the other books of Scripture present severally their own aspects of divine truth, so Canticles furnishes the believer with language of holy love, wherewith his heart can commune with his Lord; and portrays the intensity of Christ's love to him; the affection of love was created in man to be a transcript of the divine love, and the Song clothes the latter in words; were it not for this, we should be at a loss for language, having the divine warrant, wherewith to express, without presumption, the fervour of the love between Christ and us. The image of a bride, a bridegroom, and a marriage, to represent this spiritual union, has the sanction of Scripture throughout: nay, the spiritual union was the original fact in the mind of God, of which marriage is the transcript (Isa. 54. 5; 62. 5; Jer. 3. 1, &c.; Ez. 16. and 23.; Mat. 9. 15; 22. 2; 25. 1, &c.; John, 3. 29; 2 Cor. 11. 2; Eph. 5. 23 32, where Paul does not go from the marriage relation to the union of Christ and the Church, as if the former were the first; but comes down from the latter as the first and best recognised fact, on which the relation of marriage is based; Rev. 19. 7; 21. 2; 22. 17.). Above all, the Song seems to correspond to, and form a trilogy with, the 45th and 72d Psalms, which contain the same imagery: just as Ps. 37., answers to Proverbs; and Ps. 39. and 73. to Job. Love to Christ is the strongest, as it is the purest, of human passions, and therefore needs the strongest language to express it: to the pure in heart the phraseology, drawn from the rich imagery of Orientals poetry, will not only appear not indelicate or exaggerated, but even below the reality. A single emblem is a type: the actual rites, incidents, and persons of the O. T. were appointed types of truths afterwards to be revealed. But the allegory is a continued metaphor in which the circumstances are palpably often purely imagery, whilst the thing signified is altogether real. The clew to the meaning of the Song is not to be looked for in the allegory itself, but in other parts of Scripture. "It lies in the casket of revelation an exquisite gem, engraved with emblematical characters, with nothing literal thereon to break the consistency of their beauty." [*Bur.*] This accounts for the name of God not occurring in it. Whereas in the *parable* the writer narrates, in the *allegory* he never does so. The Song throughout consists of immediate addresses either of Christ to the soul, or of the soul to Christ. " The experimental knowledge of Christ's loveliness, and the believer's love, is the best commentary on the whole of this allegorical Song." [*Leighton*.] Like the curiously wrought Oriental lamps, which do not reveal the beauty of their transparent emblems until lighted up within, so the types and allegories of Scripture, " the lantern to our path," need the inner light of the *Holy Spirit* of Jesus to reveal their significance. The details of the allegory are not to be too minutely pressed. In the Song, with an Oriental profusion of imagery, numbers of lovely sensible objects are aggregated, not strictly congruous, but portraying jointly by their very diversity the thousand various and seemingly opposite beauties which meet together in Christ.

The unity of subject throughout, and the recurrence of the same expressions (ch. 2. 6, 7; 3. 5; 5. 3, 4; 2. 16. and 6. 3; 7. 10; 3. 6; 6. 10; 6. 5) prove the unity of the poem, in opposition to those who make it consist of a number of separate erotic songs. The sudden transitions, *ex. gr.*, from the midnight knocking at a humble cottage to a glorious description of the King, accord with the alternations in the believer's experience. However various the divisions assigned be, most commentators have observed four breaks (whatever more they have imagined.), followed by four abrupt beginnings (ch. 2. 7; 3. 5; 5. 1; 8. 4). Thus there result five parts, all alike ending in full repose and refreshment. We read (1 Ki. 4. 32) that Solomon's songs were " a thousand and *five*." The odd number *five* added over the complete *thousand*, makes it not unlikely that the "five" refers to the Song of songs, consisting of five parts.

It answers to the idyllic poetry of other nations. The Jews explain it of the union of Jehovah and ancient Israel; the allusions to the *temple* and the *wilderness* accord with this; some Christians, of Christ and the Church; others, of Christ and the individual believer. All these are true; for the Church is one in all ages, the ancient typifying the modern Church, and its history answering to that of each individual soul in it. Jesus " sees all, as if that all were one, loves one, as if that one were al .' "The time suited the manner of this revelation; because types and allegories belonged to the old dispensation, which reached its ripeness under Solomon, when the temple was built." [*M. Stuart.*] " The daughter of Zion at that time was openly married to Jehovah;" for it is thenceforth that the prophets, in reproving Israel's subsequent sin, speak of it as a breach of her marriage covenant. The songs heretofore sung by her were the preparatory hymns of her childhood: " the last and crowning ' Song of songs' was prepared for the now mature maiden against the day of her marriage to the King of kings." [*Origen.*] Solomon was peculiarly fitted to clothe this holy mystery with the lovely natural imagery with which the Song abounds; for " he spake of trees, from the cedar in Lebanon, even unto the hyssop that springeth out of the wall" (1 Ki, 4. 33.). A higher qualification was his knowledge of the eternal Wisdom or Word of God (Pro. 8.), the heavenly bridegroom, David, his father, had prepared the way, in Ps. 45. and 72.; the son perfected the allegory. It seems to have been written in early lite, long before his declension; for after it a song of holy gladness would hardly be appropriate. It was the song of his first love, in the kindness of his youthful espousals to Jehovah. Like other inspired books, its sense is not to be restricted to that local and temporary one in which the writer may have understood it: it extends to all ages, and shadows forth everlasting truth (1 Pet. 1. 11, 12; 2 Pet. 1. 20, 21.).

"O that I knew how all thy lights combine, and the configurations of their glorie."—*Herbert.*

Three notes of time occur. [*M. Stuart.*] (1.) The Jewish Church speaks of the Gentile Church (ch. 8. 8.), towards the end; (2.) Christ speaks to the apostles (ch. 5. 1,), in the middle; (3.) The Church speaks of the coming of Christ (ch. 1. 2,), at the beginning. Thus we have, in direct order, Christ about to come, and the cry for the advent; Christ finishing his work on earth, and the last supper; Christ ascended, and the call of the Gentiles. In another aspect, we have: (1.) In the individual soul, the longing for the manifestation of Christ to it, and the various alternations in its exper ence (ch. 1. 2, 4; 2. 8; 3. 1, 4, 6, 7) of His manifestation; (2.) The abundant enjoyment of His sensible consolations, which is soon withdrawn through the bride's carelessness (ch. 5. 1-3, &c.), and her longings after Him, and reconciliation (ch. 5. 8-16; 6. 3, &c.; 7. 1, &c.); (3.) Effects of Christ's manifestation on the believer, viz., assurance, labours of love, anxiety for the salvation of the impenitent, eagerness for the Lord's second coming (ch. 7. 10, 12; 8, 8-10, 14.).

CHAPTER I.

Ver. 1-17. CANTICLE I. — THE BRIDE SEARCHING FOR AND FINDING THE KING. —Ch. i. 2 – ii. 7. 1. Song of songs – The most excellent of all songs, *Heb.* idiom (Ex. 2). 37; Deut. 10. 14.). A foretaste on earth of the "new song" to be sung in glory Rev. 5. 9; 14. 3; 15. 2-4.. Solomon's —" King of Israel," or "Jerusalem" is not added, as in the opening of Proverbs and Ecclesiastes, not because Solomon had not yet ascended the throne [M. STUART], but because his personality is hid under that of Christ, the true Solomon (equivalent to *Prince of Peace*,). The earthly Solomon is not introduced, which would break the consistency of the allegory. Though the bride bears the chief part, the Song throughout is not her's, but that of her "Solomon." He animates her. He and she, the Head and the members, form but one Christ.[A. NEWTON.] Aaron prefigured Him as priest; Moses, as prophet; David,

as a suffering king; Solomon, as the triumphant prince of peace. The camp in the wilderness represents the Church in the world; the peaceful reign of Solomon, after all enemies had been subdued, represents the Church in heaven, of which joy the Song gives a foretaste. 2. Him — abruptly. She names him not, as is natural to one whose heart is full of some much desired friend: so Mary Magdalene at the sepulchre (John, 20. 15,), as if every one must know whom she means, the One chief object of her desire (Ps. 73. 25; Mat. 13. 44-46; Phil. 3. 7, 8.). kiss—the token of peace from the Prince of Peace (Luke, 15. 20; Peace.. "our Peace" (Ps. 85. 10; Col. 1. 21; Eph 2. 14.). of his mouth—marking the tenderest affection. For a king to permit his hands, or even garment, to be kissed, was counted a great honour; but that he should himself kiss another *with his mouth* is the greatest honour. God had in times past spoken by *the mouth* of His prophets, who hath declared the wood, so *is* my beloved among the sons. ¹ I sat down under his shadow with great delight, * and his fruit *was* sweet to my ᵃ taste.

4 He brought me to the ᵇ banqueting house, and his banner over me *was* love.

5 Stay me with flagons, ᶜ comfort me with apples: for I am sick of love.

6 His ᵇ left hand *is* under my head, and his right hand doth embrace me.

7 ⁵ I charge you, O ye daughters of Jerusalem, by the roes, and by the hinds of the field, that ye stir not up, nor awake *my* love, till he please.

8 ¶ The ᵉ voice of my beloved! behold, he cometh leaping upon the mountains, skipping upon the hills.

9 My beloved is like a roe or a young hart: behold, he standeth behind our wall, he looketh forth at the windows, ᵍ showing himself through the lattice.

10 My beloved spake, and said unto me, Rise up, my love, my fair one, and come away.

11 For, lo, the winter is past, the rain is over and gone:

12 The flowers appear on the earth; the time of the singing *of birds* is come, and the voice of the turtle is heard in our land;

13 The fig tree putteth forth her green figs, and the vines *with* the tender grape give a *good* smell. Arise, my love, my fair one, and come away.

14 O my dove, *that art* in the clefts of the rock, in the secret *places* of the stairs, let me see thy countenance, ᵈ let me hear thy voice; for sweet *is* thy voice, and thy countenance *is* comely.

15 Take us * the foxes, the little foxes, that spoil the vines: for our vines *have* tender grapes.

16 ¶ My ᶠ beloved *is* mine, and I am his: he feedeth among the lilies.

17 Until ᵍ the day break, and the shadows flee away, turn, my beloved, and be thou like ʰ a roe or a young hart upon the mountains ⁷ of Bether.

CHAPTER III.

1 *The church's fight and victory in temptation.* 6 *She glories in Christ.*

BY ᵃ night on my bed I sought him whom my soul loveth: I sought him, but I found him not.

2 I will rise now, and go about the city in the streets, and in the broad ways I will seek him whom my soul loveth: I sought him, but I found him not.

3 The ᵇ watchmen that go about the city found me: *to whom I said*, Saw ye him whom my soul loveth?

4 *It was* but ᶜ a little that I passed from them, but I found him whom my soul loveth: I ᵈ held him, and would not let him go, until I had brought him into my mother's house, and into the chamber of her that conceived me.

5 I ᵉ charge you, O ye daughters of Jerusalem, by the roes, and by the hinds of the field, that ye stir not up, nor awake *my* love, till he please.

6 ¶ Who ᶠ *is* this that cometh out of the wilderness like pillars of smoke, perfumed with myrrh and frankincense, with all powders of the merchant?

7 Behold his bed, which *is* Solomon's; threescore valiant men *are* about it, of the valiant of Israel.

8 They all hold swords, *being* expert in war: every man *hath* his sword upon his thigh, because of fear in the night.

9 King Solomon made himself ¹ a chariot of the wood of Lebanon.

10 He made the pillars thereof *of* silver, the bottom thereof *of* gold, the covering of it *of* purple, the midst thereof being paved *with* love, for the daughters of Jerusalem.

11 Go forth, O ye daughters of Zion, and behold king Solomon with the crown wherewith his mother crowned him in the ᵍ day of his espousals, and in the day of the gladness of his heart.

CHAPTER IV.

1 *Christ sets forth the graces of the church:* 8 *he shows his love to her.* 16 *She prays to be made fit for his presence.*

BEHOLD, ᵃ thou art fair, my love; behold, thou *art* fair; thou *hast* doves' eyes within thy locks: thy hair *is* as ᵇ a flock of goats, ¹ that appear from mount Gilead.

2 Thy ᶜ teeth *are* like a flock *of sheep that are even* shorn, which came up from the washing; whereof every one bear twins, and none *is* barren among them.

3 Thy lips *are* like a thread of scarlet, and thy speech *is* comely; thy temples *are* like a piece of a pomegranate within thy locks.

4 Thy ᵈ neck *is* like the tower of David builded ᵉ for an armoury, whereon there hang a thousand bucklers, all shields of mighty men.

5 Thy ᶠ two breasts *are* like two young roes that are twins, which feed among the lilies.

6 Until the day ² break, and the shadows flee away, I will get me to the mountain of myrrh, and to the hill of frankincense.

7 Thou ᵍ *art* all fair, my love; *there is* no spot in thee.

8 ¶ Come with me from Lebanon, *my* spouse, with me from Lebanon: look from the top of Amana, from the top of Shenir and ʰ Hermon, from the lions' dens, from the mountains of the leopards.

9 Thou hast ³ ravished my heart, my sister, *my* spouse; thou hast ravished my heart with one of thine eyes, with one chain of thy neck.

10 How fair is thy love, my sister, *my* spouse! how much better is thy love than wine! and the smell of thine ointments than all spices!

11 Thy lips, O *my* spouse, drop as the honey-comb: ʲ honey and milk are under thy tongue; and the smell of thy garments is ᵏ like the smell of Lebanon.

12 A ˡ garden ⁴ inclosed *is* my sister, *my* spouse; a spring shut up, a fountain sealed.

13 Thy plants *are* an orchard of pomegranates, with pleasant fruits; ᵇ camphire, with spikenard,

14 Spikenard and saffron; calamus and cinnamon, with all trees of frankincense; myrrh and aloes, with all the chief spices:

15 A fountain of gardens, a well of ᵐ living waters, and streams from Lebanon.

16 ¶ Awake, O north wind; and come, thou south; blow upon my garden, *that* the ⁿ spices thereof may flow out. ᵒ Let my beloved come into his garden, and eat his pleasant fruits.

Church's betrothal; the bride now longs for contact with *the mouth of the Bridegroom Himself* (Job, 23. 12; Luke, 4. 22; Heb. 1. 1, 2.). True of the Church before the first advent, longing for "the hope of Israel," "the desire of all nations;" also the awakened soul longing for the kiss of *reconciliation;* and further, the kiss that is the token of the *marriage contract* (Hos. 2. 19, 20,), and of *friendship* (1 Sam. 20. 41; John, 14. 21; 15. 15.). thy love—*Heb., loves,* viz., tokens of love, loving blandishments. wine—which makes glad "the heavy heart" of one ready to perish, so that he "remembers his misery no more" (Pro. 31. 6, 7.). So, in a "better" sense, Christ's love (Hab. 3. 17, 18.). He gives the same praise to the bride's love, with the emphatic addition, "How much" ch. 4. 10.). Wine was created by His first miracle (John, 2.) and was the pledge given of his love at the last supper. The spiritual wine is His blood and His Spirit, the "new" and better wine of the kingdom (Math. 26. 29,), which we can never drink to "excess," as the other (Eph. 5. 18; cf. l's. 23. 5; Isa. 55. 1.). 3. Rather, "As regards the savour of thy ointments, it is good." [MAUR.] In ch. 4. 10, 11, the Bridegroom reciprocates the praise of the bride in the same terms. thy name — Christ's *character 2nd office* as the "Anointed" (Isa. 9. 6; 61. 1,), as "the savour of ointments" is the graces that surround His *person* (Ps. 45. 7, 8.). Eccl. 7. 1, in its fullest sense, applies to Him. The holy anointing oil of the High Priest, which it was death for any one else to make (so Acts, 4. 12,, implies the exclusive preciousness of Messiah's name (Ex. 30. 23-28, 31-38; so Mary broke the box of precious ointment over Him, appropriately, Mark, 14. 5, the broken box typifying His body, which, when broken, diffused all grace: compounded of various spices, &c. (Col. 1. 19; 2. 9.); of sweet odour (Eph. 5. 2.). poured—(Isa. 53. 12; Rom. 5. 5.). therefore—because of the manifestation of God's character in Christ (1 John, 4. 9, 19.). So the penitent woman (Luke, 7. 37, 38, 47.). virgins—the pure in heart (2 Cor. 11. 2; Rev. 14. 4.). The same *Heb.* is transl. "thy hidden ones" Ps. 83. 3.). The "ointment" of the Spirit "poured forth" produces the "love of Christ" (Rom. 5. 5.). 4. (1. The cry of ancient Israel for Messiah, *ex. gr.*, Simeon, Anna, &c. (2.) The cry of an awakened soul for the drawing of the Spirit, after it has got a glimpse of Christ's loveliness, and its own helplessness. Draw me—The Father draws (John, 6. 44.). The Son draws (Jer. 31. 3; Hos. 11. 4; John, 12. 32.. "Draw" here, and "Tell" (*v.* 7,), reverently qualify the word "kiss" (*v.* 2.). me, we—no believer desires to go to heaven alone. We are converted as *individuals;* we follow Christ as joined in a *communion* of saints (John, 1. 41. 45.). Individuality and community meet in the same person. run—her earnestness kindles as she prays (Isa. 40. 31; Ps. 119. 32, 60.). after thee—not before (John, 10. 4.). King ... brought me into—(Ps. 45. 14, 16; John, 10. 16.). He is the anointed *Priest* (*v.* 3;); *King* (*v.* 4.). chambers—her prayer is answered even beyond her desires. Not only is she permitted to *run* after Him, but is brought into the inmost pavilion, where Eastern kings admitted none but the most intimate friends (Esth. 4. 11; 5. 2; Ps. 27. 5.). The erection of the temple of Solomon was the first bringing of the bride into permanent, instead of migratory chambers of the King. Christ's body on earth was the next John, 2. 21,), whereby believers are brought within the vail (Eph. 2. 6; Heb. 10. 19, 20,). Entrance into the closet for prayer is the first step. The earnest of the future bringing into heaven John, 14. 3.). His chambers are the bride's also (Isa. 26. 20.). There are various *chambers*, *plur.* John, 14. 2.). be glad and rejoice—*inward* and *outward* rejoicing. in thee—(Isa. 61. 10; Phil. 4. 1, 4.). Not in *our* spiritual frames, l's. 30. 6, 7.). remember—rather, *commemorate with praises* (Isa. 63. 7. . The mere *remembrance* of spiritual joys is better than the *present enjoyment* of carnal ones (l's. 4. 6, 7.). upright—rather, *uprightly, sincerely* (Ps. 58. 1; Rom. 12. 9;; so Nathanael (John, 1. 47;); Peter (John, 21. 17;; or *deservedly.* [MAUR.] 5. black—*viz.*, "as the tents of Kedar," equivalent to *blackness* (l's. 120. &c.; she draws the image from the black goatskins, with which the Scenite *Arabs* ("Kedar" was in Arabia Petræa) cover their tents (contrasted with the splendid state tent in which *the King* was awaiting His bride according to Eastern custom;); typifying the darkness of man's natural state. To feel this, and yet also feel one's self in Jesus Christ "comely as the curtains of Solomon," marks the believer (Rom. 7. 18, &c.; 8. 1;); 1 Tim. 1. 15, "I *am* chief;" so she says not merely, "I was," but "I am;" *still* black in herself, but comely through *His* comeliness put upon her (Ez. 16. 14.). curtains—first, the hangings and vail in the temple of Solomon Ez. 16. 10;); then, also, the "fine linen which is the righteousness of saints" (Rev. 19. 8,), the white wedding garment provided by Jesus Christ (Isa. 61. 10; Mat. 22. 11; 1 Cor. 1. 30; Col. 1. 28; 2. 10; Rev. 7. 14.). *Historically,* the dark tents of Kedar represent the Gentile Church (Isa. 60. 3-7, &c.). As the vineyard at the close is transferred from the Jews, who had not kept their own, to the Gentiles, so the Gentiles are introduced at the commencement of the Song: for they were among the earliest inquirers after Jesus Christ (Mat. 2.;); the wise men from the East (Arabia, or Kedar?) daughters of Jerusalem—professors, not the bride, or "the virgins," yet not enemies; invited to gospel blessings (ch. 3. 10, 11;); so near to Jesus Christ as not to be unlikely to find Him (ch. 5. 8;); desirous to seek Him with her (ch. 6. 1; cf. ch. 6. 13; 7. 1, 5, 8.). In ch. 7. 8, 9, the bride's Beloved becomes *their* Beloved; not however, of *all* of them (ch. 8. 4; cf. Luke, 23. 27, 28.). 6. She feels as if her blackness was so great as to be gazed at by all. mother's children—(Mat. 10. 36.). She is to forget "her own people and her father's house," *i.e.*, the worldly connections of her unregenerate state (Ps. 45. 10;); they had maltreated her Luke, 15. 15, 16.). Children of the same mother, but not the same father [MAUR.] (John, 8. 41-44.). They made her a common keeper of vineyards, whereby the sun looked upon, *i.e.*, burnt her: thus she did "not keep her own" vineyard, *i.e.*, fair beauty. So the world, and the soul (Mat. 16. 26; Luke, 9. 25.). The believer has to watch against the same danger (1 Cor. 9. 27.). So he will be able, instead of the self-reproach here, to say as ch. 8. 12. 7. my soul loveth—more intense than "the virgins" and "the upright love thee" (*v.* 3, 4; Mat. 22. 37.). To carry out the design of the allegory, the royal encampment is here represented as moving from place to place, in search of green pastures, under the *Shepherd King* (Ps. 23.). The bride, having first enjoyed communion with him in the pavilion, is willing to follow Him into labours and dangers; arising from all absorbing love Luke, 14. '6;): this distinguishes her from the formal st (John. 10. 27; Rev. 14. 4.). feedest—tendest thy flock (Isa. 40. 11; Heb. 13. 20; 1 Pet. 2. 25; 5. 4; Rev. 7. 17.). No *single* type expresses *all* the office of Jesus Christ, hence arises the variety of *diverse* images used to portray the manifold aspects of Him: these would be quite incongruous, if the song referred to the earthly Solomon. Her intercourse with Him is peculiar. She hears His voice, and addresses none but Himself. Yet it is through a veil; she sees Him not (Job, 23. 8, 9.). If we would be fed, we must follow the Shepherd through the *whole* breadth of His word, and not stay on *one* spot alone. makest ... to rest—distinct from "feedest." periods of rest are vouchsafed after labour (Isa. 4. 6; 49. 10; Ez. 34. 13-15.). Communion in private must go along with public following of Him. turneth aside— rather, one *veiled*, i.e., as a *harlot*, not His true bride (Gen. 38. 15) [GES.]; or as a *mourner* 2 Sam. 15. 30) [WEISS]; or as one *unknown*. [MAUR.] All imply estrangement from the Bridegroom. She feels estranged even among Christ's true servants, answering to "thy companions" (Luke, 22. 28,), so long as she has not Himself present. The opposite spirit to 1 Cor. 3. 4. 8. If—She ought to have *known* (John, 14. 8, 9.). The confession of her ignorance and *blackness* (v. 5,), leads Him to call her " fairest" (Mat. 12. 20. . Her jealousy of letting even "His companions" take the place of Himself (v. 7) led her too far. He directs her to follow them, as they follow Him (1 Cor. 11. 1; Heb. 6. 10, 12;): to use ordinances and the ministry: where *they* are *He* is Jer. 6. 16; Mat. 18. 19, 20; Heb. 10. 25.). Indulging in isolation is not the way to find Him. It was thus, literally, that Zipporah found her bridegroom (Ex. 2. 16.). The bride unhesitatingly asks the watchmen afterwards (ch. 3. 3.). kids— (John, 21. 15.). Christ is to be found in active ministrations, as well as in prayer (Pro. 11. 25.). shepherds' tents—ministers in the sanctuary (Ps. 84. 1.). 9. horses in Pharaoh's chariots—celebrated for *beauty, swiftness,* and *ardour,* at the Red sea (Ex. 14.; 15.). These qualities, which *seem* to belong to the ungodly, *really* belong to the saints. [M. STUART.] The allusion may be to the horses brought at a high price by Solomon out of Egypt (2 Chr. 1. 16, 17.). So the bride is redeemed out of spiritual Egypt by the true Solomon, at an infinite price (Isa. 51. 1; 1 Pet. 1. 18, 19.). But the deliverance from *Pharaoh at the Red sea* accords with the allusion to the tabernacle (ch. 1. 5; 3. 6, 7;); it rightly is put at the beginning of the Church's call. The *ardour* and *beauty* of the bride are the point of comparison ; (v. 4) "run," (v. 5) "comely." Also, like Pharaoh's horses, she forms a great company (Rev. 19. 7, 14.). As Jesus Christ is both Shepherd and Conqueror, so believers are not only His *sheep,* but also, as a Church *militant* now, His *chariots* and *horses* (ch. 6. 4.). 10. rows of jewels—(Ez. 16. 11, 12, 13.). OLEARIUS says, Persian ladies wear two or three rows of pearls round the head, beginning on the forehead and descending down to the cheeks and under the chin, so that their faces seem to be set in pearls (Ez. 16. 11.). The comparison to the horses (v. 9) implies the vital energy of the bride; this verse, her superadded graces (Pro. 1. 9; 4. 9; 1 Tim. 2. 9; 2 Pet. 1. 5.). 11. We—The Trinity implied by the Holy Ghost, whether it was so by the writer of the Song, or not (Gen. 1. 26; Pro. 8. 30; 30. 4.). "The Jews acknowledged God as king, and Messiah as king, in interpreting the Song, but did not know that these two are one. [LEIGHTON.] make—not merely *give* Eph. 2. 10.), borders of gold, with studs [i.e., spots] of silver—Jesus Christ delights to give more " to him that hath" (Mat. 25. 29.). He crowns *His own work* in us (Isa. 26. 12.). The " borders" here are equivalent to " rows" v. 10;); but here, the King seems to give the finish to her attire, by adding a *crown* (borders, or circles of gold studded with silver spots, as in Esth. 2. 17. Both the *royal* and *nuptial* crown, or chaplet. The *Heb.* for "spouse" (ch. 4. 8) is a *crowned one* (Ez. 16. 12; Rev. 2. 10.). The crown is given at once, upon conversion, in title, but in sensible possession afterwards (2 Tim. 4. 8.). 12. While—It is the presence of the Sun of Righteousness that draws out the believer's odours of grace. It was the sight of Him at table that caused the two women to bring forth their ointments for Him (Luke, 7. 37, 38; John, 12. 3; 2 Cor. 2. 15.). Historically fulfilled (Mat. 2. 11; ; spiritually (Rev. 3. 20;; and in church worship (Mat. 18. 20;) and at the Lord's supper especially, for here *public* communion with Him at table amidst His friends is spoken of, as v. 4 refers to *private* communion (1 Cor. 10. 16, 21;); typically (Ex. 24. 9-11; ; the future perfect fulfilment Luke, 22. 30; Rev. 19. 9.). The allegory supposes the King to have stopped in His movements and to be seated with His friends on the divan. What grace that a table should be prepared for us, whilst still militant (Ps. 23. 5.) my spikenard—not boasting, but *own-ing* the Lord's grace to and in her. The spikenard is a lowly herb, the emblem of humility. She rejoices that *He* is well-pleased with her graces, His own work (Phil. 4. 18.). 13. bundle of myrrh—abundant *preciousness* (Gr.) (1 Pet. 2. 7.). Even a *little* myrrh was costly; much more a *bundle* (Col. 2. 9.). BUR. takes it of *a scent-box filled with liquid myrrh*; the liquid obtained by incision gave the tree its chief value. he—rather, *it;* it is the myrrh that lies in the bosom, as the cluster of camphire is in the vineyards (v. 14.). all night—an undivided heart (Eph. 3. 17; contrast Jer. 4. 14; Ez. 16. 15, 30.). Yet on account of the everlasting covenant, God restores the adulteress Ez. 16. 60, 62; Hos. 2. 2, &c.). The night is the whole present dispensation till the everlasting day dawns Rom. 13. 12.). Also, *lit.,* night (Ps. 119. 147, 148,), the night of *affliction* (Ps. 42. 8.). cluster—Jesus Christ is one, yet *manifold* in His graces. camphire—or, *cypress.* The *hennah* is meant, whose odorous flowers grow in clusters, of a colour white and yellow softly blended; its bark is dark, the foliage light green. Women deck their persons with them. The loveliness of Jesus Christ. vineyards—appropriate in respect to Him who is " the vine." The spikenard was for the banquet (v. 12); the myrrh was in her bosom continually (v. 13; ; the camphire is in the midst of natural beauties, which, though lovely, are eclipsed by the one cluster Jesus Christ pre-eminent above them all. En-gedi

—In S. Palestine, near the Dead sea (Josh. 15. 62; Ez. 47. 10,), famed for aromatic shrubs. 15. fair—He discerns beauty in her, who had said, "I am black" (v. 5,), because of the everlasting covenant (Ps. 45. 11; Isa. 62. 5; Eph. 1. 4, 5.). doves' eyes—large and beautiful in the doves of Syria. The prominent features of her beauty (Mat. 10. 16;); gentleness, innocence, and constant love, emblem of the Holy Ghost, who changes us to His own likeness (Gen. 8. 10, 11; Mat. 3. 16.). The opposite kind of eyes (Ps. 101. 5; Mat. 20. 15; 2 Pet. 2. 14.). 16. *Reply of the Bride.* She presumes to call Him beloved, because He called her so first. Thou callest me "fair;" if I am so it is not in myself, it is all from thee (Ps. 90. 17; ; but *Thou* art fair in thyself Ps. 45. 2,). pleasant—(Pro. 3. 17) towards thy friends (2 Sam. 1. 26.). bed...green —the couch of green grass on which the King and His bride sit to "rest at noon." Thus her prayer in *v.* 7 is here granted: a green oasis in the desert, always found near waters in the E. Ps. 23. 2; Isa. 41. 17-19.). The scene is a kiosk, or summer-house. *Historically,* the literal resting of the Babe of Bethlehem and His parents on the *green* grass provided for cattle (Luke, 2.). In this verse there is an incidental allusion, in *v.* 15, to the offering (Luke, 2. 24.). So the "cedar and fir" ceiling refers to the temple (1 Ki. 5. 6-10; 6. 15-18; ; type of the heavenly temple (Rev. 21. 22.). 17. our house—see note, *v.* 16; but *primarily,* the kiosk (Isa. 11. 10,), "His rest." Cedar is pleasing to the eye and smell, hard, and never eaten by worms. fir—rather, cypress, which is hard, durable, and fragrant, of a reddish hue. [GES., WEISS, and MAUR.] Contrasted with the shifting "tents" (*v.* 5,), His house is "*our* house" Ps. 92. 13; Eph. 2. 19; Heb. 3. 6.). Perfect oneness of Him and the bride (John, 14. 20; 17. 21.). There is the shelter of a princely roof from the sun (Ps. 121. 6,), without the confinement of walls, and amidst rural beauties. The carved ceiling represents the wondrous excellencies of His divine nature.

CHAPTER II.

Ver. 1-17. 1. rose — if applied to Jesus Christ, it, with the white lily (lowly, 2 Cor. 8. 9,), answers to "white and ruddy" (ch. 5. 10.). But it is rather the *meadow-saffron;* the *Heb.* means radically a plant with a *pungent bulb,* inapplicable to the rose. So *Syr.* It is of a white and violet colour. [MAUR., GES., and WEISS.] The bride thus speaks of herself as lowly though lovely, in contrast with the lordly "apple" or citron tree, the Bridegroom (*v.* 3;); so the "lily" is applied to her (*v.* 2.). Sharou—(Isa. 35. 1,). In N. l alestine, between Mount Tabor and Lake Tiberias (1 Chr. 5, 16.). LXX. and *Vulg. transl.* it "a plain;" though they err in this, the *Heb.* Bible not elsewhere favouring it, yet the parallelism to *valleys* shows that, in the proper name Sharon, there is here a tacit reference to its meaning of lowliness. Beauty, delicacy, and lowliness, are to be in her, as they were in Him (Mat. 11. 29.). 2. *Jesus Christ to the Bride.* (Mat. 10. 16; John, 15. 19; 1 John, 5. 19.). Thorns, equivalent to the wicked (2 Sam. 23. 6; Ps. 57. 4.). daughters—of men, not of God; not "the virgins." If thou art the lily of Jesus Christ, take heed lest by impatience, rash judgments, and pride, thou thyself become a thorn." [LUTHER.] 3. *Her reply.* apple — generic term; including the golden citron, pomegranate, and orange apple (Pro. 25. 11,). He combines the *shadow* and fragrance of the citron with the *sweetness* of the orange and pomegranate fruit. The foliage is perpetual; throughout the year a succession of blossoms, fruit, and perfume (Jam. 1. 17.). among the sons — parallel to "among the daughters" (*v.* 2.). He alone is ever fruitful among the fruitless wild trees (Ps. 89. 6; Heb. 1. 9.). I sat . . . with delight—*lit., I eagerly desired and sat* (Ps. 94. 19; Mark, 6. 31; Eph. 2. 6; 1 Pet. 1. 8.). shadow—(Ps. 121. 5; Isa. 4. 6; 25. 4; 32. 2.). Jesus Christ interposes the shadow of His cross between the blazing rays of justice and us sinners. fruit—faith plucks it (Pro. 3. 18.). Man lost the tree of life (Gen. 3.). Jesus Christ has regained it for him; he eats it partly now (Ps. 119. 103; John, 6. 55, 67; 1 Pet. 2. 3,), fully hereafter (Rev. 2. 7; 22. 2, 14;); not earned by the sweat of his brow, or by his righteousness (Rom. 10.). Contrast the worldling's fruit (Deut. 32. 32; Luke, 15. 16.). 4. Historically fulfilled in the joy of Simeon and Anna in the temple, over the infant Saviour (Luke, 2.), and that of Mary too (cf. Luke, 1. 53;); typified (Ex. 24. 9-11.). Spiritually, the bride or beloved is led (*v.* 4) first *into the King's chambers,* thence is *drawn* after Him in answer to her prayer: is next received on a grassy couch under a cedar kiosk; and at last in a "banqueting hall," such as, Josephus says, Solomon had in his palace, "wherein all the vessels were of gold" (*Antiq.,* 8. 5, 2.). The transition is from holy retirement to *public* ordinances, church worship, and the Lord's supper (Ps. 36. 8.). The bride, as the queen of Sheba, is given "all her desire" (1 Ki. 10. 13; Ps. 63. 5; Eph. 3. 8, 16-21; Phil 4. 19; ; type of the heavenly feast hereafter (Isa. 25. 6, 9.). his banner . . . love— After having rescued us from the enemy, our victorious captain (Heb. 2. 10,), seats us at the banquet under a banner inscribed with *His name,* "love" (1 John, 4. 8,). His love conquered us to Himself: this banner rallies round us the forces of Omnipotence, as our protection: it marks to what country we belong, heaven, the abode of love, and in what we most glory, the cross of Jesus Christ, through which we triumph (Rom. 8. 37; 1 Cor. 15. 57; Rev. 3. 21.). cf. with "over me" (Deut. 33. 27,), "*underneath* are the everlasting arms." 5. flagons—MAUR. prefers *transl.,* "dried raisin-cakes;" from the *Heb.* root *fire, viz.,* dried by heat. But the "house of *wine*" (*Mary., v.* 4) favours "flagons:" the "new wine" of the kingdom, the Spirit of Jesus Christ. apples—from the tree (*v.* 3,), so sweet to her, the promises of God. sick of love — the highest degree of sensible enjoyment that can be attained here. It may be at an early or late stage of experience. Paul (2 Cor. 12. 7.). In the last sickness of J. Welch, he was overheard saying, "Lord, hold thine hand, it is enough; thy servant is a clay vessel, and can hold no more." [FLEMING, *Fulf. Script.*] In most cases this intensity of joy is reserved for the heavenly banquet. Historically, Israel had it, when the Lord's glory filled the tabernacle, and afterwards the temple, so that the priests could not stand to minister: so in the Christian Church, on Pentecost. The bride addresses *Christ* mainly, though in her rapture she uses the *plur.,* "Stay (*ye*) me," speaking generally. So far from asking the withdrawal of the manifestations which had overpowered her,

The Ministry of   SOLOMON'S SONG, II.   *John the Baptist.*

she asks for more: so "*fainteth for*" (Ps. 84. 2:): also Peter, on the mount of transfiguration (Luke, 9. 33,), "Let us make &c., *not knowing what he said.*" 6. The "*stay*" she prayed for (*v.* 5) is granted (Deut. 33. 12, 27: Ps. 37. 24; Isa. 41. 10.). None can pluck from that *embrace* (John, 10. 28-30.). His hand keeps us from falling (Mat. 14. 30, 31,), to it we may commit ourselves (Ps. 31. 5.). The "left" is the inferior hand, by which the Lord less signally manifests His love, than by the right: the secret hand of ordinary providence, as distinguished from that of manifested grace the "right."). They really go together, though sometimes they *seem* divided: here both are felt at once. THEODORET takes the left hand, equivalent to *judgment and wrath;* the right, equivalent to *honour and love.* The hand of justice no longer is lifted to smite, but is under the head of the believer to support (Isa. 42. 21,), the hand of Jesus Christ pierced by justice for our sin supports us. The charge not to disturb the beloved occurs thrice: but the sentiment here, "His left hand," &c., nowhere else fully; which accords with the intensity of joy (*v.* 5) found nowhere else: in ch. 8. 3, it is only conditional, "*should* embrace," not "doth." 7. Not an oath " by the roes;" but a solemn charge, to act as cautiously as the hunter would with the wild roes, which are proverbially timorous: he must advance with breathless circumspection, if he is to take them: so he who would not lose Jesus Christ and His Spirit, which is easily grieved and withdrawn, must be tender of conscience and watchful (Ez. 16. 43; Eph. 4. 30; 5. 15; 1 Thes. 5. 19,). In *Marg.* title of Ps. 22., Jesus Christ is called the "*Hind* of the morning," hunted to death by the dogs (cf. *v.* 8, 9, where He is represented as bounding on the hills, Ps. 18. 33.). Here He is *resting,* but with a repose easily broken (Zeph. 3. 17.). It is thought a gross rudeness in the E. to awaken one sleeping, especially a person of rank. my love—in *Heb., Fem.* for *Masc.,* the abstract for concrete, Jesus Christ being the embodiment of *love* itself (ch. 3. 5; 8. 7,), where, as here, the context requires it to be applied to Him, not her. She too is "love" (ch. 7. 6,), for His love calls forth her love. Presumption in the convert is as grieving to the Spirit as despair. The *lovingness* and *pleasantness* of the hind and roe (Pro. 5. 19) is included in this image of Jesus Christ.

CANTICLE II.—Ch. ii. 8—iii. 5.—JOHN THE BAPTIST'S MINISTRY. 8. voice—an exclamation of joyful surprise, evidently after a long silence. The restlessness of sin and fickleness in her had disturbed His rest with her, which she had professed not to wish disturbed "till He should please." He left her, but in sovereign grace unexpectedly heralds His return. She awakes, and at once recognises His voice (1 Sam. 3. 9, 10; John, 10. 4: : her sleep is not so sinfully deep as in ch. 5. 2. leaping—bounding, as the roe does, over the roughest obstacles (2 Sam. 2. 18; 1 Chr. 12. 8;); as the Father of the prodigal "had compassion and *ran*" (Luke, 15, 20,), upon the hills —as the sunbeams glancing from hill to hill. So *Marg.* title of Jesus Christ (Ps. 22.) "Hind of the *morning*" (type of His resurrection.). Historically, the coming of the kingdom of heaven (the gospel dispensation,) announced by John Baptist, is meant: *it* primarily is the garden or vineyard; the bride is called

so in a secondary sense. "The voice" of Jesus Christ is indirect, through "the friend of the Bridegroom" (John, 3. 29,), John the Baptist. Personally, He is silent during John's ministration, who awoke the long slumbering Church with the cry, "Every *hill* shall be made low," in the spirit of Elias, on the "rent mountains" (1 Ki. 19. 11; cf. Isa. 52. 7.). Jesus Christ is implied as coming with intense desire (Luke, 22. 15; Heb. 10. 7,), disregarding the mountain hindrances raised by man's sin. 9. he standeth—after having bounded over the intervening space like a roe. He often stands near, when our unbelief hides Him from us (Gen. 28. 16; Rev. 3. 14-20.). His usual way; long promised and expected; sudden at last: so, in visiting the second temple (Mal. 3. 1;); so at Pentecost (Acts, 2. 1, 2;); so in visiting an individual soul, Zaccheus (Luke, 19. 5, 6; John, 3. 8;); and so, at the second coming (Mat. 24. 48, 50; 2 Pet. 3. 4, 10.). So it shall be at His second coming (1 Thes. 5. 2, 3.). wall—over the cope of which He is first seen: next, He looks *through* (not *forth;* for He is outside) at the windows, *glancing* suddenly and stealthily not as *E.V.* " showing Himself") through the lattice. The prophecies, types, &c., were lattice glimpses of Him to the O. T. Church, in spite of the *wall* of separation which sin had raised (John, 8. 56:): clearer glimpses were given by John Baptist, but not unclouded John, 1. 26.). The legal wall of partition was not to be removed until His death (Eph. 2. 14, 15; Heb. 10. 20.). Even now, He is only seen by *faith,* through the windows of His Word, and the latter of ordinances and sacraments (Luke, 24. 35; John, 14. 21;); not full vision (1 Cor. 13. 12:): an incentive to our looking for His second coming (Isa. 33. 17; Tit. 2. 13.). 10, 11. Loving reassurance given by Jesus Christ to the bride, lest she should think that He had ceased to love her, on account of her unfaithfulness, which had occasioned His temporary withdrawal, He allures her to brighter than worldly joys (Mic. 2. 10.). Not only does the saint wish to depart, to be with Him, but He still more desires to have the saint with Him above (John, 17. 24.). Historically, the vineyard or garden of the King, here first introduced, is " he kingdom of heaven preached" by John baptist, before whom " the Law and the Prophets were" (Luke, 16. 16.). 11. the winter—the law of the covenant of works (Mat. 4. 16.). rain is over—(Heb. 12. 18-24; 1 John, 2. 8.). Then first the Gentile Church is called "beloved, which was not beloved" (Rom. 9. 25.). So "the winter" of estrangement also is "past" to the believer (Isa. 44. 22; Jer. 50. 20; 2 Cor. 5. 17; Eph. 2. 1.). The rising "Sun of righteousness" dispels the "rain" (2 Sam. 23. 4; Ps. 126. 5; Mal. 4. 2.). The winter in Palestine is past by April, but all the showers were not over till May. The time described here is that which comes directly after these last showers of winter. In the highest sense, the coming resurrection and deliverance of the earth from the *past* curse is here implied (Rom. 8. 19; Rev. 21. 4; 22. 3.). No more "clouds" shall then "return after the rain" (Eccl. 12. 2; Rev. 4. 3; cf. Gen. 9. 13-17.): "the rainbow round the throne" is the "token" of this. 12. flowers—tokens of anger past, and of grace come. "The summoned bride is welcome," say some Fathers, "to weave from them garlands of beauty, wherewith she may adorn herself to meet the King." Historically, the flowers, &c., only give promise; the fruit is not ripe yet: suitable to the preaching of John Baptist. "The kingdom of heaven is *at hand*," not yet fully come. the time of...singing—the rejoicing at the advent of Jesus Christ. GREGORY NYSSENUS refers the *voice* of the turtle dove to John Baptist. It with the olive branch announced to Noah that "the rain was over and gone" (Gen. 8. 11.). So John Baptist, spiritually. Its plaintive "voice" answers to his preaching of *repentance* (Jer. 8. 6, 7.). *Vulg.* and LXX. *transl.* "The time of *pruning,*" *viz.*, spring (John, 15. 2.). The mention of the "turtle's" cooing better accords with our text. The turtle is migratory (Jer. 8. 7.), and "comes" early in May; emblem of love, and so of the Holy Ghost. Love, too, shall be the keynote of the "new *song*" hereafter (Isa. 35. 10; Rev. 1. 5; 14. 3; 19. 6.). In the individual believer now, joy and love are here set forth in their *earlier* manifestations (Mark, 4. 28.). 13. putteth forth—rather, ripens, *lit.*, *makes red.* [MAUR.] The unripe figs, which grow in winter, begin to ripen in early spring, and in June are fully matured. [WEISS.] vines with the tender grape—rather, "the vines *in flower,*" *lit.*, *a flower*, in apposition with "vines." [MAUR.] The vine flowers were so sweet, that they were often put, when dried, into new wine to give it flavour. Applicable to the first manifestations of Jesus Christ, "the true Vine," both to the Church, and to individuals: as to Nathanael under the *fig-tree* (John, 1. 48.). Arise, &c.—His call, described by the bride, ends as it began (*v.* 10:): it is a consistent whole; "love" from first to last (Isa. 52. 1, 2; 2 Cor. 6. 17, 18.). "Come," in the close of Rev. 22. 17, as at His earlier manifestation (Mat. 11. 28.). 14. dove—here expressing endearment (Ps. 74. 19.). Doves are noted for *constant attachment;* emblems, also, in their soft, plaintive note, of *softened penitents* (Isa. 59. 11; Ez. 7. 16:); other points of likeness are their *beauty;* "their wings covered with silver and gold" (Ps. 68. 13.), typifying the change in the converted: the *dove-like spirit,* breathed into the saint by the Holy Ghost, whose emblem is the dove: the *messages of peace* from God to sinful men, as Noah's dove, with the olive branch (Gen. 8.,), intimated that the flood of wrath was past: *timidity,* fleeing with fear from sin and self to the cleft Rock of ages (*Marg.*, Isa. 26. 4; Hos. 11. 11:): *gregarious,* flocking together to the kingdom of Jesus Christ (Isa. 60. 8:): *harmless simplicity* (Mat. 10. 16.). clefts—the refuge of doves from storm and heat Jer. 48. 28; see Jer. 49. 16.). GES. *transl.* the *Heb.*, from a different root, "the refuges." But see, for "clefts," Ex. 33. 18-23. It is only when we are *in* Christ Jesus, that our "voice is *sweet*" (in prayer, ch. 4. 3, 11; Mat. 10. 20; Gal. 4. 6, because it is *His* voice *in* us; also in speaking *of* Him, Mal. 3. 16:); and our countenance *comely*" Ex. 34. 29; Ps. 27. 5; 71. 3; Isa. 35. 10; 2 Cor. 3. 18.). stairs—(Ez. 38. 20.). *Marg.*, a steep rock, broken into stairs, or terraces. It is in "secret places" and rugged scenes, that Jesus Christ woos the soul from the world to Himself (Mic. 2. 10; 7. 14.). So Jacob amidst the stones of Bethel (Gen. 28. 11-19:); Moses at Horeb (Ex. 3.); so Elijah (1 Ki. 19. 9-13:); Jesus Christ with the three disciples on a "high mountain apart," at the transfiguration (Mat. 17. 1; John in Patmos (Rev. 1.). "Of the eight beatitudes, five have an afflicted condition for their subject. As long as the waters are on the earth, we dwell in the ark; but when the land is dry, the dove itself will be tempted to wander." [JER. TAYLOR.] Jesus Christ does not invite her to leave the rock, but *in* it (Himself,., yet in holy freedom to lay aside the timorous spirit, look up boldly as accepted in Him, pray, praise, and confess Him (in contrast to her shrinking from being *looked at,* ch. 1. 6 Eph. 6. 19; Heb. 13. 16; 1 John, 4. 18:); still though trembling, the voice and countenance of the soul in Jesus Christ are pleasant to Him. The Church found no cleft in the Sinaitic legal rock, though good in itself, wherein to hide; but in Jesus Christ stricken by God for us, as the rock smitten by Moses (Num. 20. 11.), there is a hiding place (Isa. 32. 2.). *She* praised His "voice" (*v.* 8, 10:); it is thus that her voice also, though tremulous, is "sweet" to Him here. 15. Transition to the vineyard, often formed in "stairs" (*v.* 14.), or terraces, in which, amidst the vine leaves, foxes hid. foxes—generic term, including *jackals.* They eat only grapes, not the vine flowers; but they need to be driven out *in time* before the grape is ripe. She had failed in watchfulness before (ch. 1. 6,), now when converted, she is the more jealous of *subtle* sins Ps. 139. 23.). In spiritual winter certain evils are frozen up, as well as good: in the spring of revivals these start up unperceived, crafty, false teachers, spiritual pride, uncharitableness, &c. Ps. 19. 12; Mat. 13. 26; Luke, 8. 14; 2 Tim. 2. 17; Heb. 12. 15.). "Little" sins are parents of the greatest (Eccl. 10. 1; 1 Cor. 5. 6.). Historically, John Baptist spared not the *fox-like* Herod (Luke, 13. 32.), who gave vine-like promise of fruit at first (Mark, 6. 20,), at the cost of his life; nor the viper-Sadducees, &c.; nor the varied subtle forms of sin (Luke, 3. 7-14.). 16. mine,... his—rather, "is *for me*,... *for Him*" (Hos. 3. 3,), where, as here, there is the assurance of indissoluble union, in spite of temporary absence. Next verse, entreating Him to return, shows that He has gone, perhaps through her want of guarding against the "little sins (*v.* 15.). The order of the clauses is reversed in ch. 6. 3, when she is riper in faith: there she rests more on *her being His;* here, on *His being her's;* and no doubt her sense of love to Him is a pledge that she is His (John, 14. 21, 23; 1 Cor. 8. 3:: this is her consolation in His withdrawal now. I ..m his—by creation (Ps. 100. 3,), by redemption (John, 17. 10; Rom. 14. 8; 1 Cor. 6. 19.). feedeth—as a "roe," or gazelle (*v.* 17.); instinct is sure to lead him back to His feeding ground, where the lilies abound. So Jesus Christ, though now withdrawn, the bride feels sure will return to His favourite resting-place ch. 7. 10; Ps. 132. 14.). So hereafter, Rev. 21. 3.). Ps. 45., title, terms His lovely bride's "lilies" [HENGST.] pure and white. though among thorns (*v.* 2.). 17. Night is the image of the present world (Rom. 13. 12.) "Behold men as if dwelling in a subterranean cavern." [PLATO. *Rep.* vii. 1.] Until—*i.e.* *Before that,* &c. break—rather, *breathe;* referring to the refreshing breeze of dawn in the E.; or to the air of *life,* which distinguishes morning from the death-like stillness of *morning of night,* when the breeze arises after the heat of day (*cf. Marg.* Gen. 3. 8, wi h Gen. 18. 1,), and the "shadows" are lost in night (Ps. 102. 11:): thus our life will be the *day;*

CHAPTER V.

1 *Christ awakes the church with his calling.* 2 *She, having a taste of his love, is sick of it.* 9 *He, the Beloved of the church, described by his graces.*

I AM *a* come into my garden, my sister, my spouse: I have gathered my myrrh with my spice; I have eaten my honeycomb with my honey; I have drunk my wine with my milk: eat, O *b* friends; drink, 1 yea, drink abundantly, O beloved.

2 ¶ I sleep, but my heart waketh: *it is* the voice of my beloved *c* that knocketh, *saying*, Open to me, my sister, my love, my dove, my undefiled: for my head is filled with dew, *and* my locks with the drops of the night.

3 I have put off my coat; how shall I put it on? I have washed my feet; how shall I defile them?

4 My beloved put in his hand by the hole of the door, and my bowels were moved *d* for him.

5 I rose up to open to my beloved; and my hands dropped *with* 3 sweet-smelling myrrh, and my fingers *with* 3 sweet-smelling myrrh, upon the handles of the lock.

6 I opened to my beloved; but my beloved had *d* withdrawn himself, *and* was gone: my soul failed when he spake: I sought him, but I could not find him; I *e* called him, but he gave me no answer.

7 The *f* watchmen that went about the city found me, they smote me, they wounded me; the keepers of the walls took away my veil from me.

8 I charge you, O daughters of Jerusalem, if ye find my beloved, *4* that ye tell him, that I am sick of love.

9 ¶ What *is* thy beloved more than another beloved, O thou fairest among women? what *is* thy beloved more than another beloved, that thou dost so charge us?

10 ¶ My beloved *is* white and ruddy, 5 the chiefest among ten thousand.

11 His head *is* as the most fine gold; his locks *are* 6 bushy, *and* black as a raven.

12 His *g* eyes *are as the eyes* of doves by the rivers of waters, washed with milk, *and* 7 fitly set.

13 His cheeks *are* as a bed of spices, *as* 8 sweet flowers; his lips *like* lilies, dropping sweet-smelling myrrh:

14 His hands *are as* gold rings set with the beryl; his belly *is as* bright ivory overlaid *with* sapphires.

15 His legs *are as* pillars of marble set upon sockets of fine gold; his countenance *is* as Lebanon, excellent as the cedars.

16 *g* His mouth *is* most sweet; yea, *h* he *is* altogether lovely. This *is* my beloved, and this *is* my friend, O daughters of Jerusalem.

CHAPTER VI.

1 *The church professes her faith in Christ.* 4 *He shows her graces,* 10 *and his love toward her.*

WHITHER is thy beloved gone, *a* O thou fairest among women? whither is thy beloved turned aside? that we may seek him with thee.

2 ¶ My beloved is gone down into his garden, to the beds of spices, to *b* feed in the gardens, and to *c* gather lilies.

3 I *d am* my beloved's, and my beloved *is* mine: he feedeth among the lilies.

4 ¶ Thou *art* beautiful, O my love, as Tirzah, comely as Jerusalem, *e* terrible as an army with banners.

5 Turn away thine eyes from me, for 1 they have overcome me: thy hair *is* as a flock of goats that appear from Gilead:

6 Thy teeth *are* as a flock of sheep which go up from the washing, whereof every one beareth twins, and *there is* not one barren among them.

7 As a piece of a pomegranate *are* thy temples within thy locks.

8 There are threescore queens, and fourscore concubines, and virgins without number.

9 My dove, my undefiled is *but* one; she *is* the *only* one of her mother, she *is* the choice *one* of her that bare her. The daughters saw her, and blessed her; *yea*, the queens and the concubines, and they praised her.

10 ¶ Who *is* she *that* looketh forth as the morning, fair as the moon, clear as the sun, *and* terrible as an army with banners?

11 I went down into the garden of nuts to see the fruits of the valley, *and g* to see whether the vine flourished, *and* the pomegranates budded.

12 2 Or ever I was aware, my soul 3 made me *like* the chariots of Amminadib.

13 Return, return, O Shulamite; return, return, that we may look upon thee. What will ye see in the Shulamite? As it were the company 4 of two armies.

CHAPTER VII.

1 *A further description of the graces of the church:* 10 *she professes her faith and assurance of Christ's love.*

HOW beautiful are thy feet with shoes, O *a* prince's daughter! the joints of thy thighs *are* like jewels, the work of the hands of a cunning workman:

2 Thy navel *is like* a round goblet, *which* wanteth not 1 liquor: thy belly *is like* an heap of wheat set about with lilies:

3 Thy *b* two breasts *are* like two young roes *that are* twins.

4 Thy neck *is as* a tower of ivory; thine eyes *like* the fish-pools in Heshbon, by the gate of Bath-rabbim: thy nose *is* as the tower of Lebanon which looketh toward Damascus.

5 Thine head upon thee *is* like 2 Carmel, and the hair of thine head like purple: the king *is* 3 held in the galleries.

6 How fair and how pleasant art thou, O love, for delights!

7 This thy stature is like to a palm tree, and thy breasts to clusters *of grapes*.

8 I said, I will go up to the palm tree, I will take hold of the boughs thereof: now also thy breasts shall be as clusters of the vine, and the smell of thy nose like apples;

9 And the roof of thy mouth like the best wine for my beloved, that goeth down 4 sweetly, causing the lips 5 of those that are asleep to speak.

10 ¶ I *c am* my beloved's, and *d* his desire *is* toward me.

11 Come, my beloved, let us go forth into the field; let us lodge in the villages.

12 Let us get up early to the vineyards; let us *e* see if the vine flourish, *whether* the tender grape *6* appear, *and* the pomegranates bud forth: there will *f* I give thee my loves.

13 The *g* mandrakes give a smell, and at our gates *h are* all manner of pleasant *fruits*, new and old, *which* I have laid up for thee, O my beloved.

death, the *night* (John, 9. 4.). The *E. V.* better accords with (ch. 3. 1) "*By night*" (Rom. 13. 12.). turn—to me. Bether—Mountains of Bithron, separated from the rest of Israel by Jordan (2 Sam. 2. 29.), not far from Bethabara, where John baptised and Jesus was first manifested. Rather, as *Marg.*, *of divisions*, and LXX., *mountains intersected* with deep gaps, hard to pass over, separating the bride and Jesus Christ. In ch. 8. 14, the mountains are *of spices*, on which the roe feeds, not *of separation*; for at His first coming, He had to overpass the gulf made by sin between Him and us (Zech. 4. 6, 7.); in His second. He will only have to come down from the fragrant hill above to take home his prepared bride. Historically, in the ministry of John Baptist, Christ's call to the bride was not, as later ch. 4. 8,), "Come *with* me," but "come away," *viz.*, to meet me (v. 2, 10, 13.). Sitting in darkness (Mat. 4. 16.). She "waited," and "looked" eagerly for Him, the "great light" (Luke, 1. 79; 2. 25, 38.): at His rising, the "shadows" of the law (Col. 2. 16. 17; Heb. 10. 1) were to "flee away." So we wait for the second coming, when means of grace, so precious now, shall be superseded by the Sun of righteousness (1 Cor. 13. 10, 12; Rev. 21. 22, 23.). The Word is our light until then (2 Pet. 1. 19.).

CHAPTER III.

Ver. 1-11. 1. By night — *lit.*, "*By nights.*" Continuation of the longing for the dawn of Messiah (ch. 2. 17; Ps. 130. 6; Mal. 4. 2.). The spiritual desertion here (ch. 2. 17—3. 5) is not due to indifference, as in ch. 5. 2-8. "As nights and dews are better for flowers, than a continual sun, so Christ's absence (at times) giveth sap to humility, and putteth an edge on hunger, and furnisheth a fair field to faith to put forth itself." [RUTHERFORD.] Contrast ch. 1. 13; Ps. 30. 6, 7. ou .. the — the secret of her failure (Isa. 64. 7; Jer. 29. 13; Amos. 6. 1, 4; Hos. 7. 14.). loveth—no want of sincerity, but of diligence, which she now makes up for by leaving her bed to seek Him (Ps. 22. 2; 63. 8; Isa. 26. 9; John, 20. 17.). Four times (v. 1-4) she calls Jesus Christ "Him whom my soul loveth," designating Him as *absent*; language of desire: "He loved me," would be language of *present* fruition (Rev. 1. 5.). In questioning the watchmen (v. 3,), she does not even name Him, so full is her heart of Him. Having found Him at dawn (for throughout He is the *morning,*), she charges the daughters not to abridge, by intrusion, the period of His stay. Cf. as to the thoughtful seeking for Jesus Christ in the time of John Baptist, in vain at first, but presently after successful (Luke, 3. 15-22; John, 1. 19-34.). found him not—O for such honest dealings with ourselves (Pro. 25. 14; Jude, 12.). 2. Wholly awake for God (Luke, 15. 18-20; Eph. 5. 14.). "An honest resolution is often to (the doing of) duty, like a needle that draws the thread after it." [DUR.] Not a mere wish, that counts not the cost—to leave her easy bed, and wander in the dark night seeking Him (Pro. 13. 4; Mat. 21. 30; Luke, 14. 27-33.). the city—Jerusalem, *lit.* (Mat. 3. 5; John, 1. 19,), and spiritually, the *Church* here (Heb. 12. 22,), in glory (Rev. 21. 2.). broad ways—open spaces at the gates of E. cities, where the public assembled for business. So, the assemblies of worshippers (ch. 8. 2, 3; Pro. 1. 20-23; Heb. 10. 25.). She had in her first awakening shrunk from them, seeking Jesus Christ alone; but she was desired to seek the footsteps of the flock (ch. 1. 8,), so now in her second trial she goes forth to them of herself. "The more the soul grows in grace, and the less it leans on ordinances, the more it prizes and profits by them" [M. STUART] Ps. 73. 16, 17.). found him not—nothing short of Jesus Christ can satisfy her (Job, 23. 8-10; Ps. 63. 1, 2.). 3. watchmen—ministers (Isa. 62. 6; Jer. 6. 17; Ez. 3. 17; Heb. 13. 17.), fit persons to consult (Isa. 21. 11; Mal. 2. 7.). f und me- the general ministry of the word "finds" individually souls in quest of Jesus Christ (Gen. 24. 27, end of v.; Acts, 16. 14.); whereas formalists remain unaffected. 4. Jesus Christ is generally "found" near the watchmen and means of grace; but they are not Himself, the star that points to Bethlehem is not the Sun that has risen there; she hastens past the guide posts to the goal. [M. STUART.] Not even angels could satisfy Mary, instead of Jesus Christ (John, 20. 11-16.). f und him—(Isa. 45. 19; Hos. 6. 1-3; Mat. 13. 44-46.). held him, &c.—willing to be held; not willing, if not held (Gen. 32. 26; Mat. 28. 9; Luke, 24. 28, 29; Rev. 3. 11.). "As a little weeping child will hold its mother fast, not because it is stronger than she, but because her bowels constrain her not to leave it; so Jesus Christ yearning over the believer *cannot go*, because He *will* not." [DUR.] In ch. 1. 4, it is He who leads the bride into His chambers; here it is she who leads Him into her mother's. There are times when the grace of Jesus Christ seems to draw us to Him; and others, when we with strong cries draw Him to us and ours. In the E. one large apartment often serves for the whole family; so the bride here speaks of her mother's apartment and her own together. The mention of the "mother" excludes impropriety, and imparts the idea of heavenly love, pure as a sister's, whilst ardent as a bride's; hence the frequent title, "my sister-spouse." Our mother after the Spirit, is *the Church*, the new Jerusalem (John, 3. 5-8; Gal. 4. 19, 26); for her we ought to pray continually (Eph. 3. 14-19,), also for the *national* Jerusalem (Isa. 62. 6, 7; Rom. 10. 1,), also for the *human family*, which is our mother and k ndred after the flesh: these our mother's children have evil treated us (ch. 1. 6,), but, like our Father, we are to return good for evil (Mat. 5. 44, 45,), and so bring Jesus Christ home to them (1 Pet. 2. 12.). 5. So ch. 2. 7; but *there* it was for the non-interruption of her own fellowship with Jesus Christ that she was anxious; *here* it is for the not grieving of the Holy Ghost, on the part of the daughters of Jerusalem, Jealously avoid levity, heedlessness, and offences, which would mar the gracious work begun in others (Mat. 18. 7; Acts, 2. 42, 43; Eph. 4. 30.).

CANTICLE III. — Ch. iii. 6—v. 1, — THE BRIDEGROOM WITH THE BRIDE. Historically, the ministry of Jesus Christ on earth. 6. New scene (v. 6-11.). The friends of the Bridegroom see a cortege approach. His palanquin and guard, cometh out—rather, *up from;* the wilderness was lower than Jerusalem. [MAUR.] pillars of smoke—from the perfumes burned round Him and His bride. Image from Israel and the tabernacle (answering to "bed."v. 7) marching through the desert with the pillar of smoke by day, and fire by night (Ex. 14. 20,), and the pillars of smoke ascending from the altars of incense and of atonement; so Jesus Christ's righteousness, atonement, and ever-living intercession. Balaam, the last representative of patriarchism, was required to curse the Jewish Church, just as it afterwards would not succumb to Christianity without a struggle (Num. 22. 41,), but he had to bless in language like that here (Num. 24. 5, 6.). Angels too joyfully ask the same question, when Jesus Christ with the tabernacle of His body (answering to His bed, v. 7; John, 1. 14, "dwelt," (Gr.) tabernacled, John. 2. 21) ascends into heaven (Ps. 24. 8-10,), also when they see His glorious bride with Him (Ps. 68. 18; Rev. 7. 13-17.). Encouragement to her; amidst the darkest trials (v. 1,), she is still on the road to glory (v. 11) in a palanquin "paved with love" (v. 10;): she is now in soul spiritually "coming," exhaling the sweet graces, faith, love, joy, peace, prayer, and praise: (the fire is lighted within, the "smoke" is seen without, Acts, 4. 13:): it is in the desert of trial (v. 1-3) she gets them; (she is the "merchant" buying from Jesus Christ without money or price. Isa. 55. 1; Rev. 3. 18;); just as myrrh and frankincense are got, not in Egypt, but in the Arabian sands, and the mountains of Pale-tine. Hereafter she shall "come" (v. 6, 11, in a glorified body too (Phil. 3. 21.). Historically, Jesus Christ returning from the wilderness, full of the Holy Ghost (Luke, 4, 1, 14.). The same, "Who is this," &c. (Isa. 63. 1. 5.). 7. In v. 6, the wilderness character of the Church is portrayed; in v. 7, 8, its militant aspect. In v. 9. 10, Jesus Christ is seen dwelling in believers, who are His "chariot" and "body." In v. 11, the consummation in glory. bed—palanquin. His body, lit., guarded by a definite number of angels, "three score," or sixty (Mat. 26. 53,), from the wilderness (Mat. 4. 1, 11,), and continually (Luke, 2. 13; 22. 43; Acts, 1, 10, 11;): just as 600,000 of Israel guarded the Lord's tabernacle (Num. 2. 17-32,), one for every 10,000. In contrast to the "bed of sloth" (v. 1.). valiant— Josh. 5. 13. 14.). Angels guarding His tomb used like words (Mark, 16. 6.). of Israel—true subjects, not mercenaries. 8. hold—not actually grasping them, but having them girt on the thigh ready for use, like their Lord (Ps. 45. 3,). So believers too are guarded by angels (Ps. 91. 11; Heb. 1. 14,), and they themselves need "every man" (Neh. 4. 18 to be armed (Ps. 144. 1, 2; 2 Cor. 10. 4; Eph. 6. 12, 17; 1 Tim. 6. 12,), and "expert" (2 Cor. 2. 11.). because of fear in the night— Arab marauders often turn a wedding into mourning by a night attack. So the bridal procession of saints in the night of this wilderness, is the chief object of Satan's assault. 9. chariot—more elaborately made than the "bed" or travelling litter (v. 7,), from a Heb. root, to elaborate. [EWALD.] So the temple of "cedar of Lebanon," as compared with the temporary tabernacle of shittim-wood (2 Sam. 7. 2, 6, 7; 1 Ki. 5. 14; 6. 15-18.). Jesus Christ's body is the antitype, "made" by the Father for Him (1 Cor. 1 30; Heb. 10. 5.), the wood answering to His human nature, the gold, His divine; the two being but one Christ. 10. pillars—supporting the canopy at the four corners; curtains at the side protect the person within from the sun. Pillars with silver sockets supported the veil that enclosed the holy of holies; emblem of Jesus Christ's strength (1 Ki. 7. 21,), Mary., "silver," emblem of His purity (Ps. 12. 6;); so the saints hereafter (Rev. 3. 12,). bottom—rather, the back for resting or reclining on (Vulg. and LXX.) [MAUK.] So the floor and mercy-seat, the resting place of God (Ps. 132. 14) in the temple was gold (1 Ki. 6. 30,). covering—rather, seat, as in Lev. 15. 9.). Hereafter the saints shall share His seat (Rev. 3. 21.). purple—the veil of the holiest partly purple, and the purple robe put on Jesus Christ, accord with E. V., "covering." "Purple" (including scarlet and crimson) is the emblem of royalty, and of His blood; typified by the passover-lamb's blood, and the wine when the twelve sat or reclined at the Lord's table. paved — tesselated, like mosaic pavement, with the various acts and promises of love of Father. Son, and Holy Ghost (Zeph. 3. 17; 1 John, 4. 8, 16.), in contrast with the tables of stone in the "midst" of the ark, covered with writings of stern command (cf. John, 19. 13;); this is all grace and love to believers, who answer to "the daughters of Jerusalem" (John, 1. 17.). The exterior silver and gold, cedar, purple, and guards, may deter, but when the bride enters within, she rests on a pavement of love. 11. go forth —(Mat. 25. 6,). daughters of Zion—spirits of saints, and angels (Isa. 61. 10; Zech. 9. 9.). crown—nuptial (Ez. 16. 8-12,), (the Hebrews wore costly crowns, or chaplets at weddings,), and kingly (Ps. 2. 6; Rev. 19. 12.). The crown of thorns was once His nuptial chaplet, His blood the wedding wine-cup (John, 19. 5,). "His mother," that so crowned Him, is the human race, for He is "the Son of man," not merely the Son of Mary. The same mother reconciled to Him (Mat. 12. 50,), as the Church, travails in birth for souls, which she presents to Him as a crown (1 hil. 4. 1; Rev. 4. 10,). Not being ashamed to call the children brethren (Heb. 2. 11-14,), He calls their mother His mother (Ps. 22. 9; Rom. 8. 29; Rev. 12. 1, 2.). behold — (2 Thes. 1. 10.). day of his espousals—chiefly the final marriage, when the number of the elect is complete (Rev. 6. 11.). gladness—(Ps. 45. 15; Isa. 62. 5; Rev. 19. 7.). M. STUART observes as to this Canticle (ch. 3. 6—5. 1,), the centre of the Book, these peculiarities; (1.) The Bridegroom takes the chief part, whereas elsewhere the bride is the chief speaker; (2.) Elsewhere He is either "King" or "Solomon;" here He is twice called "king Solomon." The bride is six times here called the "spouse;" never so before or after; also "sister" four times, and, except in the first verse of the next Canticle, nowhere else; (3.) He and she are never separate, no absence, no complaint, which abound elsewhere, are in this Canticle.

CHAPTER IV.

Ver. 1-16. 1. Contrast with the bride's state by nature (Isa. 1. 6) her state by grace (v. 1-7) "perfect through His comeliness put upon her" (Ez. 16. 14; John, 15. 3.). The praise of Jesus Christ, unlike that of the world, hurts not, but edifies; as His, not ours, is the glory (John, 5. 44; Rev. 4. 10, 11.). Seven features of beauty are specified (v. 1-5,), ("lips" and "speech" are but one feature, v. 3; the number for perfection. To each of these is attached a comparison from nature: the resemblances consist not so much in outward likeness, as in the combined sensations of delight produced by contemplating these natural objects. doves—the large melting eye of the Syrian dove appears especially beautiful amidst the foliage of its native groves:

so the bride's "eyes within her locks" (Luke. 7. 44.). MAUR. for "locks," has "veil;" but locks suit the connection better: so the *Heb.* is *transl.* (Isa. 47. 2.). The dove was the only bird counted "clean" for sacrifice. Once the heart was "the cage of every unclean and hateful bird." Grace makes the change. eyes—(Mat. 6. 22; Eph. 1. 18; contrast Mat. 5. 28; Eph. 4. 18; 1 John, 2. 16.). Chaste and guileless (Mat. 10. 16, *Marg.;* John, 1. 47.). John Baptist, historically, was the "turtle dove" (ch. 2, 12.), with eye directed to the coming Bridegroom: his Nazarite unshorn hair answers to "locks" (John, 1. 29, 36.). hair ... goats—the hair of goats in the E. is fine like silk. As long hair is her glory, and marks her subjection to man (1 Cor. 11. 6-15.), so the Nazarite's hair marked his subjection and separation unto God. (Cf. Jud. 16. 17, with 2 Cor. 6. 17; Tit. 2. 14; 1 Pet. 2. 9.). Jesus Christ cares for the minutest concerns of His saints (Mat. 10. 30.). appear from—*lit.,* "*that lie down from,*" lying along the hillside, they seem to *hang from* it: a picture of the bride's hanging tresses. Gilead — beyond Jordan; there stood "the heap of witness" (Gen. 31. 48.). 2. even shorn—the *Heb.* is *transl.* 1 Ki. 6. 25.). "of one size;" so the point of comparison to *teeth* is their *symmetry* of form; as in "come up from the washing," the *spotless whiteness:* and in "twins," the *exact correspondence of the upper and under teeth:* and in "none barren," *none wanting,* none without its fellow. Faith is the tooth with which we eat the living bread (John, 6. 35, 54.), Contrast the teeth of sinners Ps. 57. 4; Pro. 30. 14; ; also their end (Ps. 3. 7; Mat. 25. 30.). Faith leads the flock to the washing (Zech. 13. 1; 1 Cor. 6. 11; Tit. 3. 5.). none ... barren— (2 Pet. 1. 8.). He who is begotten of God begets instrumentally other sons of God. 3. thread—like a delicate fillet. Not thick and white as the leper's lips (type of sin), which were therefore to be "covered," as "unclean" (Lev. 13. 45.). scarlet—the blood of Jesus Christ (Isa. 6. 5-9: cleanses the leprosy, and unseals the lips (Isa. 57. 19; Hos. 14. 2; Heb. 13. 15.). Rahab's scarlet thread was a type of it (Josh. 2. 18.). speech—not a separate feature from the *lips* Deut. 3. 9.). Contrast "uncircumcised lips" (Ex. 6. 12.). MAUR. and BUR. *transl.* "thy mouth." temples—rather, *the upper part of the cheek* next the temples: the seat of shamefacedness, so, "within thy locks," no display 1 Cor. 11. 5, 6, 15. . Mark of true penitence Ezra, 9. 6; Ez. 16. 63.). Contrast Jer. 3. 3; Ez. 3. 7. pomegranate—when cut, it displays in rows seeds pellucid, like crystal, tinged with red. Her modesty is not on the surface, but within, which Jesus Christ can see into. 4. neck— stately: in beautiful contrast to the blushing temples (*v.* 3.): not "stiff" (Isa. 48. 4; Acts, 7. 51., as that of unbroken nature; nor "stretched forth" wantonly Isa. 3. 16.); nor burdened with the legal yoke (Lam. 1. 14; Acts, 15. 10.); but erect in gospel freedom Isa. 52. 2.). tower of David—probably on Zion. He was a man of war, preparatory to the reign of Solomon, the king of peace. No warfare in the case of Jesus Christ and His saints precedes the coming rest. Each soul won from Satan by Him is a trophy gracing the bride Luke, 11. 22; (each hangs on Him, Isa. 22. 23, 24; ; also each victory of her faith. As shields adorn a temple's walls (Ez. 27. 11.), so necklaces hang on the bride's neck (Jud. 5.

30; 1 Ki. 10. 16.). 5. breasts—the bust is left open in Eastern dress. The breast-plate of the High Priest was made of "two" pieces, folded one on the other, in which were the Urim and Thummim *lights* and *perfection.*). "Faith and love" are the double breastplate (1 Thes. 5. 8., answering to "hearing the word" and "keeping it," in a similar connection with breasts Luke, 12. 27, 28.). roes He reciprocates her praise ch. 2. 9.). Emblem of *love* and *satisfaction* (Pro. 5. 19. . feed— (Ps. 23. 2.). among the lilies—shrinking from thorns of strife, worldliness, and ungodliness ;2 Sam. 23. 6; Mat. 13. 7.. Roes feed *among,* not *on* the lilies: where these grow, there is moisture, producing green pasturage. The lilies represent her white dress Ps. 45. 14; Rev. 19. 8.). 6. Historically, *the hill of frankincense* is Calvary, where, "through the eternal Spirit He offered Himself;" the mountain of myrrh is His embalment (John, 19. 39 till the resurrection "day-break." The 3d Canticle occupies the one cloudless day of His presence on earth, beginning from the night (ch. 2. 17) and ending with the night of His departure (ch. 4. 6.). His promise is almost exactly in the words of her prayer (ch. 2. 17) the same Holy Ghost breathing in Jesus Christ and His praying people, . with the difference that she then looked for His visible coming. He now tells her, that when He shall have gone from sight, He still is to be met with spiritually in prayer (Ps. 68. 16; Mat. 28. 20,', until the everlasting day break, when we shall see face to face (1 Cor. 13. 10, 12.). 7. Assurance that He is going from her in love, not in displeasure (John, 16. 6, 7.). all fair – still stronger than ch. 1. 15; *v.* 1. no spot—our privilege Eph. 5. 27; Col. 2. 10;: our duty (2 Cor. 6. 17; Jude, 23; Jam. 1. 27.). 8. Invitation to her to leave the border mountains (the highest worldly elevation) between the hostile lands N. of Palestine, and the Promised Land Ps. 45. 10; Phil. 3. 13.). Amana –S. of Anti-Libanus; the river Abana, or Amana, was near Damascus 2 Ki. 5. 12.). Shenir—The whole mountain was called *Hermon;* the part held by the Sidonians was called *Sirion;* the part held by the Amorites, *Shenir* Deut. 3. 9.). Infested by the devouring lion, and the stealthy and swift leopard (Ps. 76. 4; Eph. 6. 11; 1 Pet. 5. 8.). Contrasted with the mountain of myrrh, &c. *v.* 6; Isa. 2. 2;; the good land (Isa. 35. 9.), with *me*—twice repeated emphatically. The presence of Jesus Christ makes up for the absence of all beside (Luke, 18. 29, 30; 2 Cor. 6. 10. . Moses was permitted to see Canaan from Pisgah; Peter, James, and John, had a foretaste of glory on the mount of transfiguration. 9. sister ... spouse—this title is here first used: as he is soon about to institute the Supper, the pledge of the nuptial union. By the term "sister," carnal ideas are excluded; the ardour of a spouse's love is combined with the purity of a sister's Isa. 54. 5; cf. Mark, 3. 35. . one— even *one* look is enough to secure His love Zech. 12. 10; Luke, 23. 40-43.. Not merely the Church collectively, but each *one* the number of it Mat. 18, 10, 14; Luke, 15. 7, 24. 32., chain—necklace (Isa. 62. 3; Mal. 3. 17 answering to the "shields" hanging in the tower of David *v.* 4.). Cf. the "ornament" 1 Pet. 3. 4;; "chains" (Pro. 1. 9; 3. 22.). 10. love—*Heb. loves;* manifold tokens of thy love, much better—answering to her "better" ch. 1. 2.), but with *increased* force. An Amœbean

The Bridegroom   SOLOMON'S SONG, V.   *with the Bride.*

pastoral character pervades the Song, like the classic Amœbean Idylls and eclogues. wine —the love of His saints is a more reviving cordial to Him than wine; *ex. gr.*, at the feast in Simon's house (Luke, 7. 36, 47; John, 4. 32; cf. Zech. 10, 7. , smell of ... ointments than all spices—answering to her praise (ch. 1. 3,), with increased force. Fragrant, as being fruits of His Spirit in us (Gal. 5, 22.). 11. drop—always ready to fall, being full of honey, though not always (Pro. 10. 19) actually *dropping* (ch. 5. 13; Deut. 32. 2; Mat. 12. 34.). honey-comb— (Pro. 5. 3; 16. 24.). under thy tongue—not always *on*, but *under*, the tongue, ready to fall (Ps. 55. 21.). Contrast her former state (Ps. 140. 3; Rom. 3. 13.). "Honey and milk" were the glory of the good land. The change is illustrated in the penitent thief. Contrast Mat. 27. 44, with Luke, 23. 39, &c. It was *lit.*, with "one" eye, a sidelong glance of love "better than wine" that he refreshed Jesus Christ (*v.* 9, 10.). "To-day shalt thou be *with me* (cf. *v.* 8) in Paradise" (*v.* 12,), is the only joyous sentence of His seven utterances on the cross. smell of ... garments—which are often perfumed in the E. (Ps. 45. 8. . The perfume comes from Him on us (Ps. 133. 2.). We draw nigh to God in the perfumed garment of our elder brother (Gen. 27. 27; see Jude, 23.). Lebanon—abounding in odoriferous trees (Hos. 14: 5-7,). 12. The *Heb.* has no "is." Here she is distinct from the garden (ch. 5. 1,), yet identified with it (*v.* 16,), as being one with Him in His sufferings. Historically, the Paradise, into which the soul of Jesus Christ entered at death; and the tomb of Joseph, in which His body was laid amidst "myrrh," &c. (*v.* 6,), situated in a *nicely kept* garden cf. "gardener," John, 20. 15;) "sealed" with a stone (Mat. 27. 60;) in which resembles "wells" in the E. (Gen. 29. 3, 8.). It was in a garden of light Adam fell; in a garden of darkness, Gethsemane, and chiefly that of the tomb, the second Adam retrieved it. Spiritually, the garden is the gospel kingdom of heaven. Here all is ripe: previously ch. 2. 13,), it was "the *tender* grape." The garden is His, though he calls the plants her's (*v.* 13,), by his gift (Isa. 61, 3, end.). spring ... fountain—Jesus Christ (John, 4. 10) seated, whilst He was in the sealed tomb; it poured forth its full tide on Pentecost (John, 7. 37-39. . Still He is a sealed fountain, until the Holy Ghost open it to us (t Cor. 12. 3.). The Church also is "a garden enclosed" (Ps. 4, 5; Isa. 5. 1, &c.), Contrast Ps. 80. 9-12. So "a spring" (Isa. 27. 3; 58. 11;) "sealed" (Eph. 4, 30; 2 Tim. 2. 19.). As wives in the E. are secluded from public gaze, so believers (Ps. 83. 3; Col. 3. 3.). Contrast the open streams which "pass away" (Job, 6. 15-18; 2 Pet. 2. 17.). 13. orchard—*Heb., a paradise*, *i.e.*, a pleasure-ground and orchard. Not only flowers, but fruit-trees John, 15. 8; Phil. 1. 11. . camphire —not camphor (ch. 1. 14,), *hennah*, or cypress blooms. 14. calamus—"sweet cane" Ex. 30. 23; Jer. 6. 20.). myrrh and aloes—ointments are associated with His death, as well as with feasts John, 12. 7.). The bride's ministry of "myrrh and aloes" is recorded (John, 19. 39,). 15. of—this pleasure-ground is not dependent on mere reservoirs, it has a fountain *sufficient to water* many "gardens" (*plur.*). living—(Jer. 17. 8; John, 4. 13, 14; 7. 38, 39.). from Lebanon—though the fountain is lowly, the source is lofty; fed by the perpetual snows of Lebanon, refreshingly cool (Jer. 18.

14,), fertilising the gardens of Damascus. It springs upon earth; its source is heaven. It is now not "sealed," but open "streams" (Rev. 22. 17.). 16. Awake—*lit., Arise.* All beside is ready: one thing alone is wanted; the breath of God. This follows rightly after His death (ch. 6. 12; Acts, 2.. It is His call to the Spirit to come (John, 14. 16; ; in John, 3. 8, compared to "the wind;" quickening John, 6. 63; Ez. 27. 9.). Saints offer the same prayer (Ps. 85. 6; Hab. 3. 2.). The N. wind "*awakes,*" or *arises* strongly, *viz.*, the Holy Ghost as a reprover (John, 16. 8-11;); the S. wind "*comes*" gently, *viz.*. the Holy Ghost as the Comforter (John, 14. 16. . The W. wind brings rain from the sea (1 Ki. 18. 44, 45; Luke, 12. 54.). The E. wind is tempestuous (Job, 27. 21; Isa. 27. 8,) and withering (Gen. 41. 23.). These, therefore, are not wanted; but first the N. wind, clearing the air (Job, 37. 22; Pro. 25. 23,, and then the warm S. wind (*v.* 17;); so the Holy Ghost first clearing away mists of gloom, error, unbelief, sin, which intercept the light of Jesus Christ, then infusing spiritual warmth (2 Cor. 4. 6,, causing the graces to exhale their odour. Let my beloved, &c.—*The bride's reply.* The fruit was now at length ripe; the last passover, which He had so desired, is come (Luke. 22. 7, 15, 16, 18,), the only case in which He took charge of the preparations. his—answering to Jesus Christ's "my." She owns that the garden is His, and the fruits in her, which she does not in false humility deny (Ps, 66. 16; Acts, 21, 19; 1 Cor. 15. 10,), are His (John, 15. 8; Phil. 1. 11.).

CHAPTER V.

Ver. 1-10. 1. *Answer to her prayer* (Isa. 65. 24; Rev. 3. 20.). am come—already (ch. 4. 16;). "come" (Gen. 28. 16.). sister ... spouse—as Adam's was created of his flesh, out of his opened side, there being none on earth on a level with him; so the bride, out of the pierced Saviour (Eph. 5. 30-32.). have gathered the myrrh, &c. (Mat. 2. 11; 26. 7-12; John, 19. 39,), emblems of the indwelling of the anointing Holy Ghost, were already gathered. spice —*lit., balsam.* have eaten—answering to her "eat" ch. 4. 16.). honey-comb—distinguished here from liquid "honey" dropping from trees. The last supper, here set forth, is one of *espousal*, a pledge of the future *marriage* ch. 8. 14; Rev. 19. 9. . Feasts often took place in gardens. In the absence of sugar. then honey was more widely used than with us. His eating honey with milk indicate His true, yet spotless, human nature, from infancy (Isa. 7. 15;); and after His resurrection (Luke, 24. 42.). my wine—(John, 18. 11, , a cup of wrath to Him, of mercy to us, whereby God's word and promises become to us "milk" (Ps. 19, 10; 1 Pet. 2. 2.). "My" answers to "His" (ch. 4. 16.. The "myrrh emblem by its bitterness, of *repentance*,), honey, milk (*incipient faith*,). wine" [*strong faith*,, in reference to believers, imply that He accepts all their graces, however various in degree. eat—He desires to make us partakers in His joy (Isa. 55. 1, 2; John, 6. 53-57; 1 John, 1. 3.). drink abundantly—so as to be *filled* (Eph. 5. 18; as Hag. 1. 6.). friends— John, 15. 15.).

CANTICLE IV.—Ch. v. 2—viii. 5.—FROM THE AGONY OF GETHSEMANE, TO THE CONVERSION OF SAMARIA. 2. Sudden change of scene from evening to midnight. from a betrothal feast to cold repulse. He has gone from the feast alone; night is come; He knocks at the door of His espoused; she hears, but in sloth does not shake off half-conscious drowsiness: *viz.*, the disciples' torpor (Mat. 26. 40-43,), " the spirit willing, the flesh weak" (cf. Rom. 7.; Gal. 5.). Not *total* sleep. The lamp was burning beside the *slumbering* wise virgin, but wanted trimming (Mat. 25. 5-7.). It is *His* voice that rouses her (Jon. 1. 6; Eph. 5. 14; Rev. 3. 20.). Instead of bitter reproaches, He addresses her by the most endearing titles, " my sister, my love," &c. Cf. His thought of *Peter* after the denial (Mark, 16. 7.'. d-w—which falls heavily in summer nights in the E. see Luke, 9. 58.). drops of the night—(Ps. 22. 2; Luke, 22. 44.). His death is not *expressed*, as unsuitable to the allegory, a song of love and joy; *v.* 4. refers to the scene in the judgment hall of Caiaphas, when Jesus Christ employed the cock-crowing and look of love to awaken Peter's sleeping conscience, so that his "bowels were moved" (Luke, 22. 61, 62;); *v.* 5, 6, the disciples with " myrrh," &c. (Luke, 24. 1, 5,), seeking Jesus Christ in the tomb, but finding Him not, for He has " withdrawn Himself" (John, 7. 34; 13. 33;); *v.* 7, the trials by watchmen extend through the whole night of His withdrawal from Gethsemane to the resurrection; they took off the " veil" of Peter's disguise; also *lit.*, the linen cloth from the young man (Mark, 14. 51;); *v.* 8, the sympathy of friends (Luke, 23. 27.). undefiled — not polluted by spiritual adultery (Rev. 14. 4; Jam. 4. 4.). 3. Trivial excuses (Luke, 14. 18.). coat—rather, *the inmost vest*, next the skin, taken off before going to bed. washed . . . feet—before going to rest for they had been soiled, from the Eastern custom of wearing sandals, not shoes. Sloth (Luke, 11. 7,), and despondency (Deut. 7. 17-19.). 4. A key in the E. is usually a piece of wood with pegs in it, corresponding to small holes in a wooden bolt within, and is put through a hole in the door, and thus draws the bolt. So Jesus Christ " puts forth His hand (*viz.*, His Spirit, Ez. 3. 14,), by (Heb. *from,* so in ch. 2. 9; the hole;" in " chastening." (Ps. 38. 2; Rev. 3. 14-22, singularly similar to this passage,) and other unexpected ways letting Himself in (Luke, 22. 61, 62,). bowels . . . moved for him—it is H's, which are first troubled for us, and which cause ours to be troubled for Him (Jer. 31. 20; Hos, 11. 8.). 5. dropped with myrrh—the best proof a bride could give her lover of welcome was to anoint herself the back of the hands especially, as being the coolest part of the body,), *profusely* with the *best* perfumes (Ex. 30. 23; Esth. 2. 12; Pro. 7. 17;); "sweet-smelling" is in the *Heb.* rather, "spontaneously exuding" from the tree, and therefore the *best.* She designed also to anoint Him, whose "head was filled with the drops of night" Luke, 24. 1.). The myrrh typifies *bitter* repentance, the fruit of the Spirit's unction (2 Cor. 1. 21, 22.). handles of the lock —sins which closed the heart against Him. 6. withdrawn—He *knocked,* when she was sleeping; for to have left her *then* would have ended in the death sleep; He *withdraws* now that she is roused, as she needs correction (Jer. 2. 17, 19,), and can appreciate and safely bear it now, which she could not then. "The strong He'll strongly try" (1 Cor. 10. 13.). when he spake—rather, *because of His speaking*; at the remembrance of His tender words (Job, 29. 2, 3; Ps. 27. 13; 142. 7,), or, *till He* *should speak*. no answer—(Job, 23. 3-9; 30. 20; 34. 29; Lam. 3. 44.). Weak faith receives immediate comfort (Luke, 8. 44, 47, 48;); strong faith is tried with delay (Mat. 15. 22, 23.). 7. watchmen — historically, the Jewish priests, &c. (see note on *v.* 2;); spiritually, ministers (Isa. 62. 6; Heb. 13. 17,), faithful in " smiting" (Ps. 141. 5.), but (as she leaves them, *v.* 8,), too harshly; or, perhaps, unfaithful; disliking her zeal wherewith she sought Jesus Christ, first, with spiritual prayer, "open n." her heart to Him, and then in charitable works " about the city;" miscalling it fanaticism (Isa. 66. 5,), and taking away her veil (the greatest indignity to an Eastern lady,), as though she were positively immodest. She had before sought Him by night in the streets, under strong affection (ch. 3. 2-4,), and so without rebuff from " the wat hmen," found Him immediately; but now after sinful neglect, she encounters pain and delay. God forgives believers, but it is a serious thing to draw on His forgiveness; so the *growing reserve* of God towards Israel observable in Judges, as His people repeat their demands on His grace. 8. She turns from the unsympathising watchmen to humbler persons, not yet themselves knowing Him, but in the way towards it. Historically, His secret friends in the night of His withdrawal (Luke, 23. 27, 28.). Enquirers *may* find " *if ye find*") Jesus Christ before she who has grieved His Spirit finds Him again. tell — in prayer (Jam. 5. 16,). sick of love—from an opposite cause (ch. 2. 5) than through excess of delight at His *presence;* now excess of pain at His *absence.* 9. Her own beauty (Ez. 16. 14,), and love sickness for Him, elicit now their enquiry (Mat. 5. 16;): heretofore " other lords beside Him had dominion over them;" thus they had seen "no beauty in Him" (Isa. 26. 13; 53. 2.). 10. (1 Pet. 3. 15.). white and ruddy —health and beauty. So David (equivalent to *beloved,*), His forefather after the flesh, and type (1 Sam. 17. 42.). "The Lamb" is at once His nuptial and sacrificial name. 1 Pet. 1. 19; Rev. 19. 7,), characterised by white and red; *white.* His spotless manhood Rev. 1. 14.). The *Heb.* for *white,* is properly *illuminated by the sun,* " white as the light" (cf. Mat. 17. 2;); *red,* in His blood-dyed garment, as slain (Isa. 63. 1-3; Rev. 5. 6; 19. 13.). Angels are white, not red; the blood of martyrs does not enter heaven, His alone is seen there. chiefest—*lit.*, *a standard bearer; i.e..* as conspicuous above all others, as a standard bearer is among hosts (Ps. 45. 7; 89. 6; Isa. 11. 10; 55. 4; Heb. 2. 10; cf. 2 Sam. 18. 3; Job, 33. 23; Phil. 2. 9-11; Rev. 1. 5.). The chief of sinners needs the "chiefest" of Saviours. 11. head . . . gold—*the Godhead* of Jesus Christ, as distinguished from His *heel, i.e.,* His manhood, which was " bruised" by Satan; both together being one Christ (1 Cor. 11. 3.'. Also His sovereignty, as Nebuchadnezzar the supreme king was "the head of gold" (Dan. 2. 32-38; Col. 1. 18,', the highest creature, compared with Him, is brass, iron, and clay. " Preciousness," *Gr.,* 1 Pet. 2. 7.). bushy—*curled,* token of Headship. In contrast with her *flowing* locks (ch. 4. 1.), the token of her subjection to Him (Ps. 8. 4-8; 1 Cor. 11. 3, 6-15.). The *Heb.* is (pendulous as) the *branches of a palm,* which, when in leaf, resemble waving plumes of feathers. black—implying youth; no "rey hairs" (Ps. 102. 27; 110. 3, 4; Hos. 7. 9.). Jesus Christ was crucified in the prime of vigour

CHAPTER VIII.

1 Love of the church to Christ. 6 Vehemence of love. 8 Calling of the Gentiles. 14 Christ's coming prayed for.

OH that thou wert as my brother, that sucked the breasts of my mother! when I should find thee without, I would kiss thee; yea, I I should not be despised.

2 I would lead thee, and bring thee into my mother's house, who would instruct me: I would cause thee to drink of *a* spiced wine of the juice of my pomegranate.

3 His *b* left hand *should be* under my head, and his right hand should embrace me.

4 I charge you, O daughters of Jerusalem, *3* that ye stir not up, nor awake my love, until he please.

5 ¶ Who *is* this that cometh up from *c* the wilderness, leaning upon her beloved? I raised thee up under the apple tree: there thy mother brought thee forth; there she brought thee forth *that* bare thee.

6 Set *d* me as a seal upon thine heart, as a seal upon thine arm; for *e* love *is* strong as death; jealousy *is 3* cruel as the grave: the coals thereof *are* coals of fire, *which hath* a most vehement flame.

7 Many waters cannot quench love, neither can the floods drown it: *f* if a man would give all the substance of his house for love, it would utterly be contemned.

8 ¶ We *g* have a little sister, and she hath no breasts: what shall we do for our sister in the day when she shall be spoken for?

9 If she *be* a wall, we will build upon her a palace of silver; and if she *be h* a door, we will inclose her with boards of cedar.

10 I *i am* a wall, and *j* my breasts like towers: then was I in his eyes as one that found *4* favour.

11 Solomon had a vineyard at Baal-hamon; he *k* let out the vineyard unto keepers; every one for the fruit thereof was to bring a thousand *pieces* of silver.

12 My vineyard, which *is* mine, *is* before me: thou, O Solomon, *must have* a thousand, and those that keep the fruit thereof two hundred.

13 Thou that dwellest in the gardens, the companions hearken to thy voice: *l* cause me to hear *it.*

14 ¶ *5* Make haste, my beloved, and *m* be thou like to a roe or to a young hart upon the mountains of spices.

THE BOOK OF THE PROPHET

ISAIAH.

CHAPTER I.

1 Isaiah's complaint of Judah; 5 their universal corruption; 16 he exhorts to repentance, with promises and threatenings; 21 the prophet bewails their wickedness.

THE *a* vision of Isaiah the son of Amoz, which he saw concerning Judah and Jerusalem, in the *b* days of Uzziah, Jotham, Ahaz, *and* Hezekiah, kings of Judah.

2 ¶ Hear, O heavens, and give ear, O earth: for the LORD hath spoken, I have nourished and brought up children, and they have rebelled against me.

3 The ox knoweth his owner, and the ass his master's crib: *but* Israel *c* doth not know, my people doth not consider.

4 Ah sinful nation, a people *1* laden with iniquity, a *d* seed of evil-doers, children that are corrupters! They have forsaken the LORD, they have provoked the Holy One of Israel unto anger, they are *2* gone away backward.

5 Why *e* should ye be stricken any more? ye will *3* revolt more and more. The whole head is sick, and the whole heart faint.

6 From the sole of the foot even unto the head *there* is no soundness in it; *but* wounds, and bruises, and putrifying sores: they *f* have not been closed, neither bound up, neither mollified with *4* ointment.

7 Your *g* country *is* desolate, your cities *are* burnt with fire: your land, strangers devour it in your presence, and *it is* desolate, *5* as overthrown by strangers.

8 And the daughter of Zion is left as a cottage in a vineyard, as a lodge in a garden of cucumbers, as a besieged city.

9 Except *h* the LORD of hosts had left unto us a very small remnant, we should have been as Sodom, *and* we should have been like unto Gomorrah.

10 ¶ Hear the word of the LORD, ye rulers of *i* Sodom; give ear unto the law of our God, ye people of Gomorrah.

11 To what purpose *is* the multitude of your *j* sacrifices unto me? saith the LORD: I am full of the burnt offerings of rams, and the fat of fed beasts; and I delight not in the blood of bullocks, or of lambs, or of *6* he-goats.

12 When ye come *7* to appear before me, who hath required this at your hand, to tread my courts?

13 Bring no more vain oblations; incense is an abomination unto me; the new moons and sabbaths, the calling of assemblies, I cannot away with; *it is 8* iniquity, even the solemn meeting.

14 Your new moons and your appointed feasts my soul hateth: they are a trouble unto me; I am weary to bear *them.*

15 And *k* when ye spread forth your hands, I will hide mine eyes from you; *l* yea, when ye *9* make many prayers, I will not hear; your hands are full of *10* blood.

16 Wash *m* you, make you clean; put away the evil of your doings from before mine eyes; *q* cease to do evil;

17 Learn to do well; *o* seek judgment,*11* relieve the oppressed, judge the fatherless, plead for the widow.

18 ¶ Come now, and *p* let us reason together, saith the LORD: Though your sins be as scarlet, *q* they shall be as white as snow; though they be red like crimson, they shall be as wool.

19 If *r* ye be willing and obedient, ye shall eat the good of the land:

20 But if ye refuse and rebel, ye shall be devoured with the sword: *s* for the mouth of the LORD hath spoken *it.*

21 ¶ How is the faithful city become an

and manliness. In heaven, on the other hand, His hair is "white." He being the Ancient of days (Dan. 7. 9.). These contrasts often concur in Him (v. 10,), "white and ruddy;" here the "raven" (v. 12.), the "dove," as both with Noah in the ark (Gen. 8.). emblems of judgment and mercy. 12. as the eyes of doves—rather, as *doves* (Ps. 68. 13;); bathing in "the rivers," so combining in their "silver" feathers the *whiteness* of milk with the *sparkling brightness* of the water trickling over them (Mat. 3. 16.). The "milk" may allude to the white around the pupil of the eye. The "waters" refer to the eye as the fountain of *tears of sympathy* (Ez. 16. 5, 6; Luke, 19. 41.). Vivacity, purity, and love, are the three features typified. fitly set—as a gem in a ring; as the precious stones in the High Priest's breastplate. Rather, *transl.* as *Vulg.*, the doves *sitting at the fulness* of the stream; by the full stream; or as MAUR. (the eyes *set in fulness*, not sunk in their sockets (Rev. 5. 6,). ("seven," expressing *full* perfection! Zech. 3. 9; 4. 10.). 13. cheeks — the seat of beauty, according to the *Heb.* meaning. [GES.] Yet men smote and spat on them (Isa. 50, 6.). bed—full, like the raised surface of the garden bed; fragrant with ointments, as beds with aromatic plants [*lit., balsam.*]. sweet flowers—rather, "*terraces* of aromatic herbs,"—"*high raised* parterres of sweet plants," in parallelism to "bed," which comes from a *Heb.* root, meaning *elevation.* lips—(Ps. 45. 2; John, 7. 46.). lilies —red lilies. Soft and gentle (1 Pet. 2. 22, 23.). How different lips were man's (Ps. 22. 7)! dropping . . . myrrh—*viz..* His lips. just as the sweet dew-drops which hang in the calix of the lily. 14. rings set with . . . beryl—*Heb.*, *Tarshish*, so called from the city. The ancient chrysolite, gold in colour (LXX.), our topaz, one of the stones on the High Priest's breastplate, also in the foundation of New Jerusalem (Rev. 21.; also Dan. 10. 6.). "Are as," is pl inly to be supplied, see in *v.* 13 a similar ellipsis; not as M. STUART: "*have* gold rings." The hands bent in are compared to beautiful rings, in which beryl is set, as the nails are in the fingers. BUR. explains the rings as *cylinders* used as signets, such as are found in Nineveh, and which resemble fingers. A ring is the token of sonship (Luke, 15. 22.). A slave was not allowed to wear a *gold* ring. He imparts His sonship and freedom to us (Gal. 4. 7;); also of authority (Gen. 41. 42; cf. John, 6. 27.). He seals us in the name of God with His signet (Rev. 7. 2-4.). cf. below, ch. 8. 6, where she desires to be herself *a signet-ring* on His arm; not "graven on the palms," &c., *i.e.* on the signet-ring in His hand (Isa. 49. 16; contrast Hag. 2. 23, with Jer. 22. 24.), belly—BUR. and M. STUART *transl.* "body." NEWTON, as it is elsewhere, "bowels," *viz.*, His compassion (Ps. 22. 14; Isa. 63, 15; Jer. 31. 20; Hos. 11. 8.). bright — *lit., elaborately wrought, so as to shine*, so His "prepared" body (Heb. 10. 5.;); the "ivory palace" of the king (Ps. 45. 8;); spotless, pure, so the bride's "neck is as a tower of *ivory*" ch. 7. 4. sapphires — spangling in the *girdle* round Him Dan. 10. 5.). "To the pure all things are pure." As in statuary to the artist the partly undraped figure is suggestive only of beauty, free from indelicacy, so to the saint, the personal excellencies of Jesus Christ, typified under the ideal of the noblest human form. As, however, the bride and bridegroom are in public, the usual robes on the person, richly ornamented, are presupposed (Isa. 11. 5.). Sapphires indicate His *heavenly* nature so John, 3. 13, "*is* in heaven,"), even in His humiliation, *overlaying* or cast "over" His ivory human body (Ex. 24. 10.). Sky-blue in colour, the *height* and *depth* of the love of Jesus Christ (Eph. 3. 18.). 15. pillars—strength and stedfastness. Contrast man's "legs" Eccl. 12. 3.). Allusion to the temple (1 Ki. 5. 8, 9; 7. 21.), the "cedars" of "Lebanon" Ps. 147. 10.). Jesus Christ's "legs" were not broken on the cross, though the thieves' were; on them rests the weight of our salvation (Ps. 75. 3.). sockets of gold—His sandals, answering to the bases of the pillars; "*set* up from everlasting" (Pro. 8. 22, 23.). From the head *v.* 11) to the feet, "of fine gold." He was tried in the fire and found without alloy. countenance —rather, *His aspect*, including both *mien* and stature (cf. *Marg.* 2. Sam. 23. 21; with 1 Chr. 11. 23.). From the several *parts*, she proceeds to the general effect of the *whole* person of Jesus Christ. Lebanon — so called from its *white* limestone rocks. excellent—*lit.*, *choice i.e., fair and tall* as the cedars on Lebanon (Ez. 31. 3, &c.). Majesty is the prominent thought (Ps. 21. 5.). Also the cedar's *duration* 2. 9.). my beloved — for I love Him. my friend—for He loves me (Pro. 18. 24.). Holy boasting (Ps. 34. 2; 1 Cor. 1. 31.).

CHAPTER VI.

Ver. 1-13. 1. Historically, at Jesus Christ's crucifixion and burial, Joseph of Arimathea and Nicodemus, and others, joined with His professed disciples. By speaking of Jesus Christ, the bride does not only to her own soul, but to others note, ch. 1. 4; Mal. 3. 16; Mat. 5. 14-16.). Cf. the hypocritical use of similar words Mat. 2. 8.). 2. gone down — Jerusalem was on a hill (answering to its *moral* elevation,), and the gardens were at a little distance in the valleys below, beds of spices—(balsam) which He Himself calls the "mountain of myrrh," &c. ch. 4. 6., and again (ch. 8. 14,), the resting-place of His body amidst spices, and of His soul in paradise, and now in heaven, where He stands an High Priest for ever. Nowhere else in the Song is there mention of mountains of spices. feed in . . . gardens — *i.e.*, in the churches, though He may have withdrawn for a time from the individual believer: she implies an invitation to the daughters of Jerusalem to enter His spiritual Church, and become lilies, made white by His blood. He is gathering some lilies now to plant on earth, others to transplant into heaven (ch. 5. 1; Gen. 5. 24; Mark, 4. 28, 29; Acts, 7. 60.). 3. In speaking of Jesus Christ to others, she regains her own assurance. Lit., "I am *for* my beloved . . . *for me.*" Reverse order from ch. 2. 16. She *now*, after the season of darkness, grounds her conviction on His love towards her, more than on her's towards Him (Deut. 33. 3,. There, it was the young believer concluding that she was His, from the sensible assurance that He was her's, Tirzah — meaning *pleasant* (Heb. 13. 21;); "well-pleasing" (Mat. 5. 14;"; the royal city of one of the old Canaanite kings (Josh. 12. 24;); and after the revolt of Israel, the royal city of its kings, before Omri founded Samaria (1 Ki. 16. 8, 15.). No ground for assigning a later date than the time of Solomon to the Song, as Tirzah was even in his time the capital of the N. (Israel.;, as Jerusalem was of the S. (Judah.). Jerusalem—residence of the kings of *Judah*, as Tirzah, of *Israel* (Ps. 48. 1, &c.; 122. 1-3; 125. 1, 2.. Loveliness, security, unity, and loyalty; also the union of Israel and Judah in the Church (Isa. 11. 13; Jer. 3. 18; Ez. 37. 16, 17. 22; cf. Heb. 12. 22; Rev. 21. 2, 12.). terrible—awe-inspiring. Not only armed as a city on the defensive, but as an army on the offensive. banners—note, ch. 5. 10; Ps. 60, 4;); Jehovah-Nissi (2 Cor. 10. 4.). 5. (Ch. 4. 9; Gen. 32. 28; Ex. 32. 9-14; Hos. 12. 4.). This is the way "the army" (v. 4) "overcomes" not only enemies, but Jesus Christ Himself, with eyes fixed on Him (Ps. 25. 15; Mat. 11. 12.). Historically, v. 3, 4, 5. represent the restoration of Jesus Christ to His Church at the resurrection; His sending her forth as an army, with new powers (Mark, 16. 15-18, 20;); His rehearsing the *same* instructions (cf. v. 6, note,), as when with them (Luke, 24. 44.). overcome—*lit., have taken me by storm.* 6. Not vain repetition of ch. 4. 1, 2. The use of the same words shows his love unchanged, after her temporary unfaithfulness (Mal. 3. 6.). 8. threescore —indefinite number, as ch. 3. 7. Not queens, &c. *of Solomon,* but witnesses of the espousals, rulers of the earth contrasted with the saints, who, though many, are but "one" bride (Isa. 52. 15; Luke, 22. 25, 26; John, 17. 21; 1 Cor. 10. 17.). The one bride is contrasted with the many wives whom Eastern kings had in violation of the marriage law 1 Ki. 11. 1-3.). 9. Hollow professors, like half-wives, have no part in the one bride. only one of her mother — *viz.,* "Jerusalem above" (Gal. 4. 26.). The "little sister" ch. 8. 8) is not inconsistent with her being "the only one," for that sister is one with herself (John, 10. 16.). choice—(Eph. 1. 4; 2 Thes. 2. 13.). As she exalted Him above all others (ch. 5. 10,); so He now her. daughters ... blessed her—(Isa. 8. 18; 61. 9; Ez. 16. 14; 2 Thes. 1. 10.). So at her appearance after Pentecost (Acts, 4. 13; 6. 15; 24. 25; 26. 28.). 10. The words expressing the admiration of the daughters. Historically (Acts, 5. 24-39.). as the morning —as yet she is not come to the fulness of her light (1 Pro. 4. 18.). moon—shining in the night, by light borrowed from the sun: so the bride, in the darkness of this world, reflects the light of the Sun of righteousness (2 Cor. 3. 18.). sun—her light of justification is perfect, for it is His (2 Cor. 5. 21; 1 John, 4. 17.). The moon has less light, and has only one half illuminated; so the bride's sanctification is as yet imperfect. Her future glory (Mat. 13. 43.). army—(v. 4.). The climax requires this to be applied to the starry and angelic hosts, from which God is called Lord of Sabaoth. Her final glory (Gen. 15. 5; Dan. 12. 3; Rev. 12. 1,). The Church Patriarchal, "the morning," Levitical, "the moon;" Evangelical, "the sun;" Triumphant, "the bannered army" (Rev. 19. 14.). 11. The bride's words; for she everywhere is the narrator, and often soliloquises, which He never does. The first garden (ch. 2. 11-13) was that of spring, full of flowers and grapes not yet ripe: the second, autumn, with spices (which are always connected with the person of Jesus Christ,), and nothing unripe (ch. 4. 13, &c.). The third here, of "nuts," from the previous autumn; the end of winter, and verge of spring: the Church in the upper room (Acts, 1. 13, &c..), when one dispensation was just closed, the other not yet begun; the hard shell of the old needing to be broken, and its inner sweet kernel extracted [ORIGEN], Luke, 24. 27, 32;); waiting for the Holy Ghost to usher in spiritual spring. The *walnut* is meant with a bitter outer husk, a hard shell, and sweet kernel. So the Word is distasteful to the careless; when awakened, the sinner finds the letter hard, until the Holy Ghost reveals the sweet inner spirit. fruits of the valley—MAUR. *transl.,* "the *blooming products* of the *river*," i.e., the plants growing on the margin of the river flowing through the garden. She goes to watch the *first* sproutings of the various plants. 12. Sudden outpouring of the Spirit on Pentecost Acts, 2.,), whilst the Church was using the means (answering to "the garden," v. 11; John, 3. 8.). Ammi-nadib—supposed to be one proverbial for swift-driving. Similarly (ch. 1. 9.). Rather, *my willing people* (Ps. 110. 3.). A willing chariot bore a "willing people;" or Nadib is *the Prince,* Jesus Christ (Ps. 68. 17.). She is borne in a moment into His presence (Eph. 2. 6.). 13. Entreaty of the daughters of Jerusalem to her, in her chariot-like flight from them cf. 2 Ki. 2. 12; 2 Sam. 19. 14.). Shulamite—new name applied to her now first. *Fem.* of Solomon, Prince of Peace: His bride, daughter of peace, accepting and proclaiming it (Isa. 52. 7; John, 14. 27; Rom. 5. 1; Eph. 2. 17.). Historically, this name answers to the time when, not without a divine design in it, the young Church met in *Solomon's* porch (Acts, 3. 11; 5. 12.). The entreaty, "Return, O Shulamite," answers to the people's desire to keep Peter and John. after the lame man was healed, when they were about to enter the temple. Their reply attributing the glory not to themselves, but to Jesus Christ, answers to the bride's reply here, "What will ye see" in me? "As it were," &c. She accepts the name Shulamite, as truly describing her. But adds, that though "one" (v. 9,), she is nevertheless "two." Her glories are her Lord's, beaming through her (Eph. 5. 31, 32.). The two armies are the family of Jesus Christ in heaven, and that on earth, joined and one with Him; the one militant, the other triumphant. Or Jesus Christ and His ministering angels are one army, the Church the other, both being one (John, 17, 21, 22,). Allusion is made to Mahanaim 'meaning, *two hosts,*), the scene of Jacob's victorious conflict by prayer (Gen. 32. 2, 9, 22-30.). Though she is peace, yet she has warfare here, between flesh and spirit within and foes without: her strength, as Jacob's at Mahanaim, is Jesus Christ and His host enlisted on her side by prayer: whence she obtains those graces, which raise the admiration of the daughters of Jerusalem.

CHAPTER VII.

Ver. 1-13. thy feet—rather, *thy goings* (Ps. 17. 5.). Evident allusion to Isa. 52. 7: "*How beautiful* ... are *the feet* of him ... that publisheth *peace,*' (Shulamite, ch. 6. 13.). shoes —sandals are richly-jewelled in the E. (Luke,

15, 22; Eph. 5. 15.). She is evidently "on the mountains," whither she was wafted (ch. 6. 12.), *above* the daughters of Jerusalem, who therefore portray her *feet* first. daughter—of God the Father, with whom Jesus Christ is one (Mat. 5. 9,), "children of (the) God" of *peace*, equivalent to Shulamite (Ps. 45. 10-15; 2 Cor. 6. 18,), as well as bride of Jesus Christ. "Prince's," therefore princely herself, freely giving the word of life to others, not sparing her "feet," as in ch. 5. 3; Ex. 12, 11. To act on the offensive is defensive to ourselves. joints—rather, *the rounding;* the full graceful curve of the hips in the female figure; like the *rounding* of a *necklace* (as the *Heb.* for "jewels" means.). Cf. with the *E.V.*, Eph. 4. 13-16; Col. 2. 19. Or, applying it to the *girdle* binding together the robes round the hips (Eph. 6. 14.). cunning workman—(Ps. 139. 14-16; Eph. 2. 10, 22; 5. 29, 30, 32.), 2. navel —rather, *girdle-clasp*, called from the part of the person underneath. The "shoes" (v. 1) prove that *dress* is throughout presupposed on all parts where it is usually worn. She is "a bride adorned for her husband;" the "uncomely parts" being most adorned 1 Cor. 12. 23.). The girdle-clasp was adorned with red rubies resembling the "round goblet" (crater or *mixer*) of spice-mixed wine (not "liquor") (ch. 8. 2; Isa. 5. 22.). The wine of the "N. T. in His blood" (Luke, 22. 20.). The spiritual exhilaration by it was mistaken for that caused by new wine (Acts, 2. 13-17; Eph. 5. 18.), belly—*i.e., the vesture* on it. As in Ps. 45. 13, 14, gold and needlework compose the bride's attire, so golden-coloured "wheat" and white "lilies" here. The ripe grain, in token of harvest joy, used to be decorated with lilies; so the accumulated spiritual food (John, 6. 35; 12. 24,), free from chaff, not fenced with thorns, but made attractive by lilies (believers, ch. 2. 2; Acts, 2. 46, 47; 5. 13, 14, in common partaking of it.). Associated with the exhilarating wine-cup (Zech. 9. 17,), as here. 3. The daughters of Jerusalem describe her in the same terms as Jesus Christ in ch. 4. 5. The testimonies of heaven and earth coincide. twins—faith and love. 4. tower of ivory —in ch. 4. 4. Jesus Christ saith, "a tower of David builded for an armoury." Strength and conquest are the main thought in His description: here, beauty and polished whiteness: contrast ch. 1. 5. fish-pools — seen by BURCKHARDT, clear (Rev. 22. 1.), deep, quiet, and full 1 Cor. 2. 10, 15.). Heshbon—E. of Jordan, residence of the Amorite king, Sihon (Num. 21. 25, &c.,), afterwards held by Gad. Bath-rabbim — *Daughter of a multitude;* a crowded thoroughfare. Her eyes (ch. 4. 1) are called by Jesus Christ, "doves' eyes," waiting on Him. But here, looked on by the daughters of Jerusalem, they are compared to a placid lake. She is calm even amidst the crowd Pro. 8. 2; John, 16. 33,). nose—or, *face.* tower of Lebanon—a border fortress, watching the hostile Damascus. Towards Jesus Christ, her face was full of holy shame (ch. 4. 1, 3, notes;); towards spiritual foes, like a watchtower (Hab. 2. 1; Mark, 13. 37; Acts, 4. 13,), elevated, so that she looks not up from earth to heaven, but down from heaven to earth. If we retain "nose," discernment of spiritual fragrance is meant. 5. upon thee—the *head-dress* " upon" her. Carmel —signifying *a well-cultivated field* (Isa. 35. 2.). In ch. 5. 15, He is compared to *majestic Le*banon; she here, to *fruitful Carmel.* Her head-dress, or crown (2 Tim. 4. 8; 1 Pet. 5. 4.). Also the souls won by her (1 Thes. 2. 19, 20,), a token of her *fruitfulness.* purple—royalty (Rev. 1. 6.). As applied to hair, it expresses the glossy splendour of black hair *int.,* pendulous hair so much admired in the E. (ch. 4. 1. . Whilst the King compares her hair to the flowing hair of goats the token of her *subjection*, , the daughters of Jerusalem compare it to *royal* purple. galleries—(so ch. 1. 17, *Marg.*; Rev. 21. 3.'. But MAUR. *transl.* here, "flowing ringlets:" with these, as with *thongs* (so LEE, from the *Arabic, transl.* it) "the King is held" bound ch. 6. 5; Pro. 6. 25. . Her purple crown of martyrdom especially captivated the King, appearing from His galleries (Acts, 7. 55, 56.). As Samson's strength was in his locks (Jud. 16. 17.). Here first the daughters see the King themselves. 6. Nearer advance of the daughters to the Church Acts, 2. 47; 5. 13, end.). Love to her is the first token of love to Him 1 John. 5. 1, end.). delights—fascinating charms to them and to the King (v. 5; Isa. 62. 4, Hephzi-bah.). Hereafter, too (Zeph. 3. 17; Mal. 3. 12; Rev. 21. 9. . 7. palm-tree— Ps. 92. 12.). The sure sign of *water near* (Ex. 15. 27; John. 7. 38.). clusters —not of dates, as M. STUART thinks. The parallelism *v.* 8, , "clusters of the vine," shows it is here clusters of grapes. Vines were often trained (termed "wedded", on other trees. 8. The daughters are no longer content to admire, but resolve to lay hold of her fruits, high though these be. The palm stem is bare for a great height, and has its crown of fruit-laden boughs at the summit. It is the symbol of triumphant joy (John, 12. 13;); so hereafter (Rev. 7. 9,). breasts—(Isa. 66. 11.). i.e vine—Jesus Christ Hos. 14. 7, end; John, 15. 1.). nose—i.e., breath: the Holy Ghost breathed into her *nostrils* by Him, whose "mouth is most sweet" (ch. 5. 16.), apples—citrons, off the tree to which He is likened ch. 2. 3,). 9. roof of thy mouth—thy voice (Pro. 15. 23,). best wine—the *new* wine of the gospel kingdom Mark, 14. 25,), poured out at Pentecost (Acts, 2. 4, 13, 17.). for my beloved —(ch. 4. 10. . Here first the daughters call Him *theirs*, and become one with the bride. The steps successively are ch. 1. 5) where they misjudge her ch. 3. 11;): ch. 5. 8, where the possibility of their finding Him, before she regained Him, is expressed; ch. 5. 9 (ch. 6. 1; 7. 6, 9;); (John, 4. 42,), causing . . . asleep to speak—(Isa. 35. 6; Mark, 5. 19, 20; Acts, 2. 47; Eph. 5. 14.) Jesus Christ's first miracle turned water into "good wine kept until now" John, 2.;); just as the gospel revives those asleep and dying under the law (Pro. 31. 6; Rom. 7. 9, 10, 24, 25; 8. 1.). 10. Words of the daughters of Jerusalem and the bride, now united into one (Acts, 4. 32). They are mentioned again distinctly ch. 8. 4, , as fresh converts were being added Him, from among inquirers, and these needed to be charged not to grieve the Spirit, his desire is toward me—strong assurance. He so desires us, as to give us sense of his desire towards us (Ps. 139. 17, 18; Luke, 22. 15; Gal 2. 20; 1 John, 4. 16.). 11. field—the country. "The tender grape (MAUR. *transl.*, flowers and vines" occurred before (ch. 2. 13. . But here she prepares for Him all kinds of fruit old and new; also, she anticipates, in going forth to seek them, communion with Him in "loves." "Early" implies immediate earnestness. The villages." imply distance from Jerusalem. At Stephen's death the disciples were scattered from it through Judea and Samaria, preaching the word (Acts, 8.). Jesus Christ was with them, confirming the word with miracles. They gathered the *old* fruits, of which Jesus Christ had sowed the seed (John, 4.), as well as *new* fruits. lodge — forsaking *home* for Jesus Christ's sake (Mat. 19. 20.). 12. (Mark, 1. 35; John, 9. 4; Gal. 6. 10.). Assurance fosters diligence, not indolence. 13. mandrakes — *Heb. dudaim*, from a root, meaning *to love;* love-apples, supposed to exhilarate the spirits and excite love. Only here and Gen. 30. 14-16.. *Atropa mandragora* of Linnæus: its leaves like lettuce, but dark green, flowers purple, root forked, fruit of the size of an apple, ruddy and sweet-smelling, gathered in wheat-harvest, *i.e.,* in May. (*Mariti*, ii. 195.) gates—the entrance to the kiosk or summer-house. Love "lays up" the best of every thing for the person beloved 1 Cor. 10. 31; Phil. 3. 8; 1 Pet. 4. 11,'. thereby really, though unconsciously, laying up for itself (1 Tim. 6. 18, 19.)

CHAPTER VIII.
Ver. 1-14. 1. He had been a brother already. Why, then, this prayer here? It refers to the time after His resurrection, when the previous *outward* intimacy with Him was no longer allowed, but it was implied, it should be renewed at the second coming (John, 20. 17;); for this the Church here prays: meanwhile she enjoys *inward* spiritual communion with Him. The last who ever "kissed" Jesus Christ on earth was the traitor Judas. The bride's return with the King to her mother's house answers to Acts, 8, 25, after the mission to Samaria. The rest spoken of (*v.* 4) answers to Acts, 9, 31, that sucked... mother—a brother born of the same mother; the closest tie. 2. Her desire to bring Him into her home circle (John, 1. 41, , who would instruct me—rather, "thou wouldest instruct me," *viz.,* how I might best please thee (Isa. 11. 2, 3; 50. 4; Luke, 12. 12; John, 14. 26; 16. 13,). spiced wine — seasoned with aromatic perfumes. Jesus Christ ought to have our choicest gifts. Spices are never introduced in the Song in His absence: therefore the time of His return from "the mountain of spices" *(v.* 14) is contemplated. The cup of betrothal was given by Him at the last supper; the cup of marriage shall be presented by her at His return (Mat. 26. 29.). Till then the believer often cannot feel towards, or speak of, Him, as he would wish. 3, 4. The "left and right hand," &c., occurred only once actually (ch. 2. 6,), and here optatively. Only at His first manifestation did the Church palpably embrace Him; at His second coming there shall be again sensible communion with Him. The rest in *v.* 4, which is a *spiritual* realisation of the wish in *v.* 3 (1 Pet. 1. 8,), and the charge not to disturb it, close the 1st, 2d, and 4th canticles; not the 3d, as the Bridegroom there takes charge Himself; nor the 5th, as, if *repose* formed its close, we might mistake the present state for our rest. The broken, longing close, like that of the whole Bible (Rev. 22. 20, , reminds us we are to be waiting for a Saviour to come. On "daughters of Jerusalem," see ch. 7. 10.

CANTICLE V.—Ch. viii. 5-14.—FROM THE CALL OF THE GENTILES TO THE CLOSE OF REVELATION. 5. Who is this—Words of the daughters of Jerusalem, *i.e.*, the churches of Judea; referring to Paul, on his return from Arabia ("the wilderness.", whither he had gone after conversion (Gal. 1. 15-24.). I raised thee ... she ... bare thee—(Acts, 26. 14-16.'. The first words of Jesus Christ to the bride, since her going to the garden of nuts (ch. 6. 9, 10;); so His appearance to Paul is the only one since His ascension; *v.* 13 is not an address of Him as *visible;* her reply implies He is not visible (1 Cor. 15. 8.). Spiritually, she was found in the moral wilderness (Ez 16. 5; Hos. 13. 5;); but now she is "coming up from" it (Jer. 2. 2; Hos. 2. 14,), especially in the last stage of her journey, her conscious weakness casting itself the more wholly on Jesus Christ (2 Cor. 12. 9.). "Raised" (Eph. 2. 1-7.). Found ruined under the forbidden tree (Gen. 3.; ; restored under the shadow of Jesus Christ crucified, "the green tree" (Luke. 23. 31,'. fruit-"bearing" by the cross (Isa. 53. 11; John, 12. 24.). Born again by the Holy Ghost "there" (Ez. 16. 3-6.). In this verse, her *dependence,* in the similar verse, ch. 3. 6, &c., *His* omnipotence *to support her,* are brought out Deut. 33. 26. 6. Implying approaching absence of the Bridegroom. seal—having her name or likeness engraven on it. His Holy Priesthood also in heaven (Ex. 28. 6-12, 15-30; Heb. 4. 14;); "his heart" there answering to "thine heart" here, and "two shoulders" to "arm." (Cf. Jer. 22. 24, with Hag. 2. 23.). By the Holy Ghost (Eph. 1. 13, 14.. As in *v.* 5, she was "leaning" on Him, *i.e.,* her arm on His *arm,* while she enjoys *inward* spiritual communion with Him. The last who ever "kissed" Jesus Christ on earth was the traitor Judas. her head on His *bosom;* so she prays now that before they part, her impression may be engraven both on His *heart,* and His *arm,* answering to His *love* and His *power* (Ps. 77. 15; see Gen. 38. 18; Isa. 62. 3.'. love is strong as death—(Acts, 21. 13; Rom. 8, 35-39; Rev. 12. 11.). This their love unto death flows from His (John, 10. 15; 15. 13.). jealousy ... the grave— Zealous love, jealous of all that would come between the soul and Jesus Christ (1 Ki. 19. 10; Ps. 106. 30, 31; Luke, 9. 60; 14. 26; 1 Cor. 16. 22.). cruel—rather, *unyielding, hard:* as the grave will not let go those whom it once holds (John, 10. 28.). a most vehement flame—*lit.,* the fire-flame of Jehovah (Ps. 80. 16; Isa. 6. 6.). Nowhere else is *God's* name found in the Song. The zeal that burnt in Jesus Christ Ps. 69. 9; Luke, 12. 49, 50, kindled in His followers (Acts, 2. 3; Rom. 15. 30; Phil. 2. 17.). 7. waters—in contrast with the "coals of fire" (*v.* 6; 1 Ki. 18. 33-38.,. Persecutions (Acts, 8. 1) cannot quench love (Heb. 10. 34; Rev. 12. 15, 16.). Our many provocations have not quenched His love Rom. 8. 33-39.). if ... give all the substance ... contemned—nothing short of Jesus Christ Himself, not even heaven without Him, can satisfy the saint (Phil. 3. 8.). Satan offers the world, as to Jesus Christ (Mat. 4. 8,), so to the saint, in vain (1 John, 2. 15-17; 5. 4.. Nothing but our love in turn can satisfy Him (1 Cor. 13. 1-3.. 8. The Gentile Church (Ez. 16. 48.'. "We," *i.e.,* the Hebrew Church, which heretofore admitted Gentiles to communion, only by becoming *Judaic* proselytes. Now first *idolatrous* Gentiles are admitted *directly* (Acts. 11. 17-26.. Generally, the saint's anxiety for other souls (Mark, 5. 19; John, 4. 28, 29.). no breasts— neither faith or love as yet (note, ch. 4. 5,), which "come by hearing" of Him who first loved us. Not yet fit to be His bride, and mother of a spiritual offspring. what shall we do—the chief question in the early Church at the first council Acts, 15.). How shall "the elder brother" treat the "younger."

From the Call of the Gentiles   SOLOMON'S SONG, VIII.   *to the Close of Revelation.*

already received by the Father? (Luke, 15. 25-32.). Generally (2 Sam. 15. 16; John, 9. 4; Acts. 9. 6; Gal. 6. 10.). In the day ... spoken for—*i.e.*, when she shall be *sought in marriage* (Jud. 14. 7.), *viz.*, by Jesus Christ, the heavenly bridegroom. 9. wall ... door—the very terms employed as to the Gentile question (Acts, 14. 27; Eph. 2. 14.). If she be a wall in Zion, founded on Jesus Christ (1 Cor. 3. 11.), we will not "withstand God" (Acts, 11. 17; 16. 8-11.). But if so, we must not "build" (Acts, 15. 14-17) on her "wood, hay, stubble,"(1 Cor. 3. 12.), *i.e.*, Jewish rites, &c., but "a palace of silver," *i.e.*, all the highest privileges of church communion (Gal. 2. 11-18; Eph. 2. 11-22.). Image from the splendid turrets "built" on the "walls" of Jerusalem, and flanking the "door," or gateway. The Gentile Church is the "door," the type of catholic accessibleness (1 Cor. 16. 9.); but it must be not a mere thoroughfare, but furnished with a wooden frame work, so as not merely to admit, but also to safely enclose; cedar is fragrant, beautiful, and enduring. 10. The Gentile Church's joy at its free admission to gospel privileges (Acts, 15. 30, 31.). She is one wall in the spiritual temple of the Holy Ghost, the Hebrew Church is the other: Jesus Christ, the common foundation, joins them (Eph. 2. 11-22.). breasts ... towers—alluding to the silver palace, which the bridal virgins proposed to build on her (*v.* 9.). "Breasts" of consolation (Isa. 66. 11.); faith and love (1 Thes. 5. 8.); opposed to her previous state, "no breasts" (*v.* 8; 2 Thes. 1. 3.). Thus Ez. 16. 46, 61, was fulfilled, both Samaria and the Gentiles being joined to the Jewish gospel Church. favour—rather, *peace*. The Gentile Church too is become the Shulamite (ch. 6. 13.), or *peace*-enjoying bride of Solomon, *i.e.*, Jesus Christ, the Prince of Peace (Rom. 5. 1; Eph. 2. 14.). Reject not those whom God accepts (Num. 11. 28; Luke, 9. 49; Acts, 15. 8. 9.). Rather, superadd to such every aid and privilege (*v.* 9.). 11. The joint-Church speaks of Jesus Christ's vineyard. Transference of it from the Jews, who rendered not the fruits, as is implied by the silence respecting any, to the Gentiles (Mat. 21. 33-43.). Baal-hamon—equivalent to *the owner of a multitude:* so Israel in Solomon's days (1 Ki. 4. 20.): so Isa. 5. 1, "a *very fruitful* hill:" abounding in *privileges,* as in *numbers.* thousand pieces—*viz.*, silverlings, or shekels. The vineyard had 1000 vines probably: a vine at a silverling (Isa. 7. 23.), referring to this passage. 12. "Mine," by grant of the true Solomon. Not merely "let out to keepers," as in the Jewish dispensation of *works,* but "mine" by *grace.* This is "before me," *i.e.*, *in my power.* [MAUR.] But though no longer

under constraint of "keeping" the law as a mere letter and covenant of works, *love* to Jesus Christ will constrain her the more freely to render all to Solomon (Rom. 8. 2-4; 1 Cor. 6. 20; Gal. 5. 13; 1 Pet. 2. 16.), after having paid what justice and His will require should be paid to others (1 Cor. 7. 29-31; 9. 14.). "Before me" may also mean "I will never lose sight of it" (contrast ch. 1. 6.). [M. STUART.] She will not keep it for herself, though so freely given to her, but for His use and glory (Luke, 19. 13; Rom. 6. 15; 14. 7-9; 1 Cor. 12. 7.). Or the "two hundred" may mean a *double tithe* (two-tenths of the whole) paid back by Jesus Christ, as the reward of grace for our surrender of *all* (the thousand) to Him (Gal. 6. 7; Heb. 6. 10.): then she and "those that keep" are the same. [A. NEWTON.] But Jesus Christ pays back not merely *two tithes,* but *His all* for our all (1 Cor. 3. 21-23.). 13. Jesus Christ's address to her; now no longer visibly present. Once she "had not kept" her vineyard (ch. 1. 6.; now she "dwells" in it, not as its owner, but its superintendent under Jesus Christ, with vinedressers ("companions") *ex. gr.*, Paul, &c., (Acts, 15. 25, 26; under her (*v.* 11, 12.): these ought to obey her, when she obeys Jesus Christ. Her voice in prayer and praise is to be heard continually by Jesus Christ, if her voice before men is to be effective (ch. 2. 14, end; Acts, 6. 4; 13. 2, 3.). 14. (See note, ch. 2. 17.). As she began with longing for His first coming (ch. 1. 2.), so she ends with praying for His second coming (Ps. 130. 6; Phil. 3. 20, 21; Rev. 22. 20.). M. STUART makes the roe-upon-spices to be the musk-deer. As there are four gardens, so four mountains, which form not mere images, as Gilead, Carmel, &c., but part of the structure of the Song. (1.) Bether, or *division* ch. 2. 17.), God's justice *dividing* us from God; (2.) Those "of leopards" (ch. 4. 8, , sin, the world, and Satan; (3.) That "of myrrh and aloes" (ch. 4. 6, 14.), the sepulchre of Calvary; 4.) Those "of spices," here answering to "the hill of frankincense" (ch. 4. 6.), where His *soul* was for the three days of His death, and heaven, where He is a High Priest now, offering incense for us on the fragrant mountain of His own finished work (Heb. 4. 14; 7. 25; Rev. 8. 3, 4); thus He surmounts the other three mountains, God's justice, our sin, death. The mountain of spices is as much greater than our sins, as heaven is higher than earth (Ps. 103. 11.). The abrupt unsatisfied close with the yearning prayer for His *visible* coming shews that the marriage is future, and that to wait eagerly for it is our true attitude (1 Cor. 1. 7; 1 Thes. 1. 10; Tit. 2. 13; 2 Pet. 3. 12.).

www.ingramcontent.com/pod-product-compliance
Lightning Source LLC
Chambersburg PA
CBHW020755230426
43666CB00007B/711